Working Slavery,
Pricing Freedom

B. W. Higman

Working Slavery, Pricing Freedom

Perspectives from the Caribbean,
Africa and the African Diaspora

Edited by

Verene A. Shepherd

palgrave
New York

First Published in the United States 2002
by Palgrave – Global publishing at St. Martin's Press
175 Fifth Avenue, New York, NY 10010

Library of Congress Cataloging-in-Publication Data

Working Slavery, pricing freedom: perspectives from the Caribbean,
Africa & the African diaspora/editor, Verene A. Shepherd.

p. cm.

Includes bibliographical references and index.

ISBN 0-312-29362-3 (cloth) — ISBN 0-312-29363-1 (paper)

1. Slavery—Caribbean Area—History. 2. Slavery—Economic aspects—Caribbean Area.
3. African diaspora—History. 4. Equality—Caribbean Area—History. 5.
Civil rights—Caribbean Area—History. 6. Caribbean Area—Economic policy. 7.
Caribbean Area—Race relations. 8. Caribbean Area—Politics and government. I.
Shepherd, Verene A.
HT1105.C37 W67 2001
306.3'62'09729—dc21
2001035794

Set in Plantin Light 10/14 x 24
Text and cover design by Robert Harris
Printed and bounded in the United States of America

Contents

Section 6:   *The legacy of slavery: gender, ethnicity and occupation*

Section 7:   *The legacy of slavery: race, labour, politics and protest*

Preface

---

*T*he issues of colonisation, slavery, emancipation and freedpeople's struggles for civil rights and citizenship, continue to occupy the attention of scholars devoted to the study of the history of the Caribbean, Africa and the African diaspora. This volume of essays continues the on-going dialogue among scholars engaged in discourses of slavery and freedom at different levels. The essays illustrate that the superstructure of slave systems, their economic substructures, the fundamental and unifying characteristics of societies based on African enslavement, maturing anti-slavery consciousness and politics and the diasporic implications of Caribbean slavery are striking features of current historiography. The volume itself evolved out of an informal 'seminar' at the University of the West Indies, Mona campus at which some colleagues who wished to mark, in a significant way, Barry Higman's departure from the University of the West Indies to take up a position in his native Australia after some 28 years at the Mona campus, insisted on this modest project in recognition of his tremendous contribution to the field of slavery studies and the academic careers of many scholars. The project, of course, as the Table of Contents indicates, later expanded beyond Mona.

I am grateful to colleagues who entrusted me with the task of editing this volume, and indebted to all those who devoted time and energy to the project: the contributors; the international Editorial Advisory Committee; the anonymous reviewers, and Helen Ann Brown, Tannya Guerra, Dawn Stephenson and Carol Thompson who helped with research, correspondence with contributors, and word-processing. I thank the Mona Campus Research and Publications Fund Committee for its financial contribution towards the preparation of the volume for publication, and James Robertson for his advice on several aspects of the project.

I thank my husband, Bramwell, and my sons Duane and Deane for their continued patience and support; and Angella Lazarus, Dawn Owusu, Sylvia

Martin, Annette, Janice and Philip Brade who gave much-needed hospitality while I finalised this project in London in the summer of 2000.

Finally, I join with other colleagues in expressing appreciation for Barry Higman's contributions to the University of the West Indies. As his friend and mentor, the late Douglas Hall said of him, 'some of his innovations like the courses in Archaeology, the Social History Project and Heritage Studies, are now, hopefully, established features of our work. Others, like his well-provided "Second Breakfasts" and his seasonal "food" and "fete" occasions, in both of which he starred (as cook in one and vigorous cavorter in the other), cannot survive without him'.

Verene A. Shepherd

Introduction

VERENE A. SHEPHERD

*T*he birth of the Atlantic World as an integrated economy characterised by an enormous movement of Africans (through force) and Europeans into the Americas, hinged on the infrastructural development of chattel slavery as a specific category. Colonial exploitation, using slavery as the mode of extracting surplus value from subalterns, provided the wider market economy required by merchant capital during the seventeenth century. The emergence of Western Europe as the political centre of an Atlantic economy signalled the importance of imperial exploitation to its development, and of colonialism as the transformative engine of capitalist growth. The establishment of chattel slavery as the principal labour institution was related more to the expansion of the sugar industry, but also became critical to urban regimes and the production of non-sugar crops.

The superstructure of the slavery systems, their economic substructures, the fundamental and unifying characteristics of a society based on African enslavement, together with maturing anti-slavery consciousness and politics, are striking features of current historiography on every continent. The empirical research on the abolition of slavery has also reached an impressive level, giving rise to ever new debates and theoretical constructs. Scholars have also been preoccupied with the study of the transition from chattel enslavement to freedom, the legacies of slavery in the former slave societies, and the links that developed and cemented relationships among different geographical sections of the Atlantic World. This collection of essays by scholars working on diverse themes within the broad areas of slavery and freedom, and mostly centred on the Black diaspora in the Caribbean, continues the polemical disputes as well as reveals new data for further cross-cultural study.

The collection has multiple objectives. First, it seeks to highlight the tremendous research activity of scholars of Caribbean, Africa and African diaspora history who have brought the study of slavery and post-slavery societies into global, cross-cultural focus. Second, the expansion of the Caribbean diaspora, the resultant growing interest in the 'roots', history and culture of the people of this diaspora, and the widespread increase in the numbers of universities and colleges offering programmes and courses in Caribbean/Atlantic World history, have served to highlight the need for more pan-Caribbean, multiple-theme volumes like this. Specialist books, many arising out of doctoral theses, which are primarily microcosmic and nationalist in their perspective, will no longer be sufficient. Third, and very importantly, the volume is intended as a tribute to Barry Higman who arrived as a postgraduate student at the Mona campus of the University of the West Indies on a Commonwealth Scholarship in 1967. He went on to complete the PhD in History at Mona under the supervision of Douglas Hall, and another PhD in Geography at the University of Liverpool. He joined the staff of the History Department in 1971, resigning his Chair as Professor of History only in 1996 after close to 28 years of service, broken only by Sabbaticals and Fellowship leaves. As Douglas Hall observed shortly before he died, Barry's 'relentless pursuit of information, his meticulous arrangement of it, his growing list of publications and his unceasing intellectual curiosity brought new vigour into the [History] Department'. While at the University of the West Indies, he offered expert thesis supervision for many, as well as strong leadership as Head of Department, distinguishing his two stints as head with outstanding administrative efficiency, creative solutions, gender equity and institution-building innovations. History Day, the Heritage Studies Programme and the Social History Project remain three of his outstanding innovations. Higman has been a leading scholar in the field of Caribbean history and historical demography, particularly for the slavery period, for many decades; and his work has enabled him to annex an impressive number of honours and awards, including a Guggenheim fellowship, the University of the West Indies' Vice-Chancellor's award for excellence in research, teaching and administration and admission to the fellowship of the Royal Historical Society. Most scholars are already familiar with his pioneering work, *Slave Population and Economy in Jamaica, 1807–1834* published by Cambridge University Press in 1976 (which won him the Bancroft Prize in American History in 1977), and the follow-up work, *Slave Populations of the British Caribbean 1807–1834* published by the Johns Hopkins University Press in 1984, in which Higman ambitiously conceived the grand project of a sweeping analysis of the demographic structure of the entire slave population of the British Caribbean. That work won him the 1986

Elsa Goveia Book Prize awarded by the Association of Caribbean Historians. His training in both geography and history coalesced in *Jamaica Surveyed: Plantation Maps and Plans of the 18th and 19th Centuries*, published by the Institute of Jamaica Press in 1988. This book eventually won the Jamaica Book Industry Award for the best locally produced book in 1989. Since leaving the University of the West Indies, he has published many other works, including *Writing West Indian Histories* (Macmillan, 1999), *Montpelier, Jamaica: A Plantation Community in Slavery and Freedom 1739–1832* (Kingston, 1998), and the edited (UNESCO) volume on *Methodology and Historiography of the Caribbean* (1999). Two of these books have won awards. *Montpelier, Jamaica* got the Elsa Goveia Prize awarded by the Association of Caribbean Historians in 1999 and the Jamaica Heritage award in 2000. *Writing West Indian Histories* was awarded the Gordon K. Lewis Memorial Award for Caribbean Scholarship in 1999. His academic interests and research topics are many and varied; and this diverse research interest is acknowledged and reflected in the range of topics covered in this collection.

The twenty-three chapters, organised into two broad parts and seven sections, are arranged in a rough chronological order, allowing for an examination of the history of the Caribbean, Africa and the African diaspora from the seventeenth to the twentieth century. The first part of the volume is devoted to the early period of colonisation, plantation construction and slavery. It starts off with an essay focused on the reshaping of the economy, society and urban spaces in English-colonised Jamaica, later to become the largest producer of sugar in the English-colonised Caribbean. It was the English who in 1655 captured the island from the Spaniards, who had themselves seized it from the Tainos. The English proceeded to transform the economic and social landscape from one dominated by ranching, small-settler, mainly subsistence enterprises, buccaneering activities and limited trading links to one based on the sugar plantation system worked by large gangs of enslaved African labourers captured and forcefully transported from Africa and with an extensive commercial nexus. The establishment of the English Atlantic project in the seventeenth century with its manifestations of a colonialist ideology, racism, slavery and, later, the plantation system, had far-reaching socioeconomic and political effects. An important impact was the rise of the centuries-long struggle for liberation by Africans and their descendants who were forced into a dishonourable system of social oppression.

In Section 1, Zahedieh locates her contribution within the framework of urban centres in the Americas, in this case, Port Royal, making a comparative explanation of its rise to a position of pre-eminent commercial importance. Her article has four broad implications: first, sugar did not immediately become the economic staple of English-colonised Jamaica; second, income which was ploughed into the sugar economy was not all externally generated; third, as a commercial hub, Port Royal facilitated the integration of Caribbean commerce and caused a slight deviation from strict mercantilist policies; and finally, colonies had a fundamental economic impact on their imperial core.

The next three authors explore the nature of economic activities under slavery in Africa and its Caribbean diaspora; but they are not located within the traditional context of the sugar plantation complex. Indeed, Saunders' and Craton's analyses remind us (much as Higman, Shepherd and others have already done) that, in the case of the Caribbean, the classic plantation economy model needs to be modified. The standard interpretation of the Caribbean economy under slavery is that they were sugar plantation economies governed by an export-oriented plantation system in which inputs were imported and outputs exported primarily to the respective metropoles and mother countries; and some scholars apply the model uncritically to the entire Caribbean. However, the English were never able to fully transform the economy and society of all their colonies into that of a classic plantation system. The Jamaican economy, for example, though dominated by the sugar industry after 1750, nevertheless remained quite diversified throughout the period of slavery with proprietors earning substantial incomes from other enterprises like coffee and livestock-farming. Similarly, Saunders focuses on the Bahamas where cotton culture, not sugar, defined the experiences of the enslaved. She provides a good summary of enslaved labour in a non-sugar plantation economy, and explores the relationship between commodity production, the work regime and the demographic experiences of the enslaved. She concludes that cotton production helped to create favourable demographic characteristics in the Bahamian enslaved population.

Craton's chapter is also focused on the non-sugar plantation colony of the Bahamas, exploring in detail the dynamics of what he calls the 'Black loyalist diaspora' in the Bahamas and the contributions of these 'slave loyalists' to the economy and society of the Bahamas. The impact of these Black 'loyalists' who were relocated to the Bahamas after the end of the American War of

Independence in 1783, in Craton's view, need greater articulation. British colonialism had spread its tentacles wide, engulfing the seaboard colonies of the present United States of America. It took a war of independence to dislodge Britain and sever the imperial link; but those who could not tolerate the end of empire relocated after the war. In the case of the Bahamas, these relocated Blacks comprised the major portion of the 7,300 'loyalists' who arrived in 1783; yet, their history is less well-known than that of the 'White loyalists'. Craton examines their internal diversity and composition, their legal status, role, and impact on Bahamian economy and society, both in Nassau and in the so-called 'Out Islands'.

The section ends with the spotlight turned on West Africa. Waibinte Wariboko's chapter looks at African slavery as part of the Atlantic World continuum, tapping an underutilised source, the Church Missionary Society (CMS) documents, to provide new data on domestic slavery in New Calabar. His chapter is an important contribution to analyses of the variation in slave occupations and stresses the heterogeneous and fluid nature of domestic slavery. At the same time, he critiques the traditional interpretation of such forms of slavery as 'mild'. In addition to its revisionist perspective, he engages with the still topical issue of domestic slavery in Africa and the links between the Caribbean and Africa, specifically how forms of slavery in Africa affected the evolution of slavery in the Americas. His contribution will be of great interest to those who are interested in the comparative nature of domestic slavery in Africa and the Caribbean.

In Section 2, Monteith and Satchell examine the extent of technological experiment on the part of proprietors, more specifically, the relationship between slavery and technological advancement in the eighteenth and nineteenth centuries, an issue which has formed the basis of a long-standing debate in Caribbean economic history. They explore the extent of technological advancement on sugar and coffee estates respectively, revisiting the theoretical debate over the compatibility/non-compatibility between technology and slavery, with Satchell also looking at the extent to which such technological advances as were made affected the lives of the enslaved. Satchell examines the technological capacity of the Jamaican slave system through an analysis of technical changes or innovations in the cane sugar mill over the period 1760–1830. His view is that, contrary to the traditional belief of Marxists and some economic historians, the slave system did show a degree of willingness to adopt and adapt new technology to improve efficiency and ensure greater reliability. He goes as far as to speculate, with the limited data at his disposal, that technicians from the enslaved population were closely involved in some of the inventions. Monteith also engages with those who have argued that British Caribbean planters scoffed at improved technological innovation in the cultivation and manufacture of agricultural crops during the slavery period and that this attitude led to a decline in the British Caribbean economy. She does not entirely dismiss the view that there may have been a link between the failure to adopt new technologies and economic decline, but she argues that this conclusion should not be applied generally and uncritically. Drawing upon examples from the coffee industry, she shows that producers were not all averse to the implementation of new and improved techniques, although the extent of implementation was uneven. Some did avail themselves of the prevailing technology governing the manufacturing process. However, coffee planters were often too constrained by geographical factors and the need to minimize the cost of production to invest heavily in improved techniques in planting and processing.

The chapters in Section 3 illustrate the complexities of the societies within which slavery operated and look beyond enslaver-enslaved relationships to probe the economic basis of White power, White social relations, including the oft-neglected area of gender relations. Burnard revisits the fascinating discussion of the Manning divorce case in eighteenth-century Jamaica, showing not only the details and implications of the case for Jamaican society, but also the core/periphery constitutional and legal relations in colonial societies. The hypocritical and contradictory attitudes towards race, class and gender come through clearly in this essay. Shepherd problematises property-ownership in colonial Jamaica. She emphasises that the sugar planters were not the only property-holders and, encouraged by local geographical and economic factors, space was created for the co-existence of sugar and non-sugar proprietors; and Jamaica became involved in a complicated trading network in which England was only one participant. She contrasts the status of sugar and non-sugar producers in Jamaican society in the eighteenth and nineteenth centuries, demonstrating the ways in which the existence of proprietors not directly involved in the sugar industry complicated the social hierarchy and the distribution of enslaved and free labourers in colonial Jamaica.

The final section in Part 1 focuses on the conflicts between enslavers and the enslaved. As Bolland reminds us, a persistently thorny question in Caribbean social history is the analysis of power and resistance. Indeed, several historians have always stressed the centrality of the political dimension of social history, urging scholars to underscore the importance of conflict and hegemonic power in the analysis of the social history of rebellion and resistance. The authors in Section 4 elucidate the complex relations between hegemonic power and resistance, taking up the challenge for us to seek the dynamics of conflict in all aspects of Caribbean social history and examining Caribbean social history from the perspective of the marginalised. They point us to the ways in which the enslaved themselves were engaged in working slavery for their own benefit, negotiating and struggling to free themselves. The authors focus on the various contexts of enslaved people's resistant behaviour (even from the moment of capture) in the light of efforts to exercise control over them.

Sheridan provides an excellent synthesis of the works dealing with African resistance to capture, transportation and sale in the Americas. His chapter reinforces the strong presence of a self-liberation ethos among all socially marginalised people and provides some firm examples (for example by Olaudah Equiano and Mungo Park) of covert and overt resistance to capture and shipment from Africa by male and female captives. Hinds explores deportation as a strategy of controlling the enslaved and the response of those most affected by this strategy, the Maroons, to the attempt by colonial authorities to marginalise them. His chapter, a welcome addition to the historiography of the Maroons, explores the particular case of the Maroon War of 1795–6, tracing the experiences of those deported to Nova Scotia and later Sierra Leone. Beckles problematises 'leisure,' showing that enslaved people's dances were sites and locations for the planning of rebellions, not mere recreation. He describes and analyses the political nature of enslaved people's entertainment and leisure culture by drawing upon empirical evidence derived mostly from Barbados and to a lesser extent Jamaica. His perspective departs from traditional interpretations which suggest that the socio-cultural activities of enslaved Africans should be located within the context of actions designed and fashioned by the need to fill the empty spaces left over from the production demands upon their labour power. His interpretation is that enslaved people's leisure and recreation were not apolitical social activities; but the politics of anti-slavery was endemic to cultural activities. The enslaved perceived this relationship as well.

Part 2 of the collection focuses on the transition to freedom and the legacies of slavery in what was supposed to have been the post slave driver era when 'massa missus day' had come to an end. One of the most fundamental changes in the world economy in the eighteenth and nineteenth centuries was the transition from enslaved to free labour in the Americas. Haiti pioneered the change in the late eighteenth century, with the British Caribbean following in the period 1834–8. Emancipation was a process that transformed labour relations and reorganised Caribbean economy and politics. Despite the diverse nature of the themes covered, the main question which seems to emerge from all the authors in Section 5 is: what price freedom? More specifically, on the threshold of freedom, how did the enslaved view the attempts at amelioration and the possibilities to negotiate freedom and rights? How did the struggle for freedom reflect the contradictory nature of the slave relation itself? As Dale Tomich has pointed out elsewhere, the same social relation that shaped labour as a mass and coerced labour force also created possibilities for the enslaved to become autonomous, independent agents.[1] How did the emancipationists price freedom and work out the slave-holders' compensation packages? How did the newly freed value themselves and use this value to negotiate wages and rights? How far were they and their descendants prepared to go to actualise freedom, from the late nineteenth century? How did the elite property-holding classes and the state price freedom? How did they measure their own interests against those of working-class Africans and Asians?

Attaching a price to freedom was an essential part of the emancipation struggle, as Engerman demonstrates in his analysis of the problems and conflicts which developed over market prices on which to base the payment of compensation; for while emancipationists gave no thought to compensating the enslaved for the torture they endured through illegal capture in Africa and enslavement in the Americas, enslavers were compensated for the loss of their 'property' when slavery ended. He provides extremely useful data to help us to understand issues like the basis of and justification for compensation, the specifics of the evaluation process, the legal complications of the individual manumission procedure and the general framework of legal, state-directed emancipation. Turner explores the background to general emancipation from another angle, focusing on the role of the enslaved in their own liberation. Using Berbice (in the former British Guiana, now Guyana) as her context, she examines the amelioration proposals and slave women's resistant response to them as one way of problematising the transition from chattel-enslaved and proto-peasants to wage labour. She demonstrates that the enslaved had knowledge of their value (which Engerman referred to in his discussion of individual manumission), their price, and used this knowledge in the contests for rights and ultimately freedom.

Walvin's article prices slavery in a different way; for while British society surely benefitted from the economic resources of Africa and the Caribbean, the generation of such economic resources took a large toll on human lives. He explores the ways in which a Black Atlantic economy evolved in the slave trade and slavery eras, looks again at the debate, started by Eric Williams in 1944, about the impact of England's participation in the slave trade and slavery on society in Britain and the Caribbean.[2] His thesis is that British society was fundamentally transformed by its exploitation of Africa and Africans; and that transformation was not confined to elite life nor to the areas of banking and large industries. The fruits of empire, the products of the labour of enslaved Africans, were critical in the reshaping of the lives of ordinary British people. The presence of Africans in Britain was a constant reminder of the ways in which domestic British life was inextricably linked to Africa and the Caribbean. Yet despite the benefits which Britons derived from Africa and the Caribbean through the trade in captives and the plantation system, and the contradictions presented by Africans actually settled in the metropole, warped images and representations of Africa (another 'price of slavery') continued to inform their attitude to Africans settled in their country. It was left to Black people themselves to produce the counter-discourse to dispel the misrepresentation.

Bolland, beginning with Higman's standpoint that anti-theoretical stances have no place in Caribbean social history, and his own belief that the social history of resistance and/or opposition needs to adopt the theoretical stance of dialectical historical sociology, tests the application of de Certeau and Focault's models of resistance and opposition to hegemonic regimes for the slavery and post-slavery era. He argues that people are always located in institutions and other patterns of social relations that are marked by inequalities and discusses their responses to such inequalities within the context of opposition and resistance, using various strategies and tactics. He uses the 1823 slave rebellion in colonial Guyana and the 1930s labour rebellions in colonial Guyana and Jamaica (which occurred a century after emancipation), to help clarify the theoretical points.

The chapters in Section 6 by Shepherd, Moore, and Johnson go some way towards illuminating post-slavery and modern society in colonial Guyana and Jamaica which displayed clear legacies of the mentalities of slavery. More specifically, they point to the ethnic, class, colour and gender diversity of Caribbean societies and the ways in which people's experiences were shaped by one or more of these factors. Shepherd revisits the long-standing debate over the nature of indentured labour migration that many landholders in the British-colonised territories used to replace slavery in the period after 1838. The central question is: was indentureship a new system of slavery in Hugh Tinker's terms or the other Middle Passage in Ron Ramdin's, particularly with respect to the experiences of indentured women?[3] She provides empirical data from the passage from India, specifically from the voyage of the *Allanshaw* to colonial Guyana, to shed light on this legacy of slavery debate.

Using colonial Guyana as his example, Moore revisits a perennial issue in the analysis of the behaviour of ethnic groups in multiracial Caribbean societies: the relationship between ethnicity and economic power or economic activities. This relationship has often led to the perception that each ethnic group had inherent racial and cultural attributes which qualified it for certain kinds of occupations and economic roles. He concludes, though, that in nineteenth-century colonial Guyana there were no intrinsic racial and cultural attributes that qualified one ethnic group for certain economic roles over another. The more important factors defining ethnic roles were the over-arching political and economic structures which set the limits of ethnic participation in the economy. Any analysis of the economic power of ethnic groups in the Caribbean, especially of immigrants turned settlers, must therefore take into consideration the facilitating (or, indeed, the obstructionist) role of the state.

Johnson, drawing upon oral sources and the newspaper advertisements for domestic servants, explores the origins and the prevailing stereotypes of this occupation and the factors crucial to an understanding of the conceptualisation of women as domestic servants. She seeks to answer questions like why domestic servants were primarily young, female and of rural origin. Her chapters demonstrates that gender ideology, the exploitative nature of Jamaican society and the seeming need of middle-class employers for cheap, subservient and controllable servants played fundamental roles in constructing the prevailing profile of the domestic servant in colonial and post-colonial Jamaican society. Goodridge adds a diasporic, comparative dimension to this section, examining the role of slavery, emancipation, religion, imperialism and colonial policy in the lives of Cameroonian women. He identifies and discusses the restrictions faced by Cameroonian women, not only by slavery, but by their limited access to education and political power. The abolition of slavery was a necessary step towards Cameroonian women's liberation; but other factors were vital if these women were to experience radical changes in their socio-economic and political status. Clearly legal emancipation was not necessarily accompanied by actualised freedom for these women who had to face many obstacles in the way of their total liberation. This chapter will be of particular interest to feminist historians and other scholars engaged in the project of identifying the influences which African origins had on Caribbean women's social and economic roles.

In Section 7, Wilmot continues his excellent conversations in post-slavery politics and protest by examining the political behaviour of non-elites in one Jamaican parish. This chapter is a good contribution to the study of what social historians call 'history from below,' and underscores the extent to which post-slavery Jamaican society adjusted to new social formations which deepened its creole nature and established a political culture (helped by the church) that incorporated the urban artisans and rural settlers. Lumsden revisits the issue of the role of the Jamaican Maroons in the Morant Bay Rebellion testing the application of the two models which have been traditionally constructed to assess them. Were they freedom fighters or traitors? It was the Maroons' seeming support of the British government for more than a century, from 1738 to 1865, which has caused so much debate and given rise to the latter characterisation, which has often overshadowed their history of struggle against the White colonial regime in Jamaica in the period before 1738 to 1739 period. Her review of the role of the Maroons in the 1865 Morant Bay Rebellion will no doubt raise new questions and ensure the continuation of the debate.

Richards tries to help to break the trend of narrow academic specialisation which is threatening to reduce the field of Caribbean history to the study of individual territories, by explaining in a comparative way why elite Coloureds and Whites appropriated the leadership of the trade union movement from Black African-Caribbean people in two British Caribbean territories, particularly in the years after the 1930s labour protest. He shows that despite the marked geographical and economic divergence of St Kitts and Jamaica, both their post-slavery histories were defined by the continuation of the hegemonic control of the mostly White plantocracy or elements connected to the sugar interests; and the marginalised Black masses (at times through their organisations and leaders) adopted remarkably similar strategies in their efforts to displace this hegemonic bloc. He looks for answers to questions such as why Black politicians and labour leaders were relegated to secondary roles by the early twentieth century. To what extent did the new leaders represent the interests of the masses well and do justice to their hopes and aspirations? Did they simply take up the cause of labour to manipulate the labouring classes to serve their own narrow political ends?

Bryan examines the issue of land tenure and land use in the Dominican Republic, showing how it became a site of contest, conflict and struggle compounded by external factors relating to control and influence by the United States. Historians have consistently argued that the land question was among the most contentious issues in the post-slavery Caribbean. In many places the tensions between former owners and freed people, indeed, coalesced in issues relating to land access, price and tenure. The inflow of foreign capital and the expansion of the sugar industry in the Dominican Republic after the 1870s, resulted in land becoming contested terrain; for the traditional quasi-feudal structure of land tenure conflicted with the capitalist mode of production and the need by investors like the United States for the solidification of their economic hold on Dominican soil.

It is clear from the chapters in Section 7 that even centuries after the abolition of slavery, Caribbean peoples were still caught up in the struggle for rights and real freedom. Freed people were faced with competition for work, especially as the land-holding classes imported indentured servants to flood the labour market and depress wages. Of course, indentured and ex-indentured workers were no less exploited by the proprietors, with only some being able to escape socioeconomic marginalisation and rise to positions of socioeconomic and political importance by the mid-twentieth century. Caribbean people's agency was manifested in the contest for land, autonomy, wages, general socioeconomic benefits and political rights. Up to the 1930s, African and Asian-Caribbean people were struggling for rights, not least among these being a better price for labour and the right to organise.

Notes

1.   Dale Tomich, 'The Other Face of Slave Labor: Provision Grounds and
       Internal Marketing', in D. Tomich,   *Slavery in the Circuit of Sugar: Martinique
       and the World Economy, 1830–1848* (Baltimore: The Johns Hopkins University
       Press, 1990), pp. 259–80.
2.   Eric Williams, *Capitalism and Slavery* (Chapel Hill: North Carolina Press,
       1944).
3.   Hugh Tinker, *A New System of Slavery: The Export of Indian Labour Overseas,
       1830–1920* (London: Oxford University Press, 1974) and Ron Ramdin,   *The
       Other Middle Passage: Journal of a Voyage from Calcutta to Trinidad, 1858*
       (London: Hansib Publishers, 1994).

Part One

*Colonisation, Enslavement
and Resistance*

SECTION

Slavery and Economic Life:
Commercial, Agricultural and
Domestic Regimes

CHAPTER 1

"The Wickedest City in the World"
Port Royal, commercial hub of the seventeenth-century Caribbean

NUALA ZAHEDIEH

*T*hanks largely to the famed exploits of privateers such as Henry Morgan chronicled in sensational terms by Exquemelin and other populist writers, Port Royal was renowned in the seventeenth century as the wickedest city in the English Atlantic empire.[1] 'A sodom filled with all manner of debauchery,' exclaimed one visitor.[2] The reputation was sealed by the 'dreadful calamity' which befell the town in 1692 and was taken as clear evidence of the judgement of God.[3] A violent earthquake shook the island and Port Royal, being perched on the end of a sand spit, was within three minutes plunged to the bottom of the harbour. 'The ground opened,' reported a Quaker merchant, 'and the sea gushed up a wonderful height that in a moment almost the whole place was under water'.[4] The church, the wharves, the exchange, two of the four forts and the three principal streets were all submerged. Hundreds of people were drowned and their corpses soon began to float on the water's surface. In the words of one account, 'Great men who were so swallowed up with pride, that a man could not be admitted to speak with them, and women whose top knots seem to reach the clouds, now lie stinking upon the water and are made meat for fish and fowles of the air'.[5]

Table 1.1:   Population of English towns in America, 1680 and 1690

Towns	1680	1690
Boston	4,500	7,000
Massachusetts state	39,752	49,504
New York	3,200	3,900
New York state	9,830	13,909
Newport	2,500	2,600
Rhode Island state	3,017	4,224
Charlestown	67,700	1,200
Carolina state	1,200	3,900
Philadelphia	0	4,000
Pennsylvania state	680	11,450
Bridgetown	2,929	c.3,000
Barbados	66,000	n/a
Port Royal	2,931	4,000(est.)
Jamaica	35,000	60,000

Sources: Bridenbaugh,*Cities in the Wilderness*; Dunn, *Sugar and Slaves* (see note 9); Zahedieh, 'Trade, plunder and economic development in early English Jamaica' (see note 10).

Port Royal became the perfect vehicle for jeremiad sermons and generated a flurry of moralistic pamphlets since everyone could agree that the wicked city had got what it deserved.[6] But, of course, wickedness in the guise of abundant taverns, brothels, gambling dens and other forms of commercialised vice was found in all ports and frontier towns, even to some extent in Quaker Philadelphia. To the historian, the town's moral failings are less surprising than the rapidity and scale of its growth. As Jacob Price remarked, the basic problem facing the student of colonial American towns is 'why did the life of certain of the colonies produce relatively large towns and the life in others not'.[7] In the case of Jamaica, the question becomes why Port Royal (which was not the seat of government and, as yet, had a relatively undeveloped agricultural hinterland), was the largest town in the English Caribbean, overtaking Barbados by 1680 and outstripped by only Boston on the mainland (Table 1.1). This chapter examines this question by focusing on the economic function of the town in the island and the region, and considers the impact its

Table 1.2:   Population of Port Royal, 1661–89

Year	Whites	Blacks	Total
1661	630	40	670
1673	1,669	312	1,981
1680	2,086	845	2,931
1689 estimate	4,000	n/a	n/a

Sources: PRO CO 1/15, folio 192*Journals of Jamaican Assembly*, App. 1, p. 40; CO 1/45 folios 97–109.

development had on both Jamaica and the metropolis and how it defined its role in the imperial economy.

There was no town on the point under Spanish rule as the Spaniards had used Old Harbour west of Spanish Town as their chief port. When the English conquered the island in 1655, they decided to take advantage of the magnificent natural harbour east of Spanish Town, which is sheltered from storms and enemy attack by a ten-mile sand spit.[8] They built a fortified town, Port Cagway, at the end of the spit to guard the harbour entrance. The recorded population of the town, renamed Port Royal in 1664, grew rapidly from 740 in 1662 to about 2,000 in 1673 and almost 3,000 in 1680, making it exactly the same size as Bridgetown, although the total population of Jamaica was probably about half that of Barbados.[9] No reliable figures survive for 1692, but literary evidence makes clear that Port Royal continued to grow while Bridgetown was stable, making the Jamaican port with at least 4,000 people, the largest English town in the Caribbean (Table 1.2).

Taking the White population alone, the importance of Port Royal is even more startling. In 1680, 20–25 per cent of Whites in Jamaica lived in Port Royal, suggesting that immigrants were attracted by a range of opportunities apart from planting. Meanwhile, in Barbados a higher proportion of Whites lived in the agricultural hinterland and only 7–8 per cent lived in Bridgetown (Table 1.3). Growth was accompanied by prosperity. The average value of 49 merchants' probate inventories from the period 1686–92 is £1,789, suggesting that Port Royal may have been the richest trading community in English America.[10] As the visitor John Taylor remarked, 'the merchants and

Table 1.3:   White Population of Port Royal and Jamaica, 1662–92

Year	Port Royal	Jamaica
1662	630	3,653
1673	1,669	7,768
1680	2,086	15,000
1692	3,000–4,000 (est)	n/a

gentry live here to the height of splendour, in full ease and plenty.' Craft wages were said to be three times the level in London.[11]

Any explanation of the size and wealth of a town must, as Price indicated, revolve around its function in its regional economy. Unlike Bridgetown, Port Royal was not a government or judicial centre; nor was it a centre for processing industries; it was a port and a commercial centre, as is well reflected in the evidence about the town's occupational structure drawn from surviving seventeenth-century probate inventories. One-quarter of the 121 inventories mention that the deceased had a share in ships or trading ventures of which 65 were described as merchants, with most of the remainder in commerce-related crafts.[12]

Unfortunately, the surviving statistical information about trade is patchy, but a list of 208 ships arriving in Port Royal in the period 1668–70 demonstrates the rapid growth of commercial activity in the first 15 years of settlement and the Naval Officer's returns for the 1680s suggest around 75 entries a year compared with about 100 for Barbados.[13] Part of this commercial activity would have been similar to that in Bridgetown. Merchants in Port Royal would have imported food, wine and manufactured goods on their own or a correspondent's behalf for sale and distribution in the island. The produce obtained in exchange would be shipped to England or North America. But, whereas surviving figures suggest that Barbados produced about 10,000 tons of sugar in the 1670s and 1680s, Jamaica had barely begun sugar production in 1670 and was producing about 2,000 tons in 1680 when the population of Port Royal outstripped that of Bridgetown. Jamaica's agricultural production accelerated in the 1680s, but recent work by David Eltis suggests that Jamaican output was pegged at about half the value of that of Barbados, confirming, in his eyes, 'the well-known pre-eminence of Barbados in seventeenth-century English America'.[14]

Clearly, Barbados was indeed England's pre-eminent sugar producer but clearly too, looking at Port Royal, sugar was not the whole Caribbean story. In fact, the early settlers were not attracted to Jamaica by its future as a plantation: 'few come particularly or only to plant but to merchandize'.[15] Their interest in Jamaica was aroused by its geographical location, 'in the Spaniard's bowels and in the heart of his trade'.[16] Men had been attracted by visions of El Dorado since the first discoveries. The abundant treasure of the mines of Mexico and Peru aroused the avidity of all Europe. Spain tried to reserve this wealth for itself by declaring a monopoly of trade and navigation in the area; but what others could not have by agreement they took by force or stealth – privateers and smugglers raided and traded.[17] But the English were hampered in both activities by their lack of a suitable headquarters in the Caribbean. The English settlements which survived the early seventeenth century were all situated on the periphery of the region, where the difficulty of sailing against the prevailing winds meant (although Kalinago resistance made some islands untenable) they were safely away from Spanish harassment, but ill-placed to trade or plunder on the main. The colonists were thus confined to agricultural development by constraints imposed by geography rather than choice. Jamaica was different. It was 'in the centre of the most valuable part of the British-colonised Caribbean at an easy distance from the Spanish settlements'.[18] The island was vulnerable to enemy assault but also ideally suited for both trade and plunder.

Port Royal quickly became a base for freebooting activities against the Spaniards, attracting disorderly elements from all over the Caribbean. Unlike planting, which entailed a large capital investment and slow returns, privateering had small start-up costs and promised quick riches.[19] By 1663 Jamaica had a fleet of 15 privateers and by 1670 this had increased to over 20 with about 2,000 men.[20] Commentators all agreed that Port Royal's fortunes were founded on the servicing of the privateers' needs and a highly lucrative trade in prize commodities.[21] The Portobello raid of 1668 alone produced plunder worth £75,000 and, as Governor Lynch admitted in 1671, 'scarcely a quarter of what was shipped from the island was of its own growth'.[22] However, there were signs that the limits of growth had been reached and that the Jamaican privateers were 'overfishing', facing rising costs, higher risks and diminishing returns. The trade did not wither away after 1670 when the Treaty of Madrid promised peace and friendship between Spain and England in America but it does seem to have stabilised at a slightly lower level than the peak and other areas of economic activity overtook it in importance.[23]

Port Royal was also strategically placed for contraband trade with the Spanish colonists. Foreigners had long participated in the official Spanish colonial trade shipping on supposedly annual fleets from Seville or Cadiz to Portobello and Vera Cruz, where the goods were exchanged for rich American commodities, mainly bullion. However, profits were eroded by countless difficulties and delays, particularly as the fleets became less regular and high defence costs pushed up charges.[24] The advantages of direct trade, with Jamaica acting as a warehouse in the Caribbean were apparent to sellers and buyers. Suppliers reduced costs considerably (Peter Beckford, a Port Royal merchant, reckoned that direct trade reduced shipping and freight charges to half of what they were with the fleets), which enabled them to increase turnover and profits. The Spanish colonists could purchase goods more cheaply and dispose of their own products more regularly. The mutual attractions proved irresistible and despite the Spanish authorities' persistent refusal to condone the trade, it grew and flourished.[25] Part of the trade was conducted in Jamaica's own island-built sloops, numbering 80 by 1680.[26] Engaged in a dangerous business, the small boats (15–50 tons) were according to Thomas Lynch, 'not like those of England but of a particular build' designed for defence and were heavily armed (6–8 guns) and heavily manned (15–25 men), ensuring that Port Royal had 'abundance of seamen'.[27] Another part of the clandestine trade was conducted in English or colonial ships which called at Port Royal to strengthen crews, take on supplies and secure information.[28] By the 1690s commentators such as John Cary remarked that the attractions of the Jamaican entrepôt had diverted a substantial share of English commerce away from the traditional route to the Indies via Seville and Cadiz.[29]

The contraband trade was carried on mainly underhand in bays and creeks or the smaller towns. The larger, strongly fortified towns of Portobello, Cartagena and Havana were more difficult and risky to penetrate. The one commodity which could open their doors was slaves, for the Spaniards did not pretend to provide them for themselves, so had to turn to a middleman who did. The contractors, or *asientistas*, obtained supplies wherever possible and Jamaica was ideally suited to service them, transport costs being 20 per cent lower than they were from the rival Dutch base at Curaçao. The Royal African Company targeted this market from 1663 when it was first set up and hopes of selling slaves to the Spaniards played a substantial part in state policy towards Jamaica, the king and his brother being major shareholders. By the 1680s, the trade was substantial, the *asiento* kept an agent in Port Royal and the English African Company sold between a quarter and half of its annual supply of slaves to the Spaniards. However, it was a small group of Port Royal merchants who benefited most from these market opportunities. They bought slaves from the African Company, then sold them to the Spaniards, providing their customers with an armed convoy on their return home and accepting payment in the Spanish port. The Spaniards paid 35 per cent extra for this convenience. It was a highly lucrative and relatively safe business which was, as the planter John Helyar remarked, 'a much easier way of making money than making sugar'.[30]

Unfortunately it is impossible to quantify the value of plunder and contraband with any precision. However, their combined importance is clear. It was most obviously reflected in the unusual abundance of cash in Jamaica, which enabled the islanders to use coins as currency, rather than commodities as in other colonies. In 1683, a visitor remarked that 'there was more plenty of running cash proportionately to the number of inhabitants than is in London'.[31] Furthermore, although there are no continuous figures for bullion exports, (bullion was not recorded in local or metropolitan records), scattered estimates suggest that they were considerable. Governor Lord Inchiquin estimated bullion exports at £100,000 in 1690 compared with £88,000 worth of sugar.[32]

Port Royal's commercial success had a substantial impact on Jamaica's economic development. Although outsiders proved reluctant to make the large investment required to plant the interior, Port Royal's merchants and craftsmen patented land with enthusiasm and rather more slowly undertook the expensive work of establishing plantation agriculture.[33] Secondly, the provisioning needs of the town stimulated the development of domestic production and the internal networks of exchange which have been described by Barry Higman and Verene Shepherd.[34] In 1680 the town had almost 3,000 permanent residents, 1,500–2,000 sloopmen and the crews of about 70 visiting ships (staying between 2 and 6 months) to house, supply and entertain; and by all accounts they lived extremely well. This provided a buoyant market for small planters, pen keepers, fishermen, hunters and various other tradesmen.

The very limited amount of space available on the point was reflected in high rents (£60–80 per year for a house, which equalled rents in Cheapside in London, or £1.50 per month for a well-furnished room) and encouraged dense development.[35] F. Hanson remarked '[the town] cannot be enlarged otherwise than what the inhabitants gain by the height of their houses'.[36] Reports indicated that by 1692 there were about 600 brick houses, many four storeys high, roofed with tiles and glazed with sash windows, the only concessions to creolisation being balconies and cookhouses set apart to reduce the heat.[37] There were as many timber houses and huts for the slaves. Glass, tiles, nails and the more sophisticated furnishings were imported, as was some of the stone and marble used in the church, forts and exchange.[38] But the bulk of the necessary materials were obtained locally. In the first decade of settlement some supplies were taken from Spanish Town which had been a large and pleasant town at the English conquest but these were soon supplemented with the good quality stone and excellent timber found in the hinterland.[39] Clay works were set up to produce bricks as well as sugar pots.[40] Wattles, bamboo and lime for building; shingles and thatch for roofing, and firewood were obtained in the island and taken for use on the point. Probate inventories show that by the 1670s the town supported not only craftsmen to build houses and ships but also cabinet makers, silversmiths and comb makers, producing luxury objects from local raw materials as well as mere necessities.[41]

In the seventeenth century 35–50 per cent of income was spent on food and drink, and visitors remarked on the lavish supplies of food and drink in Port Royal.[42] The island imported large quantities of salt meats, cheese, bacon, butter and flour as well as Madeira, wine and brandy, but by the late 1670s, Lord Vaughan reported that the bulk of provisions was locally produced.[43] Port Royal held three markets (one for meat, one for fish, one for fruit and vegetables) every day except Sunday.[44] The inhabitants were supplied with 'good and wholesome meats as beef, mutton, veal, lamb, kid', which seem from the evidence in ships' accounts to have cost about 25 per cent more than in London in nominal terms by the 1680s, but given the widely acknowledged higher wages in Jamaica, meat was significantly cheaper than in London in real terms.[45] Wasteful slaughter by the English in the first years of settlement had depleted the abundant stocks of wild cattle in the 1660s. The price of a cow increased from five shillings to over £12 during the same decade. But new stocks were imported from Cuba and Vaughan reported that thanks to the high-quality pasture, numbers increased and by 1675 the price had fallen to £4 or £5 a head.[46] However, Jamaican supplies continued to be supplemented from nearby islands and livestock, meat and hides were staples in the sloop trade with Cuba and Hispaniola. Taylor considered fresh hog's flesh (wild and tame) to be the best meat found on the island. 'They salt them and smoke them to dry on a barbeque (as we do with herrings in Europe) and afterward pack it up in cabbage leaves and this they call jickt pork which proveth excellent food, will keep and yieldeth a good price at Port Royal'.[47] They were also supplied with large quantities of turtles, which at under half the price of beef was the chief meat for the 'lower sorts' and important for ships' provisions.[48] There were also plenty of fowls – 'turkies, ducks, capers, widgeon, teal, pidgeon, doves, and parratts at a reasonable rate', and daily supplies of a variety of excellent fish, 'sold cheap'.[49]

Taylor echoed other visitors in exclaiming at the island's plentiful range of fresh roots and herbs 'such as we have in Europe but also many others which those parts of Europe never saw': pawpaw, bananas, plantains, pineapples, yams (eaten by many instead of bread) and so on, giving them 'plenty of salading all round the year'.[50] Tobacco was not grown for export, as the price had fallen to a level where it was not regarded as profitable to freight it long distances, but enough was produced to supply the island 'which they spin up in rope like mulch, and then make up into rolls of 25 lb weight'.[51] Another exotic commodity was the cocoa bean with which the islanders made chocolate. When the beans were dry, they ground them very fine, mixed them with sugar, cinnamon, cloves and mace, wet them with wine and made them into cake rolls which they sold at $1 per lb in Jamaica and also exported to London. Taylor reported that after ordering into liquor, chocolate was 'every morning drunk by the luxurious planter and lecherous creolian Amazons [and] in the taverns on Port Royal you shall have about half a pint thereof for a riall'.[52] Apart from the choice fruits that adorned the tables of Port Royal the pastry cooks produced 'cheesecakes, custards, tarts etc as they sold . . . in London'. Indeed, the only thing Taylor found wanting was good, soft bread 'as we in England (through mercies) still enjoy'. They had plentiful sea biscuits (from England) and baked bread daily but 'for want of yeast and by reason of the staleness of the flour tis not comparable to our English bread and yet they sell but two small rolls thereof for a riall'.[53] Most people preferred the fresh cassava bread sold daily in the market. All in all, remarked Taylor, 'they did live with full food tables not wanting anything requisite to satisfy, delight, and please their curious appetites'.[54]

Port Royal was also well supplied with beverages, although fresh water had to be brought from across the harbour as there was none available at the point.

The gentry and merchants drank imported Madeira, wine, beer and brandy but also rum punch, and the others consumed rum punch, killdivile, rapp, perrino (cassava) and mobby (sweet potato), which was locally produced. Taylor remarked on the general hospitality and the custom of keeping a bowl of rum punch ready for visitors at all times. The port had several 'ordinaries', numerous taverns, and punch houses (or 'rather may be fitly called brothel houses'), music houses and one coffee house. Drunkenness was a problem 'by reason of privateers and debauched wild blades which come from hither'. Part of the reason was that there was little room for active recreation in the crowded town and although there was a bull and a bear for sport at the bear garden, billiards, cock fighting, and target shooting, most sociability revolved around the drinking places and very large quantities of alcohol were consumed.[55] Despite the corrective efforts of the magistrates and deterrent measures including stocks, a cage for lock-up and a bridewell, Vaughan bemoaned the damage done by alcohol causing 'disorder, poverty and disease'.[56]

Port Royal's appetites provided a lucrative market for those involved in domestic production and distribution. The 100 or so sloops based at the town carried provisions, firewood and building materials round the coast as well as engaging in fishing, turtling and trading ventures with the Spaniards.[57] The planters of Liguanea, 'the garden of Jamaica', which lay across the harbour from Port Royal on the site of modern Kingston benefited most from the market opportunities. Taylor exclaimed that:

> This is the pleasantest place on all the island being continually plantable green and flourishing for several miles together lying like one Eden, whose trees are always loaden with ripe and delicious fruits, the earth filled with choice herbs and roots and the circumambient air filled with oderous perfumes and the warbling musick of ravishing voices echoing from the slender pipes of ye ambitious nightingale . . . so that here is found most of our European products as well as the variety of American vegetables so that no part in all America can outvie it. For it not only sustains itself with all things pleasant but also sends daily to port plenty of flesh, fowls, fish, herbs, roots and fruits with milk and other quelquechoses.[58]

By 1675 this traffic had led to the growth of a prosperous settlement with about 20 'handsome and very well built' houses, some shops, a tavern and a church. The place was likely to become considerable by reason of the neighbourhood of Port Royal.[59]

But any planter with easy access to the coast and sloop transport could produce for the Port Royal market, possibly supplementing provision farming with hunting, felling timber, quarrying and some small cash crop production (cotton, ginger, etc). In 1684 a map produced by Bochart and Knollis showed 690 plantations on the island, of which 246 produced sugar and 299 were cotton/provision farms.[60] The one surviving census for the parish of St John in 1680 further illustrates the survival of small planters. The consolidating process described in Barbados was taking place and the gulf between rich and poor was widening, with not only economic but also social and political earnings being engrossed by the large planters who could afford to purchase slaves and engage in sugar production. But the small planter had by no means disappeared. The 48 families listed include nine large planters (with 77 per cent of the parish slaves), nine middling planters (with 16 per cent of the slaves) and 30 small planters (most of whom do not appear on the Bochart-Knollis map) with 6 per cent of the parish slaves and an average of two labourers each, producing cotton, provisions, cattle and so on.[61] Much of their output was no doubt produced for internal exchange and Port Royal was the major market. Thus an internal marketing system of planters, carriers and merchants developed and Jamaica did not conform to the trade patterns in classic plantation economies, which were strictly monocultural and export-oriented. The island's colonial economy was diversified and led not only to a wider range of export crops than elsewhere in the English Caribbean but offered opportunities for non-staple producers and the development of a creole economy. The economic determinism which suggests that plantation society is incompatible with a lasting White settler presence seems flawed, and recent work suggests that demographic problems rather than economic constraints should play a central role in explanations of this failure.[62]

What impact did the commercial success of Port Royal have on the metropolitan economy? Most obviously it provided a range of exotic commodities, an important supply of bullion and a demand for manufactured goods for consumption in the island and for sale in Spanish colonial markets. Colonial demand was important not only because of its quantity but also its quality: a more standardised, uniform product market provided opportunities for enhanced labour productivity through increased specialisation, improved techniques and better organisation.[63] Freighting the goods provided a major stimulus to the shipping industry and the economies of the home ports. The difficulties of financing long-distance trade, organising credit networks and securing trust between correspondents separated by the Atlantic Ocean was a major encouragement to devise ways to reduce risk by insurance, more secure paper transactions, better ways to validate reputations and what might be viewed as more modern financial techniques designed for an impersonal commercial world.[64]

Apart from the bullion trade, these effects were common to all branches of colonial trade, but another aspect of Port Royal's development which gave this frontier town a particular importance in the Atlantic World was its role as a gateway for information. Port Royal was a commercial hub where overlapped French, Spanish, Dutch and English interests. French privateers and Dutch smugglers found Port Royal more conveniently located and better equipped than their bases at Tortuga and Curaçao and were in and out of port – as were Spanish merchants and *asiento* agents – in search of slaves.[65] English and colonial ships traded in Spanish, French and Dutch ports and returned with news and information. Jamaica's policy of toleration allowed Jewish merchants with interests in Spanish colonial trade and links to Curaçao and Amsterdam to settle in the 1660s, and the community numbered 200–300 by the 1680s.[66] The town's commercial community had access to a very wide range of economic, social and political information of the type which was eagerly sought in the mother country.

The expansion and restructuring of English overseas commerce in the seventeenth century, buying and selling a much wider range of commodities in new markets beyond Europe, had depended on English merchants viewing the world afresh, having the capacity to look at a whole range of things, people and relationships in new ways and then seizing the opportunities offered. This seems to have inspired a thirst for useful knowledge, reflected in the proliferation of travel narratives and various writings in a commercial spirit of enquiry such as those of William Petty, Charles Davenant, Josiah Child, Nicholas Barbon and Houghton's *Collection for Improvement of Husbandry*, which aimed to provide a comprehensive account of the possibilities presented by trade, reflecting an anxiety to understand the world better so as to profit from it more abundantly. Visitors to Jamaica, like Taylor and Hans Sloane, could report on soils, mountains, river systems, productive potentials of the island and how they were being harnessed, and also those of competing systems with their relative strengths and weaknesses.[67] Merchants and governors reported on markets, prices, consumer preferences and commercial practices. The way in which commentators selected and filtered information for consumption in England had important commercial repercussions and in addition it affected the process of national self-definition by moulding national stereotypes or 'others'. Taylor made the Spaniards 'ambitious, proud, superstitious, lascivious, hypocrits, great thieves, unfaithful and above measure jealous of their wives'. The French of Hispaniola were 'full of compliments but empty of performances, subtle and deceitful yet stout warriors and serious people'.[68] Evidence was provided for national myth making.

How did Port Royal's commercial success founded on its function as gateway to the Spanish empire define its role in England's imperial project? As Daniel Baugh has argued, in the period between the mid-seventeenth century and the mid-eighteenth century imperial policy was directed towards encouraging the growth of maritime and financial sinews of power: a bluewater strategy. The value of empire was seen to derive from maritime commerce rather than territory and dominion, as laid out in a report to the Lords of Trade in 1686:[69]

> It being no more a secret of state now that he hath the greatest force by sea (how little soever his dominions be) hath the greatest opportunity to give law to the rest of the world . . . [and he that] hath the greatest and most constant employment for seamen must be in the hopefullest way of raising the greatest force by sea; and he that is able to find out the happiest and directest course for the promoting of all manner of commerce must pursue the surest and most rational means of giving employment and encouragement to seamen, what things being therefore understood now by our neighbours as well as ourselves; it seems not to be any way avoided [but] we must apply ourselves closely to the same concern . . . to lead a party and make ourselves foremost in this affair of shipping and commerce.[70]

This central preoccupation with commerce and shipping above territory and planting is vividly illustrated in policy towards Jamaica. There was little interest in extending the area under sugar cultivation. Contemporaries were acutely aware that preserving the profitability of any long distance trade was a perilous business. 'All the commodities which have hitherto been planted have been either produced in such gluts or great quantities or spoyled and embased so much in their qualities that they have in a short time become druggs yielding little or no price comparatively to the merchant or planter'.[71]

Those interested in promoting profitable commerce thus felt more concerned to restrict the supply of sugar than to extend it. When the Dutch expanded their sugar planting in the 1660s the English seized Saba and Eustatia and destroyed their infant plantation economies but showed no interest in retaining the land. Similarly, after the second Dutch war they exchanged the plantation colony of Surinam for New York which played an important part in Dutch commercial networks linking North America, Curaçao (the warehouse of contraband) and Amsterdam. Meanwhile, despite the certainty of offending Spain, the restored Charles II decided to retain Jamaica – seized by Cromwell – on the grounds of its strategic location.[72] As the plunder and contraband trades swelled the island's prosperity his decision was vindicated. As gateway to the Spanish empire the island not only played an important part in stimulating trade and shipping but played an absolutely pivotal role in the English Atlantic economy by providing a rich stream of bullion needed to keep the wheels of commerce turning. Although Barbados remained the pre-eminent sugar producer, Jamaica's importance in metropolitan eyes was reflected in defence priorities. Jamaica had the best naval protection, the first permanent naval base in the empire – at Port Royal after the earthquake – and even for a time in the 1680s a standing military force.[73]

Although the planting of Jamaica did not get seriously under way until the 1680s, Port Royal became the largest town in the English Caribbean, and second only to Boston in the English Atlantic. Furthermore, it was the most prosperous. The prosperity was based on its economic function as gateway to the Spanish empire – raiding, and later trading, secured Spanish gold and silver in return for slaves and manufactured goods. Wealth enabled the townspeople to build a miniature London in the tropics and provided both residents and transients with a comfortable, if notoriously debauched, lifestyle. It provided the funds to embark on plantation agriculture in the hinterland: thus the wealth of Jamaica was created out of the profits of Port Royal. And it also provided market opportunities for small planters, sloopmen and hunters, which stimulated the development of a complex network of internal exchange alongside the export economy with its metropolitan focus. The metropolis meanwhile benefited from supplies of plantation products, and above all, bullion, with the accompanying stimulus to trade and navigation and the flow of knowledge and information emerging out of the cultural fusion in the cosmopolitan port, positioned at what was effectively a crossroads between Spanish, French, Dutch and English empires. Port Royal's commercial success in exploiting its strategic location thus fed maritime and financial sinews of power and made it a focal point of seventeenth-century imperial policy making. When in 1692 a terrible earthquake plunged this 'sodom filled with all manner of debauchery' to the bottom of the ocean it punished the wicked but also destroyed a mercantilists' ideal town.

Notes

1. A.O. Exquemelin, *History of the Bucaniers* (London, 1684).
2. National Library of Jamaica (NLJ), MS 105, 'Journal of John Taylor', II, folio 509.
3. British Library (BL), Harlein MS 6,992, folio 19, 'An Account of the Earthquake at Port Royal in Jamaica Written in Two Letters from a Minister of That Place. From on Board the Granada in Port Royal Harbour', 22 June 1692.
4. Historical Society of Pennsylvania (HSP), Philadelphia, *Norris Papers*, I, Joseph to Isaac Norris, 20 June 1692.
5. Ibid., John Pike to brother, 19 June 1692.
6. Examples include, *A Full Account of the Late Dreadful Earthquake at Port Royal in Jamaica* (London, 1692); *A True and Perfect Relation of the Most Sad and Terrible Earthquake at Port Royal in Jamaica* (London, 1692); T. Doolittle, *Earthquakes Explained and Practically Improved . . . Jamaica's Miseries show London's Mercies* (London, 1695).
7. J. Price, 'Economic Function and the Growth of American Port Towns in the Eighteenth Century', *Perspectives in American History* (1974), pp. 121–186.
8. E. Hickeringill, *Jamaica Viewed* (London, 1661), p. 35.
9. For discussion of the census taken in Barbados in 1680 and comparison with the Port Royal census of the same year, see R. Dunn, *Sugar and Slaves: The Rise of the Planter Class in the English West Indies, 1624–1713* (Chapel Hill: North Carolina Press, 1972).
10. N. Zahedieh, 'Trade, Plunder and Economic Development in early English Jamaica, 1655–89', *Economic History Review*, 2nd ser., XXXIX (1986), pp. 205–22.
11. NLJ, MS 105, 'Journal of John Taylor', II, folios 500, 506.
12. Zahedieh, 'Trade, Plunder'.
13. Public Record Office, London (PRO) CO 138/1, folios 107–11, 'List of What Vessels Arrived in Port Royal, 1668–70'; CO 142/13, Naval Officers Returns, Jamaica, 1680–1705.
14. D. Eltis, 'New Estimates of Exports from Barbados and Jamaica, 1665–1701', *William and Mary Quarterly*, 3rd ser., LII (1995), pp. 637–48.
15. PRO CO 138/2, folio 117, 'State of Jamaica', 1675.
16. Hickeringill, *Jamaica Viewed*, p. 16.
17. R.D. Hussey, 'Spanish Reaction to Spanish Aggression in the Caribbean to about 1680', *Hispanic American Historical Review*, IX (1929), pp. 286–302; V. Barbour, 'Privateers and Pirates in the West Indies', *American Historical Review*, XVI (1911), pp. 526–66; K.R. Andrews, *The Spanish Caribbean: Trade and Plunder, 1530–1630* (New Haven: Yale University Press, 1978).

18. *House of Lords Journals*, XVII, p. 510, Report of Admiralty Papers Relating to Vice-Admiral Greydon, 25 March 1603.

19. Zahedieh, "A Frugal, Prudential and Hopeful Trade": Privateering in Jamaica, 1655–89', *Journal of Imperial and Commonwealth History*, 18 (1990), pp. 145–68.

20. BL Add. MS 11,410, folio 10, 'An Account of the Private Ships of War Belonging to Jamaica and Tortudos in 1663'; PRO CO 138/1, folio 105, 'A List of the Ships under the Command of Admiral Morgan', 1670.

21. PRO CO 1/23, folio 191, Richard Browne to Joseph Williamson, 17 December 1688; WAM, 11913, Sir James Modyford to Sir Andrew King, 27 December 1667.

22. PRO CO 140/1, folio 9, Thomas Lynch to Joseph Williamson, 16 June 1672.

23. Zahedieh, 'A Frugal, Prudential and Hopeful Trade'.

24. C.H. Haring, *Trade and Navigation between Spain and the Indies in the Time of the Hapsburgs* (Cambridge: Harvard University Press, 1918); J.O. MacLachlan, *Trade and Peace with Old Spain, 1667–1750: A Study of the First Half of the Eighteenth Century* (Cambridge: Cambridge University Press, 1940).

25. PRO CO 138/3, folio 407, Council of Jamaica to Lords of Trade, January 1680. N. Zahedieh, 'The Merchants of Port Royal Jamaica and the Spanish Contraband Trade, 1655–1692', *William and Mary Quarterly*, 3rd ser., (1986), pp. 570–93.

26. PRO CO 1/43, folio 59, 'Memorandum given in by the Naval Officer', 25 March 1679.

27. PRO CO 138/4, folio 115, Thomas Lynch to Jenkins, 6 November 1682.

28. PRO CO 1/43, folio 59, 'Memorandum given in by the Naval Officer', 25 March 1679. For an example of an English ship engaged in Spanish colonial trade see the case of the Cadiz Merchants in PRO HCA 30/664.

29. J. Cary, *An Essay on the State of England in Relation to its Trade* (Bristol, 1865), pp. 115–16.

30. Somerset Record Office, Taunton (SR), Helyar MS DD/WHL 1089, John to William Helyar, 16 September 1688. For extended discussion of the trade see Zahedieh, 'Merchants of Port Royal'.

31. F. Hanson, ed., *The Laws of Jamaica* (London, 1683), Introduction.

32. PRO CO 138/7, folio 19, Lord Inchiquin to Lords of Trade, 12 August 1691.

33. Zahedieh, 'Trade, Plunder'.

34. B.W. Higman, 'Jamaican Port Towns in the Early Nineteenth Century', in F.W. Knight and P.K. Liss, eds., *Atlantic Port Cities: Economy, Culture and Society in the Atlantic World, 1650–1850* (Knoxville: University of Tennessee Press, 1991), pp. 117–48. V.A. Shepherd, 'Livestock and Sugar: Aspects of Jamaica's Agricultural Development from the late Seventeenth to the early

Nineteenth Century', *Historical Journal* 34 (1991), pp. 627–43; Shepherd, 'Trade and Exchange in Jamaica in the Period of Slavery', in H. McD. Beckles and Shepherd (eds.), *Caribbean Slave Society and Economy* (Kingston: Ian Randle Publishers, 1991), pp. 111–19.

35. NLJ, MS 105, 'Journal of John Taylor', II, folio 492.
36. Hanson, *Laws of Jamaica*, Introduction.
37. NLJ, MS 105, 'Journal of John Taylor', II, folio 492.
38. Zahedieh, 'London and the Colonial Consumer in the late Seventeenth Century', *Economic History Review*, XLVII (1994), pp. 239–61.
39. BL Add. MS 11,410, folio 311, 'Jamaica Surveyed by Sir Thomas Modyford', 1663.
40. BL Egerton MS 2,395, folio 512, 'A Brief Survey of Jamaica', 1675.
41. Jamaica Archives, Spanish Town, Jamaica, Inventories, 1686–94, 1B/II/3, I-III.
42. C. Shammas, *The Pre-Industrial Consumer in England and America* (Oxford: Oxford University Press, 1990).
43. NLJ, MS 159, 'History and State of Jamaica under Lord Vaughan, 1679–80', folios 21, 57.
44. NLJ, MS 105, 'Journal of John Taylor', II, folio 492.
45. PRO HCA 15/14, 'Account Book of Swiftsure'; HCA 30/664, 'Account Book of Cadiz Merchant'.
46. NLJ, MS 159, 'History and State of Jamaica under Lord Vaughan, 1679–80', folios 21, 57.
47. NLJ, MS 105, 'Journal of John Taylor', II, folio 336.
48. PRO HCA 15/14, 'Account Book of Swiftsure'; HCA 30/664, 'Account Book of Cadiz Merchant'.
49. NLJ, MS 105, 'Journal of John Taylor', II, folio 500.
50. Ibid., folio 501.
51. Ibid., folio 447.
52. Ibid., folio 452.
53. Ibid., folio 501. The relatively high price of biscuit and bread is confirmed in ships' accounts. In 1681, the Cadiz merchant was supplied with biscuit at 20 shillings per hundredweight in London and 28 shillings per hundredweight in Port Royal. PRO HCA 30/664, 'Account Book of Cadiz Merchant'.
54. NLJ, MS 105, 'Journal of John Taylor', II, folio 501.
55. Ibid., folios 501–4. In 1671 Lynch predicted a steep fall in island revenue as the curtailment of privateering was expected to reduce liquor consumption and tax revenue. BL Add. MS 11,410, folio 382, Thomas Lynch to Earl of Sandwich, 20 August 1671.
56. NLJ MS 159, 'History and Present State of Jamaica', folio 61.
57. PRO CO 1/43, folio 59, 'Memorandum given in by the Naval Officer', 25 March 1679.

58. NLJ, MS 105, 'Journal of John Taylor', II, folios 512–13.

59. NLJ, MS 159, 'History and Present State of Jamaica', folio 50.

60. Dunn, *Sugar and Slaves*, pp. 170–2.

61. PRO CO 1/45, folio 109, 'Census of St John Parish', 1680.

62. T. Burnard, 'A Failed Settler Society: Marriage and Demographic Failure in Early Jamaica', *Journal of Social History* 28 (1994), pp. 63–82.

63. Zahedieh, 'London and the Colonial Consumer'.

64. Zahedieh, 'Overseas Expansion and Trade in the Seventeenth Century', in N. Canny, ed., *Oxford History of the British Empire*, I (Oxford: Oxford University Press, 1988).

65. Stephen Lynch arrested 53 French privateers in the taverns of Port Royal in 1688. PRO CO 138/6 folio 118, The Duke of Albemarle to the Committee of Trade, 11 May 1688. There are frequent references to Dutch ships entering port 'under pretence of want of provision', e.g. IJ, MS 105, 'Journal of John Taylor', II, folio 632.

66. PRO CO 1/27 folio 167, Lynch to Arlington, 17 December 1671; CO 138/7 folio 34, 'President and Council of Jamaica to Committee of Trade', 28 January 1691.

67. H. Sloane, *A Voyage to the Islands Madeira, Barbados, Nieves, St Christophers and Jamaica* (London, 1707).

68. NLJ, MS 105, 'Journal of John Taylor', II, folio 685.

69. D.A. Baugh, 'Maritime Strength and Atlantic Commerce. The Uses of a "Grand Marine Empire"', in L. Stone, ed., *An Imperial State at War. Britain from 1689 to 1815* (London: Routledge, 1994), pp. 185–223.

70. Bodleian Library, Oxford MS Rawl, A 478, folios 65–72, 'Advantages of Trading with Our Plantations'.

71. Ibid.

72. A.P. Thornton, *West India Policy Under the Restoration* (Oxford: Clarendon Press 1956).

73. M. Pawson and D. Buisseret, *Port Royal, Jamaica* (Oxford: Clarendon Press 1975).

CHAPTER

2

Slavery and Cotton Culture in the Bahamas*

GAIL SAUNDERS

*A*s a number of historians have demonstrated, work was central in the slaves' experience. Slavery was 'first and foremost an institution of coerced labour'.[1] Until the conference 'Cultivation and Culture: Labour and the Shaping of Slave Life in the Americas' and subsequent publications[2] emanating from it, scholars writing on slavery in North America traditionally emphasised links between the staple and the White society, the economy and mentality, but gave little attention to work and the slave society and how it shaped the lives of slaves. This was not the case for the British Caribbean as is evidenced by the work of Sidney Mintz and Douglas Hall, Barry Higman, Woodville Marshall and Michael Craton, among others.[3]

However, historians traditionally concentrated on analysing the slave domestic economy and labour on sugar plantations or sugar production. Recently there has been an effort to examine non-sugar activities and non-plantation or marginal colonies.[4]

As Higman has argued in his thorough and comprehensive study *Slave Populations of the British Caribbean*, slavery in the British Caribbean and the Americas in general 'took a variety of characteristic forms, dependent on the type of economic activity in which the slaves were employed'. He found that the material conditions of slave populations living on sugar estates were similar and were characterised by high mortality and a failure to show natural increase. On the other hand 'material conditions' of the life of slaves 'associated with coffee, cotton, cocoa, pimento, and provisions plantations, as well as wood-cutting and salt-raking, each took on a characteristic form associated with typical patterns of demographic structure and natural increase'.[5]

This chapter will examine the lives of Bahamian slaves who were involved in the growing of cotton between 1783 and 1834. It will describe how cotton was grown in the Bahamas, and how labour was organised. An attempt will be made to analyse how cotton production and its failure as a staple shaped slave life and labour in the Bahamas.

The Bahamas, like Belize, was not a true plantation colony. It never grew sugar commercially. Before the coming of the United States (US) Loyalists and their slaves to the Bahamas between 1783 and 1785, the inhabitants were principally occupied in sea-faring activities such as fishing, wrecking and turtling. They also engaged in woodcutting, mainly dye woods and other varieties such as mahogany, madeira and box wood. There was no staple crop and very little agriculture. Subsistence crops such as guinea corn, peas, beans, potatoes, yams, plantains and bananas were grown. Salt was also raked but was mainly for local consumption.[6]

Planter Loyalists who settled with the slaves mainly in the south and southeastern islands introduced the growing of cotton on a commercial scale. The crop had been planted, but in small quantities by the old inhabitants. Between 1784 and 1785 many cotton plantations were established and by November 1785, 2,476 acres of cotton were under cultivation.[7]

Initially, it seemed as though the hopes of the Loyalists would be realised. In 1785, the Bahamas produced 124 tons of cotton from 2,476 acres. During the following two years, 150 and 219 tons were produced from 3,050 and 4,500 acres respectively. Hopes were high for 1788 when 394 tons were expected from 8,000 acres. However, only 122 tons were actually produced, the remaining 282 tons being almost completely destroyed by the chenille and red bugs.[8] Despite these losses cotton production continued. In 1790, for example, 4,160 bales were exported from the ports of Nassau and Exuma, weighing 442 tons. There was an increase in 1791 when 5,163 bales were exported weighing 492 tons.[9]

Table 2.1   A Return of Sundry Articles: The production of these Islands exported from the port of Nassau to His Majesty's colonies in North America, and the United States of America, in British and Foreign vessels from the year 1794 to 1805 inclusive

Year	Lignum Vitae (tons)	Mahogany (feet)	Brazilletto (tons)	Cotton (lb)	Hides	Eleuthera Bark
1794	52½	25,700	½	3,000	224	0
1795	458	4,220	½	600	666	0
1796	756	7,724	¼	1,200	540	0
1797	277	5,380	¾	1,800	424	0
1798	1,188	700	0	0	0	0
1799	120	8,306	0	0	56	0
1800	898	1,040	0	0	200	0
1801	673	2,000	1½	600	358	0
1802	301	0	0	1,500	0	0
1803	147¼	500	0	0	0	17,309
1804	427	0	½	600	0	2,650
1805	267	12,000	0	0	0	5,900

Source: Nassau Naval Office, 5 February 1807, CO/23/51 Folio 47

However, in 1794, the chenille attacked the cotton crops of the Bahamas again and two-thirds of the cotton crop was destroyed. Four years later in 1798, cotton bugs almost totally demolished the crop and between 1794 and 1805 cotton exports were seriously diminished (see Table 2.1).[10]

Daniel McKinnen, a British traveller, noted that although the Caicos Islands, then a part of the Bahamas, had the best soil and cotton was still a staple in 1803, on most of the southern islands cotton production had declined. Of Crooked Island, where the Loyalists had settled and established about 40 plantations and planted over 2,000 acres of cotton, McKinnen states: 'I beheld some extensive fields originally planted with cotton, but which from the failure of crops were now abandoned, and had become covered with a luxuriant growth of indigenous shrubs and plants . . . I found the plantations of Crooked Island for the most part deserted.[11]

It was evident that cotton as a staple crop was a failure, although statistics show that more cotton was produced in 1809 and 1810 than in any average year between 1789 and 1799.[12] It is therefore difficult to say exactly when the decline of cotton finally set in. By 1800, however, most of the cotton planters were facing ruin. The searching questionnaire sent out to 25 of the leading cotton growers in that year by the Bahamas Government in order to determine the causes of the failure attests to this. Most attributed the decline of cotton to the exhausted state of the soil, the inexperience of the planters and injudicious planting, the attacks of the chenille and red bug, bad management and the climate.[13]

There is a dearth of literature on cotton production and until recently the work routine of slaves in the Bahamas. According to a House of Assembly report in 1826, few planters were capable of keeping records. Additionally, a large number of plantations were supervised by free people of colour and also slaves who were mostly illiterate.[14] In the absence of slave testimonies, it is necessary to depend solely on the owners' points of view. Only one journal of a Bahamian plantation has survived, as far as can be ascertained, and this only records happenings for 1831 and 1832,[15] years immediately before emancipation when cotton cultivation had drastically declined and was then 'little more than a nominal article of export'.[16]

Cotton cultivation in the late eighteenth and early nineteenth centuries was dependent on slave labour. Its production dictated the work routines of slaves, at least for a short period. One of the first tasks of the slaves was to clear the land and prepare it for cultivation. The Loyalists and their slaves established extensive cotton plantations, most on islands which had not been settled, or very sparsely so. Establishing new plantations was rigorous work. After the trees were felled and bushes cleared, the stumps and undergrowth were burnt until the field was cleared for planting. This slash-and-burn method, still used in the Bahamas today, destroyed much vegetable substance which might have been converted into excellent top soil. Besides destroying much of the mineral content of the soil, the use of manure was hardly employed, being a scarce commodity owing to the shortage of cattle.[17] William Wylly, Attorney-General, and a slave-owner,[18] complained that many of the fields laid out were too large and often not sheltered, which left the cotton plants exposed to winds. Margins were made around the fields and were often used by slaves as shelters from the sun and for cooking.

The soil in the fields was then hoed, a tedious job using primitive hand tools. Shallow holes were dug probably with a dibble stick and seven or eight seeds planted in each hole. Planting was done in rows leaving a space between each row varying from six to eight feet. Seeds were usually planted about four feet apart. Indian corn was usually cultivated between the rows of cotton. Planting took place in March and between May and September and cotton crops were harvested between seven and ten months after planting. There was usually a winter and a spring crop. Two major types of cotton were planted in the Bahamas, with seed from Anguilla and the Georgia Sea Islands. Anguilla cotton could not withstand the 'wet season' or the 'cold winds'. Georgia cotton, which was introduced later, was found to be hardier and more easily managed.[19]

In the early stages of growth, the cotton plants required close attention. Usually there were at least two weedings when all available slaves would be employed. When the plants were about eight inches high they were thinned out, leaving two of the best plants. At a height of about two feet, the cotton plants were pruned. Between three and four inches were lopped from the top; 'the extremities must be pinched off, which will force the fruit'.[20]

Cotton plants blossomed at the end of five months and formed a pod two months later. From then until the tenth month the pods ripened and burst open in three partitions displaying the cotton wool which was then gathered by hand.[21] Harvesting of cotton usually took place in January or February or March, but as all cotton did not mature at one time, gathering continued with occasional intervals to July. Charles Farquharson records in his journal that on 29 June 1831 his slaves had 'finished gathering this year's crop'. However, they were also employed in picking the lighter crop known as 'spring' cotton, referred to in the journal as 'one-one cotton'.[22]

Picking cotton was 'hard and distasteful work'.[23] On US plantations quotas had to be met. In the Bahamas, planters were anxious to gather the cotton before the rainy season. All field slaves were employed in the picking of cotton on large plantations, while on smaller estates 'all hands' were used at harvest time.[24] Shoulder baskets made of straw or cloth were probably used in the picking of cotton. It was taken from the fields either by the slaves or by horse or mule to the barns where it was stored.

The cotton was then ginned whereby the seeds were removed from the wool either by hand or by a machine. Ginning cotton required few skilled workers and unlike sugar processing, was a relatively simple operation. Before the invention of Joseph Eve's gin in about 1790,[25] a simple foot gin was used. It comprised two small rollers placed close and parallel to one another in a frame and was turned in opposite directions by different wheels which were moved by foot. The cotton was placed by hand on the rollers spiked with nails as they moved round, readily passing between them and leaving the seeds which were too large to pass through. After this process the wool was hand-picked to rid it of decayed leaves, broken seeds and damaged wool. The cotton was then packed into bales of about 200 lb and shipped to Nassau from where it was exported.

Eve's gin was a modified version of the foot gin but was turned by wind, horse, cattle or water power if there was an inlet. While it was estimated that the common gin could clean 25–40 lb of cotton in one day, Eve's gin cleaned 80–100 lb of cotton in the same time. Some plantations could gin as much as 360 lb of cotton in one day.

Besides increasing production and saving valuable time and money, Eve's gin made it unnecessary to hand-pick cotton. It also meant that the cotton was stored for brief periods, making it less exposed to dangers of rodents and other pests. Additionally, Eve's gin was less taxing on the slaves. It was said that the common gin was 'apt to rupture negroes'.

A planter, Alexander Drysdale, who used Eve's wind gin on both of his estates, congratulated Eve: 'Preparing our cotton for Market was formerly considered as the most tedious, troublesome and laborious part of the agricultural process in this country. To you we are indebted for its having been pleasant, easy and expeditious'.[26]

Wylly informed the House of Assembly in 1795 that the: 'use of this ingenious invention is equivalent to the labour of at least eight Negroes . . . it is certain that this machine attended only by two men will clean more cotton and do it in a more effectual manner than what was usually accomplished by ten negroes with the common foot Gin'.[27]

As Craton demonstrated, cotton production even before the introduction of Eve's gin 'was far less labour intensive than sugar'.[28] Sugar cultivation was a highly capitalised industry, being both an agricultural and manufacturing enterprise. A factory was necessary and it needed raw materials, that is, the sugar-cane. Large areas of land had to be planted, requiring a large labour force, some of which needed to be highly skilled in order to grow and process sugar. Sugar required one slave for every two acres as compared to one slave for five or six acres of cotton.[29]

The essential difference between cotton and sugar production was the nature of the economic system in which the slaves who were employed in the production of sugar on British Caribbean plantations were usually worked in gangs, while those who laboured on cotton plantations in the Bahamas were employed mostly by the task system. As Morgan argued, there were parallels in the experience of the Caribbean plantation and the Low-Country rice economy. In the British Caribbean, as Higman demonstrated, coffee and pimento, crops that required little supervision or regimentation, were like rice, grown by slave labour force organised by tasks rather than in gangs.[30]

It may be conjectured from Morgan's findings that the slaves who were brought by the Loyalists from the Carolinas and Georgia were already accustomed to the task system. As Morgan demonstrated, the task system by the late eighteenth century had taken deep root in the Low-Countries. The task system employed in rice cultivation was extended to the cultivation of sea island cotton.[31] Tasking became a way of life in the antebellum Low-Country.

Slave owners in the Bahamas claimed that task work as a system of labour was all they remembered. It was used to employ all slaves except those employed as domestics, sailors, trades people or in salt production. At the time of the abolition, Howard Johnson contends that salt production continued to be profitable in the closing years of slavery; it was only in the salt-producing areas that gang labour was employed on a regular basis.[32] Wylly, answering to a committee of the House of Assembly in 1815, stated: 'and whenever the nature of the work will admit of it, our Negroes are regularly tasked. The tasks are one fourth of an acre in extent, they are usually marked out by permanent stations in every field, and two, three, sometimes four slaves (but in general more than one) are put into each Task, at the discretion of the Driver according to the actual state of the fields'.[33]

From the available evidence and the frequent references to the taskable negroes, it seems that the task system predominated although gang labour was also employed. McKinnen graphically described the task system:

> Their labour is allotted to them daily and individually, according to their strength; and if they are so diligent as to have finished it at an early hour, the rest of the day is allowed to them for amusement or their private concerns. The master also frequently superintends them himself; and therefore it rarely happens that they are so much subject to the discipline of the whip as where gangs are large, and directed by agents or overseers.[34]

Gang labour was usually employed at planting, hoeing, thinning phases and harvesting times and slaves were rewarded with extra time. Wylly informed members of the House of Assembly that 'in seed time and Harvest when it would hardly be possible to assign set Tasks, they are allowed one Hour at Breakfast and two Hours at Dinner'.[35]

Farquharson seemed to have employed the gang system on his plantation. However he also rewarded his slaves for extra labour. On Saturday, 9 July 1831, he 'employed in the same way as above (weeding) one part of the gang and the other part has today to themselves having gained a day this week by extra work'.[36]

While positive incentives were offered, some coercion by owners or drivers must have been practised. But, according to Wylly, the whip was rarely used in the field. Whippings, however, were inflicted as punishment for disobedience and misdemeanour at the whipping post. Whipping was in fact the most common form of punishment for minor offences. The cowskin and cat-o-nine-tails were used in the Work House in Nassau and were probably employed on some Out Island plantations, but by 1815 the use of the cowskin had been prohibited. The cartwhip employed in the sugar colonies apparently was not used in the Bahamas.[37] Slaves also suffered confinement in the stocks for theft and disobedience, as evidenced by the publicised case of 'Poor Black Kate' in 1826.[38]

Drivers, who were chosen for reliability and loyalty, holding the highest post of the field slaves, administered punishments but were not as significant in the Bahamas as in the sugar colonies. At emancipation there were 80 drivers out of a total slave population of 10,002, representing only about 0.8 per cent of the total. In contrast, Jamaica had 14,043 head people (praedial attached), that is, those employed on lands belonging to owners and attached to the soil), listed in 1834, comprising 4.51 per cent of the total slave population.[39]

The importance of the driver varied from plantation to plantation. In the Bahamas slave-holdings were generally small. Nearly 75 per cent of slaves lived in slave-holding units of 50 or less.[40] Very often plantation owners oversaw the slaves themselves. Charles Farquharson, for example, who in 1834 had 52 slaves along with his son James, seemed to have supervised the work himself. No driver is listed for his estate.[41] On the other hand, at the Wylly plantation at Clifton in New Providence in 1818, there was a driver called Boatswain, and an underdriver, Jack, both Africans, who supervised the slaves. Boatswain was literate[42] which was very rare for a slave, and was instructed to read the prayers to the slaves on the plantation every Sunday. He was also paid a fee for teaching the slaves to read but was 'not to be paid for more than ten pupils in any one year'. Moreover, Boatswain and Jack were paid an allowance of 12 guineas a year for being drivers and additionally they were given 'a brood mare each, for the purpose of enabling them the more frequently and expeditiously to ride over the pasture grounds and other lands'.[43]

Just how many hours owners or drivers got slaves to work a year is difficult to determine. As Higman has demonstrated, it depended on a variety of factors including the type of plantation, the length of the crop season, the size of slave-holding, the use of the task system, existence of provision ground system and 'the sex, age and strength of the slaves themselves'.[44] Slave owners in the Bahamas in defending slave conditions there and protesting ameliorative measures in 1823, stated that their slaves were not overworked, rarely working over seven or eight hours.[45] In view of the system of task work and the serious decline of cotton this might have been the case, especially out of the planting and harvesting season. In 1815, Wylly informed the House of Assembly that it rarely happens that the setting sun ever leaves a negro in our Fields'.[46]

Daily routines for slaves varied according to the season and occupations changed to suit the job at hand. At the Farquharson estate, for example, when cotton was harvested, 'all hands' in gangs were usually employed. In February 1831, Farquharson devoted 11 days solely to the gathering of cotton. On some days cotton was gathered half of the day and corn picked during the other half. Other days were employed in weeding, planting, heaping and burning bush and hand-picking cotton.[47]

As Higman has demonstrated, field labourers on all types of plantations were involved in a variety of tasks in the out-of-crop season.[48] This was evident at the Farquharson estate and at Wylly's Clifton plantation and in view of the decline of cotton, was probably generally practised throughout the Bahamas. As Wylly informed the members of the House of Assembly in January 1823:

> A crop of cotton, or provisions being raised, or a few small cargoes of cedar or dye woods cut from the woods, the slaves are frequently sent, for the season, to rake and manufacture salt at the ponds; from thence they are, in due time, called back to the fields, the provision grounds, or the orchards or gardens, where fruits are raised for exportation. The produce has next to be taken to market; and a portion of the same gang become sailors for the occasion; and at other times, through the year, fishermen, wreckers . . . and even domestic servants, to attend to the business of their master's house, his cattle and other stock, for use, or for consumption or sale. Thus, with all the varieties of season and casualty, the nature of the Bahama negro's occupation changes . . .[49]

Gender division

Similarly to pen slaves on Jamaican plantations involved in driving cattle and horsekind to and from estates, Bahamian slaves were generally allowed a great deal of mobility.[50] Their occupations changed not only according to the season, but also according to age.[51] For example, among Black males, approximately 40 per cent after the age of ten worked in the field all their life until they became sick, disabled or simply too old. However, between the ages of 11 and 15, 55 per cent were in the field, but between 16 and 24 years of age, only 43 per cent. Between ages 16 and 24, about 12 per cent left the field for another occupation, probably salt production, seafaring activities or the trades.[52]

Slave-owners did not discriminate by sex, but by colour as far as female field labour was concerned. In 1834 there were nearly as many field labourers as males (see Table 2.2).[53] Among Black female slaves, about 45 per cent after the age of ten worked in the field all their life. Among Coloured females 50 per cent worked as domestics all their lives. Black slave women at their peak, that is between the ages of 16 and 39, usually worked in the field. Female slaves, as in Jamaica and the plantations in the US South,[54] were considered

Table 2.2   Occupational Distribution by Sex and Colour whole Bahamas 1834

Occupation	Black	Males Mulatto	Total	Black	Females Mulatto	Total	Grand Total
Nil	1,049	180	1,229	1,113	192	1,305	2,534
Domestic	370	58	428	1,394	181	1,575	2,003
Field	1,682	96	1,778	1,622	100	1,722	3,500
Mariner	528	57	585	–	–	–	585
Salt	496	42	538	354	26	380	918
Driver/Overseer	74	5	79	1	–	1	80
Nurse/Midwife	12	2	14	71	9	80	94
Trade/Craft	228	18	246	15	2	17	263
Sundry	8	–	8	3	–	3	11
Unknown	9	–	9	5	–	5	14
Total	4,456	458	4,914	4,578	510	5,083	10,002

Source: Calculated from RRS 1834

as valuable or more so than the slave men as far as cotton production was concerned. Farquharson employed women in every phase of the growing of cotton. McKinnen in his travels throughout the Bahamas witnessed a scene in Acklins:

> I amused myself in passing over the shrubberies at the time of gathering in the crop, which was performed with much more dexterity by the women than the men, although their utmost exertions were stimulated and put forth by the hope of a reward. One lusty female slave, with a child upon her back, gathered in between forty and fifty pounds for each day's work. [55]

Diversification

The decline of cotton and the failure to replace it with a staple caused Bahamian slave-owners to diversify. Many turned to developing salt production. Some turned to stock raising and the growing of ground provisions. Many estates became little more than subsistence farms by the end of slavery. These developments obviously affected the intensity of labour and occupational distribution in the Bahamas. Slaves were usually underemployed. At Emancipation just over half (55 per cent) of its slaves were employed in field work as compared with several sugar colonies, including Jamaica and Barbados which registered 73.3 and 70.8 per cent respectively.[56] The Bahamas' low percentage of praedial tradesmen and head people and its high percentage of slaves involved in domestic work, in shipping and working around the wharves reflected a decayed plantation system and the absence of sugar (see Table 2.3).

These economic conditions and the employment of the task system (used earlier in cotton production), as Morgan demonstrated, allowed 'the slaves a certain latitude to apportion his own day, to work intensively at this task and then have the balance of his time'.[57] If slaves completed their work by mid-afternoon they had 'leisure time to cultivate for themselves tend their stock or amuse themselves'. Although tasking could be onerous and fast-paced it had the advantage of allowing slaves some flexibility in determining the length of the work day. As Michel Rolph Trouillot stated, of 'slaves employed in the cotton era production slaves routinely used the task system to shorten the length of time spent in their masters' fields'.[58]

Slaves who worked by tasks in the Low-Country region of South Carolina and Georgia and in the Bahamas, had much time to work for themselves.

Table 2.3   Comparative Occupations in Seven British West Indian Colonies, 1834

Occupation (1 August 1834)

Praedial attached	Jamaica	Barbados	Trinidad	Antigua	Grenada	Tobago	Bahamas
Head People	14,043	1,963	1,100	593	1,164	209	68
Tradesmen	11.244	1,821	345	990	741	350	0
Inferior Tradesmen	2,635	784	333	306	278	248	0
Field Labourers	107,053	27,693	8,018	11.250	8,649	3,734	2,688
Inferior Field Labourers	63,923	15,615	2,488	6,502	5,728	3,567	1,280
Praedial unattached							
Head People	1,329	32	86	9	10	6	3
Tradesmen	1,133	224	51	39	21	5	0
Inferior Tradesmen	322	163	34	10	10	5	0
Field Labourers	11,670	2,330	1,101	472	214	74	184
Inferior Field Labourers	5,104	1,568	357	197	125	68	73
Non Praedial							
Head Tradesmen	1,759	391	92	252	95	40	162
Inferior Tradesmen	780	408	220	215	125	19	48
Head people on wharves, shipping, etc.	1,428	64	59	80	28	66	459
Inferior people on wharves, shipping, etc.	901	1,071	133	203	498	55	321
Head Domestic servants	12,883	3,816	1,678	303	350	316	1,264
Inferior Domestic servants	19,083	8,695	1,584	1,929	975	316	1,186
Children under 6 years at 1/3/1834							
Ages, diseased or otherwise non-effective	15,692	1,780	872	1,444	1,309	1,032	293
Runaway	1,075	–	–	–	–	–	–
Total	311,070	83,150	20,757	29,121	23,640	11,589	9,995

Source: T/71/851; R.M. Martin, *Colonies of the British Empire* (London, 1843)

Slaves in the Bahamas used their spare time to farm plots of land on which to grow their own provisions and to tend their animals. Some, who lived in New Providence, also had time to attend the Saturday market in Nassau and to accumulate cash. Similar to that in the Low-Country and British Caribbean colonies, a significant internal economy developed. Enslavers in the Bahamas and in the Caribbean generally were either by custom or law pledged to provide for their slaves. Certain provisions and clothing and other necessities had to be given to the slaves. To supplement the provisions, slave owners often gave their slaves extra rations. For example, Farquharson at Christmas 1832 gave each of the 'grown hands' 4 lb of pork, 4 lb of beef, a bottle of rum and 'a large cup full of sugar'. Children received half-rations of meat and sugar. Additionally, Farquharson gave his slaves 'half a sheep and 2 flasks of rum to make them a super (sic)' at the end of the corn crop. In the same year they also received the meat of two cows, one in February and the other in August.[59] Slave-owners also allowed slaves plots of land on which to grow their own provisions.[60]

The provision ground system which by the early nineteenth century was such an integral part of the Jamaican and indeed the Caribbean domestic economic system for the slaves, probably developed in the Bahamas in the latter part of the eighteenth century. No clauses relating to provision grounds appear in the early eighteenth century slave regulations. In fact, the early beginnings of the provision ground system remained obscure.[61]

However, an Act in 1767 forbade slaves to plant except on the land of their owners. This indicated that slaves in the Bahamas were accustomed to organising and planting their provision grounds.[62] By 1796 slaves, in addition to being given 'sufficient provisions' and 'proper clothing', were also given a 'sufficient quantity of land' in order to grow their own provisions. A later Act in 1824[63] reiterated this demand.

As Johnson has argued, after the collapse of cotton, the slaves 'were left with more time for productive labour of their own grounds' and the slave owners, faced with the problem of maintaining an increasing 'underemployed labour force', were 'willing to shift the burden of slave maintenance to the provision grounds since there was no crop of comparable commercial importance to replace cotton'.[64]

There is evidence that some slave-owners in the Bahamas allowed provision grounds on their plantations. Wylly, for example, directed that on his plantations at Clifton and Tusculum, 'sufficient land is set apart for the use of the people, and half an Acre is annexed to each house as the property of the occupant for time being; separate pastures are allotted for their hogs; and each head of a family is permitted to keep one sow.' This regulation seems to have been carried out. Wylly's slaves at Clifton were given two days to work on their own grounds. Each man and his 'wife' were expected to plant two acres of provisions. Wylly claimed the right to purchase 'all hogs, pigs, poultry, and eggs which the people might have for sale, and for which he is to pay Nassau prices; to be fixed by the drivers and two other men chosen by the seller'. The slaves were allowed Saturdays to take their produce, pigs and poultry, sometimes using Wylly's boat, to the Nassau market where they bartered their produce for rum by paying in corn and in cash. For work such as wall-building done on his plantations in their own time, slaves could accumulate cash.[65]

As Mintz and Marshall demonstrated, the provision ground and internal marketing systems provided the slaves latitude to participate in independent activities. Slaves 'pushed hard' to 'establish and expand' the right to produce and market independently. They also attempted to exploit their positions, creating 'intense competition' between themselves and plantation owners and managers for labour services and land resources.[66]

Nassau was the main market for slaves in New Providence and the nearby islands. Slaves, in competition with White farmers, also sold foodstuffs to local residents and 'crews of incoming ships'. On the more isolated Out Islands, slaves had intermittent opportunities to participate in the market economy. However, in some islands, it seems that local markets existed to sell products of the slaves' provision grounds.[67]

The provision ground system was particularly important in Exuma. Lord John Rolle,[68] an absentee slave master, owned five plantations at Exuma. Because of the rapid increase in the slave population and falling profits brought by the collapse of cotton, he allowed his slaves to their own provision grounds in order to provide for their families. They grew peas, beans and corn and owned poultry and some pigs. When they were given notice that they would be moved to Cat Island they objected and subsequently staged a revolt led by Pompey, a 38-year-old Black creole. Despite the fact that they were given three days to pick their crops and dispose of their animals, they resisted, not wishing to leave their provision grounds. Notice was too short; their fields were under cultivation and they wished to pick their peas and beans, thrash and pack them. The slaves also feared that their poultry would die 'if they were put on board a crowded vessel tied together'.[69]

   This act of resistance was significant as it underlined the prevailing opinion in the Bahamas that the Rolle slaves 'labour chiefly applied to their private benefit while the expense of their maintenance etc. was supplied by Lord Rolle'.[70] With no agricultural staple and a surplus labour force, the practice of the slaves maintaining themselves became common throughout the Bahamas in the closing years of slavery.[71] Despite the fact that the slaves earlier had been offered money for their crops and would have been allowed to either sell their hogs and fowls or carry them with them, if they agreed to be moved, they refused. Slave participation in the market economy support Craton's argument that 'the transition from "protopeasant" to true peasant . . . was probably more advanced in Exuma and similar Bahamian islands than any where in the British colonies'.[72]

   The Rolle and Wylly examples do not prove conclusively that the provision ground and internal marketing were systems generally employed throughout the Bahamas. However, the decayed plantation system and dire economic conditions may have encouraged the use of the system operated primarily to the slave owners' advantage. At the Farquharson estate at Watlings Island, 'Negro Ground' is referred to and there was usually a garden around each house.[73] But according to the *Journal*, slaves worked six days a week with only Sundays off. There is no indication that they used their day off to farm for themselves. Farquharson's estate, an owner-controlled plantation, therefore differed from the Rolle holdings where slaves were under the charge of a single overseer and left increasingly to their own devices.

   As Johnson argued, the decline of cotton as an export staple had implications for labour routines and the labour systems employed. The collapsed plantation system made for changes and the 'restructuring of the relationships between slaves and their owners'.[74] By the time of full Emancipation, labour tenancy and share-cropping had been adopted in the transition from slavery to free labour in the Bahamas.[75] Labour tenancy, adopted by 1828, allowed African apprentices and slaves to cultivate a plot of land for their own support and maintenance for two and a half days a week. For the remainder of the week they were expected to work for their owners. Share-cropping, introduced during the apprenticeship period, involved the apprentices making voluntary agreements to remain on the former proprietor's estate to work on liberal and beneficial terms. The usual agreement between the proprietors and their tenants was on the share system.

Without a profitable staple crop to replace cotton, and with a surplus of labour, the operation of labour tenancy and share-cropping was found to be a more satisfactory and profitable arrangement for the proprietors than directing the operation of their estates. It was an amicable solution for both the landlords and the tenants. The latter gained access to the land, while the proprietors retained the services of the ex-slaves.[76]

The self-hire-system, as Johnson argued,[77] also emerged in the Bahamas in the late eighteenth century. The collapse of cotton, the absence of an export staple to replace it and agricultural stagnation, led to the under-utilisation of the slave population. The short-lived cotton boom witnessed some redistribution of the slave labour force to cotton-producing islands. However, with the decline of cotton and the plantation system, many owners, especially those in the Out Islands, had difficulty finding work for their slaves who not only had time to tend their provision grounds, but also to hire out their own time. Governor Smyth wrote in 1831, 'many of the slaves pay a monthly sum to their owners to look out for work and employment as they please'.[78] While some slave-owners on the Out Islands, employed their slaves in cultivating foodstuff and raising livestock for the Nassau market, others transferred their under-utilised slaves to Nassau which offered greater opportunities for skilled and unskilled labour to be sold, hired out or permitted to work on the self-hire system.[79] This practice had evolved before the arrival of the American Loyalists.

Many slaves who were transferred preferred to work on the self-hire system. Slaves in the urban areas worked at a variety of tasks. Male slaves on self-hire found employment as stevedores, woodcutting and road building. They also engaged in sea-faring activities. Female slaves on self-hire were employed primarily as domestics and itinerant vendors. By the closing years of slavery 'slaves on the self-hire system dominated the urban scene'.[80] Johnson contends that the self-hire system was advantageous to both owners and slaves. Owners could look forward to cash payments and not have to supervise or supply food, clothing or shelter. Slaves recognised the system as giving them an opportunity to 'exercise extensive control over their lives'.[81] In fact, 'slave owners steadily lost their authority over slaves who were wholly dependent on waged work', and by the end of the eighteenth century 'slaves on self-hire were successfully dictating wage levels in their negotiations with prospective employers'.[82]

Some slaves, after paying 'wages' to their owners and maintaining themselves, probably saved some cash. A number of slaves indulged in leisure activities such as drinking and gambling, to which the ruling elite reacted by tightening up on regulations licensing retailers of spirits and prohibiting gambling.[83] Many slaves purchased their freedom. Higman noted that the manumission rate in the Bahamas between 1808 and 1834 was the highest in the British Caribbean for that period.[84]

Cotton production and the less arduous labour it required, in contrast to the making of sugar, helped to create favourable demographic characteristics in the Bahamian slave population. With the abrupt ending of cotton production on a commercial scale, and the subsequent diversification into salt and stock production and the growing of provisions for the Nassau market, cotton became a marginal product.

Work routines before and after the decline of cotton were organised mainly on the task system. This provided Bahamian slaves in rural areas with spare time to work for themselves. They organised and farmed their own provision grounds and engaged in an internal marketing system which was limited on the more remote Out Islands. Labour tenancy and share-cropping emerged on the Out Islands. In the urban areas, especially in Nassau, slaves hired out their time, dictated their wages and were able to acquire material goods and some cash, forming 'an incipient (and increasingly assertive) proletariat'.[85]

The failure to develop a staple to replace cotton, made for a 'loosening of ties'[86] between the slaves and the staple crop. Slave-owners found alternative methods to employ and extract labour from a steady increasing slave population. In the rural areas, where there was a shift from cotton to the growing of provisions, owners received a 'labour rent' and in the urban setting, a cash payment.[87] Slaves in both settings enjoyed much independence within slavery.

Although slave owners still had some control,[88] slaves 'operated effectively as peasants', insisting on working their own grounds on their own terms for a large part of the day. Their labour relationship with their owners by 1834 had, in Howard Johnson's words, 'moved decisively from a coercive to a contractual one', foreshadowing post-emancipation labour systems.[89]

Notes

*A version of this chapter was given at the conference 'Culture and Cultivation: Labour and the Shaping of Slave Life in the Americas' and published as 'Slave Life,

Slave Society and Cotton Production in the Bahamas', *Slavery and Abolition*, Vol. II, No. 3 (December 1990), pp. 332–50.

1.   I. Berlin and P.D. Morgan, eds., *Cultivation and Culture. Labour and the Shaping of Slave Life in the Americas* (Charlottesville and London: University Press of Virginia, 1993), p. 1. See also D. Hall, 'Slaves and Slavery in the British West Indies', *Social and Economic Studies*, 11 (1962); E. Goveia, *Slave Society in the British Leeward Islands at the end of the Eighteenth Century* (New Haven: Yale University Press 1965); K. Brathwaite, *The Development of Creole Society in Jamaica, 1770–1820* (Oxford: Clarendon Press 1971); B.W. Higman, *Slave Population and Economy in Jamaica, 1807-1834* (Cambridge: Cambridge University Press, 1976).

2.   Ibid. See also Berlin and Morgan, *Slavery and Abolition*, Vol. 12, No. 1, (May 1991), pp. 1–30.

3.   See especially S.W. Mintz and D. Hall, 'The Origins of the Jamaican Internal Marketing System', *Papers in Caribbean Anthropology*, Yale University Publication in Anthropology, No. 57 (New Haven: Yale University Press, 1960); Mintz, *Caribbean Transformations* (Chicago: Aldine, 1974); Higman, *Slave Population and Economy in Jamaica*; Higman, *Slave Populations of the British Caribbean 1807–1834* (Baltimore, MD: The Johns Hopkins University Press, 1984); M. Craton, 'Hobbesian or Panglossian? The Two Extremes of Slave Conditions in the British Caribbean, 1783 to 1834', *William and Mary Quarterly*, 35 (1978), pp. 324–56; Craton, *Searching for the Invisible Man: Slaves and Plantation Life in Jamaica* (Cambridge MA: Harvard University Press, 1978); W.K. Marshall, 'The Establishment of a Peasantry in Barbados, 1840-1920', in T. Mathews, ed., *Social Groups and Institutions in the History of the Caribbean* (Rio Piedras, Puerto Rico, Association of Caribbean Historians, 1975), pp. 84–104. See also W.K. Marshall, 'Provision Ground and Plantation Labor in Four Windward Islands: Competition for Resources During Slavery', in *Cultivation and Culture*, pp. 203–20.

4.   See V.A. Shepherd, 'Pens and Penkeepers in a Plantation Society' (PhD dissertation, Cambridge, 1988) and 'Trade and Exchange in Jamaica in the Period of Slavery', in H. Beckles and Shepherd eds., *Caribbean Slave Society and Economy*, (Kingston: Ian Randle Publishers, 1991), pp. 111–19; K. Monteith, 'The Coffee Industry in Jamaica 1790–1850', staff/post-graduate seminar paper, UWI, Mona, 1988; H. Johnson, *The Bahamas in Slavery and Freedom* (Kingston: Ian Randle Publishers, 1991). See also Johnson, *The Bahamas From Slavery to Servitude 1783–1933* (Grainesville: University Press of Florida, 1996).

5.   Higman, *Slave Populations of the British Caribbean*, p. 396.

6.   For information on the Loyalist influx see T.P. Peters, 'The American Loyalists and the Plantation Period in the Bahama Islands', (PhD thesis,

University of Florida, 1960); G. Saunders, *Slavery in The Bahamas 1648–1838*; (Nassau: Nassau Guardian, 1985), pp. 11–47, and *Bahamian Loyalists and Their Slaves* (London: Macmillan, 1983).

7. 'An Account of all Cotton Plantations in The Bahama Islands', CO 23/37/335, 1 November 1785. See also R. Millar, 'On the Cultivation of Cotton in the Bahamas', *Journal of The Bahamas Historical Society for the Diffusion of Knowledge* (May, 1835), p. 49.

8. *Bahama Gazette*, 14–21 March 1789. See also *Votes of the House of Assembly 1787-1794*; *Report of a Committee of the House*, 28 April 1789. Fausse Chenille is a worm that looks like a caterpillar. It has a long body, is variegated with beautiful colours and many legs.

9. *Bahama Gazette*, 16–20 December 1791.

10. CO 23/51/46–47. Charles Cameron to Williams Windham, 12 March 1807.

11. D. McKinnen, *A Tour through the British West Indies in the Years 1802–1803* (London, 1804), pp. 154–160. It gives a particular account of the Bahama Islands.

12. Peters, 'The American Loyalists', p. 157.

13. CO 23/39/167-211. Questionnaire and Answers sent to Planters, 7 May 1800.

14. Report on the Committee on the bill respecting Melioration, 14 November 1826. *Votes of the House of Assembly 1824–1828*, p. 63.

15. See A.D. Peggs, ed., *A Relic of Slavery. Farquharson's Journal, 1831–1832* (Nassau: Nassau Guardian 1957).

16. CO 23/91. Balfour to Stanley, 19 February 1834.

17. Questionnaire and Answers sent to Planters.

18. William Wylly, born in 1757 and called to the English bar, fought as a Loyalist in the American war of independence. Migrating to the Bahamas in 1787, he became solicitor-general in the same year. In 1797, he was promoted to attorney-general of the Bahamas. In 1818 William Wylly had 67 slaves on three plantations at the western end of New Providence. The main estate was Clifton, the largest, where provisions were raised for the slaves. The other two were at Tusculum between the present-day Orange Hill and Gambier Village, and Waterloo just west of Lightbourn Creek. The latter two estates were turned over to stock-raising. See G. Saunders, *Bahamian Loyalists and Their Slaves*, pp. 32–3, and M. Craton and G. Saunders, *Islanders in the Stream. A History of the Bahamian People*, Vol. I (Athens, GA and London: University of Georgia Press, 1992), pp. 202, 258–9, 279–302.

19. Millar 'On the Cultivation of Cotton', pp. 49–51. See also B. Edwards, *The History, Civil and Commercial of the British Colonies in the West Indies*, Vol. III (Philadelphia, 1805), p. 91.

20. Millar, 'On the Cultivation of Cotton', p. 51. See also *Farquharson's Journal*, pp. 22, 26, 27.

21. Edwards, *The History, Civil and Commercial*, p. 91.

22. *Farquharson's Journal*, p. 23. For information on harvesting see also *Bahama Gazette*, 24 December 1790.

23. E.D. Genovese, *Roll, Jordan, Roll. The World The Slaves Made* (London: Pantheon Books, 1975), p. 322.

24. See *Farquharson's Journal* for February 1831, pp. 5–9.

25. Joseph Eve was a Loyalist who settled in Cat Island. He was probably born in South Carolina and lived in Pennsylvania at the time of the American revolution and was thought to be a Quaker. See Saunders, *Bahamian Loyalists and Their Slaves*, p. 39.

26. *Bahama Gazette*, 24 December 1890 and 18-21 March, 1 May, 17 May 1794.

27. *Votes of the House of Assembly 1795–1798* (manuscript), 12 December 1795.

28. Craton, 'Hobbesian or Panglossian?', p. 349.

29. E. Williams, *From Columbus to Castro: The History of the Caribbean 1492–1969* (London: Andre Deutch 1971), p. 122, and McKinnen, *A Tour*, p. 182: McKinnen noted that 'it is generally supposed by good planters, that about five or six acres of land may be employed in the culture of Anguilla cotton to each working slave or taskable hand: but in the Georgian (or as it is properly called Persian) cotton, not more than four'.

30. Morgan, 'Work and Culture: The Task System and the World of Low Country Blacks, 1700–1800', *William and Mary Quarterly*, 3rd series, Vol. XXXIX (October 1982), p. 568; Higman, *Slave Population and Economy in Jamaica*, pp. 24–5; Johnson, *The Bahamas From Slavery to Servitude*, pp. 15–16, 49–51.

31. Morgan, 'Work and Culture', pp. 575–6. See also Berlin and Morgan, *Cultivation and Culture*, p. 582.

32. *An Official Letter from the Commissioners of Correspondence the Bahama Islands* (Nassau, 1823), p. 41. Cited Higman, *Slave Populations of the British Caribbean*, p. 179. See also Johnson, *The Bahamas From Slavery to Servitude*, p. 31.

33. CO 23/63/37–41. Report by Wylly to the House of Assembly, 26 December 1815.

34. McKinnen, *A Tour*, pp. 172–3.

35. Report by Wylly to the House of Assembly.

36. *Farquharson's Journal*, p. 24.

37. CO 23/63/39. Report by Wylly to the House of Assembly. See also the Act of 1824 (4 Geo IV c.6). This act mandated that slaves were not to receive more than 20 lashes at one time or for only one offence, unless the owner or employer of the slave, or the supervisor of the workhouse or keeper of the gaol was present.

38. *Poor Black Kate. Cruelties perpetuated by Henry and Helen Moss, on their slave Kate, in The Bahamas* (London, c. 1828). Kate was a domestic slave belonging to Henry and Helen Moss who had a plantation at Cat Island. In

July 1826 she was confined to the stocks for 17 days. During her confinement, she was beaten repeatedly. Tasks were given to her which she was incapable of performing. Red pepper was rubbed on her eyes. When taken out of the stocks, Kate was flogged and sent to the fields to work. There she died of a fever. The Mosses were found guilty of a misdemeanour and were sentenced to the jail in Nassau for five months and fined £300. A group of 28 citizens including seven members of the House of Assembly petitioned the secretary of state asking for a mitigation of their sentence. When they were released they were entertained at a public dinner. Saunders, *Slavery in The Bahamas*, pp. 160–1.

39. Saunders, 'The Slave Population of The Bahamas, 1783–1834', (MPhil thesis, University of the West Indies, 1978), pp. 259, 386.

40. Ibid., p. 198 or see Saunders, *Slavery in The Bahamas*, p. 94.

41. Saunders, 'The Slave Population of The Bahamas', p. 312.

42. CO 23/67/147–9. Wylly to William V. Munnings, 31 August 1818.

43. CO 23/67/147. Regulations for the Government of the Slaves at Clifton and Tusculum in New Providence, July 1815.

44. Higman, *Slave Populations of the British Caribbean*, p. 188.

45. *An Official Letter from the Commissioners of Correspondence of the Bahama Islands*. Cited D. Gail North, 'The Amelioration and Abolition of Slavery in The Bahamas 1808–1833' (BA thesis, University of Newcastle upon Tyne, 1966), p. 32.

46. CO 23/63/39. Report by Wylly to the House of Assembly.

47. *Farquharson's Journal*, pp. 13–24.

48. Higman, *Slave Populations of the British Caribbean*, p. 168. See also Shepherd, 'Trade and Exchange in Jamaica in the Period of Slavery', p. 113.

49. *Votes of the House of Assembly, 1821–1824*, pp. 31–2.

50. See Shepherd, 'Trade and Exchange in Jamaica in the Period of Slavery', p. 114.

51. Saunders, 'The Slave Population of the Bahamas', p. 287.

52. Ibid. About 30 per cent of coloured male slaves worked in the field their entire life after the age of ten. Approximately 25 per cent worked as mariners their entire life. Between 11 and 15, about 48 per cent were engaged in the field, but by 16 to 24 this percentage dropped to about 34 per cent; about 15 per cent had left the field to engage in mariner activities, salt and in domestic work (p. 289).

53. Saunders, 'The Slave Population of the Bahamas', pp. 273, 292.

54. Higman, *Slave Populations of the British Caribbean*, pp. 190–1; Genovese, *Roll, Jordan, Roll*, p. 319.

55. McKinnen, *A Tour*, p. 183.

56. Higman, *Slave Populations of the British Caribbean*, p. 48. See also Craton and Saunders, *Islanders in the Stream*, Vol. 1, pp. 311–13.

57. Morgan, 'Work and Culture', pp. 578, 585.

58.   M.R. Trouillot, 'Coffee Planters and Coffee Slaves in the Antilles: The Impact of a Secondary Crop', in Berlin and Morgan, *Cultivation and Culture*, p. 137.

59.   *Farquharson's Journal*, pp. 4, 5, 28, 82, 83. Cited Higman, *Slave Populations of the British Caribbean*, p. 213.

60.   Saunders, *Slavery in the Bahamas*, pp. 157–8.

61.   B. Gaspar, 'Slavery, Amelioration, and Sunday Markets in Antigua, 1823-1833', *Slavery and Abolition*, Vol. 9, (No. 1 May 1988), p. 5. See also Mintz and Hall, 'Origins of the Jamaican Internal Marketing System', p. 57.

62.   An Act for governing of Negroes, Mulattoes and Indians 1767 (MS).

63.   37 Geo. III c. 2; 4 Geo. IV. c. 6.

64.   Johnson, *The Bahamas From Slavery to Servitude*, p. 49; See Berlin and Morgan, *Cultivation and Culture*, pp. 23–4.

65.   Regulations for the Government of the slaves at Clifton and Tusculum. See Johnson, 'A Slow and Extended Abolition, The Case of The Bahamas 1800–1838', in M. Turner, *From Chattel Slaves to Wage Slaves. The Dynamics of Labour Bargaining in the Americas* (Kingston: Ian Randle; Bloomington, IN: Indiana University Press; London: James Currey 1995), p. 167. See also CO 23/67/150–1, Encl. in Munnings to Bathurst, 9 September 1818. See also folios 147–9. Johnson, ibid., p. 52.

66.   Marshall, 'Provision Ground and Plantation Labour in Four Windward Islands', p. 203. See also Mintz, 'Slavery and the Rise of Peasantries', *Historical Reflections*, 6 (1979), pp. 213–42; also Mintz and Hall, 'The Origins of the Jamaican Internal Marketing System', pp. 3–26.

67.   Johnson, *The Bahamas From Slavery and Servitude*, p. 52.

68.   John Rolle, an ardent follower of Pitt in the English House of Commons, was raised to the peerage as Baron Rolle of Stevenstone in 1796, taking the title of his uncle who had died without issue. Lord Rolle inherited the five plantations in Exuma situated in Rolleville, Rolletown, Steventon, Ramsey and Mount Thompson from his father Denys Rolle of Devonshire, England. Denys Rolle had laid out a town, Charlotia, later called Rollestown, on the eastern bank of the St John's River. The settlement comprised about 300 persons from the London slums. The venture failed as many of the original settlers fled, seeking an easier life. To some extent they were replaced by negro slaves. At the time of the evacuation of East Florida, Rolle had about 140 slaves whom he transported along with his livestock and other possessions on the *Peace and Plenty* (the name of a present-day hotel in George Town) to Exuma Island in the Bahamas. Rolle's first grant comprised two tracts totalling about 2,000 acres. The original holdings were called Rolleville and Rolletown. Later Rolle expanded his holdings to 5,000 acres in the centre of Exuma. He called the additional settlements Steventon, Ramsey and Mount Thompson.

Saunders, *Bahamian Loyalists and Their* Slaves, p. 21. See also Craton, 'Hobbesian or Panglossian?', p. 327.

69. CO 23/82/346, Police magistrate report. Enclosed in Smyth to Murray, 11 May 1830.

70. CO 23/78, 182. Cited Craton and Saunders, Islanders in the Stream, Vol. 1, p. 383. See Lewis Grant, 27 December 1828. Sir Lewis Grant was Governor of the Bahamas between 1820–1829. He arrived in the Bahamas at the end of the stormy debate over registration of slaves and was successful on getting the Registration Act passed in 1820. Before taking up his new post in Trinidad in 1829, Grant despatched of the Second West India Regiment to Exuma to quell the revolt of the Rolle slaves.

71. Johnson, *The Bahamas From Slavery to Servitude*, pp. 32, 49.

72. Craton, 'Hobbesian or Panglossian?', p. 355; Johnson, 'Slow and Extended Abolition', p. 168.

73. Saunders, *Slavery in The Bahamas*, p. 158.

74. Johnson, *The Bahamas From Slavery to Servitude*, p. 32.

75. Ibid., p. 84.

76. Ibid., p. 86.

77. Ibid., p. 33.

78. CO 23/84–134. James C. Smyth to Viscount Goderick, 2 May 1831.

79. Johnson, *The Bahamas From Slavery to Servitude*, p. 37.

80. Ibid., p. 37.

81. Ibid., 42. See also Loren Schweninger, 'The Underside of Slavery: The Internal Economy, Self-Hire, and Quasi-Freedom in Virginia, 1780–1865', *Slavery and Abolition*, Vol. 12, No. 2 (September 1991), pp. 1–22, for a discussion of the evolution of the self-hire system in Virginia.

82. Johnson, 'Slave Life and Leisure in Nassau, Bahamas 1783–1838', *Slavery and Abolition*, Vol. 16, No. 1 (April 1995), p. 55 and *The Bahamas From Slavery to Servitude*, p. 46.

83. Johnson, 'Slave Life and Leisure', pp. 56–7; See also 1795 Police Act in Duplicate Manuscript Laws of The Bahamas 1795–1799 and 1824 Slave Act, 4 Geo. IV. c. 6.

84. Higman, *Slave Populations of the British Caribbean*, p. 380.

85. Johnson, 'Slave Life and Leisure', p. 55.

86. Johnson, personal communication, 25 November 1996.

87. Johnson, 'A Slow and Extended Abolition', p. 178.

88. Craton and Saunders, *Islanders in the Stream*, p. 298.

89. Johnson, 'A Slow and Extended Abolition', p. 178; *The Bahamas from Slavery to Servitude*, p. 46.

3

Loyalists Mainly to Themselves
The 'Black Loyalist' diaspora to the Bahamas, 1783– c. 1820

MICHAEL CRATON

*I*t has long been recognised that the coming of 5,700 slaves and Free Blacks to the Bahamas after the Treaty of Versailles was quantitatively even more significant than the arrival of some 1,600 Loyalist Whites, raising the colony's ratio of Blacks from a half to two-thirds while the general influx trebled the overall population. However, the self-propagated myth that the White Loyalists totally transformed the Bahamas, and the prevalence of the type of historiography that concentrates on political events and elites, has, until recent times, underplayed the changes wrought on Bahamian society and culture by the Black majority of newcomers.[1]

Similarly, while it was recognised from the beginning that there were several types of White Loyalist migrants to the Bahamas, less stress has hitherto been placed on the distinctly different types of Black newcomers. This is partly because of the tendency of standard histories to equate all Blacks, and partly because the official records and other documentary sources identify and speak for the Whites far more clearly than for the Black, and mainly illiterate, underclasses, the majority of whom were, of course, in the eyes of the law, mere chattel property.

Though it is artificial, even ahistorical, to separate ethnic groups entirely in what is now defined as a unitary, if deeply fissured, 'slave society', this chapter concentrates on the Black immigrants to the Bahamas during the Loyalist era. This is not only to redress the imbalance in the established historiography, but to demonstrate that the Blacks were at least as varied in class, culture, motivation and their ultimate fate, as were their White fellow emigrés.[2]

In general, an important distinction has to be made between three broad categories of Black immigrants to the Bahamas in the 1780s. Those who had long been free were clearly different from those who had been recently freed to take up arms against their owners or had been promised freedom for crossing the British lines; and those who could prove or claim their freedom were even more distinct from those who unequivocally remained chattel slaves.

Other significant differences have also to be considered, in respect of the degree of control under which the incoming Blacks lived, their place of birth and domicile, and the nature and location of their employment. Some came unsupervised save by the government; some came singly and others in families; some accompanied Whites who were not their owners; while the largest number were transferred, often in large gangs, under the supervision of their owners or delegated White overseers. A minority of the Black newcomers were unacculturated Africans, while the remainder were creolised Afro-Americans, some of many generations' standing and varying degrees of ethnic mixture. A majority (and the great majority of the incoming slaves) were fieldworkers, though many of the newcomers were domestics, and a considerable number artisans. Even among the mass of chattel slaves, however, a significant number constituted an elite of more or less acculturated and trusted slaves, distinct from the usually more (allegedly) troublesome majority.

Just as important, distinctions must be made between those Blacks who arrived in the Bahamas from New York (whether or not originally from elsewhere in the mainland colonies), to be settled first (though mostly not for long) in Abaco, and those who came more or less directly from southern plantations, nearly all by way of St Augustine, Florida, to be located either in Nassau, the colonial capital, or (far more numerously) shipped out to set up plantations or work the saltpans in the Bahamas Out Islands, a half dozen of which were previously unpopulated.

Clearly, the Black newcomers from the American mainland all made an impact on the established society as on the underdeveloped economy of the Bahamas, though in notably different ways according to who they were, what they brought with them and what they found in the specific islands of their destination. It remains to be decided, however, whether (as has already been argued against the Loyalist transformation myth in general)[3] the newcomers were not at least as much changed by their new environment and the established society and culture of the Bahamas as they were able permanently to transform it.

The arrival of 'Black Loyalists': origins and composition

With the exception of the slaves belonging to Andrew Deveaux and the other adventurers from the southern mainland colonies who re-conquered Nassau from the Spaniards in April 1783 (a month after the war had ended), the first Loyalist Blacks to resettle in the Bahamas were those evacuated from New York to Abaco between August and October 1783, while New York was in the process of being handed over to the Americans.[4] The pioneer migrants were the 95 'Negroes' listed among the 250 evacuees carried in the *Nautilus* and *William* transports, which sailed from New York on 21 and 22 August 1783 and arrived ten days later at the site on the Abaco mainland (close to the modern resort of Treasure Cay), which was named Carleton after the British commander-in-chief in North America. Two larger ships followed, the *Charlotte* in September and the *Hope* in October, bringing the listed total of New York refugees to 941, of whom at least the 403 counted as 'servants' were Blacks.

A careful analysis of the lists of Blacks carried from New York to Abaco discloses their heterogeneous background and also their equivocal status on migrating or remigrating to a true slave (rather than merely slave-owning) colony.[5] In demographic respects, the 95 Blacks carried in the first two ships seemed much like a typical slave plantation population, with less than one-quarter under the age of 15, no less then 56 per cent aged between 20 and 40, and adult males outnumbering females by three to two. Yet these were in fact a more or less randomly gathered group, nearly all American rather than African-born, and none any longer strictly enslaved. Some, indeed, were highly creolised, possessing artisanal skills and even literate, which last was more than could be said for many of the Bahamian 'old inhabitants', including the poorer Whites.

The comments against each of the Black passengers disclosed that they derived from 11 of the mainland colonies, with one each from Bermuda, Barbados, Jamaica and Haiti. A fair number were said to have been born free, to have purchased their freedom, or to have been granted it by official decree. The majority were listed as 'formerly the property' of specific owners, many of them from the mainland plantation colonies, especially South Carolina and Virginia. Most were described as Blacks, but there were a few listed as Mulattos. More than three-quarters of the adults had Christian names and surnames, rather than the single names characteristic of unacculturated slaves. Fourteen of the adult Blacks were listed as couples with the same surnames, though a majority of the young children belonged to single women. However, there were several nuclear families, notably that headed by the most remarkable of all the Abaco migrants, the 'stout low man' aged 30 named Joseph Paul, a Wesleyan lay preacher (of whom more later), who was accompanied by his wife Susannah, a 'stout wench' of the same age, and their three children, aged 13, five and two.

Sir Guy Carleton had ordered lists of all Black emigrants to show the grounds under which they claimed their freedom, specifically to ensure that none who was already free, or who had come within the British lines on the promise and expectation of being made free, might subsequently be re-enslaved. The lists of all Blacks carried to Nova Scotia left no doubt that they were no longer legally owned. Yet those transported to colonies where slavery was more firmly entrenched were a more delicate matter. Consequently, in the Abaco lists (as in those of Blacks carried to the West Indies proper) against all Black persons' names were the names of White persons 'in whose possession they are now'. This (along with the general classification of Blacks as 'servants') was clearly intended to be a form of apprenticeship, or of that continued responsibility required of the former owners and managers of manumitted slaves in all plantation colonies. Potentially, though, this formula threatened the freedom of the Loyalist Blacks.

In all, 31 White owners were listed for the 95 Blacks on the *Nautilus* and *William*. Of these, twenty 'possessed' only one or two Blacks, but a handful held control of small gangs. Four Whites between them held possession of 36 Blacks from the two ships, and may well have augmented the number for whom they were held responsible from the later arrivals. In a surprising number of cases, the White person recorded as possessing a particular Black person was also listed as the former owner, even purchaser, of that individual. In such cases, particularly where the controlling White aspired to be a planter or wished to capitalise on the original investment, there was a special incentive to reduce the subject Black to absolute bondage if possible.

The status of the Blacks from New York was further compromised by the arrival in Abaco in 1784 of shipments of émigrés from St Augustine in East Florida. Totalling 650 persons, these consisted of a small number of White planter families and a majority of Black slaves. They settled some 50 miles south of the New Yorkers, at Spencer's Bight and Eight Mile Bay, where the slaves were set to clearing the bush for cotton fields and provision grounds. This style of operation was seemingly attractive to those more enterprising Whites from New York who, dismayed by the infertility of the soils in northern Abaco and the disputes among the Carleton settlers, migrated south with the Blacks in their charge, to form the rival settlement of Marsh Harbour (which became in time Abaco's mini-metropole).[6]

Success, though, came slowly for Abaco, and not from cotton plantations; and the lot of all Abaconian Blacks was generally bleak. Failing to wrest cotton from the meagre soil in a climate less suitable than further south in the Bahamian archipelago, most of the would-be planters forsook Abaco and carried their slaves and other dependent workers to other islands, particularly Long Island and the Caicos Islands. A few gave up plantership altogether, and migrated to Nassau or to new all-White settlements founded on Abaconian offshore cays (Cherokee Sound, Hope Town, Man-o-War Cay and Great Guana Cay).

Those Blacks who, like Joseph Paul, could establish their independence of a White owner and find the means also migrated to a more hopeful life in Nassau. Of those who stayed, some were left in scattered all-Black settlements on the Abaco mainland. But most were settled in separate sections of the two Abaconian townships which followed the racially bifurcated pattern long set by Nassau and Harbour Island, at Marsh Harbour and at Plymouth on Green Turtle Cay, a few miles offshore from the abandoned site of Carleton. Like the Abaconian Whites, they mainly turned to the sea for their livelihood, though some were set to grow provisions and cut timber on the Abaco mainland, more or less under the control of White owners.

Throughout the Bahamas, the Whites – whether Old Inhabitants, southern mainlanders or migrants from New York – attempted to impose a British-Caribbean pattern of racial hegemony (or at least its Bahamian variant) on the Black Loyalists. 'It is with great Pain of Mind,' wrote a sympathetic White in June 1786, 'that I, every day see the Negroes, who came here from America, with the British Generals' Free Passes, treated with unheard cruelty by Men who call themselves Loyalists. These unhappy People, after being drawn from their Masters by Promises of Freedom and the King's Protection, are every day stolen away'.[7] Yet the Abaconian Blacks, including those who had undoubtedly arrived as slaves, were particularly resistant to moves by the Loyalist Whites to entrench their domination.

When Lord Dunmore, whose 1775 proclamation when he was Governor of Virginia had first promised the mainland slaves freedom if they fought for the British, arrived in the Bahamas as governor in 1787 (a position he held until 1796), one of his first actions was to set up a tribunal to examine Blacks' claims to freedom. Whatever were Dunmore's motives, this procedure was seen by Whites and Blacks alike as a means of re-enslavement, and on Abaco at least provoked an actual armed conflict, the most serious in Bahamian history, though not the best known. 'I am just now informed from the Island of Abbaco', wrote Dunmore to Secretary of State Lord Sydney on 28 November 1787, 'that a number of outlying Negroes went about with Muskets and fix'd Bayonets, robbing and plundering, so that the White inhabitants had to collect themselves in a body and having come up with the Negroes had killed, wounded and taken most of them Prisoners, three of the latter they immediately executed'.[8]

Dunmore himself sailed to Abaco early in 1788 and convened a sitting of his tribunal to examine the claims to freedom of 30 rebellious Blacks. To the relief of Whites and dismay of Blacks, he declared all but one of them to be slaves, not free. On his return to Nassau, Dunmore claimed that his action had made Abaco permanently peaceful.[9] Yet in reality, not only did the reluctance of the Abaconian Blacks to labour for White owners contribute to the failure to establish plantations on the island, but the conflicts of the 1780s helped to entrench the racial divide that has shaped Abaco's history right up to the present day.[10]

'Black Loyalists' in the Out Islands

Those Black Loyalists who most obviously helped to reshape the Bahamas were the 3,000–4,000 slaves carried by their owners to settle and develop islands uninhabited since the time of the aboriginal Lucayans. In 1775 the Bahamas had been a maritime colony similar to but less important than Bermuda. Its small population was concentrated in Nassau's island of New Providence and the nearby Eleuthera and Harbour Island, with a mere handful of settlers in Cat Island and Exuma, and merely nominal jurisdiction over the distant Turks Islands, which were in reality much more closely connected to Bermuda. Besides Abaco, within a decade of the ending of the American war, White Loyalists and their slaves had carved up and largely cleared Cat Island, Exuma, Long Island, Watling's, Rum Cay, Crooked Island, Acklin's and the Caicos Islands, and had made the first settlements on Ragged Island, Andros and Grand Bahama, bidding fair to make the Bahamas the primary producer of sea island cotton and salt in the British Caribbean.[11]

Andrew Deveaux and his fellow freebooters pre-empted some of the best land in the new islands (Deveaux himself acquiring large tracts in Cat Island, Exuma and Long Island as well as a base in New Providence), while the majority of Loyalist planter migrants, most already transplanted from South Carolina and Georgia, remained in East Florida, nervously waiting on events. Only as it became clear that the new Spanish administration in Florida was uncongenial, and that the British government would arrange and pay for their transportation and grant them land on a headright basis, did they take ship in large numbers for the Bahamas. Many of them, however, were already crowded into Nassau when Acting-Governor Powell's official proclamation on 5 September 1785 that each planter would receive 40 acres, plus 20 acres for each of their dependents, family and slaves, began a veritable land rush to the new islands. This frenzied process was almost completed by the time that the long standing rights of the original lord proprietors were bought out in March 1787, though land transactions continued at a high level for another decade as the result of speculation, the discovery of the actual value of the lands first acquired and large-scale re-migration. Not surprisingly, Governor Dunmore and his family were the chief beneficiaries of the share-out, being able to choose prime lands in Nassau, Harbour Island, Long Island and elsewhere, 10,000 acres in all, despite not being major slave owners.[12]

With the exception of Lord Dunmore and his family, the headright system meant that it was the possession of slaves which provided the planters' chief claim to land, and thus their aspiration to wealth and status. Even more directly, it was the slaves' labour on which the planters depended. It was unlikely, though, that these forms of dependency were even tacitly acknowledged by the land-holding class, either in the pioneer period of planter optimism, when the slaves toiled to clear the fields, build the houses, roads and salinas, and in many cases learned for the first time the skills and drudgery of cotton and salt production; or in the subsequent phase (during the long last wars with France). During this latter phase when cotton cultivation failed, slaves were driven harder in the vain quest for profits, and those planters who could, left the Bahamas Out Islands for Nassau, elsewhere in the West Indies, or England, with some even going back to the United States.

Least fortunate of all were the slaves who were shifted from the hard but seasonal routine of cotton cultivation, or the increasingly diversified economy of cotton, salt and stock-raising in now familiar surroundings, to the unremitting and unhealthy toil of salt production in the southern islands; or were shipped out of the Bahamas altogether, to the harshest and unhealthiest regime of all, in the sugar plantations of Jamaica and Trinidad.[13] Yet the transfer from the mainland to the Bahamas did have important benefits for the slaves beyond their owners' control, and largely beyond their ken; and the subsequent disappointments of the planters did provide compensations for their slaves, especially for those left behind in the Bahamas Out Islands, more or less on their own.

Much work still remains to be undertaken on the distinctive features of the Loyalist slaves of the Bahamas Out Islands, particularly their culture, though a fairly convincing picture has already been put together from the governors' official correspondence, Kelsall, Rolle, Williams and Farquharson papers, the invaluable register of slave returns (1822–34), and patchy references in the local newspapers. Most thoroughly researched of all – and most useful for our understanding – were the slaves belonging to Lord Rolle settled in Exuma, though in several respects they were atypical, if not unique.[14]

Unlike the majority of Out Island slaves who had originally come from the Sea Islands or coastal plantations of South Carolina and Georgia, the roughly 150 slaves transferred to Exuma by Denys Rolle in 1784 were the survivors of the Devonshire absentee's grandiose plans in the 1760s to develop a swathe of central Florida, from a core settlement on the St John's River, close to the present city of Palatka.[15] Almost exclusively pure Blacks, rather than of mixed descent, with probably one-quarter of them African-born, the original Rolle slaves would seem to have been less creolised than the Loyalist Blacks on the average. The nature of their employment in the Florida backwoods also may have made them more independent than most from the beginning.

Yet the Rolle slaves had as healthy a balance of sexes and ages, and at least as well-established a pattern of nuclear families as the rest of the migrants, and as a consequence of their transfer to the healthier climate of the Bahamas and the gradual lightening of work imposed upon them, their increase in numbers by natural reproduction during the last half century of slavery was rapid even by the standards of the Bahamian Out Islands, the highest found anywhere in the British West Indian colonies. Under John, Lord Rolle, who succeeded to their ownership after the death of his father in 1797, the original slave-holding had doubled by 1828 and risen to 376 by 1834, making it the largest in the Bahamas at the time of Emancipation. This indicated an natural increase as high as 3.5 per cent per year. Yet the figures for the Bahamas Out Island slaves as a whole, over 2.5 per cent, were almost as remarkable; in stark contrast to the expanding sugar colony of Trinidad (which suffered a net annual decrease of 4 per cent), but also considerably higher than in any of the mainland plantation areas from which the slaves had come.[16]

The consequences of this extremely rapid growth of population, at the time (and partly as a result) of the economic decline of the Loyalists' cotton plantations, were of critical importance for the subsequent history of the Bahamas Out Islands and their population. By the mid-1820s, Lord Rolle was complaining that his slaves were almost impossible to manage and were costing far more to support than they were producing for him from their labour. Having failed to emulate several of his fellow slave owners and transfer his slaves to Jamaica or Trinidad because of a change in legislation, Rolle proposed, equally in vain, that they be allowed to go free, saving him the cost of upkeep while earning the money that would recompense him for their manumission. For their part, the Rolle slaves performed no more plantation tasks than could be enforced by the presence of troops, complained that they were receiving less than their statutory allowances and, when threatened with a transfer from Exuma to another Bahamian island, took Lord Rolle's boat and sailed to Nassau to protest to the governor.[17]

Having succeeded (despite the inevitable punishment of whipping and a spell in the workhouse) in their demand not to be transferred against their will from their now familiar lands, the Rolle slaves ingeniously played on Lord Rolle's schemes to save himself money by concocting the myth that both Denys Rolle and his son had promised them the lands to themselves once they were freed. Though no formal document to this effect was ever forthcoming, it was on this ground that the Rolle slaves took virtual possession of Lord Rolle's unsaleable lands at the time of Emancipation, and in due course they and their descendants were granted commonage rights over them in perpetuity.[18]

Such resistant behaviour and consequences, though outstanding, were by no means unique. With all the planters who could deserting the islands with their families, leaving their estates first in the hands of attorneys and managers before throwing them up altogether, most slaves did no more plantation work than they were forced to, stood on their rights and increasingly lived, in their family groups, as subsistence peasants and fishermen. After Emancipation they became share-croppers or labour tenants in the areas where Whites retained ownership, but on abandoned estates that had reverted to the Crown (or Crown lands never adopted by Loyalist planters) they were technically squatters, working the meagre soils by a rotational system of slash-and-burn agriculture, more or less in common, while trying to establish the customary system of hereditary family tenures called generation land through the legal process of establishing squatters' rights.[19]

These communities (alternatively styled 'proudly independent', 'backward', or 'products of benign neglect') naturally consisted almost entirely of persons of pure African descent. Only in the few areas where the Whites were too poor or unwilling to migrate did the descendants of White and Black Loyalists continue to coexist; not just in parallel settlements in an uneasy symbiotic relationship (as in Abaco and northern Eleuthera), but in a reciprocal mutual dependence (as on the Farquharson estate on Watling's Island, on Ragged Island, or in much of Long Island), or even, rarest of all, in that type of progressively more easy-going attitude towards social and sexual mixing that had existed before the Loyalists came on the mainland of Eleuthera and was, thereafter, to produce the distinctive phenotype referred to as 'Long Island White'.[20]

The limited and largely covert breakdown of racial taboos, along with the more general way that the Bahamian environment had led to the failure of attempted plantations and a regression to the subsistence farming and maritime activities of the pre-Loyalist era, can be cited as ways in which the Loyalist Blacks – like the Loyalist Whites – were more reshaped by existing conditions in their new home than they themselves were able to shape them. Yet the Black pioneer settlers nevertheless did have a profound impact on the history and development of the majority of Bahamas Out Islands, with effects on themselves both positive and negative.

As the Out Island Black population (augmented by the resettlement of Africans liberated from seized slave ships between 1811 and 1860) continued to increase, its lifestyle and culture became increasingly dominant in many of the islands. Yet the pressure of expanding population on meagre soils, coupled with the reconstitution of the White elite as an agro-commercial bourgeoisie based in Nassau (monopolising shipping, manufacture, trade and wage employment as well as much of the best land), meant that the price of independence was an increasingly desperate poverty.

Those descendants of Loyalist Blacks who remained on the sites first settled tended to be most locked into the pattern of dependency and exploitation. Migration to Nassau or outside the Bahamas in search of wage employment was an unsatisfactory palliative, damaging if not destructive to traditional culture and family life. Yet many Out Island Blacks did independently migrate within the archipelago, to areas and islands hitherto undeveloped, and it was here that, though the poorest of the poor, they retained the elements of an Afro-Bahamian culture in its purest form.

The most notable case was that of Andros. Largest of all Bahamian islands and ironically closest of all to New Providence, it was almost totally ignored by the Loyalist planters as being mainly swash and pine barren, with only a coastal strip of marginally cultivable soil. Its northwestern corner was first settled in the 1820s by an almost unnoticed handful of refugees from the Seminole wars under the legendary Billy Bowlegs (a delayed type of Loyalist, perhaps); its eastern shore was colonised over the following decades by an enterprising overflow of land-hungry Blacks, largely from Exuma, Cat Island and northern Long Island.[21]

Virtually untouched by the cultural influences of established church or government education system, Andros remained until modern times a land of mystery, myth and archaic survivals in the realms of language, folklore and music. To White travel writers condescendingly addicted to the non-threatening picturesque, it was the very image of Africa. To visiting scholars, however, it was more accurately seen as probably the purest survival of a Black Loyalist culture; that is, the culture of precolonial West Africa mediated through the Gullah culture of the Sea Islands of Georgia and South Carolina.[22]

The Urban milieu

Nassau, the colonial capital and mini-metropole, was the central cauldron of the changes which occurred in the Bahamas as the result of the Loyalist influx. Conditions for the Loyalist Blacks in Nassau and its island of New Providence, though generally more promising, were far more complex and at least as conflictive as those carried to the Bahamian Out Islands. In Nassau and its environs, a minimum of three distinct types of Black newcomer interacted with each other, with the old inhabitants of every shade and status, and with the Whites who wished to forge them into their own conception of an ordered society.

On the map New Providence seems a tiny island (and today is half covered by Nassau's suburban sprawl), but it is in fact scarcely smaller than Barbados, if flatter and far less fertile. Before 1775 only the parts closest to Nassau were claimed or surveyed, and even these hardly farmed. Yet after 1783, despite its sparse soil cover, bony ridges and salt marshes, almost the whole of the island was quickly taken up by White newcomers. Some were mere speculators, but most were the type of Loyalist émigré who wished to combine the style and pretensions of the slave-owning planter with the social and political consolations and rewards to be found in a colonial town, replicating as far as possible life in the hinterland of Wilmington or Beaufort, if not Charleston or Savannah. To the Loyalists' slaves, of course, fell the thankless task of clearing and farming the bush, though unlike the Out Island Blacks they did have the prospect of carrying the surplus food they produced in their own time to an urban market, of entering at least the margins of the cash economy, and the chance of mingling at weekends and holidays with a differentiated range of fellow Blacks.

Though in its way as atypical as the Rolles' Exuma holdings, the best-known and most telling New Providence slave estate was that owned by William Wylly, the Loyalist attorney-general of the Bahamas from 1789 to 1823. Originally from Georgia, Wylly came to Nassau in 1785 after a disappointing venture to Nova Scotia, and established the 500-acre Clifton plantation at the far western end of New Providence, along with the satellite holdings of Waterloo and Tusculum on the 16-mile road into Nassau. At first a conventional Loyalist planter (and opponent of Governor Dunmore), Wylly became an ardent convert to Methodism whose legalistic stance in cases involving slave ownership and transfer placed him at loggerheads with hardline Loyalists, who accused him of being soft on slavery if not an active Emancipationist.[23]

This reputation, though, was greatly exaggerated. Wylly's slaves were far healthier than those in Nassau, increasing at as fast a rate as any Out Islanders (from 40 to 67 in the decade before 1822), and they sufficiently valued their owner's regime to come to his defence with their fowling guns when he was threatened with arrest by the assembly's sergeant-at-arms in 1817. But the unique set of regulations for the slaves on his estates which Wylly published in 1815 shows him in his true colours: as a strict paternalist who made concessions to the slaves only where they strengthened the internal social order, were of direct advantage to himself, or implicitly followed the Gramscian principle that a small inoculative dose of liberalism would forestall the violent overthrow of slavery altogether.

Wylly's slaves were rewarded if they married, sustained a sound family life and zealously attended church services; but they were severely punished if they backslid. They were given provision grounds, generous time to work them and regular passes to go to market; yet in return Wylly withheld issues of food and clothing decreed by law. Similarly, he gave special privileges and even a wage (which was also technically illegal) to designated head slaves; but these were strictly conditional on unswerving fidelity and a willingness to act as a lay preacher in the slave quarters. Yet Wylly never manumitted any of his slaves, even in his will (he died in 1828). He shipped off some of his slaves to St. Vincent when he was appointed chief justice there in 1823 (four being drowned on the way). But the rest he sold to Henry Moss, one of the cruellest of Bahamian slave masters, who sent many of them to labour at the saltpans in the southern islands till slavery ended in 1834.[24]

Even before their master had left the Bahamas, Wylly's slaves had come to resist his regime, with some of the most trusted, significantly, leading the resistance. In 1818, the privileges of working three days a week on their own grounds and going to market were withheld from a slave called Caesar and several others for 'persistent skulking'. Yet in 1821 Wylly was also forced to advertise in the *Bahama Gazette* for the return of one of his trusted headmen, Boatswain, who had absconded with his wife and family to Nassau, where they were 'well known about Town', and were 'supposed to be harboured by some of the Baptist Negroes about Samuel Scriven's Meeting House'.[25]

The largest number of Loyalist slaves in Nassau itself were domestics attached to the households of White Loyalist owners, though there were also some skilled artisans such as masons and carpenters. Virtually all were Creoles and many highly creolised: baptised, formally married and even literate. Many were of mixed descent, sometimes more closely related to the Whites they served than was openly acknowledged.

Though as yet the rest are, at most, mere names in ledgers, two individuals have emerged out of the crowd to shed some light on the role of Black slaves in the domestic life of Loyalist Nassau. One is Caesar Brown (his surname the same as his owner's), the highly literate author of the only letter written by a Bahamian slave that has so far surfaced. Brown, who probably served as the family butler and coachman, wrote in 1800 to the daughter of his recently deceased master and mistress in New Jersey of his fear of being sold with the rest of the slaves because his value had been assessed too high to enable him to purchase his own freedom. The essence of the letter was to beg for help in reducing the assessment or for a contribution towards the manumission payment. But the alternative seemingly genuinely offered was more surprising; that if the Browns' daughter would take him into her employ and move him back to the United States, he would faithfully serve her 'for ever' as a slave.[26]

The story of the other domesticated Loyalist slave, Portia Kelsall, is even more remarkable, though with an equally uncertain ending. Portia was the daughter of the South Carolinian Loyalist Roger Kelsall (a widower) by his Black domestic slave Nelly. After Kelsall's death, Portia, though technically still a slave because of her mother's status, was brought up alongside her legitimate half-siblings and cousins, at first in Exuma and then, as the plantation faded, in Nassau. Occupying a social half-world somewhere between the poor relation and the genteel domestic, in 1804 Portia took employment as a lady's maid with a Loyalist family returning 'home' to England, but returned to Nassau a year later, having failed in her apparent aims either to obtain her freedom or win a suitable English husband.

As the Kelsall fortunes dwindled, Portia faced the real threat of being sold away as a slave, but her freedom (and that of her mother) was purchased by one of her half-sisters in 1807. Yet the entry of Portia and Nelly into the ranks of Nassau's Free Coloured community proved far from a step up in life for them, and a source of embarrassment for the Kelsalls. Before they lost touch altogether, the Nassau Kelsalls reported to their English relatives that while the mother and daughter made much of their previous connections, Nelly had a serious drinking problem and Portia had taken up the trade of huckster in the public market, with a disreputable male companion in tow and at least one illegitimate child.[27]

Social legislation and tensions over colour

By leaving the customary familiarity of the slave-owning household and entering the twilight world of the neither fully White nor fully free, Portia and her mother had, in fact, crossed to the other side of a world that was more polarised (in the mainland colonial and United States style) than it had ever been in the Bahamas in pre-Loyalist times. Part of the reason for the increased tension and separation, which was at its most intense in the comparatively crowded confines of Nassau and New Providence, was the sheer disparity of numbers between Whites and Blacks. Yet even more determinant was the confusion (already referred to in respect of Abaco) between the legal, the claimed and the actual status of Loyalist and other Blacks, at a time which saw cataclysmic uprisings of Free Coloureds and slaves in nearby Haiti and a 20-year war with revolutionary and Napoleonic France.

The racial situation in the Bahamian capital was not only volatile but cumulative. Increased numbers of Blacks and consequent tensions decided the ruling Whites (among whom Loyalists were now predominant) to enforce residential segregation as well as to establish a clearer definition of racial categories: yet this very segregation and more rigid classification increased the Blacks' opportunities for self-expression and further heightened tensions. Besides, as Howard Johnson has recently argued, the situation was exacerbated by the prevalence and extension of the system of self-hire among slaves as well as freed Blacks and Coloureds. A feature of Nassau's economy and society even before the Loyalists' came, self-hire became more general as cotton plantations failed, more slaves were brought or drawn to Nassau, and their will to work for wages coincided with their owners' willingness to save on their upkeep, while at the same time taking a share of their earnings.[28]

With the population of New Providence reaching 6,000, of whom only one-quarter was Whites, an Ordinance forbidding Blacks to live in Nassau's downtown core did away with the pre-Loyalist custom of domestic slaves living in quarters attached to their owners' homes (or artisans in their owners' yards). Free Coloureds formed suburban enclaves close to town, in the east and west along the shore, or just over Nassau's ridge, under Fort Fincastle or to the southwest, in what became known as Delancey Town. But they were now more separated from the Nassau Whites (including the poorer Conchy Joes along the eastern shore) than they were from the slaves. Though for the most part working downtown during the day, the majority of slaves lived in shanty yards 'over the hill', in or just south of Fort Hill or Delancey Town, in what came in time to be called Grant's Town and Bain Town.[29]

As in the coastal towns of the US mainland, the White legislators had increasing difficulties defining and controlling the Black and Coloured urban underclasses. In the earliest Loyalist years, conflicts arose from the decisions made by the tribunal set up by Dunmore to adjudicate Blacks' claims to freedom and the activities of policing patrols that were almost like White vigilante groups.[30] Yet with the added excuse of the dangers from the revolution in Haiti and from the slave and Free Coloureds arriving in Nassau as a consequence, the screws were progressively tightened.

In 1789, seemingly in response to the Mulatto uprising led by Vincent Ogé that began the Haitian revolution, the Bahamian assembly decreed that 'all free Negroes, Mulattos, Mustees and Indians should register with the Secretary their name, age, address, their family, sex and colour, under forfeit of their freedom'. Once registered, Bahamian Free Coloureds were further humiliated by being required to labour on the public roads (for a small wage), on pain of a large fine or corporal punishment if they refused. As the Haitian slaves exploded into revolution, war began with revolutionary France, and real though exaggerated slave plots were uncovered in Nassau, a whole raft of repressive legislation followed. The further importation of French slaves was banned, the militia and police were strengthened, a new jail and workhouse built and a deficiency law passed aimed at maintaining a safe proportion of Whites to Blacks. The climax of Loyalist-inspired social legislation, though, was the first Consolidated Slave Act for the Bahamas passed in May 1797.[31]

With one eye on ameliorationist sentiments in England, the new slave law started with clauses ostensibly concerned with the slaves' protection, welfare and even rights. But these were far outweighed by the concern to control, police and punish the slaves, and (more trickily, given the growing tendency to lump them together) to prevent them making common cause with the Free Coloured community. The slaves' ability to buy and sell goods and own property was severely restricted, minatory provisions were made against riotous behaviour, drinking and gambling, the carrying of items that could be used as weapons was strictly controlled and punishments for violence, even threats, directed against Whites were draconian.

Yet almost the longest section of the 1797 Act was concerned with controlling slaves' unauthorised movements. Wandering slaves without a ticket of leave were to be regarded as runaways, and any White could challenge and apprehend them by force. Slave runaways, and those slaves who harboured them, were threatened with severe punishment, though those slaves who returned runaways were rewarded. Slaves who served against rebels were promised £5 for each one killed and £10 for each captive, along with 'a Blue Cloth Coat with a Red Cross on the right Shoulder'. Even more significantly, any Black or Coloured free person who concealed a runaway or forged a ticket of leave was liable to lose their freedom and be transported, as well as 'any other punishment the court decreed short of life or limb'. Freedpeople aiding runaways to escape by boat were not only to suffer transportation themselves but were threatened with capital punishment if they returned.[32]

As elsewhere, however, such clauses are a truer indication of the actual situation than they are of the power of the legislators to control it. Slaves did in fact roam quite freely and mix socially with free Blacks and Coloureds (to whom they were, of course, often related by family ties). Many absconding slaves were indeed harboured, and a few became permanent runaways, living in the scanty bush of the New Providence interior and occasionally seen even in town.[33] There they could be easily lost in the crowd found each day round the public market and wharves, or more widely dispersed at weekends and holidays.

All in all, as Johnson has vividly shown by quoting grand jury presentments and other newspaper items, Blacks and Coloureds in post-Loyalist Nassau and New Providence defied the law to make a social life of their own, not just 'over the hill', but in the downtown streets, open spaces and harbour-front areas of Nassau itself. Besides the favourite Bahamian pastime of dancing, common to all classes, Blacks were as notoriously fond of drinking, gambling and riotous games as the less reputable Whites (against whom, of course, there were fewer restrictions). Given the perennial complaints against such activities in the press, Johnson has gone so far as to suggest that they were regulated less by the regime than by the Blacks themselves, through their increasing adherence to Christianity.[34]

The Cultural Legacy

It may be claimed that it was the Christianisation of the majority population that was the most important and lasting legacy to the Bahamas from the Loyalist Black immigrants. As we have seen, their greatest material contribution was the peopling of many previously uninhabited Out Islands and the islands' transformation, first through cotton planting and salt production, and then into a peculiar type of amphibious peasant economy. Yet it can be argued from this that it was the Bahamian environment which shaped the lives of the newcomers, rather than vice versa, and even that the Black Loyalist newcomers were simply adopting on a larger and wider scale the type of opportunistic near subsistence economy found in the long established island of Eleuthera before they arrived.[35]

Similarly, it has been shown that while the sheer number of newcomers changed the scale and pace of life in and around the colonial capital Nassau, and that the White Loyalists did what they could to enforce the bipolar system of race relations that had already developed in the mainland areas from which most of them came, these attempts were only partially successful and the social changes that occurred were more quantitative than qualitative. A greater residential separation and segregationalist laws did lead to a more independent lifestyle for Black and Coloureds free persons and slaves alike, but the social and working life they followed was essentially a more complex and conflicted extension of that found before the coming of the Loyalists.

The general cultural legacy of the Black newcomers was probably more important, though further scholarly work is needed to ascertain its form and dimensions. Indications are that the arrival of so many African-Americans from the plantation areas of the mainland south was a significant factor in determining the linguistic and folklore similarities still to be traced between modern African-Bahamians and African-Americans in southern coastal regions. Yet much more needs to be known about the culture of African-Bahamians before the Loyalist advent and about the common cultural roots they had always shared with African-American slaves. Many of the most notable Bahamian cultural traditions, such as the Junkanoo festival and goombay music and dancing, have cognate forms on the mainland, but the common roots are almost certainly African by way of the British Caribbean proper, with the mainland manifestations merely the outlying branches of a cultural diffusion.[36] Besides this, there is the difficulty posed by the fact that much of the vigour of modern African-Bahamian culture is owed to the renewal of African links by way of the liberated Africans who came to the Bahamas long after the Loyalists, between 1811 and 1860.[37]

In weighing the effects of the importation of forms of Christian worship and belief by Black Loyalists, however, one is on much firmer ground. The pre-Loyalist Bahamas was neglected and neglectful in respect of Christianity, with what ministrations there were monopolised by the established Anglican Church and directed almost solely to the respectable White population. Yet long before the end of slavery, or even that overspill of the English evangelical revival which led to the formation of missionary societies aimed at British Caribbean slaves, the Black majority of Bahamians was already well on their way to becoming what they are today, one of the most ardently Christian peoples in the world. Though it was a process paralleled among Bahamian Whites (for example, Methodist Loyalists like Wylly and Presbyterians of Scottish background), this was almost entirely the achievement of unlicensed Black nonconformist preachers, at work from the very beginning of the Loyalist influx.

This independent spiritual activity (replicated throughout the Black Loyalist diaspora, most notably in Jamaica) represented an extension of that wave of religious revivalism called the 'great awakening' that had flooded throughout the entire population of the mainland colonies in the decades before the War of Independence. If, as has been suggested, it had regenerative, even revolutionary implications for the mainland Whites, its force was redoubled for those enslaved or oppressed on racial grounds. Deeply consonant with African-Americans' own repressed spiritual legacies, it offered not only re-generation but redemption, and was naturally strong among those who fled from the plantations on promise of freedom, or were carried from the land of their bondage into a new country.[38]

The pioneer Black Loyalist evangelist (or first of whom we have certain details) was that Methodist preacher and teacher already mentioned called Joseph Paul, who landed in Abaco in 1783 and migrated onwards to Nassau shortly thereafter, where he set up a chapel and school on Augusta Street in the western suburbs. Paul, who as a boy in South Carolina had heard George Whitefield preach, was (like John Wesley himself) in favour of the reform of the Anglican Church, not breaking away from it entirely. The opportunity of finding a place on at least the margins of the established order, along with conflicts with largely unworthy rival Methodist leaders sent from the United

States in the 1790s, therefore led to Paul's defection to the Anglican Church. With an enthusiastic following among the Free Coloureds and more acculturated slaves, Paul was accepted as an Anglican catechist, his church adopted as a chapel-at-ease of Nassau's parish church (Christchurch), and his school became the first of the church-based elementary schools in Nassau funded through the charity of Dr Bray's Associates. Paul was succeeded as pastor and teacher by his son and namesake, and his church (its name changed from St Paul's to St Mary's) became a separate parish church and a centre of the ritualist revival that had such success with Nassau's Black and Coloured middle classes in the later nineteenth century.[39]

The first official nonconformist missionary arrived in Nassau in 1800. This was the Rev. William Turton, sent by the Manchester Methodist Conference on a plea from Dr Thomas Coke, the Wesleyan apostle to the British Caribbean. Turton was actually a man of colour from Barbados, and he and the White missionaries who followed him did manage to proselytise some of the more respectable Bahamian Blacks and Coloured. They had much greater success, however, with the poorer Whites previously neglected by the Established Church, and the social difficulties which Turton suffered on account of his colour (and his temerity in marrying a local White woman) were a prelude to the race–class divisions which characterised the Bahamian Methodist Church well into the twentieth century, with segregated seating (as in the Anglican churches) or even separate churches for Whites and Blacks and Coloured.[40]

If Joseph Paul and the early Methodist missionaries represented the drive towards a respectable religious revivalism among the coloured free persons and slaves, there were many more unlicensed Black Baptist preachers who carried a more ardent and all-encompassing religion to the Black majority. One of the most active, though not best known, was Frank Spence, who purchased his own freedom and built a chapel south of Fort Hill in Nassau in 1806, but had previously ministered to his fellow slaves in Long Island. There his methods and their success can be gauged by the disparaging remarks made by the Anglican Rev. Daniel Rose in 1799:

> Their preachers, Black men, are artful and designing, making a merchandise of Religion. One of them was so impious as to proclaim that he had had a familiar conversation with the Almighty, and to point out the place where he had seen him. At certain times in the year the Black preachers drive numbers of Negroes into the sea and dip them by way of baptism, for which they extort a dollar, or stolen goods.[41]

Best known of the Black Baptist preachers (and closest under the eyes of the Whites) were Sambo Scriven and Prince Williams, who ministered in the Nassau suburb of Delancey Town. Like Paul they came from the southern plantation colonies, and may have been (like George Liele of Jamaica and David George of Nova Scotia and Sierra Leone) members of the pioneer Black Baptist congregation of Silver Bluff, South Carolina, that migrated first to the British lines around Savannah, before being carried to East Florida in 1782. Baptist legend pictures them arriving independently in the Bahamas from Florida in a small boat like Irish missionary saints, and the truth does seem to be that they were both runaway slaves who later purchased their freedom. Sambo Scriven (c. 1730–1822) was much the older of the two, a Black creole, already 'well known as a Baptist Preacher' in 1785, while Prince Williams (c. 1760–1840), who seems to have been his convert and disciple, was a native African, with 'his Country marks down his face'.[42]

At first, like many other unlicensed ministers, Scriven and Williams preached in private houses or under a tree. But by 1801 they were prominent members of an Anabaptist Society that purchased two prime lots in the recently laid out Delancey Town and built the wooden chapel they called Bethel. For a few years, Scriven was the pastor and Williams his assistant, but a schism then occurred (over Williams's alleged sexual impropriety) and Williams and his followers moved a few yards down Meeting Street, to found the chapel called St John's.

Surviving many years of virtual persecution, including an 1816 act 'for the preventing the profanation of Religious Rites and false worshipping of God, under the pretence of preaching and teaching, by illiterate, ignorant and ill disposed persons', Spence, Scriven, Williams and many other anonymous preachers had converted a majority of Blacks throughout the islands well in advance of the arrival of the first White Baptist missionaries, Burton and Pearson (who had fled Jamaica) in 1833. One of the newcomers was made pastor of a grand new chapel called Zion on the northern slopes of Nassau's ridge, while Sharper Morris, who had succeeded as pastor of Bethel when Sambo Scriven died in 1822, stood down in favour of the other. The aged Williams and his congregation (along with most other native Baptists), however, would have nothing to do with this surrender of authority, their chapel being proudly rechristened St John's Particular Church of Native Baptists.[43]

Clearly the conversion of the Black and Coloured majority to Christianity through the agency of Black newcomers was made less of a radical change by the division into respectable and popular churches. Yet it is significant that it was the Baptist faith and observances that were most consonant with African beliefs and practices and which had the widest and deepest impact upon African-Bahamian culture. For a century and a half after the Loyalist era the legacies of traditional culture were strongest in those Loyalist-settled Out Islands where not only were the people most independent and least racially mixed, but the forms of popular culture were also most strongly influenced by Christian – specifically Baptist – modes. Thus, cultural anthropologists seeking the true Bahamas in the 1950s and 1960s found their richest trove of survivals in Andros and Cat Island. There survived not only folklore and folk beliefs from Africa retailed through a dialect akin to that of the Georgia Sea Islands, but a vigorous musical equivalent of the negro spiritual of the US South called antems, which combined African rhythms and storytelling with the call-and-response, hymnological style and quasi-animistic spirituality found also in the church services of the native Baptists.[44]

Notes

1. For the standard traditional history see M. Craton, *A History of the Bahamas*, 3rd edn (Waterloo: San Salvador Press, 1986). For White-oriented general histories stressing the Loyalists, see P. Albury, *The Story of the Bahamas*, (London: Macmillan, 1975); S. Riley, *Homeward Bound: A History of the Bahama Islands to 1850, with a Definitive Study of Abaco in the American Loyalist Plantation Period* (Miami, FL: Island Research, 1983).
2. This chapter relies particularly on Craton and G. Saunders, *Islanders in the Stream: A History of the Bahamian People, Vol I : From Aboriginal Times to the End of Slavery* (Athens, GA: University of Georgia Press, 1992). See also Saunders, *Bahamian Loyalists and their Slaves* (London: Macmillan, 1983).
3. Craton, 'Hopetown and Hard Bargain: The Loyalist Transformation in the Bahamas', in Ralph Bennett, ed., *Settlements in the Americas: Cross Cultural Perspectives* (Center for Renaissance and Baroque Studies and University of Delaware Press, 1993), pp. 252–82.
4. Craton and Saunders, *Islanders in the Stream*, Vol. I, pp. 179–87; Riley, *Homeward Bound*, pp. 135–66. See also S. Dodge, *Abaco: The History of an Out Island and its Cays* (Miami, FL: Tropic Isles, 1983).

5.   New York, British Headquarters Papers, 10427, f. 83, No. 2, 'Book of Negroes Registered and certified after having been inspected by the commissioners appointed by His Excellency Sir Guy Carleton . . . on board sundry Vessels on which they were embarked', quoted as Appendix D in Riley, *Homeward Bound*, pp. 266–67.

6.   Riley, *Homeward Bound*, pp. 142, 155–7, 177; Craton and Saunders, *Islanders in the Stream*, Vol. I, pp. 185–6.

7.   CO 23/26, 225, John Barry, 30 June 1786, quoted in Craton and Saunders, *Islanders in the Stream*, Vol. I, p. 187.

8.   CO 23/27, 75; Lord Dunmore to Lord Shelburne, 28 December 1787; Craton and Saunders, *Islanders In the Stream*, Vol. I, p. 187.

9.   Ibid., pp. 187–8.

10.   Dodge, Abaco: 'Independence and Separatism,' in D.V. Collinwood and S. Dodge, eds., *Modern Bahamian Society* (Parkersburg, IO: Iowa University Press 1989), pp. 48–9. Craton and Saunders, *Islanders In the Stream*, Vol. II: *From the End of Slavery to the Twenty-First Century* (Athens, GA: University of Georgia Press, 1997), Part 3, Chapter 10.

11.   Craton and Saunders, *Islanders in the Stream*, Vol. I, pp. 179–212.

12.   Proclamation by Lieutenant Governor James Powell, *Bahama Gazette*, 10 September 1785; Craton, *History of the Bahamas*, pp. 156–7; Craton and Saunders, *Islanders in the Stream*, Vol. 1, pp. 170–1.

13.   Ibid., pp. 291–6; Craton, 'Changing Patterns of Slave Families In the British West Indies', *Journal of Interdisciplinary History*, 10 (Summer 1979), pp. 1–35; D. Eltis, 'The Traffic In Slaves between the British West Indian Colonies, 1807–1833', *Economic History Review*, 2nd. ser. 25, No. 1 (1972), pp. 55-64.

14.   Craton and Saunders, *Islanders in the Stream*, Vol. I, pp. 381–93; Craton, 'Hobbesian or Panglossian? The Two Extremes of Slave Conditions In the British Caribbean, 1783-1834', *William and Mary Quarterly*, 35 (1978), pp. 226–56; 'We Shall Not Be Moved. Pompey's Proto-Peasant Slave Revolt in Exuma Island, Bahamas, 1829–1830', *Nieuwe Westindische Gids* (Spring 1983) pp. 19–35; Craton and G. Saunders, 'Seeking a Life of their Own: Aspects of Slave Resistance in the Bahamas', *Journal of Caribbean History*, Vol. 24:1 (1990), pp. 1-27, and *Indian Historical Review*, XV, 1–2 (1991), pp. 96-115; Craton and Saunders, 'On Slavery's Margins, Farquharson's Estate, San Salvador, Bahamas, 1831–2', *Slavery and Abolition*, Vol. 9, No. 2 (1991), pp. 49–72.

15.   B. Bailyn, *Voyagers to the West: A Passage in the Peopling of America on the Eve of the Revolution* (New York: Knopf, 1986), pp. 434–6, 447–51.

16.   Craton, 'Hobbesian or Panglossian?'; Craton and Saunders, *Islanders in the Stream*, Vol. 1, pp. 269–81; B. Higman, *Slave Populations of the British Caribbean, 1807–1834* (Baltimore, MD: The Johns Hopkins Press, 1984), pp. 303–78.

17. Craton and Saunders, *Islanders in the Stream*, Vol. I, pp. 381–6; Craton, 'We Shall Not Be Moved'; Craton and Saunders, 'Seeking a Life of Their Own'.
18. Craton and Saunders, *Islanders in the Stream*, Vol. I, pp. 390–1.
19. Craton, 'White Law and Black Custom: The Evolution of Bahamian Land Tenures', in J. Momsen and J. Besson, eds., *Land Development In the Caribbean* (London: Macmillan, 1987), pp. 88–114.
20. Craton and Saunders, *Islanders in the Stream*, Vol. II, Part 4, Chapter 5.
21. Ibid., Vol. 1, p. 369; D.E. Wood, *A Guide to Selected Sources for the History of the Seminole Settlements at Red Bay Cays, Andros, 1817–1980* (Nassau: Archives Department, 1989).
22. See, for example, R. Shedden, *Ups and Downs in a West Indian Diocese* (London: Mombray, 1927); K. Otterbein, *The Andros Islanders: A Study of Family Organisation In the Bahamas* (Lawrence, KS, 1966); J. Holm and A. Shilling, *Dictionary of Bahamian English* (Cold Spring, N.Y.: Lexik House Publishers, 1980).
23. Craton and Saunders, *Islanders in the Stream*, Vol. I, pp. 221–4.
24. CO 23/67, 154–60, 1815 Regulations; Craton and Saunders, *Islanders in the Stream*, Vol. I, pp. 297–303.
25. *Bahama Gazette*, 24 January 1821; Craton and Saunders, *Islanders in the Stream*, Vol. I, p. 302.
26. New York Historical Society. Misc. MSS. Brown J. Papers of John Brown and Family, New Providence, Bahamas, 1761–1835; Craton, 'The Ambivalences of Independency: The Transition out of Slavery In the Bahamas, c. 1800–1850', in R. McDonald, ed., *West Indies Accounts: Essays on the British Caribbean and the Atlantic Economy in Honour of Richard Sheridan* (Mona, Jamaica: UWI Press, 1996), pp. 274–96.
27. M.K. Armbrister, ed., 'Henrietta, My Daughter' (typescript, Bahamas Archives); Craton and Saunders, *Islanders in the Stream*, Vol. 1, pp. 233–42.
28. H. Johnson, 'Slave Life and Leisure in Nassau, 1783–1838', *Slavery and Abolition*, Vol. 16, No. 1 (April 1995), pp. 45–64; *The Bahamas In Slavery and Freedom* (Kingston: Ian Randle; London: James Currey, 1991), pp. 19–29; 'A Slow and Extended Abolition. The Case of the Bahamas, 1800-1838', in M. Turner, ed., *From Chattel Slaves to Wage Slaves: The Dynamics of Labour Bargaining in the Americas* (Kingston: Ian Randle; Bloomington: Indiana University Press; London: James Currey, 1995), pp. 165–84.
29. Craton and Saunders, *Islanders In the Stream*, Vol. I, pp. 194–5; M.F. Doran and R.A. Landis, 'Origin and Persistence of an Inner-City Slum in Nassau', *Geographical Review*, 70 (1980), pp. 185–6; Johnson, 'Slave Life and Leisure', p. 48.
30. Craton and Saunders, *Islanders in the Stream*, Vol. I, pp. 199–201.

31. CO 23130, 16–18; Minutes of Assembly, 1789, Consolidated Slave Law, 1797, Nassau Archives, Manuscript Laws, 1794–1797, pp. 265–80; Craton and Saunders, *Islanders In the Stream*, Vol. I, pp. 206–12.

32. 1797 Consolidated Slave Act, clauses 17, 19, 21, 28, 32; Craton and Saunders, *Islanders in the Stream*, Vol. I, p. 211.

33. Ibid., pp. 369-72.

34. Johnson, 'Slave Life and Leisure', pp. 48–57.

35. Craton and Saunders, *Islanders in the Stream*, Vol. I, pp. 174–6.

36. Craton, 'Decoding Pitchy-Patchy: The Roots, Branches and Essence of Junkanoo', *Slavery and Abolition*, Vol. 16, No. 1 (April, 1995), pp. 14–44.

37. Craton and Saunders, *Islanders in the Stream*, Vol. II, Chapter 1, Section 2; H. Johnson, 'The Liberated Africans', in Johnson, *The Bahamas in Slavery and Freedom*, pp. 30–54.

38. R. Isaac, *The Transformation of Virginia, 1740–1790* (Chapel Hill, NC: University of North Carolina Press, 1988); A.J. Raboteau, *Slave Religion: The Invisible Institution in the Antebellum South* (New York: Oxford Univerity Press, 1978); M. Sobel, *Trabelin' On: The Slave Journey to an Afro-Baptist Faith*, (Westport, CT: Greenwood Press, 1979).

39. Craton and Saunders, *Islanders in the Stream*, Vol. I, pp. 184–6, 195, 329, 331; C. Williams, 'The Methodist Contribution to Education in the Bahamas', (unpublished PhD thesis, University of Wales, Lampeter, 1977); T. Coke, *A History of the West Indies: Containing the Natural, Civil and Ecclesiastical History of Each Island*, 3 vols (London, 1808), III, pp. 200–3; A. Deans Peggs, ed., *Dowson's Journal: A Mission to the West India Islands*, 1810-1817 (Nassau: 1960).

40. Williams, 'Methodist Contribution', p. 227; Coke, *History of the West Indies*, I, p. 9; *Dowson's Journal*, pp. 40, 67–8, 75.

41. Quoted from SPG correspondence by C.F. Pascoe, *Two Hundred Years of the S.P.G., 1701–1900* (London: Pascoe, 1901), p. 233.

42. Runaway advertisement for the return of Sambo, who ran away from St Augustine and claimed to be free, and Prince, who absconded in Nassau, signed by planter Isaac Baillou, *Bahama Gazette*, 6 August 1785. Quoted in Craton and Saunders, *Islanders in the Stream*, Vol. I, p. 330.

43. Ibid., pp. 330–4. See also M. Symonette and A. Canzoneri, *Baptists in the Bahamas: An Historical Review* (Nassau: 1977).

44. L. Diston Powles, *Land of the Pink Pearl* (London, 1888); C.L. Edwards, *Bahama Songs and Stories* (Cincinnati, 1895); S.B. Charters, programme notes for *Music in the Bahamas*, Folkways, No. FS3845, 1959; E.C. Bethel, 'Music in the Bahamas: Its Roots, Development and Personality' (unpublished MA thesis, University of California, Los Angeles, 1978).

CHAPTER 4

Lineage Slavery in New Calabar, Eastern Niger Delta, 1850–1900

A reassessment

WAIBINTE WARIBOKO

Introduction: Statement of problem

All of the Eastern Delta states – New Calabar, Bonny, Nembe-Brass, Okrika and Opobo – illustrated many and varied purposes for which slaves were retained in most African societies in the nineteenth and early twentieth centuries. Slaves were used as trading agents, high and low political officials in the centralised sociopolitical formations, concubines and wives for lineage heads, fighting personnel for equipping and manning lineage war-canoes, servants for the performance of menial domestic and national services, and as potential sacrificial candidates to the numerous whimsical and capricious spiritual forces influencing human lives in the creeks of the Niger Delta. These Eastern Delta states were therefore slave-holding and using societies. This was principally on account of their participation in the transatlantic commerce – first in slaves (1500–1850) and later in palm oil and kernels (1830–1950) – which required an extensive workforce to operate successfully.

The contributions of slaves to the sociopolitical, economic and cultural institutions of these slave-using trading states attracted the intellectual interest of Nigeria's pioneer historians. K.O. Dike and G.I. Jones, to begin with, have given attention to the consequences of British abolition of the external slave trade; the growth, development and consequences of the successive trade in palm oil and kernels and the crucial role of domestic slaves in the internal production process of these export staples.[1] R. Horton, E.J. Alagoa and T.N. Tamuno emphasised the process of acculturating domestic slaves before their incorporation and integration into the adoptive kin group or lineage and the wider society.[2]

These earlier readings are mutually complementary in several respects. They have contributed many insights to the understanding of the relations between servile and free members of the lineage in general, and the house heads in particular. Nevertheless, these works have not paid much critical attention to the horrors of lineage slavery; and in very subtle and different ways they have idealised the lineage model of domestic slavery. One vivid example would suffice here. According to Alagoa:

> The process for the acculturation of slaves into the delta communities was such that no revolt of slaves was theoretically possible. They were ritually incorporated as children of their masters' wives and became full members of the lineages or 'war-canoe houses' [*wari*] of their masters. They were also able to achieve political authority and became heads of these houses.[3]

The above presents a number of questionable assumptions. Firstly, by stating that after the ritual of incorporation the slaves became full members of the lineage or 'war-canoe houses' [*wari*] of their masters, Alagoa presupposes that they were granted full citizenship without qualifications. Secondly, domestic slaves have been presented without any distinction as if they all enjoyed equal opportunities and access to the means of achieving economic and political power.

From the account of Comte De Cardi, a nineteenth-century trader to the Eastern Niger Delta, and other sources, including oral traditions, it is possible to decipher three fluid groups of domestic slaves. There were those who carried 'their master's pocket-handkerchief and snuffbox'. 'After some years at this duty', according to De Cardi, such slaves were:

> promoted to going down to the European traders to superintend the delivery of a canoe of oil, seeing to its being tried and gauged. This first assignment, if efficiently performed, would lead to his being sent on the same errand. The duty required a certain amount of intelligence, for he had to so look after his master's interest that the *pull-away boys* that were with him in the same canoe did not secrete any few

gallons of oil . . . nor must he allow the White trader to undergauge his master's casks by carelessness or otherwise. If he is able to do the latter part of this errand . . . that day marked the commencement of his upward career, if he was possessed of the bump for saving.[4]

According to the same source, at the end of the above trying transactions, the slave received some presents in proportion to the quantity of oil sold. Presents were in the form of cloth cut into separate pieces, each costing about 2s 6d (British sterling). If the sale amounted to about 15 puncheons of oil, the slave might get two pieces of cloth and a bunch of beads. The presents were then handed over to the slave's mother, together with all subsequent gains, until he had amassed enough property to buy his own oil. The permission to start his own trade was obtained for him by his mother from his father. Gradually, after this humble beginning, the slave soon became a man of means and could own his own canoe and slaves.

Those who achieved great heights of political and economic success belong to this fortunate group. But others, the pulla boys, were never so lucky. For the sake of convenience and the purpose of this chapter, domestic slaves have been identified in the following way. Those who began by carrying their father's snuffbox as palace boys; those at the trading posts as *fesiri* boys; and those who manned the trading canoes as pulla boys. The first, second and third groups are simply described in the consular records as the trading members of the House; however, they did not have equal opportunities within the lineage.

Alagoa and others have described the institution of lineage slavery as benign, in part because domestic slaves could rise to positions of socioeconomic and political eminence. To substantiate this, they have cited the resounding achievements of King Jaja of Opobo, George Amachree of New Calabar and Oko Jumbo of Bonny, all ex-slaves who became rulers of society and owners of slaves.[5] These men began their career either as palace or *fesiri* boys before achieving fame and success. The first contention is that there is need to look at the lives of the pull-away or pulla boys (who were in the majority), rather than concentrate historical analysis on the lives of ex-slaves who became rulers, to do a balanced assessment of lineage slavery.

The final questionable presupposition of Alagoa's analysis is that, owing to the benevolent nature of lineage slavery in the Eastern Delta states, domestic slaves had no drive (or lost the drive) to revolt against the system. Put differently, they were largely satisfied with their existential conditions politically, socially and economically because, as Alagoa went on to indicate elsewhere, 'slaves were not segregated politically and socially'.[6] The second contention is that the horrible reality of lineage slavery has been understated or set forth in restrained terms by such accounts.

Probably, the reliance on oral traditions and the Foreign Office papers – in particular the despatches of the nineteenth-century consuls, E. Hewett, H. Johnston, C. MacDonald and R. Moor, in the Eastern Niger delta – contributed to the above ideal perception of lineage slavery. This will become clearer when lineage slavery and the extra-territorial forces of change are discussed. Therefore, to reassess issues, there is need to go beyond these consular papers. The accounts of some contemporary European traders to the Delta states in the nineteenth century and the Church Missionary Society (CMS) papers are less restrained in reporting and exposing the horrors of lineage slavery. While these source materials are invaluable for this reconstruction, the much needed theoretical insights are derived from published sources on lineage slavery.[7]

To place the main discussion in perspective, the rest of the chapter is divided into the following parts: New Calabar and the lineage (*wari*) organisation; lineage slavery and the palm oil trade during the nineteenth century; lineage slavery and the extra-territorial forces of change; and the concluding remarks.

New Calabar and the lineage (wari) organisation

New Calabar was the first, among the Eastern Delta states, to engage in the slave trade with the Portuguese around the end of the fifteenth century. The Portuguese were superseded by the Dutch, who came to monopolise the New Calabar slave market. The Dutch sustained this monopoly throughout the sixteenth and early seventeenth centuries before being superseded in their turn by the English. In 1668, for example, O. Dapper, a Dutch traveller, noted that New Calabar 'was the most important place of trade for the Dutch'.[8] This view of Dapper was confirmed by John Barbot three decades later when he observed: 'New Calabar is the chief place for the trade of the Hollanders'.[9]

Around the beginning of the eighteenth century, a period coinciding with the English dominance of the slave trade, New Calabar's position was lost to the neighbouring trading state of Bonny. The latter state has since gone down in history as one of the greatest slave marts in West Africa.[10] In addition to the external trade in slaves, however, all of the Eastern Delta states participated in an internal long-distance trade with their hinterland food-producing communities on the northern fringes of the delta. Generally these agricultural communities, as distinct from the Eastern Delta fishing and trading states, belong to the Niger-Congo group of languages.

The entire economic enterprise of New Calabar, including the superstructure that supported and sustained it, revolved around the lineage, the first and basic unit of socioeconomic and political organisation. This patrilineal unit, *wari*, consisted of an initial family (the man, wife or wives, and children) and others; agnatically related persons, voluntary sojourners seeking political refuge, and large numbers of male and female domestic slaves. The overall aim of every lineage was to expand its population through reproduction and incorporation, so that its own workforce would effectively rival or surpass those of competing lineages in the body politic. In pursuit of this aim, kinship norms endorsed endogamous marriages between servile members and, occasionally, between the most industrious and successful male slaves and the free female members of the lineage.

According to extant oral traditions, Amachree, the founder of the Amachree lineage and dynasty, took advantage of these kinship norms to launch a massive integration programme of domestic slaves into his newly found lineage. This exercise took place shortly after an Okrika invasion of New Calabar had decimated the population of the city-state around the end of the eighteenth century. The above traditions have gone on to say that, by the beginning of the nineteenth century, the Amachree house had succeeded in translating this numerical superiority into political, military and economic dominance over other competing lineages in New Calabar.[11]

New Calabar and the neighbouring Eastern Delta slave-using trading states generally believed that to gain the loyalty of domestic slaves, the slave-masters (who were all males in the nineteenth century) needed to go beyond the market transaction that merely endorsed ownership of the physical, material body, the casing for the invisible and intangible human mind. This idea, for example, has been well expressed in the Eastern Delta Ijo proverb, *omoni febo bio fegha*. This means: the slave buyer does not buy the mind or the intellect – the power-house of reasoning, thinking and acting. The primary aim of acculturation, therefore, was to control the minds of domestic slaves and to reconcile them with the dominant values of the adopted kin group and wider society. Horton has described the ritual for the existential transformation of the slave at New Calabar: 'When the newly bought slave arrived in the community, the breaking-off of all previous kinship ties and the assumption of a whole series of new ties was brought home to him by means of a dramatic *rite de passage* in which his new 'mother' shaved his head clean and then give him a ritual mean. *From then on, the 'mother' was supposed to live up to her title in the fullest sense*.[12] (my italics)

Among other missionaries, Bishop Johnson was very quick to satirise the image and role of the 'mother' as portrayed in the above excerpt. To this missionary, the maternal duties did not make lineage slavery less abhorrent. His sarcasm in 1877 reads:

> (Slave) children now call 'mothers' those who shaved their heads when they were first brought down as slaves. I allow their treatment is often good and gentle, but this is only during good behaviour. And what are they, but slaves. I learnt that should any of them commit an offence, he is immediately put in irons; and for the second offence he is liable to be sold to the cannibal tribes who make savoury dishes of him.[13]

Horton has concurred with the criticism of Johnson by noting that: 'when the stupid, unadaptable slave got himself into trouble, 'mother' and 'brothers' tended to remember that they were not really of the same flesh and blood, and seldom insisted very strongly on the unfortunate man's rights. In consequence he was often mercilessly punished or deprived of his life, *where a free-born would be let off very lightly*.'[14] So in what sense is a 'mother' supposed to live up to her title in the fullest sense when she is incapable of insisting strongly on the rights of her child? This is another instance of idealisation in the published secondary literature on lineage slavery. This is also the line of separation between Horton and Alagoa on one side and Johnson on the other. More of the latter's criticism will be presented later.

Having given the above background information about the lineage and its programme of recruitment and acculturation of domestic slaves, it is time to examine the specific ways house heads related to domestic slaves in the export-import trade of the nineteenth century. The central argument here is that house heads related differently to the three groups of domestic slaves identified above.

Lineage slavery and the palm oil trade during the nineteenth century

The palm oil trade in the nineteenth century did not minimise the importance and/or exploitation of domestic slaves in New Calabar sociopolitical and economic formation. On the contrary, as the discussion below will reveal, it underscored the maximum exploitation of this underprivileged category in the social formation.

To facilitate commercial transactions with the primary producers of palm oil and kernels in the hinterland, New Calabar established ports of trade, *fesiri*, in these areas. Domestic slaves permanently resided at the ports of trade in order to purchase the export staples on a regular and daily basis. It may be recalled that New Calabar – hinterland commercial relations were based on the trust system. Under this system, New Calabar merchant chiefs – via the agency of their *fesiri* boys resident at the trading ports – passed on European manufactures (trade goods) to the hinterland primary producers in exchange for equivalent amounts of export staples. These trade goods, it has to be reiterated, were obtained on trust from European partners. Given the nature of these transactions, domestic slaves at the trading posts – that is, the *fesiri* boys as differentiated from the pulla boys – were entrusted with much capital and management responsibilities. Management responsibilities, for example, included reprocessing procured export items and putting these into firmly sealed puncheons or casks. All of these entailed some knowledge of bookkeeping and coopering.

Thereafter, the pulla boys, who manned the trading canoes, transported these casks to New Calabar. Dapper commented on these canoes in 1668: 'the negroes navigate the river Kalbarien [Kalabari] in very large canoes with twenty oarsmen or padlers on either side [*this means that it took about forty domestic slaves to man a trading canoe*], in which sixty, even eighty, men can be carried'.[15] (Italics mine).

The design of these cargo-delivery canoes, which were built for the slave trade, was improved upon to achieve greater carrying capacity for the palm oil puncheons and casks.[16] In this regard, the pulla boys could be likened to menial slaves while the *fesiri* and palace boys were the skilled ones in the trading formation.

Finally, when these puncheons or casks of palm oil arrived at the port of New Calabar, trusted retainers, chosen from among the palace slaves, superintended the delivery and sale to the European traders. We have been told that this 'duty required a certain amount of intelligence, for [the domestic slave] had to look after his master's interest . . . [so that] . . . the White trader [does not] undergauge his master's casks by carelessness or otherwise'. For the purpose of efficiency in accounting and measurement some of the palace and *fesiri* slaves were sent to the missionary boarding school when it was established in 1874. Missionary education created further differentiation among domestic slaves; this in turn facilitated social mobility among the ranks of the palace and *fesiri* slaves.[17]

Sparingly, when any of the domestic slaves engaged at the two ends of the three-tier process – that is, among the palace and *fesiri* slaves – portrayed outstanding commercial dynamism, he could be offered credit facilities by the house head to launch and expand his own trading operation. For such credit facilities, some interest, called *workbar*, was paid to the house head; this was ten per cent of the total value of every puncheon of oil sold by the domestic slave. In 1883, the servile beneficiaries of these credit facilities had cried out against this amount of interest. Thus, for example, A.F.F.P. Newns, a Colonial Officer at New Calabar, reported: 'I have seen an original communication from the traders of New Calabar [domestic slaves] to the chiefs stating that the *workbar* should be reduced, as from the 19th of February, 1883, to seven cases of gin per puncheon. Gin was then very cheap and a form of currency'.[18]

With the formal inauguration of colonial rule in 1891, the *workbar* was abolished. But the house heads were able to demand another payment from this small class of trading domestic slaves, called trade tax or house tax. As will be shown later, the colonial administration endorsed this levy in the Act of 1899. In 1904, for instance, Bishop Johnson noted: 'Members of different House holds run by chiefs pay the House tax, levied upon them for the upkeep of the House and the trading business connected with them, whether they are at home or not. That is, at the up river interior markets'.[19]

Towards the end of the nineteenth century, the exploitative socioeconomic relations described above were being challenged by the domestic slaves in New Calabar and the other Eastern Delta states. In 1910, for example, W.F. Fosbery, another colonial officer in Southern Nigeria, wrote the following concerning New Calabar domestic slaves and their masters: 'The chief source of complaint by Heads of Houses is against the trading class of members who absent themselves for a long period at the up river markets trading on their own account and who gradually became independent and throw off their allegiance to their House'.[20]

As these passages indicate, domestic slaves were in fact politically and socially segregated; they did seek to pursue an autonomous existence from the lineage; and their plight was more horrible than some accounts would want us to believe. In the next part of this chapter, the plight of slave converts to

European missionary Christianity will be discussed in order to throw more light on the central question of how truly benign domestic slavery was at New Calabar. After that, the chapter will show how the exposed horrors of lineage slavery were reported upon in very restrained terms by the nineteenth-century consuls to the Eastern Delta, in the self-interest of their administration.

Lineage slavery and the extra-territorial forces of change: the Church Missionary Society

Lineage heads at New Calabar and elsewhere in the Eastern Delta were very critical of Christianity in part because of its impact on the servile members of the lineage. Christianity dinned into the ears of these slave converts the ideals of individual freedom and rights, the equality of all persons before God and the universal brotherhood of humankind. These social doctrines were in clear opposition to the received hierarchical structure of the trading lineage or house, in which the domestic slaves were entirely subject to the control of the house head.

In a tête-à-tête with Archdeacon D.C. Crowther, a CMS proselytiser, Bob Manuel, a house head and slave-master, reported as follows in 1894: 'Those who attend church were breaking the country's laws; are taught to disobey their masters and not work when sent; and their slaves and women were actually defying and threatening them at home'.[21]

Based on the conviction that Christianity was undermining the norms and values of the traditional social order, house heads were really ruthless with slave converts. Two examples from New Calabar and Bonny will demonstrate the point.

At New Calabar two female Christians of slave origin, known as Mary and Martha, took it upon themselves to use and to wear printed cotton cloth in the community. Hitherto, a prohibition against any use whatsoever of such cloth had been imposed on the community by the tutelary deity of New Calabar, Owamekaso. Another baptised man, also reportedly a member of the servile class, had 'spent no less than one (1) pound (British sterling) to buy himself and wife, from the German shop, whatever articles he knew was against the country's law, among them an umbrella, which only chiefs and sub-chiefs were allowed to carry'.[22]

As a result of these offences, Mary and Martha were banished to two satellite New Calabar villages, Ke and Okpo. Their husbands, who were pulla boys in the house of Bob Manuel, were forced to denounce them in public; and when they eventually were allowed to return to their community, they were placed under the tutelary supervision of certain cult servants of an indigenous divinity. The male culprit, whose name or lineage identities were not given by our source, was resold into slavery.

In 1874, Bonny passed a law prohibiting 'any of their slaves or dependants from going to church on pains of heavy fines or severe punishments'; and the reason for this law was that: 'their church-going slaves being converts to Christianity, were getting independent, disobedient and refused to paddle canoes [this refers to the pulla boys] to the oil markets on Sunday'.[23]

In 1875, six Christian converts of slave origin were imprisoned for one year – November 1875 to November 1876 – by their masters for violating the above law. Among those so imprisoned, the cases of Alpha Banigo of Banigo house and Bara Hart of Hart house made sensational news because of the severity of their ordeal. According to CMS sources, these two men were: 'exposed to heavy rains and burning sun alternately; that their hands ... were handcuffed in grout, turned to the back and chained, their feet still in stock of heavy wood, and not a morsel of food . . . given them'.[24]

The protracted ordeal of these converts attracted the sympathy of the European traders in Bonny who decided to intervene. As D.C. Crowther put it:

> Some of the Europeans attending [Saint Clements church] having heard of the severe ordeals these converts of the sister church [Saint Stephens] were passing through, resolved to help by asking the united efforts of the other gentlemen supercargoes in the river, to reason with the chiefs and make known to them that such persecution and treatment of their slaves on the ground of their embracing the Christian religion cannot be tolerated, while they hold such commercial relations with them.[25]

This concerted action produced the desired result. Via the Bonny Court of Equity, a sort of commercial court in the trading states of the Eastern Delta states in the nineteenth century, the concerned European supercargoes invited the king, George Pepple, and the chiefs to discuss the matter. Consequently, these slave converts were released at 4.30 pm on 7 November 1876 on the condition that they were exiled from the community. On the request of Bishop Crowther, the European supercargoes paid their passage to Lagos where they lived in exile.

The plight of the other four prisoners also attracted comments shortly before their release. S. A. Crowther noted that they were: 'in a most pitiable condition, with overgrown hairs and nails, ribs painfully visible, feet as feeble from want of exercise and torture as to require help of friends to get up the steps, hands in handcuffs and each with a strip of rags round their loins'.[26]

The sources further reveal that, among the four persons whose horrors have been described above, one died shortly after being released from confinement. These tales of inhumane treatment drawn from Bonny and New Calabar were not isolated cases in the Eastern Niger Delta. CMS sources offer more narratives on the horrors of lineage slavery in the other trading states of Nembe-Brass, Okrika and Opobo.

De Cardi also had this to say about the horrors of lineage slavery:

> Ear cutting in its various stages, from clipping to total dismemberment; crucifixion round a large cask; extraction of teeth; suspension by the thumbs; chilli peppers pounded and stuffed up the nostrils, and forced into the eyes and ears; fastening the victim to a post driven into the beach at low water and leaving him there to be drowned with the rising tide, or to be eaten by the sharks or crocodiles piecemeal; heavily ironed and chained to a post in their master's compound, without any covering over their heads.[27]

The following observations may be made. These stories fully justify Bishop Johnson's sarcasm about the benevolent nature of lineage slavery in general, and the usefulness of the 'mother' to the acculturated domestic slave in particular; secondly, the arbitrary exercise of supreme power over slaves who proved to be deviant, or too independent, tended to make lineage slavery comparable with sugar plantation slavery in the Americas (with specific reference to master-slave relations); finally, the reported intense cruelty to domestic slaves was linked in a causal way to the need for profit maximisation in the palm oil trade. In this connection, it should be remembered that these cruelties were occurring during the years of the trade depression, 1863–1900; and they were motivated by a determination to compel the pulla boys to work on the Sabbath day.

The Christian missionaries to the Eastern Niger Delta in the nineteenth century accused the British consular administration of abetting house heads in perpetrating and perpetuating the above injustices against domestic slaves. In 1894, H.H. Dobinson, the secretary of the CMS Niger Mission, alleged as follows: 'In no place [New Calabar] have the chiefs such absolute power as here over the slaves and in this they are supported by Government who threaten to punish any slave who will not obey his master'.[28]

To evaluate the above remarks, it is pertinent to discuss the perception of the emergent colonial administration regarding lineage slavery in the nineteenth century. The discussion will be brief because the existing secondary materials on this subject – that is, the overall colonial administrative policy to the question of domestic slavery and its abolition – are fairly copious and adequate.[29] The sole purpose is to explain how and why the early consuls reported about the horrors of lineage slavery in very restrained language.

Lineage slavery and the early consuls to the Eastern Niger Delta

It has been said that the early consuls to the Eastern Delta in the nineteenth century described domestic slavery as benign in part because they carried with them concepts of slavery framed by Western intellectual and historical experience.[30] By 1877, however, this notion had come under intense criticism from Bishop Johnson when he visited New Calabar. The criticism reads:

> My language in speaking of slavery can never be apologetic; let the form it assumes be ever so mild. I have no patience with those who themselves free, would ... hide the system under the heap of mitigating pleas [this refers to the British Consuls], as if it were not a thing which deserves reprobation and total excretion. You will often hear – 'well, the masters are kind and good to them, and value them highly etc'. Not a doubt of it. They take pleasure in them just as I do in my nice breed of poultry or cattle or any other thing from which I derive my wealth. No: liberty is the birthright of every man, and no treatment can reconcile me to the idea of being deprived from my freedom.[31]

Bishop Johnson's criticism was in part informed by the tragic incidents at Bonny involving Alpha Banigo and Bara Hart. There is, therefore, evidence that these early consuls, through the critical reports of the CMS missionaries, were acquainted with the horrors of lineage slavery in the Eastern Delta.

The availability of such criticisms notwithstanding, Vice-Consul Johnston, who did a 'Report on the British Protectorate of the Oil Rivers' in December 1888, stated: 'The slaves are allowed to possess property on their own . . . *owning to its mild character* slavery offers little cause for its sudden and abrupt abolition; a change which would at present be doubtfully approved by the slaves'.[32] (my italics)

This notion regarding slave ownership of property has to be addressed or put in perspective, because it is central to this discussion. The position of house heads in the matter of property acquisition and ownership was stated by a New Calabar chief in the following terms: 'The native point of view is that members [domestic slaves] came naked into the House. Naked must they depart from it . . . However long a House member may have worked for the House the profits accruing to him are only enjoyed so long as he remains a member. Should he depart, everything reverts to the House'.[33]

In essence, the property of domestic slaves, one of the key elements that is considered benign about lineage slavery in the Eastern Delta, belonged not to the slave, but to the corporate house. The slave is only a beneficiary of corporate house property under the supervision of the house head. For this reason, the bishops of the Anglican Communion condemned the house system in the following strong terms in 1906:

> under the 'House system' liberty of action, liberty of speech, liberty of purchase, liberty to sell, liberty to marry, liberty to bequeath property, liberty to enter into a contract, save under grievous conditions, heavy to be borne, is practically denied. Apparently, the 'House system' was not made for man, but man for the 'House system'. The result is to a large extent the destruction of a spirit of enterprise, enthusiasm or devotion and the establishment of a condition of mental, moral, social stagnation, injurious alike to the individual and the Race.[34]

What Consul Johnston adumbrated in essence was that slaves in the Eastern Delta were satisfied with their status of dependency within the lineage or house. In 1895, the first consul-general of the Oil Rivers Protectorate after the inauguration of colonial rule in the area, endorsed the above perception regarding lineage slavery: 'domestic slavery and enslavement for debt have, from time immemorial, formed the basis of social life of the people, and that therefore all changes must be carried out with moderation, patience, and common sense'.[35]

Finally, Ralph Moor, the successor of Claude MacDonald, in one of his despatches to the Foreign Office in 1895, defended the perpetuation of lineage slavery in the following way: 'I do not wish to convey the idea that the present position and condition of domestic slaves, especially in the region well under Government influence, is one of suffering or hardship; for in the hundreds, I may say thousands of cases that have been inquired into there are but few where actual ill treatment has been proved'.[36]

The above reports by Johnston, MacDonald and Moor tend to prove Bishop Johnson's point that: these consuls were hiding the system under the heap of mitigating pleas. But why were the consuls, as compared with the missionaries, very restrained in their condemnation of lineage slavery? To appreciate the position of the consuls, it is pertinent to make some very brief comments about the ideological motivations of the missionaries against slavery.

The missionaries took an uncompromising doctrinal and ethical position over the question of domestic slavery and the approach to its abolition in the Niger Delta. Being led by their faith, they perceived all human souls – slave or free – as being infinitely precious in the sight of God, as God himself has signified by suffering for their redemption. To these missionaries, therefore, the human soul was divine and holy; and they interpreted this sacrosanctity of the human personality as being a sacred right to political freedom and the right to freedom of economic enterprise.[37]

On the other hand, the colonial government was motivated by economic, administrative and political considerations in formulating its perception and policy in the matter of lineage slavery. Economically, the government depended heavily on free labour for its projects in the initial years of the transition to colonial rule. This, the chiefs supplied largely from their pool of domestic slaves. In 1911, for example, Reverend Harris noted as follows: 'The maintenance of domestic slavery in certain districts of the Eastern and Central provinces, greatly facilitates the task of obtaining labour supplies today. It is obviously easier and cheaper to instruct a chief to bring 100 carriers than to engage such carriers individually; easier, but only possible under a system whereby the chiefs have possession of slaves or of a servile class'.[38]

On this question of labour, a contemporary European trader in the Eastern Niger Delta, Alex A. Cowan, further noted: 'Local labour was not procurable in 1887. It was possible at times to contract with the king or chiefs for particular work, but every day labour had to be recruited from outside'.[39]

Administratively and politically, the colonial government needed the collaboration of the slave-owning class of chiefs to rule effectively, as there was an endemic shortfall in numbers of European administrative personnel. This is borne out by MacDonald's report to the Foreign Office, when he eventually took over formal British administration of the Oil Rivers Protectorate in 1891: 'The chief, or head of the House, is also responsible for the behaviour of his slaves and for any damage done by him, or any crime they may commit. It would be impossible to administer this country without the assistance of these chiefs or heads of Houses, who have been with rare exception, most useful and loyal in helping the Queen's executive'.[40]

In addition to enlisting the support of the chiefs for administrative purposes, the colonial administration was fearful of possible anarchy if all slaves were immediately or suddenly emancipated. A combination of these factors gave rise to a very conservative programme for the eventual abolition of lineage slavery in the Niger Delta.

The colonial administration and its conservative abolition programme for lineage slavery

By December 1895, four years after the inauguration of formal British administration and five years after the Brussels international conference on arms, liquor and slavery, the Foreign Office enquired what measures MacDonald had taken respecting the issue of domestic slavery. The occasion provided MacDonald with an opportunity to discuss his programme to abolish slavery.

This programme was substantially the British Indian model.[41] This model had been evolved in India in 1843 by the East India Company, when the British government forced the reluctant company to abolish slavery in response to mounting international criticism. The chief aspect of the Indian model which MacDonald imported into the Oil Rivers Protectorate was the provisions embodied in Act V of the Indian legislation of 1843 (and especially Sections II, III and IV).

These sections dealt with domestic slavery in the following ways. Section II urged that: 'No rights arising out of alleged property in the person and services of another shall be enforced by any court'. Section III stipulated that: 'No person who may have acquired property of his own industry or by the exercise of any art, calling or profession or by inheritance, assignment, gift or bequest, shall be dispossessed of such property or prevented from taking possession thereof on the ground that such person, or that the person from whom the property may have been derived was a slave.' Finally, Section IV urged that: 'Any act which could be a penal offence if done to a free man shall be equally an offence if done to any person in the pretext of his being in a condition of slavery'.[42]

These provisions, lamentably, did not (and were not designed to) address the issue of emancipation frontally or in any serious way. They were really a compromise between the home government's demand for swift action against domestic slavery, and the more gradualist approach of the Niger Coast Protectorate administration. The administration did not enforce any of the above provisions rigorously. In fact, they did things to strengthen the sovereign powers of masters over their slaves. This example should suffice to illustrate the point.

In 1892, the pulla boys at New Calabar had refused to carry trade goods to the interior markets because they wanted to keep the Sabbath holy. This refusal directly threatened the economic basis of chiefship in the coastal trading state of New Calabar, and even the Protectorate administration became somewhat alarmed. The Vice-Consul at Degema, headquarters of the New Calabar Consulate, decided to intervene. He announced, during a consular court session at Degema, that any slave who refused to work on Sundays should be brought before him for punishment.[43]

Towards the end of the nineteenth century, the Colonial Government passed The Act of 1899 in order, as they claimed, to gradually abolish domestic slavery. In reality, however, this act continued to empower the slave-owning class. For example, the act required domestic slaves engaged in independent commercial ventures to pay the following house tax to their masters: on every puncheon of oil, a tax of 10 shillings; on every cask of kernels, a tax of 4 shillings; and on other articles of produce or commerce, a commission of 5 per cent.[44]

As these half-hearted measures generated intense campaigns against the administration locally and overseas, Moor enacted the following laws. In April 1901 the legal status of slavery was officially abolished; and to reinforce the efficacy of this, Moor also promulgated the Slave Dealing Proclamation on 17 March 1901, to take effect from 1 April. The reason for this was to make any further dealing in slaves legally punishable.[45] But to soften the anticipated impact of abolition, Moor quickly enacted the Master and Servant Proclamation on 16 March 1901, also to take effect on 1 April. The aim of this enactment was to regulate contract relations between the house heads and their apprentices whom they were encouraged to acquire for their trading businesses to and in the interior markets.[46]

However, it soon appeared that Moor still believed that it was premature to establish a free labour market in the Protectorate, or even to grant any form of unconditional emancipation to domestic slaves. Moor convened a conference with the slave-owning class at Bonny, and, in his own words, the question of slavery in the Protectorate 'was very fully gone into in all its aspects'. This meeting probably convinced him of his next move, which was in no way a departure from the gradualist approach to abolition initiated by MacDonald. On 7 July 1901, Moor wrote as follows to Secretary of State Joseph Chamberlain: 'the matter [of slavery] will require most careful and judicious handling to avoid immediate and serious difficulties which might give rise to entire dislocation in the affairs of Government, trade and control'.[47]

Thereafter, Moor devoted himself to finding ways of circumventing the abolition Ordinance against domestic slavery in Southern Nigeria. This gave birth to the famous Native House Rule Proclamation of 1901, which came into effect in January 1902. This proclamation strengthened the house heads against domestic slaves. One aim of the Ordinance, as contained in its preamble was: 'to make provision for the maintenance of the authority vested in the Heads of Houses by native law and custom'. Article 6, for example, in pursuit of the above aim stated: 'Any European or Native who knowing a Native to be a member of a House employs such Native without the express or implied consent of the Head of the House shall be liable to a fine not exceeding fifty pounds, or to imprisonment with or without hard labour for any term not exceeding one year, or to both'.[48]

Under the House Rule Ordinance it became easier, and indeed legal, to use the colonial administrative and judicial machinery to coerce domestic slaves. At New Calabar, house heads now codified rules, through the machinery of the Native Court, for the maximum exploitation of domestic slave labour. In 1906, for example, a Native Council Rule was passed stating how many days of service a domestic slave must render to his house head following a period of autonomous business activity in the interior market. This law stipulated that: 'Traders on their arrival at home from their various trading places shall remain sixteen days before again going to market in order to arrange about the business of their respective houses, and to do their share of work required to be done by the house'.[49]

This regulation was deemed necessary in order to check any avoidance of house duties under the expedient guise of absence through trading at the interior.

Domestic slaves reacted against these new and expanded powers conferred on house heads under the House Rule Ordinance. In 1906, the District Commissioner in charge of New Calabar District, D.C. Syer, noted that New Calabar domestic slaves were in the habit of fleeing to places like Old Calabar, Egwanga, Owerri and Aboh.[50] Such flights disprove the thesis of Johnston,

MacDonald and Moor that, on account of the mild nature of lineage slavery, slaves were largely unwilling to seek liberation from dependency on their house. It also proves that the existing published accounts, especially those which argued that 'slaves were not segregated politically or socially' and that after the ritual of incorporation they 'became full members of the lineages or "war-canoe houses" [*wari*] of their masters', have idealised the institution.

Conclusion

The House Rule Ordinance was eventually repealed in 1915. Before its repeal, however, the Native House Rule Amendment Ordinance was passed on 8 February 1912. The purpose of this was to set terms for the full emancipation of domestic slaves from their house heads. It stipulated: 'A member of a House shall, on ceasing to be a member, forfeit every claim and privilege of membership of the House including that of part ownership of property . . . but shall be entitled to retain all his own personal property'.[51]

This proclamation had agitated the minds of most slaves and members of the slave-owning class. Consequently, the Colonial Government had anticipated mass desertions and destabilisation of the primary units of economic organisation (the lineage) in the Eastern Delta societies. Social problems and disruptions did occur, but they were not anything approaching catastrophic levels for the lineages.

Extant records reveal that there were some people who elected to go back to their former communities. These were people who could still trace their links to their natal families, or who had suffered great political and social segregation or marginalisation. The following story about an Aro woman called Ori in Bob Manuel's house illustrates this point.

Ori was sold to Bob Manuel in 1895, together with a female baby she was then nursing. After the repeal of the house system, Ori's brother appeared to take both Ori and her daughter, who was now named Obuta Bob Manuel, back to the Aro country. But Bob Manuel refused to release Ori unless and until he was repaid the maintenance cost of Obuta for 20 years, 1895–1915. Subsequently, the matter was referred to the court. The court told Bob Manuel: 'There might be grounds for a claim for maintenance. Equally, there would then be grounds for a counter claim for wages for work done. The one would naturally be set against the other and would . . . about equalise'.[52]

Women who deserted their houses or the community, like Ori, did so for two possible reasons. Those who urged them to desert their houses had doubtless assured them of better socioeconomic opportunities in their former communities. Secondly, women without children found it easier to move from houses than those who had children. Ori had no other child except Obuta.

On the whole, social and economic conditions made mass flight impossible. The former slaves stayed behind to try to evolve more tolerable forms of socioeconomic relations within the house. In 1927, A.R. Whiteman, District Officer for Degema, reported on some of the attempts at renegotiating relations in New Calabar and Bonny. He noted:

> A regrettable feature among the New Calabar and Bonny Houses is becoming prevalent; the tendency to internal feuds and dissensions. The worst case is the Manuel House at Abonnema; the Big Harry family at Illelima and the Briggs family at Abonnema are rapidly following this deplorable lead. It is not always possible to trace how the dispute started . . . but the culminating point is litigation over family land, House property, and the succession to the headship of the House.[53]

Finally, all the available case notes suggest that, between 1915 and 1948, ex-domestic slaves acquired full rights and privileges within their lineages via the colonial judicial system. This was because they could not depend on lineage norms and conventions alone – usually subjected to the arbitrary interpretations of the house heads – to guarantee their full participation in the sociopolitical and economic activities of society as free citizens. In 1948, for example, these house heads were still urging the Colonial Government of Southern Nigeria to exclude the erstwhile servile members of society from the Native Council.[54]

Notes

The archival codes below refer to documents in the following libraries: FO means Foreign Office records at the London Public Records Office; CA3 and G3A3 refer to Church Missionary Society papers at the University of Birmingham, Birming - ham; Calprof, Rivproof, Degdist, CSE and CSO refer to papers deposited in the Enugu and Ibadan National Archives of Nigeria.

1.   K.O. Dike, *Trade and Politics in the Niger Delta* (Oxford: Oxford University Press, 1956); also see G.I. Jones, *The Trading States of the Oil Rivers* (Oxford: Oxford University Press, 1963).

2.   R. Horton, 'From Fishing Village to City-State: A Social History of New Calabar', in M. Douglas and P. Kebbery, eds., *Man in Africa* (London: Tavistock, 1969), pp. 37–58. E.J. Alagoa, 'The Slave Trade in Niger Delta Oral Tradition and History', in P. Lovejoy, ed., *Africans in Bondage: Studies in Slavery and the Slave Trade* (London: University of Wisconsin Press, 1986); T.N. Tamuno, 'The Native House Rule of Southern Nigeria', *Nigeria Magazine*, No. 93 (1967), pp. 159–68.

3.   Alagoa, 'The Slave Trade', p. 129.

4.   Comte C.N. De Cardi, 'A Short Description of the Natives of the Niger Coast Protectorate, with Some Account of Their Customs, Religion, Trade, etc', in M. Kingsley, *West African Studies* (London: Frank Cass, 1899), pp. 472–5.

5.   On King Jaja see S.J. Cookey, *King Jaja of the Niger Delta: His Life and Times 1821–1889* (New York: Nok, 1974). On George Amachree and Oko Jumbo, see G.I. Jones, *The Trading States*.

6.   E.J. Alagoa, 'Nineteenth Century Revolutions in the Eastern Niger Delta and Calabar', *Journal of the Historical Society of Nigeria*, No. 5, Vol. 4 (1971), p. 568.

7.   P. Lovejoy, 'Slavery in the Context of Ideology', in P. Lovejoy, ed., *The Ideology of Slavery in Africa* (London: Sage, 1981) pp. 11–38. Also see, S. Miers, and I. Kopytoff, *Slavery in Africa* (Wisconsin: University of Wisconsin Press, 1977), pp. 3–81.

8.   O. Dapper, 'Kalabari and the Eastern Delta', in T. Hodgkin, *Nigerian Perpectives* (Oxford: Oxford University Press, 1975), p. 174.

9.   J. Barbot, 'An Abstract of a Voyage to New Calabar or Rio Real in the year 1699', in A. Churchill, ed., *Collection of Voyages and Travels*, Vol. 5 (London: Frank Cass, 1733), pp. 455–66.

10.   Dike, *Trade and Politics*, p. 28.

11.   H.W. Brown-West, now Tienabeso, *A Short Genealogical History of Amachree 1 of Kalabari* (Yaba: Yaba Printing Press, 1956).

12.   R. Horton, 'From Fishing Village', p. 48.

13.   CA3/023/1, Bishop Henry Johnson, 'A Journey up the Niger', 14 December 1877.

14.   R. Horton, 'From Fishing Village', p. 49.

15.   O. Dapper, 'Kalabari and the Eastern Delta', p. 174.

16.   R. Smith, 'The Canoe in West African History', *JAH*, 11 (1970), pp. 515–33.

17.   W. Wariboko, 'Planting Church-Culture at New Calabar: Some Neglected Aspects of Missionary Enterprise in the Eastern Niger Delta 1865–1918', (unpublished manuscript).

18.   Degdist 3/1/3, A.F.F.P. Newns, 'Reorganisation Report on Kalabari Clan', May 1947.

19. G3A3/1905/168, Bishop Johnson, 'Journal Report', December 1904 – July 1905.
20. Calprof 14/6/82, W.F. Fosbery, 'Annual Report on the Eastern Provinces' 1910.
21. G3A3/1894/83, D.C. Crowther, 'Report of Visit to CMS Station at Obonoma [*sic*] New Calabar 19–22 May 1894'.
22. Ibid.
23. CA3/04/457, S.A. Crowther, 'A Charge Delivered at Onitsha on the Banks of the Niger', 13 November 1874.
24. CA3/04/566, D.A. Crowther, 'An Account of the Release of Two Imprisoned Converts at Bonny through the Interference of the Supercargoes in this River', 29 November 1876.
25. Ibid.
26. CA3/04/529, S.A. Crowther, to T.J. Hutchinson, 25 April 1876.
27. De Cardi, 'A Short Description of the Natives', p. 535.
28. G3A3/1894/81, H.H. Dobinson to Reverend F. Baylis, 9 July 1894.
29. S. Miers, and R. Roberts, *The End of Slavery in Africa* (Wisconsin: Wisconsin University Press, 1988); J. Grace, *Domestic Slavery in West Africa* (London: Fredrick Muller Ltd, 1975); P. Lovejoy, Transformations in Slavery (Cambridge: Cambridge University Press, 1983): P. Manning, *Slavery and African Life* (Cambridge: Cambridge University Press, 1990).
30. Miers and Roberts, *The End of Slavery*, p. 488.
31. CA3/023/1, Bishop Johnson, 'A Journey up the Niger'.
32. FO 84/1882, H. Johnston, 'A Report on the British Protectorate of the Oil Rivers', 1 December 1888.
33. CSE 8/5/82, Provincial Commissioner (Eastern Province), 'Memorandum', 9 August 1911.
34. C3A3/1907/51, J. Johnson, 'Niger Delta Pastorate and Mission work', 1906.
35. FO 2/85, C. MacDonald, to Under-Secretary of State, 17 December 1875.
36. FO2/85, R. Moor to Under-Secretary of State, 25 December 1896.
37. The passage should not be taken to mean that the CMS project in the Niger Delta was generally devoid of political motives. On the contrary, the missionaries, in partnership with the consuls, imposed British dominion in the area. My point here is that the missionary perception of lineage slavery was influenced by the underlying spiritual world view of Christianity.
38. G3A3/1911/77, Reverend J.H. Harris, 'Domestic Slavery in Southern Nigeria (Being a report to the Committee of the Anti-Slavery and Aborigines Protection Society and Correspondence), London, 5 May 1911.
39. A.A. Cowan, 'Early Trading Conditions in the Bight of Biafra', (part 2), *Journal of the African Society*, Vol. 35 (1936), pp. 53–64.
40. FO 2/84, MacDonald to the Earl of Kimberley, 18 March 1895.

41. Miers and Roberts, *The End of Slavery*, p. 12.
42. FO 2/85, MacDonald to Under-Secretary of State, 17 December 1895.
43. G3A3/1894/83, Crowther, 'Report of Visit of CMS Station at Abonnema', 19–22 May 1894.
44. FO 2/85, Moor to Under-Secretary of State, 25 December 1895.
45. CSO 4/2/1, Moor to Colonial Office, 17 March 1901.
46. Ibid.
47. CO 150/12, Moor to Joseph Chamberlain: 'Slavery in Southern Nigeria', in C. W. Newbury, *British Policy Towards West Africa (Select Documents) 1895–1914*, (Oxford: Oxford University Press, 1971), pp. 341–2.
48. CSE 8/5/82, 'Proclamation No. 26 1901: The Native House-Rule Proclamation'.
49. Calprof. 11, 'New Calabar Native Council Regulation: Native Council Rules Relating to Supervision and Regulation of Market', 1906.
50. Rivprof. 5/2/32, D.C. Syer to A.D.C. Ferguson, 'Handing over Notes, Degema District', May 1906.
51. E.J. Alagoa, *The Small Brave City State: A History of Nembe-Brass*, Appendix VI (Ibadan: Ibadan University Press, 1964), pp. 146–7.
52. Rivprof. 8/3/75, Commissioner's Office, Owerri, to District Officer, Degema, 24 March 1915.
53. A.R. Whiteman (District Officer) to F. Furguson, February 1927.
54. W. Wariboko, 'New Calabar and the Forces of Change – ca. 1850–1945', (unpublished PhD dissertation, University of Birmingham, 1991); see chapter V in particular.

SECTION II

Slavery and Technology

CHAPTER 5

Innovations in Sugar-Cane Mill Technology in Jamaica, 1760–1830

VERONT SATCHELL

A popularly held view by Marxists and some economic historians is that slavery impeded or retarded technological changes. Innovations, they argue, were incompatible with slavery.[1] This incompatibility thesis is rooted in the prevailing assumption that technological change is synonymous with technologies that are aimed at saving labour. According to the argument, then, in a slave society such as Jamaica's, with an assumed abundance of cheap coerced labour, it would be improvident to introduce labour-saving devices, as this would result in a displacement of labour. Such displaced labour, without work to fill the resultant leisure time, would engage in revolts and other acts of violence. Since there was not much evidence of the implementation of labour-saving inventions (and given the assumption that an absence of these meant an absence of technical progress), the theory concludes that slavery negated technical change.

This chapter is a contribution to the general debate on slavery and technological changes or innovations in slave societies. By presenting an analysis of empirical evidence of technological innovations which were adopted and adapted to sugar-cane mills in Jamaica during the period 1760–1830, the technical capacity of this Caribbean slave society is highlighted. Essentially the chapter examines three major data sets: the patents for invention; innovations of these and other inventions, and the diffusion of the horizontal three-roller mill in Jamaica.

The sugar-cane mill

The production of sugar for export dominated the Jamaican plantation economy throughout the period of slavery and beyond. Sugar accounted for over 80 per cent of annual exports from the island during slavery.[2] Sugar-cane planting and the manufacturing of sugar, therefore, were of extreme importance to the economy of the island. Richard Pares describes the Caribbean slave/sugar plantation as a factory set in a field, where the process of production comprised an agricultural and an industrial phase. Essentially, the planter was both a farmer and a manufacturer.[3]

The three-roller sugar-cane crushing mill could be considered the single most important machine in a sugar factory. Essentially, the successful processing of the year's crop depended heavily on its efficiency and reliability. Cut canes had to be expeditiously ground since fermentation takes place within 72 hours. Fermentation adversely affects the sucrose content and ultimately the sugar yield. Further, the sugar manufacturing process had to be completed before the start of the hurricane season.[4] Frequent breakdowns and stoppages of the mill and the unreliability of power sources could not be afforded. Time, indeed, was of the essence in sugar production and every effort had to be made to economise on this commodity.

The supervision of the mill was the responsibility of a male slave officer of the mill or boatswain. According to Thomas Roughley, it was the boatswain's duty to guarantee,

> by his presence and experience, the safety of [the mill]; to keep the mill-gang to their work; to see that the stokeholes are supplied with dry trash, the green trash taken from the mill to the trash houses, and well packed there; the mill furnished with canes by the cane carriers; the mill well braced; the cogs and gudgeons greased; the mill-bed, cases and gutterings, well washed three or four times a day, and plenty of water run to turn the water wheel. The officer should be a carpenter, who understands the formation of the mill machinery; can easily detect any fault or tameness in its members and quickly find a remedy for the defect.[5]

Indeed, the boatswain was one of the most important technicians on the sugar estate.

The task of operating the mill was assigned primarily to the women. Matthew Gregory Lewis explained the process as follows: 'the ripe canes [were taken] to mill, where the cleanest of the women are appointed, one to put them into the machine for crushing them and another to draw them out after the juice had been extracted when she throw them into an opening'.[6] The canes were passed twice between the rollers for optimum juice extraction.

Undoubtedly there was a gender bias in Caribbean plantations at least with regards to plantation jobs. While slave men dominated the skilled tasks, artisan jobs, slave women were relegated to the more menial field and factory labour.

The vertical three-roller sugar mill

From the mid-seventeenth century through to the end of the eighteenth, the vertical three-roller mill remained the principal means by which Jamaica's sugar-canes were crushed.[7] The rollers of the vertical sugar-cane mill, ranged in length from 0.76m to 1m and from 0.51m to 0.62m in diameter. They were furnished with cogwheels fixed on the upper ends and working into each other. Power was applied to the middle roller and from thence transmitted through the cogwheels to the other rollers, thus causing the other rollers to turn. The rollers were mounted in a frame consisting of two horizontal pieces, sustained by uprights. The openings of the frame contained brass bearings for the pivots of the three rollers. These brasses were capable of adjustments by means of cross keys and wedges driven through openings in their frames so as to force the rollers towards each other and retain them at unvarying distances. The spaces between the rollers did not exceed 6–9.5 mm. The second set of rollers essentially had to be set closer together than the first set because the canes, after passing through the first set, were flattened, and required a greater pressure for this second squeezing.[8] The surfaces of the rollers were fluted with shallow vertical grooves which allowed them to take a firmer grip of the cane during milling and caused the expressed cane juice to flow away from the bagasse more readily. The cane juice flowed from the canes into a pan or cup, which was formed around the rollers at the lower part by a plate of iron turned up all around at the side and placed at the bottom of the frame. At one side there was a spout to convey the juice into a pipe which led to the boiling house.

In the vertical mill the receptacle for the juice formed a small circular channel around the lower edge of each roller and a small raised rim was carried around the centre part or pivot of each roller. This prevented the expressed juice from flowing down into the bearings of the lower pivot. The weight of each roller was supported in a brass stop or bearing under the frame. In some cases friction rollers were placed underneath.[9] In the vertical mill canes passed first between the middle and one side rollers and then between the middle and the other side rollers. This operation was normally performed by hand. A slave, usually female, standing at one end, fed the mill by placing the canes between two rollers; another slave, at the other end, bent the canes as they came through, holding them in contact with the surface of the centre roller to allow them to carry the canes round by its motion.[10] This method of feeding the canes was very dangerous. Slaves' hands were often caught in the mills and had to be quickly amputated to prevent fatalities. Jean Lindsay in her study of the Pennants of Jamaica noted that accidents of this nature occurred regularly on Lord Penrhyn's estates.[11] A cutlass was invariably kept near the mill for the purpose of chopping off slaves' hands so caught.[12] The power sources applied to turn mills did not make it possible to stop these mills quickly enough to prevent serious injuries to slaves. In order to stop a waterwheel the water had to be diverted away from the wheel. The sluice gate which controlled the flow of water to the wheel, however, was some distance away from the wheel and the mill. Stopping the wheel, therefore, took much time. Windmills had no brakes and consequently could not be easily stopped. Stopping it became even more difficult when the velocity of the wind was high. Similarly, it was not easy to simultaneously bring to an immediate halt the large number of animals involved in turning a cattlemill. The steam engine could be more readily stopped by mechanically turning off the engine, thus preventing these accidents.[13] But even then, the speed at which the rollers turned prevented them from being stopped quickly enough to prevent serious accidents.

Bryan Edwards, writing in 1794, commented on the operation, economy and problems of the vertical three-roller sugar-cane mill:

> The great obstacle at [crop time] to the planters . . . [without a water powered mill] is the frequent failure or insufficiency of their mills; for though a sugar mill whether worked by water, wind or . . . cattle is a very simple contrivance great force is nevertheless requisited to make it overcome the resistance which it meets with . . . [the mill] consists of three upright iron plated rollers. The middle one to which the moving power is applied turns the other two by means of cogs. Between three rollers the canes are twice compressed . . . In Jamaica unless on high situations they [wind mills] seldom answer the expence of their erection, and the planter who

is not . . . near a copious stream of water must trust . . . a cattle mill, which is such a heavy and laborious piece of machinery that the heart sickens at beholding it work.[14]

Prior to 1794, several inventions were developed and patented locally to remedy these defects. These inventions that were effected locally, however, were not aimed at improving the plan and construction of the mill but rather at economising on power. They were therefore, incremental in nature. After this date, however, revolutionary changes were made to the mill, which were adopted locally.

Patents for invention to improve sugar-cane mill technology in Jamaica, 1760–1830

Between 1760 and 1830, the Jamaican Legislative Assembly enacted 49 Private Enabling Acts vesting in 42 petitioners or patentees exclusive property rights to their inventions for improving the methods of producing sugar and rum. Of these, 34, or 69.3 per cent, were for innovations in sugar-cane mills. The remaining portion was geared towards the process of manufacturing sugar and rum.[15] This total number of patents, granted over a 70-year period, for improvement in such an important area of the economy as sugar manu-facturing, may seem small. Indeed, it is this that has led critics to assume that there was lethargy on the part of Jamaicans in adopting and adapting new and improved techniques. Implicit in the critics' argument is that despite planters' knowledge of advances being made in England in developing new and improved agricultural techniques, many of which were relevant to Jamaica's agrarian economy, these were never transferred by patents to the island. Local and absentee planters, they argue, were indifferent to technical change. Thus they conclude that, in comparison with England, Jamaica was technically backward.[16] To what extent is this true?

Richard Sullivan, in his analysis of patents for invention issued in England, has shown that 260 agricultural patents for all farming activities were issued between 1760 and 1830. Of this total, farming activity entitled 'further processing', which parallels patents for improving sugar and rum production in Jamaica, accounted for 105. For the period 1760–1800, the total number of all agricultural patents was 98. 'Further processing' accounted for 37 per cent. 'Tilling, ploughing and planting' together accounted for 29.6 per cent of the total; 'preparing and applying manure' accounted for a paltry 3.1 per cent; 'drainage and irrigation' 12.4 per cent and 'livestock management' 14.3 per cent.[17]

Agricultural patents in England did not begin to show significant increases until the 1840s. This is clearly demonstrated by the following figures: of the 703 agricultural patents issued between 1611 and 1850, 275 or 39.1 per cent were granted during the 1840s. 'Preparing and applying manure' showed the most remarkable increase. Between 1611 and 1850 there were 57 patents in this area, the largest number being three each in 1801–10 and 1831–40. In 1841–50 alone there were 42, a fourteenfold increase. Significant increases, though not of the same magnitude as that of 'preparing manure' were made in 'further processing' 40 per cent, 'tilling, ploughing and planting' 36 per cent and 'drainage and irrigation' 33 per cent.[18]

The patent statistics for England presented by Sullivan have clearly indicated that scientific agriculture was not as remarkable as the critics suggest. It should be noted, however, that the reliability of patent statistics as an indicator of the nature and level of technological improvements in any country is under intense debate. Christine MacLeod has argued that for England, the patent statistics for the period 1600–1800 are unreliable and therefore do not indicate either inventive activity or technological change. She contends that patents came to have several other functions than just protecting property rights in inventions and that several important agricultural inventions went unpatented. Sullivan, while agreeing that patents are imperfect measures of inventions, since many inventions are not patentable, argues that they do give a good indication of inventive activity. Patents, he contends, are adopted because they contribute to productivity and patents for inventions useful to an industry indicate the potential profits inventors perceive they may make from creating inventions useful to that industry.[19] Given the state of the debate it is not clear how much weight should be placed on the patent statistics for England as given by Sullivan. On the surface, however, the Jamaican total of 49 patents granted for improvements in one area of agrarian economy, that of sugar and rum manufacturing, compares very favourably with the English total.

From the 1760s through to the 1780s, over 93 per cent of all patents granted for improving the sugar industry were geared towards improving sugar mills. The preponderance of patents for the invention of methods to improve mills seem closely related to macroeconomic events or demands, thus indicating clearly that inventions in Jamaica were demand-induced activities. The demand by local planters for efficient and reliable sugar-cane mills must be seen in light of its close relationship to sugar output/exports and consequently the economy of the wider society. This relationship cannot be overemphasised.[20]

The period 1760–79 represented the era during which over 41 per cent of all patents for 'invention of sugar-cane mills' were granted. The peak period was the 1770s, when over 23.5 per cent of these patents were issued. After this period patents in the area of mill improvements, while fluctuating somewhat, showed a definite downward trend. During the 1810–19 period patents in this category fell dramatically to 5.9 per cent, the lowest for the entire period. By the 1820s, however, the number of patents had increased to 14.7 per cent. This general downward trend in mill patents was directly related to the development of the more efficient and durable all-iron horizontal three-roller mill which was now readily available on the market.[21] This development reduced the need for the individual planter to be constantly searching for reliable mills to increase efficiency significantly. The emphasis of inventions after 1810 was on other areas of sugar production.[22]

Patents for sugar-cane mills covered several areas of milling and are classified under eight categories: first, 'new invented mill', second, 'improved mills and machinery'. These two accounted for 53 per cent of all patents granted for sugar-cane mills. Third came 'application of steam to turn cane sugar mills', which accounted for 23.5 per cent. Fourth was 'applying friction wheels to rollers and gudgeons', representing 8.1 per cent. Fifth was patents for 'machines to raise water', amounting to 5.9 per cent. Sixth came 'combination of motive forces to turn mills' 2.7 per cent; seventh 'the application of two sets of horizontal mills to grind sugar-canes', and eighth, 'machine to convey canes to mills from the mill yard', each (seventh and eighth) accounting for 2.9 per cent.[23]

Patents for 'new' and 'improved mills and machinery' were well distributed throughout the period, but while those for 'new' mills ceased after 1817, those for 'improved mills and machinery' continued until 1825, 56 per cent of which were granted between 1821 and 1825. Indeed by 1817 the diffusion of the new designed mill was evident throughout the island's sugar industry. But there was, however, the continuing need to service and improve the old-type mills belonging to planters who, for one reason or another, had not acquired the new mill but who in an effort to remain in the sugar business had to seek to increase mill efficiency.[24] This search for improvement explains the continued quest for new inventions.

'The application of two sets of horizontal rollers to a water mill' was patented in 1822, by Anders Jensen Schouberg of St George parish.[25] This method of applying a power source to turn two mills, however, was not new. During this same period many planters who had acquired steam engines were using them to power two sets of mills.[26] Schouberg then was simply extending this principle to water wheels. The general idea of utilising power sources in this manner indeed preceded the later development of multiple milling or mill tandems. Adding more rollers to mills was one of the many innovations attempted by planters to increase efficiency during this period.

Patents for adding 'friction wheels to mill machinery', to increase efficiency and power, were made between 1776 and 1788. The most important of these inventions was that of Edward Woollery, patented locally in 1774 as Woollery's improved mill, substantially increased efficiency, it was adopted island-wide. Edwards commented on this new mill:

> The great improvement, the addition to the middle roller of a lantern wheel, with trundles or wallowers . . . These act as so many friction-wheels, and their utility and importance are best demonstrated by their effect. A cattle or mule mill on the old model was thought to perform exceedingly well if it passed sufficient canes in a hour to yield from 300 to 350 gallons of juice. – The common return of a mill of Mr Woollery's construction is from 400 to 500 gallons – I have the authority to say that one of these mills in particular, which is worked with ten mules, produces hourly 500 gallons: at this rate allowing four hours out of the twenty four for loss of time, the return per diem is 10,000 gallons; being equal to 36 hogsheads of sugar of 16 cwt. for every week during crop, exclusive of Sundays – few water mills can exceed this. [27]

Although inventions aimed at improving mill technology, and, indeed, all other improvements in the sugar industry in Jamaica during this period, were primarily demand-induced, supply conditions were also operative. Kenneth Sokoloff and B. Khan argue that growth in market demand alone could not have produced much change if the level of technical knowledge previously available had not been sufficient to yield new inventions worthy of being patented.[28] The skills and knowledge necessary for patentable inventions had to be present. These skills and knowledge were evident and indeed widely distributed among the local Jamaican population.

Inventions and improvements in mill technology were not the exclusive preserves of artisans, who were normally involved in the support services of the cane sugar industry, and planters. A large cross-section of the island's population of different social and occupational classes actively sought patents for their new inventions.[29] This indicates that there were technically-inclined minds in the island constantly developing new techniques for the improvement of the island's sugar economy.

Of the total number of patentees, artisans and planters constituted the largest proportion. Artisans accounted for 50 per cent and planters 28.1 per cent.[30] Among the artisans group, millwrights accounted for 18.1 per cent. Planters and millwrights together accounted for 47 per cent of patentees. This is not surprising since planters and millwrights were intimately connected with sugar mills. Proprietors had a direct interest in developing or promoting the development of new and improved utensils, implements and processing methods aimed at increasing efficiency and productivity and ultimately enabling their enterprise to continue to be economically viable and their products competitive on the market. Millwrights, including the boatswain, were mill technicians and quite naturally they would be the ones most likely to be involved in improving existing mills and machinery and developing new models.

In addition to millwrights, the artisan group contained a wide range of other tradesmen, most of whose occupational activities were, in some way or the other, related to the plantations. An odd patentee within this group, however, was a watchmaker. In 1788, William Roach, a watchmaker of Kingston parish, received a patent for his invention of a new mill worked by a steam pump/atmospheric pressure.[31] As unconnected as the job of the watchmaker may seem in relation to sugar-cane milling and manufacturing, it is not difficult, after closer contemplation, to conceive of a watchmaker becoming involved in developing machinery for the local sugar industry. A watchmaker works with gears, cogwheels and levers, which are the essential machinery of a mill. Indeed the importance of the sugar industry cannot be overemphasised. It was the primary economic activity in Jamaica during this period; consequently it is not difficult to see all the collective minds centred upon developing new technology to enhance the sugar estates' efficiency.[32] It is also for this reason that it is not unusual for professionals, including medical doctors, to be listed among the patentees. In Jamaica, like other parts of the Caribbean, several estates were either owned or managed by professionals.

The fact that planters and artisans, especially millwrights, were the major patentees indicates that rather than being apathetic, lethargic and indifferent to developing new techniques the group most intimately connected to the business of sugar production was active and vibrant in improving existing techniques.

Role of slaves in technical improvements and inventions

Slaves were fundamental to the production processes and it is logical to assume that they played a part in technical innovations. Admittedly, their activities are difficult to ascertain, given the heavy reliance on written records and the invisibility of the slaves' views in such sources.

Nevertheless, slaves were the principal artisans, and they worked in foundries. My considered view here is that the slaves actively participated in inventing new techniques and equipment pertinent to the sugar industry. My position is based on two premises. First (as stated before), slaves were the principal artisans in the island. In Jamaica there was a paucity of White artisans, so there developed an almost total reliance on the artisan slaves. Planters relied heavily on slave labour for all aspects of plantation life; it is for this reason that Douglas Hall concludes that the slave was a 'multi-purpose tool'.[33] Barry Higman notes that at the time of emancipation in 1834 compensation was paid for 17,873 artisan slaves, representing 5.74 per cent of the total slave population. These included blacksmiths, millwrights, coopers, wheelwrights, masons, plumbers, carpenters, coppersmiths and engineers.[34] Over 9 per cent of the slaves on Edward Long's estates were artisans, on Braco estate artisan slaves accounted for over 5 per cent of the total slaves.[35]

It has been shown above that in the sugar manufacturing processes the mill engineer was an experienced slave. His was a highly technical and responsible position. He had to see to it that the mill was in good repair at all times. It is quite likely that he implemented technical innovations to make his mill more efficient and less likely to breakdowns during the crucial period of crop-time. The successful milling of an entire crop rested on his shoulders.

Second, the slaves came from an area of Africa that had a highly developed, complex and sophisticated metallurgy industry. Candice Goucher has shown that the West African coast, from where the bulk of the British Caribbean slaves were drawn, had developed complex skills in working iron and wrought iron. According to her, many of the Africans who were transported to the new world were skilled blacksmiths. Thus Africa exported not only labourers but also skilled technicians.[36] Indeed locally in Jamaica, Africans – slave and free – were master blacksmiths working on the estates and in foundries. Their activities included the manufacturing and repairing of plantation equipment, including mills and mill rollers; as well as making arms and ammunition. Two, of the leading foundries in the island during the period under review were those of John Reeder and William James. Reeder's foundry operated in the parish of St Thomas-in-the-East until 1793, and employed over 300 African-Jamaicans, including slaves, who, according to him, 'were perfect in every branch of the iron manufacturing'.[37] James began operating his foundry in the parish of Kingston in 1817. He had in his employment 37 Black young apprentices, 21 slaves, one Coloured journeyman and two Whites.[38] He reported in 1829 in a petition to the House that owing to his use of locals (mostly slaves) in his foundry, he was able to:

> perform all manner of foundry work the greater portion of which cannot be performed by any other establishment in the island . . . in consequence of that improvement [he] is enabled to manufacture and repair all manner of machinery, steam engines &c. thereby obviating the necessity which previously existed of sending to Great Britain for a variety of those articles for the use of the plantations &c.[39]

The slaves' technical background and their occupation of key technical areas of sugar manufacturing, provided them with excellent positions to develop improved techniques. As chattel, however, they could not acquire property rights or monopolies or patents for inventions that they might contrive; so slave inventions probably were unpatented, though it is not improbable that owners patented inventions originated by their slaves. But it could be argued that slaves' input was minimal as they had nothing to gain from inventing new techniques. They might even have used opposition to innovation as a technique of resistance. In fact Hall argues that one of the reasons for the seeming unwillingness of planters to innovate was the feeling held by them that slaves might deliberately inflict damages on estate equipment in the field.[40] Nevertheless, I maintain here that given the pivotal role of the slaves in the sugar manufacturing process, they were in the best position to make such inventions. Of course, until more evidence is unearthed, this view can only be tentative and speculative. One must await the findings of ethno-archaeologists in this area.

Innovations

It has been stated above that Woollery's mill was widely adopted in the island and other minor innovations were implemented in existing mill technology;

but planters did not stop there. Efforts were continually being made to develop and implement new technology to improve mill performance. For example, to improve the grinding capacity of estates, planters found it expedient to operate more than one sugar mill. The norm was for an estate to be equipped with two mills, but there were several estates on which three and as many as four sugar mills existed. James Robertson's 1804 map, for example, shows that in that year there were 1,116 mills on 830 estates. Each of these mills either used the same power source or a combination of power sources. Thus an estate might have one or more cattle or water mills, a wind and a cattle mill, a water and a cattle mill, a wind, water and a cattle mill and so on. Later in the early nineteenth century, with the wide introduction of steam as a power source for mills in Jamaica, steam engines came to complement other existing power sources on estates. This practice of using more than one mill was to ensure the speedy and efficient processing of the crop. Animal power was considered inefficient but because of its lower initial cost and locational flexibility it was normally the first choice on newly established estates. However, as soon as planters were financially able they opted for more efficient power sources. Thus on mature or well established estates, whenever an animal mill was used it was in combination with other sources of power and was normally used as a back-up rather than a complement.[41] One very important innovation associated with the extensive use of animals to power mills was the development of the local livestock industry. By the early eighteenth century pen-keeping became a prop to the sugar industry, satisfactorily supplying draft animals and mill animals.[42]

To reduce the number of accidents while feeding the mills planters employed the dumbturner during the late eighteenth century. The dumbturner was a circular piece of framework or screen, which was fixed to the upper and lower frames which encompassed the middle roller at the back. This frame received the canes as they passed through the first time and held them in contact with the middle roller until the ends returned between the other pair of rollers.[43]

The timing of the dumbturner was no accident. It coincided with two significant developments of this period: firstly, the constant disruption in the supply of slaves caused by continuous warfare, and secondly, the continued debate in Britain on the efficacy of the slave trade. In fact, by 1803, the abolitionist forces in the British Parliament had begun making successful and decisive gains which culminated in the total abolition of the British slave trade in 1807. With abolition, the price of slaves fluctuated and the effective slave labour force began to diminish. A slave whose productivity was prematurely cut, say for example through amputation of an arm during milling, was a liability to the planter, in that the planter was still responsible for the upkeep of that slave whose productive capacity was drastically reduced. Before abolition of the slave trade a maimed slave could be easily replaced through purchase on the slave market. With abolition and with it the inelasticity of slave labour supply, such a replacement was difficult. Given this situation planters had to take measures to preserve their investment in labour. The implementation of the dumbturner was one such innovative measure. Ralph Walker and James Falconer's inventions to prevent accidents to slaves while milling, patented in 1788 and 1818 respectively, were indeed a direct response to the economic loss planters encountered with accidents such as the amputation of a slave's hand. Whereas Falconer's invention was implemented on two estates in Westmoreland where it was reported that they 'appeared . . . perfectly adapted to the purpose',44 it has not been established whether or not Walker's invention became an innovation. The estates on which Falconer's inventions were applied have not yet been identified. It seems quite evident that economic considerations, namely, loss in the planters' investment and reduction in the productivity level of slaves, prompted the development and implementation of the dumbturner in Jamaica.

The first Industrial Revolution significantly improved the sugar-cane mill. By the early 1800s iron had replaced wood in mill construction. Wooden frames gave way to all iron frames. The rollers, which formerly were formed from hardwood and covered with iron plates or steel, were replaced by hollow cylinders of cast iron in the 1820s. These technical innovations were evident in Jamaican sugar-cane mills.

The most significant and indeed the most revolutionary improvement in mill technology, however, came in 1794 with the invention of the horizontal three-roller mill by John Collinge.

The horizontal three-roller mill in Jamaica

The earliest record of a mill of this design is to be found in a drawing in 1754, made by Smeaton for a Mr Gray, planter of Jamaica. It was marked 'not executed'.45 However, in so far as this type mill was actually designed, presumably on the instruction of Gray, is clear evidence that Jamaican planting interests were active in seeking to develop new methods to improve the sugar business. Collinge's 'invention', therefore, must be seen as the practical culmination of an idea conceived earlier by a local planter.

The rollers of the horizontal mill measured about 1.5–1.8m in length and 0.76m in diameter. They were arranged in a triangular form one above and two below, their centres forming the vertexes of an isosceles triangle. In this position they were secured in a housing or headstock. Power was applied to the upper roller. By a system of gearing, similar to that of the vertical three-roller mill, the other rollers were simultaneously turned. The two lower rollers were placed close to each other and moved in opposite directions. They were placed in a cistern which collected the cane juice as it was extracted.[46]

Once the horizontal arrangement of the rollers had been adopted the cane mill received its present form. The changes, which ensued over the succeeding 50 years, according to Noel Deerr, were concerned primarily with reducing the headstock to a sound engineering model, permitting it to withstand the power of steam and multiple milling, thus making it more efficient and productive.[47]

The horizontal three-roller mill presented several advantages over the old vertical type. It was more durable and the transmission mechanisms much better; consequently it lightened the work of mill animals. The horizontal mill allowed for a better distribution of the canes, avoided a concentration of wear and tear at one point and exerted pressure on only one of the shafts. The rollers could be fed broadly from gravity chute over a greater width of roller, resulting in a more even wear. According to Porter, it was not unusual to find the rollers in vertical mills wearing out in one part, while the rest of the surface remained perfect. The method of feeding also resulted in greater safety as hands did not have to come near the mills; consequently, the dumbturner could be dispensed with.[48] The horizontal mill was also more readily adapted to steam power, which was becoming common in the island by the beginning of the nineteenth century.[49] By the early 1800s, this new horizontal three-roller mill was manufactured entirely of iron and sold in bulk by the chief tool concerns of England and the United States.[50]

Compared to the vertical three-roller mill the horizontal mill was much more expensive. The price of vertical three-roller mills supplied by John Rennie, was between £640 and £650, payable in four months. The cost of a horizontal mill supplied by the same firm was £850, approximately 30 per cent higher than that of the vertical design. It was however, sold on the same terms as that of the vertical mill.[51]

By 1815 the horizontal three-roller mill was well diffused in Jamaica and the Caribbean despite its higher price. It would appear that its utility and the several advantages it presented over the vertical type made it more attractive to the planters. Several pieces of evidence indicate the rapid diffusion of this type of mill in the island. First, this is demonstrated in a letter sent in 1815 by Boulton and Watt to Messrs Davidson and Graham, consignee for several Jamaican estates. The consignee had ordered a steam engine to power a vertical mill on a Jamaican estate. Watt replied to the effect that such a request was unusual for the Caribbean, since estates operated horizontal mills. As a result his engines were designed to power this type mill. To fill this order, the firm had to make adjustments to the engine shafts. Because of this additional work, the engine cost much more than normal.[52] Secondly, Leonard Wray, in his discussion on power sources and mill machinery in Jamaica during the early 1830s, referred to the vertical mill as 'the old time vertical mill'.[53] Thirdly, records of the firm of Messrs Fawcett, Preston and Company of Liverpool, one of the leading manufacturers and suppliers of the new designed mill to the Caribbean, indicate that between 1813 and 1817, it received orders for 63 horizontal mills but only 11 of the vertical design.[54]

In addition to Fawcett, Preston, there were several other mill manufacturers in England supplying this new designed mill to the island. For example, Messrs R. Dobbinson and Company of Bristol, John Rennie of London and Low Moore. Rennie and Dobbinson and Company were the chief millwrights manufacturing mills for the Watt engines sent to the island. There is preserved on the site of the old works of Ellis Caymanas estate, in the parish of St Catherine, an iron horizontal mill made in 1825 by Low Moore bearing the serial number 904 EC 16. 3. 25. With the exception of the missing top roller the mill is in a relatively complete form.[55] Because of the unavailability of data on these companies locally, the number of mills of this design sent to the island by them remains unknown.

The evidence, however, clearly suggests the rapid diffusion of this mill in Jamaica and demonstrates the planters' eagerness to implement a new technique which promised greater efficiency in sugar-cane juice extraction despite the extra costs. The implementation of the horizontal three-roller mill is indeed a good example of planters manifesting true capitalist tendencies. They were making rational economic decisions. Indeed they must have calculated the opportunity cost in rejecting the old vertical model for the new designed mill, despite the higher costs involved.

Conclusion

Between 1760 and 1830, the three-roller sugar-cane mill underwent significant changes in Jamaica. Before 1794 this was somewhat incremental in nature, since the major thrust was geared towards increasing the power and efficiency of the vertical three-roller mill. Planters recognising the close relationship between mill efficiency and the success of a year's sugar crop, and the general inefficiency of the vertical type mill, sought for improvements. Consequently several inventions developed locally and overseas, aimed at improved cane mills, were adopted and adapted. The invention of the horizontal three-roller mill in 1794, which revolutionised sugar-cane mill technology, did not go unnoticed. As soon as it was invented, planters readily adopted this innovation, to the extent that by 1830 the vertical mill was almost obsolete. This new design mill was first conceived by a Jamaican planter as far back as 1754. There is no doubt that planters expended immense capital in improving the old vertical three-roller mill and in acquiring the newly designed type.

These innovations in mill technology represented the technical and investment capabilities of the Jamaican slave society and seriously challenges the views on planter conservatism.

Notes

1.   See for example E. Genovese, *The Political Economy of Slavery: Studies in the Economy and Society of the Slave South* (New York: Random House, 1976); M. Fraginals, *The Sugar Mill: The Socio-Economic Complex of Sugar in Cuba 1760–1860* (New York: Monthly Review Press, 1976); L. Ragatz, *The Fall of the Planter Class in the British Caribbean 1763–1833* (New York: Octagon Books, 1963).

2.   B.W. Higman, *Slave Population and Economy in Jamaica 1807–1834* (Cambridge: Cambridge University Press, 1976), p. 13.

3.   R. Pares, *Merchants and Planters* (Cambridge: Cambridge University Press, 1960), p. 23.

4. In the Caribbean, the hurricane season begins in June and continues through to November annually.
5. T. Roughley, *The Jamaica Planters' Guide* (London, 1823), pp. 338–9.
6. M. Gregory Lewis, *Journal of a Residence Among the Negroes in the West Indies* (London, 1816), p. 43.
7. G. Richardson Porter, *The Nature and Properties of the sugar-cane with Practical Directions for the Improvement of its Culture and the Manufacture of its Products* (London, 1830), pp. 140–6; J. Daniels and C. Daniels, 'The Origins of the sugar-cane Roller Mill', *Technology and Culture*, 29:3 (1988), p. 531; R. Sheridan, *Sugar and Slavery* (Exeter: Ginn, 1976), p. 114.
8. Porter, 'Nature and Properties', pp. 531–3; N. Deerr, 'Evolution of sugar-cane Mill', *Transactions of the Newcomen Society*, 21 (1940/41), p. 7.
9. Porter, 'Nature and Properties', p. 145.
10. Ibid., p. 142.
11. J. Lindsay, 'The Pennants and Jamaica, 1665–1805', *Transaction of the Caernarvonshire Historical Society*, 43 (1992), p. 53.
12. V. Satchell, 'Technology and Productivity Change In the Jamaican Sugar Industry 1760–1830', (unpublished PhD thesis, University of the West Indies, Mona 1993, p. 177).
13. J. Stewart, *A Description of a Machine or Invention to Grind sugar-canes by the Power of a Fire Engine* (Kingston, 1768), pp. 6-8; Satchell, 'Technology', pp. 177–8.
14. B. Edwards, *The History Civil and Commercial of the British Colonies in the West Indies* (London, 1794), p. 228.
15. Satchell, 'Technology', p. 85.
16. Ragatz, 'Fall of the Planter Class', pp. 57–8.
17. R. Sullivan, 'The Timing and Pattern of Technological Development in English Agriculture 1611–1850', *Journal of Economic History*, 38:2 (1978), p. 306.
18. Sullivan, 'Timing', p. 306.
19. C. MacLeod, 'The 1690s Patents Boom: Invention or Stock Jobbing', *Economic History Review*, 34:4 (1986), pp. 549–71; R. Sullivan, 'The Revolution of Ideas: Widespread Patenting and Inventions During the English Industrial Revolution', *Journal of Economic History*, 50:2 (June 1990), p. 358.
20. K. Sokoloff and B. Khan in their study of patents for inventions in the United States similarly argue that inventions in that country were essentially demand-induced activities: Sokoloff and Khan, 'The Democratization of Invention During Early Industrialization: Evidence From the United States 1790–1846', *Journal of Economic History*, 50:2 (1990), pp. 365–7.
21. Satchell, 'Technology', p. 100.

22. The first modern horizontal three-roller mill was designed by John Smeaton in 1754 for a Mr Gray, a Jamaican sugar planter. Nothing seemed to have come of this until 1794 when John Collinge began making these mills in bulk, and so popularised this type of mill. For a full discussion on the development and diffusion of the horizontal three-roller mill see Deerr, 'Evolution', pp. 1–9; Daniels and Daniels, 'Origins', pp. 496–533; Fraginals, 'Sugar Mill', pp. 56, 101.

23. Satchell, 'Technology', pp. 93–5.

24. Ibid., p. 100.

25. The machine made use of two sets of horizontal rollers instead of the vertical rollers and dumbturner. See patent of Anders Jensen Schouburg, *Votes of the Hon. House of Assembly of Jamaica* [JHAJ], 15 November 1822, p. 110.

26. Satchell, 'Technology', p. 103.

27. Edwards, 'History Civil', pp. 228, 262–3.

28. Sokoloff and Khan, 'Democratization', p. 367.

29. Patentees included artisans, planters and professionals.

30. Satchell, 'Technology', pp. 116–17.

31. *Journal of the Honourable House of Assembly of Jamaica* [JHAJ], 15 December 1788.

32. Satchell, 'Technology', pp. 118–19.

33. D. Hall, 'Slaves and Slavery in the British West Indies', *Social and Economic Studies,* 11 (1962), pp. 312.

34. Higman, *Slave Population and Economy,* p. 38.

35. M. Craton, J. Walvin and D. Wright, eds., 'Edward Long Describes his own Estate in Jamaica', in *Slavery, Abolition and Emancipation: Black Slaves and the British Empire, A Thematic Documentary* (London: Longmans, 1976), pp. 102–3.

36. C. Goucher, 'African Hammer European Anvil, the History of Iron Technology in the Caribbean', seminar paper presented at the Department of History, University of the West Indies, Mona, Seminar Series (April, 1990), p. 2.

37. Goucher, 'African Hammer', p. 8.

38. See petition of William James of Kingston, founder, in *Votes,* 27 November 1829, pp. 118–19.

39. Petition of William James, p. 119; proprietors of sugar estates in their petition to the House in support of James attested to his claim of being able to perform all types of metal work locally, JHAJ, 24 November 1830, p. 78.

40. Hall, 'Slaves', p. 309.

41. See Robertson's map of Jamaica (1804), *The National Library of Jamaica.*

42. V.A. Shepherd, 'Problems in the Supply of Livestock to Sugar Estates in the Period of Slavery: An Example From the History of Spring Sugar Plantation in the Parish of St. Andrew, Jamaica c. 1700–1800', paper presented at

Department of History, Staff/ Post Graduate Seminar, University of the West Indies, Mona, Jamaica (May 1987), p. 3.

43. Deerr argues that the dumbturner was invented in 1805 by a Mr Bell, a Barbadian planter, Porter contends, however, that Jacques François Dutrone La Courte in the late eighteenth century promoted a similar device, called by the French *doubleuse*. The *doubleuse* served essentially the same purpose, guiding the bagasse of the first set of rollers and returning them through the second set. Edwards, however, made reference to the dumbturner in his description of the sugar-cane mill, thus indicating that it was in use prior to 1805. Presumably this was of the earlier La Courte models. It would appear, therefore, that the 1805 invention by Bell was the first among the British Caribbean planters. See Deerr, 'Evolution', pp. 5–7; Porter, 'Nature and Properties', pp. 144–5; Edwards, 'History Civil', pp. 223, 227. For a discussion of the development of the mill and dumbturner, see Daniels and Daniels, 'Origins', pp. 494–5, 531; Fraginals, 'Sugar Mill', pp. 102–3.

44. Satchell, 'Technology' pp. 179–80.

45. Deerr, 'Evolution', p. 4; Daniels and Daniels, 'Origins', p. 534; Higman, *Jamaica Surveyed: Plantation Maps and Plans of the Eighteenth and Nineteenth Centuries* (Kingston: Institute of Jamaica, 1988), p. 141.

46. Deerr, 'Evolution', p. 5; Daniels and Daniels, 'Origins', pp. 494–5; Porter, 'Nature and Properties', pp. 144–5; Fraginals, 'Sugar Mill', pp. 102–3.

47. Deerr, 'Evolution', p. 5.

48. Porter, 'Nature and Properties', 144–5; see also Fraginals, 'Sugar Mill', pp. 101–3.

49. Deerr, 'Evolution', p. 5; Fraginals, 'Sugar Mill', pp. 101–5.

50. Deerr, 'Evolution', p. 5; Fraginals, 'Sugar Mill', p. 101.

51. Letter Book, John Rennie to Boulton and Watt, No. 23/17/5, 22 February 1810; No. 23/17/6, 2 March 1810, *Boulton and Watt Collections (B&W Coll.)*; Letter Book, John Rennie to Boulton and Watt, No. 23/13/128, 17 December 1824, *B&W Coll.*

52. Letter Book, John Rennie to Boulton and Watt, No. 40, 3 June 1815, *B&W Coll.*

53. L. Wray, *The Practical Sugar Planter; A Complete Account of the Cultivation and Manufacture of the sugar-cane According to the Latest and most Improved Processes* (London, 1848), p. 291.

54. Deerr, 'Evolution', pp. 4–5.

55. Satchell, 'Technology', pp. 314–16.

Planting and Processing Techniques on Jamaican Coffee Plantations, during Slavery

KATHLEEN E.A. MONTEITH

British Caribbean planters have been accused of scoffing at improved technological innovation with respect to the cultivation and manufacture of agricultural crops during the slave period. Prominent among those who have held this view is L.J. Ragatz, who charged that the adoption of a wasteful agricultural system by planters was a contributory factor to the decline of the West Indian economy. On the other hand, Douglas Hall, William Green and R. Keith Aufhauser have indicated that this issue should be viewed within the context of the adaptability of new and improved techniques to peculiar geographical locations and the socio-economic circumstances of the period. The discussion has led to a more general debate concerning the relationship between slavery and technology, questioning whether technological improvements were incompatible with slavery. At the same time, recent work examining productivity change in the Jamaican sugar industry between 1760 and 1830 has revealed that sugar producers were not averse to implementing new and improved techniques in the field and factory during the slave period.[1]

This chapter's focus is an examination of the planting and processing techniques pursued by coffee planters in Jamaica in the period 1790–1838. This is with a view to a better understanding of one of the factors which led to the demise of coffee production at the plantation level in the nineteenth century. It relies on the views of the respected French émigré and St Domingue coffee planter, P.J. Laborie, who had been invited to make his observations and recommendations to the Jamaican coffee planting community. It also makes use of the observations by contemporaries of the period, as well as documentary evidence in plantation journals and estate maps.

Coffee by the early nineteenth century had grown in importance in the Jamaican plantation economy. In this period coffee became the second most important export crop after sugar and its derivatives, largely as result of the St Domingue (Haiti) revolution (1792–1804). The protracted warfare in that French colony caused a severe dislocation in the production and export of agricultural crops, resulting in a scarcity of supplies to the world market. Hence the rapid rise in prices, along with a reduction in duty on imports into Britain, provided the impetus for a dramatic expansion in production and exports from Jamaica. Between 1790 and 1795, exports from Jamaica increased from just below 2 million lb to 5 million lb. By 1805 they amounted to just under 24 million lb. Peak exports occurred in 1808 when they reached 30 million lb, though the highest exports, 34 million lb, were recorded in 1814. This figure is deceptive, since it included accumulated stocks of coffee which planters were unable to sell due to the French blockade of the continent between 1807 and 1814. Between 1820 and 1830 exports from Jamaica averaged 23 million lb, and by 1834, they stood at 19 million lb. By 1838 coffee exports had fallen to 13.5 million lb. This meant a decline in exports by 55 per cent between 1808 and 1838.[2]

A combination of factors accounted for this decline before 1838. These included an overall decline in the price for coffee on the world market after 1800, caused by increased production and supplies from other coffee-producing areas within and outside the British empire. Prices also declined as a result of changes in British fiscal policy in the 1820s and 1830s, which reduced the preferential rates of duty accorded to British colonial coffee entering Britain. As prices declined, many planters in Jamaica were unable to compete effectively because of high production costs.[3]

This chapter suggests that a major contributory factor to these high production costs were the production methods utilised by coffee planters in Jamaica in the period 1790–1838.

In the early nineteenth century, coffee plantations in Jamaica were located in all the parishes. However, the majority were to be found in the eastern parishes of Port Royal, St Andrew, St David, St Thomas-in-the East and St George, numbering 281 or 42 per cent of the total of 686 in existence in 1800. A significant number of properties were also to be found in the parishes of Clarendon, St Ann and St Elizabeth, which together accounted for 175 properties, or 25 per cent of the total. All these parishes possessed the environmental factors necessary for coffee culture. Coffee required a cool climate, and it was therefore necessary to cultivate it at considerable elevations above sea level. Altitudes between 3,000 ft and 5,000 ft, which are associated with temperatures between 65° and 73° are regarded as being ideal for the cultivation of coffee. In Jamaica cultivation was generally at these altitudes, particularly in the eastern parishes where the Blue Mountains are located. In the western parishes, plantations occupied lands which rose between 1,000 ft and 3,000 ft and between 2,000 ft and 3,000 ft, particularly in the May Day and Don Figuero mountains.[4]

The soil conditions in these regions were generally suitable for coffee cultivation. In the eastern section of the island, particularly in the Blue Mountains, the soil was of a dark brown, gravelly loam, formed on shales and conglomerates and possessing the properties necessary for coffee culture. However, because of the steepness of the mountains in this area, the soils were prone to be washed away during heavy rainfall, thereby rendering them infertile. In the central and western parishes, coffee was grown in the red limestone and black marl soils which were also suitable for its cultivation.[5]

Planting techniques

Once planted, coffee had a productive life which could span 12–30 years, and the method of planting was regarded as being the single most important factor in the eventual level of production achieved on plantations. Laborie, who visited Jamaica in the 1790s, recommended that saplings be planted in holes 9–12 inches in diameter and 15–18 inches in depth. He also suggested that the holes be prepared at least two months before planting. This was to ensure the proper preparation of the soil, exposing it to the sunlight and air necessary for the proper root development and penetration of the coffee plant.[6]

Notwithstanding, planting techniques pursued by the coffee planters in this period were antiquated, as planters were content to force a large pointed stick into the ground, move it around and then insert the sapling along with some mould as fertiliser. Also, planters generally relied on seedlings that germinated in the shade under the parent plant. While these could be transplanted, usually in taking up these seedlings the roots were damaged, and the sudden exposure to the sun and air in their new location caused the retardation of full bearing by as much as two years. Saplings cultivated in nurseries were more suitable, since they were grown in conditions similar to those in which they would be transplanted.[7]

Maintaining the fertility of the soil in which coffee was grown was very important, since the development and productivity of the plant could be affected by insufficient nutrient intake. Hence, the practice of soil conservation measures was of vital importance if plantations were to remain productive. The layout of the coffee fields was an important aspect of soil conservation. The usual mode of planting was to line the fields in squares of 8 ft spacing, making it possible for at least 680 plants to occupy 1 acre of land. Under conditions of average soil fertility the competition for nutrients would be too great if the spacing was less than 8 ft per square. This led to poor yields from the plants. In the case of high soil fertility, the overcrowding of plants also resulted in poor yields because of the rapid depletion of the nutrients in the soil. Hence, it was important for planters to assess the soil conditions of their properties before deciding upon the spacing of the plants in the fields.[8]

The declivity of the land also had to be considered when deciding upon the measure of spacing of the coffee plants since improper spacing could result in rapid soil erosion. A spacing of 9 ft square was recommended for level to gently sloping lands. On more steeply sloping lands, where soil erosion was more likely to occur, it was recommended that spacing be 9 ft along contoured lines.[9]

There is no indication that coffee planters in Jamaica during the eighteenth and nineteenth centuries terraced or contoured their lands, in spite of plantations occupying declivitous land areas. Edward Long, writing in the 1770s, recommended that the practice should be adapted on sugar plantations located on declivitous land. However, he made no reference to its adoption on coffee plantations which were generally located on high mountain ranges and slopes exceeding 20°.[10] The statements by Laborie are in themselves confusing. With reference to the establishment of the coffee settlement on declivitous land, he stated that 'amphitheatres or platforms rising one above the other be cut into the ground so as to give the ground a level effect'. However, in reference to coffee fields occupying very steep land, Laborie stated:

the grounds . . . are liable to break off and fall down . . . By some of these falls, 5000–6000 coffee trees have at once been known to be carried away. Sometimes more consistent and compact grounds though equally steep happen to slide off from rain water, which after penetrating upwards, creeps in, dilutes and dissolves the soil under ground on account of the great declivity. I know no means of preventing this.[11]

So it seems that planters knew of the technique and felt that it could only be applied to areas required for siting buildings, and did not feel obliged to apply it to the fields. This precarious situation was also aggravated by improper methods of weeding, which served to loosen the soil in steep locations, causing it to be easily swept away during heavy rainfall. In such locations it was preferable to have weeds pulled up by hand, and where it was necessary to dig with tools, it was important that the earth be returned and pressed down where it had been loosened.[12] However, the practice on coffee plantations was to use hoes for weeding purposes. This had adverse effects, since it increased the rate of erosion by loosening the topsoil and also destroyed the surface-feeding roots of the plants.[13] Thus as a result of the failure of planters to introduce methods to prevent soil erosion, a significant number of plantations, especially in the eastern parishes of Jamaica, had to be abandoned very early in the period, as they were rendered unproductive. At least 78 coffee plantations went out of production or were sold between 1805 and 1815. The committee of the House of Assembly in Jamaica in 1815 noted in reference to these plantations that, 'the fields, once productive have gradually been abandoned and are altogether unfit; they do not even throw up nor can they be made to yield a grass fit for rearing cattle'.[14]

One technique which planters were aware of but failed to use on a consistent basis was the application of fertiliser to coffee fields. The only time that coffee plants received any form of fertiliser was at the time of planting. The regular application of fertiliser was particularly important, given the fact that each crop of coffee removed significant portions of nutrients from the soil. For example, a crop of 560 lb of clean coffee per acre consisted of approximately 30 lb of nitrogen, 6 lb of phosphorus, 30 lb of potassium and 22 lb of other minerals. Without a good supply of organic matter the friability and granular structure of the soil, which was important to the plant's continued productivity, suffered.[15]

During the nineteenth century, fertilisers were not available commercially and planters had to rely on local substances. Sugar producers depended on refuse, cane trash and ashes from the boiling and still houses. Other substances included mud from ponds which received wastes from the manufacturing process, lime and shell-laden sea sand. However, the most commonly utilised substance was manure produced by the estates' livestock. Coffee planters had at their disposal coffee pulp, leaf mould and manure from the plantations' livestock. Richard Ormrod notes that most planters resented the necessity of fertilising their fields, since it was very time-consuming. For example, accumulated manure had first to be heaped up in the stock pen, then loaded on to carts and transported to the fields to be placed in each hole during planting. Sugar-cane planters got around this by adopting the method of fly-penning. This technique involved the fencing of the estates' non-working livestock on fallow fields with movable or flying pens. In this way the animals were left for two or three weeks in a particular spot to spread their dung and urine throughout the enclosure, working it into the soil with their hooves.[16]

It was virtually impossible to implement this method on coffee plantations in Jamaica, given the rugged character of the lands. In addition, coffee plantations did not utilise as large a number of livestock as sugar estates. Hence it would have been very difficult to practise fly-penning with too few animals. Ormrod refers to Thomas Roughley's estimate of at least 80–100 head of cattle required to adequately fertilise 30 acres of land over an eight-month period. In any event, even if coffee properties occupied gently sloping lands and had at their disposal sufficient livestock with which to fly-pen, the method was impractical. This was because coffee shrubs were perennial, and fly-penning would have resulted in the animals causing considerable damage to the plants.[17]

Thus, coffee planters, if they were serious about applying fertiliser to their fields, had to rely on the more time-consuming practice of slaves being assigned to administer fertilisers to the plants. This, however was not done, and what resulted was a patchy appearance, with significant portions of the plantation in ruinate. For example, Windsor Lodge in Port Royal and extending into Saint David covered 336 acres of which only 74 acres were in coffee. A plan of the plantation reveals several acres occupied in pasture, interspersed with ruinate, which Barry Higman notes hinted at a cycle of soil exhaustion and replacement. Land-use patterns depicted on maps of coffee plantations, indicate that the area in ruinate was positively correlated with the area in coffee. This suggests that as one area became worn out, planters simply shifted cultivation to another.[18] The planters' explanation was simply that 'coffee plantations are worn out. Coffee is planted in what is called virgin soil and can only be planted once'.[19]

The plantation works

In Jamaica the coffee works occupied a relatively small area of an average of 1.7 acres, in contrast to an average of seven acres occupied by sugar works. This difference was largely because the coffee works complex involved less elaborate structures and machinery in comparison to what was found on sugar properties. Very little change was noted in the area occupied by the works during the slavery period and beyond. This can be explained by the fact that there was very little change in the technology and scale of operations of coffee works during this period in Jamaica.[20]

The positioning of the works complex

The rugged character of coffee lands in Jamaica placed a great deal of pressure on the ideal model of plantation layout as recommended by Laborie in his manual. This model had the location of the works, village and great house at the centre of the plantation. According to Laborie, 'it appears more eligible that building be more laborious either from the carriage of materials or from the trenchings necessary to level the spot, than to fix in a place from which the future plantations will be greatly distant'.[21]

Laborie's concern was therefore with the distance between the fields and works. His other concern was with maintaining labour discipline. He stated that with the siting of the settlement near a public road, travellers might disturb 'the interior order and discipline of the Negroes'.[22] However, Laborie also recognised that at the centre the ground might be too steep. Besides, planters might prefer to locate their complex in close proximity to a water source, timber and stone. But Laborie still maintained that 'where every necessary thing does not lie contiguous', it would be preferable to give up those accessory conveniences rather than to abandon a central location of the works, especially if the water could be conducted through a pipe.[23]

However, on Jamaican coffee plantations the coffee works were rarely located at the centre. Higman has shown that the ability or inability of planters to place their coffee works in a central position was not dependent upon the topographical constraints associated with most coffee regions in Jamaica.

Instead, planters preferred to position their works in the vicinity of rivers if they were present on their plantations in order to facilitate the easy tapping of water-power for mills. The advantage of this was that costs of production were kept minimal, since pipes were not needed for conveying the water to the mills. However, to position the settlement in a central location would mean that the distance between the fields and the mills would be minimised in the long run, though the shifting nature of cultivation in response to soil exhaustion meant that efficiency and profitability would vary from time to time. Where mills were animal-powered, they tended to be shifted to follow the focus of cultivation.[24]

The works: machinery, buildings and the processing of coffee

Depending upon the scale of operations, the coffee works could range from the very basic and rudimentary to more sophisticated outlays. As such, the methods utilised in the processing of the crop on large plantations tended to be different from those on smaller properties.[25]

Processing coffee involved the removal of the outer skins, pulp and the inner parchment in order to expose the marketable coffee beans inside. Before the 1790s, coffee in Jamaica was commonly cured by first drying it in the state that it was picked from the trees, instead of first removing the outer coverings. Patrick Browne, writing in the 1770s, referred to plantations in Jamaica on which berries 'were left soaking in their clammy juices to dry, but slowly in a damp air, in many parts of the island'.

This practice continued into the nineteenth century on some plantations such as Industry in the parish of St George. This method of curing was referred to as the 'in cherries' method.[26] This method was likely to be adopted by plantations operating on a very small scale, thereby making it too expensive to invest in mills, or because of a lack of sufficient water, which was vital for the removal of the outer skins and pulp before drying.

This technique was considered primitive for a number of reasons. The drying time of the berries was extended by as much as three times the length it took to dry them without their outer skins and pulp, and so more time had to be spent in attending the berries on the barbecues. Also the berries were likely to ferment too much, thereby affecting the quality of the final product. The barbecues were also liable to decay more rapidly as a result of the fermentative gum from the berries dissolving the lime used in their construction. Laborie noted, however, that coffee dried in this way usually weighed 13 per cent more than if dried without the outer skins, and therefore were more likely to fetch a higher price, since coffee was sold according to weight. Coffee planters who utilised this method probably assessed the costs involved in relation to the prices that they could fetch for their beans if of a reasonable quality.[27] Thus, these planters adopted a calculated risk in response to their operating scale, energy supply and market price.

The best method of curing coffee was known as the drying in parchment method or the wet process. This involved the removal of the outer skins and pulp before the coffee was put to dry by a machine known as a pulper or grater.[28] Alec Haarer notes that the principle of the pulping machine included in the wet process of preparing coffee was to force the seeds, causing them to fly out through the apertures, while the skins of the fruit were pulled away. Since the berries were fed continuously into the machine by gravity, the operation could only be successful if the seeds were held in their slippery mucilaginous coverings, and if the skins of the fruit were soft and ripe enough to burst open. Therefore, it was important that the berries fed into the hopper were all properly ripe. If the berries were under-ripe or partially dried, blockage would result, or the berries improperly pulped, beans crushed and a great deal of pulp would pass through along with the pulped beans. Such a situation could adversely affect a vast amount of the crop. In cases where stones were gathered up with the coffee berries from the ground, the machine was in danger of being damaged, making the grater ineffective by damaging the sharp points.[29]

There is evidence that pulping machines were used by coffee planters in Jamaica, though it is not possible to ascertain the models and types commonly used. The machines were fairly inexpensive, valued at only £10 throughout the period.[30]

The building in which the mill was housed was known as the pulping mill house. Laborie recommended that the building be 40 ft in length and 20 ft in breadth in order to facilitate four manually operated pulpers. At Hermitage in St Elizabeth, the mill house was 40 ft square, but housed only one pulper. The building contained a floor with wooden gutters, usually 6 inches square. This floor was positioned over the mill, upon which the coffee berries were first laid, then conducted through the gutters to the mill. Laborie advised that 'in very steep grounds, there being a good terrace wall, it might be one and close to the cut hill, so that the labourers were able to get onto the floor on a level'. The mill or mills were placed over the gutters, which led into basins or cisterns. Laborie also suggested that the basins should be 8–10 ft square and 18–20 ft deep, so that the labourer whose responsibility it was to turn the coffee did not have water above his knees. Conduits led water into the basins. From there, water was carried into lesser vessels which contained the floating scums from the mills which had been carried along by water in a gutter. A sluice allowed water when taken up to carry the coffee and scums from their basins to their respective draining platforms or barbecues.[31]

This general plan was evident at both Oldbury in Manchester and Malvern in St Elizabeth. Both plantations were located in parishes where the supply of water from streams and rivers was limited, and hence, on both properties tanks were erected for the purpose of catching and supplying water to the works. At Oldbury, the tank, with a capacity for 59,000 gallons of water, had gutters leading from it to the pulping house, washing cisterns and barbecues.[32]

Draining platforms, barbecues and kilns

The draining platforms were built in such a way that coffee was spread out evenly under the impulse of the running water which conveyed the beans from the pulping house. The borders to the fore of the platforms were fitted with outlets and grates to allow water to pass but prevent the coffee from escaping.

Draining platforms were not necessary where there was plenty of running water. In such a situation, 'all the platforms or barbecues were arranged under the washing basin on both sides of a canal through which the water passed with the coffee. By means of sluices, the coffee was then conveyed to the various barbecues for drying'.[33] After 24 hours on the draining platforms, the coffee, which was by then white in appearance, was taken to the barbecues, where it was spread out to dry in the sun. The ideal location for barbecues was in close proximity to the pulpery. This may not have been always possible, basically because of two factors. To obtain the advantages of gravity flow and water supply, the pulpery and tanks were often sited on lower slopes and in valleys. These locations were not suited for the positioning of barbecues, since these areas usually had mists hanging over at night, thereby prolonging the drying process. It was preferable to have barbecues located on high ground, where the air was drier and windy, and where full advantage of the drying effects of the sun could be taken.[34]

Drying by barbecues was labour-intensive, for it meant that slaves had to be constantly tending to the beans, periodically raking them to ensure that their surface areas were adequately exposed to the sun. Some plantations used both kilns and barbecues for drying.[35]

The most obvious advantage in using kilns was the convenience of drying coffee during rainy weather. The kiln consisted of a covered building made primarily of masonry. The coffee was placed on several trays in layers inside the building, which was heated by a fireplace. The heat was diffused throughout the kiln from this fireplace by copper tubing and flues. Because this building was covered, the utilisation of the kiln precluded the necessity of earnestly sweeping coffee to shelter into rounds or bassicots in the middle of the barbecues, whenever rain or dew threatened.

Another advantage of the kiln, was that the drying time was also considerably shortened. The kiln designed by Dr Bryan Higgins in the early 1800s was capable of drying 4,000–5,000 lb of pulped coffee within 18–20 hours. Pulped coffee spread out on barbecues generally took between six and seven days to dry under the most favourable conditions. Labour was also conserved, since the kiln required only half the number of labourers for tending coffee on barbecues, which was usually 12–14 persons. It was also argued that kilns were less expensive, being at least a quarter of the total cost of erecting barbecues. The prevention of pilferage of coffee was another advantage to planters, since they could be locked. It was argued that the slaves' work in the kiln was less laborious than on the barbecues.

Improvements in the efficiency of the kiln were developed by Higgins in the early 1800s. His design was adopted at Vaughansfield in St Thomas, and was found satisfactory. Improvements involved less fuel, and a more even distribution of heat throughout the kiln, thereby ensuring proper drying. Higgins reported that a Mr Woolfrys and Mr Lagourgue were interested in the new design. However, there is no evidence to suggest how widespread the use of kilns was in Jamaica during this period.[36]

Coffee house or store

Coffee stores were generally found located near by the pulping mill house and the peeling mill house. In this building, coffee was not only stored, but slaves were employed there to sift, cull and weigh coffee. Hence the building had to be of adequate size in order to facilitate all these activities. Laborie recommended that the building be 60 ft in length and 34 ft in width. Such a building would have the capacity to store at least 200,000 lb of coffee along with scums and pickings. At Lapland in St James, the store was much smaller, being 20 ft square. Since coffee is hygroscopic, it was important that the product was protected from moisture and rain, as well as from pungent odours, all of which could affect its quality. Hence it was important that coffee stores possessed features that would ensure adequate protection of the crop while in storage on the plantation. Thus the buildings were made basically of masonry lined with rafters along the walls in order to keep the air inside dry. The floors were made of boards, with openings all around to facilitate the free passage of air underneath. Numerous windows were necessary in order to provide for the easy passage of dry air, especially important after a shower of rain, so as to absorb any moisture and dampness left behind. This design described by Laborie was evident at Oldbury.[37]

Coffee stores were fitted with tables for picking or culling, as it was sometimes referred to. Laborie recommended that these tables be edged with a 'lath about an inch high and if there was a bottomless box in the middle, supported upon small triangles with feet of two inches high'. From this box, from slides underneath, coffee was taken to be picked. In front of each picker was a hole, 'under which a bag was hung and kept open by nails', into which the more marketable coffee was thrown. The triage was bagged and either retained for plantation use or sold locally. It is not known whether tables such as the one described by Laborie were used on Jamaican plantations, as inventories merely listed the presence of picking tables, giving no indication of their design.[38]

Peeling mill house

At the peeling mill house, the activities of removing the husk or parchment took place. This building was an expensive one, as it had to be large enough to hold both the peeling and winnowing machines. At Oldbury there were two separate buildings located beside each other for these functions. Laborie suggested a building of 36 ft square in which the winnowing machine was placed in a gallery, leaving enough room for the peeling mill. On most Jamaican coffee plantations, especially in the Manchester and St Elizabeth region, the mill houses were circular structures, suggesting the importance of animal power, as well as the fact that the peeling and winnowing processes were conducted separately.[39] The peeling machine consisted of a circular trough of about 10–12 inches deep and 10–12 ft in diameter. It was usually made of hardwood, or masonry, paved with large flat stones. The grinder, peeler or wheel made up the other part of the machine. This was made of very heavy wood, and was 6 ft in height, 12–14 inches thick in the centre and about 4 inches in circumference. An axle-tree or tail was passed through it, with one end fixed to the trough in a way that facilitated easy rotation. A fork was fitted behind the axle-tree in the trough, so that as the axle-tree was taken around in a circular direction, the coffee was pushed to the middle to fall under the wheel and so be peeled. It was estimated that it would require at least four or six horses, working for nine hours, to peel 2–3 tierces of coffee. While the peeling mill house was fairly costly, averaging £400 to be built, most properties seem to have had one.[40]

The winnowing machine or fanner was frequently used on coffee plantations in general. The structure described by Laborie consisted of a machine enclosed within a wooden box, having two openings. The structure was designed to separate the chaff which was produced during processing from the beans. The machine itself consisted of a fan with four plates made of tin or thin planks mounted upon an axle-tree at the end of which was a toothwheel. There was also another wheel which provided increased velocity to the machine when activated. The coffee and chaff entered the machine through its hopper to fall upon a sieve. This sieve was set in motion by means of an oval pulley and a wooden spring, which caused the unbruised coffee to be tossed into a gutter, since it was unable to pass through the sieves. The coffee beans, having been rid of their outer coverings and parchment, passed through the sieve to another positioned below it. From there, the beans slid into a box as the chaff was blown away through another opening. While it is not certain whether models of the kind described by Laborie were utilised, it was evident that planters accepted the principle of the use of fanners as part of the production process.[41]

Water-powered mills on coffee plantations in Jamaica

The pulping, peeling and winnowing machines were all adaptable to being water-powered with the use of a water-wheel. The water-wheel was common in Jamaica during this period. However, it is not possible to provide an estimate of the relative importance of water-powered mills because of the unavailability of data.[42] Only a few coffee plantations in the eastern parishes have been identified with water-mills. However, it was inevitable that in parishes such as St Elizabeth and Manchester, the incidence of animal-powered mills would be greater, given the fact that there were very few streams and rivers present from which water power could be accessed. Animal power would also have been convenient, since numerous coffee plantations in those parishes combined coffee production with livestock rearing.[43]

The use of water-powered mills on coffee plantations meant that a greater degree of efficiency in the production process was possible. The operations of the pulping, peeling and winnowing machines were synchronised, thus cutting down on the number of labourers required to operate the mills, while at the same time producing double the amount possible from a common mill in a given time. However, a prohibitive factor in the adoption of water-powered mills on plantations must have been the economies of scale of particular plantations. Water mills were only economically feasible on plantations capable of producing at least 60,000 lb of coffee annually.[44]

Conclusion

Jamaican planters in the nineteenth century generally chose the most ideal locations in which to engage in coffee production, but their agricultural practices left much to be desired. Planting methods were generally substandard, contributing to a rapid depletion of soil nutrients, which meant less than average yields per plant on plantations. In addition, there was little appreciation of the necessity of contouring the lands upon which their plantations were located. This was in spite of the fact that many occupied lands of a declivitous nature. As a result, many coffee properties in Jamaica exhibited extensive soil erosion, rendering them unproductive very early in the history of the industry. Indeed, there was a general acceptance within the industry that coffee lands would eventually wear out, and as such, the industry exhibited a cycle of soil exhaustion and replacement, as cultivation was periodically shifted to virgin soil, leaving behind tracts of ruinate land. In that regard, the charge by Ragatz that planters in the British Caribbean were wasteful in their agricultural practices was applicable to coffee planters in Jamaica in the late eighteenth and early nineteenth century.

At the same time, it was evident that most coffee planters availed themselves of the prevailing technology governing the manufacturing process. However, there existed variations in the methods of processing which were related to the scale of operations. Generally the larger properties were outfitted with the more sophisticated machinery and equipment, and the smaller ones utilised rudimentary forms of processing.

In general, planters were keen on minimising costs at the processing stage. This was evident in the decision to position their coffee works in close proximity to a water source if it was present on the property. Wherever possible, water-powered mills were utilised, which offered a level of synchronisation within the various processing stages. This meant a greater degree of efficiency. However, the extent to which water-mills were used was dependent upon the availability of a water source. Hence, properties located in parishes that were deficient in rivers continued to rely on the less efficient animal-powered mills. At the same time, economies of scale would also have been a factor which planters would have had to consider when making the decision to introduce water-powered mills.

Notes

1.   L.J. Ragatz, *The Fall of the Planter Class in the British Caribbean 1763–1833. A Study in Social and Economic History* (New York: American Historical Association, 1928), pp. 56, 57; Ragatz, 'Absentee Landlordism in the British Caribbean 1750–1833', *Agricultural History*, 5 (1931), pp. 7–24; R.K. Aufhauser, 'Slavery and Technological Change', *Journal of Economic History*, 34:1 (1974), pp. 42–4; W.A. Green, 'The Planter Class and British West Indian Sugar Production, Before and After Emancipation', *Economic History Review*, 26:4 (1973), pp. 448–9; D. Hall, 'Slaves and Slavery in the British West Indies', *Social and Economic Studies* 11 (1962), pp. 305–18; M. Fraginals, *The Sugar Mill, The Socioeconomic Complex of Sugar in Cuba, 1760–1860*, trans. Cedric Belfrage (New York, London: Monthly Review Press, 1976) and R. Scott, 'Explaining Abolition: Contradiction, Adaptation and Challenge in Cuban Slave Society 1860–1866', *Comparative Studies in Society and History*, 26 (1984), pp. 83–111. See also V. Satchell, 'Technology and Productivity Change in the Jamaican Sugar Industry, 1760–1830' (unpublished PhD thesis, UWI, Mona, 1993).
2.   K.E.A. Monteith, 'The Coffee Industry in Jamaica, 1790–1850' (unpublished MPhil thesis, UWI, Mona, 1991), pp. 15–20, 202–6.
3.   Ibid., pp. 214–34.
4.   Ibid., pp. 35–6.

5.   Ibid., pp. 37–8.
6.   F. Thurber, *Coffee. From Plantation to Cup: A Brief History of Coffee Production and Consumption* (New York, 1884), p. 5; R. Baird, *Impressions and Experiences of the West Indies and North America in 1849*, Vol. 1 (London, 1850), p. 148; R.I. Moss, *A Guide to Coffee Culture in Jamaica* (Jamaica: Department of Agriculture, 1956), p. 24. Baird's estimate is 12–60 years; *Radnor Coffee Plantation Journal*, January 1822–February 1826. MS 180, National Library of Jamaica (NLJ); P.J. Laborie, *The Coffee Planter of Saint Domingo* (N.P. c. 1799), pp. 114–17.
7.   Moss, *A Guide*, p. 25; Laborie, *The Coffee Planter*, p. 117; J. Lunan, *Hortus Jamaicensis*, 2 vols (Jamaica *Gazette*, 1814), Vol. 2, p. 215; Thurber, *Coffee*, p. 140; Moss, *A Guide*, p. 24.
8.   Moss, *A Guide*, pp. 7–8; Laborie, *The Coffee Planter*, p. 49; Moss, *A Guide*, pp. 14–15; Thurber, *Coffee*, p. 6; B. Edwards, *The History, Civil and Commercial of the British Colonies in the West Indies*, 5 vols, 6th edn (New York: AMS Press, 1966), Vol. 1, p. 341.
9.   Moss, *A Guide*, pp. 14–15.
10. E. Long, *History of Jamaica*, 2 vols (London: Frank Cass, 1970), Vol. 1, pp. 446–7. See also B.W. Higman, 'Jamaican Coffee Plantations, 1790–1860: A Cartographic Analysis', *Caribbean Geography*, 2 (1986), p. 77.
11. Laborie, *The Coffee Planter*, pp. 33–4.
12. Ibid., p. 117.
13. *Radnor Journal*, July–December 1822; Moss, *A Guide*, p. 52; A.E. Haarer, *Modern Coffee Production* (London: Leonard Hill, 1962), p. 415.
14. *Further Proceedings of the Honourable House of Assembly of Jamaica* (London, 1816), pp. 34–5, 99–100.
15. Lunan, *Hortus Jamaicensis*, p. 215; Thurber, *Coffee*, p. 139; Moss, *A Guide*, p. 49.
16. R.K. Ormrod, 'The Evolution of Soil Management Practices in Early Jamaican Sugar Planting', *Journal of Historical Geography*, 5:2 (1979), pp. 160–1; Laborie, *The Coffee Planter*, pp. 144–5; Moss, *A Guide*, p. 25.
17. *Select Committee on the West Indian Colonies. West Indies.1. Sessions (1842)* (Shannon: Irish University Press, 1968), p. 417; Higman, *Jamaica Surveyed: Plantation Maps and Plans of the 18th and 19th Centuries* (Kingston: Institute of Jamaica Publications, 1988), p. 164; Ormrod, 'The Evolution of Soil Management', p. 161; T. Roughley, *The Jamaica Planter's Guide*, (London, 1823), pp. 97–119; Moss, *A Guide* p. 24.
18. Thurber, *Coffee*, p. 139; Higman, 'Jamaican Coffee Plantations', p. 83; Higman, *Jamaica Surveyed*, p. 174.
19. G. Eisner, *Jamaica 1830–1930. A Study in Economic Growth*, (Westport, CT: Greenwood Press, 1974), p. 303.

20. Higman, 'The Spatial Economy of Jamaican Sugar Plantations: Cartographic Evidence from the 18th and 19th centuries', *Journal of Historical Geography*, 13 (1987), pp. 17–39; Higman, 'Jamaican Coffee Plantations', pp. 78–9.

21. Higman, 'Jamaican Coffee Plantations', p. 77; Laborie, *The Coffee Planter*, p. 37.

22. Laborie, *The Coffee Planter*, p. 13.

23. Ibid.

24. Higman, 'Jamaican Coffee Plantations', p. 80.

25. S. Stein, *Vassouras. A Coffee County, 1850-1900* (Cambridge, MA: Harvard University Press, 1957), p. 36.

26. Laborie, *The Coffee Planter*, p. 45; Haarer, *Modern Coffee Production*, p. 239; Edwards, *History Civil*, p. 345; P. Browne, *The Civil and Natural History of Jamaica* (London, 1789), p. 163; J. Kelly, *Jamaica in 1831* (Belfast, 1838), p. 19; W. Dean, *Rio Claro, A Brazilian Plantation System* (Stanford, CA: Stanford University Press, 1976), pp. 37–8.

27. Laborie, *The Coffee Planter*, pp. 46–7; Dean, *Rio Claro*, p. 38.

28. Laborie, *The Coffee Planter*, pp. 45–9; Haarer, *Modern Coffee Production*, p. 239.

29. Haarer, *Modern Coffee Production*, p. 239; Laborie, *The Coffee Planter*, p. 52.

30. Inventories, Liber 103, folios 16, 33, Jamaica Archives, Spanish Town; *The Royal Gazette*, October 1805, December 1808, January 1812.

31. Laborie, *The Coffee Planter*, pp. 60, 74; NLJ, MS 250, Letterbook of John Wemyss, Hermitage Estate 1819–1824. St Elizabeth, letter dated 12 April 1820.

32. Higman, *Jamaica Surveyed*, pp. 186–8; NLJ, Oldbury Works Plan, MS Manchester 121.

33. Laborie, *The Coffee Planter*, pp. 81–2.

34. Laborie, *The Coffee Planter*, pp. 52–3; Haarer, *Modern Coffee Production*, p. 254.

35. Laborie, *The Coffee Planter*, p. 54; Oldbury Works Plan, Jamaica House of Assembly Journal, 1796 (Kingston), 2 November 1796, pp. 496–7.

36. B. Higgins, *From Observations and Advice for the Improvement of the Manufacture of Muscovado Sugar and Rum. To which is added a Description of a new Kiln for Drying Coffee* (St Jago de la Vega, n.d.), pp. 221, 223, 318, 323.

37. Oldbury Works Plan, *JHAJ* 1796, pp. 496–7; Laborie, *The Coffee Planter*, pp. 87–8, plates 4 and 5, Oldbury Works Plan.

38. Laborie, *The Coffee Planter*, p. 60; JA, Inventories.

39. Laborie, *The Coffee Planter*, p. 88; Oldbury Works Plan; Higman, *Jamaica Surveyed*, p. 187.

40. Laborie, *The Coffee Planter*, pp. 57–8; J. Humber, 'Description of a New Mill for Peeling Coffee', *Jamaica Almanack 1841* (Kingston, 1841), p. 50.

41. *The Royal Gazette*, October 1805, December 1808, February 1809. An advertisement by a John Green informed the public of 'twenty coffee fanners of the best construction for sale'; Laborie, *The Coffee Planter*, p. 59.
42. Laborie, *The Coffee Planter*, pp. 86–7; Higman, *Jamaica Surveyed*, p. 164.
43. J. Robertson, *Map of the County of Surrey 1804* (Kingston, 1804); *The Royal Gazette*, March 1812, May 1806, October 1805; Higman, 'Jamaican Coffee Plantations', p. 84.
44. Laborie, *The Coffee Planter*, pp. 86–7.

SECTION III

*Race, Class, Gender and Power
in Caribbean Slave Systems*

CHAPTER 7

'A Matron in Rank, A Prostitute in Manners'[1]

The Manning divorce of 1741 and class, gender, race and the law in eighteenth-century Jamaica

TREVOR BURNARD

On 13 April 1739 an unusual petition came before the members of the Jamaican House of Assembly. One of its leading members, a Kingston merchant, Edward Manning, petitioned the House to be allowed to dissolve his marriage to Elizabeth Manning, née Moore, so that 'He might be enabled to contract matrimony with any other woman'.[2] Manning claimed that his wife had committed adultery with another member of the House, Ballard Beckford, scion of the richest family in the island. A high-powered committee of the House was convened to 'report the facts and their opinion thereof'. On 27 April the committee reported. It declared itself satisfied that Beckford and Mrs Manning had cohabited since Mrs Manning's elopement, stated that 'adultery must be concluded', and called 15 witnesses to enquire into the circumstances of Mrs Manning's elopement. The House agreed that 'a crime had been committed against the very source and foundation of society' and Beckford was expelled from the House 'for flagrant and public offence against the order and peace of the community in general'.

But between the beginning of the case and the expulsion of Beckford, an odd twist occurred. Late on 27 April, one witness, Mrs Elizabeth O'Hara, Mrs Manning's former maidservant, was recalled for examination and gave extremely scandalous evidence. Mrs O'Hara claimed that her mistress had violated one of the most sacred taboos in Jamaican society, that which forbade sexual contact between White women and Black men. Mrs Manning was forced to petition the House about these new allegations. Although the House lectured Mrs Manning that her petition was 'scandalous, groundless, and highly reflecting on the honour and justice of the House', it allowed her counsel on 5 May 1739 to interrogate a further eight witnesses. In the end, however, the Assembly passed a bill that dissolved the Mannings' marriage and allowed Manning the right to remarry. The bill went to Jamaica's Council which sent the bill back to the Assembly, asking that the clause enabling Mr Manning to remarry be deleted. The Assembly refused, the Council relented, and the governor, Edward Trelawny, an erstwhile business partner of Manning, gave his assent on 12 May 1739.[3] The bill then went to the Board of Trade in London who asked for the opinion of the Lords of the Privy Council. Finally, on 16 July 1741, the Lords Justice in Council in Whitehall met and disallowed the Act providing for Manning's divorce, commenting that such an Act 'was the first such from the colonies' and that, moreover, 'the adultery was not positively proved'.[4] From this point, we lose track of events but from a letter written by Governor Trelawny to British Prime Minister, Henry Pelham, on 13 April 1749, it appears that the Assembly was 'affronted with the repeal of the law that divorced Mr Manning' and was only with difficulty persuaded from demonstrating that it 'had a mind to show that they would not be so us'd by their mother'.[5] Manning seems also to have been determined to see his ties with his wife severed. An unsuccessful appeal by Beckford to the Privy Council against a decision by the Jamaican Grand Court that he should pay Manning an unspecified sum for damages arising from 'criminal conversation' indicates that Manning pursued other alternatives to a parliamentary divorce after his private bill for divorce was disallowed in London.

The Manning divorce fascinates for a number of reasons. First, it is, as the Privy Council judgement declared, the only divorce in this form from a British colony before the American revolution and as such offers interesting insights into the legal procedure of gaining divorce in early modern British America.

Second, the case is revealing about colonial pretensions about usurping metropolitan authority. The Manning divorce was one of many attempts by a Jamaican Assembly to show itself the equal of the British Parliament. As such, it is a striking example of constitutional definition at work in the early modern British empire. An analysis of the divorce allows for an examination into the way in which constitutional authority was contested between metropolis and periphery and demonstrates the degree to which an assertive local elite was willing to insist on its right to define for itself what laws it would follow. I do not concern myself with such issues here but mention them in order to signal the constitutional importance of this case. Jamaican legislators saw the case as a way to signal to metropolitan authority the Assembly's belief that it was a tropical equivalent of the House of Commons, willing to assume and exercise the powers of that body 'as nearly as the circumstances of the Country cou'd allow, apprehending themselves to have an inherent right so to do as English subjects'.[6]

Third, the detailed testimonies of witnesses into the state of the Manning marriage provide a window into the complex intersections between class, race and gender in an eighteenth-century plantation society, in particular, the sensational evidence presented at the conclusion of the first day of hearings and the subsequent attempt by Mrs Manning to counter the allegations made against her is highly instructive about the status of women in early Jamaica. The ambivalent position of lower-class unfree women in a society increasingly divided into wealthy free Whites and oppressed unfree Black and mulatto slaves is made abundantly clear through the testimony of Mrs O'Hara. I have found no other instance in the records of eighteenth-century Jamaica where a person like Mrs O'Hara, a female White servant in a caste society, has her voice heard. This case should be situated, I believe, within a changing mid-eighteenth-century discourse on White women's sexuality in which White women were desexualised and where differences between White women were elided. It intersected, moreover, with another discourse over settlement in which White Jamaicans came to doubt whether Jamaica would ever become fully settled by Whites. Finally, the Manning case is important because so much of what actually happened is unclear. As in other legal cases involving women explored by early modern historians,[7] a number of perfectly plausible but contradictory interpretations about how the Mannings' marriage fell apart can be put forward. The indeterminacy of historical meaning in complex texts is fully realised in this case.

An Adulterous Affair

The Manning divorce was a *cause célèbre* in mid-eighteenth-century Jamaica. According to George Bridges, the local newspaper entertained its readers for weeks with 'the amusing details' of the divorce bill.[8] The case was news not just in Kingston but throughout the island: when one of the witnesses in the case was asked at Beckford's north-side plantation what news there was from town, he immediately regaled his listeners with an account of how Mrs Manning had run away and how Mr Manning had disowned her in a newspaper advertisement. Unfortunately, copies of the newspaper of the time and contemporary gossip and comment about the case in private letters have not survived. The only source for the details of the Manning divorce available to us is the legislative record of the Assembly's deliberations over the bill. Although the evidence is remarkably detailed compared with the usual bare summary of the Assembly's deliberations (the case takes up 24 closely printed pages in which the evidence of the 23 witnesses in the case is reported at considerable length), much that we would like to know is hidden from us, probably forever. We do not have, for example, any testimony from Mrs Manning. Nor was any testimony by slaves, who surely would have been privy to the truth or otherwise of Manning's allegation, permitted. More important, the questions asked witnesses by the Assembly were directed towards particular issues that are not necessarily the issues that modern historians would now consider most important. The evidence about the Mannings' marriage that survives was shaped by what questions, never clearly described in the legislative record, the Assembly wanted answered. Thus, the historian is forced to speculate about the lacunae that remain concerning the case.

Nevertheless, the essential facts and issues in the case are clear. On 18 March 1739, Mrs Manning left her husband's plantation estate after a disagreement with him, visited her friends, Mr and Mrs William Peete, in Kingston, and then left from the Mannings' Kingston residence for Spanish Town, in the company of Beckford. Beckford and Mrs Manning then removed to Beckford's north-side plantation. After learning of the elopement, Manning placed an advertisement in the *Jamaica Courant* warning people not to give Elizabeth Manning any credit for goods that she might want to purchase. Manning claimed before the House that this elopement was evidence that Beckford and his wife had committed adultery. Beckford denied this, claiming no impropriety on his part. Mrs Manning was not called to testify and was not allowed to do so, despite her complaint that she had 'not had a chance to be heard'. Through her counsel, she denied vehemently, however, Mrs O'Hara's accusation that she had slept with a number of Black men and was allowed to interrogate witnesses about Mrs O'Hara's reliability and trustworthiness. The case fell, therefore, into two distinct sections. At first, the Assembly was concerned about the details of the elopement and whether adultery had taken place. They concluded that adultery could be proven. They next had to decide, following Mrs Manning's petition to them, whether Mrs O'Hara had a character sufficiently trustworthy that her accusations against Mrs Manning could be believed. They made no decision regarding this matter but as Francis Fane, counsel to the Board of Trade, remarked in his report to the Lords Justices in Council, the fact that Mrs O'Hara's claims were not 'recited in the Act as part of her Crime' made him think 'that there was not much Credit given abroad to that piece of evidence'.[9]

The Assembly had five questions it wanted answered. First, it wished to establish whether one of its members had injured the honour of another member and in so doing had cast a slur upon its good reputation. The Assembly was a body jealous of its own privileges and was insistent on Assemblymen maintaining proper respect for its honour. More crucial to the Assembly than establishing whether his wife had cuckolded Mr Manning was whether one of its own members, Beckford, had misled the Assembly or had exposed it to public contempt. The Assembly's primary objective was to determine whether Beckford should be expelled from the House and this was the matter upon which it adjudicated well before it agreed to pass a bill dissolving the Mannings' marriage. It did not find that Beckford had lied to the Assembly, the worst offence of all, but it did agree that 'a crime had been committed' by Beckford 'ag'st the very source and foundation of society' and that he should be expelled'.

The second point upon which the Assembly sought an answer was whether Manning was entitled to a divorce through a private Act of Assembly. The committee of the House charged with investigating whether Manning had a case presumably dealt with this issue. Their deliberations are not reported but the committee evidently decided that Manning was able to bring a case because the Jamaica Assembly was an institution analogous to the House of Commons with the same powers in its own area as the British Parliament had in Britain. They also accepted Manning's claim that his only remedy against his wife's adultery was a parliamentary divorce, despite the fact that Manning also had a remedy under the common law under the action of trespass legislation extended to 'criminal conversation', where damages, often very substantial, could be sought from a wife's seducer. The committee accepted that obtaining a private bill was Manning's only remedy because Jamaica lacked any ecclesiastical courts where a petitioner might sue for a separation from his wife *a menso et thoro* (from bed and board), allowing all the rights offered under a private bill except the right to remarry.[10] That the committee accepted Manning's arguments suggests that the Assembly was as interested in issuing a challenge to imperial authority in regard to its own constitutional pretensions as it was concerned about seeing justice done to Manning.[11]

Third, the Assembly wanted to know whether the facts supported Manning's petition. That Beckford and Mrs Manning had eloped was clear. Less certain was the degree of familiarity between Beckford and Mrs Manning. They were certainly very close; to a degree that witnesses felt was improper. Several witnesses commented that they had seen the two hugging and kissing and Elizabeth Tibbett, a servant, had observed them on a piazza 'with Mrs Manning against the wall and [Beckford] against her'. Were they having an affair? Mrs O'Hara and Mrs Manning's cousin believed so, as did Manning. Francis Moore reported that Manning 'had several times suspected his wife of "criminal conversation" and had remonstrated with her, her brother Henry and her best friends'. Adultery, however, was difficult to prove. Neither Mrs O'Hara nor Mrs Manning's cousin had seen adulterous acts and Elizabeth Tibbett admitted that although she had seen Beckford and Mrs Manning pressed together she 'could not observe any motions and never saw her clothes up or his breeches down'. Although a self-serving witness, Beckford also insisted that no adultery had taken place. Witnesses noted that Mrs Manning slept in a different room from Beckford at Beckford's plantation and Dr Dennis stated that he saw no familiarity between the two there except 'what was very modest and what might pass between any modest lady and honourable gentleman'.

Adultery was more difficult to prove in Jamaica than in Britain. Elite people in both countries lived in a very public world, always under the gaze of domestics even in their most intimate moments. But in Britain domestics were White servants, who were allowed to testify in court. In Jamaica, domestics were enslaved Africans who were not permitted to bear witness against enslaved Whites. As Lawrence Stone has described in entertaining detail, servants could be relied upon to know every secret of their master and mistress and to retail these secrets in court.[12] Household slaves in the establishments of Mr Manning, Mr Peete and Francis Moore, where indiscretions were alleged to have occurred, would have known the exact nature of the relationship between Beckford and Mrs Manning; but they were prevented from revealing their secrets because of the strictly enforced prohibition against allowing slave testimony.

At the very least, Mrs Manning and Beckford were wildly indiscreet. Three of Mrs Manning's cousins felt that she and Beckford had been too close, and Mrs Manning's friend, Mrs Stephenson, finding the two talking in 'too Free and familiar manner', had gone with another friend to remonstrate with Mrs Manning about 'her familiarity and indiscretion'. Mrs O'Hara, a hostile witness, declared that Mrs Manning had told her at Christmas that she intended to leave her husband for Beckford. Adultery was at least an intention, if not an established fact.

Fourth, the Assembly sought to discover whether Mrs Manning's abandonment of the family home could be explained for reasons besides adultery. Was there, for example, evidence that Manning was a cruel and unreasonable husband? No one thought so. Every witness considered that Manning was a good husband: he was 'fond and indulgent' and never 'used Mrs Manning ill'. Francis Moore even produced an affectionate letter from wife to husband. The only complaint that Mrs Manning could legitimately have against her spouse was that he was jealous of other men, especially Beckford. But given the evident intimacy between Beckford and Mrs Manning, Manning had good reason to be jealous.

Mrs O'Hara's allegations about events that she believed occurred in February and March may have changed the usually indulgent Manning's attitude. Whether Mrs O'Hara was a reliable witness was the final area about which the Assembly sought answers. If she could be trusted, her damning accusations against Mrs Manning would render almost irrelevant the question whether she and Beckford were in an adulterous relationship. By the mid-eighteenth century, sexual relations between Black men and White women were strictly proscribed by custom if not by law.[13] As John Stedman noted half a century later, 'should it be known that any European female had an intercourse with a slave' the woman 'is forever detested and the slave loses his life without mercy – such are the despotic laws of men over the weaker sex'.[14] For a woman of the rank of Mrs Manning, the daughter of a leading planter, sister of a future governor and wife of a leading merchant and Assemblyman, such interracial coupling would disgrace her beyond any possible hope of redemption. In her second testimony before the Assembly, Mrs O'Hara amplified on her earlier refusal to 'swear no further' when asked whether Mrs Manning had had 'criminal conversation' with anyone else besides Beckford. Mrs O'Hara now claimed that she saw Black men often go into Mrs Manning's chamber and heard them 'kiss and smack'. She believed that 'negro fellows' had slept with Mrs Manning and told a story about coming into her room with the Mannings' young child, Neddy, and seeing Mrs Manning and a slave driver, Jemmy, together on the bed. Surprised, little Neddy called out 'Mamma Hara, man there under bed', but Mrs Manning, Mrs O'Hara alleged, scolded her son, saying 'You little saucy dog, hold your tongue'.

Mrs Manning, according to Mrs O'Hara, enjoined her to 'let what she heard and knew be a secret and die with her'. Mrs Manning put her faith in the wrong person. Sometime in January or February, Mrs O'Hara told Thomas Moone and his wife, tavern-keepers with a property called, appropriately enough, Cuckold's Point, about Mrs Manning's indiscretions. Mrs Manning also came to hear about the calumnies against her. In late February or early March, Mrs Manning arrived at the Mannings' country estate in a distressed condition, and informed a merchant guest, John Mereweather, that Mrs O'Hara had accused her 'of a familiarity with negroes', crying out 'Good God, could she be suspected with her own slaves?' Mereweather advised Mrs Manning to tell her husband about Mrs O'Hara's slurs, which she did, and Manning, supporting his wife, dismissed Mrs O'Hara 'with as great resentment as any gentleman could show, without breaking the peace'.

Could Mrs O'Hara be believed? If so, this would be as good proof as physical evidence of Mrs Manning's infidelities. But the general opinion of Mrs O'Hara's character was poor. Both Mereweather and John Endter said she had an indifferent character, and James Cunningham called her 'a noisy woman'. One especially damaging accusation against Mrs O'Hara was that she had borne a bastard child. Moore related a story told to him by a female slave that the slave had seen 'a little thing of about four or five inches that moved' and that Mrs O'Hara had 'thrown or knocked it against the wall'. Thomas Egan, with whom Mrs O'Hara had boarded five years previously, added that she habitually drank. But significantly, witnesses, except for Endter, did not think her a liar although they characterised her as a scold, a tattletale, a busybody and mischief-maker. Moreover, Endter only thought her a liar because she wrongfully accused him of stealing seashells, a trivial offence that Endter vehemently denied committing. Egan, who knew her best, and who thought little of her, did not consider her to be a liar or a thief. That the Assembly decided not to include Mrs O'Hara's allegations within the body of the Act dissolving the Mannings' marriage suggests that they did not believe her to be telling the truth. But if not supporting her claims, they did not specifically discount them. Mrs O'Hara's explanation of why she felt it necessary to bring these damaging accusations forward (that she felt it her duty, based on Psalm 50, verses 17–22, to instruct and reprove Mrs Manning about her conduct) may have been correct.

Why did Mrs O'Hara say what she did? She argued that she felt impelled by her conscience to do so. Two other reasons, however, suggest themselves. First, she may have acted out of vindictiveness. Mrs O'Hara and Mrs Manning had fallen out. By accusing Mrs Manning of a gross violation of Jamaica's moral code, Mrs O'Hara was able to harm her. But if Mrs O'Hara had wanted to make difficulties for Mrs Manning, all she had to do was confirm Manning's suspicions about his wife's involvement with Beckford. As Manning was already suspicious about Beckford's relationship with his wife, confirming his suspicions would achieve Mrs O'Hara's revenge very effectively. All that she achieved by her accusations about Mrs Manning and her male slaves was her own dismissal.

But Mrs Manning may not have been the only target. Mrs O'Hara had a fraught relationship with slaves, as well as with Mrs Manning. As a single White female domestic, Mrs O'Hara did not fit within eighteenth-century Jamaican society. The principal divisions within Jamaican society were between White and Black and between slaves and Free. The two divisions easily became conflated: White freed people versus Black unfree people. Mrs O'Hara was White but she was not properly Free, in the sense of being an independent householder. Her status was not sufficiently high to gain respect either from Whites or from Blacks and her personal character aggravated the situation. Slaves would have noticed that Mrs O'Hara was not held in high esteem within White society and would have recognised that she was someone whose authority over them they need not accept. Moreover, they resented her propensity to interfere in slave affairs. She had told Francis Moore, for example, that two White servants had frequently lain with a Black girl. Presumably, this caused trouble not only for the servants but also for the Black girl. The reaction of slaves towards Mrs O'Hara's mischief-making was to defy her tenuous authority over them. She told Mrs Champney that Mrs

Manning had given her authority to whip slaves at the Mannings' pen, but the fact that she had to ask to be able to exercise what was automatically assumed a White prerogative speaks volumes about her weak authority. She was unable to control slave behaviour. Egan noted that when living at his residence Mrs O'Hara had 'made an unusual noise scolding negroes' while Mrs Champney related Mrs O'Hara's comment that the Manning slaves were 'very impudent'. Slaves' lack of respect for this single, White woman went so far as to include physical violence. Mrs O'Hara told the Moores a 'lamentable story' in which a 'negro wench' had 'flung a brick' at her when she attempted to whip a male slave, declaring that if she did whip this man 'she should never whip anybody again'. Such threats were seldom idle in a society that punished such utterances by slaves severely. Mrs O'Hara, therefore, felt threatened by slave behaviour. She may have decided to seek revenge against 'impudent Negroes', whom she denounced specifically by name, by implicating them in a very serious crime in a society where punishment of slaves for trivial offences was brutal and punishment for major offences was barbaric.

Evidence and Interpretations

The Manning divorce case is intriguing in part because determining what actually happened in 1738 and 1739 in the Manning household is so uncertain. Three plausible interpretations of the known facts can be made. The commonsense interpretation is that Mrs Manning and Beckford were indeed having an affair. Mrs Manning's conduct with Beckford certainly suggested an adulterous relationship. Yet, as the Lords Justice commented, adultery could only be assumed, not proven. A second interpretation, especially given Mrs O'Hara's second testimony, was that Mrs O'Hara was determined to wreak revenge on her recent employer, using any means possible. The way in which evidence relating to the elopement was presented supports this interpretation. At first Mrs O'Hara was content to focus on Mrs Manning's indiscretions with Beckford. She proffered damning evidence against Mrs Manning, accusing her of having declared her love for Beckford and having stated that she intended to leave her husband for Beckford. Complicitous lovers, therefore, according to Mrs O'Hara, prearranged Mrs Manning's elopement in March 1739.

Mrs O'Hara constructed her initial narrative very carefully. She wanted to show both that she was a devoted and committed servant and that Mrs

Manning was indeed adulterous. She declared that she thought of Mrs Manning 'as her own child' and that Mrs Mannings' conduct had cost her 'many a salt tear'. She presented herself as a faithful retainer, reluctant to say what she did but compelled to do so because of Mrs Manning's 'imprudence'. The extent to which her evidence was carefully crafted is best seen in her very partial account of how she left the Mannings' service. Other witnesses suggested that Manning was dismissed by Mrs O'Hara, but she described her departure as resulting from her disquiet about Mrs Manning's behaviour. She claimed, moreover, that she remained a favourite of Mrs Manning until leaving the Mannings' service and that Mrs Manning had 'proposed several times' to her that she follow her mistress to Beckford.

Undoubtedly, although this is mere speculation, Mrs O'Hara stepped down from her interrogation well pleased with how she had preserved her reputation as a loyal servant and also ensured that Mrs Manning be suspected of adultery. The rest of the day's proceedings would have been a grave disappointment. No one else was as convinced of Mrs Manning's adultery as Mrs O'Hara and, worse, little firm evidence was presented that confirmed Mrs Manning's guilt. Consequently, Mrs O'Hara might have decided to try a new tack. Accusing Mrs Manning of cavorting with slaves refocused the Assembly's attention on Mrs Manning's deficiencies.

But attributing Mrs O'Hara's evidence solely to her desire for revenge is problematic. Telling people of her suspicions about Mrs Manning and her slaves had already cost Mrs O'Hara her job. Making such an accusation to the Assembly led to a lengthy character assassination of Mrs O'Hara herself in the highest court in the country. If she had wished to incriminate Mrs Manning, she did not need to make up a story about sleeping with slaves. She needed merely to elaborate on Mrs Manning's behaviour with Beckford.

The third, least likely, interpretation of what happened is that Mrs Manning did have affairs with slaves or, alternatively, that Manning believed reports that his wife had affairs with slaves. Four pieces of evidence lend support to this theory. First, Mrs O'Hara did not need to bring forward a lurid story about interracial sexual activities in order to incriminate Mrs Manning. If Mrs O'Hara is to be believed, she revealed her accusations reluctantly and only after much soul searching. Second, Mrs O'Hara had no reason to believe that the Assembly would be willing to recall her for examination once she had given evidence. She was not permitted to give testimony on 5 May when her character was maligned in public, and thus should have told all that she knew at her first interrogation. Moreover, repeating these accusations did not help her situation. Mrs O'Hara had strong incentives to keep her thoughts on Mrs Manning's behaviour with slaves to herself. Telling people what she knew, after all, led to dismissal, ridicule and public humiliation.

Third, Manning's decision to seek an absolute divorce in front of the Legislative Assembly can be explained if, despite his public defence of his wife, he in fact believed his dismissed servant's claims. Allowing himself to be cuckolded by a fellow White man was one thing; having a wife produce a Mulatto heir was quite another. An absolute divorce would prevent such a possibility. Similar sets of circumstances in eighteenth-century America led to male demands for absolute divorces. The first bills for private Divorce Acts in post-revolutionary Maryland and Virginia were given to men whose wives gave birth to Mulatto infants.[15] Certainly, Manning held no lasting grudge against Beckford. In the heated political atmosphere of the 1750s, the two became allies and were both appointed to Jamaica's highest body, the Council, in September 1754. Both were suspended from the Council on the same day, 4 December 1756, after disagreements with the newly appointed governor. Ironically, but perhaps not coincidentally, that governor was Mrs Manning's brother, Henry Moore.[16]

Finally, the behaviour of both Beckford and Mrs Manning on and after 18 March 1739 can be explained just as easily as a reaction to Manning's rage against a wife consorting with male slaves as a prearranged plan by lovers to set up together. A plausible alternative to Manning's narrative of the events of 18 March goes as follows. On 18 March, the Mannings quarrelled at their Snow Hill property over Mrs O'Hara's assertions. The quarrel became so fierce that Mrs Manning fled back to Kingston where she poured out her troubles to the Peetes and to Beckford, who was supping with the Peetes that night. Beckford, acting in the place of Mrs Manning's absent brother, decided that the honourable action was for him to spirit her away from her abusive husband. Mrs Manning went home to pack while Beckford waited fretfully at Francis Moore's house until 11 pm. The two fled for Spanish Town and then for Beckford's plantation on the north-side where, as all witnesses agreed, they behaved in a most circumspect manner. Such a narrative lends support to Beckford's claim, in front of an Assembly that was more concerned about a member lying to it than about 'flagrant' offences against public order, that he had not carried Mrs Manning away but was providing her with a residence before she could be rescued by her brother. Beckford may have been merely an intermediary in a dispute between husband and wife over Mrs O'Hara's allegations.

White Women in a Patriarchal Society

The Manning divorce case allows us to view two significant, though usually unrelated, issues in the history of early Jamaica. First, it shows the extent to which colonial legislators were prepared to push the authority of their own legislatures. We have not dealt with constitutional issues here but their importance in this case needs to be stressed. Second, the Manning case offers rare insight into the assumptions about gender, race and class that governed White Jamaican thinking in the eighteenth century. It emphasises the extent to which Jamaica was a highly patriarchal society in which White women were seriously disadvantaged. The aftermath of the case illustrates the handicaps White women faced in a society designed almost solely for White men. Neither Beckford nor Manning suffered much from the scandal of the divorce. Beckford was expelled from the House but returned to the Legislature in 1749 as a member for St Mary's parish. Between 1754 and 1756 he was a Councillor. He died, wealthy and honoured, on 24 May 1760 in St Catherine, leaving a wife and a young daughter.[17] Manning's subsequent career was even more impressive. He established himself as the leading political spokesman of Kingston's merchants and as one of Jamaica's major political power-brokers. In the mid-1750s, he was at the centre of a prolonged conflict over where to situate the island's capital and was elected Speaker of the House, the most powerful position in the island below that of Governor, in the highly faction-alised Assembly of 1755. Briefly a Councillor in 1756, he died with an estate of over £60,000. He did not remarry but did form a liaison with a free Mulatto woman named Elizabeth Pinnock, with whom he had two daughters. The strength of the double standard in Jamaica is obvious in the ready acceptance of Manning's open concubinage with a Coloured woman and the utter condemnation of even the possibility of Mrs Manning entering into a relation-ship with a Coloured man. White men but not White women were Free to form relationships with Coloured people outside marriage and to favour their Coloured concubines with substantial bequests in their wills. Manning, for example, left Elizabeth Pinnock a healthy annuity of £50, along with a house worth £350 and 11 slaves.[18]

If the subsequent histories of the male principals in this case are reasonably clear, the same is not true for the women centrally concerned in the divorce. The only information I have found about Mrs O'Hara after the case is that she married Jonathan Deverell, a tavern-keeper, on 28 July 1740 and that she buried her husband in Kingston Parish Church seven months later.[19] She vanishes from the record after this desultory reference. That so little can be found about her is perhaps not surprising given her lowly status, but it is substantial compared with that on the well-born Mrs Manning. Apart from the detailed testimony about her marriage and its dissolution preserved in the journal of the Assembly, no other evidence of her life remains except for a note about her baptism in 1715 in the Vere Parish Register and a mention of Elizabeth Manning in the Kingston Parish Register as the mother of her short-lived son, Edward Moore Manning.[20] Mrs Manning is not mentioned in the wills of her husband, brother and cousins and Beckford does not mention her in his will.[21] She simply vanishes from the historical record as if she were invisible.

The historical invisibility of Mrs O'Hara and Mrs Manning after the divorce case – a case, moreover, where each indulged in guerrilla warfare against the other, to the mutual detriment of both – is testimony to the growing invisibility of White women in eighteenth-century Jamaica. Heavily outnumbered by White men within the White population,[22] intimidated by their slaves and by their responsibilities in a society that did not recognise them as full participants,[23] reduced to sexual and economic impotence as a result of the importance of Black and Coloured women,[24] by the mid-eighteenth century White women were anomalies in a society that was divided on strict racial and gender lines. Mrs Manning and Mrs O'Hara came from vastly different social stations and became determined foes but the result for each in the aftermath of the case was remarkably similar. Both had their reputations destroyed. As was so often the case in early modern divorce proceedings, women fared very badly.[25] That was hardly surprising within a legal system that gave virtually no recognition to women. Mrs Manning was not called to give evidence on her own behalf and was only allowed to have her counsel interrogate witnesses after submitting to an indignant lecture from the Assembly that they had 'shewed Mrs Manning all the indulgence that the nature of her case would admit'. Mrs O'Hara was permitted to give evidence against Mrs Manning but was not permitted to testify on her own behalf, despite the many attacks made on her character. The subordination of White women's interests to those of men in a highly patriarchal society is clearly illustrated by Mrs Manning's and Mrs O'Hara's lack of control over judicial proceedings.

The treatment of this episode by the few historians to write about it also shows how White women have been written out of Jamaican history.[26] The only historians to mention the Manning divorce are the early nineteenth-century Tory clergyman and ardent pro-slavery advocate, George Bridges and, more recently, the Caribbean historian and poet, Kamau Brathwaite.[27] Neither do justice to the women involved in the case. Bridges fulminated against Mrs Manning as 'a beautiful female, a matron in rank, a prostitute in manners and who never shared the passion she inspired'. Mrs Manning, he insisted, was highly exceptional as since her time 'the daughters of Jamaica have [had] an unimpeachable conjugal faith'. Believing that White women were chaste paragons of virtue, domesticity and respectability, Bridges was at pains to distinguish Mrs Manning from what had become by his time a well-established stereotype of the respectable, refined and very passive plantation lady. Incapable of envisioning a White woman able to exercise her own sexuality, Bridges allocated most of the blame for Mrs Manning's 'shamelessness' on her husband: 'for though a philosopher may pity and forgive the infirmities of the female nature, contemptible must be the man who feels and yet endures the infamy of his wife'. Mrs Manning may have been 'infamous' but Bridges conceived limits to her 'infamy'. He made no mention of Mrs O'Hara's claims at all. Clearly, the notion of a well-born White woman succumbing to the charms of Black men was beyond his comprehension.[28] Kamau Brathwaite, however, who made passing mention of the Manning case in a general survey of Caribbean women, gave credence to nothing except Mrs O'Hara's claims, alleging that Mrs Manning engaged in a number of sexual activities with Black men and that indeed she 'was something of a nymphomaniac'.[29] Brathwaite's suggestion that sexual relations between Black men and White women did exist may be more appealing to a modern audience than Bridges' paternalistic denial of such a possibility, but his presentation of the case is no less misleading, concentrating as he does, just like Bridges, on the aberrant nature of Mrs Manning's sexual activities.

Whether Mrs Manning was a nymphomaniac, a 'prostitute in manners', or an upright matron, unfairly maligned, is of little importance. What is important is how hard it is to see White women outside the stultifying prisms that have enveloped them since the mid-eighteenth century. Neither Mrs Manning nor Mrs O'Hara is 'seen' as they actually were because the image of the White

Creole woman occupies a very curious position within Caribbean historiography. The White Creole woman raises questions about what Elizabeth Nunez-Harrell calls the 'paradoxes of belonging' because she is portrayed as 'a sort of freak rejected by both Europe and England, whose blood she shares, and by the Black Caribbean people, whose culture and home have been hers.'[30]

The first White women in Jamaica were depicted as naturally lascivious, either 'whores by origin' or affected by the tropical climate that 'so changes the Constitution of its Inhabitants, that if a Woman land there chaste as a Vestal, she becomes in forty-eight hours a perfect Messalina'.[31] Echoes of this early imagery of the debauched White woman of lowly origins remain in the characterisation of Mrs O'Hara as sexually loose. But this once common image lasted no longer than did dreams of White settlement. Jamaica was transformed in the first third of the eighteenth century into a highly productive slave society where Blacks vastly outnumbered Whites and where Whites prospered economically but failed dismally demographically.[32] By mid-century, perceptive observers could see that Jamaica was not likely to become a White settler society as in British North America but was instead likely to become a society dominated numerically and eventually politically by Free Coloureds, if not Black slaves.

As Jamaica's population became increasingly Black dominated, patriarchal concerns about unregulated White female sexuality were replaced by an obsession with the sexuality of Coloured women, 'hot constitution'd Ladies' who made 'no scruple to prostitute themselves to Europeans'. Black women became the object of White male fantasies and fears, being seen as scheming Jezebels, possessed of almost superhuman sexual 'tricks, cajolements and infidelities'. In love, Edward Long asserted, Coloured women were 'far more perfectly versed than any adept of the Drury'.[33] As the sexuality of Black women was enhanced, that of White women was diminished. White women were ideologically desexed and made passive. They became icons of domesticity and maternity rather than sexual beings. Moreover, all social distinctions between White women were collapsed in this fresh representation. All women except the passive plantation lady were erased from the historiographical gaze. Women like Mrs O'Hara became invisible in Jamaican history because they did not fit into this rigid and limited conception of what constituted White womanhood.[34] White women's role became entirely reproductive, their importance arising solely from the role as the progenitors of future generations of White male patriarchs.[35] Seen in this light, Mrs Manning's inability to have a direct say in events of crucial importance to her future and her reputation, despite her extensive connections within the Jamaican ruling elite, is not surprising: an elite White woman having active sexual agency was already by 1739 beyond the comprehension of White men. Nor is it surprising that Mrs O'Hara's attack upon Mrs Manning focused on White interracial mixing and raised perhaps White men's greatest fear, that the purity of White dominance might be diluted by the presence of racially mixed people with wealth who were legally considered White. The superordinate position of the White male patriarch in a slave system predicted upon the interplay between race, sex and gender and in which White women were important only as the vehicles for the reproduction of free people had to be preserved at all costs.[36] One of those costs, as this case perhaps demonstrates, was an increased marginalisation and erasure of White women's presence and agency.

Notes

1. The quote in the title comes from a description of Mrs Elizabeth Manning by the Rev. George Bridges, a misogynist, high Tory, pro-slavery clergyman, writing in the early nineteenth century. G.W. Bridges, *The Annals of Jamaica*, 2 vols (London, 1827), Vol. II, p. 43.
2. The Manning divorce case can be found in the *Journals of the Assembly of Jamaica* (JHAJ),7 vols (Kingston, 1798) Vol. 3, pp. 474–98. All references to the case will be from this source unless otherwise noted.
3. G. Metcalf, *Royal Government and Political Conflict in Jamaica, 1729–1783* (London: Longmans, 1965), pp. 85, 92–4.
4. British deliberations can be found in CO 137/23, fols. 60, 130 and in W.L. Grant and J. Munro, eds., *Acts of the Privy Council, Colonial Series*, 6 vols (London: HM Stationery Office, 1908–12), Vol. 3: pp. 681–3.
5. Cited in J.P. Greene, 'Edward Trelawny's "Grand Elixir"': Metropolitan Weakness and Constitutional Reform in the Mid-Eighteenth-Century British Empire', in R.A. McDonald, ed., *West Indies Accounts: Essays on the History of the British Caribbean and the Atlantic Economy in Honour of Richard Sheridan* (Kingston: University Press of the West Indies, 1996), p. 93.
6. E. Long, *The History of Jamaica . . .*, 3 vols (London, 1774; reprint Frank Cass, 1970), Vol. 1, p. 9. The constitutional pretensions of the mid-eighteenth-century Jamaican Assembly can be traced in the following works by J.P. Greene: *Peripheries and Center: Constitutional Development in the Extended Polities of the British Empire and the United States, 1607–1788*

(Athens, GA: University of Georgia Press, 1986), pp. 7–54; 'The Jamaica Privilege Controversy, 1764–66: An Episode in the Process of Constitutional Definition in the Early Modern British Empire', *Journal of Imperial and Commonwealth History*, 22 (1994), pp. 16–53; 'Edward Trelawny's "Grand Elixir"', pp. 87–100.

7.   See, for example, N.Z. Davis, *The Return of Martin Guerre* (Cambridge, MA: Harvard University Press, 1983).

8.   Bridges, *The Annals of Jamaica*, Vol. II, p. 43.

9.   CO 137/23 fol. 61.

10.   Important studies of eighteenth-century divorce procedures include L. Stone, *Road to Divorce: England 1530-1987* (Oxford: Oxford University Press, 1990) and R. Phillips, *Putting Asunder: A History of Divorce in Western Society* (Cambridge: Cambridge University Press, 1988).

11.   Why Edward Manning wanted a private bill for divorce rather than other remedies is unclear, but may have had something to do with the recent death of his only child, Edward Moore Manning, who had died, aged two and a half, on 13 February 1739 (Kingston Parish Register, The Armoury, Island Record Office, Spanish Town, Jamaica). He may have also chosen divorce in this form for pecuniary reasons. Francis Fane noted that the Act providing for the Manning divorce allowed Mrs Manning 'only a small settlement of £100 per annum whereas her fortune is £3,000, her husband is exceeding rich, and there are no children'. CO 137/23 fol. 60. Fane to Board of Trade, 12 May 1740. Political considerations may have influenced the Assembly's decision. Manning was the leading merchant in the island, an important Assemblyman, and, most importantly, a friend and business partner of Trelawny. Jamaican politics was notoriously factionalised, with the principal division being between the merchants of Kingston and planters based in Spanish Town. Beckford was a member of the most powerful planter family in the island but the Beckford family's influence may have been temporarily in decline in 1739 following the recent deaths of its two most important family members, Peter and Thomas Beckford, and in the absence of Peter's heir, William Beckford, who was making a grand tour of Europe. Mrs Manning was perhaps better connected than her husband, being a member of the powerful Moore clan, but her principal supporter, her brother and future governor of Jamaica, Henry, was also not on the island: he had joined his close friend, William Beckford, in Europe. For a useful account of the politics of Trelawny's governorship, see Metcalf, *Royal Government*, pp. 58–108.

12.   Stone, *Road to Divorce*, pp. 21–30.

13.   B. Bush, *Slave Women in Caribbean Society 1650–1838* (Kingston: Heinemann Publishers (Caribbean), 1990), pp. 111–12.

14. R. and S. Price, *Stedman's Surinam: Life in an Eighteenth-Century Slave Society* (Baltimore and London: Johns Hopkins University Press, 1988), p. 242.

15. M. Salmon, *Women and the Law of Property in Early America* (Chapel Hill, NC: University of North Carolina Press, 1986), p. 66.

16. Metcalf, *Royal Government*, pp. 126, 139.

17. 30 March 1749, JHAJ, Vol. 3, p. 144; 24 May 1760, St Catherine Parish Register of Deaths, JA, Spanish Town, Jamaica.

18. Inventory of Edward Manning, 1758, Inventories, Vol. 36, Jamaica Archives; will of Edward Manning, 1754, Wills, Vol. 30, fol. 176, Island Record Office, Spanish Town, Jamaica; C 109, fol. 338, Public Record Office, Chancery Masters' Exhibits, Chancery Lane, London , UK.

19. Kingston Parish Register.

20. Vere Parish Register, Kingston Parish Register, The Armoury, IRO.

21. Wills, IRO.

22. R.V. Wells, *The Population of the British Colonies in America before 1776: A Survey of Census Data* (Princeton: Princeton University Press, 1975), pp. 196, 201, 294.

23. See, for example, letters by Mrs Mary Elbridge complaining about the difficulties faced by women in managing a plantation and slaves. Spring Plantation Correspondence, AC/WO 16 (17) e; 16 (22) a, Woolnough Papers, Ashton Court MSS, Bristol Record Office, Bristol. Mary Elbridge to Henry Woolnough, 29 June 1739; Mary Elbridge to John Elbridge, 29 January 1740.

24. T. Burnard, 'Inheritance and Independence: Women's Status in Early Colonial Jamaica', *William and Mary Quarterly*, 3rd ser., 48 (1991), p. 112.

25. Phillips, *Putting Asunder*, pp. 122–3; Salmon, *Women and the Law of Property*, pp. 65–6.

26. For an account of how White women have been subsumed within the experience of other groups in Caribbean history, see H. McD. Beckles, 'White Women and Slavery in the Caribbean', *History Workshop Journal*, 36 (1993), pp. 66–81.

27. Long makes no mention of the Manning divorce in his lengthy contemporary history of Jamaica, despite being connected to Elizabeth Manning by marriage. Long's wife was the sister of Elizabeth's brother, Sir Henry Moore.

28. Bridges, *Annals of Jamaica*, Vol. II, p. 43.

29. K. Brathwaite, 'Caribbean Woman during the Period of Slavery', 1984 Elsa Goveia Memorial Lecture, Department of History, University of the West Indies, Cave Hill, 1985.

30. E. Nunez-Harrell, ' "The Paradoxes of Belonging": The White West-Indian Woman in Fiction', *Modern Fiction Studies*, 31 (1985), pp. 281–2.

31. E. Ward, *A Trip to Jamaica With a True Character of the People and the Island* (London, 1698), p. 16; [William Pittis], *The Jamaica Lady; or the Life of Bavia* (London, 1720), p. 35.

32. Burnard, 'A Failed Settler Society: Marriage and Demographic Failure in Early Jamaica', *Journal of Social History*, 28 (1994), pp. 63–82.

33. W. Smith, *A New Voyage to Guinea . . .* (London, 1744), p. 146; Long, *History of Jamaica*, Vol. 2, pp, 328, 331. 'Drury' was where London prostitutes plied their trade.

34. Hilary Beckles describes how this enduring stereotype of White Creole women arose and demonstrates how insufficient an image it is of what White women actually did, in 'Sex and Gender in the Historiography of Caribbean Slavery', in V.A. Shepherd, et al., eds., *Engendering History: Caribbean Women in Historical Perspective* (Kingston: Ian Randle Publishers, 1995), pp. 125–40.

35. K. Butler, *The Economics of Emancipation: Jamaica and Barbados, 1823–1843* (Chapel Hill, NC: University of North Carolina Press, 1995).

36. Beckles, 'Sex and Gender', pp. 130–1.

CHAPTER 8

Land, Labour and Social Status

Non-sugar producers in Jamaica
in slavery and Freedom

VERENE A. SHEPHERD

Studies of Jamaica's political economy have been deeply influenced by the ideology of the sugar plantation complex as a result of the dominant position of sugar in the island's economy from the mid-eighteenth to the mid-nineteenth century. Contemporary and modern writers have stressed the superordinate position occupied within the sugar plantation structure by those who depended on the sugar industry for their wealth. This group, referred to variously by some historians as the plantocracy or sugarocracy (even though other economic sectors were represented in the government and among the elite), arguably owned and controlled most of the means and markets of production and influenced the political life of the island.[1] Until recently, analyses of proprietors other than the sugar planters were generally absent from the historical works on Jamaica; for among students of rural history, enquiry into class and race dynamics outside of the sugar plantation per se has been consigned to a position of secondary significance. In fact, slavery came to be associated almost exclusively with sugar in the context of a diversified economy and society that featured other export agricultural activities. Similarly, the study of the sugar planter elite has been considered more socially significant that the study of other producers. This is understandable; for in a tradition of scholarship that has tended to focus on the dominant sugar economy throughout the majority of the European-colonised Caribbean, non-sugar-producing units represented a divergent pattern of social and economic development. Furthermore, it was the sugar plantation which defined the societies and economies of the majority of the colonised Caribbean until the late nineteenth century.

Nevertheless, this heavy focus on the sugar-planting sector has masked the importance of non-sugar producers in Jamaica, an island which sustained a greater degree of diversification than its counterparts in the Eastern Caribbean. In Jamaica, a more varied topography enabled the emergence of an important group of smaller-scale proprietors engaged in the cultivation of commodities other than sugar-cane. The most important of these were the food producers, and livestock and coffee farmers, who, for the most part, occupied land unsuitable for cane growing. Along with the sugar planters, the coffee and livestock farmers controlled most of the cultivable land in the island in the period of slavery. With the decline of sugar and coffee in the period after 1845, the island's agricultural economy became dominated by the banana barons and livestock, primarily cattle farmers.

Douglas Hall's explanation for this marginalisation of non-sugar producers in the historiography is that 'in our early rush to the goldmines of information, [historians] took the larger veins and did not search for the smaller, though perhaps equally rich capillaries of data'.[2] Historians were, of course, also influenced by better and more accessible documentation on the sugar industry and the sugar planters.

Yet it is clear from works done by Kamau Brathwaite, Barry Higman, Douglas Hall and others that small settlers, numbering about 4,000 in 1792, who produced commodities other than sugar, played an important role in the Jamaican pre-emancipation economy.[3] In the seventeenth and early eighteenth centuries, during the early period of economic development, livestock farmers were more numerous than those engaged in sugar and had an important political voice. Their political importance only declined after the rise of the sugar industry and the expansion of the sugar-growing elite, after which they were hardly to be found in the colonial legislature. Nevertheless, the possibilities remained for those without capital to invest in sugar to continue to engage in livestock farming, coffee production and provision farming. Indeed, the coffee farmers contributed to the export trade and the livestock farmers, along with enslaved food producers, were largely responsible for the maintenance of a vibrant, internal, inter-property trade during slavery.[4] The livestock farmers supplied valuable plantation inputs and provided outlets for some of the estates' output. Indeed, as evidence of their importance in the period of slavery, Higman, using quantitative analysis, found that in 1832 the majority of the enslaved were not located on the sugar estates, but were distributed among coffee farmers, livestock farms (called 'pens'), the wharves, the towns, jobbing gangs and food-producing units.[5]

Despite their importance to the economy, however, non-sugar producers were hardly ranked among the island's colonial elite after the mid-eighteenth century. The sugar plantation after all generated its own distinct system of social relations and a class system. Plantation society developed and sustained its own characteristic and highly stratified system of class, colour, race and gender relations. In addition, in this society status also derived from the ownership of large acreages of land, large numbers of chattel and the cultivation and export of sugar. Non-sugar producers tended to own smaller acreages and numbers of enslaved people; but they did attempt, some successfully, to challenge this institutional arrangement of sugar plantation society and by the late nineteenth century were representing a real political challenge to the traditional sugar-planting sector.

This chapter seeks to develop further this theme of the relationship between land use and social status among Jamaica's agriculturists and to outline the effects of the concentration of land in the hands of the large and small proprietors on the labour force. It uses the example of the livestock farmers (styled pen-keepers in colonial Jamaica) to show how non-sugar producers, in contrast to the pre-sugar era, were marginalised from the late eighteenth century, only beginning to regain their socioeconomic and political status after the abolition of slavery and the decline of the sugar sector. It will be shown that during the height of slavery, even those small-scale local proprietors who were White were relegated to secondary roles and remained ancillary to the sugar sector. The dominant sugar sector, indeed, exploited those dependent on it, thereby reinforcing its superordinate position. Elite social status was accorded only to those White proprietors who were large land holders, had a large enslaved labour force, produced for export and used their dominant position in the economy to also control the island's politics.

Before and after sugar: the development of pens

The livestock farmers (hereafter referred to as 'pen-keepers') along with the coffee farmers were the most significant proprietors other than the sugar planters in Jamaica in the period of slavery. Pen-keeping predated both coffee farming and sugar cultivation in Jamaica. The Spaniards had maintained a ranching economy in the island up to 1655. This was consistent with their early economic activities in Cuba and Puerto Rico where *hatos, criaderos* and *corrales* were numerous in the pre-plantation era.[6] After the English captured the island from the Spaniards, they maintained this industry for a while before converting lowland pasture lands to sugar estates. A large number of pens re-emerged on lands not used for cane. By 1782, there were around 300 pens in the island owned mostly by colonists who did not have the resources necessary to invest in the sugar industry. Rearing animals in enclosures called pens suited their financial resources, given the low initial capital outlay required for the establishment of these types of property.

Before the development of the sugar industry on a large scale, the pen-keepers were elite White men, many with large grants from the Crown but who had not yet accumulated the resources to establish large sugar estates. By the mid-eighteenth century, however, pen-keepers were primarily Free Coloured men and White men from the lower strata of the segmented White group who could not make the switch to sugar. The only White elites who reared livestock were those large sugar barons who maintained satellite pens to service their own estates. On the whole, then, by the end of the eighteenth century, the pen-keepers were those who, on the basis of either race or class, were accorded a social position below the sugar owners. Many of them were attorneys and overseers. There were very few female pen-keepers, especially among the White population; they were more likely to be freed Blacks and freed Coloureds. Both male and female pen-keepers were further marginalised because they were primarily Creole and resident.

A characteristic of Jamaica plantation society was the large degree of absenteeism among its sugar planters; yet absenteeism was socially significant and a mark of wealth. Indeed, the aim of most Caribbean proprietors was to make enough money in the colonies to enable them to return to Europe to live in style. It would seem that the returns from dedicated livestock farming were not substantial enough to enable these proprietors to follow in the steps of the sugar planters. In addition, as many pen-keepers were overseers or attorneys on sugar estates, their jobs kept them pretty much tied to the island. Calculations based on the Accounts Produce show that at the time of emancipation, about 35 per cent of the pen-keepers resided in Britain.[7] As John Bigelow observed, pens were categorised as moderate-sized farms; and 'it would not be worthwhile for a non-resident to keep up the supervision of a moderate-sized farm 3,000 miles from home'.[8] He continued: 'nothing less than the profits of a very large estate could compensate . . . for the trouble and expenses of keeping up a force of attornies [sic] agents and bookkeepers, and for the absence of that personal devotion to its management which none but a proprietor ever feels'.[9]

While the sugar planters and coffee farmers had their own independent economic dynamic, participating in the direct export trade, the livestock farmers were heavily dependent on the sugar estate sector. The estates represented their main outlet for animals used in the sugar mills; for the majority of Jamaican sugar estates utilised cattle mills during slavery. Such economic dependence might suggest a close interaction socially, between planters and pen-keepers; but this did not seem to have been the case. The system of social stratification precluded such inter-sectional mixing and testifies to the lack of homogeneity in White society.

Social and political position

Brathwaite has stressed that in Jamaica phenotype affinity did not seem to have been a sufficient guarantee of elite status.[10] The history of pen-keepers would seem to support this. White pen-keepers, particularly those who were overseers and managers, were clearly socially differentiated from the top echelons of White sugar planter society and typically represented a contradictory location within the class configuration of the eighteenth and nineteenth century Jamaican slave system. Neither Brathwaite's nor M.G. Smith's account of White society in Jamaica listed such Whites among the elite or principal Whites. According to Smith, principal Whites formed a closed social class from which secondary Whites, Coloureds and Blacks were vigorously excluded.[11] The fact that most White males were in the habit of keeping Coloured or Black mistresses should not be taken as an indication that these women were accepted unreservedly in White society and accorded any higher social status.

The bases of such social marginalisation and the evolution of a group of non-elite Whites were the result of economic and social factors, some of which were peculiar to colonial settings. From the mid- to late-eighteenth century, pens were considered to be less prestigious properties and could not at first attract White workers, as the wages paid their managers were lower than wages paid on the sugar estates. J.B. Moreton emphasised that 'grass pens were considered as despicable objects for enterprising individuals to hunt after, nor would any man accept the management of one who had hopes of preferment on sugar plantations'.[12] He stressed that managers and overseers of sugar estates would not even associate themselves with people in similar occupations on the pens.

Relationships of superordination and subordination were also clearly discernible between principal and secondary Whites according to Smith's formulation. This was because a significant number of Jamaican pen-keepers, ranked among the secondary Whites, were also overseers and attorneys. It is well documented that occupational difference functioned as a factor in social stratification in plantation societies.[13]

Free Coloured and free Black property owners, were ranked lower down on the social scale. In their case, social status was derived not simply from their being small-scale producers, but also because of race and colour. It did not matter if economically they were among the elite of their own group. Thus, those who were substantial property owners and who were more than four generations removed from their African mothers often applied to be regarded as White, thereby changing their race and class classification.

Among the White males, who traditionally appropriated the position as the ruling class in Caribbean plantation societies, there was differential access to political power. It was the elite White sugar planters who dominated the political life of the island, being more numerous in the legislature than any other economic sector. The absence of most other classes from political positions, especially at the level of central government, stemmed from a combination of race, colour, class and gender factors. Before they achieved full civil rights in 1830 (and unless they successfully applied for privileges) Free Coloured farmers were barred from voting or being elected to any high office. By 1830, the enslaved were so successfully undermining the plantation system that the Whites sought to ally themselves with the Free Coloureds in an effort to strengthen the forces of control in the island. They were quite aware that the Free Coloureds themselves had a vested interest in maintaining the slavery system.

Female property owners were all excluded from active participation in government. Patriarchy was a vibrant social ethos in all the colonies, and factors relating to gender, therefore, dictated the political marginalisation of female property owners regardless of race and colour. Women were affected by the sexist attitudes which considered it unseemly for them to be involved in such a public sphere as government. In any case, they were not considered by men to possess the intellectual capacity to be involved in politics. White women seem to have been, nevertheless, quite active in sending petitions to the Assembly when unfavourable legislation was passed which affected their economic welfare. Free Coloured women were similarly affected by the sexist attitude of Free Coloured men who, according to Sheena Boa, excluded them from the Free Coloured civil rights movement.[14]

Secondary Whites, among whom rural pen-keepers were numerous, were clearly deemed to be politically subordinate to the principal Whites. White pen-keepers were among those likely to be on the margins of the political process. They could vote as they had the property qualification; but pen-keepers were not normally to be found in central government. They were more likely to get into the local parish vestries, particularly in parishes in which they were widely distributed. Their virtual exclusion from the House of Assembly caused them to be powerless and unable to influence legislation to protect their economic activity. For example, they were unsuccessful in getting the Assembly to increase significantly the duties levied on imported animals in order to protect the local industry from competition, or to lower the taxes imposed on breeding stock. With respect to the latter, the sugar planters apparently paid only one-third of the sum levied on the pen-keepers. Upward social mobility could be achieved if the pen-keepers invested the profits generated by the pens in the purchase of coffee and/or sugar plantations. A comparison between the social and political position of the pen-keepers and the coffee farmers will serve to reinforce the association between export production and status.

The political location of the pen-keepers seems to have been divergent from that of the coffee farmers. Politically, the coffee farmers fared better than the pen-keepers although they displayed similar social characteristics which determined social and political marginalisation within plantation society. For example, coffee farmers were also predominantly resident and suffered the same stigma attached to living in Jamaica instead of in Britain. In fact, more coffee farmers than pen-keepers resided in the island. Kathleen Monteith records that in 1799, 90 per cent of the 519 coffee proprietors resided in

Jamaica.[15] By 1800, the number of absentee coffee farmers had increased; but still, in that year, 478 of 607 properties were owned by residents.[16]

However, because the coffee farmers were more involved in production for export, the elite members of the group were accorded a somewhat higher social status in plantation society than even the White pen-keepers. Furthermore, a larger number of coffee farmers were members of the House of Assembly, a position which hardly any pen-keeper achieved until the later period of slavery. This meant that, unlike the pen-keepers, the coffee farmers were involved more directly in the decision-making process. Coffee farmers, unlike the pen-keepers, were also not usually in an antagonistic relationship with the dominant planter class, conflicting over import duty on imported animals, land, etc. There was no competition between sugar planters and coffee farmers over land; for sugar and coffee occupied completely different zones. The coffee farmers were less likely to be economically exploited by the sugar planters or be affected by unfavourable legislation passed in the House of Assembly.[17]

There is no doubt that the pen-keepers contributed much to the domestic sector and to the maintenance of the sugar estates; but despite their importance in creole society they were never able to challenge successfully the institutional arrangement of the sugar planter-dominated society. Non-sugar producers, except where they formed an alliance with the sugar planter class, seem to have been relegated to secondary roles and social positions in a society dominated by the sugar sector. It is undeniable that for some of these producers their ascribed social position derived from race, colour, gender and class factors; but it would be safe to say that the nature of their primary economic activity and their lesser participation in the sugar industry were crucial contributory factors.

Ownership of property in chattel

The ownership of enslaved people also conferred status on Jamaican proprietors who regarded enslaved people primarily as valuable assets that increased their wealth. A large enslaved population also enabled planters to establish and maintain larger estates. In Jamaica, most of the enslaved were located outside the physical context of the sugar estates. Around 1832, as Higman has shown, 49.5 per cent of the enslaved population were located on the sugar estates and 50.5 per cent were distributed among non-sugar units, the towns, jobbing gangs and the wharves.[18] The pens only controlled 13 per cent of the total enslaved population.[19] The average estate employed more of the enslaved than any of the other agricultural units. Sugar planters had an average of 1,036 acres of land and 223 enslaved persons (with a range up to 600).[20] The pen-keepers' properties averaged 825 acres during slavery [21] and an average of 99 enslaved persons with a range up to 295.[22]

There is very little evidence which would indicate how those enslaved regarded their differential location on the pens as opposed to on sugar estates. Certainly enslaved males on the pen had greater mobility as they drove cattle, horses and mules to distant markets; and the work regime was less regimented. But we do not know, for example, whether the enslaved felt that they had a higher or lower social status than their counterparts on the estates, or whether such differences in location functioned in the social hierarchy of enslaved populations.

Aspects of the social behaviour of enslaved people in the US South can probably throw some light on the subject of the enslaveds' perception of their own social position if they belonged to a large planter or a small-scale settler or producer. Narratives of enslaved people indicate that they were quite aware of the different status of various landed proprietors and perceived their own status in relationship to the wealth of their owners. Some of their observations indicate that they reacted to their location according to the work regime, type of crop and status of their owners. Harriet Tubman indicated that when those enslaved on Mr Brodas' small plantation of cotton and corn in Maryland learned that they were to be sold, they ran away. The reason she offered was that: 'They were afraid of the living death that awaited them on the rice fields, on the great cotton plantations, the sugar plantation, in the Deep South'.[23]

After being temporarily moved from a small cotton plantation in Mississippi to Memphis, Tennessee, Louis Hughes observed of his new 'and more splendid' surroundings that the enslaved sent with him: 'really seemed pleased, for strange to say, the slaves of rich people always rejoiced in that fact. A servant owned by a man of moderate circumstances was hooted at by rich men's slaves. It was common for them to say: "Oh! don't mind that darkey, he belongs to po'r White trash".'[24]

Frederick Douglass observed that the enslaved often became embroiled in arguments over whose master was the richest, smartest, etc. The rationale was that: 'they seemed to think that the greatness of their masters was transferable to themselves. It was considered as being bad enough to be a slave; but to be a poor man's slave was deemed a disgrace indeed!'[25]

Comparisons: the post-slavery period

The abolition of slavery in the British-colonised Caribbean in 1834 and the ending of that system of neo-slavery euphemistically called the Apprenticeship system in 1838 ushered in far-reaching changes in the economy and society of Jamaica. More specifically, these developments led to the further decline in the fortunes of the traditional landowners and saw the emergence of a new class of land barons among people previously concentrated in commercial and professional fields. Unlike in the period of slavery, land in Jamaica became associated after the 1840s with non-sugar activities, specifically the cultivation of banana, citrus, cocoa and coconuts, and the expansion of the cattle industry. While in the period of slavery non-sugar producers like the pen-keepers had occupied an inferior social position in relation to the so-called 'sugarocracy', such landholders were members of the elite in the period after 1845.

Economic and social changes: the decline of the sugar industry

While there have been disagreements among historians from Lowell Ragatz and Eric Williams to William Green, J.R. Ward and Seymour Drescher over whether the decline of the sugar plantations set in around the 1750s, 1770s or later towards 1834,[26] there seems to be little controversy over the claim that after the 1840s and 1850s the sugar plantation as a dominant economic and social unit was on its way out in Jamaica.

In 1849 Governor Charles Grey of Jamaica was still maintaining that sugar was 'the produce which is raised for exportation [and that sugar] is beyond all comparison the chief object of the agriculture of Jamaica'.[27] By 1854, however, Governor Barkly was arguing the opposite to Grey, noting in his correspondence to the Duke of Newcastle that 'unsuccessful sugar cultivation may be said to be confined to three or four districts of limited area possessed of peculiar advantage. Elsewhere it would seem to be at its lowest ebb',[28] and by 1860, William Sewell was observing that 'the [sugar] plantocracy of Jamaica is a thing of the past'.[29]

Table 8.1:   Share of exports of major products, 1883

Product	Amount	Value £	% of Exports
Sugar	33,392 hhds.	614,283	39.65
Rum	22,742 puns	295,645	19.09
Coffee	66,238 cwt	133,535	8.62
Fruit	–	124,269	8.02
Pimento	76,022 cwt	112,817	7.28
Dyewood, etc.	34,532 tons	103,034	6.65

Source: Hand Book of Jamaica, 1833, p. 363

Qualitative statements by governors and visitors to the island relating to the decline of the sugar plantations and other agricultural units are supported by quantitative data which show that whereas there had been 670 sugar plantations in the island in 1830, between 1846 and 1869 432 plantations were abandoned. By 1882, the island had 188 sugar estates and by the 1890s sugar was important only in the parishes of St James, Hanover and Westmoreland.[30] An 1884–5 agricultural report from a previously important sugar parish, St Thomas, is particularly insightful and was reflective of the general situation in the sugar parishes by this date. The report stated that: 'the area from the Plantain Garden River District to Port Antonio was once covered with flourishing sugar estates but is now utilized as grazing pens. Fifteen large sugar estates only are in operation'.[31]

Islandwide the area under sugar cane had been reduced from 47,440 acres in 1869 to 26,121 acres in 1900.[32] Furthermore, whereas in 1770 sugar accounted for 76 per cent of the island's exports and rum and molasses 13 per cent (making 89 per cent from sugar and its by-products), by 1870 sugar contributed 44.5 per cent to the value of total agricultural exports. By 1900, it contributed 11 per cent. By contrast, crops other than sugar were contributing an ever increasing percentage of the total exports, especially after 1880.[33] The exception was coffee which declined as an estate crop in the immediate post-slavery period. Indeed, by 1865, 75 per cent of the coffee estates had been abandoned and by 1879 the rest had declined in output and value and exports.[34] In 1770, agricultural exports other than sugar contributed only 11 per cent to the total value of exports. But by the second half of the nineteenth century their performance had improved.

The increasing importance of the non-sugar producers had been noted from 1854. In that year Governor Barkly, after detailing the decline of sugar, coffee and livestock farms, which had dominated the agricultural landscape during slavery, observed that while the large plantations and the pens were in trouble, small settlers producing a variety of other commodities were doing better.[35] Indeed, by 1883, as Table 8.1 illustrates, rum, coffee, fruit, pimento and a variety of woods contributed 49.66 per cent of exports.

The rise of the banana industry, the banana barons and the re-emergence of the pen-keepers

It was the banana industry and the expanded livestock industry more than any other rural economic activity which eventually outpaced sugar. In contrast to the period of slavery, land in Jamaica became increasingly concentrated in the hands of the banana barons and the new pen-keepers in the late nineteenth and early twentieth centuries. The *Handbooks of Jamaica* (HBJ) show that there were over 450 of such planters and pen-keepers by the early twentieth century;[36] and the banana barons and the pen-keepers emerged as the new agro-elite.

Banana

Before the 1870s banana cultivation had been confined to the peasantry, who contributed much to its widespread use as a fruit and as food (cooked when green). In fact in 1879, there was only one large banana plantation in the island. By 1900, however, the large banana plantation had become a dominant feature of the rural agricultural landscape.[37] Small banana farmers did not entirely disappear, but most of the good banana lands were by then in the hands of large-scale producers. Many banana plantations were established on former sugar lands and there seems to have been a direct relationship between the abandonment of sugar estates and the increase in the number of banana estates in north-eastern Jamaica. In 1900, close to 190 former sugar estates had been turned over to banana, and the number of banana plantations had increased from 113 in 1893 to 435 by 1910. There was also a dramatic increase in the number of stems being exported. In 1873, 38,689 stems were exported.

Table 8.2:   Contribution of major staples to total agricultural exports, 1870–1900
(% value)

Crop/export	1870	1880	1884	1890	1895	1900
Sugar	44.5	30.5	26.1	13.1	12.9	10.8
Rum	19.3	15.7	19.8	11.0	10.1	7.2
Coffee	15.1	20.9	11.1	15.7	19.3	7.8
Logwood	–	11.9	13.2	21.3	20.4	4.8
Banana	0.06	1.95	11.01	24.57	17.36	25.6
Pimento	–	8.0	4.3	4.5	5.1	9.7
Other (minor) crops	21.04	11.05	14.49	9.83	14.84	24.1

Sources: V. Satchell, *From Plots to Plantations* (Kingston, 1990), p. 46; *Hand Book of Jamaica, Agricultural Reports*, 1880–1900.

In 1873 this increased to 440,642 stems. By 1884, 1 million stems were being exported and by 1900, 11 million stems were sold abroad.[38]

Banana estates first proliferated in parishes which had experienced the most drastic decline of the sugar industry: the parishes of St Mary, Portland and St Thomas. By 1890, not one large sugar estate was still in operation in Portland. Many St Mary planters had also long abandoned sugar cultivation. By 1910, the process of conversion of sugar estates into banana plantations had extended beyond these parishes to St Ann, St Catherine and parts of Trelawny, St James, Hanover, St Elizabeth and Clarendon, where the natural conditions for banana-growing were less favourable but where they still brought higher returns than the sugar-cane they replaced.[39] Table 8.2 indicates that while sugar declined in its contribution to the share of exports, banana increased its share.

Table 8.3 gives an indication of the increase in the acreage under banana and the decrease in the land devoted to sugar-cane cultivation.

There were many factors that attracted investors to the banana industry. In the first place, significant profits could be secured from banana cultivation. Second, banana required a comparatively low capital outlay when compared with sugar. Capital could thus be in the form of reinvested profits from the professions and trades. This encouraged many Jewish merchants and professionals to invest in land. Only later did corporate channels from the United

Table 8.3:   Acres in banana and sugar-cane, 1891–1900

Year	Acres in banana	Acres in cane
1891	9,959	32,487
1892	14,860	32,486
1893	17,297	31,555
1894	18,528	31,284
1895	18,847	30,971
1896	19,227	30,036
1897	19,760	28,764
1898	23,405	27,123
1899	25,184	26,121
1900	27,543	25,616

Source: *Hand Book of Jamaica,* 1906; G. Eisner,*Jamaica 1830 –1930,* p. 206.

States, such as the United Fruit Company and the Boston Fruit Company, become heavy investors. A third factor was that land for the establishment of banana plantations could be bought at a much reduced cost. While abandoned estate lands were not made available to the ex-slaves, they were sold relatively cheaply to the new investors, particularly as they were no longer being considered prime sugar lands. A fourth factor was that banana plantations required no capital equipment, most of the current expenses going into the payment of wages. The use by the banana barons of contract immigrant workers whom they paid extremely low wages further helped them to keep their production costs low. The import of Asians took place within the context of an expanding labour force and reduction in the plantations' demand for labourers. This effectively kept wages low and assured the planter class of a steady nucleus of resident plantation workers whose labour time they could control more effectively.[40]

The banana barons, who along with pen-keepers formed the new agro-elite in post-slavery Jamaica, were distinct from the old sugar-planting elite. In other words, they were not simply old sugar planters now investing in another crop, but were from quite a different section of the society. In fact not many of the old sugar planters or their descendants were still connected with planting by the end of the nineteenth century. Those who remained in agriculture showed a strong disinclination to go into banana cultivation. They considered this a step down the social ladder, fruit-growing being dismissed as 'a backwoods, nigger business'.[41] Those sugar planters who reluctantly made the shift to banana still devoted a part of their land to sugar-cane, investing the profits from banana to keep the sugar industry going.

Many of the new land-owners, such as the Jewish investors, had been engaged in commercial or professional activities not specifically linked to the sugar industry, and had not invested in landed property until banana offered a good investment opportunity. In fact Jews had only obtained their full civil rights in the nineteenth century. By the 1890s the list of banana proprietors included several Portuguese Jewish names.[42]

The typical banana baron tended to own smaller units than the earlier sugar planters. In 1893 the average size of a banana plantation was 75 acres. By 1892 it had increased to 123 acres, though of course some planters owned much larger individual units. Higman's cartographic analysis indicates that large holdings of 1,000 acres and over had declined after the abolition of slavery. While in 1850 there had been 755 such holdings, in 1900 there were 456.[43]

The banana barons, unlike non-sugar producers in the period of slavery, were not at all marginal to the political process. They were active in local and central government and held offices previously associated with the sugar barons. John Pringle, for example, who was educated in Scotland at Aberdeen University, held several high offices in Jamaica. These included custos rotolorum for the parish of St Mary, chairman of the St Mary Parochial Board, justice of the peace for the parish, chairman of several boards, and member of the Privy and Legislative Councils of the island.[44]

Pens and the new pen-keepers

The abolition of slavery and the decline of the sugar industry had an impact on the livestock industry. Early indications of change in this industry were the reduction in the number of pens after 1838 either through sale or abandonment, and the increasing reports of decline by Stipendiary Magistrates and managers of pens. The attorney for Thatchfield Pen in St Elizabeth, one of the foremost pen parishes, noted in the mid-nineteenth century that: 'the death of pen-keeping seems to have made a great impression against the place';[45]

and the accounts of the stipendiary magistrates working in St Ann reflected a similar opinion.[46]

The decline of the original pen-keepers was reflected in the drastic reduction of pen accounts in the post-slavery period. In 1840, there had been 152 pen accounts. By 1845 there were 129 such accounts and by 1900 only 21.[47] Another indication of decline was the clear fall-off in profits mentioned frequently in the reports of governors, stipendiary magistrates and individual pen-keepers, and reflected in the Crop Accounts and Accounts Current (which, of course, have to be used with caution as they are so incomplete). The 14 complete sets of Accounts Current which survive for the period 1840–5 show that receipts from the sale of livestock and other goods and services generally declined while payments for goods and services increased. The accounts which were sampled for the post-1845 period indicate a similar trend, the majority showing that payments exceeded receipts. The labourers' wage bill was always a significant – at times the largest – part of payments made by the pen-keepers. Other heavy items of expenditure were the overseer's salary, the attorney's 6 per cent commission on sales, family annuities and household expenses.[48]

The pen-keepers were quick to attribute their declining fortunes to what they termed the 'labour problem'. Despite strong counter-evidence represented by the contribution of the enslaved to the export and local economies in the eighteenth and nineteenth centuries and the ex-slaves' vigorous efforts to establish a viable peasantry, planters and pen-keepers persisted in characterising them as lazy. One overseer, Stephen Harmer, unflatteringly observed in 1842 that freed people preferred to 'lay down under their plantain trees and sleep sounder than work for fair wages'.[49]

There was, arguably, a clear reduction in the labour force on the pens after 1838. Salt Pond Pen in St Catherine had 45 apprentices up to 1838, but by 1840 the pen's labour force numbered 15. Similar drastic reductions occurred on other pens. Retreat Bannister and Ann Castle pens in the parish of St Dorothy had a total labour force of 280 during 1834–8. The average daily turnout on each pen then had been 60 in the great gang and 25 in the second gang. From August to December 1838 the average attendance for both gangs was 25 on each pen. Fort George pen had 200 workers at the time of emancipation. In January 1843, the pen had just over 150 workers, though only 64 seem to have resided on the pen. The working population numbered 88 by March and 58 by December of that year.[50]

The factors which determined the movement of labourers from the various properties have been keenly debated by scholars. At the centre of the debate is whether push or pull factors should be accorded primacy in explaining this movement. While the pull theory, as advanced by planters and pen-keepers, was the staple of the historiographical tradition and was linked by modern writers of the pull school to land availability or scarcity, the push school as articulated by the late Douglas Hall, O. Nigel Bolland, Swithin Wilmot, Michel Rolph Trouillot, Verene Shepherd, Woodville Marshall and Thomas Holt has been steadily gaining ground and is being supported by firmer empirical base.51 The research being done on the pens indicates that there was initially no large-scale exodus of labourers. The movement was gradual, as evidenced by the gradual reduction in the wage bill each year. The journals of the manager of Fort George Pen in the parish of St George also bear testimony to this notion of gradual withdrawal. Neither the Accounts Current which detail the wage bill nor Fort George Pen records tell us definitively the reasons for the gradual withdrawal; but it would seem from comments made by the manager of that pen and the record of eviction and rent payment that the conflict over rents was a factor in the movement of labourers.[52]

The reports of the stipendiary magistrates in the years immediately following the termination of the apprenticeship system provide us with more reasons. It would seem that a primary reason was the conflict over task and daily labour. During most of the apprenticeship period, labour was guaranteed and work on pens could be accommodated within the 40½ hours of compulsory labour. Stipendiary Magistrate Davies reported that: 'the pens have suffered very little by the diminution of the hours of labour under the present system'.[53]

Stipendiary Magistrate Laidlaw reporting from St Ann, the foremost pen parish, confirmed Davies' report, observing that 'there has been very little need in the pen areas for extra labour, the time allowed by law being in general sufficient for the species of cultivation required'.[54]

Other reports from magistrates in other parishes generally supported Davies' and Laidlaw's observations.

By 1837, however, the situation had changed. The pens first lost the services of jobbers on whom they had relied to do extra work. This meant that the resident pen labourers were asked to fill the gap created by the withdrawal of jobbers. The pen labourers refused to do such extra jobs. After 1838, also the pen labourers began to demand task work, long being resorted to on the sugar estates; but the pen-keepers generally refused to acquiesce to the workers' demands for task work. Their reason was summed up by Stipendiary Magistrate Laidlaw, who noted: 'the various sorts of labour required on pens renders it difficult to resort to task work, and it is not therefore genuinely practiced in this . . . district'.[55]

The refusal of pen workers, particularly the women, to labour on a daily basis, was yet another factor explaining their movement off the pens.

Some former pen workers sought jobs on the sugar plantations that were offering task and seasonal work. The wages on sugar estates were not appreciably higher than wages on the pens. It would appear, then, that it was the difference in the terms of labour in the post-slavery period and not differential wage rates which determined the shift from pens to sugar plantations by some of the former pen workers.

The refusal of the pen-keepers to allow the workers to remain on the pen with the customary Free use of their houses and grounds, their charging of exorbitant rents for houses and grounds and pasturage facilities, their resistance to the sale of lands to the workers, their insistence on daily (instead of task) work and weekend work, their tendency to evict labourers for a variety of reasons, combined with freed people's utilisation of alternative job opportunities, all hastened the trek from the pens.

There were, however, more easily identifiable reasons for the decline of pen-keeping in the island. A reason for the loss of profitability was that the pens lost the sugar estate and the coffee plantation markets, once their primary markets for working or planters' stock. Governor Charles Grey observed in 1849: 'the estates in the high grounds which are called Pens and are laid out almost entirely in pasture, have been intended mainly for the raising of horned cattle, horses and mules for the use of the sugar and coffee estates. These are suffering due to the diminished demand for working animals on sugar and coffee estates which are in decline'.[56]

The supply of planters' stock to the estates for use in the cattle mills had, of course, been one of the factors responsible for the expansion of pen-keeping in eighteenth century Jamaica. In 1763 there had been 34 windmills, 150 water-mills and 382 cattle mills in the island, indicating a large market for animals on the estates.[57] By 1804, the number of cattle mills had increased to 656 or 61 per cent of the total number of mills.[58] In the post-slavery period, by contrast, those estates which remained in operation increasingly switched to steam mills. The use of steam power had commenced in the island around 1768 but had never been general. Only about one-tenth of Jamaica's estates were equipped with steam engines in the three decades before abolition,[59] but they were rapidly installed thereafter. By 1906, only one sugar estate in the island was still using a cattle mill.[60]

The decline in their main markets caused the pen-keepers to sell animals to the butchers, often at a reduced price. Indeed, it was the anticipated expansion of the consumer market for fresh beef after 1838 which had acted as an incentive for some pen-keepers to remain in operation. The hope was that the large freed Black population would now buy fresh beef instead of the 'old slave food'; but this hope was not realised as not only did the peasantry keep their own small stock which supplied them with meat, but they continued to buy the cheaper salted and pickled fish.

With this declining internal market for animals and with the external market still in its infancy, more pen-keepers either abandoned their properties and sold out or increased their attempts to further diversify their economic activities and expand their sources of income. In addition to the sale of animals, pens were collecting money for the impounding of stray animals and from the sale of wood, coffee, citrus, hides and horns. They even sold agricultural tools and clothing material to the Freed people and collected rents for the use of the pasture, the use of the grindstone, and for houses and provision grounds used by the African-Jamaican labourers.[61]

The pen accounts indicate clearly this trend among the surviving pens to earn more from the sale of products other than livestock. Whereas 19 of the 38 pens belonging to absentee owners which indicated the value of goods sold in 1860 collected more money from the sale of animals than from other goods and services, only 11 of the 30 returned in 1880 still earned most from the sale of animals. Of the 21 accounts for 1900, eight collected more from animal sales than from any other product.[62] The Accounts Produce also indicate that fewer and fewer transactions were carried out between the pens and the estates. So, that both types of properties clearly became less and less dependent on each other.

From the 1870s, however, attempts were made to revive the pen-keeping industry in Jamaica and by 1900 there were some 307 pens with over 100 head of livestock.[63] The increased possibilities for the development of the meat and dairy industries and for the export of cattle and horses to Cuba and the Eastern Caribbean were incentives for this trend. Some pens were also occasionally exporting animals to the United Kingdom, the United States, Italy, France, Gibraltar and South America.[64]

There were four main trends in the efforts to re-establish the pen-keeping industry in post-slavery Jamaica. First, existing pen-keepers expanded their acreage, buying additional lands. Second, new investors bought up abandoned sugar estates and turned them over to cattle-rearing. As an indication of this tendency, the governor's Agricultural Report of 1884 pointed out: 'the area from the Plantain Garden River District to Port Antonio was once covered with flourishing sugar estates but is now utilised as grazing pens. Fifteen large sugar estates only are now in operation'.[65]

Third, but least noted, sugar planters turned their land over to pasture; and fourth, pen-keepers who had switched to other enterprises such as logwood in the immediate post-slavery period now switched back to livestock farming. This was the case of pen-keepers in St Elizabeth, like George Forbes, in the face of declining reserves of logwood in the late nineteenth century. The manager of Forbes' pen, Thatchfield, advised his employer in 1871 that the pen should once more be stocked with animals (which they had sold a few years back) because: 'cattle is what will pay [on Thatchfield pen] for it has the expectation of being the best fattening pen in the parish'.[66]

By 1893, unlike in the period of slavery, the majority of livestock were located on the pens. In that year the pens had a total of 78,951 head of cattle and 18,912 horses and mules, compared with the estates' 24,612 and 4,361 respectively.[67]

The increase in grass cultivation islandwide was also phenomenal, the acreage in guinea grass moving from 110,705 in 1869 to 124,193 in 1900. The land in common pasture also increased from 222,790 acres in 1869 to 353,588 acres in 1900. Compared with sugar-cane cultivation which engrossed 29,182 acres and banana cultivation which occupied 62,685 acres in 1908, grazing lands comprised 615,685 acres.[68]

As was the case with the banana farmers, the majority of the members of what may be termed the penocracy, were not simply reorganised former sugar planters. In any case because of the traditional association of pen-keeping, by the old sugar elite, with a lower social position, this activity would not have been acceptable socially to some of them. That is not to say such a shift in activity by sugar planters never took place; for there had been an interplay of cattle and cane from the days of slavery. But this had not been a widespread occurrence. During slavery some sugar planters had also invested in pen-keeping, but not as their primary income-generating activity.

The newly established pens seemed to have been on average larger than the banana plantations. In 1908, those with over 100 head of livestock had an average of 615 acres, though not all of this land was always in pasture.[69] Male pen owners were in the majority, with females comprising just 9 per cent of the group by the turn of the twentieth century. The male members of the new group of pen-keepers were primarily resident on their properties but the female members were primarily absentees.[70] Female pen-keepers may now have been Freed from the stigma of owning livestock farms, but continued to be affected by other social factors which barred them from being integrally a part of the island's government. Male pen-keepers, on the other hand, became more and more visible in local and central government in the late nineteenth and early twentieth centuries. Before the 1870s the list of jurors and vestry men rarely identified the occupation of officeholders as pen-keepers. They would identify them as planters even though independent checks on the names in these lists (such as in wills and inventories) reveal that some of those listed as planters were really pen-keepers. By the end of the nineteenth century and into the twentieth century, such lists identified occupations more correctly, listing those who were pen-keepers or planter/pen-keepers.

On the St Elizabeth Jury List of 1883 and 1884, 17 men were actually identified as pen-keepers. This list contained the names of 110 planters, 17 pen-keepers, 55 store or shopkeepers and 122 professionals. In 1885, 22 pen-keepers were identified as jurors and in 1891, 32.[71] *The Blue Books of Jamaica (BBJ)*, *Votes of the House of Assembly* and the Legislative Council Minutes all reveal that pen-keepers were more visible as office-holders in the post-slavery period. They held such positions as parish custos, attorney-general, receiver-general, member of the House of Assembly, Speaker of the House of Assembly, Clerk and Deputy Clerk of the Supreme Court and member of the Executive Committee. They were active in local government and central government, and held positions in both the Lower and Upper Houses.[72]

Finally, it must be noted that the revival of pen-keeping and the transition of banana cultivation from an essentially small-farming crop to an estate crop had a negative impact on the labouring, specifically African-Jamaica population. As Veront Satchell has shown, the tendency after 1880 was for the concentration of land into large holdings and as land was consolidated in the hands of large land-holders this affected the growth of the peasantry. This peasantry had been increasing rapidly since the 1840s; but the expansion of pen-keeping and the shift in banana cultivation from a peasant crop to an estate export crop served to displace the peasantry from land they previously rented. Agricultural reports for 1897 show that the small banana cultivators were losing their land to the large land barons. In St Thomas, for example, only 168 acres were in the hands of the small banana growers. The 20 large banana estates in that parish controlled some 12,000 acres of land. Similarly in Portland, in 1897, there were 35 large banana plantations and small farmers had only 735 acres of land. In St Mary there were 41 large banana estates. There, the peasantry controlled 4,245 acres of banana land.[73] The re-emergence of the large plantations resulted in a reduction in the efforts of the Crown colony government to increase land holding among the peasantry. The plantation sector, by reasserting its hold on prime agricultural lands, contributed to the deterioration in the conditions of the African-Jamaicans and the ex-indentured Indian labourers. The re-emergence of an influential plantation sector resulted in a return to dependence on the estate for labour at subsistence wages. This dependence on the estate led to destitution and poverty because wages were constantly reduced in an attempt to rationalise production and keep command over the labour force.

The solutions sought, emigration and rural-to-urban migration, were only partially successful in alleviating their condition. For those who returned to the estates, their positions were threatened by the importation of Indian indentured immigrants.

In conclusion, this chapter has tried to show that although the Jamaican slave society was characterised in a generalised sense by a dichotomy of classes – the White exploiting class and an exploited Black and Coloured class – it displayed significant intra-class diversities. In the case of the Whites, internal socioeconomic and political differentiation and antagonistic economic activity lend support to the notion that Caribbean plantation societies were not characterised by a homogenous White 'race', forming the ruling class. Political positions were dominated, but not exclusively held, by sugar planters as a few non-sugar producers gained seats in the House of Assembly, the traditional bastion of sugar power. But in general, non-sugar producers marginalised in this society which equated ownership and control of a sugar estate with high social status. The coffee farmers more than the pen-keepers were able to challenge this marginal position. In the case of the pen-keepers, their efforts were diminished by external factors relating to the state of the sugar market and their economic dependence on the sugar estate and coffee markets for the sale of animals and food. In the case of the Free Coloured pen-keepers, responses to their subordinate position represented individualistic and pragmatic strategies for upward social mobility, such as the application for privileges and the acquisition of the higher-status sugar estate in a society where social position was determined not only by class, but by race, colour and gender. They used their education and accumulated resources to seek acceptance in White elite society, not to challenge the dominant ideology. The coffee farmers, by having an alliance with the sugarocracy, also achieved upward social mobility.

In the post-slavery period, the sugar planter class that had upheld and sustained this system of stratification was displaced by merchants and professionals turned banana planters, and livestock farmers. In the post-slavery period, then, while the sugar plantocracy declined in importance, it was those proprietors growing banana and cocoa and rearing livestock who came to dominate the agricultural economy and who formed the new agro-commercial elite.

Notes

1.   See, for example, G. Beckford, *Persistent Poverty: Underdevelopment in Plantation Economies of the Third World* (New York: Oxford University Press, 1972).
2.   D.G. Hall, 'Planters, Farmers and Gardeners in 18th Century Jamaica', Elsa Goveia Memorial Lecture, UWI, Mona, 1987, p.1.
3.   K. Brathwaite, *The Development of Creole Society in Jamaica 1770–1820* (Oxford: Clarendon Press, 1976); B.W. Higman, *Slave Population and Economy in Jamaica* (Cambridge: Cambridge University Press, 1976).
4.   See V.A. Shepherd, 'Trade and Exchange in Jamaica in the Period of Slavery', in H. Beckles and Verene Shepherd, eds., *Caribbean Slave Society and Economy: A Student Reader* (Kingston: Ian Randle; London: James Currey, 1991), pp. 111–19; and K. Monteith, 'The Coffee Industry in Jamaica, 1790–1850', Staff/Graduate Seminar Paper, UWI, Mona, 1988. See also V.A. Shepherd and K.E.A. Monteith, 'Non-sugar Proprietors in a Sugar Plantation Society', *Plantation Society in the Americas*, v: 2, 3 (Fall 1998), 205–225. Special issue on *Slavery Without Sugar*, guest editor V.A. Shepherd.
5.   Higman, *Slave Population and Economy in Jamaica*, p. 16.
6.   Francisco A. Scarano, 'Congregate and Control: The Peasantry and Labor Coercion in Puerto Rico Before the Age of Sugar', *New West Indian Guide: Special Issue on Changing Sugar Technology and the Labour Nexus*, 63: 1–2 (1989), 23–40; and F. Knight, *Slave Society in Cuba in the Nineteenth Century* (Madison: University of Wisconsin Press, 1970).

7. Jamaica Archives (JA), I/B/11/4, Accounts Produce, 1834. Accounts Produce were returned annually by overseers or attorneys to their absentee employers. They recorded the production and sale of commodities. They were different from the Accounts Current, which returned both receipts and payments.
8. J. Bigelow, *Jamaica in 1850*, (London, 1851), p. 104.
9. Ibid.
10. Brathwaite, *The Development of Creole Society in Jamaica*, pp. 105–150.
11. M.G. Smith, 'Social Structure in the British Caribbean around 1820', *Social and Economic Studies*, 1:4 (1955), 55–79.
12. J.B. Moreton, *Manners and Customs in our West India Islands*, (London, 1790), p. 58.
13. See, for example, Elsa Goveia's analysis in *Slave Society in the British Leeward Islands at the end of the 18th Century* (New haven: Yale University Press, 1965)
14. Sheena Boa, 'Free Black and Coloured Women in a White Man's Slave Society', M.Phil, UWI, Mona, 1985, p. 202.
15. Monteith, 'The Coffee Industry in Jamaica', 1988, p. 1.
16. Ibid
17. Ibid., p. 21 and Shepherd and Monteith, 'Non-Sugar Proprietors'.
18. Higman, *Slave Population and Economy*, p. 16.
19. Ibid
20. Higman, 'The Internal Economy of Jamaica Pens, 1760–1890', *Social and Economic Studies*, 38, 1 (1989), 72.
21. V.A. Shepherd, 'Pens and Penkeepers in a Plantation Society: Aspects of Jamaican Social and Economic History, 1740–1845', Ph.D Diss., Cambridge 1988, Chapter 4.
22. Ibid
23. Ann Petry, *Harriet Tubman, Conductor on the Underground Railroad* (New York: Harper Collins, 1971), pp.7–8.
24. Autobiography of Louis Hughes (Milwaukee, 1897), p. 63.
25. *Narrative of the Life of Frederick Douglass an American Slave* (Boston, 1845), p. 37.
26. L.J. Ragatz, *The Fall of the Planter Class in the British Caribbean 1763–1833*, (New York: Octagon Books, 1928).
27. Public Record Office, London. C.O. 137/302, Charles Grey to Earl Grey, Despatch No. 31, Sept. 3, 1849.
28. C.O. 137/322, Despatch No. 24, Feb. 21, 1854.
29. W.G. Sewell, *The Ordeal of Free Labor* (London: Frank Cass, 1968), p. 188.
30. *The Blue Books of Jamaica (BBJ)*, 1869, p. 43; 1882, pp. x 4–x 6; 1885–6, pp. x 2–x 4 and 1889–91, pp. x 4–5.
31. *Handbooks of Jamaica (HBJ)*, 1884–5, p. 231.
32. *BBJ*, 1870, pp. 44–45 and *HBJ*, 1908, p. 398.

33. *HBJ*, 1883, pp. 363–65 and Veront Satchell, *From Plots to Plantations* (Kingston: I.S.E.R., University of the West Indies, Mona, 1990), p. 46.

34. *HBJ*, 1883, p. 364.

35. C.O. 137/322, Barkly to Newcastle, Feb. 21, 1854.

36. National Library of Jamaica, (NLJ), MS 65, 'List of Planters and Penkeepers compiled from Mr. Espeut's List'. This list gives an idea of the parishes in which these landowners lived. Only the initials and surnames appear on the list so that it is impossible to identify the female landowners.

37. *HBJ*, 1897, p. 413, *HBJ*, 1902, p. 378 and G. Eisner, *Jamaica 1830–1930: A Study in Economic Growth* (Westport, Connecticut: Greenwood Press, 1974), pp. 256–57.

38. *HBJ*, 1882–1902, Agricultural Reports, 1879–1900.

39. *HBJ*, 1902, p. 378 and *HBJ*, 1912, pp. 430–8.

40. For a discussion of Asian immigration in particular, see V.A. Shepherd, *Transients to Settlers: The Experience of Indians in Jamaica, 1845–1950* (Leeds and Warwick: Peepal Tree & The University of Warwick's Centre for the Study of Asian Migration, 1994).

41. Eisner, *Jamaica 1830–1930*, p. 313.

42. *HBJ*, 1908, pp. 406–410.

43. B.W. Higman, *Jamaica Surveyed: Plantation Maps and Plans of the 18th and 19th Centuries* (Kingston: Institute of Jamaica Publication, 1988), p. 17.

44. *Who is Who in Jamaica*, 1916, p. 116.

45. JA, Private Deposit 4/100, Gunnis Papers.

46. *Parliamentary Papers (PP)*, (212) xxv, *Half Yearly Agricultural Reports*, 1840, pp. 4–22.

47. JA, *Accounts Produce Returns*, IB/11/4/83-91 and New Series, 1.

48. JA, *Accounts Produce and Accounts Current*, IB/11/4/83, New Series 2 and IB/11/5/46–53.

49. NLJ, MS 765, Stephen Harmer to Saul Harmer, March 16, 1842.

50. PP (158) xxxv, *Correspondence Relating to the Negro Population of Jamaica*, Appendix E, p. 64, NLJ, MS 274a, Fort George Pen Journals and V.A. Shepherd, 'The Effects of the Abolition of Slavery on Jamaican Livestock Farms, 1834–1845', *Slavery and Abolition*, 10, 2(1989), 188–211.

51. W.A. Green, *British Slave Emancipation: The Sugar Colonies and the Great Experiment, 1830–1865* (Oxford: Clarendon Pres, 1976), D.G. Hall, 'The Flight from the Estates Reconsidered', *The Journal of Caribbean History*, 10, 11 (1978), Hall, 'Fort George Pen, Jamaica: Slaves, Tenants and Labourers', 11th Conference of Caribbean Historians, Curacao, 1979; O.N. Bolland, 'Systems of Domination after Slavery: the Control of Land and Labour in the British West Indies after 1838', *Comparative Studies in Society and History*, 23, 4 (1981), S. Wilmot, 'Emancipation in Action: Workers and Wage Conflicts

in Jamaica, 1838–1840', *Jamaica Journal*, 19, 3 (1986); M.R. Trouillot, 'Labour and Emancipation in Dominica: Contribution to a Debate', *Caribbean Quarterly*, 30, 3, 4 (1988); V.A. Shepherd, 'The Effects of the Abolition of Slavery on Jamaican Livestock Farms, 1834–1845', *Slavery and Abolition*, 10, 2 (1989); W.K. Marshall, *The Post-Slavery Labour Problem Revisited*, The 1990 Elsa Goveia Memorial Lecture, UWI, Mona, Jamaica, 1991 and T.C. Holt, *The Problem of Freedom: Race, Labor and Politics in Jamaica and Britain, 1832–1938* (Baltimore: The Johns Hopkins University Press: Baltimore, 1992), Chapter 4.

52. Shepherd, 'The Effects of the Abolition' and Fort George Pen Journals, NLJ, MS 274

53. C.O. 137/214, Enclosure in Despatch No. 259, Governor Sligo to Lord Glenelg, Jan. 1, 1836.

54. C.O. 137/219, Enclosure in Despatch No. 90, Governor Smith to Lord Glenelg, April 4, 1837.

55. C.O. 137/219, 1, Henry Laidlaw to Governor Smith, Enclosure in Despatch No. 90.

56. C.O. 137/302, Enclosure in Despatch No. 31, Barkly to Newcastle, Dec. 31, 1853.

57. C.O. 700/16, Simpson's and Craskill's Map of Jamaica, 1763.

58. J. Robertson, County Maps of Jamaica, 1804, NLJ, Map Collection.

59. J.R. Ward, *British West Indian Slavery, 1750–1834: The Process of Amelioration* (Oxford: Clarendon Press, 1988), p. 101.

60. *HBJ*, 1908, pp. 406–412.

61. This increasing diversification is indicated clearly in the Accounts Produce.

62. JA, Accounts Produce IB/11/4/93–99, 1860–79 and New Series, vols. 1 & 2, 1879–1927.

63. *HBJ*, 1908, pp. 412–17.

64. Trade Statistics, *BBJ*, 1885–86, pp. u 49 – u 115; *BBJ*, 1887–88, pp. u 50 – u 107; *BBJ*, 1888–89, pp. u 52 – 110 and *BBJ*, 1891–92, pp. u 61–62.

65. *HBJ*, 1884–85, p. 231.

66. JA, Private Deposit 4/110, Anderson to Forbes, March 30, 1871.

67. *HBJ*, 1893, p. 289.

68. *HBJ*, 1882, pp. 363–65 and *HBJ*, 1908, p. 397.

69. *HBJ*, 1908, pp. 412–17.

70. Ibid., pp. 413–19.

71. JA, 2/10/1. Vestry Minutes, and Municipal Board Minutes, 113, 1891, St Elizabeth.

72. *BBJ*, 1840–62; *Votes of the House of Assembly of Jamaica, (JHAV)* 1859–1865 and *Legislative Council Minutes*, 1880–1892.

73. *HBJ*, 1897, pp. 412–13.

IV

Contesting Slavery:
Causes and Consequences

Resistance and Rebellion of African Captives in the Transatlantic Slave Trade before becoming Seasoned Labourers in the British Caribbean, 1690–1807

RICHARD SHERIDAN

Much has been written in recent decades about the resistance and rebellion of African-American slaves against their owners. In his book on African-American slave revolts in the New World, Eugene D. Genovese writes that 'the extraordinary scholarship of recent years has finally laid to rest the myth of slave docility and quiescence'.[1] His lengthy bibliographical essay lists the authors and their books and articles which he considers '[i]ndispensable for the historical context of revolts and of modern slavery generally'. Approximately 300 authors and their publications are classified according to geographical region, ranging from Brazil to Canada and extending from the early Spanish conquest to the end of slavery in Cuba and Brazil in the 1880s. Genovese does not discuss the 'non-insurrectionary forms of resistance nor even such insurrectionary forms as the impressive shipboard revolts in the slave trade', contending that while these subjects are important in themselves and bear on the themes of his book, they 'would only extend the text without essentially affecting the argument'.[2]

Contrasted with the abundance of historical studies of African-American revolts is the paucity of studies of resistance and rebellion in West Africa and on the vessels which carried the cargoes of forced migrants to the plantation and mining colonies of the Americas. Included among the reasons for the lack of these studies are the generally small groups of African captives who were involved, the wide dispersal of their actions over time and space, the individual and covert nature of much of the resistance and the lack of surviving records.

There are, however, four studies by Darold Wax, William Piersen, Winston McGowan and Richard Rathbone, that address the nature and causes of resistance and rebellion before the arrival of the captives in the Americas.[3] Wax, in his article of 1966, notes that Africans first resisted being captured and enslaved in their homeland, and that every stage in the transatlantic traffic was marked by behaviour which was uncooperative and belligerent. After recounting the case histories of resistance from the interior of Africa to the coast and continuing on the Atlantic crossing or Middle Passage, Wax concludes that resistance in the North American slave trade was real and occurred with regularity. Piersen's 1977 article sheds new light on fear, depression and religious faith as causes of suicide among new slaves, extending from capture and enslavement in Africa to the Middle Passage and early life and death in the Americas. A paramount cause of suicide, he claims, was the captives' fear of being eaten by white cannibals. McGowan, whose article of 1990 focuses upon resistance to the Atlantic slave trade in West Africa, writes that much attention has been devoted to the origin and growth of the trade, its organisation, volume, profitability, impact upon Africa and the Americas, abolition and suppression. But he claims there has been little scholarly focus on resistance to the trade in West Africa. After delineating the forms of resistance and their efficacy, he concludes by asserting that the pattern of resistance which began in Africa was ultimately the evidence of the determination of the human spirit to triumph over adversity. By a culture of resistance, Rathbone means the actual evidence of physical attempts to prevent the forcible removal of African people from their home environment. In his article of 1985 he finds that the 'frequency of escapes, rebellions both successful and unsuccessful, and the intelligence about places of safety for the fugitive, suggest a mounting challenge not only against the Atlantic trade but also against indigenous institutions of slavery'.

It should be noted that resistance to capture and enslavement was both non-violent and violent. The captives expressed their resentment either in a covert and indirect manner which fell short of violent behaviour, or they resorted to violent resistance. Covert resistance took such forms as refusing to walk and carry loads in caravans or coffles, refusing to be shackled with leg- and arm-irons and chains, refusing to enter boats and ships, running away, committing suicide, inflicting injuries or self-mutilation, and refusing to eat. Exacting vengeance by violent means took such forms as poisoning with herbs, destroying property such as slave ships and their component parts, resorting to conspiracies and collective violence or rebellion by wielding knives, cut-lasses, or firearms taken from their oppressors.

Before becoming seasoned to labour in the mines and on the plantations of the New World, the ordeal of slavery involved the Africans in the following stages or categories: (1) enslavement; (2) journey to the coast; (3) the Middle Passage which can be subdivided into (4) coasting, (5) ocean crossing; (6) sale and transfer; and (7) seasoning or adjusting to American environments. As Johannes Postma points out: '[n]ot all slaves, not even those who survived the whole ordeal were subjected to all these categories, but some may have had to undergo the same experience more than once'.[4]

Although the greater part of American slaves came from the coastal ethnic groups in West Africa, they came increasingly from the interior parts of the continent as the trade expanded during the eighteenth and early nineteenth centuries. Those who came from the interior can be divided into two distinct groups: first, those who were born as slaves from enslaved mothers, and secondly, those who were born free but afterwards, by various means, became slaves. Some of the latter had been sold by relatives to secure food in time of famine. Others were free people who had been enslaved for committing such crimes as adultery or dealing in witchcraft. But most of the slaves shipped overseas had been free men and women who had been deprived of their liberty as a result of organised slave-raiding expeditions or kidnapping. The late Walter Rodney, an authority on slavery in Africa, writes that '[i]n the long run, West Africans were reduced to a state of "sell or be sold"'. To be able to sell slaves the African rulers had to be strong, and to be strong they needed to get firearms from the Europeans. 'This can be described as a "vicious circle"', he writes. 'It does not entirely excuse the African rulers who helped the Europeans, but it explains how in the end they were not so much the partners of the Europeans but rather their servants or lackeys'.[5]

Enslavement

Olaudah Equiano, later given the name Gustavus Vassa, was the only African slave who became sufficiently proficient in English to write his autobiography. He was born in 1745. His home was in the interior of what is now Eastern Nigeria, and his language was Ibo. His father was an elder in the community and owned numerous slaves. The people in his village feared losing relatives and friends to kidnappers and raiders who sold their victims into slavery. Equiano wrote that precautions against kidnapping and raids included the building of circular walls around each house and having children climb trees to watch for kidnappers. Furthermore, he noted, 'Our whole district is a kind of militia; on a certain signal given, such as the firing of a gun at night, they all rise in arms and rush upon their enemy'. One day when all the adults were working in a field some distance from the village, the ten-year-old Olaudah and his younger sister were kidnapped by two men and a woman who climbed over the walls, 'and in a moment seized us both, and without giving us time to cry out or make resistance they stopped our mouths and ran off with us into the nearest wood'. Later when he was separated from his sister he was left in a 'state of distraction not to be described'. He cried and grieved and did not eat anything for several days except the food his captors forced into his mouth.[6]

After many days of travelling and numerous changes of masters, Olaudah came to the banks of a 'large river' which was probably the Niger. He was put into one of the many canoes, and with other captives, 'we began to paddle and move along the river'. He summed up his long and eventful journey by saying that he 'continued to travel, sometimes by land, sometimes by water, through different countries and various nations, till at the end of six or seven months after I had been kidnapped I arrived at the sea coast'.[7]

The first object that met Olaudah's eyes was the sea, 'and a slave ship which was then riding at anchor and waiting for its cargo'. These filled him with astonishment, which was soon converted into terror when he was carried on board. 'I was immediately handled and tossed up to see if I were sound by some of the crew', he wrote, 'and I was now persuaded that I had gotten into a world of bad spirits and that they were going to kill me'. When he looked round the ship he 'saw a large furnace or copper boiling and a multitude of black people of every description chained together, every one of their countenances expressing dejection and sorrow. I no longer doubted of my fate; and quite overpowered with horror and anguish, I fell motionless on the deck and fainted'.

When he had partly recovered he asked the fellow Africans who had brought him on board 'if we were not to be eaten by those White men with horrible looks, and faces, and loose hair. They told me I was not'. Soon after he was put down under the deck where the stench of the hold 'was so intolerably loathsome that it was dangerous to remain there for any time'. Olaudah became so sick and low that he was unable to eat and wished for 'the last friend, death' to relieve him. One day at sea when the slaves were on deck he witnessed three of his countrymen make it through the nettings and jump into the sea, 'preferring death to such a life of misery'.[8]

Olaudah was landed at Barbados and soon after shipped off to Virginia where he worked for a time on a plantation and later on a sloop trading from North American ports to the Caribbean islands. As with his experience in Africa, he was traded from one owner to another until he earned enough money to purchase his freedom in 1766. Thereafter he engaged in trade with the islands and the Mosquito Shore of Central America. Later he was the hairdresser on a ship that toured the Mediterranean, joined an expedition to explore the northeast passage in arctic waters, was converted to Calvinism, and in November 1786 was appointed commissary for stores for freed slaves in the colony of Sierra Leone. He returned to England the following year to write his autobiography and work against slavery. He died in London on 30 April 1797. For the purposes of this chapter, Equiano's life story illustrates the various forms of non-violent resistance in the transatlantic slave trade, with the widespread fear of kidnapping and raids on his home village, the actual kidnapping of the author and his sister, their separation and being passed from one owner to another, the terror he felt when boarding the slave ship and his mistaken belief that he would be eaten by white cannibals, the suicide of three of his countrymen who jumped overboard, and in later years his joining in the campaign to abolish the slave trade.[9]

Mungo Park (1771–1806), was a Scottish explorer of the interior of West Africa and especially the Niger river. In June 1795 he ascended the Gambia river some 200 miles to the British trading station of Pisania. From there he entered the then unknown interior of the continent, and after a number of difficulties and life-threatening experiences, reached the Niger and traced the course of that great river. He reached Pisania again in July 1797, returned to Scotland, married and practised medicine. On his second exploration in West Africa he was drowned in an attempt to escape from hostile natives.

Park learned much of the working of the slave trade in the interior of Africa, including the resistance of the captives and precautions taken by their captors. One of his important insights had to do with prisoners taken in war. 'All these unfortunate beings are considered as strangers and foreigners', he wrote in his *Travels in the Interior of Africa*, 'who have no right to the protection of the law, and may be treated with severity, or sold to a stranger according to the pleasure of their owners'. Slaves of this description were bought and sold in regular markets. In the eye of the African purchaser, according to Park, the slaves increased in value in proportion to the distance from their native kingdom,

> for when slaves are only a few days journey from the place of their nativity, they frequently effect their escape, but when one or more kingdoms intervene, escape being more difficult, they are more readily reconciled to their situation. On this account, the unhappy slave is frequently transferred from one dealer to another, and he has lost all hopes of returning to his native kingdom.[10]

Park noted that the captives who were purchased by Europeans on the coast of Africa were chiefly of this description. They were brought down in caravans from the inland countries.

Journey to the coast

Philip D. Curtin says that the key institution for moving goods, including slaves, overland in Africa was the caravan or coffle. It was a highly variable institution, ranging from less than 100 to 600–800 slaves, together with guards, porters and donkey drivers, which raised the number to as many as 2,000 people. To secure the slaves they were tied together with leather cords, chains or ropes, sometimes with a Y-shaped piece of wood fastened with the fork round the neck of one slave and the stem resting on the one behind. Besides being fettered, the slaves were required to carry heavy loads upon their heads and to walk quickly.[11]

Mungo Park joined a coffle in 1797 that departed Kamalia, near Bamako in what is now Mali, and ended at the Gambia river port of Pisania, a distance of 330 miles, which together with the boat trip to the mouth of the river amounted to nearly 600 miles. The overland part of the journey extended over 51 days. On the departure, the coffle consisted of 27 captives, later increased to 35. They were fastened by a rope round their necks, four of them to a rope. The number of free people and domestic slaves amounted to 38, making a total of 73. On the first day two female slaves were so much fatigued they could not keep up with the coffle. They were severely whipped and dragged along. When they became sick and vomited it was discovered they had eaten clay, which Park said was a practice by no means uncommon among Africans. He could not confirm whether they had eaten the clay because of 'a vitiated appetite, or from a settled intention to destroy themselves'. A few days later, after travelling all day in the hot sun, many of the slaves who had loads upon their heads were very much fatigued and 'some of them *snapt their fingers*, which among the Negroes is a sure sign of desperation'. They were immediately put in irons.[12]

Park expressed his appreciation for the help accorded him by the slaves as they approached the end of their tedious and toilsome journey. He was touched by the fact that 'the poor slaves, amidst their own infinitely greater sufferings, would commiserate mine'. They frequently brought water to quench his thirst and at night collected branches and leaves to prepare him a bed in the wilderness. 'We parted with reciprocal expressions of regret and benediction', he wrote. 'My good wishes and prayers were all I could bestow upon them, and it afforded me some consolation to be told, that they were sensible I had no more to give'.[13]

On the coast of Africa the captives were held in custody in forts and castles and at trading posts for weeks or months till the arrival of ships bound for America. Special prisons called 'barracoons' were built for the men and women. At Cape Coast Castle, headquarters of the Royal African Company on the Gold Coast, the prison could accommodate over 1,000 slaves. Since it was dangerous both for the health of the slaves and their good order, and also costly to feed them for long periods, they were frequently rented out to local farmers, in which circumstances it was not uncommon for them to take flight either singly or in groups.[14]

The Middle Passage

The 'Middle Passage' was the second leg of the triangle trade whereby British manufactures, firearms, rum, etc were shipped to West Africa to exchange for slaves, ivory, gold and other commodities; the slaves then being transported to the North American and Caribbean colonies to produce sugar, rum, tobacco, rice and cotton, which products were carried to markets in Great Britain and North America. The Middle Passage was beset with appalling experiences for the slaves and White crews in crossing the Atlantic Ocean. There were the dangers of crew and slave mutinies, shipwreck, storms, calms, shortage of water and food, epidemic disease and death. Captives were packed into the lower decks 'like books on a shelf', according to a contemporary observer. The overcrowded ships were notorious for their unsanitary conditions and constant danger of disease and death. Those who died were thrown overboard, and some slaves committed suicide by jumping into the sea and by refusing to eat. On many voyages the coasting phase of the Middle Passage presented dangers approaching in severity those encountered on the ocean crossing. Tropical diseases might take off so many White crew members that slaves met with little resistance in winning their freedom. At the same time, mutineers on coasting vessels were sometimes aided by shore-based Africans in their struggle for freedom. It was an axiom that the dangers of slave resistance and rebellion, as was also the case with morbidity and mortality, escalated with the length of the stay on the coast.[15]

Many captains of slave ships believed that the time of embarkation was the most dangerous phase of the triangular voyage. They noted that the enslaved captives resisted their forced removal from their homeland, refusing to board the canoes and boats that carried them from shore to ship. As a consequence, many of the recalcitrant captives were severely beaten. Captain Thomas Phillips of the *Hannibal* described the embarkation of a group of captives he had purchased at Whydah on the slave coast in 1693 as follows:

> The negroes are so wilful and loth to leave their own country, that they have often leap'd out of the canoes, boats and ships, into the sea, and kept under water till they were drowned, to avoid being taken up and saved by our own boats, which pursued them, they having a more dreadful apprehension of Barbados than we can of hell . . . We have likewise seen divers of them eaten by the sharks, of which a prodigious number kept about the ships in this place, and I have been told will follow her hence to Barbados, for the dead negroes that are thrown overboard in the passage.[16]

'There are fairly detailed accounts of 55 mutinies on slavers from 1699 to 1845', according to Daniel P. Mannix and Malcolm Cowley, 'not to mention passing references to more than a hundred others'.[17] Drawing chiefly on the magisterial four-volume collection of documents on the slave trade which was edited and compiled by Elizabeth Donnan, the author of this study has counted 64 plots and mutinies on English and North American slave vessels from 1693 to 1807, or about one every other year. Ten of these incidents occurred in the Gambia river, nine each on the Gold Coast and Sierra Leone, six are designated 'Coast of Africa' or 'Coast of Guinea', five each at Bonny, Middle Passage, and West Indies; and 15 left no record of the trading station or area in Africa where they obtained slaves.[18]

The changing organisation of the transatlantic slave trade affected the frequency and impact of slave plots and mutinies. During the period 1663–92 the English trade with West Africa was chiefly in the hands of chartered companies that were granted a legal monopoly to buy and sell slaves. By building forts and castles and keeping supplies of slaves on hand, they were able to supply the vessels engaged in the trade at fairly short notice, especially during periods of warfare in Africa when captives were plentiful. However, after the Royal African Company's monopoly was rescinded in 1692, large numbers of free traders or interlopers entered the African trade. Donnan says there is little question but that mutinies 'became much more common as the trade fell into the hands of independent traders, who probably were more careless in their supervision of the Negroes, and who carried smaller crews in comparison with the size of their cargoes than had the company'.[19]

Slave trade records show that elaborate precautions were taken to prevent mutinies, although they were not always enforced sufficiently to avoid fatal consequences. There was a mutiny on the *Don Carlos* of London, James Barbot master, which departed from the Congo river for Jamaica on 1 January 1701. About 5 leagues distant from the departure point the slaves broke off their shackles and armed with knives and clubs, murdered one of the crew and wounded five others. Twenty-seven or twenty-eight slaves were either killed or jumped overboard and drowned. The mutiny broke out despite such precautions as 'narrowly searching every corner between decks, to see whether they have not found means, to gather any piece of iron, or wood, or knives, about the ship'. On 7 October 1725 the Bristol owner of the slaver *Dispatch* issued written instructions to Captain William Barry, part of which read as follows:

> So soon as you begin to slave let your knetting [or fence on the main deck] be fix'd breast high fore and aft and so keep 'em shackled and hand Bolted fearing their rising or leaping Overboard, to prevent which let always a Constant and Carefull watch be appointed to which must give the strictest Charge for the preservation of their Own Lives, as well as yours and on which the Voyage depends, which per

sleeping on their Watch has often been fatal and many a good Voyage (which otherwise might been made) entirely ruin'd.[20]

The Gold Coast was a major scene of European activity in West Africa, first attracting traders to its supplies of gold and later chattel slaves. 'By the early years of the eighteenth century', writes J.D. Fage, 'there were on the Gold Coast about twenty-five major stone or brick-built forts, together with about the same number of trading posts or "lodges", crammed together on about 250 miles of coastline'. These forts and trading posts were possessed by English, Dutch, French, Danish and Brandenburgers, of which the English held the greater number. The Europeans who occupied these coastal trading centres changed the lives of the African peoples who surrounded them and indirectly the larger region beyond. In contrast with the slaves who travelled great distances to Senegambia river ports on the Upper Guinea coast, K.G. Davies says that those brought to the Gold Coast 'seem to have come mostly from within three or four hundred miles of the sea'.[21]

Two accounts of mutinies at or near the Gold Coast merit brief attention. On 25 September 1729 the *Boston News Letter* learned by way of Antigua that the *Clare* galley, Captain Murrell master, after completing her cargo of slaves and departing from the coast of Guinea for South Carolina, had a mutiny on board. The slaves rose and made themselves 'Masters of the Gunpowder and Fire Arms'. The captain and ship's crew took to the longboat and got ashore near Cape Coast Castle. 'The Negroes ran the Ship on Shore, within a few leagues of the said Castle, and made their escape'. Another mutiny was reported in the *Boston News Letter* of 7 May 1747. It took place on a Rhode Island vessel which was off Cape Coast Castle with a number of slaves and a considerable quantity of gold dust. The slaves found an opportunity and killed the captain and all the crew except for two mates who jumped overboard and swam ashore and saved their lives. What became of the vessel and the slaves was not mentioned in the news item.[22]

That the mutinies on the Gold Coast may have reached an epidemic scale in the early 1730s is suggested by the report of a sloop belonging to Glasgow in which the mate and most of the crew were killed when the slaves rebelled. The report went on to say:

Several of our [Bristol] Ships lately come from the [Gold] Coast have met with dangerous Repulses by the Negroes rising, to quell whom the Sailors were obliged to kill several, and some of them lost their Lives in the Expedient; a Sickness too in that climate has been very fatal to some of our Ships' Companies, and carried off many. What with the Negroes rising, and other Disappointments, in the late Voyages thither, have occasioned a great reducement in our Merchant's Gains.[23]

Captain William Snelgrave was the author of *A New Account of Some Parts of Guinea and the Slave Trade*. His narrative is concerned chiefly with events in 1719, 1726–7 and 1729–30. He made his first voyage to Africa in 1704 as purser on board the *Eagle Galley*, of London, commanded by his father. Later, as captain of numerous slave ships, he said he made it his principal care to have the African captives kindly used, to strictly charge his White crew to treat them with humanity and tenderness, which he claimed had the effect of keeping them from mutinying and preserving them in health. The sturdy men slaves were coupled together with irons at the time of their purchase, but the women and children were unfettered. Soon after sailing from the coast all the men were unfettered. Furthermore:

> They are fed twice a day, and are allowed in fair Weather to come on Deck at seven a Clock in the Morning, and to remain there, if they think proper, till Sun setting. Every Monday Morning they are served with Pipes and Tobacco, which they are very fond of. The men *Negroes* lodge separate from the Women and Children: and the places where they all lye are cleaned every day, some White Men being appointed to see them do it.[24]

Snelgrave devoted a section of his book to the slave mutinies that occurred on board the Guinea vessels to which he was attached. The first occurred in 1704 at Old Calabar, a leading slave trading port to the east of the Niger Delta. Some 400 captives were on board but the crew on duty was reduced to only ten because of deaths, sickness and fetching wood fuel from the shore. 'All the circumstances put the *Negroes* on consulting how to mutiny', he wrote, 'which they did at four a clock in the Afternoon, just as they went to Supper'. Some of the men slaves grabbed the chief mate and attempted to throw him overboard, but they were attacked by the sentries who were on duty at the time. Upon examination it was found that 'there were not above twenty Men Slaves concerned in this Mutiny, and the two Ringleaders were missing, having, it seems, jumped overboard as soon as they found their Project defeated, and drowned'. A slave who was shot by a sentry was cured by the surgeon, and another slave who intervened to save Snelgrave's father who took part in the altercation was given his freedom.[25]

Snelgrave said he had been on several voyages when there had been no attempt made by the slaves to mutiny. He believed it was owing chiefly to the kind usage accorded the slaves and his officers' care in keeping a strict watch. On the other hand, he had met with 'stout, stubborn People amongst them, who are never to be made easy'. They were generally some of the Akan-speaking Coromantees, a nation of the Gold Coast. In the Caribbean these people were regarded as the most intransigent, most feared and admired of all Africans who were brought to the Americas in chains. They were said to be grateful and obedient to a kind owner for whom they were diligent workers, but implacably revengeful when ill treated. They generally led the not infrequent servile revolts in the islands.[26]

'The danger of mutiny was greatest', write Mannix and Cowley, 'when all the slaves on board belonged to a single tribe, especially if it was one of the warlike tribes from the Gold Coast'.[27] Snelgrave told of a Coromantee-led mutiny in 1721. He and his officers had purchased a 'good many' of these people and were obliged to secure them very well in irons and watch them closely. Nevertheless, they mutinied despite little prospect of succeeding. There were near 500 captives on board, of whom 300 were men. To guard them there were 40 officers and men, all in health. After securing the men slaves below deck they began to make a 'great noise'. Snelgrave bid them to be quiet. After quieting down, he asked, 'What had induced them to mutiny?' whereupon they answered by way of his translator that Snelgrave 'was a great Rogue to buy them, in order to carry them away from their own Country, and that they were resolved to regain their Liberty, if possible'. Snelgrave then explained that if they had gained their liberty by escaping on shore, they would only be recaptured by their countrymen and sold back into slavery. They seemed convinced by this argument and begged forgiveness, promising for the future to be obedient. But several days later they were discovered to be plotting again, proposing to procure an axe to cut the line securing the ship to the anchor. Again they were foiled without serious repercussions. He was happy the affair ended peacefully, for he realised that 'these People are the stoutest and most sensible *Negroes* on the Coast: Neither are they so weak as to imagine as others do, that we buy them to eat them, being satisfied we carry them to work on our Plantations, as they do in their own Country'.[28]

Evidence from agents, sources, traders

Senegambia is a geographical term for the region between the Senegal and Gambia rivers on the west coast of Africa. In the eighteenth century and afterwards the territory was chiefly dominated by the French, but the British held a narrow strip of land along the Gambia which is the only river of Africa navigable by ocean vessels at all seasons for more than 200 miles from its mouth. In Senegambia, which is part of the Upper Guinea Coast, the slave trade was both an overland and a riverine trade, penetrating into the Western Sudan, part of what is today the country of Mali. The Portuguese were the first Europeans to arrive on the Upper Guinea Coast in the mid-fifteenth century, at a time when the Mohammedan Mandigas were well established in the region as traders in gold, ivory and increasingly by African slaves.[29]

The Gambia river and adjacent lands attracted English explorers and traders in the latter part of Elizabeth I's reign and under James I and Charles I. Responding to the demand for African slaves to grow tobacco and sugar canes in the North American and Caribbean colonies, the Restoration government of Charles II chartered the Company of Royal Adventurers Trading to Africa in 1663, to be succeeded in 1672 by the Royal African Company. Davies, historian of this company, notes that it was not enough for European traders to wait at the mouths of the Gambia and Senegal rivers for trade to come to them. Instead, 'small outposts were settled at strategic points, especially up-river. At each, one or two English factors with the help of a few slaves were stationed with a supply of trading goods periodically replenished from the base' at James Fort on the island by the same name at the mouth of the Gambia river.[30]

Francis Moore was the Royal African Company's agent based at James Fort from 1730 to 1734. He travelled up and down the Gambia, supervising the 13 English factors along the river, expediting supplies of trade goods and organising the shipment of slaves to overseas markets. In his *Travels into the Inland Parts of Africa*, Moore wrote of the risks of the river trade, noting that

> for all the time a slave ship was delayed in completing a cargo it ran the Hazard of the Sickness and Rebellion of those Slaves he already has, they being apter to rise in a Harbor than when out at Sea; since if they once get Masters of the Ship, in the River, their Escape to Shore is almost certain, by running the Ship aground; but at Sea it is otherwise, for they must have the Assistance of the White men, or perish.[31]

Moore knew of several instances of ships that were lost because most of the crew had been sick or on shore and consequently unable to guard the slaves. As a case in point, on 4 September 1742, the slaves of the *Mary Galley*, of London, then in the Gambia river, rose in rebellion, murdered the ship's crew and confined the captain and mate in the cabin for 27 days before they made their escape. The ship was driven ashore, plundered and destroyed.

Other reports of mutinies in the Gambia river indicate it was a dangerous place to obtain slaves. In July 1759 it was reported that the *Snow Perfect*, Captain William Potter master, of Liverpool, was 'cut off by the Negroes in the River Gambia and every Man on board murdered; and the vessel lost'. Later in the same year there was an account of a sloop commanded by Captain Ingledieu that was 'slaving up the River Gambia'. It was attacked from the shore by about 80 Africans. Finding himself desperately wounded and likely to be overcome and 'fall into the Hands of such merciless Wretches', the Captain 'discharged a Pistol into the Magazine, and blew her up, himself and every Soul on Board perished'.[32]

The Portuguese, who were the first Europeans to reach the Sierra Leone river in 1460, penetrated inland regions and established trading stations on the coast and up the many rivers and creeks between the Senegal and Sierra Leone rivers. With the growth of the transatlantic slave trade, independent traders were attracted to the many coastal inlets and offshore islands which offered secluded anchorages for their ships. No European nation dominated the Sierra Leone region by means of a monopolistic trading company. Instead, as Fage observes, 'this part of the Gambia coast was a happy hunting ground for slave traders of many nations'.[33] They conducted what can be called a coasting and boating trade, moving from one anchorage to another and sending out boats manned by crew members and carrying trade goods to purchase slaves from European and mulatto factors and African village headmen.

John Atkins was a surgeon in the Royal Navy who was attached to the warships *Swallow* and *Weymouth* on a voyage to Africa, Brazil and the West Indies. While anchored at Sierra Leone, he went ashore to view the purchase of slaves. His attention was drawn to a slave called 'Captain Tomba' who 'seemed to disdain his Fellow-Slaves for their Readiness to be examined . . . and refused to rise and stretch out his Limbs, as the Master commanded'. For this behaviour Captain Tomba was whipped unmercifully, which he suffered with remarkable courage. On board the ship which purchased him, Captain Tomba 'combined with three or four of the stoutest of his Country-Men to kill the Ship's Company, and attempt their Escape, while they had a Shore to fly to'. They nearly succeeded when they found the White men on watch asleep, but two of the latter awakened in time to spread the alarm and the mutiny was suppressed. Three of the rebel slaves were sentenced to cruel deaths and two others, one of whom was Captain Tomba, were whipped and scarified, which punishment was customarily meted out to 'Rogues of Dignity'. A woman who took part in the conspiracy was 'hoisted up by the Thumbs, whipp'd, and slashed with Knives, before the other Slaves till she died'.[34]

The story of John Newton, the slave trader who became an Anglican divine, is encapsulated in the lyrics of the famous hymn he wrote in later life:

Amazing grace! how sweet the sound!
that saved a wretch like me;
I once was lost but now am found;
Was blind, but now I see.

Newton was born in London in 1725, the son of a master of a ship in the Mediterranean trade. His mother, who gave him some religious training, died in 1732. Having had little education, he went to sea with his father from 1737 to 1742. He was impressed on board a naval vessel in 1743, and soon after deserted, was captured and degraded from the rank of midshipman to common sailor. Subsequently he was transferred to a slave ship which took him to the coast of Sierra Leone. In the years from 1748 to 1754 he made four voyages from England to West Africa and the British Caribbean and North America, the first as mate and the other three as master.[35]

In later years Newton recalled that he was led from degrading debauchery and free thinking to conversion to Christianity as a result of the ordeal of a voyage when he feared for his life. He devoted his leisure time to a rigorous programme of self-education, mastering Latin, studying Greek and Hebrew and the Bible and adopting a Calvinistic view of theology. On the ships he commanded he suppressed swearing and profligacy, and read the Liturgy twice on Sunday with the crew. In 1764 he became an Anglican priest and was appointed curate of the parish of Olney, Buckinghamshire, where he was a close friend of the poet William Cowper, with whom he collaborated in publishing the *Olney Hymns*. From 1780 until his death in 1807, Newton was Rector of St Mary Woolnoth Church in London, alongside the Bank of England in the heart of the metropolis. Newton attracted large congregations and his church was the centre of a widespread evangelical movement. According to Herbert Lockyer, 'His piety, zeal, warm heart and candour gained him the friendship of a reformer like William Wilberforce, who, through Newton's influence came to abolish slavery'.[36]

Slave resistance and rebellion are topics which Newton described and analysed in his writings and testimony. Appearing before a committee of the House of Commons in 1790, he was asked, 'Were the Men Slaves in general fettered during the Middle Passage in your voyages?' He replied, 'Always; I never put them out of irons till we saw the land in the West Indies'. To the question, 'Did the precaution appear to be necessary for the security of the ship?', he answered, 'I think the ship would not have been safe without it; it was the universal custom at that time'. Furthermore, he was asked, 'Did the Slaves ever plot, or attempt to rise in your vessel?' He answered, 'I remember two or three plots, but they were happily discovered in time, in the ships that I was master of; I was mate of a ship in which there was an insurrection where one White Man was killed, and three or four of the Negroes'.[37]

One of the plots occurred on the voyage of the *Duke of Argyle* which got underway from Liverpool to the coast of Africa on 20 August 1750. Newton recorded in his *Journal* on 8 October that the carpenter had marked off the slaves' rooms or compartments below the deck and begun to build the bulkheads to separate the sexes. The gunner was said to be making cartridges for the carriage and swivel guns. Two months later he noted that four swivel blunderbusses had been installed in the 'barricado', which, with the two carriage guns, Newton believed, would 'make a formidable appearance on the main deck, and will, I hope be sufficient to intimidate the slaves from any thoughts of an insurrection'.[38]

However, the barriers and guns failed to intimidate the slaves. The plot was discovered on 20 May 1751, when the *Duke of Argyle* was three days out of the Sierra Leone river with 174 slaves bound for Antigua in the British Caribbean. A young slave had been let out of irons partly because of a large ulcer and partly for his seeming good behaviour. He had given the slaves below deck a large marling spike. Newton later discovered that 'near 20 of them had broke their irons' and that the plot was 'exceedingly well laid, and had they been let alone an hour longer, must have occasioned us a good deal of trouble and damage'. By the afternoon of 27 May all the men's irons had been secured again and six of the ringleaders had been punished.[39]

Another plot was discovered on the snow *African* which Newton commanded. He sailed from Liverpool on 30 June 1752 to the windward coast of Africa in company with the *Adlington*, another slaver. The *African* was anchored off Sierra Leone on 11 December 1752 when Newton recorded in his *Journal*:

> By the favour of Divine Providence made a timely discovery to-day that the slaves were forming a plot for an insurrection. Surprised 2 of them attempting to get off their irons, and upon farther search in their rooms, upon the information of 3 of the boys, found some knives, stones, shot, etc., and a cold chisel. Upon inquiry there appeared 8 principally concerned to move in projecting the mischief and 4 boys in supplying them with the above instruments. Put the boys in irons and slightly in the thumbscrews to urge them to full confession.

The following morning Newton examined the men slaves and punished six of the principals, of whom four were put in collars.[40]

Although no plots or insurrections occurred on the third voyage which Newton commanded, the same was not true of other slavers on the coast of Africa. Going ashore in Sierra Leone on 2 December 1753, he learned that the snow *Racehorse* from Liverpool had been cut off and recovered from the native Susas. Five days later he was informed that the *Adventure*, of London, which had been near five months on the coast had been run on shore by the slaves in an insurrection and totally lost. One member of the crew was killed and another wounded.[41]

In a few cases the slaves resorted to poisoning and passive resistance on the slavers Newton commanded. On his first voyage he was alarmed to learn that some of the men slaves had found means to poison the water in casks on the deck. This, however, was a false alarm. From further investigation he learned that they had 'only conveyed some of their country fetishes, as they call them' into the casks with the intention 'to charm us to death'. Newton noted that when crew members went ashore and became sexually involved with native women, they were prone to quarrel with the latter's menfolk, and 'if not killed on the spot, they were frequently poisoned'. Only one case of a slave committing suicide by jumping overboard is recorded, but since the reprinted version of Newton's *Journal* is abridged, it is possible that there were other cases of this form of passive resistance.[42]

In later life Newton sought to instruct the public about the causes and consequences of slave insurrections in his pamphlet, *Thoughts Upon the African Slave Trade*. He observed that about two-thirds of a cargo of slaves were males. When 150 or 200 stout men, torn from their native land, many of whom had never seen the sea, much less a ship, till a short space before they had embarked, who had, probably, the same natural prejudice against a White man, as we have against a black; and who often brought with them an apprehension they are bought to be eaten, they could not be expected to tamely resign themselves to their situation. He wrote that it was 'always taken for granted, that they will attempt to gain their liberty if possible. Accordingly, as we dare not trust them, we receive them on board, from the first as enemies; and, before their number exceeds, perhaps, ten or fifteen, they are all put in irons'. Insurrections, Newton believed, were always premeditated:

> for the men slaves are not easily reconciled to their confinement and treatment; and, if attempted, they are seldom suppressed without considerable loss; and sometimes they succeed, to the destruction of the whole ship's company at once. Seldom a year passes, but we hear of one or more such catastrophes; and we likewise hear, sometimes of Whites and Blacks involved, in one moment, in one common ruin, by the gunpowder taking fire, and blowing up the ship.[43]

Journey to the Caribbean

Once the complement of slaves was filled, the vessel with its human cargo weighed anchor and sailed from the coast of Africa. Some captains made a point of sailing at night when the slaves were below deck and unable to see their homeland for the last time on their one-way forced migration to the Americas. Some captains removed the shackles and chains from all slaves after getting out of sight of land, but others kept the men in irons the entire voyage, while the women and young children remained free of fetters. The slaves' alleged ignorance of navigation was regarded by some captains as a safeguard against mutinies on the high seas. However, John Atkins noted that examples of risings and killing a ship's company were not wanting as a result of the slaves' fear of being eaten by their new masters in America. Added to the slaves' use of force on vessels at sea was the passive resistance which took the form of suicide, self-starvation and poisoning.[44]

Two case studies of violent and non-violent resistance on the Middle Passage merit brief mention. Captain John Bruce wrote that his ship was at sea after slaving at the Gambia river, Goree and Sierra Leone. One night he learned that an attempt was made by some of the men slaves to remove their shackles. He ordered an officer to go down and examine them. Finding 'two stout men' had got their irons off their feet, he handcuffed them and sent them on deck. They were ordered to the other side of the deck while a further search was made below. But a few minutes afterwards, to the captain's great surprise, 'they plunged into the sea together, and were drowned, notwithstanding all possible means were used to save them'.[45]

On 14 February 1785 the *New York Packet* reported a catastrophe on a schooner that had sailed from Newport, Rhode Island to the coast of Africa. On the return it was met at sea by a vessel bound for Bristol, England, 'without Sails, had only 15 negroes on board and those in a very emaciated and wretched condition, having doubtless been long at sea. The negroes it is supposed had rose and murdered the Captain and Crew; after which many of the blacks must have died. Those found on board were carried into Bristol'.[46]

The case of the schooner *Nancy* involved several slave risings, widespread sickness among crew members and condemnation of the ship by officials in the West Indies. In June 1807 the *Nancy* had sailed from Charleston, South Carolina, to the Senegal river and purchased a cargo of about 80 slaves. Four or five days after departing the Senegal the slaves rose while they were being fed. Several of them seized the captain but were forced to release him and be driven below the main deck by the mate and crew members with small arms. By the time the *Nancy* reached the British Caribbean all but two of the crew were disabled by sickness, and outside assistance to prevent further mutiny was imperative. A British tender put an officer and five men on board and ordered the *Nancy* into the British island colony of Tortola. There the schooner was 'condemned to His Majesty, pursuant to the Act of Parliament made for abolishing the Slave Trade'. Having been landed on British soil, the slaves were accordingly restored to their freedom.[47]

Arrival and sale

Acts of resistance persisted until the slavers from Africa arrived in the harbours of the Caribbean islands. Writing from the British sugar island of St Kitts on 7 April 1737, Captain Japhet Bird of the *Prince of Orange*, of Bristol, noted, 'At our Arrival here, I thought all our Troubles were over, but on the contrary I might say that Dangers rest on the Borders of Security'. Three weeks previously Bird had discovered a great deal of discontent among the slaves on his ship. The discontent continued until the afternoon of 16 March, 'when to our great Amazement above a hundred Men Slaves jump'd over board, and it was with great Difficulty we sav'd so many as we did'. Out of the whole, the loss was 33 'of as good Men Slaves as we had on board, who would not endeavour to save themselves but resolv'd to die, and sunk directly down'. Many more were taken up almost drowned and later some of them died. Captain Bird learned after the calamity that one of the victim's countrymen in Africa had come on board and in a joking manner had told the slaves they were first to have their eyes put out, and then to be eaten, 'with a great many other nonsensical Falsities'.[48]

As a slave ship came in sight of land in the Caribbean the captives were prepared for sale by being cleaned and oiled to hide any scars or skin blemishes. The cargo was advertised in a local newspaper, specifying the number of slaves imported, the country or countries of origin and day of sale. One method of sale called the 'scramble' had the planters come on board the vessel and physically mingle with the slaves and select those to be purchased. The planter-historian Bryan Edwards wrote that 'it frequently happened, when slave ships were scarce, that such crowds of people went on board and began so disgraceful a scramble, as to terrify the poor ignorant Africans with the notion that they were seized on by a herd of cannibals, and speedily to be devoured'. To obviate these noisy, greedy and disgraceful proceedings, the legislature of Jamaica enacted that the sales be conducted on shore and that care be taken not to separate different branches of the same African families.[49]

Having purchased a parcel of slaves, the planter or his overseer escorted them to the plantation which was to become their home and workplace. Here they were branded with their owner's initials. They underwent what was called the 'seasoning', a period of acclimatisation and adjustment to a life of forced labour. One doctor-planter observed that not less than one-quarter of the slaves exported from the coast of Africa to the British Caribbean died within three or four years from their arrival. He enumerated the causes of death, consisting of diseases acquired on the Middle Passage, change of climate, poor diet, hard labour, severe treatment, suicide and running away. Severity in the form of harsh rebukes, threats and chastisements by White overseers was said to create disgust and terror, causing some slaves to commit suicide and others to run away.[50]

Approximately 2,400,000 African slaves were imported into the British Caribbean from 1627 to 1807, of whom about four-fifths were retained for labour in the islands. Numerous contemporary and modern writers have testified to the inability of the slave population to reproduce itself, with the consequent need for new slaves from Africa to keep up the labour force. John Newton, who had first-hand knowledge of slavery on both sides of the Atlantic, contended that slavery was much milder in Africa where the people had 'no land in high cultivation, like our West India plantations, and therefore no call for that excessive, unintermitted labour which exhausts our slaves; so on the other hand, no man is permitted to draw blood even from a slave'. High mortality among plantation slaves resulted from despondence, disease, accidents, malnutrition, and the harsh labour regimen. On the other hand, before the anti-slavery movement the planters seldom encouraged family life and slave reproduction, finding it cheaper to buy than to breed. It is true that British Caribbean slavery became less harsh during the second half of the eighteenth century, but even then it was only in the island of Barbados that the slave population achieved a condition of natural increase by the second decade of the nineteenth century.[51]

Abolition of the British slave trade was achieved by an Act of Parliament in 1807, after long years of agitation by abolitionists in public meetings, sermons, pamphlets, petitions, and debates in Parliament. In recent decades there has been a vigorous new debate whether abolition was achieved by outside or inside organisation and action, that is, agitation by religious, humanitarian, and political leaders in Britain, or by the resistance and rebellion of the slaves in the British Caribbean. In fact, both outside and inside forces contributed to the final victory, however, the role of the slaves has attracted growing interest and stimulated much scholarly endeavour. In his study of resistance to slavery in the British Caribbean, Michael Craton observes that the African contribution to African-Caribbean slave resistance was both pervasive and complex; that there were common elements in responses to enslavement in Africa, the Middle Passage, and the Caribbean. Both African and African-Caribbean Indians responded to enslavement by such non-violent forms of resistance as committing suicide, running away, and malingering. Slaves on shipboard mutinied when the captain and most of the crew were sick or on shore visits, much like their counterparts on the understaffed sugar plantations of absentee proprietors. Ringleaders of failed maritime mutinies frequently resorted to suicide, as did plantation slaves in the British Caribbean. Ships at anchor off the coast or in the rivers of West Africa were sometimes destroyed by slaves who rose up and cut the cables to run them aground, while plantation slaves frequently destroyed their masters' property, setting fire to cane fields and killing livestock. The Akan-speaking Coromantees, those 'stout, stubborn People' from the Gold Coast, were notable leaders of both maritime mutinies and slave revolts in the British Caribbean. To a considerable extent, it can be argued that instead of separating the people of West Africa and the Caribbean, the transatlantic slave trade served as a bridge to join together the oppressed peoples in common resistance to chattel slavery. Although resistance and rebellion seldom achieved the ends sought by their perpetrator, the very acts of flight and rising up in bloody rebellion were testimonies to the determination of the human spirit to triumph over adversity.[52]

Notes

1. E.D. Genovese, *From Rebellion to Revolution: Afro-American Slave Revolts in the Making of the Modern World* (New York: Vintage Books, 1979), pp. xxiii, 139–66.
2. Ibid.
3. D.D. Wax, 'Negro Resistance to the Early American Slave Trade', *Journal of Negro History*, Vol. LI, No. 1 (January 1966), pp. 1–15; W.D. Piersen, 'White Cannibals, Black Martyrs: Fear, Depression, and Religious Faith as Causes of Suicide Among New Slaves', *Journal of Negro History*, Vol. LXII, No. 2 (April 1977), pp. 147–59; W. McGowan, 'African Resistance to the Atlantic Slave Trade in West Africa', *Slavery and Abolition*, Vol. 11, No. 1 (May 1990), pp. 5–29; R. Rathbone, 'Some Thoughts on Resistance to Enslavement in Africa', *Slavery and Abolition*, Vol. 6, No. 3 (December 1985), pp. 3–22. See also D.P. Mannix and M. Cowley, *Black Cargoes: A History of the Atlantic Slave Trade, 1518–1865* (New York: Viking Press, 1962), pp. 108–111; James Walvin, *Black Ivory: A History of British Slavery* (London: Harper Collins, 1992), pp. 233–7.
4. J. Postma, 'Mortality in the Dutch Slave Trade, 1675–1795', in H.A. Gemery and J.S. Hogendorn, eds., *The Uncommon Market: Essays in the Economic History of the Atlantic Slave Trade* (New York: Academic Press, 1979), pp. 239–60.
5. W. Rodney, *West Africa and the Atlantic Slave Trade*, published for the Historical Association of Tanzania, Paper No. 2 (Nairobi, Kenya, 1969).
6. P. Edwards, ed., *Equiano's Travels: His Autobiography: The Interesting Narrative of the Life of Olaudah Equiano or Gustavus Vassa the African* (New York: Frederick A. Praeger, 1966; first published 1789), pp. x–xvii, 8–9, 15–16. There is now increasing debate on the authenticity of Equianos alleged African birth and his first-hand knowledge of capture in Africa and experience of the Middle Passage.
7. Ibid., pp. 17–24.
8. Ibid., pp. 25–30.

9.   Ibid., pp. 30–59.
10. M. Park, *Travels in the Interior of Africa*, (London: J.M. Dent & Sons, 1907), pp. 220–1.
11. P.D. Curtin, *Economic Change in Precolonial Africa: Senegambia in the Era of the Slave Trade* (Madison: University of Wisconsin Press, 1975), pp. 272–3.
12. Ibid., pp. 170–1, 273–4; Park, *Travels in the Interior of Africa*, pp. 252–5.
13. Park, *Travels in the Interior of Africa*, pp. 272–3.
14. A.W. Lawrence, *Trade Castles and Forts of West Africa* (Stanford, CA: Stanford University Press, 1964), pp. 86, 132, 158, 166, 185, 189–90, 222; McGowan, 'African Resistance to the Atlantic Slave Trade', pp. 17–18.
15. Postma, 'Mortality in the Dutch Slave Trade', pp. 241–2; Wax, 'Negro Resistance', pp. 4–8; R.B. Sheridan, *Doctors and Slaves: A Medical and Demographic History of Slavery in the British West Indies, 1680–1834* (Cambridge: Cambridge University Press, 1985), pp. 115–26.
16. McGowan, 'African Resistance', pp. 18–19; 'A Journal of a Voyage made in the Hannibal of London, Ann. 1693–1694', in E. Donnan, ed., *Documents Illustrative of the History of the Slave Trade to America, Vol. I: 1441–1700* (Washington, DC: Carnegie Institution of Washington, 1930), p. 402.
17. Mannix and Cowley, *Black Cargoes*, p. 111; J.A. Rawley, *The Transatlantic Slave Trade: A History* (New York, 1981), p. 299.
18. Donnan, *Documents*, I, II, III, IV. In his research on the British slave trade, 1785–1807, Stephen D. Behrendt finds that of 11,051 deaths of crew members in the Liverpool slave trade, 1785–1807, an estimated 146 were killed by slaves and that two (or perhaps three) were captains. See Behrendt, 'The Captains in the British Slave Trade from 1785 to 1807', *Transactions of the Historic Society of Lancashire and Cheshire*, 140 (1991), pp. 132–9; and 'The British Slave Trade, 1785–1807: Volume, Profitability, and Mortality', (unpublished PhD thesis, University of Wisconsin-Madison, 1993), p. 345. The author is indebted to him for supplying him with data and references for this chapter.
19. Donnan, *Documents*, II, 361, n. 17. K. G. Davies, *The Royal African Company* (London: Longmans, Green, 1957), pp. 38–46, 179–80, 226–7;
20. 'James Barbot's Voyage', Donnan, *Documents*, I, pp. 451–8; 'Instructions to Captain William Barry', ibid., II, pp. 327–8.
21. J.D. Fage, *A History of West Africa* (Cambridge: Cambridge University Press, 1969), pp. 74–5; Davies, *Royal African Company*, pp. 226–8.
22. 'News Items Relating to the Slave Trade, 1729', Donnan, *Documents*, IV, p. 274; 'Notices of Sales, 1739–1741', ibid., III, p. 51, n.4.
23. *Boston News Letter*, 9 September 1731, quoted in Donnan, *Documents*, II, p. 431, n.l.

24. W. Snelgrave, *A New Account of Some Parts of Guinea and the Slave Trade* (London, Frank Cass, 1971; first published 1734), pp. 162–4.

25. Ibid., pp. 165–8; A.J.H. Latham, *Old Calabar 1600–1891: The Impact of the International Economy Upon a Traditional Society* (Oxford: Clarendon Press, 1973), pp. 17–30.

26. Snelgrave, *New Account of Guinea*, p. 168; M. Schuler, 'Akan Slave Rebellions in the British Caribbean', *Savacou*, Vol. 1, No. 1 (June 1970, published in Jamaica); M. Craton, *Testing the Chains: Resistance to Slavery in the British West Indies* (Ithaca, New York: Cornell University Press, 1982), pp. 25, 75–8, 96, 99–104.

27. Mannix and Cowley, *Black Cargoes*.

28. Snelgrave, *New Account of Guinea*, pp. 168–72.

29. Rodney, *A History of the Upper Guinea Coast 1545–1800* (Oxford: Clarendon Press, 1970), pp. 1–18; Curtin, *Economic Change in Precolonial Africa*, pp. 59–68.

30. Davies, *Royal African Company*, pp. 38–46, 216–22.

31. F. Moore, *Travels into the Inland Parts of Africa* (London, 1734), reprinted in Donnan, *Documents*, II, pp. 402–12; *South Carolina Gazette*, 24 October 1743; Donnan, *Documents*, IV, p. 296.

32. 'News Items Relating to the Slave Trade, 1759', Donnan, *Documents*, IV, p. 374.

33. Fage, *History of West Africa*, pp. 52–8, 72–3; A. Falconbridge, *An Account of the Slave Trade on the Coast of Africa* (London, 1788), p. 18; Mannix and Cowley, *Black Cargoes*, pp. 75–7.

34. J. Atkins, *A Voyage to Guinea, Brazil, and the West Indies in His Majesty's Ships, the Swallow and Weymouth* (London, Frank Cass, 1970; first published 1735), pp. 41–2, 71–3.

35. L. Stephen, ed., *The Dictionary of National Biography* (Oxford, Oxford University Press 1917), Vol. XIV, pp. 395–8.

36. Ibid., pp. 395–8; *Out of the Depths; The Autobiography of John Newton*, introduction by Herbert Lockyer (New Canaan, CT: 1981); B. Martin, *John Newton: a Biography* (London: William Heinemann, 1950).

37. *British Parliamentary Papers*, 1790-91, XXIX (698), 'Report from the Select Committee of the House of Commons on the Slave Trade; with Minutes of Evidence', evidence of John Newton, pp. 142–4.

38. J. Newton, *The Journal of a Slave Trader 1750-1754*, ed. with an introduction by B. Martin and M. Spurrell (London: Epworth Press, 1962), pp. 10, 22.

39. Ibid., pp. 54–5.

40. Ibid., p. 71.

41. Ibid., pp. 87–8.

42. Ibid., pp. 56, 75, 101.

43. J. Newton, *Thoughts Upon the African Slave Trade* (London, 1788), included in Martin and Spurrell, eds., *Journal of a Slave Trader*, pp. 102–13.

44. Atkins, *Voyage to Guinea, Brazil*, pp. 175–6.

45. A. Benezet, *Some Historical Account of Guinea* (London, Frank Cass, 1968; first published 1771), pp. 129–31.

46. 'Dr. Samuel Hopkins to Moses Brown, 1787', Donnan, *Documents*, III, p. 341, n. 6.

47. 'The Case of the Nancy, 1807', ibid., III, pp. 394–9.

48. 'Letter on Board the Prince of Orange of Bristol', ibid., II, pp. 460–1.

49. B. Edwards, *The History, Civil and Commercial, of the British Colonies in the West Indies* (Dublin, 1793), Vol. II, pp. 115–16.

50. [Dr David Collins], *Practical Rules for the Management and Medical Treatment of Negro Slaves, in the Sugar Colonies* (London, 1803), pp. 44–52; O. Patterson, *Sociology of Slavery: An Analysis of the origin, development and Structure of Negro Slave Society in Jamaica* (London: McGibbon and Kee; reprinted, Rutherford, NJ: Fairliegh Dickinson University Press, 1969), pp. 262–71.

51. Rawley, *Transatlantic Slave Trade*, pp. 427–34; R.B. Sheridan, 'Africa and the Caribbean in the Atlantic Slave Trade', *American Historical Review*, Vol. 77, No. 1 (February 1972), pp. 17–35; Newton, *Thoughts Upon the African Slave Trade*, in Martin and Spurrell, eds., *Journal of a Slave Trader*, pp. 107–8.

52. Craton, *Testing the Chains*, pp. 23–8; B.W. Higman, *Slave Populations of the British Caribbean 1807–1834* (Baltimore: The Johns Hopkins University Press 1984), pp. 72–77, 100, 115–16, 303–4.

'Deportees in Nova Scotia'

The Jamaican Maroons, 1796–1800

ALLISTER HINDS

Although the history of the Maroon War of 1795–6 is well documented,[1] the experiences of the Maroons who were deported to Nova Scotia at the end of the war, and the circumstances which led to their removal from that province to Sierra Leone, are yet to be adequately addressed. Only R.C. Dallas and Mavis Campbell have considered these issues to date. However, despite the usefulness of their work, the former underestimates the role of the Maroons in the events which led to their removal from Nova Scotia, while the latter is a documentary history. This chapter attempts to help fill this void in the Maroon historiography by examining the contribution of the Jamaican House of Assembly, Governor Wentworth and others in Nova Scotia and the Maroons themselves, to the circumstances which culminated in the decision to move the Maroons from Nova Scotia to Sierra Leone.

At the end of the Maroon War of 1795–6 a treaty was signed by General Walpole, commander of the British forces during the war, and Colonel Montague James, chief of the Maroons. This treaty was ratified by the Jamaican House of Assembly on 28 December 1796. According to the terms of the treaty the Maroons were to: seek His Majesty's pardon; settle on lands deemed appropriate by the Governor's Council; and finally, agree to give up all runaway slaves. There was also a secret clause in the treaty in which

Walpole assured the Maroons who surrendered that they would not be deported from Jamaica. Walpole told Governor Balcarres: 'I was obliged to accede on my oath, I promised a secret article that they [the Maroons] should not be sent off the island'.[2] Having made this commitment on 24 December 1796 Walpole told Balcarres: 'if I might give you an opinion, it should be that they [the Maroons] should be settled near Spanish Town, or some other of the large towns in the lowlands, the access to spirits will soon decrease their numbers and destroy that large constitution which is nourished by an healthy mountainous situation'.[3] Walpole had clearly expected Balcarres to honour the commitment he had made to the Maroons.

But as Campbell points out, Balcarres had no doubt whatever over the policy to be pursued with respect to the Maroons who surrendered.[4] He gave them a three-day ultimatum to comply with the terms set out in the treaty, a deadline which was impossible for them to meet, and subsequently used their non-compliance as a justification for deporting them. Balcarres' policy on deportation was endorsed by the Colonial Office through the colonial secretary, the Duke of Portland,[5] and some members of the Jamaican House of Assembly.

The official decision to deport the Maroons was endorsed by a joint committee of the House of Assembly and Council[6] which was set up by Balcarres to look into the 'disposal' of the Maroons. This committee recommended the following: that the 31 Maroons who surrendered at Vaughnsfield under the proclamation of 8 August 1795, together with those who surrendered between 1 January 1796 and 10 March 1796 should be deported to a country in which they would be free. It added, that this was to 'secure the island against the danger of their return'. It noted also that the cost of their journey and their maintenance should be at public expense for a reasonable time after their arrival at their destination.[7] Despite the machinations of Balcarres, it is clear that the Maroons were deported because the imperial and colonial authorities felt that they constituted a threat to the security of the island. Although this view was no doubt reinforced by the ongoing rebellion in neighbouring St Domingue, it was not unanimous. When the report of the joint committee was presented to the House of Assembly for its approval on 27 April 1796, 21 members were in favour of its recommendations and 13 were opposed.[8]

Before the Maroons were deported from Jamaica two possible destinations for settling them were seriously considered by the House of Assembly, Sierra

Leone and Nova Scotia. According to Jamaica's agent in London, Robert Sewell,

> it was at first conceived that the coast of Africa was (on account of its general climate) a suitable situation for them, and I understand some application was made in that respect to the Sierra Leone and African Companies, neither of which were disposed to admit them, till at length the former intimated they were not averse to receive them provided that they were sent in different periods, from time to time, in small numbers, or a few families at a time, but not all at once.[9]

The ambivalence of the Sierra Leone and African Companies was hardly surprising. The application to settle the Maroons was received at a time when the publication of new marriage laws in Sierra Leone had triggered violent reaction from the settlers in the colony. According to J.W.L. Walker, the latter talked loudly of the violation of their religious rights, of their liberty of conscience being infringed, and 'the call there was to resist such acts even to blood'.[10] In these circumstances the directors of the companies were naturally reluctant to admit mutinous settlers, such as the Maroons, because they feared that they would have joined the rebel settlers.[11]

Nova Scotia was a logical choice because it was one of the locations in Canada used some years earlier by the British, to settle Black Loyalists following the American War of Independence.[12] It was also recommended by Colonel Quarrell, a member of the House of Assembly, who had recently travelled through upper Canada. J.C. Hamilton claims that Quarrell was impressed with the large cultivated districts, beautiful towns rising in the forests north of Lake Ontario and the provisions which were being made to extend a system of self-government.[13]

Although it considered possible options for settling the Maroons slated for deportation, the decision on their destination was the prerogative of the British imperial government, not the Jamaican House of Assembly. Despite the antecedents which recommended it, initially, the Maroons were sent to Nova Scotia because of expedience, rather than choice. According to Wentworth of Nova Scotia, Balcarres told him that the Maroons were in three ships in Port Royal Bay awaiting the king's decision on their destination, when a scarcity of provisions and the convenience of getting transport forced him to send them to another port.[14] Balcarres therefore requested that they be permitted to anchor at Halifax, 'until His Majesty's pleasure is signified'. Balcarres added that indications were that the intention of His Majesty would have been known in about three weeks' time. The exigencies surrounding the deportation of the

Maroons were also evident in the fact that Governor Wentworth 'had never been consulted on the propriety of sending the Maroons to Nova Scotia, nor had any official knowledge there of until they arrived'.[15] The 549 Maroons who were deported reached Nova Scotia on 22 July 1796 after six weeks at sea. About three weeks later, following discussions between Wentworth and the Duke of Portland, it was decided to settle the Maroons there.[16]

The inability of the Jamaican legislature and Wentworth to resolve differences over the provisions which were made for the maintenance of the Maroons in Nova Scotia, provided an important context for developments which led to the removal of the Maroons from Nova Scotia to Sierra Leone. The principle governing Maroon subsistence was laid out in a resolution of the Joint Committee of the Council and the House of Assembly dated 20 April 1796. It stated that the Maroons were to be maintained at the expense of the Jamaican public for a reasonable time after they reached their final destination. Moreover, before their arrival in Nova Scotia, Quarrell, the Commissary-General for the Maroon deportees, was given a £10,000 line of credit by the Receiver-General, as part of a £25,000 grant from the Commissioner of Public Accounts for the upkeep of the Maroons.[17] With the resolution of the joint committee as its guide, on 7 December 1796 a Committee of the House of Assembly recommended that financial support for the Maroons from the Assembly should be terminated on 22 July 1798,[18] (two years after the Maroons arrived in Nova Scotia). It also suggested that comfortable subsistence (an exact figure was not provided) should be allowed until 22 July 1797, and for the next year until July 1798, a sum of £10 should be allotted for each man, woman and child.[19] This formula was subsequently adopted without modification by the Jamaican House of Assembly. It was also at the centre of the dispute which developed between the Jamaican House of Assembly and Wentworth.

In retrospect problems were inevitable. Even though the financial terms and conditions which governed the settlement of the Maroons was a matter of profound importance to the people of Nova Scotia, the Jamaican legislature did not discuss them with either the governor of Nova Scotia or the Assembly for the province. It simply imposed its terms on the governor and people of Nova Scotia. The Jamaican Assembly fixed the time period for which it was prepared to accept responsibility for the maintenance of the Maroons in Nova Scotia. It also placed a limit on the funds it was prepared to advance to the latter's cause in the final year of the scheme it devised. As far as the Jamaican legislature was concerned, the Maroons were deported for rebellion against the State, and the funds for their subsistence were not an entitlement, but evidence of the humanity and magnanimity of the Assembly. Further, it expected that the Maroon deportees would have become self-sufficient through 'labour and industry' within a short space of time. From the viewpoint of the Nova Scotians, the most troublesome aspect of the Jamaican Assembly's plan was the fact that the people of Nova Scotia were expected to absorb costs, if its financial provisions proved inadequate in 1798 (a mere two years after the arrival of the Maroons in the province). The Colonial Secretary, the Duke of Portland, deemed it unwise, illiberal and unjust for the Jamaicans 'to suppose they could intend to prescribe a definite limit to that which could not but of necessity depend upon events which human foresight could not provide for'.[20] As far as Wentworth was concerned, the scheme was unacceptable. In May 1797 he made it clear to Quarrell, that 'the sum proposed by the House of Assembly in Jamaica, is greatly inadequate . . . nor will it be possible for them [the Maroons] to remain in this province without a more ample and longer continued support'.[21]

The Jamaican House of Assembly was clearly not deterred by Wentworth's threat. After expressing some dissatisfaction with the manner in which he was dispensing the funds set aside for the maintenance of the Maroons since their arrival in Nova Scotia (in June 1796), the 'business of settling the Maroons . . . was delivered over to Lieut. Gov. Sir John Wentworth'[22] in July 1797. According to Sewell, the Jamaican Assembly contended that up to this point in time (July 1797) it had spent about £41,000 on the settlement of the Maroons. It felt that 'the magnitude of this expenditure . . . would have left no more than a moderate provision for the subsistence of the Maroons for a short time, in aid of their labours . . . and a further supply of ten pounds sterling for each man, woman and child'.[23] In addition to surrendering direct responsibility for the Maroons to Wentworth, the Jamaican Assembly gave him the £5,580 which it had intended to spend on the Maroons for the period between July 1797 and July 1798. This sum was insufficient. Between July 1797 and December 1797, Wentworth spent no less than £10,695.[24] Moreover, he complained to the Colonial Secretary that Jamaica did not take measures to pay the bills drawn by Quarrell, and that the latter had exhausted his credit, leaving the Maroons without supplies.[25]

The Jamaican House of Assembly was clearly not perturbed by Wentworth's complaints; if anything, it became more recalcitrant. In December 1797 members of the Assembly passed a resolution 'that they would on no account whatever provide any more money for the subsistence of the Maroons transported by this country and received in Nova Scotia by the governor of that province'.[26] The hard line taken by the assembly cast a shadow over the future of the Maroon deportees in Nova Scotia. Moreover, the dispute also took its toll on the Maroons. They were left unattended and according to Sewell, 'because of their inactivity and their inability to support themselves, the Maroons have turned to violence and as such have stirred up the people of the province'.[27] Nevertheless, Sewell felt that the Jamaican Assembly should not have been made a scapegoat for 'any want of police within Sir John Wentworth's government'. The Colonial Secretary's view of this issue was nearer to Wentworth's than that of the Jamaicans. Consequently, he recommended that Lord Commissioners of the Treasury pay the bills drawn by Wentworth from the account of Jamaica. He added that Wentworth was well aware of the dreadful evils which must follow if the Maroons were left without the means to support themselves. He contended that even though the police in Nova Scotia were competent they 'may be totally incompetent to avert the calamities so properly noticed by Sir John'.[28] He concluded 'it is utterly impossible that the Maroons can be allowed to remain there, or in any other part of His Majesty's Dominions unless they are subsisted by Jamaica as long as is necessary'.[29] Not surprisingly, by the middle months of 1798 the impasse between the Jamaican House of Assembly and the governor of Nova Scotia had triggered disturbances among the Maroons which were considered a threat to the security of the province. Moreover, it was clear that neither the Colonial Secretary nor Wentworth was willing to maintain the Maroons in Nova Scotia if the Jamaican Assembly refused to provide financial support for as long as was necessary.

The dispute between the Jamaican House of Assembly and Wentworth deteriorated further at the close of 1798. In a report to the House of Assembly on 19 December 1798, the Maroon committee (which was established by the Assembly) accused Wentworth of squandering the money which was provided for the settlement of the Maroons. The Committee claimed that he created 'a system for maintaining in indolence a large body of transported rebels . . . the foundation of an expensive establishment, which it was never in the contemplation of the legislature to form'. It also accused Wentworth of failing to provide an account of his disbursements of the funds for the maintenance of the Maroons for the last 15 months. It contended that the sums set aside for the welfare of the Maroons were sufficient but they were wasted unprofitably.[30] By January 1799 it was clear that a resolution of the conflict between the Jamaican House of Assembly and Wentworth was unlikely. As a result the British Government, through the Under Secretary of State at the Colonial Office, Mr King, initiated talks with the chairman of the Sierra Leone Company about the prospects for moving the Maroons to Sierra Leone. In June 1797 Portland informed Wentworth that because of the great expenses incurred in maintaining the Maroons in Nova Scotia and the doubts surrounding their ability to subsist on their own in the near future, the king of England was advised that 'that part of the coast of Africa which is in the neighbourhood of Sierra Leone would be the most proper place, in which the Maroons could be settled'. He added further that 'the necessary measures for that purpose have been already taken'.[31]

Despite its importance, the feud between the Jamaican Assembly and the governor of Nova Scotia was not the only contributory factor to the events which resulted in the departure of the Maroons from Nova Scotia. The Maroons and the inhabitants of the province also contributed significantly. Given that prior arrangements were not made for their settlement, the Maroons were initially encamped behind Citadel Hill in Halifax, the capital of Nova Scotia. Wentworth was advised that accommodation for the Maroons did not exist in Halifax; consequently they could not stay there. He was also warned against building barracks in the town to accommodate them because of the uneasiness it would have created among some inhabitants and the expense involved.[32] As a result of this it was decided to accommodate them in Preston, a township about five or six miles from Halifax where there was 'a number of vacant houses and small lots of cleared land, which had been occupied by the black people sent to Sierra Leone, and by disbanded soldiers'.[33] There was fuel available all round the settlement and enough land was already cleared for the cultivation of potatoes and other root crops, and a road was cut through the settlement. In addition there was plenty of fish available. It was on this basis that Preston was chosen to settle the Maroons. Wentworth was keen on settling the Maroons before winter set in because they had to make preparations for cultivating in the following spring. By the first week in October 1796 the Maroons had moved from Halifax to their settlement in Preston. Although the dispersal of the Maroons among the local inhabitants was considered, it was not implemented. This was primarily because Wentworth felt that it was impractical and unwise in light of the prejudices which had built up because of accounts given about the Maroons. In addition, he believed that it would have been too expensive.[34] Thus, the Maroons were settled in a manner which made it easy for them to retain the sociopolitical structures and attitudes which they brought with them from Jamaica. As the Report of the Maroon Committee put it, they were kept together in 'a body forming a distinct colony, and preserving all the habits and prejudices of Maroons [in Jamaica]'.[35] At Preston they were given land lots ranging between 30 and 100 acres and by December 1796 all the lots were distributed.

The Maroons' first winter was, according to T. Chamberlain, director of agriculture, 'as severe as we ever had'.[36] In addition, the frost remained on the ground until May 1797. Wentworth claimed that 'having been terrified and alarmed with the length and extreme severity of the last winter', the Maroons concluded that they could not live in Nova Scotia in comfort and wanted to be removed to a warmer country.[37] Wentworth promised to transmit their wishes to His Majesty and 'if it should be commanded to remove the Maroons from this country there may be time to accomplish such commands before the ensuing winter'.[38] The Maroons took this as a commitment by Wentworth to have them removed from Nova Scotia.

Wentworth raised Maroon expectations about the possibility of their removal to warmer climes and Quarrell gave them a destination, Sierra Leone. He claimed that the increasing cold made the Maroons 'particularly some of the bad subjects, very peevish and discontented and that three or four families had petitioned to be sent to a warmer climate, these happened to be the most turbulent and troublesome'.[39] Quarrell explained, 'as the Duke of Portland had said that the Sierra Leone company had offered to take a few families, I was desirous of getting rid of them, that others might be better accommodated and more readily colonised in this country'.[40] He added: 'I herein stated that a transport ship was offered by His Royal Highness Prince Edward, and I readily assented to their embarkation; when suddenly the governor made them an unexpected visit and I found afterwards that they had little desire to go'.[41] Quarrell's response to the plight of the Maroons was much more substantial than the promise Wentworth made to them in early January. Thus it reinforced their belief that it was possible for them to go to Sierra Leone.

The impact of their first winter upon the Maroons was captured succinctly, in a letter to Walpole, commander of the British forces in the Maroon War of 1795–96, dated 10 January 1797, which was written on behalf of Smith, a Maroon leader.[42] The letter pointed out that Smith was instrumental in bringing the Maroons to terms and ultimately to this inclement region. Walpole was told:

> Sir, you may not have felt the region of a North American winter, it is almost as great as Europeans can bear, and to a degree unknown in England. Let me add to assist your imagination that the thermometer has been this day at 15 below zero Fahrenheit – conceive if you can, the feelings of a West Indian constitution in such a climate. I am unable so to compare otherwise than from information, the present with the former state of the Maroons. But when I consider them as deprived of their rum, their sugar and their tobacco which habit had rendered almost necessary for life – their fruits, their vegetables and almost everything that could constitute its luxuries . . . I conceive them to be as destitute of every particular that can make life desirable.[43]

The writer added that during the winter the Maroons did not leave their houses except when driven by necessity, but 'sitting around their stoves they drag on the most melancholy existence'. Enquiries about their health were met by 'the silent shivering thing of the men and the clamorous complaints of the women', accompanied by the cries of children from pain hitherto unfelt. The writer questioned how a Maroon father was supposed to provide for his family of three or four wives and half a dozen children in these circumstances. It noted also that the culture of potatoes, the sowing of wheat for his harvest, his winter stock of vegetables and hay were studies a Maroon head of household was yet to begin and at too advanced an age to learn.

While writing the letter the writer claimed to have witnessed an event 'which had too strong and disciplined feelings not to be noticed'. He stated 'two days ago a general assembly of the Maroons desired to speak to Mr Quarrell'. They told him of their situation in this country and not only their dread of being obliged to remain in the cold, but the fears of their wives and children. Then they pleaded that for the sake of their families 'remove us, if our crimes deserve such punishment, let us rather be hanged; hang every man that bore arms, only let our women and children reside in a warmer climate where existence maybe desirable'. Apart from the physical discomfort and mental anguish they experienced in adjusting to the Canadian winter, the predicament of the Maroons was exacerbated by their unwillingness to adjust to the new material culture of cultivating winter crops and vegetables.

Although the letter suggests that many experienced extreme depression, the Maroons were not fatalistic. Even though the details are patchy, available evidence suggests that they also made organised and calculated attempts to force the colonial authorities to send them to Sierra Leone. The Maroons in Preston organised a general work stoppage during the winter of 1796–7.[44] According to Chamberlain, during the first winter the Maroons complained of stomach cramps and refused to work. Dr. J. Oxley, a surgeon, examined the Maroons and concluded that it was all a farce. He theorised that the thought of striking may have inoffensively entered the mind of one man, 'but when the same thought was all at once impressed upon the minds of nearly one hundred, scattered three or four miles round the woods here, it showed an evil genius of the first order was by some means or another, very influential'.[45] He added that when the strikers were threatened with a stoppage of their allowance to force them to work they laughed. He revealed that 'Maroons would break open stores, kill the cattle, and take anything they could lay their hands on rather than be starved into compliance'. Oxley claimed that the seeds of 'absolute rebellion have been sown in the minds of those unhappy people, and they have been artfully led into an obstinate refusal to work'.[46] He said when Palmer, Fowler, O'Connor and several other Maroons broke rank and resolved to work in the spring of 1797, they went at once to Wentworth with Quarrell and Chamberlain, and claimed that they feared for their lives. Oxley said that the opposition to work was so strong and the determination to leave Nova Scotia so great that 'acts of violence were committed by some against others for planting potatoes'.[47] He added that in about the second week of June 'Mr. Quarrell wearied out by those continued excuses and seeing nothing but cockfighting and every other species of debauchery, going forward',[48] ordered Chamberlain to get the Maroons to work. The Maroons' resistance finally crumbled when Quarrell sent some of them to Boydville, a town close to Preston, and placed 150 Maroons under Chamberlain with strict orders not to feed those who did not work. According to Chamberlain the Maroons said that they would sooner starve than work, 'a few indeed, went without their allowance from Saturday to Wednesday, and there ended their resolution to my cruelty'.[49]

In June 1798 Benjamin Gray, the clergyman who worked among the Maroons, reported that as a result of the 'malignant influence of the climate' the Maroons became extremely discontented 'and at length an agreement was entered into, and . . . attended with a dreadful religious ceremony, wherein the parties mutually bound themselves to encourage and support alone a scheme for their removal from this country'.[50] He said that the tenor of the compact was to try to weaken the confidence of the Jamaican government in

Wentworth's views of the Maroons and to convince the Assembly that they could no longer exist in Nova Scotia. As a result of the compact the Maroons refused to work, attended neither public worship or private Bible classes and were always ready to tell tales of oppression and suffering to anyone willing to listen to them.

The Maroon strategy to force their removal did not only involve refusal to work. On 4 April 1798, eight Maroon leaders petitioned Quarrell when they heard that he was due to leave Nova Scotia to return to Jamaica, 'to lay before the House of Assembly in Jamaica, their distress, their contrition and sorrow for past offences'.[51] They acknowledged the justice of their banishment, but wanted to be removed 'to some other country, more congenial to people of their complexion'. They claimed that 'the length and severity of the last two winters have been such, as almost to drive them to despair'.[52] In June 1799 Chamberlain informed Quarrell that the Maroons got word that their petition was presented and that the prospects for their speedy removal were good. As a result 'they were universally declared against ever making any improvements in Nova Scotia'.[53]

While it is clear that the Maroons themselves conceived of schemes to force their removal from Nova Scotia, it is equally clear that they got support from individuals who were either sympathetic to their cause or stood to benefit from their departure. According to Colonel Howe, who replaced Quarrell, the Maroons' reluctance to work was inspired by the fact that Alexander Ochterlony, Quarrell's former deputy, had encouraged them to believe that their deportation from Jamaica was a breach of the treaty with Walpole and that they could have expected to be removed from Nova Scotia to some part of the island of Hispaniola, Guadeloupe, the Cape of Good Hope or Sierra Leone. He added 'they have expressed such expectations to me frequently saying . . . put arms in our hands and land us anywhere in a warm climate and we will soon make a settlement and room for ourselves'.[54] Howe accused Ochterlony of poisoning the minds of the Maroons against remaining in Nova Scotia. He contended 'I believe it will be fully established . . . that no measure has been left untried by Mr Ochterlony, to effect the removal of the Maroons'.[55] He claimed that if they were sure that the efforts of their friends could not effect their removal, they would then be brought to a proper sense of their situation. Despite this he noted that some Maroons who were prepared to work were reluctant to do so for wages less than those given to White men.[56]

In July 1799, J. Moody of Annapolis county and member of the Nova Scotian House of Assembly, testified that he had frequently heard Ochterlony declaring that he would dissuade the Maroons from working on plantations. He also claimed that Ochterlony felt that the Jamaican legislature, the government and Wentworth 'were all highly to blame, and unjust in placing the Maroons in a country and a climate so different from that which they had been removed'.[57] As a result, Ochterlony actively encouraged the Maroons to seek removal from Nova Scotia. He was not the only one to encourage them along these lines. In his report to Balcarres on the Maroon settlement, Quarrell stated that 'many of the inhabitants, and more particularly some members of the Assembly of Nova Scotia, disappointed in engaging the Maroons upon indentures, and on other proposals to settle them, began to be very clamorous, and sent a message to the governor to enquire what was to be done should Jamaica discontinue supplies and whether they would be a burden on the province'.[58] The members of the Nova Scotian House of Assembly were most likely the persons who made the Maroons privy to official correspondence. Chamberlain made an amazing revelation. He pointed out that in 1799, in addition to receiving information that their petition was presented to the Jamaican House of Assembly, 'journals of the House of Assembly [Jamaican], with its appendix, has been shown them and the horrible practices of the governor, and others under him, to ruin the Maroons are pretended to have come to light; it is now impossible to calculate the end of the mischiefs'.[59] Quarrell testified also that some neighbouring settlers wanted the Maroons to leave in order to inherit their homes on easy terms, or because they feared that 'by their [the Maroons] becoming labourers, a reduction in the price of labour'.[60] Ochterlony noted that the Maroons 'were more fully convinced by the stories told them by the few White people settled around them [in Preston], who were continually holding before them their own miserable situation as the inevitable result of their remaining'.[61]

The Maroons also made it difficult for their settlement in Nova Scotia to succeed by resisting the attempts which were made to socialise them. According to Wentworth because the Maroons were 'accustomed to war, and the uncultivated savage manners of a warm island country, they have much to learn towards the good use of the benefits provided for them'.[62] He argued that among 'the best means of advancing their civilisation, was immediate instruction in Christian religion, reading, writing and arithmetic'.[63] To this end he appointed a chaplain and a teacher from the Church of England, with an assistant, to reside among the Maroons to 'perform public worship, and teach all those that are capable'.[64] He was convinced that this act would have enabled the Maroons to claim 'the rules and comforts of social life'. This attempt at acculturation was a dismal failure. In October 1797 it was reported that despite the questionable incentive of a bottle of rum to every four Maroons who attended church, the clergyman never had a congregation of an average of more than six Maroons. In any event they did not attend church during the winter.[65] In 1798 it was reported that the Maroons had selected Sundays and other holidays 'for the express purpose of gaming, cock-fighting and debauch-ery'.[66] B.G. Gray, the clergyman, claimed that Christianity failed to make an impact because even though they attended church 'a great many of the Maroons were so far unacquainted with our own language, as not to compre-hend fully what was addressed to them from the pulpit'.[67] The Maroons objected to Gray's involvement in their marriage and burial ceremonies. Gray said that their interments were generally 'the occasion of festive excess, while what we proposed in exchange, was conducted with the deepest solemnity, and excluded the slightest indecorum'.[68] He added that he warned them against burying their dead about their dwellings because bodies could be unearthed when they were tilling the land, so he offered them a place in the church yard. He contended that in the case of marriage there was even greater opposition because 'they allowed for polygamy' and 'they part with their interest in their wives, upon compensation being made'.[69] By 1800, therefore, the Maroons, acting either on their own accord or in collusion with some of the inhabitants of the Nova Scotia, had undermined the viability of their settlement in the province.

The Maroons' clamour for removal to Sierra Leone was also assisted by the fact that their agitation coincided with a period in which both the settlers and the indigenous Africans had launched a serious challenge to the authority of the company directors who were administering the settlement.[70] Thus, the directors welcomed a petition from the Maroons who sought their support in an effort to leave Nova Scotia. In response, they proposed to arrange a home for the Maroons in the neighbourhood of Sierra Leone. Although they were concerned that they might join the settlers rebelling against them, the company directors were prepared to accept this risk. They offered to accept the Maroons because they believed that as British subjects 'the Maroons' presence would encourage the British Government to assist in Sierra Leone's defence and other expenses'.[71]

In the final analysis their offer was accepted by the Duke of Portland because he had grown impatient with the failure of the Jamaican and Nova Scotian Assemblies to resolve the problems which plagued the Maroon settlement in Nova Scotia. In addition, Portland also saw the Maroons who wanted to go to Sierra Leone as possible reinforcements to assist the Colonial Authorities in combating the rebels.[72] Thus eventually he asked the 'company to make appropriate arrangements and ordered Wentworth to prepare the Maroons for the Trans-Atlantic crossing'.[73] On 6 August 1800, 551 Maroons left Nova Scotia for Sierra Leone. Their departure signalled the end of an experiment which failed. It failed not only because the Colonial Authorities in Jamaica and Nova Scotia were unable to reconcile their differences over the problems which emerged in the creation of the Maroon settlement, but also because the Maroons refused to adjust to living conditions in Nova Scotia.

Notes

1. See for example R.C. Dallas, *The History of the Maroons*, (Longman and Rees, London, 1803), vols. 1 and 2; Vera Rubin and Arthur Tuden eds., *Comparative Perspectives on Slavery in New World Plantations Societies*, (New York Academy of Sciences, 1976); Mavis Campbell, *The Maroons of Jamaica 1655–1796*, (Trenton New Jersey, Africa World Press, 1990) and Campbell, *Nova Scotia and the Fighting Maroons: A Documentary History*, (College of William and Mary, Williamsburg Virginia, 1990).
2. Jamaica Archives (JA)1B/5/1/41. House of Assembly Journals December 1795 – November 1796. Gen. Walpole to Gov. (Private) Dec. 24, 1795.
3. Ibid., Walpole to Lieut. Gov. Old Maroon Town December 24, 1795.
4. Campbell, *The Maroons of Jamaica*, pp. 235–237.
5. He felt that the "very defence which from their local situation and other causes they have been able to make against such a superior force, renders it essential that the island should be secured against the possibility of a similar insurrection." He continued, that this would have been best achieved "first, by not restoring them to their district, and secondly by placing them in such a situation within the island, (if it cannot be done out of it), which it would be preferable as will from its nature incapacitate them from contriving further mischief."
6. It was comprised of three members of the Council and nine from the House of Assembly.

7.   JA. 1B/5/1/41. House of Assembly Journals Dec. 1795 – Nov. 1796. House of Assembly members to the Council April 20, 1796.

8.   Ibid., April 27, 1796.

9.   JA. 1B/5/14/2. Committee of Correspondence (C. of C.) Out letter Book of Agents in England. Stephen Fuller and Robert Sewell 1795–1801. Robert Sewell to C of C July 6, 1796.

10. J.W. Walker, *The Black Loyalists: The Search for a Promised Land in Nova Scotia and Sierra Leone 1783–1870*, (London: Longman & Dalhousie University Press, 1976), p. 208.

11. Ibid., p. 229.

12. Ibid., Ch. 2. pp. 18–39.

13. J.C. Hamilton "The Maroons of Jamaica and Nova Scotia," *Proceedings of the Canadian Institute*, Toronto, April 1890, pp. 260–269.

14. JA. 1B/11. Votes of the Assembly 1799–1800. J. Wentworth. Statement of Facts respecting the settling of the Maroons in Nova Scotia, June 27, 1799.

15. Ibid., Michael Wallace declared this upon oath to S.S. Blower, Chief Justice of Nova Scotia, June 24, 1799.

16. The testimony of Alexander Ochterlony taken before the Committee of the House of Assembly, December 18, 1799.

17. JA 1B/11. Votes of the Assembly 1795–96. Extract from Report of the Committee of the House of Assembly of Jamaica, December 17, 1796.

18. JA 1B/11. Votes of the Assembly 1795–96. Extract from Report of the Committee of the House of Assembly of Jamaica, December 17, 1796.

19. JA 1B/11. Votes of the Assembly 1795–96. Extract from Report of the Committee of the House of Assembly of Jamaica, December 17, 1796.

20. Ibid. Votes of the Assembly 1798–99. Portland to Sewell, March 11, 1798.

21. M. Campbell, *Nova Scotia and the Fighting Maroons*, Wentworth to Portland, May 7, 1797: C.O.217/68, p. 36.

22. Ibid., Committee of Correspondence Out Letter Book. Agents in England Stephen Fuller and Robert Sewell 1795–1801. Robert Sewell to C of C, March 9, 1798.

23. JA. 1B/11. Votes of the Assembly 1798–99. Sewell to Portland, June 25, 1798.

24. Ibid., Report of the Maroon Committee presented December 19, 1798 at the sitting of the Assembly.

25. Ibid., Extract of letter from Wentworth to the Duke of Portland, November 4, 1798.

26. JA. 1B/5/13/1. Committee of Correspondence Out Letter Book 1794–1883. June 23, 1798.

27. Ibid., Committee of Correspondence Out Letter Book 1795–1801. Robert Sewell to the Duke of Portland, June 25, 1798.

28. Ibid., Duke of Portland to Robert Sewell, July 2, 1798.

29. Ibid.
30. JA. 1B/11. Votes of the Assembly 1798–99. Report of the Maroon Committee presented December 19, 1798 at the sitting of the Assembly.
31. Campbell, *Nova Scotia and the Fighting Maroons*, Portland to Wentworth June 10, 1799, (secret), p. 130.
32. JA. 1B/11. J. Wentworth, "Statement of Facts respecting the Settlement of the Maroons in Nova Scotia", June 27, 1799.
33. Ibid., Michael Wallace, Treasurer of the Province of Nova Scotia declared to S.S. Blower, Chief Justice of Nova Scotia, June 24, 1799.
34. Ibid., J. Wentworth Statement of the Facts respecting the Settlement of the Maroons in Nova Scotia, June 27, 1799.
35. Ibid., Report of the Maroon Committee presented December 19, 1798 at the sitting of the Assembly.
36. Ibid., T. Chamberlain to Wentworth Preston, June 20, 1797. The Maroon's first winter was reputed to be the longest and most severe since the British occupation in 1749.
37. Ibid., Wentworth to Col. Montague James and Capt. Smith and the Maroons resident at Preston. Undated.
38. Ibid.
39. JA 1B/11. Votes of the Assembly 1800–1801. Mr Quarrell to the Chairman of the Maroon Committee, June 24, 1799.
40. Ibid.
41. Ibid.
42. JA. 1B/5/14/2. Committee of Correspondence Out letter Book of the Agents in England 1795–1801. Extract of a letter from Halifax to Gen. Walpole, January 10, 1797.
43. Ibid. In "The Maroons of Jamaica and Nova Scotia", J.C. Hamilton claims that the Maroons also complained about the absence of wild hogs to hunt and yams, bananas and cocoa.
44. The nature of the jobs done by the strikers was not given. However, archival documents suggest that the Maroons at Preston were paid to undertake a variety of tasks such as: woodcutting, road building, fencing land, picking stones and clearing land for the cultivation of oats and potatoes.
45. JA. 1B/11. Votes of the Assembly 1798–99. T. Chamberlain to Wentworth, June 20, 1797.
46. Ibid.
47. Ibid. J. Oxley to Wentworth June 16, 1798.
48. Ibid.
49. Ibid., Chamberlain to Quarrell, August 7, 1798.
50. Ibid., Benjamin Gerrish Gray to Wentworth, Preston June 18, 1798.

51. JA. 1B/11. Votes of the Assembly 1798–1799. The Maroons Capt. Montague James, Col. Smith, Maj. Jarret, Capt. Smith, Capt. Charles Shaw, Capt. Dunbar, Capt. D. Shaw, and Capt. J. Harden to Quarrell, April 20, 1798.
52. Ibid.
53. Ibid., T. Chamberlain to Quarrell Preston, June 10, 1799.
54. Ibid., Howe to Wentworth, June 8, 1798.
55. Ibid.
56. Ibid.
57. Ibid., Moody, J., of Annapolis County and member of the House of Assembly. Declared under oath July 22, 1799 to S.S Blowers Chief Justice of Nova Scotia.
58. Ibid., Quarrell to Balcarres, January 27, 1798.
59. Ibid., T. Chamberlain to Quarrell Preston, June 10, 1799.
60. Ibid., Oath of William Quarrell taken before the Committee of the Assembly investigating the Maroon settlement in Nova Scotia. Undated.
61. Ibid., The testimony of Alexander Ochterlony taken before the Committee of the Assembly investigating the Maroon settlement in Nova Scotia, December 18, 1798.
62. JA. 1B/5/1/41. House of Assembly Journals December 1795 to November 1796. Wentworth to Balcarres, October 10, 1796.
63. Ibid.
64. Ibid.
65. JA. 1B/14/2. Committee of Correspondence Out Letter book of Agents in England. Stephen Fuller and Robert Sewell 1795-1801. Halifax, October 26, 1797. The correspondents were not given.
66. Ibid., Howe to Wentworth, June 8, 1798.
67. Ibid., Votes of the Assembly 1795–96. Benjamin Gerrish Gray to Wentworth, Preston, June 18, 1798.
68. Ibid.
69. Ibid.
70. J.W Walker, *The Black Loyalists*, pp. 230–235.
71. Ibid. p. 230.
72. When the Maroons arrived in Sierra Leone, they were welcomed as an addition to the Governor's forces and the terms and conditions of settlement were quickly arranged with them. See E. Martin, *The British West African Settlements 1750–21*, (Longmans 1927), pp. 133–37 and Walker, *The Black Loyalists*, pp.230–35.
73. Walker, *The Black Loyalists*, p. 230.

'War Dances'

Slave leisure and anti-slavery in the British-colonised Caribbean

HILARY McD. BECKLES

The continuous rhythm of commodity production on the Caribbean slave plantation was but one aspect of its organisational culture. Outside the economic sphere of bell-driven productive activities, the social life and cultural work of slave communities swayed to different kinds of sounds. While the day-life of slaves was fashioned by a persistent struggle to survive debilitating hard labour under an unrelenting tropical sun, their night-life beneath softly caressing moons was textured by an irrepressible pursuit of leisure, entertainment and ontological freedom.[1]

Enslaved Africans valued highly, and guarded keenly, their cultural worlds. As a consequence, they placed a premium on the social time and space required to explore, express and ritualise artistic and recreational activities. As the social frontier of individual colonies receded, and cultural expressions evolved and settled into popular creole formations, the routine of dances and festivals came to typify the highlights of Caribbean nights. Traditional African, as well as new creole forms of entertainment, were discernible cultural manifestations of Black communities.

Music and dance, above all, constituted the bridge over the troubled waters that connected Africa-born persons and their creole progeny.[2] The linkages of these cultural encounters, however, represented much more than the passionate pursuit of pleasure; they were encoded with noises of spiritual ideological liberation and invoked the voices of cosmological redemption. Dances, as musical parties were called, embraced persons other than those gathered for a fun-filled time; they also provided masks for slaves to share opinions on the issues of the day, such as British anti-slavery debates and slave-owners' responses, and to consider and organise for revolutionary self-liberation.

The objective of this examination is to describe and analyse the political nature of slaves' entertainment and leisure culture by drawing upon empirical evidence derived mostly from Barbados and to a lesser degree Jamaica. The argument departs from assertions commonly found in the historiography of slavery that the sociocultural activities of enslaved Africans can best be understood as actions designed and fashioned by the need to fill the empty time-space that remained from the productive demands upon their labour power. Instead, the argument is advanced that the politics of anti-slavery was endemic to cultural activities, and that this relationship was understood to varying degrees over time and place by significant sections of the slave-owning population. Furthermore, it problematises and critiques the view of slave leisure and recreation as apolitical social activities that followed periods of supervised work, constituting essentially forms of respite and recuperation from production schedules.

Eurocentric accounts of the visible aspects of slaves' entertainment and leisure culture provide glimpses into the political environment and cosmologies of the plantation world. Descriptions of their recreational activities, and to a lesser extent devotional practices, underscore the importance to them of cultural and philosophical expressions within the social contexts of enslavement. They indicate, furthermore, how the enslaved used sociocultural events and activities to display and promote coherent anti-slavery attitudes and actions. The inevitable interaction of ritualised culture and political ideology within these circumstances magnified and disseminated symbolically various representations of resistance. Culture was a primary area of anti-slavery discourse, and dances took centre stage in the social and institutional infrastructure of resistance.[3]

The political dimension of slave leisure sheds significant light on the process of creolisation and illuminates the fact that over time and space the changing social and economic relationships between enslavers and slaves was determined by considerations of power and perceptions of self-interest. Orlando Patterson's seminal work on Jamaican slave society suggests that there was nothing phenomenal about the existence of a popular entertainment culture among slaves, and indicates that it was linked, in terms of time-space dimensions, to the evolving political economy of slave-ownership. 'To break the routine of their harsh daily existence', he states, 'the slaves participated in various forms of recreation whenever they had the opportunity'.[4] Furthermore, he notes, 'recreation was largely sporadic, taking place on week nights or weekends when they would dance and sing'.

The demographic aspect of creolisation expressed itself in terms of a greater cultural determination and autonomy among slaves. By the end of the eighteenth century, African and creole cultural forms were distinguishable in terms of performance and use of instrumental technology. The evidence suggests, however, that together they constituted a melange that cemented successive generations over time, and gave social unity to the cultural diversity that creolisation generated. African creative, popular cultures stood face to face with the institutional structure and social designs of slavery and mocked it, mimicked its representatives and challenged its moral authority. In these ways anti-slavery ideology was manifested in the social praxis of slaves' recreational and entertainment activities. While for slaves the time frames and space available for these actions were negotiable with slave-owners, the ideological contents were not.

In general, what held true for one society was also the case in others across imperial lines. Neville Hall reported as much in his analysis of slave culture in the Danish Virgin Islands, though he seemed more certain of the opinion than most scholars that European social hegemony prescribed and constrained African expression. For him, the ability of slaves to participate in recreational activities was a gift from benevolent but politically pragmatic slave-owning entrepreneurs. 'Despite the all-encompassing nature of slavery in these islands', he added, 'it is nevertheless true to say that the slaves' occupational spread and the nature of the work routine allowed many slaves to have discretionary time'.[5] The politics of concession, he concludes, enabled this time to be subdivided into various usable packages for slaves' self-fulfilment. Howard Johnson's work on the Bahamas shows that slave-owners sought effective control over the way slaves made use of this time, and that contests over autonomous cultural activity, particularly the nightly dances, gained intensity over time.[6]

Hall's approach and conclusion invoke the need to explore at length the nature of slaves' collective inputs into the dialogue over the use of discretionary time as a resource, and to make fuller assessments of the social ideas they promoted within the dynamic cultural systems of the plantation. At the outset, serious problems can be identified with an analytical tendency that interprets leisure activities among slaves as primarily mundane, sensual escapism rather than creative cultural and political work. Furthermore, important evidence is ignored when approaches to slaves' recreational culture do not consider their general anti-slavery posture and the sophisticated epistemologies that informed it. Recent work in popular cultural studies, for instance, has sharpened our focus on these issues, and suggests, in most cases, the need for revisionist approaches in which slave leisure can also be seen as advanced cultural and political work whose meaning requires specific epistemological terms of reference for comprehension.[7]

There is no doubt that for some slave-owners the musical extravaganzas of Blacks had all to do with jollity, fun, distraction and respite from productive labour. Entertainment activities were considered by them as low community engagements of a culturally inferior people seeking release from drudgery. They argued, Kamau Brathwaite tells us, that slaves were brutes; they dismissed their music as noise, and believed that their so-called artistic expressions spoke exclusively of 'sexual misconduct and debauchery'. The slaves, they surmised, 'could produce no philosophy that reached above the navel'.[8]

Representations of the black body, above and beneath the navel, within pro-slavery British Caribbean literature indicate the extent to which the physical and sexual aspects of the slavery discourse tortured and tore European consciousness. African dance styles, even of a devotional or sacred nature, were sexualised and de-intellectualised by Whites who found the interface of languid and jerky movements aesthetically problematical. Some, however, were sufficiently sensitive, or paranoid, to interpret African dance performance, then, as anti-slavery ritual constructions that ridiculed their slave-owning world and promoted revolt. Eurocentric sexualisation and politicisation of African dance performance produced two distinct types of literature: one that generated sociomoral representations of the African inherent character; the other that sought the identification of attitudes and practices of insubordination and resistance.[9]

Black sexual aesthetic and ideological revolt furthermore emerged as the common elements of the cultural discourse that underpinned the voluminous pro-slavery literature. Slave-owners' fear of anti-slavery expression, both physical and ideological, led them to target slave dancing, for example, as liberated bodies in action. Dancing as a recreational institution, therefore, attracted the attention of legislators. But it was the dance, as a social institution, that assumed political dimensions within the Black community as a place where plans were made to turn the world upside down. While dancing became a metaphor for spiritual independence, the dance, as an institution, provided contexts for the formulation of political strategies.

Robert Dirks disagrees. He accepts that 'slaves expressed their ethnic identities and outlook on European culture most clearly in music and dance', but is unwilling to accept that discernible relations exist between the ontological aspects and quests for social freedom. He limits the notion of the black saturnalia to ritual display of cultural mimicry, and does not locate within the culture of the Black community any discourse about alternative political and social orders. The upsurge of slave rebellions around the festive periods of Christmas and Easter, when dances and festivals abound, he accounts for in terms of the rumbustiousness that followed sudden increases of nutrition levels, excess alcohol consumption and 'the extraordinary license handed them by the planters'.

'The effect of this nutritional boost and the availability of other fresh sources of nourishment', Dirks concludes, 'was nothing short of explosive'. While much of 'the energy went into jolly sport', outbursts of violence 'was a typical ecological and nutritional' response.[10] Dirks' understanding of slave behaviour, therefore, denies the Black community any kind of political 'mind', and certainly removes them from an association with epistemological processes. In this regard, his thinking corresponds closely to aspects of Eurocentric thought found especially in eighteenth-century pro-slavery literature.

Slave-owners' opinions about slave culture, however, were neither consensual nor stable over time. There were extreme differences of opinion and considerable volatility in responses. On the plantations many Whites imagined a plot of slaves to be the outcome of every social gathering and sought to outlaw and disband group encounters. Such persons were particularly hostile to the slaves' use of the drum, the beating of which they considered a form of subversive language. The passing of legislation against the free use of some drums, which criminalised a major element of the slaves' cultural firmament, was therefore a significant sociopolitical offensive against Blacks. Brathwaite noted that the political function of slaves' music was the cause of the 'banning of drumming or gatherings where drumming took place'. Slave-owners in Barbados were first to legislate, in 1688, setting a pattern for other English colonists to follow. One hundred years later, William Dickson reported from Barbados that the sound of the 'coromantin drum' still brings 'terrors' to the White community who 'panic' on the few occasions that it is heard.[11]

The evidence suggests, rather, that slave-owners attempted to adopt reconciliatory approaches in dealing with organised slave culture. Details of their searches for an understanding of it leap from the evidence. Furthermore, their articulation of complex ideological representations of slave life indicates that they were as much concerned with comprehending all social environments as they were with production efficiency. The changing of attitudes and policies with respect to slave culture characterised their pro-slavery ideology, and constitutes a well-located window through which to view the dynamics of social management in the slave society.

Karl Watson's assertion, for instance, that planter-sponsored slave leisure activities assisted in fostering among slaves and slave-owners a sense of community[12] should be understood within the contexts of pro-slavery literature and opinion. He speaks in terms of a social contract between slaves and slave-owners in which the former were granted autonomy with respect to cultural activities in return for a commitment to non-violent searches for betterment.[13] Such an arrangement, however, could not promote feelings among the enslaved of being ideologically and culturally integrated within the White community. While some slave-owners must have received considerable affectionate responses from slaves for adopting a conciliatory approach to their cultural demand, the strength of anti-slavery sentiment transcended such impulses and assured ultimately the existence of clashes over the terms and meaning of freedom. The intimate sharing of leisure time and space demanded by popular culture was not influential enough for slave-owners and slaves to be cemented by a common sense of community interest, despite the impressive body of evidence which suggests that on such occasions discipline and social decorum did prevail.

Over time slave-owners in most places came to recognise that cultural activity within the slave community were organisationally and ideologically informed by the general expressions of endemic anti-slavery consciousness. The social contract between slave-owners and slaves intimated by Watson was evidently discarded from time to time by the eruption of rebellion and the placement of freedom in its fullest legal sense at the top of individual and community agenda. Social autonomy offered slaves at the bargaining table by slave-owners was received and understood as a prerequisite for general emancipation. For them, an amelioration of living conditions was no end in itself, but the precursor for the reconstruction of social life. The crisis of the social contract, then, resulted from a shift in consciousness in which slaves perceived that social concessions were not acceptable as substitutes for freedom.

Essentially, because the life experiences of slaves were charged by cosmologies in which anti-slavery considerations were paramount, the conflict between slaves and slave-owners over the definition, possession, and use of time, as well as methods of arbitration and settlement, revealed the distinct way in which the central paradigm of slavery and freedom was contested. By their cultural actions slaves raised and problematised not only the issues of identity, autonomy and social justice, but matters relative to art, oral literature, performance, music and dance. It was a discourse that centred slaves' claim to, or assumption of, humanity in the disease-ridden, life-and-love destructive plantation environment, where good physical and mental health were as rare as personal legal liberty. It indicated, furthermore, the extent to which slaves worked hard and long at devising and designing ways and means of producing a dynamic social culture of their own. This process of creation and self-definition required considerable conceptual innovation, political initiative, and psychological and social adjustment to relations of power in which even their personage was legally denied. Their quest for an autonomous systemisation of cultural organisation, together with owners' monopolistic management of their labour power and time, constituted two discrete worlds of politics held apart, in spite of an internal creolising synthesis, by attitudes that emanated from popular anti-slavery consciousness.

The entertainment culture of slaves: contradictory perspectives

Colourful descriptions and informed observations of the entertainment culture of slaves are scattered throughout the textual records of persons who set out to communicate to reading audiences the lifestyles of Blacks in bondage. During his early nineteenth-century visit to the British-Colonised Caribbean, Frederick Bayley, for example, took care to record what enslaved Blacks had to say about the evolving terms and conditions of their cultural lives. Special note, he tells us, was taken in seeking to understand and report their reactions to social constraints imposed by slave-owners. The reality of slavery, he concluded, should be perceived as located somewhere between slave-owners' intention – with regard to regulation and control – and the degree of refusal and assertion on the part of the slaves. He recognised, even if unwittingly, that the continuous remaking of the relationship between slave-owners and slaves made for incompleteness in the specific victories sought by both groups. Independent ownership of time by slaves, he intimates, was central to the contradiction that constituted an important part of the discourse of slavery and freedom.[14]

While eavesdropping on a conversation between 'two black boys' in Barbados, Bayley was privileged to an aspect of the cultural making of slave life. The exposure offered him the opportunity to occupy a reference point with which to view slaves' anti-slavery ideology as far as it related to issues of resource ownership and redistribution, and the politics of leisure. He reported the conversation as follows:

> 'If massa been know somting he would lick me dis night self'
> 'Whar far?'
> 'You sabe, daddy Quaco da gib one ball to-night
> And I bin tief one dollar for buy wine.'
> 'Dat like me. I bin take from misses, one young fowle, and two bottle portar.
> She bin hab friends last night, and she will tink de gentlemen drink um.'[15]

Following this invitation, Bayley continued his investigations. One conclusion the evidence clearly suggests, he stated, is that in Barbados masters are 'greatly plundered' by their slaves of such things as 'poultry, porter, wine, and sometimes money, for the purpose of carrying them to entertainments, which the negroes give among themselves'.[16] References such as this constitute but part of the sociopolitical framework within which Europeans interpreted the social culture of enslaved Africans. They indicate, furthermore, the material circumstances under which an oppressed and highly regulated people sought to come to terms with the entertainment element of organised culture. Unfortunately, Bayley erected no signposts that may guide towards the political foundations of such cultural practices.

On the plantations practical considerations of a managerial nature often dominated the reflections of slave-owners on matters of this kind. In general, their actions suggest a belief that it was necessary to requite their human chattel with brief periods of free time, the use of which they invested with some measure of autonomy. The principal issue here is slave-owners' reluctant realisation that human chattel had the irreparable flaw of possessing a physical and social being which required time for rest, reflection and recreation. This recognition had clear implications for labour productivity, social stability and rates of property depreciation. It had little to do with slave-owners' ideology and labour policy softening in the face of slaves' assertion of right to a social life.

A major contradiction, then, existed between the slaves' insistence upon a social right to a long life, and slave-owners' economic claims to their lifelong labour. Only in a few instances could slaves perceive a direct social and material interest in plantation work. In cases where part of the product of estates above normal levels of subsistence was shared with slaves, terms of agreements did not recognise any right by slaves to reduced labour. As a result, labour relations seemed irretrievably unjust once slavery existed as the principal coercive social framework. Equity within slavery, then, could not be achieved. Liveable arrangements required constant negotiation, intricate psychological adjustments, and at times the use of open force and terrorism on both sides. The politicisation of slaves' leisure time, and the criminalisation of much of their cultural action by slave-owners, were therefore issues of prime importance that indicated the precise natures of public governance.

First, the concessions; inclement weather, Sundays and Christian holidays were considered just reasons by slave-owners, during much of the eighteenth and nineteenth centuries, to withdraw slaves from mainline production. This model, however, did not apply to slaves across occupational categories. Senior domestic artisan, supervisorial slaves on the estates, as well as many urban slaves, experienced a different rhythm in their labour-leisure cycle. What integrated their diverse experiences and attitudes, however, was the swift manner with which they relocated custom to the realm of rights around which an intense political dialogue emerged.

Once slaves had settled the matter of a right to leisure time, attention shifted to the more testing and vexing question of the manner in which it could be legitimately organised, and the degree to which slaves could attain specific forms of autonomy. These were issues, moreover, that could not be operationalised within the confines of individual plantations. They touched upon the central issue of general control and regulation. Slaves would wish to travel to other plantations or towns in order to participate in planned events, which in turn problematised seemingly peripheral issues such as group movement and dress codes. In many colonies dress restrictions were put in place in order to prohibit slaves appearing in society with lavish finery. Legislators were as much concerned with enforcing provisions against unregulated movement as they were with these sumptuary laws that sought to tone down a celebratory culture in which slaves decorated themselves with silks, fine jewellery and lace.

The absence of any major slave revolt in Barbados during what has been described as the long and turbulent eighteenth century seemed to enhance the creation of an environment within which slave-owners gradually moved towards a relaxing of internal controls in order to facilitate the slaves' development and promotion of a vibrant leisure culture. Organised leisure activities, as was also the case with family and kinship patterns, transcended the spatial dimensions of single plantations and indicated the inescapable social reality that slaves had consciously fashioned a life of their own beyond their owners' corporate boundaries. While frequent bloody armed mass conflict between masters and slaves in other major plantation colonies was the order of things, Barbados was characterised and represented as a place where non-violent, individualised resistance had gained paramountcy within the politics of anti-slavery. The relationship between the absence of organised, large-scale militant conflict and the establishment of a widespread and well-structured entertainment culture among slaves, therefore, was understood as sequential by slave-owners on the island and elsewhere.

Watson's perspective on the 'world the slaves made', however, does offer an instructive and valuable instrument of analysis. He invokes the notion of a moral economy in enslaver-enslaved relations that gave primacy to collective negotiation over terms and conditions of labour and leisure.17 Responding to flexibility in managerial authority, Watson intimates, slaves appreciated the wisdom in seeking to convert privileges into rights as the basis of a long-term accumulationist strategy. He argued, moreover, that slaves ultimately abandoned anti-slavery ideology: 'In giving a general assessment of the reaction of enslaved people in Barbados to their situation, one must note the functional importance of compliance. It was on the basis of acceptance of the status quo that the system functioned. The whole slave system began as a coercive one, but developed into a system of consent'.[18]

Watson did not take into consideration the extent to which slaves in Barbados were in fact reacting to a perception of the highly organised slave-owners' military power structure which had crushed their insurrectionary attempts in 1675 and 1692. Nor did he take into account the manner in which slaves sought to maximise social benefits while at the same time maintaining a firm commitment to general emancipation. One major privilege, or liberty, slaves enjoyed increasingly was less restricted off-plantation movements. From the early eighteenth century, in spite of the frequently expressed concern of imperial governors, Barbados slave-owners moved in the direction of operating a relatively relaxed system of travel monitoring. Slaves were allowed to traverse the extremities of the island at nights and on weekends, in order to attend dances and markets, and to maintain kinship and friendship relations. This was done in large measure without the aid of passes or tickets which slave-owners had issued to their slaves in earlier times as proof of their legitimate travel.

The development that saw evening dances become a visible part of slave culture owed its existence and popularity, to reduced levels of social regulation. One manifestation of this understanding, Dickson reported at the end of the eighteenth century, was the busy nature of highways during the nights and early mornings as slaves sought to take full advantage of their leisure time. 'Their contubernal connections are unlimited as to number and local situations,' he stated. 'Both sexes are frequently travelling all night, going to or returning from a distant connection, in order, without sleep, to be in due time to go through a hard day's labour, after their nocturnal adventures'.[19] Such pursuits, he tells us, included family gatherings, sexual relations, economic exchange, as well as the organisation and enjoyment of dances and festivals.

In 1790, G. Franklyn supported Dickson's observations concerning the movements of slaves in pursuit of leisure. 'Nothing will', he said 'at any time, restrain them from pursuing their amours or their amusements. Dancing they are passionately fond of; and they will travel several miles, after their daily labour is over, to a dance, and after dancing the greatest part of the night, they will return to their owners' plantations and be in the field at the usual hour of labour'.[20] Dr. George Pinckard's observations during 1795–6, were similar: 'They are passionately fond of dancing and the Sabbath offering them an interval from toil, is, generally, devoted to their favourite amusement; and, instead of remaining in tranquil rest, they undergo more fatigue, or at least more personal exertion, during their gala hours of Saturday night and Sunday, during any four days of the week'.[21]

Slave-owners took it for granted that these movements and gatherings would be used for activities other than the organisation of rebellion. Some suggested, in support of this arrangement, that unless slaves were allowed the right to travel in pursuit of their social and economic business they would run away, sabotage production and ultimately revolt. An eighteenth-century commentator reported that 'it was commonly observed that, after they had so diverted themselves, they went through their work with greater courage and cheerfulness without expressing any weariness, and did all things better than if they had rested all night long in their huts'.[22] Watson suggests, furthermore, that 'apart from considerations of leniency and custom, planters were in general not opposed to regular dances because, in their view, productivity was greater than under a regime of denial'.[23] His reading of this social development led him to the conclusion that slaves, in the process of accumulating specific sociocultural rights, had capitulated with respect to the revolutionary attainment of freedom.[24]

Crop-over

At the centre of slaves' entertainment culture during the eighteenth century were the annual crop-over festival and weekend dances. Bayley tells us that anti-slavery Whites who spoke of the 'groans of the negroes' would not believe the spectacle of 'an assembly of these oppressed people on their grand day of jubilee, which they call "CROP OVER"'.[25] The crop-over festival, he continued, begins on the 'day on which the last of the canes are cut on a sugar plantation', during which 'flags are displayed in the field and all is merriment'. To initiate the ceremony, 'a quart of sugar and a quart of rum are allowed each negro on the occasion', after which 'all authority, and all distinction of color ceases; black and White, overseer and book-keeper mingle together in dance'.[26] On the plantations, he added, 'it was common on occasions of this kind to see the different African tribes forming a distinct party, singing and dancing to the gumbay', a spectacle removed by the process of creolisation and the popular use of fiddles instead of drums.[27]

   The festival spirit of 'crop-over', was a British Caribbean affair. Mrs Carmichael who witnessed the closing years of the slave system in St Vincent and Trinidad, wrote in 1833 that crop-over festivals were universal. Dirks notes, in addition, that the Jamaican crop-over, rather than coming at the end of the harvest, was often put off until the conclusion of sugar making, when the slave gangs assembled around the boiling house, dancing and roaring for joy. The overseer would distribute salt fish and rum, and the 'feast would be followed by a ball'.[28] These planter-sponsored harvest-home celebrations allowed slaves an opportunity to ritualise their relationships to the plantation world with song and dance, one aspect of which was captured by satirical colonial literature such as this 1754 poem by Nathaniel Weekes, a White creole Barbadian:

> There's not a slave,
> In spite of slavery, but is pleased and gay
> For this is their delightful, darling time!
> On all sides, hear the Dialogue obscene,
> The last Night's Theft, the adulterous Intrigue,
> And all the scandal of unmanner'd Tongue.
> While some, to cheer their Toil, and laugh the Hours
> In merriment away, forth from their Throats,
> The Barb'rous unintelligible song.
> Unmusically roared.

Descriptions of Barbados' crop-over celebrations, though few in number, are quite graphic in detail. In 1798, Sampson Wood, manager of Newton Plantation in the Christ Church parish, reported that after the crop he would gather the slaves and give them a 'dinner and a sober dance'. The reason he gave in justifying the financial expenditures was that it was 'a celebration of Harvest Home after the crop'. On the Codrington plantation, owned by the Church of England, the policy was adopted in 1819 to celebrate 'crop-over' with a holiday for slaves.[29]

Generally, there were two types of crop-over dances: those organised by, and held within, slave-owners' households; and those convened by the slaves – with or without their owners' permission. With respect to Barbados, Pinckard offers limited comments on the second type. The slaves, he stated, 'assembled in crowds upon the open green, or in any square or corner of the town, and forming a ring in the centre of the throng, dance to the sound of their beloved music'.[30] Trewlawny Wentworth, however, added more details:

> Music and dancing, the negroes love to their heart's core, although of late years, they have been taught by the missionaries to believe that they are inconsistent with morality. At the time to which we are referring, dancing was frequent in the negro-houses in an evening, and once a week, a more general assemblage took place under the auspices of one negro, who invited people from the neighbouring estates. On such occasions, it was customary to ask leave of their master to ensure a license for a greater duration of their obstreperous mirth, which, from the usual vicinity of his dwelling to the negro-houses, he must necessarily hear.[31]

Wentworth also commented on the political and economic aspects of slaves' entertainment activities, and stressed that slave dances were not illegal when officially sanctioned by masters and mistresses.

Legal gatherings were permitted under the slave codes of most Caribbean colonies, and it was 'expedient', Wentworth stated, for owners to 'admit them according to the character of the applicant'. Providing entertainment was also 'profitable to the negroes', and slave-owners tried to regulate activities so as to 'avoid monopoly' by any one slave on the estates. With respect to the financial arrangements, he states:

> Each negro coming to the assembly paid half a bit, or a bit, in order, partly, to meet the expense of a fiddler, who commonly charged as much as four and five dollars; and who, if not to be found among themselves, was always to be engaged from among the slaves upon some other estate. If it happened, that the negro giving the entertainment has inferior accommodation, he would borrow a more eligible spot from another, the dancing taking place in the house, and in the adjoining plot of ground.[32]

Bayley's description of crop-over fetes, which he said were usually held in 'a negro hut', speaks to slaves' commitment to an independent cultural order. According to him, 'tea and coffee are first handed round, after which the musicians, consisting of perhaps three fiddlers, a tambourine player, and a man who beats an instrument called a triangle, commence playing, and the dancing continues for a while in the most lively and spirited manner'. 'After the dancing', he added, 'the group sits down to the supper table, the contents of which have all been stolen from the masters or mistresses'. 'After supper', he continues, 'the parties separate and each return to his home; the masters know nothing of the matter; but if by chance, any of them are charged the next day with having been on such an excursion, they do not hesitate in declaring that they never left the house, and assert, with the most imprudent assurance, their total ignorance that even such an occurrence was to take place'.[33] These accounts offer insights into the social environment in which slaves carved a celebratory and entertainment culture. They suggest the extensive nature of social and artistic expression, and indicate how the enslaved used cultural events and processes to legitimately display and promote an oppositional vanguard.

Dance parties and slave uprisings in Barbados and Jamaica

Slaves, then, never abandoned their hope for general emancipation. The dance party as an institution provided an opportunity for slaves to organise concrete anti-slavery politics. In this regard, two types of gatherings were discernible:

those at which slaves ventilated disaffection in a general sort of way; and those that constituted a critical part of the fabric of revolutionary planning. It may be said that these categories were political stages in anti-slavery rather than organisational types, but some dances were organised specifically for the purpose of planning revolution and others were social gatherings innocent of anti-slavery issues. Official data on the 1816 Barbados slave rebellion and the 1824 Jamaica slave conspiracy illustrate the different natures and functions of slave dances, and locates slaves' subsequent experiences within criminal law and the judicial system.

On Easter Sunday, 14 April 1816, shortly after Barbados slave-owners had taken the opportunity of the debate over William Wilberforce's slave registration bill to reaffirm their unwavering pro-slavery stances, over 10,000 slaves took to arms in an act of revolutionary self-liberation. The rebellion started in the parish of St Philip, the largest in the colony, and quickly spread throughout most of the southern and central parishes of Christ Church, St John, St Thomas, St George and parts of Bridgetown in St Michael. Minor outbreaks of arson, but no skirmishes with the militia, also occurred in the northernmost parish of St Lucy. In geopolitical terms, more than half of the island was engulfed by the insurrection. The rebellion was short-lived. Within four days, it was effectively squashed by a joint offensive of the local militia and garrisoned imperial troops; included among the latter were the slave soldiers of the 1st West Indian Regiment. Mopping up operations continued during May and June, and martial law, imposed about 2.00 am, Monday, 15 April, was lifted on 12 July. An estimated 1,000 slaves lost their lives in battle and as a result of executions ordered by courts martial that found them guilty of rebellion. Also, 123 prisoners not condemned to death by the courts martial were subsequently deported to Sierra Leone as convicts by order of the governor in Council.[34]

Slave-owners claimed that they were shocked by the suddenness of the rebellion, and argued that the extensive social and cultural liberties granted slaves ought to have protected them from such an onslaught. Robert Haynes, a prominent planter and Assemblyman, stated in a letter dated September 1816: 'The night of the insurrection I would and did sleep with my chamber door open, and if I had possessed ten thousand pounds in my house, I should not have had any more precaution, so well convinced I was of their (slaves) attachment'.[35] This attitude seemed to have been widespread throughout the White community, though references were often made to the 'mischief' slaves got up to on account of the many opportunities for gathering in large numbers occasioned by frequent night dances and parties.

Among those who had called earlier for tighter security was Governor Leith. Not being a Barbadian, Leith was accused by creole planters of being obsessed with notions of Black uprising. Following the rebellion he informed the Secretary for Colonies about the danger of slave-owners' long-held complacency: 'The planters of Barbados who have flattered themselves that the general good treatment of the slaves would have prevented them resorting to violence to establish an elusion of material right, which by long custom sanctioned by law has been hitherto refused to be acknowledged, had not any apprehension of such a convulsion'.[36] When the Assembly established an investigative Commission to report on the causes of the revolt, Whites expected that considerable attention would focus on the issue of slaves' cultural life and its sociopolitical implication. In this regard the report did not disappoint. It detailed the degree to which the slave population enjoyed extensive mobility throughout the colony, and explained this in terms of slave-owners' willingness to allow them to develop cultural and kinship rights. It referred to the complex network of slave communications and the degree to which information passed between town and country and through the estates that separated them.[37]

Several depositions were received by the Commissioners in which the view was expressed that the revolt was hatched within the context of the slaves' cultural infrastructure. Edward Thomas, manager of Bayley Plantation, home of Bussa, the principal leader of the rebels, informed the Commission that he had long provided many free days for the slaves to have dances which, unfortunately, opened their appetite for greater rights. Joseph Gittens, manager at the nearby Padmore estate, supported this line of argument:

> Long before the Insurrection, it appeared to me that the slaves were inclined to presume upon and to abuse the great indulgences granted them by Proprietors and Overseers, such as, permitting them to have dances frequently on Saturday and Sunday evenings – all of which induced them to assume airs of consequence, and put a value on themselves unknown amongst the slaves of former periods.[38]

Both Gittens and Padmore assumed that the anti-slavery positions of slaves, and their opinion that freedom had to be fought for, were made possible as a result of social relations facilitated by cultural developments.

Thomas Nurse, chief overseer at the River estate, argued that excessive social liberty and material comfort were the principal triggers of rebellion. It is a 'fact well known', he informed the Commission, that slaves 'have had frequent dances and feasts, at which all were well (and some expensively) dressed'. Thomas Stoute, manager at Mapps estate, also explained the outbreak of violence in terms of the slaves' extensive social activities. He told the Commission: 'I conceive, as far as I am able to judge, that the Insurrection was produced by the negroes (in the first instance) abusing those indulgences which, for many years past, owners of slaves in this Island had been in the habit of granting them, such as having constant parties and dances on Saturday and Sunday evenings (at which they were most gaily attired)'.[39]

James Maycock, practising physician in the parishes most physically affected by the revolt, a graduate of the University of Edinburgh, shared these opinions. His deposition states that 'the frequency of dances, and other meetings of that kind, no doubt, enabled the disaffected to mislead their associates'.[40] Maycock accused 'elite' slaves of propagandising less informed field hands with respect to the contents and time frames of Parliamentary emancipation debates, using dances as fora for the planning of such political action. He attributed 'the Insurrection, in a great degree, to the number of officers, tradesmen, and other favoured persons, on plantations.' 'These persons', he said, 'generally possess considerable influence and having extensive connections, had thereby the means of communication, of concert, and of secrecy; and it is certain that they were the first to be deluded themselves, and were afterwards the principal agents to delude others'.[41]

Privileged slaves, Maycock added, misrepresented to field hands the Slave Registration Act of 1814 as the general emancipation legislation. Lewis Young, Maycock's medical colleague, also an estate owner, advanced a similar account of the rebellion. He told the commissioners:

> As to the causes which produced the Insurrection, I am of the opinion that it was partly owing to the increased wealth and means of information of the slaves, who, from their manual labour having been materially lessened within the last few years, by the employment of horned cattle, carts, and ploughs, to perform the most laborious parts of the business, and from the great efforts made by Owners and Overseers, not only to keep them in health, but to make them comfortable – granting them many indulgences – suffering them to keep cattle, and some own houses – to have large dwelling houses – great and frequent entertainments, with dancing, costly apparel, trinkets, etc. – had become more impatient of restraint ...[42]

Barbadian slave-owners were suggesting, in part, that earlier reforms and ameliorative action had created the context for increased leisure activities among slaves, and were mindful that abolitionists were of the opinion that the considerable social autonomy slaves experienced constituted proof of their readiness for general emancipation. For slave-owners, then, it was necessary to demonstrate the irresponsibility of Blacks, with respect to their management and proper use of free time, as the basis of their rejection of the abolitionists' notion of inevitable gradual emancipation.

Confessions taken from rebel slaves before the courts martial, and from the depositions of slave witnesses confirmed that revolutionary organisation was made possible on account of the frequent contact at social gatherings. The confession of Daniel, carpenter at the River estate where hundreds of slaves were involved, appeared as a principal document of the report. Daniel reported possession of first-hand knowledge of the main leaders of the rebellion: Bussa, Cain Davis and Sarjeant. Cain Davis, he said, had come to his home and apprised him of early plans, and that the next time they met was at a dance on Good Friday night at the River estate to make final plans for the revolt. This dance was attended by Bussa, Jackey, Johnny Cooper and other leaders.[43]

Similar reactions were reported by Jamaican slave-owners with respect to their slaves' possession and use of free time. On the 28 January 1824 charges 'to enter into a rebellious conspiracy, for the purpose of obtaining, by force and violence, and by acts of resistance to the lawful authorities of [the] island, the freedom of themselves, and other such slaves' were heard in a Montego Bay, Jamaica, court-house. The prisoners, Richard Allen, Trelawny, Robert Galloway, Garrett Rainie, Philip Haughton, William Stennett, John Cunningham, Archy Bucknor, Mary Ann Reid, James Kerr, William Kerr, Corydon, James Campbell and Providence, were represented by Hon. Samuel Jackson and William Quarrell before a jury of 12 White men (three merchants, six planters, two wharfingers and a carpenter). Seven counts were levied against the accused, the fifth, sixth and seventh of which drew attention to three, and possibly more, dances and pre-Christmas parties, they attended for the 'dangerous purpose of exciting, encouraging, and maintaining each other, and other slaves in endeavouring by force, to obtain their freedom'.[44]

The prosecution for the Crown sought indictment not for rebellion, but for a rebellious conspiracy. The first four counts were framed under the 46th clause of the island's slave code, and related to 'being at a meeting for an unlawful and dangerous purpose'. The remaining three counts were with respect to the 51st clause, 'being at meetings without the knowledge of the owner or overseer'. The prosecution spoke of the illegality of the dances within the contexts of their unauthorised and rebellious nature. The slaves, all from Unity Hall and Spring Garden estates in the parish of St James, were presented as clandestine political agents with revolutionary intentions.

Parties and dances were advanced as the social events within which anti-slavery designs were organised. Reference was made specifically to two dances held at Mary Ann's house and one at John Cunningham's in the pre-Christmas period, but general mention was made of gatherings as early as August when it was common to celebrate the yam harvest. Mary Ann's home was described as a regular dance venue with slaves from distant estates attending to drink rum and dance into the early hours of the morning. Both slaves and free persons, Black, Coloured and White, gave evidence for and against the accused in the case which was presided over by Hon. Samuel Vaughan, a judge and planter of elite social standing.

It was a trial in which Jamaican slave-owners seized an opportunity to debate the extent to which slaves had established a social life of their own, as well as an occasion to publicly ventilate their responses to Wilberforce's assault upon colonial society. In court proceedings slaves were described as having attained extensive social freedom, and Wilberforce was termed 'a base traitor' by the prosecution.[45] Images of slaves freely holding nightly parties and interrupting their dancing to drink 'Wilberforce's health' during the Christmas season were constructed for the jury by the prosecution; the defence sought to establish that slave parties were entirely permissible under the law, and that while there could have been some loose talk, typical of the season and often alcohol-inspired, there was no evidence of real conspiracy. The slaves, in summary, were not rebellious, but 'were merry-makers, mere dancers'.[46]

The jury was not convinced fully by the argument of the defence. They were instructed by Judge Vaughan that dances were permitted by the slave laws, and that free men of good character often attended such gatherings. The legal question before them, however, was whether these night dances were protective cover for the planning and encouragement of 'sedition, conspiracy or rebellion'. Several witnesses, Judge Vaughan noted, provided evidence that slaves did state at the dances in question that with respect to freedom they 'would fight for it', and that 'they and the Whites are now on a footing'.[47] 'All these expressions', he instructed the jury, 'must be termed criminal and rebellious', but he implored them 'to consider that there was no overt act of rebellion proved; no proof of a sword being drawn, nor a threat against a White except by implication'. 'In rebellion', he concluded, 'you must have an overt act', but in this case not concluded, 'there is only a disposition in the mind, a propensity of mind to crime'.

It took one hour of deliberations for the 12-man jury to reach its verdict after the three-day trial. Trelawny, William Kerr, James Campbell, John Cunningham and Philip Haughton were found guilty of the fifth, sixth and seventh counts of the indictment. Richard Allen, Robert Galloway, Garrett Rainie, William Stennett, Archy Bucknor, Mary Ann Reid, James Kerr and Croydon were found guilty of the seventh count. Providence was found not guilty. For 'attending meetings for the dangerous purpose of obtaining [their own] freedom, and the freedom of others by force', Trelawney and the others were sentenced to be transported off the island for life. Richard Allen and others were sentenced to various terms of hard labour and corporal punishments. Mary Ann Reid, 'in consideration of her sex' was ordered to serve four months hard labour in the workhouse.[48]

Conclusions

Barbadian slaves, then, were executed in large numbers on conviction for using dances as venues for the planning and staging of anti-slavery revolution, while a few of their Jamaican counterparts were sentenced to terms of hard labour, transportation and corporal punishments for thinking and carelessly talking at parties about self-liberation. In the latter case, the relations between language, culture and ideology enabled the judiciary to probe into an area of philosophy that provided a context for the meaning of resistance. A slave was not considered to be in a state of rebellion by virtue of harbouring recognisable anti-slavery thoughts, or even by the social articulation of such thoughts. Rebellion required actual physical action, as well as conscious organisation and planning.

The law, it seemed, had interest in a very limited understanding of language as a signifier and symbols of political ideology. Insubordinate attitudes and refusal mentalities were considered natural and therefore inevitable by the law, even though slave-owners and the White community in general did interpret such behaviours and states of consciousness as rebellious and acted punitively in accordance with notions of self-protection. The relationship between a slave-owner's subjective reading of a slave's mind, and the legal protection of the slave from owner tyranny, created a grey area within which more slaves lost their lives than the records available suggest.

The entertainment culture of slaves, therefore, constituted a slice of every-day life over which the contest between hegemonic consensus and popular resistance was played out. Slave dances were also attended by White persons, as well as Free Blacks and Free Coloureds, whose pro-slavery agendas and ideologies were known to their slave hosts. Ideologically, then, the formal context of leisure organisation was complex, with the free and the enslaved moving to the beat of different drums. In this sense, the slave party was in part an aspect of the pro-slavery apparatus that had to be internally subverted in order to serve anti-slavery purposes. For these reasons, the judge and jury at Montego Bay found it necessary to untangle the threads in order to separate the guilty from the innocent, the rebels from the revellers.[49]

Dances, then, were events designed for social amusement and recreation, as well as venues for political conscientisation and organisation. The notion of a social contract between slave-owners and slaves was ultimately a figment of some slave-owners' imagination, since freedom in its fullest legal sense was never removed from the top of the slaves' agenda. Slave-owners' misrepre-sentation of the impact of paternalistic ideology was also in part the result of unfamiliarity with the nature and role of cultural action in plantation-based African-derived ontologies. While cultural activity among slaves took on an overt leisure-pleasure format, ultimately the process of celebration was about freedom from constraints, real or imagined, and the search for, or idealisation of, autonomy – the antithesis of slavery. Slave-owners had, once again, proceeded with assumptions of their race and class superiority that excluded the possibility of a closer interpretation of Black social culture within the organic context of the evolving anti-slavery struggle. Finally, the condition of slavery, enslaved Blacks seemed to be stating, was no more than a transitory state.

Notes

1.   See K. Brathwaite, *The Folk Culture of the Slaves in Jamaica* (London: New Beacon Books, 1970); R. Dirks, 'John Canoe: Ethnohistorical and Comparative Analysis of a Carib Dance', *Actes du XLII Congrès International des Américanistes*, 6 (1979), pp. 487–501; R. Dirks, 'Slave Holiday', *Natural History*, 84: 10 (1975), pp. 84–90; J. Handler and R. Corruccine, 'Plantation

Slave Life in Barbados', *Journal of Interdisciplinary History*, 14, 1 (1983), pp. 65–90; S. Mintz, 'The Plantation as a Socio-Cultural Type', in *Plantation Systems of the New World*, Social Science Monograph, 7 (Washington, DC: Pan American Union, 1959); M. Craton, 'Decoding Pitchy-Patchy: The Roots, Branches and Essence of Junkanoo', paper presented at the 26th Annual Conference of the Association of Caribbean Historians (Puerto Rico, 1994).

2.   Dirks, *The Black Saturnalia: Conflict and its Ritual Expression on British West Indian Slave Plantations* (Gainesville, FL: University Presses of Florida, 1987), p. 145; S. Wynter, 'Jonkonnu in Jamaica: Toward an Interpretation of Folk Dance as Cultural Process', *Jamaica Journal*, Vol. 4. No. 2, (1970), pp. 34–48; J. Bettelheim, 'Jamaica Jonkonu and Related Caribbean Festivals', in M. Crahan and F. Knight, *Africa in the Caribbean* (Baltimore: Johns Hopkins Press, 1979), pp. 80–100; R. Rath, 'African Music in Seventeenth-Century Jamaica: Cultural Transit and Transmission', *William and Mary Quarterly*, 3rd ser., L:4 (October 1993), pp. 700–26; Mintz and R. Price, *An Anthropological Approach to the Afro-American Past: A Caribbean Perspective* (Philadelphia: ISHI, 1976).

3.   See, for example, how Africans mobilised their economic culture: H. Beckles, 'An Economic Life of Their Own: Slaves as Commodity Producers and Distributors in Barbados', in I. Berlin and P. Morgan, eds., *The Slaves' Economy: Independent Production by Slaves in the Americas* (London; Frank Cass, 1991), pp. 31–48; M. Turner, 'Slave Workers, Subsistence and Labour Bargaining: Amity Hall, Jamaica, 1805–32', Berlin and Morgan, in *The Slaves' Economy*; Mintz, 'Caribbean Market Places and Caribbean History', *Nova Americana*, 1 (1980–1), pp. 333–44; Beckles and K. Watson, 'Social Protest and Labour Bargaining: The Changing Nature of Slaves' Responses to Plantation Life in 18th Century Barbados', *Slavery and Abolition*, 8 (1987), pp. 272–93.

4.   O. Patterson, *The Sociology of Slavery: An Analysis of the Origins, Development and Structure of Negro Slave Society in Jamaica* (London: MacGibbon and Kee, 1967), pp. 230–59. See also H. Johnson, 'Slave Life and Leisure in Nassau, Bahamas, 1783–1838', paper presented at the 26th Annual Conference of the Association of Caribbean Historians (Puerto Rico, 1994), pp. 1, 9.

5.   N. Hall, 'Slave use of their "free" time in the Danish Virgin Islands in the Later Eighteenth and Early Nineteenth Century', *Journal of Caribbean History*, Vol. 13 (1980), p. 22. See also Brathwaite, *The Development of Creole Society in Jamaica, 1770–1820* (Oxford: Clarendon Press, 1971), pp. 295–6.

6.   Johnson, 'Slave life and leisure', op. cit.

7.   S. Arutuniev, 'Cultural Paradigms: The Process of Change Through Cultural Borrowings' *Cultures*, Vol. 5. No. 1 (1978), pp. 94–5; J. Dumanazedier, *Sociology of Leisure* (Oxford: Oxford University Press, 1974); P. Burke,

Popular Culture in Early Modern Europe (London: Routledge, 1979); J. Walvin, *Leisure and Society* (London: MacMillan 1978); R. W. Malcolmson, *Popular Recreations in English Society, 1700–1850* (Cambridge: University Press, 1973); G. Turner, *British Cultural Studies: An Introduction* (London: Routledge, 1990), pp. 180–215; H. Cunningham, 'Class and Leisure in Mid-Victorian England', in B. Waites et al., eds., *Popular Culture: Past and Present* (London: Croom Helm, 1982), pp. 64–91; J. Fiske, *Understanding Popular Culture* (Boston: Unwin Hyman, 1989); S. Hall, 'Cultural Studies: Two Paradigms', in A. Bennett, et al., eds., *Culture, Ideology and Social Process: A Reader* (London, Open University Press, 1981), pp. 19–37; C. Mouffe, 'Hegemony and Ideology in Gramsci', in Bennett, *Culture, Ideology*, pp. 219–34.

8.   Brathwaite, *Development of Creole Society*, p. 220.
9.   See S. Stuckey, *Slave Culture: Nationalist Theory and the Foundations of Black America* (New York: Oxford University Press, 1987), pp. 7–27; 'Through the Prism of Folklore: The Black Ethos in Slavery', *Massachusetts Review*, 9 (1968), p. 427; J.H. Aimes, 'African Institutions in America', *Journal of American Folk-Lore*, 18 (1905), p. 15.
10. Dirks, *Black Saturnalia*, pp. 145, 168, 170–1.
11. Brathwaite, *Development of Creole Society*, p. 220; 'An Act for the Better Governing of Slaves, 1688', in R. Hall, *Acts Passed in the Island of Barbados from 1643 to 1762 Inclusive* (London, 1764), pp. 112–7; W. Dickson, *The Mitigation of Slavery* (London, 1814) Watson, *The Civilised Island, Barbados: A Social History, 1750–1816* (Barbados, 1979, n.p.), pp. 85–6.
12. Watson, *Civilised Island*, p. 80.
13. Ibid., pp. 92–3.
14. F. Bayley, *Four Years Residence in the West Indies* (London, 1830).
15. Ibid. p. 69.
16. Ibid. p. 305.
17. Watson, *Civilised Island*.
18. Ibid.
19. Dickson, *Mitigation of Slavery*, pp. 155–6.
20. G. Franklyn, *Reply to R. B. Nicholls' Letter to the Treasurer of the Society Instituted for the Purposes of Effecting the Abolition of the Slave Trade* (London, c. 1790) p. 56.
21. G. Pinckard, *Notes on the West Indies*, 3 vols (London, 1806), Vol. I, p. 263.
22. Cited in Watson, *Civilised Island*, p. 83.
23. Ibid., p. 84.
25. Ibid.
25. Bayley, *Four Years Residence*, p. 436.
26. Ibid.

27. Ibid.
28. Mrs A.C. Carmichael, *Domestic Manners and Social Conditions of the White, Coloured and Negro Population of the West Indies*, 2 vols (London, 1833), Vol 1, pp. 175–6. Dirks, *Black Saturnalia*, pp. 146–7.
29. See Watson *Civilised Island*, p. 84.
30. Pinckard, *Notes*, pp. 263–4.
31. T. Wentworth, *The West India Sketch Book* (London, 1834), Vol. 1, pp. 65–7, 228–30; Vol. II, pp. 240–2, 282.
32. Ibid.
33. Bayley, *Four Years Residence*, pp. 69–71, 437–8.
34. Beckles, 'The Slave Drivers' War: The 1816 Barbados Slave Uprising', *Boletin del y Estudios Caribe Latinamericanos* No. 39, (December 1985), pp. 85–111; 'Emancipation by Law or War! Wilberforce and the 1816 Barbados Slave Rebellion', in D. Richardson, ed., *Abolition and Its Aftermath: The Historical Context, 1790–1916* (London: Frank Cass, 1985), pp. 80–105; Craton, 'Proto-Peasant Revolts'? op. cit.; C. Levy, 'Slavery and the Emancipation Movement in Barbados, 1650–1833', *Journal of Negro History*, 58 (1970), pp. 1–12; Craton, *Testing the Chains: Resistance to Slavery in the British West Indies* (Ithaca, NY: Cornell University Press, 1982), pp. 254–67.
35. Robert Haynes to Thomas Lane, 23 September 1816; Newton Estate Papers, 523/781, Senate House Library, London University.
36. CO 28/85, fol. 8, Governor Leith to Lord Bathurst, 29 April 1816.
37. *The Report from a Select Committee of the House of Assembly Appointed to Inquire into the Origins, Cause, and Progress of the Late Insurrection of April 1816* (Barbados, 1818). For an independent report of the rebellion, see anon., An Account of the Late Negro Insurrection which took place in the Island of Barbados on Easter Sunday, 14 April 1816. New York Public Library, MSS Division.
38. *The Report from a Select Committee.*
39. Ibid., p. 51.
40. Ibid., p. 53.
41. Ibid.
42. Ibid., p. 55.
43. Ibid., pp. 26–7.
44. *Report of the Trial of Fourteen Negroes at the Court-House, Montego Bay, January 28, 1824 on a Charge of Rebellious Conspiracy* (Montego Bay, 1824), pp. 4–5.
45. Ibid., p. 43.
46. Ibid., p. 49.
47. Ibid., p. 31.
48. Ibid., p. 54.
49. Ibid., p. 4.

Part Two

Massa/Missus Day Done?

SECTION

V

Pricing Slavery, Pricing Freedom

'The 11 o'clock flog'
Women, work and labour law in the British Caribbean

MARY TURNER

The British imperial government began to dismantle the slave labour system in its colonies in the mid-1820s. Under pressure from the abolitionists and with the full support of the West India Committee, it set out a reform programme which defined significant changes in the slave labour laws and made special provisions to implement them. The proposed slave labour laws set out new terms for slave labour, regulated work place discipline, legalised and expanded certain customary civil rights the slaves had won, and appointed a full-time official, a Protector of Slaves, to implement the law. The declared aim of the reform package was to 'prepare the slaves for freedom'.

Planters in the Representative Colonies consistently opposed the amelioration policy. The Jamaica Assembly, which controlled the largest single unit of slaves in the British Caribbean, at first refused to even consider the proposed reforms, claiming the imperial government was trespassing on its constitutional privileges. Planters in the Crown Colonies, conquered from the Spanish and Dutch during the Revolutionary Wars (Trinidad, Demerara-Essequibo and Berbice) were scarcely more enthusiastic, but commanded less constitutional power. In Trinidad the imperial government implemented its model reform package by Order in Council in 1824; and in Demerara-Essequibo and Berbice on the South American mainland, new slave labour laws reflecting imperial guidelines were in place by 1826.

The co-operation of the Crown Colonies was facilitated by the fact that in the colonial legal structures which the British took over from the Dutch and the Spanish there was an official whose duties included guardianship of the slaves. In the mainland colonies the *fiscals* and in Trinidad the *procurador fiscal*, continued to function in this capacity, consistent with the terms of conquest, after the British take-over. The appointment of a Protector of Slaves, therefore, was not an innovation, but an adaptation of an established office. In Trinidad the existing *procurador fiscal* in fact took over as Protector.

The re-definition and implementation of the slave labour laws mark with some precision the moment of articulation between one system of labour extraction and another: chattel slavery into wage slavery. On the one hand, the existing laws reflect the slave labour system as established for perpetuity; on the other, the new laws devised by the first industrial imperial state, point the way to wage work.

This chapter investigates the impact of the new laws on slave workers, particularly on women slave workers in Berbice. It reviews first the cases they brought against their owners and managers under the old slave laws before the Fiscal and then reviews the cases brought under the 1826 Code before the Protector. Berbice is the only mainland colony where the records allow this comparison to be made. No records of slave grievance cases, or of the Fiscal's summary judgements made were kept in Demerara-Essequibo. Records exist for Berbice only because in 1819 Henry Beard, a qualified lawyer, was for the first time appointed President of the Courts of Civil and Criminal Justice; he persuaded the Fiscal, H.M. Bennett, that he should voluntarily (since no regulation compelled him to do so) record the cases he dealt with as guardian of the slaves. Bennett partially complied by making 'notes for his own satisfaction' of his investigations, but omitted to record his judgements except on the very rare occasion when cases were referred to a higher court. His deputy, J.M. Scott, was more conscientious and noted both investigation and judgement. These records, in conjunction with the detailed reports the Protector of Slaves was required by law to submit to the local and imperial government, provide the basis for this investigation.[1]

Berbice was the last of the three colonies the Dutch established on the shoulder of South America and the slowest to develop. In economic terms its performance was quite outclassed by the sugar plantation dominated colonies of Demerara-Essequibo, which in the 1820s constituted the colonies' economic heartland. Berbice by comparison remained a frontier province. Its population in 1830 was almost 90 per cent slaves and totalled only 23,000 people who were thinly spread along the coast and the upper reaches of the Berbice river and Canje creek. Many plantations there were isolated as many as 40 miles from the nearest government outpost. As much as half the slave population was African born and was held, characteristically, in large-scale holdings of 200 or more workers. The economy was comparatively diversified: sugar production occupied less than 50 per cent of slave workers (compared with 80 per cent in Demerara-Essequibo) coffee, cotton, provision and cattle production engaged most of the rest.[2]

Work conditions in Berbice, as in Demerara-Essequibo, were vitally influenced by the fact that the coastal plain was below sea level. Plantations there were polders, land claimed from the sea, and maintenance of sea defences, drains and canals constantly demanded strenuous digging and building work from the slave gangs. At the same time, in contrast to the island territories, there was no sugar harvest period; the mills could be kept turning throughout the year, making the demand for night work in the factories continuous.[3]

Women slaves, who constituted slightly less than half the work force, were valued on the estates primarily as field and factory workers: supervisory roles and skilled work were male preserves. Women shared in the heaviest work and this conflicted with their role in reproduction. It is not surprising to find that the birth rate in Berbice, as elsewhere in the British Caribbean outside Barbados, was significantly below the death rate. Self-interest consequently encouraged owners, particularly after 1807 when abolition of the slave trade cut off their reserve army of African labour, to provide sick care. By the 1820s Berbice was comparatively well supplied with doctors with one for every 900 slaves employed by slave-owners at a fixed annual rate and some estates had hospitals.[4]

The statute laws regulating slave labour were embodied in a few local Ordinances that dealt with slave discipline and subsistence rights. The maximum punishment for workplace offences was set in 1810 at 39 lashes, the Biblical standard and pass laws in 1804 and 1806 confined slaves to the estate unless they had written permission from their owner. In 1806 their rations were defined as two full grown bunches of plantain weekly (nursing children excepted), or two common coffee baskets full of cassava or yam. To secure this supply, coastal estates were to grow 75 plantain trees per slave or 60 on the rivers where the plantain grew better. Fines were fixed at 1,000 and 2,000 guilders for the first and second offence and criminal prosecution for the third, a punishment schedule that suggests a law more honoured in the breach than the observance. A few slaves also had the use of small plots, though these were not common on poldered land, to supply fruit and vegetables; in contrast to some of the island economies, however, market outlets for any surplus were limited.

The Ordinances were supplemented by customs, a form of Common Law, which embodied slave rights established by tradition under pressure from the slaves, or rights which had been conceded by the Dutch and continued to be recognised by government officials. The slaves' customary rights included the right to own most forms of personal property except firearms and small boats which were useful for escape along the rivers; a customary right to be either sold in families, or separated by consent; the right to give evidence in criminal cases, but not on oath; and a right, limited by works of necessity only, to Sunday free from forced labour as well as Christmas holidays. This right was widely established by law or custom throughout the British Caribbean by the end of the eighteenth century and, when occasion arose, was defended in Berbice by the Fiscal. Customary rights, however, tended to be fragile and slave workers had to act on their own behalf to defend them.[5]

The Fiscal consequently administered a system with few legally defined pains and penalties. He had undefined discretionary power to punish the slaves for petty offences with flogging and imprisonment in a 'summary but moderate way'. And he took legal action against owners and managers found in breach of regulations. To facilitate this he enjoyed a general brief which entitled him to enter all properties where slaves were working to check the extent of grounds growing provisions, the scale of food and clothing supplied, the condition of estate sick houses and of the slave population in general.

The Fiscal's salary was 3,000 guilders a year plus fees and an under-sheriff and six 'dienaars' or justice officers assisted him. Bennett was a substantial slave-owner with a half interest in two sugar estates with a slave population of 288, together with ten domestics in his New Amsterdam household. He combined in his person every level of authority over slaves.[6] The lack of a systematic and comprehensive slave labour law, decision-making at the highest level in the hands of a slave owner and the tradition of non-accountability, were problems the 1826 Ordinance was intended to resolve.

The pre-1826 records used here show that the Fiscal and his deputy dealt on average with three cases a month and noted one-third with judgements.[7] These cases represented only a small proportion of the work-place disputes which occurred. As the case histories outlined below demonstrate, plaintiffs often made their grievances known to their manager, attorney or owner, even the local burger officer who combined the functions of magistrate and military officer, before requesting a pass from their manager to visit the Fiscal. Such disputes characterised the day-to-day working of the slave labour system throughout the Americas and helped to shape customary law and the informal contract terms on which slave labour was exacted. The slaves' ultimate weapon in these disputes was collective withdrawal of labour, or strike action; 'going to bush' pitted their ultimate ownership of their labour power against the owners' punishment capacity in efforts to shape their terms of work: hours worked, work loads, punishment norms and food supplied.[8]

In Berbice, appeal to the Fiscal offered an additional, constitutional-legal route to achieving these ends. The slaves' right to lay grievances before a high-ranking, salaried government official, legitimised and, arguably gave added value to their estate-based struggles. This was more particularly the case since, under the Dutch system, owners and managers were penalised for failing to resolve conflicts on the estates; they paid 12 guilders for every slave worker who appeared before the Fiscal, which made collective complaints expensive, and more than double that (25 guilders) for each slave punished at the town jail for lodging a complaint judged unfounded. The cases the slaves brought for redress to the Fiscal and, subsequently, to the Protector of Slaves, illuminate the working of the estate-based labour bargaining system and raise the question, in what ways did the 1826 Slave Code impact on these processes?[9]

Women slave workers went to the Fiscal with charges against owners, managers and, on occasion, slave drivers. They acted individually and collectively; sometimes in a group with other women on behalf of themselves, or of the whole work force and sometimes with their male co-workers. In the latter case a man was usually spokesperson and women spoke in support. Groups of men appearing at the Office conveyed an element of threat, a hint of the physical force slave workers implicitly commanded – a factor which had added value after the August 1823 rebellion in neighbouring Demerara. All-women collective protests to the Fiscal were comparatively rare and comprise only one in every eight of the total. They posed, arguably, a different sort of threat by showing that slave workers of the very lowest rank had been driven to combine and protest. Women, both individually and collectively, often opened up the process with managers and attorneys, or attempted to win redress when their men-folk had failed. In some cases, as at Reumzigt, for example, they filled both roles. Reumzigt was a coffee property on the Berbice river with some 80 workers where punishment levels were first protested to one of the estate attorneys by an 11-man delegation. He sent them back to the estate to have their grievances flogged out of them, and to make sure the job was properly done and to preserve the authority of the gang's resident driver, floggers were hired to do the job. The delegation was then put in the stocks, making two punishments for one protest.

The workers then tried a different tack and sent one individual pregnant woman to see the second attorney who ordered her flogged as well. The manager was unwilling to do this and put her in the stocks to be 'fed sparingly' for a week. Methods of local redress had been exhausted, therefore, when the manager knocked down and kicked a woman because her box of coffee beans was not picked clean enough. At this point a four-woman delegation went to the Fiscal. They complained on behalf of the whole workforce that for every trifling offence, such as a single unsound bean in a box of picked over coffee, earned flogging. They brought a box of coffee beans to show the standard they thought acceptable. The record does not, unfortunately, reveal what the outcome of this protest was. No judgement was recorded and as was frequently the case, no law applied to it. The Fiscal's frequent practice in such circumstances was to tell the manager to moderate his conduct and give notice of a complaint to his employer. The case exemplifies, however, all the customary and legal methods available to slave workers in the absence of a resident owner to protest their work conditions and the roles played by women workers in this process.[10]

Women worker disputes with managers revolved around the issues taken up by the men: punishments, task size, overwork, Sunday work, sickness and work, food and clothing, separation of families and parent rights, sale or hire of their persons as individuals, or collectively. To these were added disputes concerning pregnancy, child rearing and sexual services. Most cases involved more than one issue since once before the Fiscal, workers often took the opportunity to state all their grievances. Their fundamental purposes, however, were clear; they sought to limit the use of coercion and limit the demands on their labour power. The cases dealt with below illustrate both workplace conditions and the extent of legal redress available before the 1826 Ordinance was implemented.

The task-work system characteristic of Berbice and all the mainland colonies was a key focus of manager-worker conflict. Tasks were defined by managers and regulated, at best, by custom. Defined as a quantity of work, the task system notionally rewarded the industrious with free time and automatically penalised the lazy; in practice, it allowed managers to set tasks which filled the regular working day and then measure and punish shortfalls without necessarily taking into account weather and soil conditions which affected the quantity of labour needed. New managers also used the system to intensify labour exaction by setting higher production standards. The 11 o'clock flog was integral to task work; it took place when, after the morning's work was done and the slaves were due for their two-hour 11 am to 1 pm break, it was found that less than half the task had been completed. The threat of the 11 o'clock flog sometimes drove slaves to work through their break in the hope of avoiding punishment.[11]

At Prospect sugar estate worker discontent covered the entire spectrum of worker grievances, but was brought to a head by the task issue and the 11 o'clock flog. The manager's work and punishment regime had already prompted an all-male delegation to the attorney and cuts in rations had sent a woman to complain to him also; neither appeal was successful and the female petitioner was flogged. The women were sparked into action by an 11 o'clock flog. They were employed relieving and supplying canes and found behind hand with their task. The manager said the task was one row of 49 roods (a rood being 12 feet) and they had only done 15 by break time. They claimed the work went slowly because the ground was dried out and had first to be watered before they could chop it and plant the cane. As they explained to the driver, if the cane was not properly planted they would be flogged for that. At noon the manager, who clearly thought they were under-exerting themselves, sent the headman, the highest authority in the slave village, to go and flog each of the strong (not the weak, or pregnant) women 12 lashes each.

The women made it clear that the manager's regime at Prospect maximised workloads and minimised subsistence. They were obliged to do night work at the mill for sugar manufacture, to bring firewood in from the canal mouth, to do occasional work, such as moving a corn store in the evening. On Sundays they had to collect firewood for the kitchen and steam engine as well as grass. At the same time individual workloads had been increased; for example, only four instead of five workers were employed to move megasse from the mill. The manager also deprived them of their rations; the attorney supplied their two bunches of plantain each week, but one was used to feed the stock together with all the molasses, and they were never issued tobacco, or rum. Even the sick were kept on short rations and received no fish.[12]

Once the slaves had stated their case the Fiscal or his deputy either visited the estate to collect evidence, or called witnesses, including owners, attorneys, managers, drivers and slave workers not involved in the delegation, to his office. His power to redress grievances was strictly limited. He could rule the size of the task was reasonable, but where he found it unreasonable he could do no more than suggest reduction. He could condemn a punishment regime as 'excessive' and declare the manager 'too frequently inflicted punishment without sufficient cause'. But if no evidence indicated that any one flogging exceeded the upper limit of 39 lashes he could only tell the manager to moderate his conduct and advise his employer to dismiss him if he failed to do so.[13]

Of the charges brought by the women at Prospect, Sunday work breached acknowledged custom and another related to subsistence standards customarily afforded by the estate. Attorney and manager defended themselves as best they could. The manager professed not to know Sunday work was not customary in Berbice so he was simply continuing a practice he found operating when he took over the estate. In any case, he argued, the workers expending more labour could 'easily' move the twenty cords of wood in question over six nights. And he had 'paid' the slaves for overwork on the corn store with baskets of corn.

It is quite possible that Sunday work was customary at Prospect; but slave workers subjected to new managers usually tried to resolve old grievances as well as win new concessions. And the exchange of additional rations, or of free time, or cash for additional work, was a well-established custom in Berbice as elsewhere. In this case, however, the exchange of corn for extra work simply aggravated the slaves' grievances about subsistence.

The ration issue was very sensitive both between workers and managers and between owners and managers because managers were commonly suppose to embezzle plantation supplies for their own profit. The managers in this case stoutly defended themselves. The overseer supplied a certificate of supplies issued to the slaves and the driver backed up the manager's denial that slave rations went to the stock. Nevertheless, it is clear that the manager was making economies. The slaves got two bunches of plantains one week and one bunch plus seven pounds of rice or 25 ears of corn on alternate weeks. Plantains were, however, more nutritious than corn or rice, having twice the calorie content. The customary rum ration was cut and distributed only as a reward, a system that penalised average and elderly workers, and tobacco was no longer distributed. Customary standards of subsistence had been cut, but not below legal standards.[14]

The Fiscal used the occasion to condemn the 11 o'clock flog as 'premature'; he considered punishment for an unfinished task was appropriate, but only at the end of the working day and not before. He affirmed the slaves' right to be free from work on Sundays. The plaintiffs, however, were reprimanded for complaining to him instead of to their master. By doing so they showed a lack of proper respect for a master who 'supplied their wants plentifully'. The women accepted defeat and made the necessary signals of regret and apology. The case had given them a political platform, obliged their bosses to defend themselves, cost the attorney Mr Ross 72 guilders, affirmed their right to a work-free Sunday and sent a warning signal to the manager about punishments and food supplies.

The case neatly exposes how the system worked. The Fiscal's chief role was to mediate conflict in the best interest of slave property owners, sparing the manager legal prosecution and reinforcing where possible the attorney's authority. Managers were warned in no less than 42 judgements recorded by the deputy Fiscal between 1822 and 1823 that any further complaint of equivalent ill treatment by their slaves would lead to prosecution. There is only one recorded instance, however, where a slave's complaint prompted an owner's immediate punishment and this involved a man who, at the behest of his wife, flogged, put in the stocks and threatened to put a chain round the neck of a slave woman who had supplied him with sexual services. This combination of harsh punishment and sexual exploitation prompted a 600 guilder fine. But when slaves complained that the manager at Plantation Scotland had at various times taken over no less than 11 slaves wives, he was only reprimanded and his employer advised to dismiss him.[15]

Excessive workload and punishment regimes were often combined with underfeeding and ill treatment of the sick. Two female and three male delegates from the aptly named sugar estate Plantation Profit, with its daily 11 o'clock flog of 25 lashes, its stocks full of people and a fish ration once a month, said when they complained of sickness they were flogged first then dosed with salts and camomile. One of the plaintiffs had asked for a blister (which would have kept her in hospital some days) and was flogged by the manager who said he would blister her backside; another was told 'the stocks is your physic'. Punishment and neglect of sick workers prompted numerous complaints from both men and women. As the judgements recorded by the Acting-Fiscal demonstrate, however, his powers were limited to recommending medical care, reprimanding managers for flogging the sick or dismissing the complaint as frivolous.[16]

The workload, punishment, subsistence and health problems women slave workers shared with men were multiplied by their role as mothers. Once the slave trade was cut off, the reproduction of the slave workforce became, notionally, a priority for owners throughout the British Caribbean and more particularly in colonies such as Berbice with an internal frontier to exploit. But notional long-term benefits for owners inevitably tended to take second place to the immediate needs of plantation production and profit. Pregnant women labourers necessarily in the later months worked at reduced capacity while nursing women labourers threatened a longer-term loss of hours in the field. The conflictive demands of work and reproduction which led in England, for example, to infants being born at the bottom of mineshafts, were intensified under slavery by the use of the whip.

Some estates in Berbice, as the cases outlined above indicate, made concessions to pregnant workers, and modified workloads, deployed them in jobs suited to their capacity and punished them in the stocks rather than by flogging. But the evidence makes it abundantly clear these were not standard practices. Managers were more likely to take the attitude that 'they were not there to mind babies'. They forced women by threats of violence – one promised 'to break her belly with a foe-foe pounder', a stout wooden stick used to process plantain – to continue their regular work routine and subjected them with sadistic zeal to standard punishments.

Occasionally such managers were brought to justice. This happened at Plantation L'Esperance coffee estate, where Rosa, who was far advanced in pregnancy and protested she was too big to stoop, was sent to pick coffee. She had to do so on her knees. It was task work and at 11 am when the driver checked, none of the women had picked their quota. The manager ordered him to lay all the women out on the coffee-drying platform and flog them one after the other. When the driver got to Rosa he stopped and said, 'This woman is rather big with child'. The manager said, 'Give it to her till the blood flies out'. The bush whip, the *carracarra*, had broken by then so he used a doubled cart whip. The next day Rosa was sent to the field again, but had labour pains and was allowed to go to the hospital. The doctor examined her and declared sitting down would not be good for her. Many miscarriages, he considered, came from women taking no exercise and contracting lazy habits. So Rosa was sent back to the field. The next day she miscarried.

It was a hard labour and the midwife had to force it. Three women as well as Rosa and her husband saw the child; it was perfectly formed as she was near term, but born dead 'with one eye out, the arm broken, and a stripe visible over the head which must have been done with the double whip'. The parents told the manager the baby was dead, the father dug the grave and one of the helpers at the birth carried the body out. The next day the doctor saw Rosa and said, 'I suppose you have been eating green pines'.

The Fiscal heard evidence from all the actors involved and took particular care to get one witness to confirm the manager's order to 'flog her till the blood comes'. This case prompted instant action: the manager was immediately suspended and prosecuted. Despite a judicial system characteristically arbitrary in dealing with such cases he was eventually sentenced to three months in jail, fined 200 pounds and dismissed from his post.[17] Flogging women could induce a miscarriage at any stage of pregnancy and the question arises, did confinement in the stocks do the same? Two witnesses in one case, including the slave sick nurse attendant, testified this happened to a woman in the early stage of pregnancy who was put in the hospital stocks for a week for attacking a slave driver.[18]

When babies arrived safely and survived the initial hazards of death from disease, mothers faced the problem of securing time to nurse. Some managers allowed nursing women a shorter working day so they could feed the infant before work and at noon as well as in the evening; others insisted infants be weaned early and left in the care of women too old for field work. On No. 6 Canje Creek sugar estate, the latter system applied and one worker named Laura, who claimed her child was weakly and left the field to feed it, was flogged. She complained to the Fiscal and requested assistance to carry out what the minutes term 'this natural favour'. The manager, called to the office to give his account, claimed that time at the beginning and end of the day (one and half hours) was allowed for nursing and four nurses were supplied. Further, 12 children had been raised in the last two years which showed the method succeeded. None of this addressed Laura's problem of feeding her weak child at noon, but the Fiscal was evidently satisfied that nursery care at No. 6 Canje Creek met customary standards and the infant was left to take its chances.[19]

Slave workers as parents also turned to the Fiscal when they saw their children harshly punished and underfed. This happened at Plantation Leldenrust where a couple brought charges against their owner on behalf of their four children and themselves. The children had insufficient allowances, inadequate clothing and regular flogging with a bush rope. The Fiscal found one of the boys with marks of severe beating on his posterior and the other, as his mother put it, 'lingers very much'. The parents were themselves forced to work until 4 pm on Sundays, got no holidays, half rations and short cloth allowances.

The Fiscal's investigation revealed that the parent's complaints represented the problems of the entire workforce. He called the slaves together with their owner and made it clear that they were entitled to Sundays free from work, entitled to their rations and bush rope was not to be used. The clothing question, however, was not addressed and no penalty was imposed on the owner. To implement his instructions the Fiscal in this case relied on the slave workers themselves, who were instructed to complain to their nearest burgher officer if the owner did not comply. Although the children stood to benefit together with the rest of the workforce if these changes were implemented, they had no special right to protection by their parents or the law. The assumption was that children raised to the age of five were likely to survive one way or another and in any case property rights were paramount.[20]

Slave workers also looked to the Fiscal to punish managers who sexually exploited their wives and to prevent the break-up by sale of the nuclear family and of their kin and village units. Separation of families by sale contravened acknowledged custom in Berbice, but fear of sale and separation were pervasive, fed not only by local transfers, but by the export trade to Demerara. Slave sales disrupted not only nuclear families but kin groups and village communities as a whole, as well as reviving memories barely a generation old of the traumas of forced migration. One group, sold from their homes, hired out and then threatened with separation protested to the Fiscal that they were 'sent about like new negroes'. Such complaints, which challenged property rights, were considered offensive. Slaves were told to obey their owners on pain of exemplary punishment at the jail.[21]

The evidence here makes clear that the Fiscal presided over a conglomerate of estate-based labour extraction systems barely regulated by law or custom over which he exerted very limited powers. Such powers as he had were, according to the recorded judgements, used more often to dismiss complaints and punish the plaintiffs than to redress grievances. Judgements in favour of slave plaintiffs, moreover, meant at best partial redress; managers were usually only reprimanded, or warned that prosecution was possible but actual prosecutions were rare.[22] Investigation by the Fiscal, however, requiring evidence from managers as well as workers, sometimes on the estate with the full knowledge of the workforce, may have had some effect. The fact that slave workers utilised the system suggests it may have done so.

The slaves' protests outlined here made clear what legal changes were needed to improve their work conditions: legally limited workloads, work time and punishment schedules; adequate and secure subsistence: provisions for sickness, pregnancy, nursing and parenting: protection for family, kin and community groups from division by sale. Slaves also wanted the right to be sold to another employer and the right to secure the dismissal of managers who failed to apply the law. The slave workers' immediate needs required the labour laws to be more comprehensive and rigorously impose new limits on their owners' and managers' personal power.

From the imperial government's point of view, however, the aims and purposes of restructuring the slave laws were more far-reaching and complex. To dismantle chattel slavery meant beginning the transition to wage work, preparing slave workers and slave-owners to become servants and masters, employees and employers. This process required first and foremost that owner-slave relationships be defined by law and systematically applied to both parties by enhancing the powers of the colonial state. The imperial government's 1824 blueprint consequently made implementation of the law its priority. Within the proposed new structural framework the labour laws modified customary methods of slave labour exaction and introduced elements of wage work. Imperial government proposals also took cognisance of the need, on the one hand, to award slave workers new statutory rights that adumbrated citizen status and, on the other, accustom owners to conceding such rights. And to reinforce and sanction ideological change in both classes the imperial government invoked the influence of the church and suggested regulations to facilitate the slaves' religious instruction.

The 1826 Berbice Slave Code reflected in essentials the imperial government's blueprint. Drawn up under the energetic direction of the Lieutenant-Governor, Henry Beard, by his appointed Council between 21 July and 30 September 1826 and put into effect on 1 November, the 44-clause Code incorporated substantial segments of the imperial government's 1824 Order in Council, as well as elaborating local innovations and caveats.[23]

The Code, following the Order in Council, gave primacy to the implementation of the law. It endorsed the appointment of a full-time, salaried Protector of Slaves to hear charges brought by slave workers and slave-owners against each other and either deal with them summarily by applying the fines and punishment defined in the new regulations, or by referring cases to the courts. To assist the Protector in fulfilling his duties the administration of the colony was reorganised. The entire province was divided into districts based partly on divisions established by the Dutch; in each district the governor appointed one or more Civil Magistrates to take over all the civil duties of the Burgher Officers who retained solely military functions. The Magistrates were designated Assistant Protectors of the slaves and bound to obey the Protector's instructions.[24]

The new administration clearly articulated with pre-existing structures. The Fiscal's part-time role as Protector of Slaves became a full time office and the Burgher Officers who had from time to time been called on to act as his assistants, were superseded by Civil Magistrates officially charged to do so. To maximise local support for the new Protector and the new Code, the Lieutenant-Governor chose of a new Raft of Civil Magistrates. The Magistrates, however, who were fined 2,000 guilders if they turned down their appointment, were unpaid. The new structures marked a clear expansion of local authority and were directly responsive to the imperial government. An English official, David Power, was appointed Protector at a salary of £1,000 sterling a year to be paid by the Colonial Government. In due course the Civil Magistrates were superseded by full-time Assistant Protectors of Slaves.[25]

The Governor ordered the new Magistrates to promulgate the law by visiting all the estates in their districts to read and explain it in person to the slaves so as 'to remove any erroneous expectations which they may have formed of anything being in contemplation regarding their state and condition beyond the provisions of this Code'. Where managers were delegated to perform this function they were obliged to report that they had done so to the magistrate. Comments on its reception were to go directly to the Governor.[26]

Implementing the new law nevertheless presented serious problems. As Protector Power told the Colonial Secretary it would go against the 'uniform experience of mankind' to expect that 'legislation so novel and so opposed to the ordinary prepossessions of those upon whose instrumentality its efficiency mainly depended' would be effective on 'mere promulgation'. Power feared he could count neither on the co-operation of planters and Magistrates, nor the support of the Fiscal and the Courts of Civil and Criminal Justice when he tried to put the law into effect.[27] But the 1826 law and his own appointment expanded the Colonial State's authority to mediate between owners and slaves. The number of cases dealt with almost doubled (an average of five rather than two-three a month), investigations were regularly carried out on the estates rather than in the Protector's office, and most significantly, despite substantial legal costs, cases against owners and managers were referred to the courts. The processing of implementing the rule of law between owners and slaves had begun.

The new Code, again in conformity with imperial guidelines, targeted the problem of labour discipline. It limited the use of the whip and defined alternative methods of punishment. The whip, a focus of slave complaints and of anti-slavery propaganda, symbolised the physical brutality, the barely restricted personal power owners exercised at the workplace and the archaic nature of the labour extraction methods which characterised chattel slavery. The Code eliminated the 11 o'clock flog for all slave workers by making it illegal for slave supervisors even to carry a whip in the field on pain of a 600 guilders fine. It prohibited flogging of women on pain of a 1,400 guilder fine, or one to six months in jail, and imposed new regulations on the flogging of male slaves. Flogging was to be administered the day after the offence was committed and in the presence of witnesses, either one free person, or six slaves and the number of lashes was limited to 25 on pain of a 900 guilder fine, or six months in jail.

The Code then spelt out alternative punishments which could be used for both women and men: solitary confinement for no more than three days with, or without work, in a place licensed by a medical practitioner, confinement, solitary or otherwise, for one hour at noon: confinement in the public stocks for up to three hours for each offence by day: in the house stocks, with seats, for up to six hours, or in bedstocks for confinement at night. Food was to be supplied to women held longer than 12 hours. For women estate workers alternative punishments included wearing handcuffs, distinguishing dress, or lightweight collars. Corporal punishments continued to be legal, however, for slave children under the age of 12 to the degree customary for free children.

To implement these regulations managers and owners were corralled into a self-policing exercise, set out in the 1824 Order in Council, which was extended in Berbice to cover domestic, hired and jobbing slaves. All owners, or managers of more than six slaves had to keep a Punishment Record Book to record within 48 hours of inflicting punishment, the offence, the witnesses as well as time and place of punishment. This record was to be sworn on oath before the civil magistrate every quarter, submitted to the Protector and forwarded to the Colonial Office.

The new regulations appear to have benefited slave workers. The Protector dealt with fewer complaints about punishment than the Fiscal had done although, interestingly, such complaints continued to comprise about 25 per cent of the total. Women workers represented only three per cent of these cases, which all related to punishment in the stocks, not illegal flogging. The removal of the whip from the field impacted significantly on the proportion of complaints from male workers about punishments for protesting against workloads and tasks, which were reduced from one in every three or four to one in every nine or ten cases.

According to the records the new laws also reduced the intensity of workplace punishments. The maximum number of lashes inflicted on men for 'disobedience' and for 'insubordination' from July to December 1827 was 75; in 1830, just before a revised code went into effect, it was 25 and by that date two-thirds of male as well as female slave workers were punished by the stocks and imprisonment.[28] The maximum punishments for women for the same offences in the period 1829–30 was reduced from 71 hours in solitary to four hours in the public stocks for 'disobedience' and from three days in solitary confinement to six hours in the public stocks for 'insubordination'.[29] These modifications benefited owners and managers by minimising work-time lost. But the scale of punishments in relation to the offence, whether in reduced numbers of lashes, or reduced hours of confinement still measured the grossly inflated powers in the hands of estate managers to punish for offences described only in the most general terms. It is easy to see why the overall rate of slave complaints about punishments remained the same.

Estate-based discipline was, nevertheless, backed up by a new method of summary punishment which was placed in the hands of the Protector and the Civil Magistrates, the treadmill. The treadmill, introduced in British prisons to discipline convicted criminals in 1818, was rapidly imported into the Crown Colonies and installed in Trinidad in 1824. The severity of the punishment it inflicted depended in part on how the machine was regulated in terms of weight and speed and it easily became an instrument of brutal torture.[30] Time on the treadmill in New Amsterdam's jail provided an adjunct in Berbice to summary punishments administered on the estates and for women workers who obdurately opposed their owners and managers it substituted for flogging. The Protector sentenced women to it on only one occasion in the period 1826–30 but it was also used by the Civil Magistrates. Eight days on the treadmill, one woman complained, made her very weak and it readily promoted miscarriages.[31] So the modern instrument available to the fledging colonial state authorities to inflict physical punishment on workers judged ill-disciplined was no less ferocious than the archaic instrument it partially replaced.

The regulation of labour time and the introduction of modern labour incentives paralleled the regulation and modernisation of labour discipline. The customary 12-hour working day for field slaves with two hours for meals and the customary six-day working week, ending by sunset on Saturday and beginning sunrise on Monday became the legal standard enforceable by fines. Some customary exceptions, however, in the length of the working week were legalised, the most important of which was work needed for 'the preservation of crops'. On sugar estates this meant boiling-off cane juice produced on Saturday and potting on Sunday: turning and drying cotton and coffee already picked, but not cured and picking cotton and coffee during harvest. Enforceable statutory limits on the slaves' working time were in themselves innovative. More significantly, however, following imperial guidelines, the 1826 Code ruled that slave workers not engaged in sugar production were to be paid wages in cash, not kind for such 'additional exigible labour' at rates set by the Protector. The rates were set at 11.5 pence (sterling) for field workers for one to four hours' work while artisans boiler-men and drivers earned 11.5 pence for one-two hours and one shilling 4.5 pence for two-four hours. Owners failing to pay a slave on these terms faced a 50 guilder fine.

The 'wages in cash for overwork' clause built on the well-established Americas-wide custom of paying slaves for overwork in cash, kind or free time; the women at Prospect, for example, who moved the corn store were paid in baskets of corn (see above) and the complaints about overwork frequently made to the Fiscal may have reflected lack of payment. It is interesting that the new regulation did not lead to a rash of wage claims: wages were claimed just once before the Protector, by ferrymen flogged for refusing a Sunday fare. This may reflect the fact that cash was in short supply and paper money widely relied on.[32] In practical terms the regulation may have served to secure the slaves more regular and possibly more adequate payments of wages in kind.

The significance of the clause, however, extends beyond its immediate practical effects; to require the exchange of cash for work struck at the heart of the slave labour system which in essence denied labour exchange value. Making wages for slaves a legal requirement in certain circumstances precisely paralleled the abolition of flogging for women and both innovations planted a marker pointing the way to replacing an archaic with a modern system of labour exaction. The attack on the central feature of chattel slavery was complemented by measures intended to make adjustments to the relative status of owners and slaves. The 1826 Code, again following imperial guide-lines, awarded the slaves a range of civil rights, which their owners were necessarily obliged to acknowledge. Slaves acquired a statutory right to attend church and receive religious instruction; a right to marry; to qualify to give evidence in court; to become substantial property owners and, most signifi-cantly, to purchase manumission. In practical terms these rights were little exercised. Religious instruction was available from one London Missionary Society minister and, on Sunday afternoons only, from one Anglican clergy-man. Sunday markets were, nevertheless, closed at 11 am to allow exercise of this right without curtailing the working week. In these circumstances slaves rarely married, or qualified to give evidence in court. And of the substantial new rights opened up to slaves as potential property owners, to own land, cattle, agricultural implements, furniture and money which could be deposited on interest in a Savings Bank, the slaves commonly utilised only the right to claim payment from their debtors for goods sold to them. Women traders in particular regularly went to the Protector to claim small debts. In the same way the right to manumission proved useful only to a few privileged slaves. Nevertheless, these clauses shifted the legal parameters of slave-owner rela-tions simultaneously awarding new rights and curbing old privileges in an effort to influence the ideological formation of both classes.[33]

The impact of the 1826 Code on the slaves' terms of work, the main focus of this study, is complex; it generated new problems and left old ones unresolved. The 12-hour day was defined for 'field workers' and the question arose as to whether it applied to field workers engaged in sugar manufacture.

Sugar estate owners were specifically exempted from the obligation to pay their slaves for overwork and the lack of clarity in this definition allowed them to continue night work. Women workers first protested this practice; four women from Plantation Smithson's Place charged they had cut cane by day and tied and carried megasse by night. At the inquiry the head boiler confirmed that they got no more than three hours sleep a night. They took refuge in being sick, but were punished as malingerers and put in the stocks in solitary confinement over the three-day Christmas holiday. Within weeks workers from Plantation Canefield corroborated their complaint where the manager instituted night work at his own discretion. Night work was better organised at 'Canefield'; the slaves worked alternate shifts changing over at 12 pm. But the question remained, was night work legal?

The issue was taken up during Power's absence while on leave in England by his deputy, Charles Bird, who called for opinions from the Fiscal, Bennett and the King's Advocate, M. Daly. The slaves, Bennett urged, were not engaged in night work on the manager's inclination, but from the necessity of maintaining production levels. It would be impolitic and detrimental to prevent it. Daly dissented. On appeal to London the Colonial Secretary briskly opined, a year after the women protested, 'This defect in the law cannot be too speedily remedied'. He ordered a supplementary ordinance to define the slaves' hours for repose each night and punishments for their owners.[34]

Confusion in the definition of the working day was compounded by the lack of any legal definition of the task scale. In contested cases the Protector, like his predecessor the Fiscal, determined judgement and on this issue the owners were prepared to use his services. At Plantation Overyssel for example, where a new manager had taken over, the 18 workers in the 'strong women's gang' went on strike one Monday morning. They refused to begin weeding the 12-by-72 feet task the driver measured out for them on the grounds they would do 'no more than in Mr. Downer's (their previous owner) time'. They claimed they were defending their customary workload. When mediation by a neighbouring planter proved ineffective, the owner called in the Protector.

On the estate Power listened to all parties. The women maintained the task was 'too much' while the manager claimed their task was eight feet shorter than other estates required and produced certificates from neighbouring planters to prove it. He claimed further that a task 80 feet long could be completed in seven hours. The driver backed management and accused some women of intimidating the rest. But all the women stuck to their point. Power concluded that this was a collective effort to reduce the workload and was determined to crush such combinations. He sent the four women identified as ringleaders to jail for seven days for three sessions a day on the treadmill. The rest spent their weekend locked up in the sick house under threat of losing their Christmas holiday and Christmas presents.

The proprietor was well satisfied with this judgement, which from his point of view had the 'happiest effect'. The women completed the task 'with ease', their holidays and presents were restored and the four sentenced to the treadmill subsequently apologised to him at the Protector's office. Once resistance was quelled and production restored on his own terms, the owner tried to convince the women their behaviour had been irrational; who, he asked, had put them up to it? But the women, who evidently thought that attempting to reduce their workload was rational, kept their own counsel.[35]

Slave workers' rations, their regular wages in kind, were not improved by the 1826 legislation, but complaints about short ration supplies featured in 25 per cent of complaints to the Fiscal dropped sharply after 1826, possibly because the likelihood of prosecution increased and penalties were enhanced. The slaves' frequently contested customary right to run poultry and small stock on estate land was made dependent on the owners' express permission. Slave sick care was improved in the sense that the new Code made licensed doctors, 'commodious' estate hospitals supplied with medicines and attendants mandatory on every estate on pain of a 600 guilder penalty and hospital procedures were tightened up. Patients' names, diagnoses and treatments were to be registered by the medical attendant on pain of a fine for each omission. As a result, when slave complaints revealed that managers had dosed them because no doctor was available, their owners were recommended for prosecution by the Protector for failing to supply 'a legally qualified medical practitioner'.[36] But delivery of medical care remained a problem. Slave complaints that they were denied treatment, worked and punished when sick continued; but the Protector, like the Fiscal, could only investigate, refer to the doctor and request the owner to act on his advice.

Substantively, benefits to women workers began and ended with the prohibition of flogging. Pregnant women continued to charge they were overworked and ought not to be put in the stocks; but, like the sick, they could only be sent to the estate doctor for examination and re-definition of their task.[37] Nursing and parental rights continued to be contested with managers and slave families continued to be exposed to separation by sale. While the

Code prohibited the separation of husbands and wives, but only families (husbands and wives with children under 16) sold for debt were to be sold in the same lot, to the same person and the responsibility for implementing the rule was placed on the Marshal and his clerk in charge of the sale. The onus of proof lay with the slave family in question until such time as planters submitted records of marriages and births to the Protector. Slave families sold in the ordinary way continued dependent on the 'acknowledged usage of the colony'.

Slaves continued to claim other rights on their own behalf before the Protector, just as they had before the Fiscal. They wanted some control over their occupation and disputed job changes imposed by managers and owners, particularly when they were sent from home as task workers to other estates. They wanted the right to change employer by being sold. This claim was made not only by individuals, but by slave worker communities. Delegates from a workforce of more than a hundred slaves sold as a group by their owner in England to a neighbouring estate, told the Protector they knew perfectly well the life they would lead under the manager there and requested public sale. Better the chances of the saleroom than the certainties of an 'indifferent' management.[38] More frequently slave workers claimed the right to be sold as a community. The law afforded them no assistance in this, so it is not surprising that some abandoned legal-constitutional methods of appeal in favour of strike action; the whole 226-strong workforce at Catherine's burg, for example, retired to the bush determined not to be sold separately.[39]

Slave workers making these claims challenged the owners' right to use their persons as property, the legal premise that sanctioned chattel slavery. In doing so they sharply illuminated the limitations of the 1826 Code which did no more than slightly adjust the parameters in which their struggle continued. These limitations were also established in statistical terms by the massively detailed documentary evidence the Protector and his assistants garnered from the 'Punishment Record Books'. Systematising and implementing the slave labour law revealed more fully than ever before the terms on which slave labour was exacted. The Colonial Office officials, who closely supervised the dismantling process and commented in detail on the Protector's reports, were forcibly struck by the sheer number of punishments inflicted on the workforce and by the fact that year after year the number showed no sign of diminution. Between 25–33 per cent of the total population were affected, almost one-third, by flogging and all for minor infractions of workplace discipline. The figures abundantly confirmed the superiority of a labour system 'where man is left either to work, or want'.[40]

Viewed in historical perspective the Code and its implementation outlined here exposes the ways in which the law which aimed to dismantle the slave labour system, engaged with the regulations intended to perpetuate it. The new law modified and regulated workplace discipline, partly replacing archaic with modern disciplinary measures, set limits to the hours of labour, aimed to translate workers' customary payments in kind for overwork into mandatory, legally fixed cash payments. It nudged slave workers and slave owners toward wage work. In society at large the law proclaimed the slaves' right to elements of citizen status, signalling the abolition of slave status.

The 1826 Code is also significant in that its provisions and omissions indicate continuities between traditional chattel slavery and the wage work system which replaced it. The particular needs of women workers at the workplace, the prohibition of flogging aside, were ignored. Subsistence was kept at the same low level, prefiguring minimal wage rates. And perhaps most significantly, implementing the labour laws both before and after abolition meant punishing, by different methods, workers who withdrew their labour and collectively protested their terms of work.

Notes

1.   Parliamentary Papers, House of Commons (PP HC) 1825 XXV 476 Further
      Papers relating to Slaves in the West Indies: Demerara and Berbice (hereafter
      SWI), H.M. Bennett to Henry Beard, 19 February 1825.
2.   B.W. Higman, *Slave Populations of the British Caribbean, 1807–1834*
      (Baltimore and London: The Johns Hopkins University Press, 1984), pp. 63,
      77, 104–5.
3.   Ibid., p. 183.
4.   There were 31.4 births per thousand in Berbice compared with 52.3 per
      thousand in Barbados 1817–34; Ibid., pp. 76, 262, 270.
5.   Commissioners of Criminal and Civil Justice (CCJ), Appendix A, pp. 144–5;
      A. Thompson, *Colonialism and Underdevelopment in Guyana 1580–1803*
      (Bridgetown, Barbados: Carib Research and Publications Inc., 1965), pp.
      114–21; Higman, *Slave Populations*, pp. 180, 205–9.
6.   PP HC 1828 XIII, 577 Second Report of the CCJ in the West Indies and
      South America, Appendix J, p. 250, Appendix A, pp. 91, 148; D.J. Murray,

The West Indies and the Development of Colonial Government, 1801–1834 (Oxford: Clarendon Press, 1965), p. 86.

7. SWI 144 cases in all were dealt with February to June 1819: July 1820 to December 1823.

8. M. Turner, ed., *From Chattel Slaves to Wage Slaves: The Dynamics of Labour Bargaining in the Americas* (London: James Currey; Bloomington and Indianapolis: Indiana University Press, 1995), Introduction, pp. 1–32.

9. 1 pound sterling = 1.4 guilders. CCJ, Appendix A., p. 90.

10. SWI, 18 July, 1823.

11. Higman, *Slave Populations*, p.180; SWI, 3 March, 10 November 1823.

12. SWI, 4 September 1823.

13. SWI, 3 March, 10 December 1823.

14. Thompson, *Colonialism and Underdevelopment in Guyana*, p. 123; Higman, pp. 205, 209.

15. SWI, 2 July, 14 August, 23 August 1822.

16. SWI, 21 October 1823.

17. SWI, 10 June 1819; Extract from Register of the Proceedings of the CCJ, 1819, CO 116/139, cited in E.V. da Costa, *Crowns of Glory Tears of Blood: the Demerara Slave Rebellion of 1823* (New York and Oxford: Oxford University Press, 1994), p. 328, note 129.

18. SWI, 14 June 1819.

19. SWI, 4 June 1819.

20. SWI, 15 March, 17 April 1819.

21. SWI, 15 October, 1821.

22. Of the judgements recorded by the Deputy Fiscal 44 cases resulted in punishment for the plaintiffs or dismissal of their cases.

23. CO 111/102, Beard to Earl Bathurst, 21 July 1826, no. 13, 14: 1826 Slave Code, *Berbice Royal Gazette*, 30 September 1826, folio 166.

24. CO 111/102, Beard to Bathurst, 23 October 1826, no. 30.

25. CO.111/102, Beard to Bathurst, 31 August 1826, no. 24; 22 September 1826, no. 27; PP HC 1830–1 XV 262, Protectors of Slaves Reports (PSR 262) Murray to Beard, 1 September 1829. Experience in Trinidad demonstrated that this post could not be trusted to a colonial official. The appointment of Civil Magistrates also modified the precedent established in Trinidad where the existing officials, called Commandants of Quarters, were simply transformed into Assistant Protectors.

26. CO 111/102, Beard to Bathurst, 23 October 1826, Encl. 3 Circular to Magistrates.

27. PP HC 1829 XXV 335, PSR 335, David Power to Beard, 1 September 1828.

28. PSR 335, List of Offences committed by Male and Female Slaves in the Colony of Berbice, 1 July–31 December 1827, pp. 38–9; PSR 262, Abstract

of Offences committed by Male and Female Plantation Slaves in the Colony of Berbice 1 July–31 December 1829, pp. 103–9.

29. PSR 262, Abstract of Offences . . . 1 July–31December 1829, pp. 103–9; Abstract of Offences, 1 January–14 May 1830, pp. 119–20. The Magistrates played a comparatively small role awarding slave punishments. In the six months 1 July–31 December 1829, for example, out of more than 5,000 punishments inflicted the Magistrates determined only 37, and of these only 4 affected women. 'False complaints' and 'riotous behaviour' earned them up to two weeks' solitary, or 14 nights in the bedstocks. Male 'insubordination' earned 70 lashes from the Magistrates and neglect of duty, one of the most common charges brought against all slave workers, 80 lashes.

30. W.L. Burn, *Emancipation and Apprenticeship in the British West Indies* (London: Jonathan Cape, 1937; reprint 1970), pp. 282–3.

31. PSR 262, 16 September 1828.

32. Wood ms.

33. Higman, *Slave Populations,* p. 381; PSR 262, Charles Bird to Beard, 1 March 1830.

34. PSR 335, Bennett to Bird, 2 January 1828: Murray to Beard, 24 November 1828.

35. PSR 262, 12 December 1829.

36. PSR 262, 12 February 1829.

37. PSR 262, 29 March 1830.

38. PSR 262, 31 December 1829.

39. PSR 262, 7 November 1828.

40. PSR 262, Murray to Beard, 1 September 1829; Power to Beard, 1 September 1829.

Pricing Freedom

Evaluating the costs of emancipation and of manumission*

STANLEY ENGERMAN

The economic expansion of slavery and slave societies in the Caribbean in the first part of the nineteenth century can be indicated by several measures, including the output of sugar and other commodities, the continued import of slaves from Africa wherever it was still legally permitted by the metropolitan powers, and the rising prices paid for slaves, both for those bought and sold internally and those new arrivals purchased from Africa. In general, prices reflected the value of the slaves to their owners, and were based upon the expected future outputs of slave labour, the expected longevity of the slave (either due to individual mortality or to the general ending of slavery), and the costs of subsistence or 'maintenance'. The rising prices not only demonstrated the increasing profitability of slavery, but they also were thought to have increased the difficulties of any system of ending slavery or of freeing individual slaves by manumission, since the costs of the compensation to be paid to slave-owners to free the slaves had also risen.[1] In addition to these higher costs, as discussions of abolition and manumission increased there were a number of interesting conceptual issues that arose to confound these debates.

In this chapter I will examine some discussions in and about the British Caribbean in the first third of the nineteenth century, to see what was considered to be the basis of compensation as well as to understand how the specifics of the evaluation process were to be implemented. The general issue of the circumstances that would make compensation justifiable has long been important in many societies, but my principal focus here regarding slaves is on the logic of the economic arguments presented, and what issues were employed by those debating the means of evaluation. Clearly this begs several of what some would argue are the most important philosophical issues relating to any compensation scheme. First, should the slave-holders be entitled to receive any compensation, from the slaves or from the government, given the ultimate immorality of the system? It was frequently argued that the original slave capture was a theft, and therefore that slaves were to be regarded as stolen property.[2] In subsequent payments for, and ownership of, the slave the nature of the process of acquisition was known to the purchasers, who, it was argued, had knowingly accepted stolen goods. In contrast, the argument for compensation was that slave ownership had long been legal according to the British government (who in many ways had encouraged its expansion), and that the slave-owners had behaved in good faith, given what the government had permitted. Thus, it was argued, the possible change in property rights regimes would penalise individuals who had been law-abiding (and, it might be argued, by now were making, at most, only normal profits, since the major benefits had probably gone to earlier captors and owners).[3] The slave-owners of the 1830s could present the emancipation movement as among the first major drives against a specific form of private property, a form of confiscation that, it was argued, would soon be applied to owners of other types of privately owned property.[4]

A second question, for which the answer seemed, unfortunately, to be very obvious at the time, was whether the slaves should be compensated, since it was they who had earlier lost their rights and suffered losses of income as well as having been compelled into unfavourable working conditions.[5] Yet, while sometimes used as an argument against paying compensation to slave-owners, the case for compensating the slaves was seldom proposed as a serious possibility, by the British or any other slave-holding power, nor was there any serious argument proposed for compensating serfs.[6] Several of the questions about who should be compensated and how, have remained central to much of the economic discussion in subsequent years concerning government policies towards business, including antitrust actions, where questions of whether to pay, who should be paid and how much compensation should be paid still persist. The problems become particularly acute when there have been sales among individuals, so that the present asset owners are not those involved in the initial transaction where the basic change in ownership or in property values took place.

There were two issues where the role of prices and compensation were important to the study of the economics of slavery and abolition. The first concerns the nature of the process of legal emancipation which ended the legal status of enslavement. These were generally legislated by the national or metropolitan government, and applied to slave-owners and slaves within a specific geographic area. The second was the manumission of individual slaves by individual slave-owners, providing freedom to the slave. While some manumissions were by grant from individuals or the state and costless to the slave, in many cases the slaves were given the right to purchase themselves at some agreed price, generally close to the market evaluation.[7] The rights to manumission and the procedures to realise it were regulated by metropolitan, national or state governments and varied, for example, between the colonies of the Iberian nations and those of the Northwest European nations, but the specific decisions were made by the slaves and their owners. As part of the amelioration measures of the early 1820s, British Caribbean slaves were granted rights to obtain compulsory manumission. This meant that they could request from the protector of slaves an appraisement of their value to set the price that they would pay their master to acquire freedom. As we shall see, there were several legal complications in this procedure, which influenced the nature and costs of these measures.

Legal complications of emancipation and compensation

The policies for legal emancipation of slaves in the Americas took a variety of forms regarding both the appropriateness of whether any compensation was to be paid and also as to the specific forms that it could take. In no case, however, did slaves receive any compensation, while in some cases there was no compensation paid to slave-owners. These latter cases include the two largest slave-holding nations, the US and Brazil, as well as Haiti, where emancipation and independence was achieved by slave revolt.[8] In the US and Brazil, although property rights in slaves were lost, the owners of slaves did not lose their ownership rights in land although, as had been argued by slave-owners in the emancipation debates, ending slavery often meant a loss in the value of these lands. Various forms of non-immediate emancipation were implemented in other areas. In some areas, emancipation was not granted to those already born, but only to those born after a specified date, who were to be considered free and would gain complete freedom upon reaching a specified age, the precise age varying by nation.[9] There is some indication that the age of complete freedom was selected to equalise the incomes expected to be produced by the slave and the costs to their owners of rearing the slave, thus providing the owner sufficient returns to meet the necessary payments of the costs of rearing the slaves.[10] This, in effect, meant evaluating the slave at zero at birth. As pointed out elsewhere, this could mean a loss in value for the mother, due to the removal of the economic returns from her childbearing capacity, but it was one that would not be substantial relative to the overall slave price.[11]

Another approach was to free all slaves at some future date, effectively truncating some parts of the slave-earning stream, and thereby reducing the capital value of the slave to the owner. This type of measure did give rise to concerns about the treatment by their owners of those who were too young to be able to cover their rearing costs, and gave rise to discussions to determine how best to allocate these costs among owner, slave and taxpayers in general. In general, the compensation could be paid directly to slave-owners, in the form either of cash or bonds from the government, or in the form of the labour time provided by the freed. Questions remained concerning how close was the relation between the politically bargained for and determined amount of compensation and what would have been the full and complete compensation due to slave-owners, since political bargains need not necessarily end up agreeing with the market price. The British system of emancipation, one that was followed by several other countries, combined the payment of some cash compensation, based on relative slave prices among islands, and a period of compelled plantation labour called 'apprenticeship'.[12] The fact that this period of compelled labour would increase the returns to slave-owners was recognised in Parliament, and was considered to be a part of the compensation allowed (in addition to providing the ex-slaves with education in proper work habits). The return to slave-owners could have been further raised by their taking advantage of the limited period of returns, leading to a more intensive work effort and more limited care, relative to the longer-term conditions under slavery.[13]

Thus compensation could be paid in funds or some equivalent in labour time; emancipation could be immediate or deferred; and, obviously, the actual compensation could vary in relation to full compensation, depending upon the balance of political power in the government at the time of the legislated emancipation. The nature of the political activities of the anti-slavery movement, and the expectations as to their possible success, had major implications for the pattern of changing slave prices. These actions affected the market evaluations, particularly if it were thought that a weakening or ending of the institution would occur in the not-too distant future.[14] This concern with declining slave values had been manifest earlier, at the start of the nineteenth century, in the British Caribbean. The British Caribbean interest called for some compensation to be paid if the British were to end the slave trade. An argument was made that if the British government could end the slave trade, they would also have the power to end slavery, and that was the real aim of abolitionists despite their denials. It was the possibility of future loss, as well as the present problems, that greatly concerned the slave-owners' interests.[15] While ending the slave trade could raise the value of slaves in the colonies, thus benefiting present slave-owners, it would also have an important political negative in at least preventing growth in the number of slave-owners. No compensation was paid on the ending of the slave trade, for whatever reasons, but there had been compensation allowed for some losses in the first of the major regulations of the slave trade, Sir William Dolben's Act of 1788.[16] The provision for payment to shippers who suffered loses as a result of the Act was presumably to apply only to those ships still in transit after the legislation's passage, who could not avoid the influence of the legal change. In 1799, William Pitt suggested preventing the use of newly imported slaves on uncleared land which the Jamaica agent interpreted as leading to a form of compensation to slave-owners.[17]

The principle of compensation to slave-owners had earlier been discussed, as the slave-owners frequently pointed out. The possibilities of compensation had been raised after the American revolution, and was the basis of long political discussions within the US and between the US and Britain after the American revolution. The US request, which was originally for the restoration of the slaves, shifted to compensation for the loss in value suffered by their owners, because of the British unwillingness to reverse the freedom granted to these slaves. But compensation for those slaves evacuated by the British in 1783 was never agreed to, in part because of the anti-slavery attitude of the American negotiator, William Jay, and it soon become a dead issue.[18] The claims of revolutionary war Loyalists for compensation for assets, including slaves, confiscated by the Americans were met, but by the British, not by the Americans. After the war of 1812, as a result of the Treaty of Ghent, the US owners were compensated by the British for slaves that had been removed from the US. The payments were based on individual claims, and at prices that seemed to reflect market values, with a sharp differential between the reimbursement price per slave for Louisiana in contrast with the prices for slaves from Virginia, Maryland and Georgia.[19] The British Caribbean interest, in dealing with Parliament, noted subsequently that the American planters 'had been compensated when they had slaves taken from them during the late War [War of 1812] and not restored at the Peace'.[20]

Reactions to reform and expected emancipation

The various changes and reforms introduced concerning slaves and in the relations between governments and slave-owners had an important impact on slave-owners. Planters feared that reforms such as were included in the amelioration codes of the 1820s, which included restrictions on punishments and requirements for compulsory manumission, would lower property values. These could cause a direct economic loss to slave-owners and also, because of the further effects upon compensation based upon market values, could be quite costly to slave-owners. The difference between the value of slaves if the system were left unchanged, and the value of slaves when legislation imposed obligations on slave-owners, reflected the power of the metropolitan government to influence the price of slaves and, some argued, the prospective future profitability of slavery.[21]

Similarly, at the time of emancipation as well as earlier, government policy on tariffs on foreign sugar affected Caribbean planter incomes, with the specific direction and magnitude influenced by the elasticity of demand.[22] The limitations introduced on intra-island sales of slaves beginning in 1805 meant a lowering of slave prices (and, after emancipation, of labourer wages) and an increased slave population in the older islands, with higher prices and fewer slaves in the newer areas.[23] This wedge in slave prices between the older and newer parts of the British Caribbean led to some conflicts at the time of the determination of compensation procedures in 1833, with disagreement as to whether compensation should be based on the number of slaves or on the value of slaves.[24] The newer areas did come out ahead in amounts of compensation, since the relative compensation was based on the market prices of slaves, leading to the large intercolonial differentials in the proceeds received by slave-owners.

The basis of the market prices of slaves to be used for compensation also became the subject of parliamentary debate. Presumably the best estimate to use would be the market values at the time of legislation, if emancipation were unanticipated, since that price would presumably be based on the absence of any expectational influence of future limits to, or endings of, the slave system. Given the extensive prior debates, this would have been a rather uncertain calculation, and the decision was made to base the relative slave evaluations on the average prices for 1822–30, without any adjustments for differences in age and sex of those sold.[25] It was argued that these years were before the major onslaught on slavery, although some claimed, correctly, that it was with the 1823 expansion of the anti-slavery movement that slave prices started to fall.[26] Thus it was argued by the slave-owning interests that the particular period chosen was one with already lowered prices, and also, in regard to equity among colonies, that this decline was not uniform across areas. Presumably no overall agreement could be reached, given the different patterns of slave price changes, and in the differences resulting from the choice of number of years as well as the specific years of slave prices to be examined.[27]

Also important in the parliamentary debates were the differences between slave-owners and the government regarding the appropriate amount of compensation for the losses in property values of the slave-holder. These were influenced by standard arguments concerning the economic impact of slavery and its abolition. The crucial point was the different interpretations of the willingness of the ex-slaves to work on plantations after they were freed, and the impact that this would have on the value of the land and capital used on plantations. Given the lack of opportunity to legally import more slaves or to legally coerce freed slaves into plantation work, the slave-owners expected the emancipation process to reduce the amount of plantation labour, except perhaps for those few areas where the labour-land ratio was so high, and/or where the government controls could be so strong, that leaving the plantation sector was not a viable option for ex-slaves. The impact of the labour-land ratio on labour costs can be seen in the comparison of the level of slave prices prior to emancipation and the relative wages rates after freedom.[28] High slave prices, as in Trinidad and Colonial Guyana, were followed by high wages, and, in Barbados, low slave prices were followed by low wages. In Barbados there was both a continued plantation sector and also, because of the wage differentials, a labour outflow to elsewhere in the British Caribbean. The labour shortage problem in Trinidad and Colonial Guyana was to be solved, decades later, by labour inflows of indentured labourers, primarily from India.

To the extent that it was believed that plantation labour was possible only with the legal controls of slavery, the ending of slavery would mean that the slave-owners would lose not only the direct value based on the labour productivity and cost differences between free and slave labour, but also the inframarginal losses in value to land and capital due to the reduction of the labour supply.[29] As land-owners had anticipated, their losses from ending slavery exceeded those embodied in the value of the slave. This is why they had argued that the basis for compensation should have included these additional amounts. The behaviour of land values and the changes in regard to other assets used by slaves in most ex-slave areas (in the British colonies and elsewhere) indicates the accuracy of these expectations of ex-slave behaviour. Thus, as J.R. Ward has argued, the planter's loss at the time of emancipation was greater than the difference between the slave's market evaluation and the sum of cash compensation and the labour value of the apprenticeship.[30] The slave-owner's rights to land ownership continued, but ending slavery made land worth less to the land-owners.

Because of these complexities, it is rather difficult to evaluate the full set of benefits and costs to land-owners due to emancipation.[31] While it can be argued that the returns to the market value of slaves were approximately equivalent as a percentage of slave value across regions, the economic adjustments to freedom differed considerably. In Barbados, for example, the value of land probably declined relatively little, and the cost of labour remained low. There was some transfer of surplus from slave-owners to ex-slaves, but overall the former slave-owner's loss was probably relatively small. At the other extreme, at least before the attraction of indentured labour, was Colonial Guyana, where the value of land declined dramatically and there was little ability to maintain plantation labour. The arrival of indentured labour for plantation work meant enhanced land values, but there were costs to acquiring this labour. Part of the costs were paid by the colony, and part by the land-owner using the labour. While indentured labour reduced the losses faced by land-owners, it is possible that because of the time necessary for the adjustments to occur, the loss to the Guyanese slave-owners was greater than that for those in Barbados, although the differences in the compensation paid per slave did serve to offset the costs of the subsequent adjustments.

Manumission

In most slave societies, provisions were made to allow slaves to be legally freed individually, via the process of manumission. In general, however, although some slaves acquired freedom, the existence of the slave system and its continuation seemed minimally affected. The magnitude and the terms of manumission differed quite dramatically across the Americas (and elsewhere).[32] The rates of manumission tended to be higher in the Spanish and Portuguese colonies than elsewhere. Manumission frequently meant the granting of the rights to slaves to purchase their freedom rather than the free granting of freedom to the slave.[33] Manumissions could take the form of a gift by the owner, whether now or in the future; be conditional, either contingent on the behaviour of the slave or the mortality of the owner; or by self-purchase, at some agreed upon price between slave and owner. The price paid in some of the manumissions did not necessarily reflect the actual market price at any given date, but rather some mutually acceptable sum, presumably between zero and the market price (or perhaps even above that), depending on the bargaining relations and concerns of slave and master.

The issue of the market price did become an important consideration when manumission was made compulsory in some of the colonies by the British government in the 1820s. Manumission was to be granted, at a price agreed upon by appraisers, who would presumably base their price upon market evaluations.[34] A fair appraisal was necessary to prevent a slave-owner from requesting too high a price for manumission, while allowing the owner what seemed to be a fair return on his slave.[35] In 1824, as part of its amelioration programme, the Colonial Office presented Orders in Council for Trinidad, imposing compulsory manumission on slave-owners.[36] This permitted slaves to purchase their freedom at a price set by the legal process. By suggesting a market evaluation for the slaves, it was implied that the full magnitude of the loss to the slave-owner was reflected in the price, and also that the slave-owner would be able to replace this labourer at a comparable price. Manumission would thus be anticipated to hold the owner's income and wealth unchanged.

For most cases the procedure seemed to have worked out in an acceptable manner under the existing conditions, for both slave-owners and slaves, with relatively few cases of requested manumission requiring intervention on the part of government officials. Under the law a limited number of slaves were able to purchase their freedom, at prices acceptable to their owners, although this alternative was available to only a few slaves. Some general criticisms were raised about the particular prices to be paid by the manumittee, however, reflecting arguments similar to those that would be made later at the time of overall emancipation. This disagreement on the evaluation for manumission was based on the generally perceived unwillingness of freed labour to work on plantations. This meant that there would presumably be additional losses to slave-owners, due to declines in the value of land and capital.[37] But whereas in the case of an overall emancipation such a decline in the values of land and capital would be expected, this outcome need not be anticipated where only a small fraction of the slaves were freed, since there would presumably be other slaves still available at the current market price. To use the present-day economists' parlance, outcomes would differ between a general equilibrium analysis and a partial equilibrium analysis, that is, for changes which affect a large part of the market in contrast with those changes that affect only a small part of the market. Clearly, the initial price changes will be smaller, and the quantity of labour supplied adjustment less, where only a few slaves were manumitted than when all slaves were granted freedom.

This analytical distinction arose in a rather interesting and unusual case of compulsory manumission in Trinidad in the 1820s. This episode led to a debate that presented the basic arguments concerning the use of slave prices to determine the amounts to be paid for compensation. While previous appraisements came in at about the market price, and did not give rise to complaints, in the case of Pamela Munro the evaluation was at an estimated double the market price.[38] The mother of the potential manumittee complained to the Protector of Slaves about this injustice, which obviously denied the intent of the manumission procedure, and might ultimately be used to preclude any manumissions. The resulting correspondence included the appraisers, the Protector of Slaves, Earl Bathurst of the Colonial Office and the governor of Trinidad, and spelled out different approaches to the evaluation of slaves for purposes of manumission. This discussion flows through *Parliamentary Papers*, *Colonial Office Papers* and *Hansard*, with opinions based on the presumed answers to various economic questions, including the valuation of assets when there are economies of scale, the work attitudes of slave and free labour, the role of economies of scale in plantation production, and the effects of limitations on importing of more slaves on slave prices. Was the payment to compensate for the decline in the value of an asset, or was it to replace the asset in the production of an equivalent amount of output, even if the free labour situation required a higher payment to get labour than if slave labour had continued? These possibilities will not necessarily lead to the same answer, depending on whether there was alternative labour available and what would be required to pay them to perform work similar to that done by the slave, and this problem did seem to arise whenever compensation claims were at issue.[39]

The Protector of Slaves had brought this case to the attention of the governor, who expressed concern that such a high price would have 'deprived [slaves] of the chance they formerly enjoyed of obtaining their freedom for a fair but moderate valuation'.[40] Governor Woodford, also claimed that if the prices had risen it was 'obviously the effect of the prohibition . . . of bringing any Slave to the Colony', a clear reference to the limits on the inter-island slave trade, linking that decision to the problem of slaves, including Pamela Munro, being manumitted. In response to queries about how they made their valuation, the two appraisers argued that Bathurst had written that the valuation for purposes of manumission should be based 'on a fair estimate of the loss which the owner may sustain', thus providing the planter with 'an adequate compensation'. Bathurst (who later claimed that his argument had been misunderstood by the appraisers) had said that if it:

> be found that the Slaves thus manumitted altogether abandon their owners, and refuse to work as free persons, the owner not having the means, by reason of the Abolition Act, to supply the loss of his slaves, and not being able to engage any free labourers for his sugar plantations, the price which must then be assigned to the loss of each Slave must have a direct reference to that state in which the plantation will be placed by the progressive reduction of the means of conducting it.

Using this argument as the basis for their evaluation, the appraisers claimed that:

> it being notorious that in this Colony Slaves so manumitted altogether abandon their owners, and that it is impossible to engage or contract with any free labourer for any settled term of work, and that the few which are to be procured come and go as suits their own caprice, so that no dependence can be placed upon them, would have felt themselves bound to value the said Pamela Munro at the sum of twelve hundred round Mexican dollars, to secure to her owner an adequate compensation, had she been attached as a field labourer to an estate; – but the said Pamela Munro being a domestic, the undersigned have recurred to other data by which to establish her value, and finding that she is in the prime of life, healthy,

and in possession of many valuable qualities, so that her services could not be replaced by the hire of any other Slaves in the Colony at a less sum than six round dollars per month, in which case the Slave so hired is fed, clothed, and insured against all depreciation of her capital value from death or disease; and further, that the minors (Pasca) who now own the said Pamela could immediately hire her out, and obtain that remuneration for her services.

They went on to suggest that, 'as an alternative', 'she be allowed to receive her manumission whenever the Protector of Slaves can find and purchase, with the means of the mother, another female Slave equally good and valuable in every respect to be given to the minors (Pasca), in compensation for the loss of the services of the said Pamela Munro'.

Why the presumed market price would be below the replacement cost is not explained here, but the non-pecuniary aspects of free labour decisions would explain the non-availability of free labour to work on sugar plantations at the same price as slave labour. The cause of the possible differentials in slave prices, however, is not examined.

Bathurst's response was more lengthy and detailed in presenting the economic arguments, starting with the claim that the appraisers 'have proceeded on an entire misapprehension and misapplication of the instruction by which they profess to have been guided'. Rather,

> It had reference to the eventually progressive value of Slaves, after a sensible reduction of the number employed on each plantation; to the growing difficulty of replacing them by purchase, in consequence of corresponding reductions on other plantations; and, lastly, but more essentially, that instruction proceeded on the contingency of its being eventually proved by experience that free labour is not applicable to the culture of plantations in the West Indies. It therefore had an express reference not only to field labour but to field labour in 'a sugar plantation', as being that particular description of labour to which it was contended free labour was peculiarly inapplicable. All these considerations were not brought forward as what should affect existing valuations, (except so far as they might affect the price at which a substitute could be actually purchased according to the current prices of the Colony,) but as what were allowed to form reasonable objections to an uniform price being now fixed for what might be the appraisements which eventually ought to be hereafter assigned to the manumission of Slaves.
>
> The appraisers, professing to be governed by these instructions, have given immediate effect to those prospective considerations, and have applied them to what they would at any time be the least applicable, namely, to the manumission of a domestic Slave.[41]

Bathurst then pointed out the general principles by which the appraisement should be made:

> Generally speaking, the market price of Slaves is the fairest criterion of their value, and it is that by which the appraisers should principally regulate their valuations. The various considerations mentioned in the instruction above referred to, were not brought forward to supersede this criterion, but as those which might progressively affect the market price, and thereby make the fixing now an uniform price objectionable. By the term market price, it is not intended to refer to special sales which may have taken place under special circumstances, but to that price for which a Slave *bona fide* equivalent could be purchased at the period of the appraisement, and in that case whether the proprietor receives an actual substitution of an equivalent Slave, or a sum of money, for which at his option an equivalent Slave can be procured, his interests are equally preserved. Even under the supposition that no equivalent Slave could be procured, the principle of appraisement would in no degree be changed. The price of the manumission in that case would be a sum which would be either an equivalent for the increased expense which the proprietor would incur from employing a free person in services in which it is known by experience that free people can be employed, or as a compensation, whatever may be the loss of the Slave's labour in those services for which it may be found that free labour will not be available, or in those for which free labour may be only partially or inadequately substituted.
>
> The manumission price therefore of Pamela Munro ought not to exceed the price for which 'another female Slave equally good and valuable in every respect' could be procured for the minors Pasca. And if the appraisers had been able to form any definite opinion of the price of such a Slave, that amount is the price which they ought to have awarded as the price of Pamela Munro.

The Protector of Slaves, Henry Gloster, wrote a concurring letter to Governor Woodford, which described the implications of the upward trend in slave prices, but also claimed that the appraisers had misunderstood the principles of the manumission process:

> The appraised value of Slaves manumitted by the Chief Judge under the provisions of the Order in Council for the first eighteen months after the Order came into operation, does not average much more than one half of the general average for the last twelve months.
>
> The selling or market price of Slaves however has not experienced a commensurate rise, and therefore it is evident that the magnitude of the appraisements lately made are not occasioned by the encreased value of Slaves.
>
> It is also certain that the market price will rise in proportion to the decrease of the number or difficulty of procuring plantation Slaves. It is therefore unjust to

add to the real value or market price of the Slave purchasing his freedom, a portion of the value of the Estate to which the Slave is attached, until it becomes impracticable to continue the cultivation of the Estate in consequence of the impossibility of procuring a substitute for the Slave who is to be enfranchised.

The principle, that the value of the Slave should be estimated at the amount of the capital required to yield a revenue equal to the hire which could be obtained for the Slave, is evidently fallacious, from the fact, that every day instances occur of Slaves being bought for four hundred dollars, or eighty-six pounds thirteen shillings and four pence sterling, who, as Mr. Burnley mentions, may be imme-diately hired at the rate of six dollars, or one pound six shillings sterling per month, fed, clothed, and the capital guaranteed; the corresponding capital to which, at six per cent (the ordinary rate of interest in Trinidad), is one thousand two hundred dollars, or two hundred and sixty pounds sterling (the appraised value of Pamela Munro). Yet surely it could not be pretended, that the latter sum was the real value of a Slave which had been bought for one-third of the sum a short time before, and which could not be re-sold at an advanced price.

This, I submit, proves that the market price is the only just and fair criterion for determining the value of a Slave.

Yet, since the law stated that the appraised value of the slave was solely to be determined by the appraisers and could not be changed, the high appraisal was maintained. To the best of our knowledge, at this higher price Pamela Munro was not able to obtain her freedom.

In addition to these disagreements, there was some discussion within the Colonial Office that are of interest as early statements about the evaluation of what would later be called, by economists, human capital. Several of these were probably written by the economist R.J. Wilmot-Horton, who was to achieve some fame for his writings on colonial policy.[42] Among the several points stressed by Wilmot-Horton was the role of specific training, and the variations in the value of labour for specific purposes and in particular locations:

for the value of a Slave may partly depend upon aptitudes which habit has given & which the change of owners would throw out of use. A servant who has grown up and lived long in a family may be of some use in that family though of little or none in any other and consequently of little or no value in the market. The Slave's fellowship with the gang which he has lived peaceably with, and has been assorted with in labour, his trained pliancy to particular modes of discipline, his knowledge of his owner's, manager's, overseer's and Driver's tempers and theirs of his, every circumstance which rests in the slave a local and incommunicable value constitutes a difference between his value in possession and his value in exchange. How far the appraisers may be allowed to take this difference into their estimate appears to be a question of difficulty.

But there is something more questionable in the case (probably of more frequent occurrence) in which the unwillingness proceeds from some actual advantage which the owners could get by the Slave which others could not get & which therefore the market-price will not cover. Loss in these cases is either to be sustained by the owner or paid for by the Slave. The loss is not of a direct pecuniary interest, yet of advantages and conveniences which are worth money. Now if it were possible to devise means for ensuring in each case a fair estimate of these advantages the principle of full compensation would seen to require that according to this estimate a price should be paid for them. But this is perhaps scarcely possible.

The market is the surest criterion though it be not in all cases a perfect one, and all that the appraisers can do with safety is to estimate the marketable qualities of the Slave & fix the price which in the best of their judgement he would bring by auction. It has been objected that the Slave might be a cooper or a wheelwright, the only one on the estate, the loss of whose services might disarrange the whole operations of the Planter; since there might be very few coopers or wheelwrights in the Colony, & the planter might be unable to procure a substitute. But it is submitted that the principle of appraisement by market-price meets this objection. If wheelwrights are more scarce than other Slaves it must be owning to some accident which has disturbed the proportion between the demand and supply of wheelwrights. But be they as scarce as they may they are always to be had for money. Everything which is saleable will be sold if he who wants it will bid high enough. Wheelwrights therefore though dear would still have their market price, & an appraisement which should conform to this market price would set a compensating value upon the Slave.

Wilmot-Horton returned to these questions in other places. In debate in the House of Commons in 1828, he cited that the difficulties in getting an appropriate appraisal 'turned on one point; namely the degree of probability of the owner being able to supply the place of his slave'.[43] His problem was aggravated by the fact that 'free labour would not found as effectual as the labour of slaves in the production of sugar', since in sugar production 'the work should be continuous, that there should be no interruption, that the labourers should be available in all periods'. And, in the 1826 volume attributed to him, *The West India Question Practically Considered*, he argues that the:

loss [to the master] will be measured by a comparison between the profit which the labour of that Slave produced to his master, after deducting the expense of his maintenance, and the profit which the master will derive from the labour of a free black, after deducting the wages which it will be necessary to give, in order to induce such free black to execute the duties previously performed by that Slave . . . The case in which there will be the highest amount of compensation will be that in which the services of the Slave can neither be replaced by the purchase of another Slave within the colony (the only opportunity for such purchase permitted by law), or by the services of a free black labourer; and in that case, the principle of compensation will extend to a definite proportion of the property of the planter, who will be obliged to throw out of cultivation part of that soil . . .[44]

Wilmot-Horton goes on to point out that if the abolitionists were right, and free labour can replace slave labour, and be more productive, then no compensation need be paid. In an essay in the *Quarterly Review* in 1825, the authors list arguments which claim that the ending of slavery could be costless to British Caribbean planters, but they remain rather sceptical, and go so far as to argue that those arguing for the advantages of free labour 'allow themselves a latitude very nearly approaching to criminality'.[45]

The Order-in-Council regarding manumission in Demerara and Berbice (British Guiana), authored by Bathurst, had further comments about what might have influenced the value of a slave. The order specified that 'on the appraisement of a slave, the slave appraisers are to take into consideration the physical strength of the slave and mental acquirements, and absolute value of the slave to the owner, the loss which such owner would sustain by the loss of his services'. Also noted was the fact that slave children are valued at low prices, because 'they would be valued according to their ages'. More specifically, Major T. Moody suggested consideration of 'the sinews, the age, the height, strength, and appearance of the man', as well as 'a knowledge of the slave's value in use to a particular master', in determining the value of the slave.[46]

Conclusion

In this chapter, I have dealt with several issues relating to the evaluation of slaves, both for cases of individual manumissions and for the ending of the slave system itself. The debates on evaluation have been of interest, also, for discussions of legal questions relating to property rights and the nature and direction of compensation claims when the government introduces changes in the legal arrangements under which society operates, and also for examinations of the evaluation of what is now called human capital. That the slaves were willing to 'accept' these terms of manumissions, and to pursue this end for themselves no doubt served as a divisive safety-valve, perhaps removing some of the more talented slaves from the slave community, at least as reflected by labouring skills. The ability to accumulate funds sufficient to pay the market prices of the time suggests both that slave-owners did not obtain the 'full' surplus value from their slave labourers and that the nature of the incentive schemes provided to influence slave behaviour had more complexities than sometimes argued.

Two general points are of interest for further study. One, is the concern with market evaluations of slaves in determining the prices for manumission and for estimating the costs of emancipation of the slave populations when compensation was paid to slave-owners. This payment of some compensation to American slave-owners was a frequent practice, with the notable exceptions of Haiti and also the US, Cuba and Brazil, these being among the last of the slave powers to free their slaves. Second, is the general belief that compensation was to be paid for changes in property rights, it seldom being argued and never implemented that those who bore the burden of enslavement should be compensated. This general belief is one that, while predominant at the time, has undergone rather dramatic changes in the present century, with the discussion of compensating past and present victims of society's injustices. Although few of these current cases involve the property rights aspect that existed under slavery, the changing recognition of the legal rights to own property in other people has meant a shift in beliefs about the nature of compensation to be paid.

Notes

*For comments and discussions on these issues I should like to thank Seymour Drescher, David Eltis, Linda Levy Peck, Sherwin Rosen and Robert Steinfield.

1. While the price to be paid for manumission may have increased, if the share of the rising productivity which underlaid the rising price provided the slaves were unchanged, then the ratio of income to price would remain constant and the time-cost of manumission would not vary. This point was discussed in evaluating the legal provision for compulsory manumission in Trinidad in 1824. See W.L. Mathieson, *British Slavery and its Abolition, 1823–1838* (London: Longman, Green, 1926), pp. 150–1; 176–9.

2.   For examples of the use of the imagery of slavery as theft, see, among
      numerous sources, Edmund Burke, in *Hansard* (1789), Vol. 28, 96–7; O.
      Cugonao, *Thoughts and Sentiments on the Evil of Slavery* (London, 1787), pp.
      39–41, 70–4; and W. Garrison, 'Declaration of Sentiments of the American
      Anti-slavery Convention', in *Selections from the writings and speeches of William
      Lloyd Garrison* (London, 1852), pp. 66–71. Garrison argues, further, that 'if
      compensation is to be given at all, it should be given to the outraged and
      guiltless slave, and not to those who have plundered and abused them'.
3.   Actually, given the nature of the various markets in which slaves were
      purchased and sold, and the markets for the crops produced by slaves, the
      probable main beneficiaries were the captors of the slaves in Africa and the
      consumers of the slave-grown products. See R. Fogel and S. Engerman, *Time
      on the Cross: the Economics of Negro Slavery*, 2 vols (Boston: Little Brown,
      1974), Vol.1, pp. 244–6; Vol. 2, pp. 160–2. No one seems to have suggested
      that either the consumers or the Africans directly bear the costs of, or benefits
      from, the proceeds of emancipation. For an interesting discussion of what
      appeared to be the limited gains from the initial enslavement in Africa, see P.
      Curtin, 'The abolition of the slave trade from Senegambia', in D. Eltis and J.
      Walvin, eds., *The Abolition of the Atlantic Slave Trade: Origins and Effects in
      Europe, Africa, and the Americas* (Madison, WI: University of Wisconsin Press,
      1981), pp. 88–94.
4.   The possibility of changing sentiments leading from government
      encouragement to government prohibition was highlighted in the cases of the
      slave trade and slavery, and was central to claims of compensation. If the
      government could change the laws regarding any asset, presumably even the
      national debt and all other assets were at possible risk. See *The Port of Spain
      Gazette*, 2 July 1833, which notes that it should be 'remembered that the first
      attack on the right of West India property was considered by all reasonable
      persons as bordering on madness', and then sarcastically added the hope 'that
      the same equitable consideration will be extended to the National creditors as
      has been dealt out to the West India Colonies'. In the 1832 parliamentary
      debates Lord Wynford argued that if the government were able to force
      masters to abandon their property in slaves, that 'once adopt that principle,
      and there was an end of all property' (*Hansard*, 1832, Vol. 12, 630).
      Moreover, these concerns were heightened by the impression that the earlier
      advocates of abolishing the slave trade who denied 'that there was any
      intention on their parts to follow it up by any proposition for abolition of
      slavery', had been somewhat deceitful. See the speech of the Duke of
      Wellington in *Hansard* (1833, Vol. 18, 1180–1194). The idea of
      compensation for the loss in assets had been discussed earlier in Britain, and
      some compensation had been paid for losses in value and/or ownership rights.

In the complex settlements in the Restoration of 1660, for example, some holders of church lands were provided some compensation for their being dispossessed. See G. Holmes, *The Making of a Great Power: Late Stuart and Early Georgian Britain, 1660–1722*, (London: Longmans, 1993), p. 36. For a general point about the early role of compensation for deaths, in British law, see A. Harding, *A Social History of English Law* (Baltimore: Penguin Books, 1966), pp. 13–17. In the US, Congressional legislation in 1796, in an attempt to bring some peace to the frontier, provided compensation to either Indians or whites for losses of property caused by the other, a system that was ended only in 1920. The compensation was to be paid by the party causing the damage, but if they were unable to, by the Federal government. See L. Skogen, *Indian Depredation Claims, 1766–1920* (Norman, OK: University of Oklahoma Press, 1996).

5. Frequently slave-owners were compensated for the execution or transportation of their slaves resulting from criminal activity. For discussions of the payment of compensation related to market prices, see, among many sources, U.B. Phillips, 'Slave crime in Virginia', *American Historical Review*, 20 (January 1915), pp. 51–68; M. Kay and L. Cary, *Slavery in North Carolina, 1748–1775* (Chapel Hill, NC: University of North Carolina Press, 1995), pp. 87–94, 239–55; and D.B. Gaspar, 'Slave importation, runaways, and compensation in Antigua, 1720–1729', in J. Inikori and Engerman, eds., *The Atlantic Slave Trade: Effects on Economies, Societies and Peoples in Africa, the Americas and Europe* (Durham, NC: Duke University Press, 1992), pp.301–20.

6. See J. Blum, *The End of the Old Order in Rural Europe* (Princeton, NJ: Princeton University Press, 1978), pp. 357–417, for discussions of the various compensation schemes proposed to accomplish the abolition of European serfdom. Under serfdom the freed serfs often acquired land but they generally were required to pay for it. At times, it is argued, they were forced to pay too high a price, an additional form of exploitation undertaken as a cost of obtaining freedom. See E. Domar, 'Were Russian Serfs Overcharged for Their Land by the 1861 Emancipation? The History of One Historical Table', *Research in Economic History*, Supplement 5, (September 1985), pp. 429–439. The Dutch did have a proposal to have ex-slaves explicitly bear the costs of the compensation paid to slave-owners, but this provision did not enter the final emancipation scheme. See M. Kuitenbrouwer, 'The Dutch Case of Anti-slavery: Late and Elitist Abolitionism', in G. Oostindie, ed., *Fifty Years Later: Anti-slavery, Capitalism and Modernity in the Dutch Orbit* (Pittsburgh, PA: University of Pittsburgh Press, 1996), pp. 75–6. In abolishing seigniorial tenure in Quebec in 1854, compensation was paid to land-owners, primarily via funds coming from the taxpayers of Quebec, particularly those in urban areas. See M. Percy and R. Szostak, 'The Political Economy of the Abolition

of Seigniorial Tenure in Canada East', *Explorations in Economic History*, 29 (January 1992), pp. 51–68, and W. Munro, *The Seigniorial System in Canada: a Study in French Colonial Policy* (London: Longman Green, 1907), pp. 224–51.

7.   The Spanish system of manumission, which became the basis of the compulsory manumissions in the British colonies, included the use of appraisers of slave values and the holding of funds (the *coartación*) for the slave to enable him or her to achieve the price of self-purchase. An external appraisal was required to avoid the problems of moral hazard, of slaves working ineffectively to set a low price or of owners demanding a high price in order to preclude any successful manumissions. On Cuba, see H. Aimes, 'Coartación: a Spanish institution for the advancement of slaves into freedom', *Yale Review*, 17 (February 1909), pp. 412–31, and also E. Goveia, *The West Indian Slave Laws of the 18th century* (Barbados: Caribbean Universities Press, 1970), pp. 14–17; F. Knight, *Slave Society in Cuba in the 19th century* (Madison, WI: University of Wisconsin Press, 1970), pp. 130–1; R. Scott, *Slave Emancipation in Cuba* (Princeton, NJ: Princeton University Press, 1985), pp. 13–15; H.S. Klein, *Slavery in the Americas: a Comparative Study of Virginia and Cuba* (Chicago, IL: University of Chicago Press, 1967), pp. 196–201; and L. Bergad, et al., *The Cuban Slave Market* (Cambridge: Cambridge University Press, 1995), pp. 122–42. For manumissions in Portuguese Brazil, see K. Mattoso, *To Be A Slave in Brazil, 1550–1888* (New Brunswick: Rutgers University Press, 1986), pp. 155–76; S.B. Schwartz, 'The Manumission of Slaves in Colonial Brazil: Bahia, 1684–1745', *Hispanic American Historical Review*, (*HAHR*) 54 (November 1974), pp. 603–35; and M.Karasch, *Slave Life in Rio de Janeiro, 1808–1850* (Princeton, NJ: Princeton University Press, 1987), pp. 335–69. See M.I. Finley, *Economy and Society in Ancient Greece* (Harmondsworth: Penguin Books, 1983), pp. 116–66; K. Hopkins, *Conquerors and Slaves* (Cambridge: Cambridge University Press, 1978), pp. 115–71; and Y. Garlan, *Slavery in Ancient Greece* (Ithaca, NY: Cornell University Press, 1988), pp. 73–83, on self-purchase manumissions in ancient Greece, and K.R. Bradley, *Slaves and Masters in the Roman Empire* (New York: Oxford University Press, 1987), pp. 81–112, on Rome. In Greece, Garlan indicates, the price for self-purchase was 'a price that presumably corresponded roughly to the market value of the slave' (Ibid., p. 75). The option existed in Greece to provide 'a slave to take his place' (Ibid., p. 78), an alternative frequently existing in other slave societies. For a survival of the method of self-purchase to early twentieth-century West Africa, see P. Lovejoy and J. Hogendorn, *Slow Death for Slavery: the Course of Abolition in Northern Nigeria, 1897–1936* (Cambridge: Cambridge University Press, 1993), pp. 1–126. For serf self-purchase in Russia, see P. Kolchin, *Unfree*

Labour: American Slavery and Russian Serfdom (Cambridge, MA: Belknap Press, 1987), pp. 142–8, 189–91; and D. Field, *The End of Serfdom: Nobility and Bureaucracy in Russia, 1855–1861* (Cambridge, MA: Harvard University Press, 1976), pp. 191–9. For other areas and times in Iberian countries, see W. Sharp, *Slavery on the Spanish Frontier: the Colombian Chocó, 1650–1810* (Norman, OK: University of Oklahoma Press, 1976), pp.142–7; Schwartz, *Sugar Plantations in the Formation of Brazilian Society: Bahia, 1550–1835* (Cambridge: Cambridge University Press, 1985), pp. 157–8, 256–8; M. Nishida, 'Manumission and Ethnicity in Urban Slavery: Salvador, Brazil, 1808–1888'. *HAHR*, 73 (August 1993), pp. 361–91); C. Hünefeldt, *Paying the Price of Freedom: Family and Labour among Lima's Slaves, 1800–1854* (Berkeley, CA: University of California Press, 1994), pp. 66–79; F. Bowser, 'The Free Person of Colour in Mexico City and Lima: Manumission and Opportunity, 1580–1650', in Engerman and E. Genovese, eds., *Race and Slavery in the Western Hemisphere* (Princeton, NJ: Princeton University Press, 1975), pp. 331–68; and L. Johnson, 'Manumission in colonial Buenos Aires, 1776–1810', *HAHR*, 59 (May 1979), pp. 258–79. See also the discussion, including the French areas, in Klein, *African Slavery in Latin America and the Caribbean* (New York: Oxford University Press, 1986). The basic point in most cases is that the intended price for manumission generally varied with the market price. For US discussions of the general issue of self-purchase, see the contributions of John Cimprich and Whittington B. Johnson in R. Miller and J. Smith, eds., *Dictionary of Afro-American Slavery* (New York: Greenwood Press, 1988), pp. 430–2; 661–3, S. Matison, 'Manumission by Purchase', *Journal of Negro History*, 33 (April 1948), pp. 146–67; K. Stampp, *The Peculiar Institution: Slavery in the Anti-Bellum South* (New York: Vintage Books, 1956), pp. 96–7; Genovese, *Roll, Jordan, Roll: The World the Slaves Made* (New York: Pantheon Books, 1974), pp. 392, 406; S. Whitman, *The Price of Freedom: Slavery and Manumission in Baltimore and Early National Maryland* (Lexington, KY: University Press of Kentucky, 1997); and K. Hanger, *Bounded Lives, Bounded Places: Free Black Society in Colonial New Orleans, 1769–1803* (Durham, NC: Duke University Press, 1997); and, on legal issues, A. Watson, *Slave Law in the Americas* (Athens, GA: University of Georgia Press, 1989); and J. Schaeffer, *Slavery, the Civil Law, and the Supreme Court of Louisiana* (Baton Rouge, LA: Louisiana State University Press, 1994), pp. 1–6, 220–49.

8. There was some indemnity paid by the free Haitians to the French in 1825, in terms of both tariff preferences as well as sums of money. The presumed reason was the previous failure to compensate French slave-owners and land-owners for their losses in the Haitian revolution. This was a basic condition for French recognition of Haiti. The terms were reduced over time

by the French, until the Haitians were able to meet them. See R. Rotberg, *Haiti: the Politics of Squalor* (Boston, MA: Houghton Mifflin, 1971), pp. 66–102, 398–9. The terms of the agreement are reprinted in the *Annual Register* (1825), 143–7. In 1825 the French themselves provided indemnification to those former émigrés whose property had been nationalised during the Revolution. See M. Boffa, 'Émigrés', in F. Furet and M. Ozouf, eds., *A Critical Dictionary of the French Revolution* (Cambridge, MA: Belknap Press, 1989), pp. 324–36.

9. For discussions of these issues see Fogel and Engerman, 'Philanthropy at Bargain Prices: Notes on the Economics of Gradual Emancipation', *Journal of Legal Studies*, 3 (June 1974), pp. 377–401, and Engerman, 'Emancipation in Comparative Perspective: a Long and Wide View', in Oostindie, *Fifty Years Later*, pp. 223–41.

10. In proposing such a scheme of post-natal gradual emancipation, the eminent Virginia jurist, St George Tucker, claimed that 'the loss of the mother's labour for nine months, and the maintenance of a child for a dozen or fourteen years, is amply compensated by the services of that child for as many years more, as he has been an expense to them (95)': St G. Tucker, *A Dissertation on Slavery with a Proposal for the Gradual Abolition of it, in the State of Virginia* (Philadelphia, 1796). Thus the slave-owners would not be able to claim that they were being deprived of their property without 'just' compensation. See also E. McManus, *Black Bondage in the North* (Syracuse, NY: Syracuse University Press, 1973), pp. 160–79, and A. Zilversmit, *The First Emancipation: the abolition of slavery in the North* (Chicago, IL: University of Chicago Press, 1967) on the northern United States. They indicate that these legal provisions regarding manumission were to make it worthwhile for the owner to care for slaves, thus reducing the costs to the taxpayers. In general this type of gradual emancipation was frequently discussed and proposed, and was suggested as the possible means of British emancipation. Note that Britain's 1834 freeing of those slaves under six, or born after the start of apprenticeship, shifted the rearing costs from the owners to the ex-slaves (thus adding further to the benefits of slave-owners). See Article XIII of *An Act for the Abolition of Slavery throughout the British Colonies* (28 August 1833).

11. See the discussion in Fogel and Engerman, 'Philanthropy', and *Time on the Cross*, pp. 67–86.

12. The compensation was paid based on market values, and not paid on the per slave basis that those on islands with lower slave prices advocated. Some argued the injustice of using the per slave value basis since, they claimed, they had taken excellent care of their slaves, who were able to grow in numbers, and thus have a lower price than in areas where treatment was harsher. See B. Taylor, 'Our man in London: John Pollard Mayers, agent for Barbados, and

the British Abolition Act, 1832–1834', *Caribbean Studies*, 16 (October 1976), pp. 60–84, as well as the correspondence of the Jamaica agents (Jamaica Archives [JA], Spanish Town) in the early 1830s. This issue of basing payments on the numbers of slaves as opposed to slave values arose also in the cases of the French and Dutch emancipation. See A. Cochin, *The Results of Emancipation* (Boston, 1863), pp. 143–50, 396–401; and Cochin, *The Results of Slavery*, (Boston, 1863), pp. 221–5.

13. It was, therefore, no accident that British apprenticeship ended two years earlier than scheduled, after giving rise to a renewed set of complaints in England as well as from the slaves in the British Caribbean.

14. It was frequently argued that it was only after 1823, with the passage of amelioration acts and the increased activity of the anti-slavery movement, that slave prices began to fall in most of the colonies. See the discussion in Engerman, 'Economic Change and Contract Labour', in Richardson, ed., *Abolition and Its Aftermath* (London: Frank Cass, 1985), pp. 225–44. The French deliberately used earlier years, in 'an epoch when emancipation was not talked of (1825–1834)' to evaluate slave prices. See Cochin, *The Results of Emancipation*, p. 146.

15. See, e.g., [Earl of Sheffield], *Observations on the Project for Abolishing the Slave Trade* (London, 1790), pp. 50–1: 'At present the object is, an indirect and future abolition of *slavery*, and a direct and immediate abolition *of the slave trade*'. Perhaps the future actions would be legislated abolition, perhaps a dying out of slavery because of the demographic impact of ending the slave trade.

16. See the discussion in D. Porter, *The Abolition of the Slave Trade in England* (Hamden: Archon, 1970), pp. 30–51, 125–39. See also J. Lo Gerfo, 'Sir William Dolben and "the Cause of Humanity": the Passage of the Slave Trade Regulation Act of 1788', *Eighteenth Century Studies*, 4, (Summer 1973), pp. 431–51; F.E. Sanderson, 'The Liverpool Delegates and Sir William Dolben's Bill', *Transactions of the Historic Society of Lancashire and Cheshire*, 124 (1972), pp. 57–84 on the compensation provision of Dolben's Act, which appointed several commissions to evaluate the claims for compensation made by 'Individuals who may sustain Losses in consequence of this Act'. For a note about the limited implementation of this provision, see S. Behrendt, 'The British Slave Trade, 1785–1807: Volume, Profitability and Mortality' (unpublished PhD thesis, University of Wisconsin, 1993, p. 28). This was discussed in *Hansard* (1788, Vol. 27, 649–651). The issue of whether Parliament's responsibility for imposing losses via its actions required indemnification of losers was noted in many debates. See, e.g. [Earl of Sheffield], *Observations on the Project*, p. 50, and the discussion in J. Oldham, 'New Light on Mansfield and Slavery', *Journal of British Studies*, 27 (January

1988), pp. 45–68. Sheffield claimed this was a 'new doctrine', 'that compensation is not to be made for private property, diminished or destroyed for public views, by act of Parliament'. This point arose frequently in the parliamentary debates related to slavery and the slave trade. See William Pitt's discussion in *Hansard* (1792, Vol. 29, 1145–46), which points out that all commercial regulations affect people, and if compensation were always required, no new taxes, expenditures, etc, could ever be introduced by Parliament. Burke argued both that compensation was not needed as slavery was 'a system of robbery' and that those in the slave trade knew that the government had the right to withdraw its approval from that which it had previously 'authorised and protected', (*Hansard* 1789, Vol. 28, 96–7). On the iniquitous nature of slavery, but the need, if sanctioned by law in the past, to compensate slave-owners, see J.S. Mill, *Principles of Political Economy*, 2 vol.; (New York: 1895; first published 1848), Vol. I, pp. 298–300. Compensation, however, need not be paid for all changes in government policy, particularly if policy was known to be variable. This issue of governmental legislation has remained an essential legal problem. See, e.g., recent difference of opinion between Justice Scalia and Justice Blackmun, in *Lucas* v. *South Carolina Coastal Council* (Supreme Court of the United States, 1992), which distinguishes between the actual taking of property by the government and the imposition of financial losses on the owner of the asset. In 1872, the US Supreme Court ruled (*White* v. *Hart*) that while no compensation was to be paid for slaves, payment for 'slaves sold before emancipation' was required, pointing to the importance of maintaining the validity of previously made contracts. See H. Hyman, *The Reconstruction Justice of Salmon P. Chase in Re: Turner and Texas v. White* (Lawrence, KS: University of Kansas Press, 1997), pp. 157–8.

17.   See Letters of the Jamaica agents, 8 April 1799, where the compensation is seen to result from a resumption of the use of the 'uncultivated patented Lands'. See also the comments made by Pitt (*Hansard*, 1799–1800, Vol. 34, 561–4).

18.   See the brief discussion of this negotiation in S. Bemis, *Jay's Treaty: a Study in Commerce and Diplomacy* (New Haven, CT: Yale University Press, 1923), pp. 63, 284, 289, 357. See also F. Ogg, 'Jay's Treaty and the Slavery Interests of the United States', *Annual Report of the American Historical Association for the Year 1901*, 2 vols (Washington, DC: Government Printing Office, 1902), Vol. 1, pp. 273–99.

19.   See the correspondence in *American State Papers*, Vol. 5, 214–21, 801–29; Vol. 6, 339–55, 372–3, 637–8, 745–53, 821–2, 855–63, 882–92, 950–2. See also F. Updyke, *The Diplomacy of the War of 1812* (Baltimore, MD: Johns Hopkins University Press, 1915), pp. 399–405; J. Moore, *History and Digest of*

the International Arbitrations to which the United States has been a Party, 6 vols (Washington, 1898), Vol. 1, pp. 350–90.

20. See 'Petition of the several Planters, . . . now residing in Antigua', to Parliament, 28 June 1831 (Kingston, 1831). These planters also claimed 'a right to be fully paid, not only for their slaves but for their lands and extensive Plantation Buildings which will be rendered of no value to your Petitioners when they are deprived of the labour of their Slaves'.

21. This influenced, in principle, not only the amount to be paid, but also the allocations among colonies. A debate also emerged about the choice of the particular years for which to obtain price data for purposes of apportioning compensation. In addition to arguing for compensation based on the number of slaves, Jamaica opposed the particular choice of years used, arguing that earlier years would have provided a fairer division. An 1840 proposal made for French emancipation, not adopted, was to use the average rate of sale in each colony during a ten-year period of prosperity when emancipation was not yet talked about (1825–34), with compensation to be paid one-half in money and one-half in labour. (The final measure was part cash, part bonds.) There was another interesting suggestion made in this period in regard to French emancipation, but not utilised, based on the difference between daily free wages and daily slave costs, multiplied by 250 working days per year multiplied by a five-year period. See Cochin, *The Results of Emancipation,* pp. 59–73, 143–53. Also discussed were the owners' demand for indemnity for loss in value of land and other property due to the freeing of slaves, and the issue of whether it was the slaves who deserved compensation. The compensation payments per slave varied by colony, the relatives based ultimately upon prices of slaves sold in judiciary sales after 1840. Ibid., pp. 146–9; S. McCloy, *The Negro in the French West Indies* (Lexington, KY: University of Kentucky Press, 1966), pp. 141–59.

22. On this point, see Curtin, 'The British Sugar Duties and West Indian Prosperity', *Journal of Economic History,* 14 (June 1954), pp. 157–66, and Fogel, et al., eds., *Without Consent or Contract: the Rise and Fall of American Slavery: Evidence and Methods* (New York: W.W. Norton, 1992), pp. 168–90.

23. This led to a claim that the ability of slaves to manumit themselves was unfortunately limited by the inability of the newer areas to obtain more slaves from the older areas, thus raising their prices. The impact on the older areas was, however, seldom discussed. For an attack on the policy of restricting the internal slave trade, see the 1831 comments of Mill, *Newspaper writings, August 1831–October 1834* (Toronto: University of Toronto Press, 1986), pp. 347–50, (The original publication was the *Examiner,* 18 September 1831, pp. 594-595), who claimed that 'the ruin of the [older] colony would be partly alleviated, if its proprietors were permitted to dispose of their slaves to those

who are suffering for want of them'. This policy, he argued, would be a
benefit to British taxpayers.

24. See, e.g., the points in *Hansard* (1833, Vol. 20, 628–32). It was claimed that
     compensation helped those areas which were better off. The inverse of this
     argument, that emancipation was easier to accomplish in Barbados than in
     Trinidad, was made by Colonel Torrens (*Hansard*, 1833, Vol. 19,
     1263–1266).

25. While the Act of Abolition 1833 contained considerable detail about the terms
     of apprenticeship, and about the logistical aspects of the payment of
     compensation, the relatively brief discussion of the calculation of the amounts
     to be paid to slave-owners was mainly to the effect that the apportionment
     among the colonies would be based on 'Prices for which, on an Average of
     Eight Years ending on the Thirty-first Day of December [1830], slaves had
     been sold'. These 'average values' did not distinguish by age and sex, but only
     by whether they were praedial attached ('usually employed in Agriculture or
     in the Manufacture of Colonial Produce . . . upon Lands belonging to their
     Owners'); praedial unattached, who worked upon Lands not belonging to
     their Owners; or non-praedial labourers. Since the total sum to be paid to
     slave-owners was fixed at £20 million, the average values were used as an
     allocation mechanism among the islands and did not represent the amount to
     be received as compensation. The ratio of compensation to 1822–30 values is
     usually estimated to have been about 45 per cent, but some have argued for
     higher (or lower) amounts. For recent discussions of compensation, see K.M.
     Butler, *The Economics of Emancipation* (Chapel Hill, NC: University of North
     Carolina Press, 1995), and R. Lobdell, 'The Price of Freedom: Financial
     Aspects of British Slave Emancipation', (unpublished Association of
     Caribbean Historians conference paper, 1996). For a listing of the value of
     compensation for slaves from the different islands, see Engerman, 'Economic
     Change and Contract Labour in the British Caribbean', in Richardson,
     Abolition and Its Aftermath.

26. See Engerman, 'Economic Change and Contract Labour'.

27. In the discussions of the 1830s other possible schemes of compensation were
     noted, whereby some of the disagreements would possibly be papered over.
     These included; the rate of profit (which would presumably allow for
     differences in land values); the amount of exports (posing problems
     dependent on whether food was locally produced or imported); or original
     cost (as a way to equalise the values of slaves). On the limited debates
     concerning compensated emancipation in the US, see B. Fladeland,
     'Compensated Emancipation: a Rejected Alternative', *Journal of Southern
     History*, 42 (May 1976), pp. 169–86. Other cases of compensated
     emancipation existed. The Danish compensation magnitude was comparable

with the earlier slaves prices for two small British islands, Antigua and Tortola, near the Danish West Indies, which had relatively low prices. The form of the compensation was intended to include 12 years of labour under a form of apprenticeship, but a labour strike terminated that at once. In 1852, there was a small cash payment per slave made to owners. See Cochin *The Results of Emancipation*, pp. 389–94; W. Boyer, *America's Virgin Islands: a History of Human Rights and Wrongs* (Durham, NC: Carolina Academic Press, 1983), pp. 35–60; and N. Hall, *Slave Society in the Danish West Indies* (Mona: University of the West Indies Press, 1992), pp. 30–3, 54–5. The Swedish emancipation had compensation paid by the government, apparently based on an earlier proposal that had suggested using slave prices based upon three age categories. See Cochin, *The Results of Emancipation*, p. 395, and E. Ekman, 'Sweden, the Slave Trade and Slavery, 1784–1847', *Revue Française d'Histoire d'Outre-Mer*, 62 (1975), pp. 221–31. There had been numerous plans discussed for Dutch abolition between 1835 and the ultimate success that took effect in 1863. Among these proposals, in 1857, were plans to have freed slaves contribute to a fund to pay the costs of the emancipation, and also the payment of an indemnity to slave-owners for the decline in the value of land and buildings due to the freeing of slaves. Neither entered into the final plan which had compensation paid by the government plus a ten-year apprenticeship. The compensation per slave varied by colony, and the terms of apprenticeship also varied between Suriname and the other colonies. Cochin suggests that the average payment per slave in the English colonies was adopted by the Dutch. See Cochin, *The Results of Emancipation*, pp. 396–401, and Kuitenbriouwer, 'The Dutch Case'. See also Cochin, *The Results of Slavery*, pp. 221–5, and P. Hiss, *Netherlands America: the Dutch Territories in the West* (New York: Duell, Sloan and Pearce, 1943), pp. 106–8, 207.

28. Compare the compensation data from the *Parliamentary Papers* (*PP*), presented in N. Deerr, *The History of Sugar*, 2 vols (London: Chapman and Hall, 1949, 1950), p. 306, with the wage data for 1839–50 in W.E. Riviere, 'Labour Shortage in the British West Indies after Emancipation', *Journal of Caribbean History*, 4 (May 1972), pp. 1–30, who draws mainly upon *Parliamentary Papers* and *Colonial Office Papers*. This information was frequently available also in contemporary publications such as *The Colonial Magazine and Commercial Maritime Journal*, edited by R. Montgomery Martin.

29. This was pointed out at the time. It was, for instance, clearly stated by Sir Robert Peel in the 1830 debates on slavery. In discussions on what should be the amount of compensation, he asked: 'Was the country to recompense the owner for the direct loss he would sustain in his slave, or from the

consequential loss he must suffer in his property and plantations?' To these 'grave and serious questions' he, however, provided no answers. (*Hansard*, 1830, Vol. I, 1063). Not surprisingly, the Jamaica agent also argued that freeing slaves would reduce the value of land and buildings, and thus some of the losses to planters would not be compensated under the existing schemes: (see, e.g., Letters of the Jamaica Agents, 20 April 1832).

30.   See J.R. Ward, 'The Profitability and viability of British West Indian slavery, 1807–1834', (unpublished paper), for the presentation of this argument.

31.   In July 1833, Secretary Stanley commented that: 'The question was not about the principle of compensation, but about its amount. There was great difficulty in ascertaining what the amount should be, because the calculations depended upon a variety of considerations, and a small mistake in a minute particular would throw them all wrong'. These considerations included: the net effect of reducing hours owed planters while still imposing the full costs of labour maintenance on them, and 'the deduction . . . for the sum to be paid, depending upon the rate of interest in consequence of the money being advanced immediately'. (*Hansard*, 1833, Vol. 19, 1198). Stanley also pointed out 'that the system of apprenticeship formed part of the compensation by which the planter was to be indemnified'.

32.   For a general discussion of the process and meaning of manumission, see O. Patterson, *Slavery and Social Death* (Cambridge, MA: Harvard University Press, 1982), pp. 209–96. Self-purchase manumission has been described as far back as Greece and Rome, and it played a role at least as late as early twentieth-century British West Africa. See note 7.

33.   On the patterns of manumission in the Americas, see F. Tannenbaum, *Slave and Citizen: the Negro in the Americas* (New York: Alfred Knopf, 1946).

34.   See the Colonial Office discussions on this issue in the 1820s (CO 295 and 320) often reprinted in *PP*, and also CO 884/1 'Compulsory Manumission' (1826). On the Trinidad background, see B. Brereton, *A History of Modern Trinidad, 1783–1962* (Kingston: Heinemann, 1981), pp. 52–75. For an extended discussion of the compulsory manumission policy, see A. O'Donnell, *Compulsory Manumission or an examination of the actual state of the West India Question* (London: John Murray, 1827). See also Mathieson, *British Slavery and its Abolition*, pp. 183–7. There was an interesting parliamentary discussion of this issue in (*Hansard*, 1828, Vol. 18, 1023–1048).

35.   There was also concern with the moral hazard problem that might arise from the slave's market value being established on the basis of his conduct and productivity, providing a slave seeking to be manumitted an incentive (as long as his income was not directly related to productivity) to rendering himself of less value. While it was argued that prior knowledge of the productive capacities of slaves would permit slave-owners to judge

expected value more accurately, such information might not have been available to the appraisers.

36. See the Draft of the Orders in Council for Improving the Condition of the Slaves in Trinidad, *PP*, 1824, Vol. 24, Provisions 29–34. *Papers Relating to the Slave Trade, 1823–1824*, (Shannon: Irish University Press (IUP), 1969), Series of British Parliamentary Papers subject on Slave Trade, Volume 66. As a result of the Orders in Council there were a total of 588 manumissions between June 1824 and December 1827, with generally little disagreement arising, or at least reaching the governor's office. Of these, 409 involved purchase ('for valuable consideration'), 155 were gratuitous and 24 by will. Relative to the preceding period the big increase was in the number purchased. See *PP*, 1828, Vol. 27, 118–20 (IUP, Vol. 76).

37. See the discussions in *PP*, 1826–27, Vol. 26 (IUP, Vol. 73); 1828, Vol. 25 (IUP, Vol. 75), relating to Trinidad, and to Berbice and Demerara.

38. This seems the only such case that occurred in this period in Trinidad (or elsewhere in the British colonies). Note the discussion of the relation between the increase in the price of manumissions and in Trinidad slave prices in *PP*, 1828, Vol. 27, 116–17 (IUP, Vol. 76); 1829, Vol. 25, 78–9 (IUP, Vol. 76).

39. See, for example the recent debate in Britain concerning payments to farmers as part of the 'mad-cow' controversy. Offered compensation based on the value of those cows previously owned, farmers requested compensation based on the cost of acquiring new, disease-free, cattle. See *The Economist*, 30 March 1996, pp. 53–4.

40. The discussion here and in the next several paragraphs come from the *PP* copies of Colonial Office letters, 1826–27, Vol. 26, 265–71 (IUP, Vol. 73); and *Colonial Office Papers*, CO 295 and CO 320. There is a brief discussion of the issue of manumission and the case of Pamela Munro in the *Port of Spain Gazette*, 1 August 1827, taken from the *Trinidad Guardian* of 17 July 1827. See also the discussion of this case in N. Titus, 'Amelioration and Emancipation in Trinidad, 1812–1834', (MA thesis, UWI, St Augustine, Trinidad, 1974), pp. 191–9.

41. *PP*, 1826–27, Vol. 26, p. 268. The specific problem of price rises as the result of manumission-induced reductions in the labour supply was sometimes discussed, but generally to make the argument that fewer slaves would mean the ending of the plantation system.

42. See *The West India Question Practically Considered* (London: 1826). R.N. Ghosh presents a discussion of Wilmot-Horton's role in the colonisation debates of the time in 'The colonisation controversy', *Economica*, 31 (November 1964), pp. 385–400.

43. *Hansard* (1828, Vol. 18, 1026–1027).

44. Wilmot-Horton, *The West India Question*, pp. 88–9. A statement received 15
     August 1829 in regard to compulsory manumission (CO 320/6) points out
     'that shortly after the date of Lord Bathurst's Despatch of February 1826, Mr.
     Wilmot Horton published a Pamphlet which, though anonymous, was the
     avowed production of his Pen, and . . . enforced the argument introduced into
     the Despatch to show that the Trinidad Law afforded the Owner an adequate
     compensation for the loss of his Slave; although, in certain contingencies, it
     would be the duty of the State to come to the Slave's assistance'. It is also
     noted that the pamphlet 'was naturally ascribed' 'some degree of official
     authority' 'from the situation which the writer then occupied in this
     Department'.
45. 'West India Colonies', pp. 567–71. According to Frank Fetter, 'The economic
     articles in the *Quarterly Review* and their authors, 1809–52, 11', *Journal of
     Political Economy*, 66 (April 1958), p. 161, this article was authored by Sir
     Robert John Wilmot-Horton and Charles Rose Ellis in 'West India Colonies',
     Quarterly Review, 30 (January 1824), pp. 559–87.
46. *PP*, 1828, Vol. 25, 33–67, 72 (IUP, Vol. 75). There is an excellent discussion
     of the problem of evaluating what would now be called specific human capital
     in CO 320/1, #108, noting the distinction between 'the slave's value to his
     master and his exchangeable value'. See also *PP*, Ibid, 48. Some pointed to
     the value of 'moral character' and its influence on others. *PP*, Ibid., 27, 28.

CHAPTER

14

Black and White

Slaves, slavery and British society, 1600–1807

JAMES WALVIN

*T*he history of the Black community in Britain has attracted serious and growing intellectual attention over the past 25 years.[1] The consequent scholarship has been important at a number of levels, most notably for an understanding of the longevity of Black Britain and for accepting the complexity of racial attitudes displayed by the host British society. It is tempting to argue that, at any point from, say, the mid-seventeenth century onwards, in the varied British contacts with Africans and their British-born descendants, the British were bemused and curious. There is plenty of evidence which illustrates the British unease and hostility towards a developing Black community. As the Black presence in Britain grew – in size, in ubiquity and in the public's awareness – there is an abundance of detail to paint a picture of a curious host society coming to terms, reluctantly and generally with bad grace, to people they viewed as unalterably different and alien.[2] In words which clearly spoke for many of his fellow Blacks, Ignatius Sancho wrote in 1779; 'I am only a lodger, and hardly that'.[3]

Historians of Britain's Black community have, for a generation, provided us with ever more details: about its size, its location, its evolution and social consequences. But in focusing on the local and the specific – in seeking to draw the outline of a community which was British – there has been a temptation to lose sight of key, defining characteristics of that community. It is important to recognise that the growing British awareness of Black life was shaped not simply (perhaps not even largely) by a face-to-face contact with Blacks in Britain, but rather by those expansive and thoroughly pervasive links which evolved between Britain and its vast slave-based Atlantic economy. Put simply, and crudely, the awareness of Africa and Africans was shaped as much by the growing economic importance of trading and manufacturing links with Africans on both sides of the Atlantic as it was with Blacks who found themselves cast adrift in Britain itself. More than that, it seems clear enough that Blacks in London, the nub of the Atlantic slave empire, were in touch with friends and associates on the other side of the Atlantic. Olaudah Equiano, for example, had African friends in London, the Caribbean, Charleston, Savanna and Philadelphia.[4]

From the blizzard of scholarly papers and books which has swirled around the Eric Williams thesis, a few widely accepted simple truths have emerged. Few can surely doubt, now, the critical importance of the Atlantic slave system in the transformation of the British economy after 1650.[5] Of course even this Atlantic economy, in all its vastness, did not thrive in isolation, and it cannot easily be abstracted from the much broader contours of British economic involvement with Europe and Asia.[6] It was not always easy to distinguish the broader benefits of imperial trade, to India for example, from the rewards to be gained from the Atlantic empire. But the critical mass of trade to and from West Africa and the slave colonies of the Americas was a powerful force in shaping British economic well-being – and that long before the first signs of modern industrial growth could be detected. Ever more economic activities in Britain were shaped, directly or indirectly, in order to satisfy the voracious material and commercial demands of the trade to Africa and to the slave colonies. More and more people, throughout Britain, found their material well-being (in many cases, their material livelihoods) dependent on the slave-based Atlantic economy.

Few were more aware of this fact than that early generation of Caribbean historians whose task was both to describe and defend the slave system. Edward Long was one of many who sought to underline British dependence on the Atlantic slave system. It is proper, he wrote,

> to begin with the Negro trade, which is the ground-work for all. The Negro slaves
> are purchased in Africa, by the British merchants, with a great variety of woollen

goods; a cheap sort of fire-arms from Birmingham, Sheffield and other places; powder, bullets, iron bars, copper bars, brass pans, malt spirits, tallow, tobacco-pipes, Manchester goods, glass beads; some particular kind of linens, ironmongery and cutlery ware; certain toys, some East India goods; but in the main with very little that is not of British growth or manufacture.

Long also recited the obvious fact that British Caribbean plantations were equipped and serviced by the British economy; from the hats on the slaves' heads to the ale and cider on the planters' tables.[7] Whites at Worthy Park in 1789 took delivery of 'A Box with a Cheshire Cheese'. To anyone who has worked on plantation ledgers and inventories, the point is obvious and irrefutable.[8] Early abolitionists had to devise answers to the obvious fact that the slave system seemed to be good for British economic well-being.

The most immediately obvious consequence of British economic links to the Atlantic slave system was the simple growth of shipping. There was a remarkable proliferation of ships, port facilities and an expanding labour force of British sailors whose prime activity, over some 150 years, was to nurture the economic and social complexities of the slave system.[9] It is true of course that the ships involved in the slave system represented only a part of Britain's overall maritime fleet. Nonetheless, the numbers were enormous. Between the end of the trading monopoly of the Royal African Company in 1698 and abolition in 1807, some 11,000 British ships left Britain to trade in Africans. In the course of the eighteenth century, the British transported three million Africans. London led the way, followed by Bristol and then, by 1750, Liverpool dominated the trade. Almost one-half of British slave ships in the eighteenth century were Liverpool-based. By the last years of the British slave trade, perhaps three-quarters of all the British slave trade was fitted out in Liverpool.[10] Thousands of ships, tens of thousands of sailors, plied their trade within the Atlantic slave economy. Yet such statistics can serve to hide a much deeper and more broadly-based involvement.

In dozens of ports there were few merchant houses, local traders and manufacturers who did not, at some stage, direct at least part of their commercial efforts to the slave trade, even though the main thrust of their commercial activities might lie elsewhere. Quakers alone spurned the opportunities afforded by slavery – and even then not always comprehensively. Few could resist the temptation to dabble in slavery, even as a marginal sideline to their main commercial preoccupations. This picture, of the ubiquitous spread of slaving interests into the fabric of British life after 1660, is reinforced when we look closer at the slave ports themselves.

Understandably a great deal of attention has been devoted to the major slave-trading ports; to London, Bristol and Liverpool. But that concentration has often deflected interest from the extraordinary number and range of ports involved in the African trade. We now know that a host of smaller ports were lured into the Atlantic trade, small towns whose local merchants, investors and tradesmen pooled their relatively meagre savings and expertise to finance a slave ship. The names of those ports often cause surprise. Poole and Lyme Regis, Whitehaven and Lancaster, Chester and Preston: these are not towns which are automatically associated with British slave trading. Yet all and more involved themselves (their town-fathers, shopkeepers, craftsmen and the much deeper rural hinterland to which they had commercial and economic links) in the lucrative speculations of trading to and from Africa.[11] One small result of this trade, from small and sometimes isolated British ports, was that Africans, enslaved and free, found themselves cast ashore in the most unlikely of British communities.[12] We thus find Africans living across the length and breadth of Britain in the eighteenth century.

The commercial centres of the African trade were of course the major ports and the capital. But local research has piled detail upon detail of the irresistible and pervasive lure of Africa. In the years of British Atlantic dominance, all sorts and conditions of people from across provincial Britain looked to profit from slavery, assembling finance, expertise and commercial interests from a remarkable range of local people and interest groups. Men and women of all ages were generally keen to invest in slaving ventures. Though few were prepared to commit themselves uniquely to the African trade, many were willing to invest at least part of their money and skills in the slaving system. In Lancaster, a string of men in their early 20s – drapers, upholsterers, grocers, apothecaries, apprentices even – invested in local slaving voyages. Older investors came from the grocery, rope-making and wine-selling trades.[13] These investors came from varied business interests, but it seems clear enough that the slave trade held a special appeal for men in the towns' wholesale and manufacturing concerns. Trade to and from Africa (and that meant slaving) had a virtually universal economic appeal which went far beyond those groups of men who were uniquely Africanist in their dealings. Moreover, such ventures attracted capital from well beyond the towns' limits, drawing upon a deep geographic hinterland. Lancaster's trade, for instance, involved a variety of inland villages. Slave ships from Preston and Poulton were partly financed by flax merchants from Kirkham. Manchester textile merchants sunk money into slavers in a number of Lancashire ports. Slave ships from Chester attracted investments from local ironmongers, glove-makers and rope-makers.[14]

When we look at the origins of goods which ships loaded for Africa and the Americas we begin to see a trading network which stretched from the slave port itself deep into the regional heartland. When the *Hope* cleared for Africa from Lancaster in 1792 her cargo contained rice (from South Carolina), knives from Liverpool, salt from Nantwich, brass and wire from Cheadle, cotton from Manchester, sails from Kirkham, flagons from a Lancaster tea-merchant, foodstuff from a local grocer, earthenware from Preston, chests made by a local cooper and a variety of Asian textiles transshipped by Liverpool merchant houses.[15] This simple example could be repeated for most ships which sailed for Africa and thence to the Americas.

Variants of a similar story could be repeated, on the coast of Africa, to provide a litany of British (and Asian) goods unloaded at crucial points along the slaving coasts – and all to make trade and barter with African middlemen for the coffles of Africans destined for the barracoons of the Americas. Now, the point here is not to offer a miniature economic history of the slave trade, but to trace that trade back to its British roots. However we analyse the topic in the years from the mid-seventeenth century onwards, there is a convergence of data which takes us back to the British heartlands. British producers, merchants and manufacturers became ever more intimately linked into a lucrative dependency on the Atlantic trade. What British people knew and valued of Africa was its fundamental economic importance. The slave coasts (and their own trading hinterlands) provided a remarkable market for British goods and items transshipped through Britain. In return, it yielded apparently limitless supplies of servile African labour to tap the luxuriant wealth of the Americas.

It would then be wrong to imagine that the critical relations between Black and White, between Britain and Africa, were necessarily forged primarily by face-to-face dealings in Britain; by personal, visual experience, of one side staring at and working with the other. Rather, those relations emerged from a more complex trading nexus which bound Black and White together in an economic interdependence which utterly transformed the lives of both.

The most obvious agent for this process of change were those articles of trade which became the vital bargaining counters throughout the world of the

Atlantic economy. Historians of Africa have been at pains to stress the complex nature of the export trade from Africa throughout the period.[16] Yet to illustrate the broad range of African exports is not to minimise the importance of the trade in African humanity; that devastating westward surge of millions of reluctant peoples from a vast (and changing) region of coastal and interior Africa. Again, there is no need to recite the accepted figures here, but we can simply repeat the destruction and convulsions attendant on that process for a series of African societies, many of them unknown to the Europeans. And at the heart of this phenomenon lay the voracious European appetite for Africans. In return, Africa absorbed imported British goods. Of course, long before the British had become involved, complex consumer tastes had developed on the African coast, demanding (and getting) from European traders a range of materials goods (many trans-shipped from Asia) in return for slaves. First under the monopolistic Royal African Company and, after the opening of the trade in 1712 a growing number of slave traders imported a huge range of British (and Asian) material goods and luxuries to West Africa.

The volume and variety of those imports were remarkable. While the statistics for firearms have impressed historians,[17] other British goods were perhaps even more important. On the eve of abolition for example, more than a third of a million pieces of textiles were imported into the slaving region annually and similar figures could be rehearsed for other European slave trading nations.[18] French wines and brandy, rum from the Caribbean, tobacco from the Chesapeake, thousands of pipes from manufacturers scattered across Britain (and Holland), tens of thousands of tons of sugar from the British Caribbean, all this and more poured into West Africa in return for yet more African slaves. It was a remarkable irony that the fruits of slave labour in the Americas – sugar, rum and tobacco – should find their way back to West Africa and on to the westbound slave ships; slave-made produce shipped back and forth across the Atlantic in order to accumulate and then pacify yet more cargoes of Africans.

The trading pattern on the African coast was replicated in the Americas. There too British goods formed the crucial lubricant of local social and economic life. The plantations of colonial America, especially the sugar colonies of the Caribbean, were utterly dependent on Britain for supplies of labour and for most items of daily life and sustenance. Even that inflow of goods direct from colonial North America to the British Caribbean was controlled and directed within the broader imperial system of protection.

Local White elites in the islands – planters, merchants and military – continued to depend upon Britain for the basics of life. Indeed it was this dependence on Britain which, ultimately, prevented the British Caribbean territories going the way of independence in the political ferment after 1776.

Both Black and White were dependent on imported British goods throughout the slave islands. Even in so luxurious and fruitful a habitat as the Caribbean, the basic slave foodstuff was imported saltfish from the Newfoundland fisheries. A similar story emerges when we look at the cargoes of those ships which sailed direct from Britain to the slave colonies. One estate ledger after another documents the arrival from Britain of prodigious volumes of British goods and agricultural produce. The annual accounts of Worthy Park estate in Jamaica for 1789, for example, lists the following goods imported from Britain; mosquito nets, copper boilers, strainers, metal goods, saddles and furniture, hats for the slaves, porter (for the Whites), coal, lime, lead, stationery, nails and shingles, chains and tools for the field, seeds for the gardens, cheese from Cheshire, oil, paint, gunpowder, cork and blankets, medicines, rope and tarpaulin. Food and candles came direct from Ireland.[19]

No one doubts the extent of the dependence of the slave societies on the flow of British goods into the islands. Daily life, at home and at work, for Black and White, pivoted on imported goods. Clothing was imported (though made up generally by slaves); houses were imported in the form of timber or in frames from New England. Much of the hardware of domestic life was imported. Even the manuals for management – how to control the slaves, how to manufacture local produce – were imported from Britain.[20] This ought not to surprise us of course. After all, for much of the period, the labour force itself was imported. What is surprising, however, is the degree to Caribbean slaves, like West African middlemen, became addicted to the material artefacts of the outside world. Both regions were, in effect, part of a broader Atlantic world of material consumption. The history of modern material consumption has focused primarily on modern Europe and North America, but it is a story which was also evident in the slave islands; slaves, like their free British contemporaries, became consumers. Indeed some of the most telling evidence about the onset of the consumer revolution of the seventeenth and eighteenth centuries can be found not so much in Britain itself but on the very fringes of colonial settlement and trade. There, the British cultivated the habits of consumption – the desire for – alien, imported material goods among local peoples. This was as true in West Africa as it was in the Caribbean (and indeed it was striking among the Indian peoples of northeastern America).[21]

When commentators looked into the slave quarters of the Caribbean they were sometimes amazed, by the late eighteenth century, to see artefacts they had not expected. When they were able, slaves began to accumulate possessions. Bryan Edwards reported in 1793 that some Jamaican slaves 'have larger houses with boarded floors, and are accommodated (*at their own expence* it is true) with very decent furniture: a few have even good beds, linen sheets, and mosquito nets, and display *a shelf or two of plates and dishes of queens or Staffordshire ware*'.[22] (author's italics)

Solid furniture, decent bedding, costly pottery – and all acquired by the slaves. This surely was a remarkable testimony to the seductive power of material consumption. The purpose here, however, is not to discuss that important process. Yet it does have important implications for my thesis, for what we are witnessing is the development of a desire among slaves for artefacts disgorged by a range of British producers. British goods were to be found in slave quarters, just as the fruits of slave labour – the tropical staples – had, by the same period, entered the homes and the social lives of most British people. Black and White had become locked together in a process of material consumption, the prime aim of which was the enhancement of British material well-being.

The produce of distant colonies had fundamentally transformed daily British life. A number of significant domestic and public British routines which are thought to be utterly British were in fact shaped by the fruits of distant empire. Sidney Mintz has brilliantly captured the story for sugar.[23] But a much broader account needs to be told: of key tropical staples transforming the cultural fabric of British life in the years after 1650. Sugar was clearly central because, without it, other tropical produce would have remained unpalatable to Western taste. It was no accident that the three main drinks, tea, coffee and chocolate, which travelled the social route from elite fashion to the universal and commonplace, did so in the company of sugar. In each of their remote (and widely separated) natural habitats, those drinks were enjoyed locally in their naturally bitter form. Aztec chocolate had been consumed with spices and chillies; Yemeni coffee was drunk thick and Black, and Chinese tea was served with no additives. In all cases, it was the ability of the British from the 1630s onwards, to conjure forth increasing volumes of sugar, from the cornucopia of their slave islands, which provided the key to the rising consumption and ever increasing popularity of those bitter drinks. And that, of course, was made possible by Africans.

Sugar poured into Britain – and thence to Europe – in remarkable volumes. Cane sugar, once the costly preserve of society's elite and prosperous, quickly became the necessity of the common people. It was helped on its way by the remarkable proliferation of shops throughout the British Isles. In recent years, historians of the rise of consumption have spent a great deal of time looking for the outlets of consumer goods. And while it is tempting to be impressed by that dazzling array of shops housed in London, more eye-catching and more varied even than Paris, the real transformation was taking place in provincial Britain. Shops began to appear in the remotest corners of the nation, in Welsh villages and remote Highland settlements. Often of course they were little more than a counter in the front room of a local cottage. But the fact that they existed is important. So too, for our purposes, is the question of what they sold.

The humblest of shops in mid-eighteenth-century Britain provided customers with the fruits of distant colonies. Tobacco, tea and sugar were, above all other commodities, the basic items on even the most sparsely stocked shelves. Research on shop inventories tells a similar story from one side of the country to another. Tropical staples provided a quick turnover, a reasonable profit margin, were sold in very small amounts to working people and were also sold on credit; shops in effect acted as banks for the local poor. Needless to say, Adam Smith, was among the first to spot the trend; small shops were responsible for breaking and dividing crude and manufactured produce into such small parcels as suited the occasional demands of those who wanted them. Such shops were ideal for working people, enabling a man to purchase his subsistence from day to day, or even hour to hour, as he wanted it.[24]

This pattern was truly national. On the eve of the American war, tropical staples could be had anywhere in Britain. More prosperous folks ordered their goods direct from the great London import houses. Twinings were happy to dispatch four hundredweight of sugar along with 60 lb of tea to the account of Lord Duncan Alex Ross in Perth. William Stout, shopkeeper in Lancaster, bought most of his sugar and tobacco from Liverpool and Bristol.[25] Provincial shopkeepers everywhere tried to promote their tropical staples by undercutting local rivals, by advertising their wares in the local press and by puffing their produce, often by dismissing their opponents. One Edinburgh shopkeeper told locals that his tea was cheaper than those on South Bridge as his shop rent is not one-third of theirs.

Long before Napoleon's famous aphorism took root, the role of shopkeepers had been appreciated by Adam Smith. 'To found a great empire for the sole purpose of raising up a people of customers, may at first sight appear a project fit only for a nation of shop-keepers. It is however, a project altogether unfit for a nation of shop-keepers; but extremely fit for a nation governed by shop-keepers'.[26]

Even more remarkable, surely, is the fact that the basis of much of this shop trade was providing the British consumer with tropical staples. These fruits of distant empires so quickly established themselves as features of British life that it is easy to overlook their novelty and the degree to which they shaped key features of British social experience. What could be more British than a sweet cup of tea? What was more typically British, by the late eighteenth century, than the crowded coffee house, centre of male conviviality, thick with current gossip or political discussion, but thick too with tobacco smoke from the pipes of Virginian tobacco passed around the tables? What could be more genteel than the afternoon tea party, hosted by a fashionable lady, displaying her finest china (some of the best now made in Europe, by Meissen, Sèvres and Wedgwood)? What could be more British than a labourer's tea-break? Of course each of these social habits was a freak of historical circumstance, shaped by the accidents of history and the peculiarities of imperial history. But each of them was also made possible by Africa and by the efforts of African slaves toiling in the Americas.

These social habits began life in Europe as the preserve of the wealthy. Sugar, once an exclusive item within the reach of a small, well-to-do elite was by the mid-eighteenth century to be found in the meanest of homes. Tobacco, initially the fad of the wealthy, had by the early eighteenth century, become an addiction among even the very poor. In both cases we can plot the rise of these staples by the data about the implements used to consume them. Cheap clay pipes, production of which formed a minor industry, were ubiquitous. Teapots, cups and sugar bowls were universal (though they were available of course in costly format for the luxurious displays of society's elite). Indeed when social investigators scrutinised the poor towards the end of the eighteenth century, especially in the crisis decade of the 1790s, they gazed in irritable disbelief at the plebeian attachment to imported tropical staples.[27] The poor would go to any length to secure sugar, tea and tobacco. When, in those moments of desperation (which were to become all too frequent), the poor could not afford even the cheapest of tea, they poured hot water over burnt bread to simulate the drink.[28]

Behind the story of these various staples there lay a major social revolution at work: the transmutation of the luxurious into a common and ubiquitous necessity. It was, of course, one aspect of a much more broadly based consumer revolution which tied together peoples in different parts of the globe: in West Africa, in the American colonies, even in remote Indian communities of the Americas.[29] Further, this evolution of tropical consumption also helped to shape – even to define – distinct social and gender roles. By the late eighteenth century the ingestion of tobacco had come to be a masculine habit; ladies were expected to use it only as snuff (Marie Antoinette received more than 50 (gold) snuff boxes among her wedding presents), but even snuff soon faded from the inventory of female respectability. If an artist wished to portray an image of a dirty old crone, stripped of all traces of femininity, he had only to put a pipe in her hand to convey the message. Though doctors were aware of tobacco's consequences – it was already infamous for forcing men to expectorate and spit – it had become a defining feature of masculinity itself. Men smoked; ladies refrained. Tobacco was at its most public in the coffee and ale house (both of which sold tobacco). Here, again, was a forum for those displays of masculine behaviour which seem so familiar today but which, to a marked degree, were shaped by the addiction to tropical staples in the years after 1600.

Both in the home and in public, key areas of sociability evolved around the public and private consumption of tropical staples. It happened very quickly. The hallmark of social class served to create distinctions in the way staples were consumed by different social groups. The labourer's clay pipe seemed far removed from the French Queen's gold snuff boxes. Nobility's silver sugar bowls seemed unconnected to the pinch of sugar hiding in a cracked pot in a poor home. Yet they were, in essence, one and the same thing. More than that, they were all made possible by Africa.

Each of these habits, the socially defining characteristics of late eighteenth-century Britain – habits which helped shape the contours of masculinity, femininity and even nationality – were rooted in African sweat. Those millions of Africans shipped across the Atlantic were transported, overwhelmingly, to work in the production of tropical staples. More specifically, some 70 per cent of all Africans deposited in the Americas were destined, initially at least, for the sugar fields. We know that as the American colonial economies matured, as local society became ever more sophisticated, more and more slaves slipped out of the labouring mould, taking up that host of skilled and semi-skilled jobs spawned by local society. But the purpose behind their importation was, primarily, the production of staples for European consumption. And to that end, imported Africans transformed the face of the Americas.

In the welter of statistics which has characterised (and often blurred) the study of the Atlantic slave trade, one central issue is often overlooked. Until the 1830s – until, that is, the great waves of European migrations westwards – the typical migrant to the Americas was an African. Of course the word 'migrant' is inappropriate; they were slaves. Nonetheless, it needs to be stressed that if we add up the data for migrations to the Americas as a whole, we are left with an indisputable and seminal fact. It was the African, the African slave, who was the pioneer of American settlement until the early nineteenth century. Of the 8.5 million people settled in the Americas up to the 1820s, only 2.5 million were White; the rest were Africans.[30] Thereafter, the forces of abolition and the westward migrations of poor Europeans altered the pattern quite dramatically.

The pattern was of course uneven, across time and space. There were regions of the Americas where Africans and their local-born were unusual. Elsewhere, the White man was exceptional. In parts of South Carolina, throughout the Caribbean and into Brazil, visitors were struck by the African-ness of the human environment. In the fields, in their villages, in their cabins, straggling to and from work, in local markets, on the quaysides, local slaves reminded outsiders of Africa. It was no accident that slave communities in the Caribbean were often described as 'African villages'. And in the confusion of different languages and creole among the slaves, outsiders again heard the sounds of Africa.

In the British debate which flowed back and forth, from the 1760s onwards, about the slave trade and slavery, a debate which spawned an amazing welter of publications on the slave colonies (and which underpinned much of the early Black writing in Britain), images of Africa were rarely far from view. The plantocracy, in league with British economic slaving interests, asserted the utter indispensability of African labour. We know of course that some islands and some regions (notably Barbados and North America) had already moved to a local self-sufficiency in slaves. But in general the slave empire seemed unworkable without its umbilical links to Africa. Those tropical staples which had become indispensable to Western life, especially sugar, needed Africans. The West India lobby also agreed that the slave trade and slavery yielded material bounty to Britain, and, at the same time, was the agency for the civilising of Africa and Africans. Chattel slavery, it was claimed, was the only means available to intrude among Africans and their descendants the institutions of Christian civilisation, of language, of faith, of family and social habits – and of course of obedient application to work. Here was self-interest masquerading as a civilising process. Moreover, it was an argument which disguised the brutal crudities involved (but which others were, at the same time, ever more alert to and alarmed about). Throughout the debate about the slave trade – much later about slavery – images of Africa were dangled before the reading public. Often they were mythical, sometimes absurd and generally uncomfortable. And it was here that Africans in Britain began to play their distinctive role.

The work of Black writers provided a literary counterpoint to the racist assertions of plantocratic scribes. More than that, Blacks scattered across Britain formed a living contradiction of the baser charges levelled by the same plantocratic lobby. In that range of attainments and human qualities (and despite imputations to the contrary) here were people of the most varied kind – warts and all – who owed little resemblance to the grotesque caricatures drawn by the slave lobby. They offered, personally and collectively, a refutation of the basic points which underpinned plantocratic ideology. The simplest point (one which seems in retrospect scarcely necessary to make) is that this Black presence asserted an irrefutable humanity. In a world which had for some centuries past profited from the philosophy that Africans were consigned to the edges of humanity, this simple point was seminal. What, after all, was the point of the famous Wedgwood medallion ('Am I not a man and a brother?'), if not to assert a shared humanity?

The Atlantic slave colonies had thrived – had been brought into being and nurtured – by a philosophy which denied that premise. The law, maritime and commercial usage, plantocratic management and colonial governance, all and more viewed the African as an object; a chattel like most others. Of course, we know that this proposition was riddled with inconsistencies, contradictions and problems. Nonetheless, the chattel status of Black humanity was the very foundation of colonial prosperity. Yet in the diversity of work and attainment, in the social and economic independence which emerged within the Black community, there was irrefutable proof to the contrary.[31] Of course this fact was even more striking in the Americas. The Black presence, with all its weaknesses and foibles, its human shortcomings and failings, provided varied refutation of everything the slave lobby stood for and was struggling to maintain.

The West India lobby had developed into a powerful force in Britain. Their wealth was legendary and stood in sharp contrast to the general material hardship of the Black community. Like Indian nabobs, returning planters shamed even the boldest of local *arrivistes* by their lavish displays of wealth. In major urban areas and fashionable watering holes, the planters, those 'uncouth whales of fortune', were to be counted among Smollett's 'upstarts of fortune'; the 'planters, negro-drivers and hucksters from the American plantations, enriched they know not how'.[32] Their presence in Britain was a pale reflection, distorted by distance and cultural variation, of life in the colonies; of a prospering White elite and an impoverished and struggling Black labour force. Time and again it was to this issue, this contrast, that Black writers and spokesmen turned in the debate about slavery unleashed in Britain after 1787.

Few doubted that Britain had benefited enormously from its Atlantic slave empire. When Edwards published his classic account of the British Caribbean in 1789, the dedication (to George III) simply asserted that the British Caribbean had become the principal source of the national opulence and maritime power.[33]

Yet it could not have been brought to pass without Africa and without the armies of Africans cast ashore throughout the Americas as the assault troops of European invasion and settlement.

One of the most important lessons we have learned about Black history over the past 30 years or so is its centrality to the unfolding of the Atlantic economy in the years after European encroachment into the Americas. In the complex development of the Americas – that devastation of native peoples, the conquest of key regions and the tapping of American wealth by labour ferried in from Africa – a formula emerged which was with varying local differences to serve Europeans well in other parts of the globe. Luxuriant land cleared (mainly by disease) of its native inhabitants, European management and finance and servile labour: here was a formula which converted great swathes of the Americas to the lucrative production of tropical and semi-tropical staples. It also rendered the Western world addicted to that range of commodities (tobacco, coffee, chocolate, sugar and, indirectly, tea) which in time came to be a defining characteristic of Western life itself. Yet each of those ubiquitous, national habits was dependent, in one form or other, on Black labour. Each was impossible without the slaves of the Americas. Yet it was one of the ironic curiosities of eighteenth-century life that these staples, and the habits they spawned, were enjoyed, in domestic privacy or in public, without too much thought about their origins. Because they were imported from such great distances, it was easy to imagine that the people who made it all possible were out of sight and out of mind. The purpose here is to suggest that the people whose toil created these staples hovered over British life in the form of the cultural habits which the staples made possible.

I have tried here to stress that the development of Britain's Black community in the seventeenth and eighteenth centuries was one of the more obvious and persistent reminders that domestic British life had become inextricably linked to the fate and efforts of distant peoples on both sides of the Atlantic. At one level this was obvious. But, like so many obvious points, it is occasionally in need of repetition. Indeed in the continuing search for the detailed history of Black Britain, there is a danger that the broader defining context will be lost. And that context is the history of Atlantic slavery. The domestic, British experience can be wrested from the broader story of the Atlantic economy only by sleight of hand, or by seriously damaging the real history of Blacks in Britain. The real importance of Black British history is the bridge it enables us to build between the apparently local and the global; between domestic Britain and worldwide aggressive British economic and political activities in Africa and the Americas.

Notes

1.   For the latest work on the history of the Black community see R. King, et al., *Ignatius Sancho. An African Man of Letters* (London: National Portrait Gallery, 1997); G. Gerzina, *Black England. Life before Emancipation* (London: John Murray, 1995); N. Myers, *Reconstructing the Black Past: Blacks in Britain, 1780–1830,* (London: Cass, 1996); S.J. Braidwood, *Black Poor and White Philanthropists* (Liverpool: Liverpool University Press, 1994).

2.   This was the broad thesis of my own, initial work in this field in *Black and White. The Negro and English Society, 1555–1945* (London: Allen Lane, The Penguin Press, 1973). I now think that argument to have been overstated.

3. Letter 105, 7 September 1779, P. Edwards and P. Rewt, eds., *The Letters of Ignatius Sancho* (Edinburgh: University of Edinburgh Press, 1994), p. 186.
4. See J. Walvin, *An African's Life. The Life and Times of Olaudah Equiano, 1745–1797* (London: Cassell, 1998).
5. For a recent debate, see J.E. Inikori and S.L. Engerman, eds., *The Atlantic Slave Trade. The Effects on Economics, Societies, and Peoples in Africa, the Americas, and Europe* (Durham, NC: Duke University Press, 1992).
6. J. Walvin, *Fruits of Empire. Exotic Produce and British Taste, 1660–1800* (London: Macmillan, 1997).
7. E. Long, *The History of Jamaica*, 3 vols (London, 1774), Vol. I, pp. 491–3.
8. 'Supplies Imported from London in the Betsey, Capt Lewis'; 'Supplies from Cork and Bristol, 1787, 1788, 1789'. See also 'Inventory of household furniture . . . at the Overseers House, August 21st 1787', all in Jamaica Archives (JA), *Worthy Park Plantation Register, 1787–1791*, Spanish Town.
9. For shipping statistics, see I.K. Steele, *The English Atlantic. An Exploration of Communication and Community* (Oxford: Oxford University Press, 1986). See also introductory essays in D. Richardson, ed., *Bristol, Africa and the Eighteenth-Century Slave Trade to America*, 4 vols, 1698–1807 (Bristol: Bristol Record Society Publications, 1986–1996), pp. xxxviii-xlvii.
10. D. Richardson, 'Liverpool and the English Slave Trade', in A. Tibbles, ed., *Trans-Atlantic Slavery. Against Human Dignity*, (Her Majesty's Stationery Office, London, 1994). See also D. Eltis and D. Richardson, eds., *Routes to Slavery* (London: Frank Cass, 1997).
11. For two good case studies of small-town slave trading see N. Tattersfield, *The Forgotten Trade* (London: Cape, 1991); M. Elder, *The Slave Trade and the Economic Development of 18th-century Lancaster* (Halifax: Ryburn, 1992).
12. M. Elder, ibid, p. 144.
13. Ibid, p. 127.
14. Ibid. Ch. III.
15. Ibid, Appendix A, pp. 211–12.
16. P.D. Curtin, *Economic Change in Pre-Colonial Africa: Senegambia in the Era of the Slave Trade* (Madison: University of Wisconsin Press, 1975).
17. J.E. Inikori, 'The Import of firearms into West Africa', in J.E. Inikori, *Forced Migration. The Impact of the Export Slave Trade on African Societies* (London: Hutchinson, 1982).
18. Inikori and Engerman, eds., *Atlantic Slave Trade*, Appendix I, pp. 173–4; J.M. Postma, *The Dutch in the Atlantic Slave Trade, 1600–1815* (Cambridge: Cambridge University Press, 1990), pp. 103–4.
19. JA, *Worthy Park Plantation Register, 1787–1791*.

20. See list of books delivered to Thomas Thistlewood in Jamaica, April 1771, in D. Hall, *In Miserable Slavery. Thomas Thistlewood in Jamaica, 1750–1786* (London: Macmillan, 1989), p. 225.

21. J. Axtell, 'The First Consumer Revolution', in J. Axtell, ed., *Beyond 1492. Encounters in Colonial North America* (New York: Oxford University Press, 1992).

22. B. Edwards, *The History of the British Colonies in the West Indies*, 3 vols (London, 1801), 3rd edn, Vol. III, p. 165. We need to recall, of course, that Edwards was making a political as much as a social point; that is, that slaves were able to improve themselves.

23. S. Mintz, *Sweetness and Power. The Place of Sugar in Modern History* (London: Viking, 1985).

24. Quoted in H.C. Mui and L.H. Mui, *Shops and Shopping in Eighteenth Century England* (Kingston, Ontario: McGill-Queens University Press, 1989), p. 6.

25. Ibid., pp. 8–9, 48, 223–5.

26. A. Smith, *The Wealth of Nations*, Vol. II, Bk. iv, Ch. 7. Pt. iii (London: J.M. Dent; New York: E.P. Dutton, 1910).

27. F. Eden, *The State of the Poor*, 3 vols (London, 1797), Vol. I, pp. 496; 535.

28. E.P. Thompson, *The Making of the English Working Class* (London: Gollancz, 1963), p. 308.

29. For the latest essays on the consumer revolution, see J. Brewer and R. Porter, eds., *Consumption and the World of Goods* (London: Routledge, 1993).

30. P. Manning, *Slavery and African Life* (Cambridge: Cambridge University Press, 1993), p. 37.

31. R.A. McDonald, *The Economy and Material Culture of Slaves. Goods and Chattels on the Sugar Plantations of Jamaica and Lousiana* (Baton Rouge, LA: Lousiana State University Press, 1993).

32. Quoted in M.D. George, *Hogarth to Cruikshank*, (London: Allen Lane, The Penguin Press, 1967), pp. 151–3.

33. B. Edwards, *The History of the British Colonies*, Vol. I, Dedication.

'The Hundredth Year of our Emancipation'

The dialectics of resistance in slavery and freedom

O. NIGEL BOLLAND

Power, resistance and opposition

Barry Higman insists, correctly, that 'Antitheoretical stances . . . have no place in Caribbean social history',[1] but in most Caribbean social history theoretical perspectives remain implicit. Higman has himself made important contributions to issues of theory and method in Caribbean social history, not least in the ways he taught a generation of students at the University of the West Indies.

One of the persistently thorny questions in Caribbean social history concerns the analysis of power and resistance, or the political dimension of social history and the variety of ways that authority is formulated, implemented, maintained and challenged. Higman affirms the centrality of this dimension in Caribbean social history and defines it, appropriately, in the broadest terms: 'The importance of conflict and hegemonic power are obvious enough in the social history of rebellion and resistance, but it is necessary to extend these theoretical political notions to all areas – historical demography, architecture, religion, sport, humour – without exception'.[2] Thus, Higman challenges us to seek the dynamics of conflict in all aspects of Caribbean social history or, to put it another way, to understand Caribbean social life in terms of the dynamics of conflict. In this chapter I will attempt to elucidate the complex relations between hegemonic power and resistance, using examples of labour struggle during the periods of slavery and freedom.

My starting point is the work of Michel Foucault and Michel de Certeau. Foucault emphasises the 'strictly relational character of power relationships', and proposes that 'where there is power, there is resistance, and yet, or rather consequently, this resistance is never in a position of exteriority in relation to power'.[3] De Certeau expands on this point in his book *The Practice of Everyday Life*,[4] which suggests some fruitful perspectives for analysing and under-standing the dynamics of power and resistance in Caribbean social history. One reason why de Certeau's work is so promising is that he focuses on ways that the politically weak may resist the strong, and particularly on ways that the weak make do with what is available in the 'imposed terrain' to which the established order restricts them. He uses a spatial metaphor to distinguish between the strategies of the strong and the tactics of the weak. De Certeau defines a strategy as 'the calculation (or manipulation) of power relationships that becomes possible as soon as a subject with will and power . . . can be isolated. It postulates a place that can be delimited as its own and serve as a base from which relations with an exteriority composed of targets or threats . . . can be managed'. In contrast, he defines a tactic as

> a calculated action determined by the absence of a proper locus. No delimitation of an exteriority, then, provides it with the condition necessary for autonomy. The space of a tactic is the space of the other. Thus it must play on and with a terrain imposed on it and organised by the law of a foreign power. It does not have the means to keep to itself, at a distance . . . It does not, therefore, have the options of planning general strategy . . . It operates in isolated actions, blow by blow. It takes advantage of 'opportunities' and depends on them, being without any base where it could stockpile its winnings, build up its own position, and plan raids. What it wins it cannot keep . . . a mobility that must accept the chance offerings of the moment, and seize on the wing the possibilities that offer themselves at any given moment.[5]

In short, de Certeau contrasts strategies and tactics by defining the latter as

> an art of the weak . . . Power is bound by its very visibility. In contrast, trickery is possible for the weak, and often it is his only possibility, as a 'last resort' . . . The

art of 'pulling tricks' involves a sense of the opportunities afforded by a particular occasion . . .

Lacking its own place, lacking a view of the whole . . . limited by the possibilities of the moment, a tactic is determined by the absence of power.[6]

This passage has great resonance for students of Caribbean social history, not least because of the reference to pulling tricks. Anansi, the spider trickster of West African tales, who 'play fool fe catch wise', became the folk hero of slaves and their descendants throughout the Caribbean. De Certeau's use of the metaphor of the sea, 'slipping in among the rocks and defiles of an established order',[7] also has special resonance in the Caribbean. Above all, though, de Certeau's discussion of the 'practice of everyday life' is important because he emphasises there are many ways that the dominated and oppressed people in a society may shape their own culture and make their own history by subverting the goals and structures of their oppressors, even when they lack power. He explains why the actions of the weak are frequently, perhaps generally, invisible, particularly when we usually rely for our evidence on documentation written for and left by the strong. Perhaps inevitably, when seeking evidence of resistance to oppression, social historians seize on the great events, the large-scale confrontations, such as massive rebellions and strikes, not only because these are most obviously defiant but also because they are usually the best documented. But de Certeau reminds us that it may have been the less audible 'murmurings' and the hidden actions that eroded the system of domination, over long periods of time, like the sea on the rocks. The weak, in innumerable and ingenious ways, may resist even while hiding their resistance, as they smuggle in their hidden agendas and infiltrate the systems of domination, like sappers burrowing under an apparently almighty castle. For obvious reasons, resistance in social contexts of extreme domination, such as slavery and colonialism, is often not externally manifested, so the modes of action of those people whose status is subordinate – because of their enslaved or racial status, their gender or their class – often conceal their real contributions to the formation of culture, including political culture. Their contributions are no less important, however, simply because they are obscured, unsigned and unacknowledged by posterity.

Two further points may be made regarding the value of de Certeau's perspective for Caribbean social history. The first concerns his distinction between resistance and opposition,[8] which is related to the contrast between strategy and tactics. A system of domination can be resisted, in this narrower sense, only when a dominated group has enough of a base of its own that it can develop a strategy of resistance. In contrast, then, those who are so weak that they have no 'space' of their own may resort only to the tactics of opposition from within the system. De Certeau's distinction between resistance and opposition, like that between strategy and tactics, enables us to view with greater clarity the various kinds of action undertaken against systems of domination. The more complete the domination, the harder it is for any group to have the space, or sufficient sense of exteriority from the system, to be able to resist the system as such. More common, therefore, will be the varieties of everyday practice that constitute opposition but which do not amount to resistance. Simply put, resistance in this more specific sense can occur only when the weak have enough sense of their own distinct possibilities, of their own potential strength in relation to the strong, that they can actually conceive of overpowering them, and hence of devising strategies to do so. More generally, the weak must acknowledge their weakness, and the impossibility of overpowering the strong, and must consequently resort to the more limited tactics of opposition. Much of what historians of the Caribbean have referred to as 'resistance', therefore, is not resistance so much as opposition in de Certeau's terms. This does not reduce the importance of the actions of the weak, however, as their accumulated acts of opposition over long periods of time may be more successful in changing a system of domination than a full-frontal attack that risks all.

In their eagerness to move away from versions of slavery that characterise the slaves as passive victims of oppression, some accounts appear to portray almost every action, or inaction, on the part of the slaves as a form of resistance. Michael Craton, a leading scholar of Caribbean slave rebellions, acknowledges the problem of where to draw the line when he denies 'proposing the obvious absurdity that even accommodation by slaves was a form of resistance'.[9] But he distinguishes between different forms of resistance in terms of 'a fatal division between unacculturated Africans and the local-born creoles',[10] as if this division determined whether they adopted strategies or tactics of resistance. Thus, Craton writes,

> We would define distinctively creole forms of slave resistance as those attempts to achieve freedom that did not necessarily involve the destruction of, or even separation from, the predominant economic system in favour of a reconstituted African lifestyle ... But many creole slaves had rather less radical and more rational aims: simply to widen the ambit of freedom already won within the plantation

system, by becoming resident free wage labourers or, best of all, predominantly peasants with the opportunity to work for fair wages when they wished.[11]

The key point of distinction, however, is not whether the protagonists were Africans or Creoles, but rather how the scope and purpose of their actions were affected by the character of the power relationships in which they were engaged. Whether as Africans, Creoles, Indians, slaves, indentured workers, wage workers or peasants, most working people in the Caribbean have been engaged, as Walter Rodney wrote, in 'both struggle and accommodation'.

> Struggle was implicit in the application of labour power to earn wages or to grow crops, while accommodation was a necessary aspect of survival within a system in which power was so comprehensively monopolised by the planter class. Some persons resisted more tenaciously and consistently than others; but there was no simple distinction between those who resisted and those who accommodated.[12]

We may not be able to make a simple distinction between those who resisted and those who opposed, any more than 'between those who resisted and those who accommodated', but de Certeau's conceptual distinction contributes to greater clarity in understanding varieties of what are broadly called the 'arts of resistance',[13] thereby avoiding the pitfalls of the antinomy of resistance and accommodation.

The second point concerns de Certeau's rejection of the social atomism so prevalent in the dominant bourgeois culture, that posits the individual as the elementary unit of society. In contrast to such reductionism, de Certeau's analysis of everyday practices 'shows that a relation (always social) determines its terms, and not the reverse, and that each individual is a locus in which an incoherent (and often contradictory) plurality of such relational determinations interacts'.[14] The common illusions that society is merely an aggregate of individuals, and that individuals are coherent personalities with great freedom of choice about how they interact, have affected the way historians seek to uncover patterns of resistance. All too often we seek heroic leaders among the enslaved, as if we need to know such leaders in order to understand why people resisted. De Certeau reminds us of the more ambiguous, but perhaps no less courageous, practices of everyday life through which countless people wore away at the systems of their domination. When the colonisers and slave owners succeeded in imposing their will and their system on those whom they oppressed they were often blind to the persistence of opposition, particularly when they could not pin the responsibility on to individuals. De Certeau reminds us, therefore, at one and the same time, that resistance and opposition, like domination itself, is always a matter of social relations that cannot be reduced to individuals, and also that the very status and situation of the oppressed encourages social acts of opposition, just as, on the reverse of the coin, power corrupts people into the false faith of individualist autonomy.

In short, the social history of resistance and/or opposition in the Caribbean needs to adopt the theoretical stance of dialectical historical sociology, beginning with the premise that people are always located in institutions and other patterns of social relations that are marked by inequalities. Indeed, it is precisely – and nothing more than – the persistence of peoples' activities in recognisably structured ways that constitutes institutions and society. We must avoid, on the one hand, the pitfall of reifying society and institutions such as slavery. And, on the other hand, we must also avoid the trap of reifying the individual because, as Roger Bastide points out, 'these individuals are not independent creatures but are interrelated by complex webs of communication, of domination-subordination, or of egalitarian exchange. They are a part of institutions, which have rules for action, norms and organization'.[15] Nor should we reify culture. These concepts – 'individual', 'institution', 'society' and 'culture' – are abstractions that refer to aspects of a mutually constitutive and continually changing sociocultural system. Social life is essentially practical activity, and people are essentially social beings. Consequently, 'society consists of the social relations in which people engage in their activities, and is not reducible to individuals ... Culture and society, in the form of traditions, ideas, customs, languages, institutions, and social formations, shape the social action of individuals, which in turn maintains, modifies, and transforms social structure and culture'.[16]

I will now use examples from two periods in Caribbean history to help clarify these theoretical points: first, the great slave rebellion in Demerara in 1823, and second, the strikes and labour rebellions that occurred in Guyana and Jamaica, among other British Caribbean colonies, in the 1930s, a century after legal emancipation. In dialectical relation to the hegemonic power of the planter class, enslaved Africans and Creoles, and wage workers and peasants of African and Indian descent, sought to remake their world, albeit in ways that were profoundly shaped by their relations and experiences in that world.[17]

The Demerara Rebellion, 1823

Emilia Viotti da Costa, in her detailed account of the great slave rebellion in Demerara in 1823, refers to the nature of the slaves' responses in terms that echo Marx's famous statement about men making their history under circumstances transmitted from the past.[18]

> Torn from kin-centred or tributary societies, with their rules, norms, and decorum, slaves had been forced to redefine their identities in slavery – though not merely as slaves. From scripts brought from their pasts, modified by their new condition and environment, slaves wove new narratives about the world, created new forms of kinship, and invented new utopias. They did not try simply to re-create their past, but to control their present and shape their future. In their day-to-day interactions with masters and missionaries, they appropriated symbols that originally were meant to subject them and wrought those symbols into weapons of their own emancipation. In this process they not only transformed themselves and everyone around, but they also helped to shape the course of history.[19]

Viotti da Costa portrays the slaves, like the slave-owners and missionaries, as being shaped but not entirely determined by their different cultural heritages and current social circumstances. As conscious agents, the enslaved Africans and Creoles, no less than free Europeans, had a sense of 'rules, norms, and decorum', and the fact that they did not coincide with those imposed upon them in their role as slaves provokes their opposition.

Viotti da Costa outlines her theoretical perspective:

> Identities, language, and meanings are products of social interaction, which takes place within a specific system of social relations and power, with its own rituals, protocols, and sanctions. The material conditions of peoples' lives, the way human and ecological resources are utilised and distributed, the concrete ways power is exerted, are as important in shaping identities, defining language, and creating meanings, as the social codes that mediate experience or the conventions used to define what is real. In fact, material conditions and symbolic systems are intimately connected.[20]

From this perspective, Viotti da Costa examines the changing conditions in slaves' lives in the two decades prior to the Rebellion. In those years, the incorporation of the colony into the British empire led to massive capital investment and increased commodity production, which shifted from cotton and coffee to sugar, at the same time that the import of new slaves from Africa ended. These broad changes led the slave-owners and their managers to impose longer hours and a faster pace of work, closer supervision and more frequent punishments, and fewer allowances of food, clothing, provision grounds and other privileges. Slaves were also more likely to be separated from their kin and friends in these times.[21] In short, the slaves' lives deteriorated in a number of ways. What their owners viewed as privileges, however, the slaves had begun to perceive as rights, so they protested against encroachments. Thus, the fundamental contradiction between the enslavers and the enslaved was accentuated in this period in several ways and the balance of power was repeatedly contested in everyday practice.

Central to the relations between slaves and slave-owners, of course, were the questions of obedience, justice and the duties of work. We generally have to infer the slaves' hidden transcript from their reported behaviour, and some public records are good enough for the historian to achieve insight into how they thought and what they sought. Thus, Viotti da Costa concludes:

> From these records it becomes clear that while masters dreamt of total power and blind obedience, slaves perceived slavery as a system of reciprocal obliga-tions. They assumed that between masters and slaves there was an unspoken contract, an invisible text that defined rules and obligations, a text they used to assess any violation of their 'rights'. Slaves expected to perform a 'reason-able amount of work', to be defined according to customary rules and adjusted to the strength and competence of individual workers. In exchange, they felt entitled to receive an allowance of food and clothing according to custom, to be given time enough to have their meals, to have access to land and 'free' time to cultivate their gardens and provision grounds, to go to the market and to the chapel, and to visit relatives and friends. They felt they were entitled to the produce of their gardens and provision grounds, and that they should be paid for services they rendered on their 'free' time. They expected to be relieved from work, to receive some kind of assistance when sick, and to be given food and clothing allowances in their old age. They also believed they should not be punished if they accomplished their tasks and behaved according to the rules, and that punishment itself should not go beyond the limits of the 'acceptable'. In addition, women felt entitled to nurse their babies according to their habitual practices, and to have some control over their children. The Demerara slaves' 'public transcript' could be summed up in a few words: all slaves should perform according to their abilities, and all should be provided according to their needs. And whenever this norm was violated and the implicit 'contract' was broken, they felt entitled to protest.[22]

The slaves' hidden transcript changed, by becoming more public or by including new expectations, as social circumstances changed. For example, when missionaries sought to require slaves to attend their Sunday services, some slaves were encouraged to press for their 'right' to have Sundays off work. So slaves' conception of their rights, of what they owed their owners and what was due to them, of what was fair and unfair, was increasingly a matter of complaint and contestation. Yet the rebels in 1823 do not appear to have sought to destroy the plantations, kill all the Whites and take over the colony. Only a few Whites were killed, apparently when they shot at slaves and the slaves fired back, and a few slaves who sided with their owners were beaten or put in stocks by the rebels.[23] Most rebels did not have a clear idea of what they sought for their future, or of what they were supposed to do, and many probably joined for quite personal and particular motives. Viotti da Costa is therefore correct to call this uprising a rebellion, in the sense that the rebels sought to correct particular abuses in the system rather than to over-throw the entire system. Yet their dreams and actions, like those of Maroons, pushed not only at the margins of slavery but also at its essential ideology. 'The system of authority characteristic of the slave system required the humiliation of the slaves',[24] while their rebellious actions declared their inal-ienable humanity in the shaping of their society and the making of their history. The Rebellion forced the slave-owners to consider their slaves' motives, desires, plots and organisations, when the system would have preferred to deal with them as mere tools of production. Nor were things the same after such a rebellion, when

> the slaves returned to their day-to-day forms of resistance . . . The slaves had been defeated, but had not surrendered. They continued to fight their battles in their usual ways . . . [until slavery was abolished]. Ex-slaves and ex-masters entered the new contests over the meaning of freedom. The struggles of the past would lead them into the future.[25]

Viotti da Costa gives us a richly detailed history of the Demerara Rebellion, and she also helps us understand the social dynamics of a whole world in which the complex web of interrelations between the slave-owners and the enslaved, the colonial officials and the missionaries, was implicated in shaping a future after slavery was legally abolished. The former slaves and slave-owners who entered this new legal situation brought with them a whole complex of attitudes, values, identities, notions of rights and entitlements out of the period of slavery. 'The meaning of freedom, for both owners and slaves, was historically and dialectically interconnected with the system and experience of slavery, but in different ways, so we should not assume that the former slaves shared the dominant conception of freedom',[26] the liberal-bourgeois concept of freedom held by the planters, merchants, colonial officials and missionaries. This dominant version of freedom, which appeared in the context of the rise of the liberal state and the capitalist economy, 'meant submission only to the impersonal forces of the marketplace and to the rational and uniform con-straints of law'.[27] These market forces and colonial laws helped to perpetuate the poverty and powerlessness of the former slaves and indentured workers and their descendants in the British Caribbean. This kind of freedom, which denied the majority of people civil rights or economic security for over a century after emancipation, was really 'a new form of domination, albeit one more limited and disguised than the naked domination of slavery. Those who had formerly been slaves, it seems, aspired to a kind of freedom that their legal emancipation appeared to promise, but that could not be achieved in the societies where they lived'.[28]

Strikes and protests in Guyana, 1935, and Jamaica, 1938

Slaves and former slaves, indentured workers and former indentured workers, and their descendants, resorted to their day-to-day forms of resistance while periodically engineering major strikes, protests and even rebellions during the decades after 1838. These protests were largely spontaneous, unable to depend on or to create organised labour. In the so-called Ruimveldt Riots in Colonial Guyana in 1905, for example, the strikers had few resources with which to sustain their struggle. Yet such efforts should not be dismissed as failures because, even when they did not achieve their goals, 'it was through political struggle that the working people (and the middle class) clarified their identity and tested their relationship with other classes and strata'.[29] Such struggles, then, helped provide a basis for the great series of labour rebellions that swept through the British Caribbean between 1934 and 1939, through which working people won, and were able to make use of, the legal right to organise trade unions.[30] Organised labour became the basis of mass political parties and the achievement of universal adult suffrage, beginning in Jamaica in 1944. Then, in a process of constitutional decolonisation, stages of self-government followed, leading to independence for almost all the British Caribbean colonies, again beginning with Jamaica in 1962.

The outlines of these efforts, and their results in legal and constitutional reforms, are widely known, but the long-term continuities in authoritarian tendencies and democratic aspirations within the political culture are less clearly understood.[31] The modest point I will make here is simply that, 100 years after their legal emancipation, the descendants of slaves (and, in some places, of indentured workers also) made comparable demands about similar issues, sometimes using the idiom of slavery. In de Certeau's terms, these are examples of opposition rather than resistance, but through their incremental effects they contributed to a broad range of political and social changes throughout the region.

The first example is a strike in Colonial Guyana, part of the widespread labour unrest on sugar estates in September and October 1935.[32] On 15 October, a crowd of workers on Plantation Farm, led by a former policeman named Joseph Barlow, shouted at the manager, 'We want more money'. When the manager said their demands were unreasonable, they shouted, 'Slavery done long time', and became 'threatening'. The next day two overseers were assaulted and by 18 October police were stationed on the estate and the overseers were sworn in as special constables. By 22 October work was returning to normal, and this seems to have been a minor incident among the extensive 'disturbances'. However, this example shows that some of the unrest on the Guyanese estates was about how the workers were treated, as well as about their wages and working conditions. One of the workers on Plantation Farm, a shovelman named Soobrian Singh, gave evidence that workers felt that they could not ask for more money because if they did the overseer and driver 'would tell such a man "no work for you"', so they could only make demands when they were emboldened as a group: 'when the strike come on they get a little pluck otherwise the game would have continued so always'. Barlow himself testified that they had planned to strike, having decided on 12 October that if they were not told the price of work for new tasks on 15 October they would strike. Further, he objected that the manager had implied that if they did not like the price they should take their wives to the bars in Georgetown where they could earn money as prostitutes. 'I turned to him and said, "Oh, you take us then to make slaves", and he said yes if we does not know that we are still slaves. I said if we are slaves then nobody goes to work and I will see that no man work.' Barlow, who was described as 'a capable and industrious worker', and who as a former policeman was probably less intimidated than many other workers, said he went about persuading people to stop working because of these insults.

What is striking about this example, one of many from Colonial Guyana in 1935, is that the workers responded to a variety of problems and that it was the fact that they began to act together that emboldened them to persist. In 1935, management still sought to keep workers in line through intimidation and in the event that workers became more demanding, the overseers, many of whom were White, would be sworn in as special constables. In the absence of legal or accepted ways for the workers to express their grievances or make demands, their actions were quickly defined as 'threatening' or as a 'riot'. Employers and managers, who were often racially distinct from their workers, armed themselves and called for armed police as soon as a labour dispute began and many of them were enrolled as volunteers as special constables to reinforce the regular police. These men, therefore, were given licence by the state to use violence against the workers. The police forces, regular and special, consisted of officers and volunteers who were largely White or near White, from the privileged sectors or from outside the colony, while the rank and file were brown and Black. They were not only the front line of protection for capitalist property in the colonies, but were also the visible embodiment of racial privileges and hierarchy, which were maintained through violence as in the days of slavery.

The ready use of armed force to intimidate workers involved in a labour dispute itself became an issue as workers struggled for the right to express and negotiate their grievances. The workers demanded wage increases and better working terms and conditions, of course, but they were provoked into action also by the attitudes and abuse of drivers, overseers and managers, who carried on in ways that were reminiscent of the systems of slavery and indenture. The workers, naturally, were sensitive to this and in 1935 a good deal of their militancy and some of their symbolic acts of opposition, such as the ritual humiliation of hated supervisors, were focused on the issue of the abuse of authority.[33] Their struggle, like that of the slaves and indentured workers, was simultaneously over material and economic issues and for 'rights at the work place, including the right to be treated with respect as human beings'.[34] These workers, by demanding decent and respectful treatment as human beings, were linking the more specifically workers' rights, such as the right to negotiate and organise, to demands for broader rights as citizens, such as being free from abuse and racial discrimination. Their view of themselves as free people, and their resentment at being treated as if they were still in bondage a century after the abolition of slavery, was inseparable from their sense of the dignity and respect that they, like all other people, deserved.

The second example is from Jamaica in 1938. Early that year a group of peasants in the rural parish of Clarendon, led by Robert E. Rumble, had formed the Poor Man's Improvement Land Settlement and Labour Association (PMILSLA).[35] Rumble, a poor peasant who had worked in Cuban cane fields in the 1920s, returned to Jamaica in 1932, and by 1937 was writing about 'the oppression of these iron-handed landowners in these parts of Clarendon'. He declared, 'We want no more landlords'. The PMILSLA, claiming to have a membership of 800, petitioned the governor on 23 April 1938:

> We are the Sons of slaves who have been paying rent to Landlords for fully many decades, we want better wages, we have been exploited for years and we are looking to you to help us. We want a Minimum Wage Law. We want freedom in this the Hundredth year of our Emancipation. We are still economic Slaves, burdened in paying rent to Landlords who are sucking out our vitalities.

Though Rumble, like so many peasants in other contexts, appealed to the higher authority as if it were a benevolent power above the local landlords, his tone was radical, and the demand for a minimum wage reflects the imminent proletarianisation of the Jamaican peasantry and the discourse of modern labour reform. Many peasants believed, moreover, that 99-year leases had been given to landlords at the end of apprenticeship and that the land was due to pass to its rightful owners, the descendants of the slaves. This radical interpretation expressed the peasants' class grievances and their historical desire for compensation, as well as further politicising them.

Rumble's organisation did not extend beyond Clarendon and it was swallowed up in the general labour rebellion that erupted on 29 April 1938 at the Frome estate in Westmoreland and then spread throughout the island. On 25 May, the *Jamaica Standard* reported that tenants in upper Clarendon, encouraged by the PMILSLA, were refusing to pay rent to their landlords and that in anticipation of acquiring formal ownership on 1 August, they were putting up fences and were even offering to pay taxes on their land in advance. Shaken by the great labour rebellion, the colonial government and capitalists were anxious that the hundredth anniversary of emancipation would bring new disturbances and land invasions by people who believed that rights in land should revert to them. In June and July, the Colonial Office staff and Acting-Governor C.C. Woolley were taking this possibility seriously. J.H. Emmens of the Colonial Office wrote:

> In the Clarendon district there had been a no-rent campaign since the beginning of the year, and labourers have already staked out their plots and endeavoured to induce Government tax-collectors to accept land-tax on these plots in order to establish a claim to them at zero hour. It is said that owners who will not hand over are to be massacred . . . If this is true it would explain the anxiety of the Officer administering the Government to have a warship available on 1st August.[36]

There is no evidence that any widespread plot existed, however, and the fear of a massacre of landlords was clearly paranoia, similar to that commonly exhibited by slave-owners. On 3 August Woolley reported:

> August 1st passed off very quietly, much to my relief. I think the people understand now that we are not going to tolerate any further disturbances. We took every precaution of course and the Police, military and some 2,000 Special Constables took up 'battle' positions. There were no attempts at seizure of land as had been anticipated . . . I think the worst is over, although there is a tremendous amount of mopping up to be done.[37]

It would not have escaped the descendants of slaves that on the hundredth anniversary of emancipation Jamaica resembled an occupied territory, as thousands of armed agents of the colonial state ensured the security of the great land-owners' property. Undoubtedly, many of them would have been intimidated by this show of force. Part of the government's 'mopping up' involved Rumble. To silence Rumble, the government arrested him on charges of committing an act of public mischief by inciting people to abstain from paying rents that were legally due. He was tried in December 1938 and sentenced to six months' hard labour.[38]

The PMILSLA's demands for free land and better wages reflect the ambivalent class consciousness of people who are part peasant and part proletariat.[39] During the days of slavery and apprenticeship access to provision grounds was important for symbolic and social as well as material reasons. What Woodville Marshall says for the Windward Islands was true also in Jamaica and elsewhere:

> From the slaves' perspective, their own-account activities were as important as coerced labour in defining their status, their humanity and their notions of

freedom. Perhaps it is not too fanciful to suggest that humanity and freedom may have been equated by them with own-account activities. Further, they may have concluded that their forced involvement in plantation labour was the factor which constrained their exploitation of the potential in proto-peasant activities, and was therefore the critical limiting factor on their acquisition of freedom and full expression of humanity.[40]

In 1938, as in 1838, many Jamaicans who felt abused, exploited and insecure in plantation labour sought a degree of independence from the estates through having access to a plot of land. Such access would provide them with the means to grow their own subsistence, with more bargaining power because they would be less dependent on estate labour, and not least, with a sense of greater control over their social life. Many Jamaican workers in the 1930s had experienced a transition from poor peasant to rural wage earner, or from rural to urban life, but many experienced the reverse also because the state of Jamaica's economy produced great insecurity, and thousands of workers migrated back and forth in the desperate search for a little work and/or a bit of land. Though the Rebellion of 1938 began with a dispute over wages on a sugar estate, many of the people who became most involved were banana workers and small peasants in the parishes of St Ann, St Mary, Portland and St Thomas. Whereas the waterfront workers and sugar workers in the Rebellion organised traded unions and sought higher wages and more job security, the small peasants were attracted by Woolley's promise of a 'New Deal', a land settlement scheme that was hastily announced on 6 June. Banana workers, unlike waterfront workers, still hoped to avoid proletarianisation, so the promise of a land settlement scheme appealed to them and the Colonial Government calculated that granting them access to plots of land would not only keep the rural poor from starvation but would also deter further unrest.[41]

These two examples suggest that the so-called push and pull factors that were apparent in the early years of the post-slavery period were closely interrelated, may have reinforced each other,[42] and persisted for at least a century after the abolition of slavery. On the one hand, the former slaves and indentured workers and their descendants continued to struggle with the persistently oppressive and exploitative conditions on the estates, as they sought higher wages, better working conditions, more secure jobs and more respect by their employers and supervisors. On the other hand, many of the former slaves and indentured workers and their descendants continued to view access to land as a means to achieve more material security, independence from oppressive supervision, and a greater degree of dignity and control within their community. For some this may have appeared as a choice, but for many it was not so much an alternative as a balance to be sought between two activities and roles, neither of which alone offered enough in terms of material or social progress. The desire for land persisted, in part, because tension and unrest persisted on the estates, and such tension and unrest were endemic because the social and economic structures and political culture of the plantation system continued to reflect the inequalities and injustices of the slavery period during which the planter class had so comprehensively monopolised power. These elements of the system of domination are central among 'the long continuities'[43] of Caribbean culture and society.

Conclusions

Conflict and resistance are important in Caribbean social history because of the persistence of hegemonic power to which they are dialectically linked. Among the multiple and pervasive ways that power is exerted are the shaping of social codes, identities, relationships and the creation of cultural values, meanings and even language itself. It is scarcely surprisingly that societies that developed as extreme systems of domination, based as they were on conquest, slavery, colonialism, racism and the plantation's monopoly, also exhibit endemic patterns of opposition and resistance. De Certeau's distinctions may help historians of the Caribbean understand why opposition is so common while resistance, in his sense, is quite rare. The extraordinarily pervasive and persistent character of the system of domination in the Caribbean has at once made it hard for any group to find enough space from which to mount resistance, while ensuring that virtually everyone, in some way or other, would be engaged in a form of opposition. The oppositional tactics to which the weak must resort sometimes yield beneficial results in the short term, and may contribute, little by little, to long-term transformations. However, as Kevin Yelvington points out, 'given the nature of the overarching power relationships, the utilisation of these tactics provide [sic] a basis of further attempts to subordinate the subordinate in the long run. This is the operation of a historical dialectic'.[44] Thus, for example, slaves who feigned stupidity in order to go slow reinforced their owners' stereotype of the 'Quashie' personality that was an aspect of their ideological oppression. Likewise, women who flirt with men may do so in order to manipulate power relations in their favour, in the sense of seizing an opportunity to gain a particular advantage, but in so doing they also reinforce a general system of expectations concerning sexuality and gender that oppresses them.[45] Also, workers who achieve the recognition of their trade union as a legitimate bargaining agent are accepting a compromise with the system that exploits them because the labour laws are an expression of the dominant class forces of capitalism. Perhaps, if we see the space of social action as relative, we may see that what appears as strategy at one level is tactic at another. Thus, for workers to win unionisation within a factory provides them with some space from which they may strategise resistance within the factory, but in relation to the wider society unionisation remains a tactic of the weak because it continues to acknowledge the subordination of the working class within the capitalist system.

The dialectical perspective helps us to analyse the political dimension of social history and understand more precisely why 'emancipation was unfinished business'.[46] Real human emancipation, as distinct from a change of legal status, is not an event but a continuing process, a long-term process in which everyone has a part to play.

Notes

1.   B.W. Higman, 'Theory, Method and Technique in Caribbean Social History', *Journal of Caribbean History*, 20 (1985–6), p. 20.
2.   Ibid., pp. 20–1.
3.   M. Foucault, *The History of Sexuality*, Volume 1: *An Introduction*, trans. R. Hurley (New York: Allen Lane, 1978), p. 95.
4.   M. de Certeau, *The Practice of Everyday Life*, trans. S.F. Rendall (Berkeley: University of California Press, 1984). I have utilised this work previously, in 'Creolisation and Creole Societies: A Cultural Nationalist View of Caribbean Social History', in *Intellectuals in the Twentieth-Century Caribbean*. Volume 1: *Spectre of the New Class: The Commonwealth Caribbean*, ed. Alistair Hennessy (London: Macmillan Caribbean, 1992), pp. 50–79. I am intellectually indebted to my colleague Gary Urton for drawing my attention to Michel de Certeau's work some years ago, and to the stimulation of R. D.E. Burton and K. A. Yelvington's work which encourages me to keep thinking about it. And I thank Ellie Bolland and two anonymous reviewers for their helpful criticisms of the first version of this chapter.
5.   De Certeau, *The Practice*, pp. 35–8.
6.   Ibid.

7. Ibid., p. 34.
8. I am grateful to R. D.E. Burton for drawing this to my attention; see his *Afro-Creole: Power, Opposition and Play in Jamaica, Trinidad and Haiti* (Ithaca, NY: Cornell University Press, 1997).
9. M. Craton, *Empire, Enslavement and Freedom in the Caribbean* (Kingston: Ian Randle, 1997), p. 191.
10. Ibid., p. 194.
11. Ibid., p. 195.
12. W. Rodney, *A History of the Guyanese Working People, 1881–1905* (Baltimore: The Johns Hopkins University Press, 1981), p. 151.
13. J.C. Scott, *Domination and the Arts of Resistance: Hidden Transcripts* (New Haven: Yale University Press, 1990).
14. De Certeau, *The Practice*, p. xi.
15. R. Price, 'Foreword' to R. Bastide, *The African Religions of Brazil: Toward a Sociology of the Interpenetration of Civilisations*, trans. H. Sebba (Baltimore: The Johns Hopkins University Press, 1978), p. x.
16. Bolland, 'Creolisation and Creole Society', p. 65.
17. As a disclaimer, I must point out that these are simply examples and that this is not a survey of resistance and opposition in Caribbean history. My examples are chiefly about people (mostly men) of African origin; others have described how Indian indentured workers resisted oppression and women engaged in distinctive forms of struggle during slavery and after. See, for example, K. Haraksingh, 'Control and Resistance among Overseas Indian Workers: A Study of Labour on the Sugar Plantations of Trinidad, 1875–1917', *Journal of Caribbean History*, 14 (1981), pp. 1–17; R.E. Reddock, *Women, Labour and Politics in Trinidad and Tobago: A History* (London: Zed Books, 1994); and V.A. Shepherd, 'Control, Resistance, Accommodation and Race Relations: Aspects of the Indentureship Experience of Indian Immigrants in Jamaica', in D. Dabydeen and B. Samaroo, eds., *Across the Dark Waters: Ethnicity and Indian Identity in the Caribbean* (London: Macmillan Publishers, 1996), pp. 65–87.
18. 'Men make their history, but they do not make it just as they please; they do not make it under circumstances chosen by themselves, but under circumstances directly found, given and transmitted from the past'. K. Marx, 'The Eighteenth Brumaire of Louis Bonaparte', in *The Marx-Engels Reader*, ed. by R.C. Tucker (New York: W.W. Norton, 1972), p. 437.
19. E. Viotti da Costa, *Crowns of Glory, Tears of Blood: The Demerara Slave Rebellion of 1823* (New York: Oxford University Press, 1994), p. xvii.
20. Ibid., pp. xv–xvi.
21. Ibid., p. 40.
22. Ibid., p. 73.

23. Ibid., p. 201.

24. Ibid., p. 291.

25. Ibid., pp. 291–2.

26. Bolland, 'The Politics of Freedom in the British Caribbean', in F. McGlynn and S. Drescher, eds., *The Meaning of Freedom: Economics, Politics, and Culture after Slavery*, (Pittsburgh: University of Pittsburgh Press, 1992), p. 140.

27. T.C. Holt, '"An Empire Over the Mind": Emancipation, Race, and Ideology in the British West Indies and the American South,' in J.M. Kousser and J.M. McPherson, eds., *Region, Race, and Reconstruction*, (New York: Oxford University Press, 1982), p. 286.

28. Bolland, 'The Politics of Freedom' p. 143.

29. Rodney, *A History of the Guyanese Working People*, p. 220.

30. Bolland, *On the March: Labour Rebellions in the British Caribbean, 1934–39* (Kingston: Ian Randle, 1995).

31. Bolland, *The Politics of Labour in the British Caribbean: The Social Origins of Authoritarianism and Democracy in the Labour Movement*, (Kingston: Ian Randle, 2001).

32. From CO 111/732/60036, the 'Report of the Commission of Enquiry into the 1935 Disturbances', 24 August 1936, pp. 27–8.

33. Ibid., p. 25.

34. Bolland, *On the March*, p. 180.

35. The following information and quotes about Rumble and PMILSLA are drawn, unless otherwise noted, from K. Post, *Arise Ye Starvelings: The Jamaican Labour Rebellion of 1938 and Its Aftermath* (The Hague: Martinus Nijhoff, 1978), pp. 248–9.

36. CO 137/827/68868, Minute by J.H. Emmens, 23 June 1938.

37. CO 137/826/68868, Act.-Gov. C.C. Woolley to Sir Henry Moore, Assistant Under Secretary in charge of West Indian Affairs, 3 August 1938.

38. R. Hart, *Rise and Organise: The Birth of the Workers and National Movements in Jamaica (1936–1939)* (London: Karia Press, 1989), p. 96.

39. R. Frucht, 'A Caribbean Social Type: Neither "Peasant" nor "Proletarian"' *Social and Economic Studies*, 16:3 (1967), pp. 295–300.

40. Marshall, 'Provision Ground and Plantation Labour: Competition for Resources', paper presented at the 20th annual conference of the Association of Caribbean Historians, St Thomas, VI, (1988), pp. 38–9.

41. Bolland, *On the March*, p. 156.

42. Marshall, 'The Post-Slavery Labour Problem Revisited', Paper presented at Elsa Goveia Memorial Lecture, (Department of History, UWI, Mona, 1991), p. 12.

43. Marshall, '"We be wise to many more tings": Blacks' Hopes and Expectations of Emancipation', in H. Beckles and Shepherd, eds., *Caribbean Freedom:*

       Society and Economy From Emancipation to the Present, (Kingston: Ian Randle, 1993), p. 20.

44.   K.A. Yelvington, *Producing Power: Ethnicity, Gender and Class in a Caribbean Workplace* (Pennsylvania, PA: Temple University Press, 1995), p. 229.

45.   Ibid., p. 175.

46.   Marshall, 'We be wise', p. 20.

The Legacy of Slavery:
Gender, ethnicity and occupation

The 'Other Middle Passage?'

Nineteenth-century bonded labour migration and the legacy of the slavery debate in the British-colonised Caribbean

VERENE A. SHEPHERD

*I*n 1858 the ship *Salsette*, captained by E. Swinton, set sail from India bound for the island of Trinidad in the Southern Caribbean with 324 Indian contract workers on board. The voyage lasted 108 days and at the end of it, 124 of the emigrants had died, an average of more than one per day.[1] It may have been this exceedingly high mortality rate and the distressing experiences of the emigrants, so graphically outlined in Captain Swinton's journal (along with the comments of his wife Jane who had also been on the *Salsette*), that led Ron Ramdin to title his book based on this voyage, *The Other Middle Passage*. Ramdin's use of the term 'Middle Passage' in this context does not, of course, refer simply to that leg of the journey from the West African coast, but the whole passage from India, from Calcutta or Madras, around the Cape of Good Hope, up to St Helena and across to the Caribbean; and is meant to capture the horrors of a system of emigration that many scholars feel replicated many aspects of the trade in African captives. Thus, the book adds to that genre of historical writing that seeks to compare the journeys from India with the Middle Passage of enslaved African captives that preceded Indian labour migration.

The tendency to compare Indian emigration (lasting from 1838 to 1917 in the Caribbean), with African slavery is not new. Anti-slavery and anti-immigration forces on both sides of the Atlantic since the second quarter of the nineteenth century had opposed the relocation of Indians to Caribbean, South African, Fijian and Mauritian sugar plantations on the grounds that the scheme proposed was nothing more than a revival of slavery. This neo-slavery or legacy of slavery theme was picked up by Joseph Beaumont, who was Chief Justice of Colonial Guyana from 1863 to 1868 and who was removed from office because of his empathy for the cause of Indian indentured servants, in his book *The New Slavery*.[2] Beaumont, in justifying why he described Indian indentureship as the new slavery, said that indentureship was not simply a matter of:

> an occasional defect here or excuses there but it is that of a monstrous rotten
> system rooted upon slavery, grown in its stale soil, emulating its worst abuses and
> only the more dangerous because it presents itself under false guise, whereas
> slavery had a brand of infamy obviously displayed upon its forehead.[3]

The neo-slavery debate revived in the historiography in the 1970s with Hugh Tinker's *A New System of Slavery*[4] and continued into the 1980s and 1990s with the spotlight turned on the mortality rate at sea[5] and the treatment of the immigrants on the plantations. Briefly, the neo-slavery thesis proponents argue that the passing of the Abolition Act in 1833, the end of slavery in the British-colonised Caribbean in 1834 and apprenticeship in 1838 did not end systems of domination. On the contrary, the White-dominated elite attempted to recreate slave relations of production and maintain the old slavery mentalities in its organisation of the socioeconomic and political environment. In trying to replace enslaved labour, the ruling/land-holding class seemed to have turned to the most familiar model of labour control – slavery. Thus, just like enslaved Africans before them, some Indians were taken from India against their will; some, mostly women, were kidnapped; recruits were kept in holding depôts before embarkation and shipped in cramped quarters; female Indians were sexually abused by the crew and subjected to harsh conditions of servitude on Caribbean plantations. Other features pointed out are that indentured Indians were not housed, fed or medically treated in an adequate fashion, so that the mortality rate was high in some territories; immigrants lacked proper sanitary facilities on the estates; and were subject to a wide range of rules, infraction of which incurred fines and prison terms. As with enslaved peoples, Indians were not free to move without passes and were anchored to the estates by restrictive contracts. Like enslaved African women, Indian women were sexually abused not only on the high seas, but also by plantation managers, mostly White. Above all, Indians responded to indentureship with a range of resistance strategies much like enslaved peoples, although there were no major labour protests aimed at ending the indentureship system in the way in which slave rebellions targeted freedom. Anti-emigration arguments, like the emancipatory rhetoric of the 1820s and 1830s, centred on the conditions of women.

Not all scholars support the neo-slavery thesis, some arguing counter to Beaumont and Tinker that no matter how harsh conditions were for Indians (with practice often departing from official regulations laid down for their care and treatment), their emigration and indentureship could never approximate the brutality and wretched conditions of Africans, captured and shipped to the Caribbean from the sixteenth to the nineteenth centuries particularly as outlined in the accounts of slaver captains and traders like Alexander Falconbridge, Captain Canot and Jose E. Cliffe.[6] David Eltis has been the most recent scholar to insist on the unique severity of the slave trade, though he admits that this line of argument 'goes against much of the literature on the shipping of indentured servants and convicts in the seventeenth and eighteenth centuries and the transportation of contract labour from Asia in the nineteenth'.[7] But he has supporters. Opponents of the view that Indian emigration and indentureship were slavery revived argue that, unlike the case of Africans, no wars were waged to secure Indian workers; for the most part, recruitment was not carried out in such a way as to disrupt families and cause death; more care was taken to regulate all aspects of the system, from recruitment to shipment and allocation to estates. Additionally, the passage from India was not attended with the same level of mortality as occurred on slavers, except in isolated cases and usually in the pre-steamship age. Only already dead or suicidal Indians ended up overboard. No Indian was deliberately thrown overboard to lighten the load of the ship. With respect to shipping, strict regulations were laid down to regulate the size of the ships, the space allocated to each emigrant and the rations to be served. In a concerted effort to stave off anti-slavery agitation and the charge that Indian emigration resembled the Middle Passage of slavers, great efforts were made to avoid overcrowding on emigrant ships; and members of the crew were paid gratuities based on each person landed alive to encourage better care on each voyage. Moreover, there was a major legal difference between slavery and servitude. Under slavery, the enslaved was chattel, the legal property of another person. S/he could be bought and sold, exchanged or used to settle debt. Indentured workers, on the other hand, sold their labour time, not their person; and no matter how low, regular wages were paid. Indian families were not broken up deliberately through sale or forced relocation and parents were not deprived of authority in the care of their children.

Several other areas of difference between slavery and Indian servitude have been isolated. Whereas slavery was for life, the indentured Indians worked under contracts (admittedly fraudulently lengthened at times), at the end of which they were freed from servitude. They could reindenture, although most chose not to do so. While admittedly rules were broken, immigration laws prohibited routine flogging. The status of indentureship was not passed on from mother to child; and children could not normally be pressed into indentureship before they were teenagers. Children could also not be located away from their mothers or parents. Comparatively few aspects of the Indian culture were forcefully suppressed on the estates. Finally, unlike enslaved Africans, Indians had civil rights. This fact was stressed by the commission appointed in Colonial Guyana after the Leonora protests of 1869.[8] While confirming the existence of abuses, the commission concluded that Indians had civil rights unlike enslaved people before them. Additionally, indentured labourers were not as 'natally alienated' as enslaved Africans.[9] Repatriation was enshrined in the immigration regulations and while these regulations were not honoured in all respects, there was a significant degree of circulation among Indians; a cycle of emigration, return and re-emigration that kept many linked to their homeland.

Since the 1980s, some scholars have added the specific conditions of Indian women to the general debate over the nature of indentured servitude. While some argue that the Indian woman's experience of emigration and indentureship was one of 'sexploitation', others claim that despite elements of 'sexploitation' akin to slavery, Indian women had far more to gain. Pieter Emmer, for example, holds that emigration was of significant material benefit to women escaping from 'an illiberal, inhibiting and very hierarchical social system in India'.[10] Charles Doorly, Protector of Emigrants in the Madras presidency, had expressed a similar view in 1915, remarking 'I am convinced that emigration is a blessing to a large number of the women we send, and opens to them a way of escape from lives of misery, poverty and prostitution'.[11] The first perspective, which echoes Beaumont's and Tinker's neo-slavery thesis, is most clearly articulated in the work of Rhoda Reddock, Jeremy Poynting and Jo Beall. After studying the fraudulent and abusive elements of labour migration, Beall, using data from Natal, argued that Indian women suffered 'ultraexploitability'; Reddock concluded that their whole experience was one of 'freedom denied', and Poynting that they experienced 'multiple oppression'.[12]

For the most part, however, the dichotomising discourse on slavery and indentureship that emerged in the aftermath of the abolition of slavery when the search for an alternative labour force intensified has not focused sufficiently on recruitment practices and the voyages from India, the discussions being based heavily on the plantation experience. More specifically, most of those who have pushed the neo-slavery perspective in relation to Indian migrant women's experiences, (arguing that Indian women suffered gender-differentiated exploitation), have located their arguments within the context of women's experience as workers on Caribbean plantations, or their encounter with White and Indian masculinity and gendered tyranny on estates and in the private sphere. But if the conditions of indentured women are to be critical to the neo-slavery thesis that seeks to compare their experiences with those of African women on Middle Passage slavers, more data on such conditions on the 'other Middle Passage' need to be excavated. The excavation of gender-differentiated data in the pre-plantation phase of the indentureship journey, particularly in the area of sexual exploitation on nineteenth-century ships, is thus the primary objective of this chapter. In this regard, the chapter represents a contribution to that genre of historical writing, already fully developed by slavery scholars, that focuses on the exercise of social power and authority through the medium of sociosexual manipulation by empowered males over subaltern women.[13] This focus on women is a reflection of the long-range impact of the historiographical revolution of the 1960s and 1970s which resulted in a pluralisation of the discourse on subaltern people's experiences, and the new attempt by academic feminists, in the aftermath of the emergence of women's history, to target the masculinist project that served to disarticulate the subaltern as woman.

In order to set the stage for the comparative assessment of Indian women's experience of the journey from India, the chapter begins by rehearsing the establishment of the trade in African captives and Indian contract workers, moves on to review the outlines of the capture and recruitment and the sexual disparity in the two trades, and then proceeds to compare the conditions under which the two sets of 'human cargo' were transported to the Caribbean. Such a comparison will no doubt provide ammunition both for those who support and those who oppose the 'neo-slavery' thesis; for differences and similarities are equally stark. The chapter ends with a case study of one Indian woman's experience of rape on the 'other Middle Passage', concluding that this one case captures graphically both the similarities and contrasts between slavery and indentureship.

Background: the two trades in human cargo

Commerce bound India to the Caribbean in the nineteenth century much as it did Africa to the Caribbean in the preceding three centuries. In both cases, the trade fluctuated with European policies and demands. In both cases, Europeans established varying degrees of permanence on the soil,[14] though they were more successful in controlling land in India than in Africa during the operation of the transatlantic trade in enslaved African captives. In both cases, capture and recruitment were conducted through middlemen who penetrated the interior. Unlike India, though, the sovereignty of African states was unimpaired by the presence of Europeans. On the whole the political power of the African states reigned supreme over both outsiders and indigenous peoples. Europeans only administered the forts until later partition and political control of Africa in the late nineteenth century. In both cases, sugar plantations were the primary recipients of imported labourers, though they were used in other enterprises.

While the Iberians pioneered the trade in African captives with other nations following suit (but with Portugal controlling a large share up to the nineteenth century), it was the British who pioneered the Indian indentureship system in the Caribbean. Britain, of course, later surpassed most nations in the eighteenth century in terms of her market share in the trade in African captives. In discussing the recent quantitative findings based on the CD-ROM database on the transatlantic slave trade, David Eltis notes that 'the British (including British colonials) and the Portuguese account for seven out of ten transatlantic slaving voyages, and carried nearly three-quarters of all slaves who embarked in Africa. Broadly, the Portuguese were dominant before 1640 and after 1807, with the British displacing them in the intervening period'.[15] Within the Caribbean, it was colonial Guyana that introduced the first batch, eventually importing 238,909 Indians between 1838 and 1917. This figure represented 55.6 per cent of the total of 429,623 Indian immigrants imported to the colonial Caribbean, and only Trinidad, which imported 33.5 per cent of the total number, came close to Guyana's figure.[16] This figure, of course, was a drop in the bucket compared with the numbers of Africans shipped across the Atlantic. Scholars continue to debate this so-called numbers game, but all agree that somewhere between 9.6 million and 15.4 million Africans reached the Americas, with millions more dying in the process of capture and shipment.[17] Unlike the trade in Indians, Guyana and Trinidad were comparatively minor players in the trade in African captives, Jamaica and Barbados receiving the majority of captives transported to the British-colonised territories. Eltis has shown that for the period 1519–1867, Jamaica and Barbados received 11.2 per cent and 5.1 per cent of the trade respectively, compared to 4.2 per cent for the Guianas and 3.2 per cent for the British Windward Islands and Trinidad combined.[18]

As was the case with the shipping of African captives, the relocation of Indians to colonial Guyana and the wider Caribbean was characterised by a sexual disparity. Scholars of the slave trade have shown that, despite regional variations (with a significantly high proportion of women exported from the Bight of Biafra or present south-east Nigeria), overall less than 40 per cent of enslaved African captives were female (compared with over 60 per cent in the trade to Muslim areas), though women came to be over-represented in field labour assignment in all importing territories.[19]

The sexual disparity among Indian emigrants was especially marked during the early years of the scheme. There were only 14 women among the first shipment to colonial Guyana in 1838, and this situation improved only gradually. By 1856, 38.2 per cent of the 5,004 imported to colonial Guyana were females, well above the average of 16 per cent shipped from Calcutta to all colonies in that year. The records of the Colonial Land and Emigration Commission (CLEC) show that in 1857, females comprised a high of 69.6 per cent, decreasing thereafter to 27.2–47.7 per cent between 1858 and 1866.[20] The sexual disparity was not confined to colonial Guyana. Only 11 per cent of the 261 immigrants imported to Jamaica on the first Indian emigrant ship, the *Blundell,* comprised women. If girls are added, the female percentage increases to 15 per cent. In 1863, the *Alnwick Castle* to Trinidad carried only 14.6 per cent females out of its 460 emigrants and the *Golden City,* of the same year, 13.4 per cent.[21] The excess of males over females among Indian emigrants was also noted in Suriname where slavery was abolished in 1863 and immigration began in 1873. The 1872 treaty between the Dutch Parliament and Britain respecting emigration from India stipulated that a 50:100 female:male ratio was to be maintained.[22] This was later lowered to 40:100, as it was for the British-colonised territories as recruiters could not meet the higher quota. This unfavourable, and frequently below quota, female:male ratio led the British government to seek a workable solution by imposing standard ratios. These ratios fluctuated between the 1850s and the 1860s, being at various times 25:100 and 50:100. The female:male ratio finally settled at 40:100 for most importing territories, but dispatching the requisite proportion of females for the colonies was a perennial problem for all concerned. The records indicate that a great effort was made to conform to the ratios set after 1860. For example, the female:male ratio on the *St Kilda* to colonial Guyana in 1871 was 57.8:100. The ratio never fell below 40:100 on the ships which sailed for that territory in 1872, with this allowable ratio also being maintained during 1873.[23] But, as in the case of the slave trade, kidnapping was also used to secure Indian women for Caribbean plantations. Indeed, by the early 1870s, kidnapping had reportedly become prevalent in recruiting districts of Allahabad and the North West Provinces, though this never approximated the extent perpetuated during the capture of Africans. Falconbridge indicated in 1788 that 'there is great reason to believe, that most of the negroes shipped from the coast of Africa, are kidnapped'.[24] The newspaper *The Pioneer of India* carried a report in 1871 about an attempted kidnapping of an Indian woman in Allahabad by four peons, Gohree, Baldeo, Raoti and Rumzan. The woman was to be sent to Jamaica. The men were convicted and sentenced to prison terms ranging of 6–12 months.[25]

The other Middle Passage?

After being captured and recruited, both male and female Indians, accompanied by *chaprasis*, were taken to the depôts in the area of first recruitment, then transported by train to final embarkation depôts either in Calcutta or in Madras. There were about ten emigration agencies serving the various colonies individually or in combination in Calcutta in the 1880s, but only four or so depôts: the Mauritius depot at Bhowanipur, the Demerara depôt at Garden Reach and others at Ballygunj and Chitpur. Each was staffed by an emigration agent, doctors, clerks, watchmen and sweepers. These depôts, all built on the same pattern, were not in the healthiest of spots, with grave implications for the health of those accommodated in them. They were surrounded by a high wall to prevent uncontrolled movement in and out and contained a number of barracks with bungalows for the staff. Accommodation was sufficient to provide for two shiploads at any time in the larger depôts. Emigrants spent on average one to three weeks waiting to be shipped, although in extreme cases, they could wait up to three months, as was the case with slavers. These depôts, however, bore no resemblance to the dehumanising slave barracoons or 'castles' on the West African coast, though in both cases, women were exposed to sexploitation. On arrival at the depôts,[26] each recruit was told to bathe and issued with a change of clothing while the old clothes were washed and returned.

Since the process by which Indians were obtained for transportation was dogged by fraud, attempts were made by the various emigration officials to ensure that emigrants had voluntarily signed on for emigration. Despite the improvements and efforts to tighten control over the process, fraud and deception were never eliminated completely from the process. Many found themselves on ships bound for places they had not opted to go to; and on journeys longer than they had been made to believe, at times leading to protest action usually described by British officials as 'mutiny'. For example, there was a so-called 'mutiny' by emigrants on the ship *Clasmerden* from Calcutta to Guyana in 1862. The ship was forced to stop in Pernambuco in Brazil. The emigrants reportedly 'mutineed' because they claimed that they had been misled about the length of the voyage.[27]

At the embarkation depôts, emigrants were given several medical examinations by the native doctor and the government-appointed European doctor, to ensure that they were fit to undertake the long journey to the Caribbean. The women were not given as detailed an examination as the men for two reasons: one, officials wanted few obstacles in the way of female emigration and opted for a cursory examination; and two, for cultural reasons, the detailed examination of women by male doctors was unacceptable to the women and the men, especially husbands. By the early twentieth century agitation had increased for the appointment of female depôt doctors to examine women. Part of the preparations included administering the appropriate vaccinations and allowing the recruits to sign their indenture contracts. The emigrants were also issued with clothes for the journey, a pair of woollen trousers, jacket, shoes and a cap for males, and a sari, two flannel jackets, one woollen petticoat, a pair of worsted stockings and shoes for females. With the exception of the sari, these clothes were not those of the typical rural Indian. In response to complaints before 1860s of inadequate clothing, in 1867 calls were made for an additional petticoat to be issued to the women.

Once the emigrant was certified as fit for agricultural labour and embarkation, an emigration certificate was signed to that effect for each one by the Surgeon-Superintendent and the depôt surgeon and countersigned by the protector of emigrants at the port of embarkation and the emigration agent for Guyana. This certificate, duly signed and countersigned, was delivered to each emigrant. It contained the emigrant's name, father's name, age, caste, height, name of next of kin, marital status and name of partner if applicable, distinguishing marks and place of origin in India. Each emigrant also had a 'tin ticket' or identification disk placed around the neck or arm, and an embarkation number; and these details have allowed many descendants to trace their immigrant ancestors. Once all the preparations were complete, emigrants were put on board the ships for their voyage to the Caribbean.

Captured Africans had a vastly different experience. They were shackled and marched to the coast in slave coffles. Many died on the way. Those who survived the journey were accommodated in barracoons, euphemistically called 'castles' along the West African coast, where they sometimes had a long wait before being stowed on slavers bound for the Caribbean. As Cliffe records, at times there was insufficient food to feed those waiting to be shipped out. Women were exposed to greater sexploitation while in the barracoons than Indian female recruits endured at the depôts. A few days before embarkation, women, like men, had their heads shaved; and if the cargo belonged to more than one owner, they were branded with pieces of silver wire or small irons fashioned into the merchant's initials, 'heated just enough to blister without burning the skin', according to Captain Canot's account.[28] The captives were then taken out to the slaver in canoes or small boats. Women and men were stripped of their clothes as they boarded the ships.

Indian recruits were transported from Calcutta (like those also from Madras) in ships specially selected to participate in the Indian labour migration scheme. They were also placed under the care of crew members who were instructed in their responsibilities towards those in their care. A primary concern of those who decided on the ships to be used and the crew to be hired was the necessity of avoiding any charge that Indian emigration was a new system of slavery.

Specific standards relating to size, space, crew, diet and medical stores were laid down for ships accepted to participate in the Indian labour migration scheme. In general, the ships were larger in tonnage than those used in the transatlantic trade in enslaved Africans. Indeed, Herbert S. Klein records that between 1782 and 1788, the size of ships engaged in transporting enslaved Africans to Jamaica averaged just 172 tons.[29] The average size increased to 236 tons between 1791 and 1799 and 294 tons between 1800 and 1808. The average number of captives carried per ship in these same periods was 396, 328 and 289 respectively.[30] The Parliamentary Slave Trade Regulating Acts of 1788 and 1799 had reduced the number of captives per ton ratio as a way of reducing the overcrowding and high mortality on slavers; for to compensate for inevitable deaths, slavers had been packed way over their capacity. After 1799, the regulation provided for one captive per ton as opposed to 2.6 per ton previously.[31] The tonnage of ships also rose after 1788, though few ever approximated the size of emigrant ships.[32] Still, Eltis holds that the density on slave ships remained higher than on ships carrying other people. For the seventeenth century, such ships rarely carried in excess of 150 people.[33]

The *Whitby* to Guyana in 1838 was among the smallest ships used in the trade in Indian contract labourers, being just 350 tons. By the 1850s, a larger class of ships was being used. Some, like the *Ganges*, owned by James Nourse, was 839 tons. The Nourse Line became the principal carrier to the Caribbean, although Sandbach, Tinne and Co. was also involved. From the 1880s ships increased in size, being 1,600 tons or larger. Between 1884 and 1888 Nourse brought seven iron ships into service, which were 1,700 tons each. Steamships made the voyage in less time. For example, the first steamship to Guyana, the *Enmore*, took just 49 days.[34] The journey on sailing ships could take up to three months, sometimes longer. The *Silhet* took 96 days to reach Jamaica in 1878 and the *Lightening*, 112 days. Despite their longer sailing time, sailing ships were never totally replaced, and in 1895, there were still 22 of them in service. The average Middle Passage slaver from West Africa had taken 2–3 months in the early sixteenth century; but by the mid-nineteenth century they averaged 4–6 weeks.[35] Though some ships passed through the Suez Canal, the usual journey, such as the one made by the *Allanshaw* in 1885, was round the Cape of Good Hope.

Emigrant ships had to be well ventilated, and from the 1860s were required to be supplied with lifeboats, fire appliances and other rescue equipment. No firearms or flammable material were allowed on board. Poor ventilation which would have led to unbearable stench (as on slavers), and heavy loss of life during possible shipwrecks or other disasters were conditions which those involved in the trade of Indian labourers wanted to avoid.

Emigrant ships were required to carry an adequate number of crew and workers to look after the ship and its passengers, but the ratio of crew-to-ton on slave ships was much higher than on these emigrant ships (and also higher than on ships from Africa not carrying slaves). Once the ship had embarked all the 'passengers', the crew was mustered on the quarterdeck and reminded of their duties on the voyage. In addition to the Surgeon-Superintendent (perhaps the highest authority on board) and the Captain, there were several other officers and crew: a compounder or dispenser, an assistant compounder; a third officer who issued supplies and clothing; an engineer; ordinary sailors; sweepers or topazes; cooks selected from the higher Hindu castes on board, hospital attendants and sirdars. These sirdars were usually second-time emigrants who knew the ropes and were appointed one for each 25 emigrants. Sometimes there was a nurse for the ship's hospital, drawn from among the emigrants on board. Some ships, like the *Allanshaw* had other categories of crew like steward, first, second and third mate and boatswain. The Captain's responsibility was limited to navigation, supervision of the crew and his ship. He had supreme responsibility in the event of a disaster, but he often listened to the Surgeon-Superintendent. In fact, it was the latter who decided if the captain and crew would receive their gratuities. A poor report from the surgeon could not only affect gratuities, but the future of ships and personnel employed in the trade from India.

The ship's surgeon was crucial to the voyage and great effort was made to select competent and experienced ones. As Basdeo Mangru observed, the rate of mortality among the emigrants depended considerably on the care, competence and character of the surgeons employed. The positive correlation between competent surgeons and low mortality on some ships did not escape the attention of emigration officials.[36] Despite the acceptance among all involved that the role of the surgeon was crucial to the success of the Indian labour migration scheme and that the best qualified ones were to be selected, the surgeons were inevitably a mixed group of competent and not so competent men. Some of the surgeons had a wealth of experience in the Australia service. Some were former army doctors; others were inexperienced men employed in the Indian medical service and Indian jails. As was the case with the ships' doctors under slavery, not many qualified surgeons wanted to participate in this 'disagreeable trade'. Falconbridge, in discussing the surgeons on slavers had observed that: 'it may not be improper here to remark that the surgeons employed in the Guinea trade, are generally driven to engage in so disagreeable an employ by the confined state of their finance'.[37] Strained finances may have been a major reason for the Surgeon-Superintendents of emigrant ships, though their salaries were far from attractive. Indeed, the low remuneration may have been one factor militating against the ability of emigration officials to secure more competent surgeons. Surgeons-Superintendent received a gratuity per head on those landed alive with an increase in proportion to the number of voyages undertaken. A Surgeon-Superintendent like Edward A. Hardwicke on the *Allanshaw* would have received a higher rate of gratuity than some others, as he had undertaken around nine voyages in this service.[38] This per head pay was lower than was paid to those transporting emigrants to Australia; consequently the better ones gravitated towards the Australia service. They were guaranteed a free return passage to India or England; but they were not entitled to a pension, free outfits or continued employment in the service. Besides gratuities, surgeons proceeding to the Cape of Good Hope or Australia were given fixed sums of £40 and £60 respectively, claimable within a specified period, in lieu of return passage.

The continued difficulty of attracting competent surgeons resulted in an increase in their pay by the late 1860s when it went up from eight shillings a head landed alive to ten shillings for the first voyage, 11 shillings for the second as long as the surgeon's conduct was deemed satisfactory; and 12 shillings for subsequent voyages. On the voyage, they were supposed to attend to the medical care of the emigrants on board the ship, making sure to detect and treat illnesses before they assumed epidemic proportions. They were to keep up the spirits of the emigrants by encouraging them to sing and dance, and supervise the cooking and serving of food. Because of the difficulty of attracting competent surgeons to the Indian labour migration trade, infractions of the rules laid down for their conduct were often overlooked; still there were cases, however infrequent, of withholding of gratuities and outright dismissal. Some carried out their duties diligently, others did not. Captains on slavers also stood to lose part of their pay for excessive loss of captives; but as allowance was made for death through resistance, a loophole was created to lessen their financial loss.

Up to the 1850s, and like in the case of slavers, males and females had been separated on board without any attention to family, but unlike on the Middle

Passage, this was later modified. The strict spatial separation by gender had been maintained on the grounds of decency and to reduce the spread of sexually transmitted diseases by limiting or trying to prevent sexual contact. It was the negatives of this arrangement which dictated later modifications. The negatives stressed were that: families or couples were separated and that there was an increased likelihood of sexual harassment of women by sailors. Indian men, the supporters of modification argued, were crucial to protect Indian wives on board. Consequently, by the 1860s, single men and women were separated but couples were kept together. Single women were placed aft, followed by married couples and children amidships. Single men were placed in the forward part of the ship. On the ships involved in the trade of enslaved Africans, women and girls had been placed between decks, followed by boys on the same deck, with men in a separate compartment.

Regulations were laid down regarding clothes and diet, the space allocated to each emigrant and the sleeping arrangements. The food supplies provided for Indians conformed to caste and religious preferences and were different from the yams, horse beans, rice, corn, small quantities of beef and pork and palm oil-based sauce served to enslaved Africans on the Middle Passage. By the 1870s, meat (mostly fresh mutton) had been introduced into the diet on board where previously dried fish had been the choice. Dried fish was still recommended for the first few weeks of the voyage when unstable sea conditions made cooking difficult; but fresh meat was to be cooked thereafter. Increased portions of rice, flour, ghee and dhall were implemented in 1871. The cook was usually drawn from among the highest Hindu castes on board in an effort to avoid caste conflicts; but such conflicts could not be avoided completely. Furthermore, the choice of Hindu cooks (and at times what they chose to serve) offended Muslims, usually a minority on emigrant ships. Twenty Muslims on the *Jura* bound for Guyana in 1891 reportedly refused to eat because the sheep had been killed by a Hindu. The food was thrown overboard. On arrival of the ship *Grecian* in Georgetown in 1893, the agent general of immigration reported that three Muslims had been 'placed in irons' on the voyage on 17 September 1892 for inciting the other immigrants not to eat the food issued to them because the meat was pig, and beef not fit for Mohammedans.[39]

The use of space on emigrant ships was regulated as a result of the concern about avoiding the overcrowding and high mortality so associated with slavers in the Middle Passage. In 1842, the numbers allowed on board were related to the size (tonnage) of the ships, one emigrant per 2 tons. By 1845, this was abandoned in favour of the cubic measurement of 70 square ft or 12 superficial ft for each emigrant. The CLEC was insistent that sufficient space should be allocated to allow for 'respiration and motion' and that such space should be such that a 'full grown man' of about an average height of 5 ft 6 inches 'might lie down, supposing no system of berthing be adopted [and] move about without much inconvenience'.[40] Despite the opposition from some quarters, Act XIII of 1864 reduced this to 10 superficial ft for each adult. Increased numbers could be carried by this reduction. This again caused overcrowding and inadequate ventilation, and so was reversed by the CLEC to the 1845 space for adults. The allocation of 10 superficial ft was retained for children. No upward limit of numbers was actually stipulated, but preference was shown for larger vessels with better ventilation and space for recreational facilities than smaller vessels. There had been an attempt to stipulate that emigrant ships should not carry more than 300–350 contract labourers on board, but this had been abandoned in 1860 on the grounds that not only did it increase the cost of passage, but it restricted the emigration agent's selection to small ships which could not be as well fitted or ventilated for comfort as large ships.

The space allocated for Indian emigrants as well as the spatial organisation of those on board showed vast differences when compared with slavers on the Middle Passage. Indeed, Eltis concludes that ships carrying all other categories of people (convicts, indentured servants, fee-paying passengers) carried far fewer people and were less closely packed than did slave ships.[41] On one eighteenth-century slaver of 235 tons, 25 ft wide across the beam and 92 ft long between the decks , the division into compartments for men and women (not counting space taken up by the platforms) was as follows:

Storeroom	= 15 ft [no captives]
Men's compartment	= 45 ft
Women's compartment	= 10 ft
Boys' compartment	= 22 ft

On account of the expectation of a sexual disparity, slavers always allocated a smaller space for women. 'But at the same time', wrote Falconbridge in his account of the Middle Passage, the enslaved Africans 'are frequently stowed so close, as to admit of no other posture than lying on their sides. Neither will the height between decks, unless directly under the grating, permit them the indulgence of an erect posture, especially where there are platforms, which is usually the case'.[42]

He explained further that: 'These platforms are a kind of shelf, about 8 or 9 feet in breadth, extending from the side of the ship towards the centre. They are placed nearly midway between the decks, at the distance of two or three feet from each deck. Upon these the negroes are stowed in the same manner as they are on the deck'.[43]

Space was cramped, as eye-witnesses related. Captain Canot had this to say of one such slaver:

> I returned on board to aid in stowing 108 boys and girls, the eldest of whom did not exceed 15 years. As I crawled between decks, I could not imagine how this little army was to be packed or draw breath in a hold but 22 inches high. I found it impossible to adjust the whole in a sitting posture; but we made them lie down in each other's laps, like sardines in a can, and in this way obtained space for the entire cargo.[44]

Cliffe concurred:

> They make 2–3 slave decks in a vessel, which has perhaps 6 feet between her deck and her beams above. There would be three tiers of slaves stowed away. Sometimes there are no slave decks and slaves sleep on casks . . . the slaves are jammed in . . . They are packed in upon their sides, laid in, heads among legs and arms, so that it is very difficult frequently, until they become very much emaciated so as to leave the room, for them to get up alone, without the whole section moving.[45]

For the most part, then, 'the captives could not individually turn from side to side – the whole section had to turn; and when they were so tightly packed, they could not go on deck for air and to be washed'.[46] Such appalling accommodation conditions were not repeated on the emigrant ships.

Initially, emigrants slept on mats on the floor of the ship. In 1866 a recommendation was put forward by Dr Pearse, Surgeon-Superintendent on the *Oasis,* for raised wooden platforms instead of mats. This was in an effort to improve health and reduce the mortality on ships; but it is unclear if this recommendation was effected on all ships involved in the indentured labour trade.

Strict rules were laid down to regulate the conduct of the sailors towards the emigrants. For example, when they were mustered on board as the ship *Allanshaw* started its journey in 1885, the crew was reminded that 'any member of the crew found amongst the emigrants talking to, or interfering with, or molesting them in any way, will be fined one month's pay each offence'; and one of its sailors, the 22-year-old African-American man, Robert Ipson, seemed to have been reminded about this constantly by the Captain and Surgeon-Superintendent.[47] Fraternising between the crew and Indian women was especially forbidden. The hatchways were guarded, especially that section leading down to the single women's quarters. Men were forbidden to enter this section of the ship and this applied to both fellow emigrants and crew, whose quarters were usually in the forecastle, next to the prow. Some surgeons ensured that the decks below were well lit, especially the female section, to prevent what they termed 'promiscuous intercourse'. This was unlike during the Middle Passage when the crew was not prevented from raping Black female captives. Falconbridge noted that 'on board some [slave] ships, the common sailors are allowed to have intercourse with such of the Black women whose consent they can procure'. But, 'permission' was neither always sought, nor granted. He noted further that 'the Officers are permitted to indulge their passions among them at pleasure, and sometimes are guilty of such brutal excesses, as disgraces human nature'.[48] The strict legislation regarding protecting women from the crew and single male emigrants makes it clear that there was a real fear that emigrant women were always in danger of sexual assault. Indeed, Moses Seenarine recently concluded that 'the entire "coolie ship" was an unsafe place for single females, as well as married women, as they were frequent targets of sexual attacks'.[49]

Regulations required that adequate food be provided for the emigrants. The sirdar received and distributed daily rations and supervised the cooking and sanitary arrangements in addition to his other role of maintaining discipline and promoting the emigrants' general welfare. By 1885 there were trained cooks on board the ships, and this development decreased the sirdar's duties somewhat. As on the Middle Passage slavers, emigrants were normally fed twice per day, though unlike African captives, Indian emigrants mostly took their meals on deck as long as the weather was good. Breakfast was served by nine a.m. and the evening meal between five and six p.m. The fear of African captives jumping overboard, despite the netting, caused slavers to be reluctant to have them on deck, especially the men. They were thus fed on deck as little as possible. Cliffe noted that on one ship 'someone . . . takes the food down below deck and pass out to each'. But as none of the crew liked the job 'as the place is so filthy, whoever has to go carry out the job as quickly as possible and sometimes does not move along to each slave to make sure each gets food. Those furthest from the hatchways at times get no food'.[50] On some ships, they were given water three times in each 24 hours, a half pint each. Water was never adequate, however.

The Indian emigrants, though, were encouraged to be on deck as much as possible and, like enslaved Africans, to entertain themselves by dancing, singing and playing games. Adult men and women were provided with chillum pipes and women were provided with combs and other supplies for their comfort. Pipes and tobacco had also been circulated among captive African men and women.

Every attention was supposed to be given to the health of those on board, particularly with a view to maintaining as low a death rate as possible in order not to repeat the high death rate of the slave trade. While enslaved Africans on slavers had been provided only with slop buckets, emigrants' ships were fitted out with water closets, separate ones for men and women and the crew by 1885. This not only prevented their quarters from being smelly from excrement, but also reduced the spread of diseases on account of a filthy environment. Emigrants were encouraged to bathe at least once per week, to keep active and to oil themselves with coconut oil weekly. After the near disastrous 1856/7 emigration season in which the death rate on ships from Calcutta to the Caribbean ranged from 6 per cent on the *Wellesley* to 31 per cent on the *Merchantman*, an average of 17.27 per cent, regulations were improved with a positive impact on the death rates which fell to 3 per cent by the 1862/3 season. Apart from enormously high death rates when accidents happened, as in 1858 when 120 out of 324 emigrants on the *Salsette* to Trinidad died en route; and in 1865 when the *Fusilier* was wrecked at Natal with a total loss of life of 246 (including those who died from fever on the voyage to Natal) and the *Eagle Speed* was wrecked at the mouth of the Mutlah river with 300 lives lost, in general, by 1885, the mortality rate was much lower. It was 3.26 per cent on the *Jorawur* which landed in Guyana in December 1884 and under 3 per cent on the *Allanshaw* of 1885. The mortality rate was lower on ships sailing from Madras (an average 0.9 per cent in the 1850s) than on those which sailed from Calcutta. Among the improvements were better medical examination and selection of prospective recruits at the emigration depot in India, improved ventilation; separate compartments for the sick; recruitment of experienced surgeons capable of dealing with diseases and illnesses on board; improved water and better diet on board. By 1885, the

The Other Middle Passage

average mortality was 2.5 per cent on ships to Colonial Guyana, and it was to become even lower by 1890, as Table 16.1 shows.

Table 16.1   Mortality at sea: voyages to Colonial Guyana, 1871–90

Year	%	Year	%
1871	1.60	1881	2.68
1872	4.74	1882	1.46
1873	5.56	1883	0.64
1874	5.58	1884	2.04
1875	1.12	1885	2.50
1876	1.08	1886	1.41
1877	1.52	1887	1.59
1878	3.30	1888	1.82
1879	1.55	1889	1.50
1880	1.34	1890	1.41

Source: D.W.D. Comins, 'Note on Emigration . . . to Guyana, 1893', in Tinker, *New System of Slavery*, p. 165.

Philip Curtin has noted that 'the cost of the slave trade in human life was many times the number of slaves landed in the Americas', with shipboard mortality ranging from a low of 13 per cent to a high of 33 per cent.[51] Eltis also notes regional differences for the seventeenth and eighteenth centuries, showing that almost one-third of the captives leaving the Bight of Biafra ports (the majority female), between 1663 and 1713 never made it to the Americas, whereas in no other region was the ratio higher than one-fifth.[52] Even though shipboard mortality rates on Middle Passage slavers decreased by the nineteenth century, averaging 14 per cent according to Eltis's analysis,[53] this was still a far higher figure than that for nineteenth century emigrant ships. Despite the strict regulations governing the treatment of emigrants on board ships to colonial Guyana and other importing territories, such rules were flouted constantly and flagrantly. In 1862, for example, charges were brought against the Surgeon-Superintendent of the *Persia*, Mr Chapman, for cruelty to the emigrants on board.[54] In 1863 those on the *Clasmerden* who had staged a 'mutiny', forcing the ship to stop in Brazil, complained that the surgeon, A.N.

Watts, had been drunk for most of the voyage and had not carried out his duties satisfactorily. His gratuity was eventually reduced as punishment from 10 shillings to 2 shillings per emigrant landed alive.[55] On the *Jorawur* of 1884, complaints of indiscipline, lack of authority and drunkenness on the part of the captain were made. There were complaints on several voyages that the food was inadequate, that potato, milk and pumpkin spoiled on the way and that food designated for the emigrants was at times siphoned off for the crew. There were also reports that the water taken on board was contaminated, and that emigrants were physically punished by crew. On the voyage of the *Main* to Guyana in 1888, several crew members breached the rules proscribing physical punishment of emigrants and proceeded to shackle and handcuff those they regarded as having committed offences. Whereas African men were routinely shackled and handcuffed on the Middle Passage slavers, regulations surrounding Indian emigration were that emigrants were to be put in irons only in extreme cases of indiscipline. But the interpretation of what constituted extreme indiscipline was left up to the crew. Putting emigrants in irons was also allowed if they threatened to jump overboard to commit suicide as several high-caste Indians had done on the *Foyle* of 1887, following the example of Podrath Singh, because they claimed to have been 'polluted' by being touched by a low-caste sirdar[56], or if they were deemed insane. The eight men and five women who had been handcuffed complained to the agent general of immigration upon arrival in Guyana that they thought the punishment had not fit the so-called crimes. One of the women had been handcuffed, for example, for lighting her 'haka' (chillum pipe) and smoking in between decks.[57]

Despite the insistence of the emigrants on the majority of ships that they were well-treated, few voyages were incident-free. The logbooks kept by the surgeon and captain of the ship *Allanshaw* were full of incidents in which the crew abused the emigrants. For example, the 'coloured boatswain' had struck Auntoo on the shoulder with a rope; Juggessar and his wife had been verbally abused and threatened by Robert Ipson; Ipson had abused others, including the cook and 'Kalu/Kaloo no. 289' whom he had pushed and kicked on 30 September, leading Kalu to say to two of his compatriots Janki and Bhadaya (interpreted for Ipson by a sailor, Templeton) that Ipson might have been one of those who had raped the young woman, Maharani; Nandhal had been struck with a rope by the engineer; Palukdhan had been struck by the sailor John Smith; O'Brien had deliberately thrown a 6-lb tin of mutton at the Indian

women on deck; Beharie's [Behary?] thumb had been cut by the cabin boy
Clentworth who was subsequently punished, leading to a near mutiny by the
crew; and several sailors had been accused of annoying the hospital inmates
'when they came aft to muster at 8 pm [on 23rd August] by making ugly noises
with their mouths at the doors and windows'.[58] The brutality on slavers and
the unrelenting application of force was much worse, leading to constant
resistance on the Middle Passage by captives who hated the crew and their
captors with a passion. They not only committed suicide, refused to eat and
threatened the crew with violence, but on several occasions attempted to take
over the ship and return to Africa. Resistance and full-scale revolts on
nineteenth-century Indian emigrant ships were far fewer, and indeed, these
ships were not as heavily armed as slavers.

The regulations against fraternising between crew and female emigrants
and proscribing sexual relationships between crew and Indian women were
also flouted constantly. Unlike during the Middle Passage when perpetrators
were usually White, the sexual exploitation of women in this period did not
reflect only White, but also Black and Indian masculinity in action; for the
emigrant ships hired non-European crew. A few positions, like that of sirdars,
were held by high-caste Indian men and a few cases have surfaced in the
manuscript sources of these sirdars molesting women on board. Even though
there was no love lost between European and non-European, especially
African and Caribbean, crew, as is indicated by the frequent outbreaks of
conflicts between them, and the equally frequent requests by the Surgeons-
Superintendent of the ships that Black crew members be replaced by Europeans, the actions of both groups towards Indian women reveal that indentureship, like enslavement, manifested signs of gendered tyranny on the part
of those who exercised and abused their power over the subalterns they were
exclusively employed to protect. Although the duty of the crew and officers
was to see to the health and comfort of the emigrants aboard the ships engaged
in the trade in contract labourers, they often held out rights as privileges as a
way of forcing compliance among the women. Above all, the actions of Black
and White men towards Indian emigrant women on the ships destined for the
Caribbean demonstrated that the roots of the racist and ethnic tensions which
later characterised the host societies in which Indians settled, were deeply
embedded in the voyage from India and did not suddenly emerge in the region.
The White crew, both officers and rank-and-file sailors, harboured a certain
contempt for Indians as a race, perhaps a racial attitude towards other

ethnicities inherited from enslavement and strengthened by British imperialism in India and the emigrants as a class. One Surgeon-Superintendent, Dr R. Whitelaw, noted in his diary of 1882 that 'there is a great tendency among officers, apprentices and men (if European) to consider the coolies [*sic*] a people who may be pushed about, abused and annoyed at will'.[59] Ipson articulated clearly that he did not know what all the fuss about the emigrants was about; that he 'had been in emigrant ships before and with as many as 800 on board and never so saw so such a damned fuss as these was made on board of this ship about them'.[60] Their views about lower-caste women, whom they characterised frequently as prostitutes, were clearly seen in their treatment of female emigrants on the voyages and came out strongly in the evidence given at several official inquiries launched over the period of the existence of indentured labour migration when complaints about sexual assault and other misconduct of the crew could not go unnoticed or pushed under the mat. The rather 'democratic' spread of the practice among the men in charge of the ships, as this section will demonstrate empirically, reflected a certain amount of acceptance of it.

The complaints about the abuse of emigrant women by Black men were seen in the reports of emigration officials and ships' surgeons. Indeed, one argument used by the surgeons who called for the reduction in the number of Black men employed as crew on Indian emigrant ships, or their total elimination, was the usual ethnic stereotype that they had an 'incorrigible addictedness to sexual intercourse'. This view was articulated strongly by the Surgeon-Superintendent of the *Moy* which landed in Jamaica in June 1891 and whose crew apparently consisted mostly of Black men. He wrote in his report: 'the greatest difficulty was experienced during the voyage in preventing intercourse between the [Black crew] and the female passengers . . . I concur in thinking that on account of their generally incorrigible addictedness to sexual intercourse, negroes [*sic*], if so employed, should be in a minority on a cooly [*sic*] emigrant ship'.[61]

Individual Black men were at times implicated, as the case on the *Allanshaw* will indicate later. Other examples have come to light. The Agent General of immigration, in summarising all the data relating to the voyage of the *Avon* to Guyana in 1892/3 for transmission to the Colonial Office, reported that it had come to his attention that Steed, an African crew member 'had so often been cautioned against interfering with or molesting the immigrants that the Surgeon-Superintendent, on arrival at St Helena requested the Inspector of

Emigrants to have [him] removed from the ship'. The inspector refused to take this drastic action on the basis that no actual assault had taken place and so no legal charge could be brought against Steed.[62]

Although some Surgeons-Superintendent complained that Black men were more likely than White men to molest women on board emigrant ships and used this argument to justify their call for a White only or predominantly White crew, a higher proportion of the complaints about the sexual abuse of emigrant women by officers and rank-and-file crew on emigrant ships to the Caribbean was directed at European men. The surgeons themselves were infrequently implicated, based on complaints made by the emigrants on arrival at their destination. My research has uncovered more evidence of 'sexploitation' on the ships destined for Guyana than on those destined for other Caribbean territories. This may be a reflection of the uneven nature of the contents of the reports submitted by emigration officials and surgeons. It could also be explained by the fact that far more reports exist for Guyana which outpaced any other receiving territory in the region, and was the destination of numerous ships from Calcutta and Madras.[63]

The major sources of evidence are enclosed with the correspondence between the emigration agents and the CLEC for the period 1854–60 and with the correspondence between the colonial governors and the Colonial Office officials. It was customary for all reports of the surgeons and Agents General of Immigration or Emigration (Protector of Immigrants or Emigrants in some territories) to be forwarded to the Colonial Office, and these have proved to be a wealth of information on the issue of the abuse of women. The Guyanese Agents-General of Immigration's reports are replete with complaints of 'misconduct' on the part of the Surgeons-Superintendent, captains and other crew; for immigrants were usually encouraged to lodge such complaints on arrival in the colony. Such complaints were made against Dr Wilkinson on the *Bucephalus*, Dr Galbraith on the *Devonshire*, Mr Simmonds on the *Royal George* and Dr Cook on the *Assaye* – all to Guyana. The Captain of the *Thetis* was said to have indicated that he had no intention of interfering when the Indian women and the sailors on the ship engaged in sex; and the Surgeon-Superintendent of the *Canning* of 1860 lost a part of his gratuity because he was accused of getting three women drunk so that they could not testify against him. On that same ship, two sailors had 'violently assaulted' women to have sex with them, yet no one found out who the individuals were so that they could be punished.[64] The crew on the *Dovercastle* to Guyana in

1871 was accused of 'misconduct' towards the women on board. The CLEC complained that as long as the water closets were placed where they were (in the forepart of the ship) 'these things will happen'. T.W.C. Murdoch of the CLEC, in a letter to R.H. McCade, indicated further that 'we have always maintained the impropriety of so placing them, notwithstanding the opposition for several years of the Indian Authorities'.[65] There were complaints that the drunken captain of the *Jorawur* of 1884 and the crew and the steward of the *Grecian* of 1885 molested the women.

Dr Atkins, Surgeon-Superintendent on the ship *Silhet* to Guyana in 1882, was said to have formed a relationship with the female emigrant Janky despite the fact that Deemohammed, a sirdar, had staked his claims to her previously. Predictably, Atkins was absolved of any 'illicit intercourse' with Janky during the voyage and was later allowed to marry her, a highly unusual occurrence for the nineteenth century. On arrival in Guyana, Atkins requested the cancellation of Janky's indenture on payment of the required sum. After this was agreed, but before final permission to marry was granted, a contract was drawn up 'securing to the wife control over the sum of £250 deposited on her behalf by the husband with the Acting Administrator General, to be applied for the benefit of the said wife as he and his successors should think proper'. The sum was invested with the Receiver-General. Janky was given a letter addressed to Messrs. W. & H. Brand of 109 Fenchurch St in London, who were agents of the Administrator General's Department. This letter instructed them to give Janky any advice she needed in the event of her husband's absence or death.[66] They were married in Georgetown, Guyana by the Minister of St Andrews Church and Atkins was directed to present himself to the emigration agent on arrival in London where he proceeded to take Janky.

Such complaints about the surgeon, captain and other crew on emigrant ships were not confined to Guyana, but applied to Jamaica and Trinidad as well. An early case to come to light on a voyage to Jamaica involved Dr Prince, Surgeon-Superintendent of the *Ravenscraig* of 1861. In addition to having been accused of excessive drunkenness on the voyage, Prince was said to have committed 'criminal assaults' on some of the Indian women 'under circumstances of an extremely aggravated nature'.[67] As the alleged offences were committed before the Atlantic crossing, and as was usual in such cases, the ship stopped at St Helena where the governor ruled that there was sufficient evidence against Prince. He ordered that Prince be sent to Jamaica under arrest and be relieved of his duties. On arrival in Jamaica, however, the police magistrate and other officials released Prince on the basis that there was not enough evidence to convict him. They paid him his salary and gratuities as per his contract. The police magistrate and his supporters felt that even if such intercourse had taken place between Prince and the women on board, 'it is clear that it must have been with their consent'.[68] How they came to this conclusion is unclear; but it was not unusual for lower-caste women from India, as African women enslaved in the Americas had been, to be regarded as loose and promiscuous and incapable of being raped.

The reports of voyages to Trinidad also contained complaints about illicit intercourse between crew and emigrant women. Complaints were made in this regard about the *Nerbuddah* of 1885. Complaints also originated among emigrants to Mauritius and one Dr R. Brown was actually dismissed from the Mauritius service after four voyages when he was reported for drunkenness and pulling off the clothes of female emigrants.

It should also be pointed out that Indian women also suffered abuses at the hands of Indian men on board as domestic violence was not unheard of in instances where people tried to live as couples and families on board. On the *Artist* to Guyana in 1874, there was 'a murderous assault on a woman by her husband', who was subsequently 'put in irons to be dealt with upon landing'.[69] While on the journey of the *Silhet* to Guyana in 1883, the male emigrant Gazee and his wife had an argument. She complained, and the third officer hit Gazee and threatened him with further action if he continued to ill-treat his wife. The Surgeon-Superintendent's report indicated that Gazee seemed to have believed that he had 'a prescriptive right' to ill-use his wife.[70]. Perhaps Gazee's attitude was reflective of the caste and gender hierarchies which were organising principles of the Brahminical social order and which resulted in the subordination of women.

A male emigrant on the *John Davie* in 1885 reportedly tried to rape a young girl. He was beaten, even though corporal punishment was not supposed to be carried out on emigrant ships. The Surgeon-Superintendent, however, felt justified in breaking the regulation in view of the gravity of the offence. The man was given six lashes 'with a moderately hard rope on the buttocks'.[71]

The protector of immigrants in Trinidad reported that a woman, Bhag-wandie, a passenger on the *Nerbuddah* of 1885, had jumped overboard 'after she had been assaulted by a man . . . who appears to have slept with her several nights during the voyage'. It turned out that this man was Indian, a sirdar, who had also stabbed her in her side with a bayonet. He was arrested on arrival.[72] Several Indian sirdars and Lascars were also accused of molesting Indian women on this voyage.

One woman's experience of 'sexploitation'

The most telling example of sexploitation of an emigrant woman is that of the 20-year-old Maharani who embarked on the *Allanshaw* for colonial Guyana in 1885 and who was allegedly raped and died before the ship arrived in the Caribbean. Maharani, given emigrant number 353, whose next of kin was stated as her father 'Pargas', was one of 660 other contract labourers who boarded the ship in the early morning hours of 24 July 1885. Sixteen others died on this journey of three and a half months to the southern Caribbean. Seven men, two women and one infant died from cerebro-spinal fever which reached almost epidemic proportions in the early part of the voyage; one man committed suicide by jumping overboard; one child died from being 'overlain by the mother', two died from pneumonia; one died from 'pernicious anaemia' and one from enteritis.

As far as can be ascertained from the documents, 11 weeks out of India, specifically on the morning of 24 September 1885, Maharani was found lying on the deck suffering from fever and complaining of a pain in her arm. The ship's surgeon at first simply medicated her and sent her back to her quarters. Her condition, however, worsened overnight and the next day she was admitted to the ship's hospital for further examination and treatment. A few days later, on 27 September, at around 10.30 am, she died. Shortly afterwards, two women, Moorti and Mohadaya, confided in the surgeon that Maharani's death was probably associated with her rape by one or more of the sailors. This they based on information gleaned from Maharani before she died. Dr Hardwicke not only performed a post-mortem examination on the body, but also conducted an on-board investigation in order to ascertain the cause of death and the veracity of the rumours of rape. He concluded that rape was possible, though the medical and non-medical evidence appeared inconclusive. He reported the alleged perpetrator, Ipson, to the colonial officials in St Helena, the revictualling point for the ship; but again, no action was taken on the basis that there was insufficient proof of 'criminal assault'.

Nevertheless, on the arrival of the ship in colonial Guyana, the governor ordered a full-scale investigation into the matter, particularly in light of the failure of the police case against Ipson to hold. Maharani's death thus gave rise to a nine-day investigation involving some 22 witnesses, including some of the emigrants. These testimonies illuminate the systemic violence that was a part of colonialism and indentureship and which later played out on colonial plantations, and remind us of what has been left out of the traditional discourses of sex, gender, race and power in the study of Caribbean history.

Still, despite the allegations of rape and the elaborate investigation into the journey of the *Allanshaw* and the circumstances of Maharani's death, no one was ever charged specifically with her death or convicted of rape. The official cause of death was said to have been trauma and shock to the nervous system; and even though the Surgeon-Superintendent of the ship, Dr Hardwicke, conceded that rape could have triggered these physical effects, the Commissioners ruled that the evidence was thin. Ipson, of course, denied the charges levelled against him; and even though he was not a favourite of the ship's Captain or the Surgeon-Superintendent, and was even initially arrested by the police in Guyana, he escaped prosecution for the offence.[73]

Despite the negative outcome of the case, it revealed two interesting trends. First, unlike during the period of slavery, freedom had created the conditions under which litigation was contemplated for cases of suspected rape, even though, much as today, few women secured victories. Second, by the late nineteenth century, the ideological terrain upon which indentured labour migration was constructed was firmly in place; and representations of not only gender, but also of racial inequality, had already found roots in the colonial setting both in India and the Caribbean.

An important issue to note in Maharani's case is that the racialised ideological justification for sexploitation, that is that subaltern women were 'naturally promiscuous' and thus 'could not be raped', had not undergone fundamental changes in the post-slavery period. It is well known that under slavery, Black women were characterised by White society as 'natural' prostitutes and enslavers had no qualms about raping their 'property'. While after 1838, as opposed to under slavery, litigation was now contemplated in cases of alleged rape, clearly then, as now, rape was a hard case to prove within the context of the prevailing patriarchal and gender ideology. Despite the evidence of *Allanshaw* crew members William Lee and James Grant that they had heard some sort of a struggle or 'scuffle' on the night of Maharani's ordeal, the Commissioners ruled, on the evidence of the Surgeon-Superintendent, that that there was no evidence of a scuffle or that anybody had held Maharani to enable the defendant(s) to commit such an assault; that 'even the appearance of the woman after death repudiated the idea that she had been criminally assaulted by any man'. They preferred to believe that if she had been taken to the forecastle, the scene of the crime, she had been carried there without 'struggling or attempting to cry out', and that while there, Ipson and others of the crew 'had connection with her, if not with full at least with forced consent on her part, the latter being more probable from the previous modest and retiring character of the woman'. They even found something in the medical evidence to further their notion that what happened to Maharani was consensual. The medical evidence, they claimed, 'leads to the inference that the cause of death was inflammatory action in or near the womb, which might have been caused by sexual excess or excitement'. Similar views had been expressed in the case involving Dr Prince of the *Ravenscraig* and the sailors on the *Canning*. The ruling on the behaviour of the sailors towards Indian women on the *Canning* was that, at least in one case, prostitution was involved. Even if this were true, that sailors were not supposed to be encouraging prostitution on board emigrant ship seems to have been overlooked.[74]

The only high-ranking official who supported the charge of rape was Dr Robert Grieves, who, in a separate report, declared that he could not go along with the conclusions of his colleagues on the Commission which they had presented to the governor. He stated that he found the whole circumstances surrounding the death of Maharani extremely painful and that he believed that 'the present enquiry, held at considerable length and with all obtainable thoroughness, [with some of the witnesses even being reluctant to come forward] conclusively proves that there were occurrences on board the *Allanshaw* on this voyage, disgraceful in their character and serious in their consequences'.[75] The responsibility for these incidents, he argued, must rest somewhere, especially as everyone from the Captain and the Surgeon-Superintendent downward testified that it was by no means a satisfactory voyage and that several incidents of misconduct had occurred. In his considered view, 'it is evident that in respect of the relationship between the men and women on board, there was a considerable amount of feeling, and that there were rumours on the ship of undue intimacy between some of the Officers and the "Coolie women".[76]

There was, therefore, no doubt in Dr Grieves's mind that 'her death was caused by inflammatory action in or near the womb and that this inflammation was attributable to sexual excess committed by several men, [and not "sexual excitement" as in the Commissioners' summary report]. His personal conclusion was uncompromising: the death of Maharani was due to her being sexually abused by a number of the crew'.[77]

Still, the outcome was not surprising. Only infrequently were those accused of committing offences (sexual or otherwise) on emigrant ships convicted; and even then, rank-and-file crew were more likely than the higher officers to be the ones fined, censured or imprisoned. Yet, the correspondence between the emigration agents and the CLEC for the period 1854–60 are replete with actual cases of misconduct on the part of the Surgeons-Superintendent, showing that it was not only the sailors who tended to molest emigrant women.

The Surgeon-Superintendent of the *Allanshaw,* Hardwicke, was himself accused of misconduct the year after Maharani's death. Predictably, he was not found guilty. In 1886, Aladin, a male emigrant on the ship *Foyle* on which Hardwicke was again the Surgeon-Superintendent, complained to the agent general of immigration on arrival in Guyana that Hardwicke had taken 'indecent liberties' with his wife, Asserum.[78] Apparently Aladin had formed an alliance with Asserum at the depôt in Calcutta where she had been 'given' to him by her mother. They proceeded to register this 'marriage' before the magistrate as required and to live as a couple on the voyage. Predictably, after a more detailed enquiry, the Agent General of Immigration claimed that Aladin could not prove that any sexual intercourse had taken place. For 'all that Aladin could testify to was that on one occasion he saw Dr Hardwicke sitting in the Chart Room with Asserum on his lap and with his hands on her breasts'. Chamela corroborated this, though she added that 'I never saw him doing anything except holding her breasts outside her clothes'. Asserum herself denied that Hardwicke had molested her. She further stated that Aladin had not treated her well on the voyage and that she had never really slept with him and had no wish to live with him as his wife in Guyana or to be located with him on the same estate. Dr Harwicke, in his defence, claimed, and the agent general of immigration seemed to believe him, that he was only treating Asserum the way he treated all children. The fact that she was someone's wife, although only 15, did not seem to deter him.[79] The result of the enquiry was that Hardwicke was not penalised in any way, although the agent general of immigration did concede that the manner in which he treated Asserum was 'objectionable' and he should be warned not to behave in this way with a girl that age.

Conclusion

The objective of this chapter has not been to marginalize the experiences of indentured emigrants on what has been termed 'The Other Middle Passage', because that 'Passage' might not be a perfect match when compared with the 'First Middle Passage'. The rationale of the chapter is that the debate over how best to categorise the indentureship system has not sufficiently incorporated data on the recruitment and shipment of the emigrating Indians, both supporters of, and opponents to, the 'neo-slavery' thesis basing their arguments on the indentureship experience. The chapter has revisited the voyages from India and incorporated new data that must form part of the debate over slavery and indentureship. The comparative assessment of the two Middle Passages attempted might not be as systematic as it should be; but it should still be clear from this partial analysis that Eltis' view of all non-slave trade voyages might not be far off the mark. At the same time, there must be some sympathy for the neo-slavery perspective, given the fact that while vigorous attempts were made in the post-slavery period to institute a system of labour recruitment and migration that would be a vast improvement over the transatlantic trade in enslaved Africans, such attempts were not entirely successful. The passage from India, as Maharani's case has illustrated, was certainly no cruise of voluntary passengers.

Notes

1.   R. Ramdin, *The Other Middle Passage: Journal of a Voyage from Calcutta to Trinidad, 1858* (London: Hansib, 1994).
2.   J. Beaumont, *The New Slavery: an Account of the Indian and Chinese Immigrants in British Guiana* (London, 1871).
3.   Beaumont, *The New Slavery*, p. 14.
4.   H. Tinker, *A New System of Slavery: the Export of Indian Labour Overseas* (Oxford: Oxford University Press, 1974).
5.   See, for example, J. McDonald and R. Shlomowitz, 'Mortality on Chinese and Indian Voyages to the West Indies and South America, 1847–1874', *Social and Economic Studies*, 41:2 (1992).
6.   See J.E. Cliffe's evidence before the Select Committee of the House of Commons, London, in *An Exposition of the African Slave Trade, from the year*

1840, to 1850, inclusive. Prepared from the official documents and published by the direction of the Representatives of the Religious Society of Friends (Philadelphia, 1851); M. Cowley, ed, *Adventures of an African Slaver: being a true account of the life of Capt. Canot, trader in gold, ivory and slaves on the coast of Guinea: his own story as told in the year 1854 to Brantz Mayer* (Cornwall Press, USA: Albert & Charles Boni, Bonibooks, 1935); A. Falconbridge, *An Account of the Slave Trade on the Coast of Africa* (London, 1788).

7.   D. Eltis, *The Rise of African Slavery in the Americas* (Cambridge: Cambridge University Press, 2000), p. 117.

8.   British Parliamentary Papers (PP) 1871, XX (C393), *Report* of the British Guiana Immigration Commission, 1870–1.

9.   For an elaboration of the thesis of 'natal alienation' as a characteristic of enslaved Africans, see O. Patterson, *Slavery and Social Death: A Comparative Study* (Cambridge, MA: Harvard University Press, 1982).

10.   P. Emmer, 'The Great Escape: the Migration of Female Indentured Servants from British India into Suriname', in D. Richardson, ed, *Abolition and its Aftermath* (London: Frank Cass, 1985), pp. 245–66.

11.   CO 571/3, Minute Paper 54685, 'Notes on the Methods of Recruiting Emigrants in the Madras Presidency', 6 November 1915.

12.   J. Beall, 'Women under Indenture in Colonial Natal', in S. Bhana, ed., *Essays on Indentured Indians in Natal* (Leeds: Peepal Tree Press, 1991), pp. 89–115; R. Reddock, 'Indian Women and Indentureship in Trinidad and Tobago: Freedom Denied', in H. Beckles and V.A. Shepherd, eds., *Caribbean Freedom* (Kingston: Ian Randle, 1993), pp. 225–37; J. Poynting, 'East Indian Women in the Caribbean: Experience and Voice', in D. Dabydeen and B. Samaroo eds., *India in the Caribbean* (London: Centre for Caribbean Studies, University of Warwick, Hansib, 1987), pp. 231–63.

13.   See, for example, Beckles, *Centering Woman: Gender Discourses in Caribbean Slave Society* (Kingston: Ian Randle, 1999); B. Bush, *Slave Women in Caribbean Society, 1650–1838* (London: James Currey, 1990); D. Hall, *In Miserable Slavery: Thomas Thistlewood in Jamaica, 1750–86* (London: Macmillan, 1989).

14.   K.O. Dike, *Trade and Politics in the Niger Delta, 1830-1835: an Introduction to the Economic and Political History of Nigeria* (Oxford: Oxford University Press, 1956), p. 7.

15.   D. Eltis, 'The Volume and Structure of the Transatlantic Slave Trade: A Reassessment', paper presented at the Conference on Enslaving Connections: Africa and Brazil during the era of the Slave Trade, York University, Toronto, Canada, 12–15 October 2000, p. 4, and Eltis, et al., The Transatlantic Slave Trade: a database on CD-ROM (New York: Cambridge, 1999).

16.   W. Look Lai, *Indentured Labor, Caribbean Sugar* (Baltimore, MD: The Johns Hopkins University Press, 1993).

17. For various perspectives on the numbers of Africans who were captured, shipped to the Americas and died before arrival in the Americas, see P.D. Curtin, *The Atlantic Slave Trade: a Census* (Madison: University of Wisconsin Press, 1969); P. Lovejoy, 'The Volume of the Atlantic Slave Trade: a Synthesis', *Journal of African History*, 23 (1982), pp. 473–501; J. Inikori and S. Engerman, 'Introduction: Gainers and Losers in the Atlantic Slave Trade', in J. Inikori and S. Engerman, eds., *The Atlantic Slave Trade: Effects on Economics, Societies and Peoples in Africa, the Americas and Europe* (Durham, NC: Duke Universty Press, 1992), pp. 1–21; Inikori, *The Chaining of a Continent* (Mona: *Institute of Social and Economic Research Publications*, 1992); Eltis, *The Rise of African Slavery* 'Volume and Structure', and Beckles and Shepherd, *Slave Voyages* (Paris: UNESCO, 1999).

18. Eltis, 'Volume and Structure', Table 3, p. 36.

19. Eltis, *Rise of African Slavery*, pp. 85–113; Eltis 'Volume and Structure', and Beckles and Shepherd, *Slave Voyages*, pp. 42–4.

20. CO 386, Colonial Land and Emigration Committee (CLEC), Letter Books, 1857–1866.

21. Ibid., Vol. 99.

22. R. Hoefte, *In Place of Slavery* (Gainsville, FL: University of Florida Press, 1998), p. 31.

23. CO 386/97, CLEC Correspondence, 1869–1874.

24. Falconbridge, *Account of the Slave Trade*, p. 13.

25. CO 386/93, S. Walcott of the CLEC to R.G.N. Herbert of the Colonial Office, 14 October 1871.

26. Tinker, *A New System of Slavery*, p. 137.

27. CO 386/95, T.W.C. Murdoch of the CLEC to Frederick Rogers of the Colonial Office, 26 February 1863.

28. *Adventures of an African Slaver*, p. 107.

29. H.S. Klein, *The Middle Passage* (Princeton, NJ: Princeton University Press, 1978), pp. 143–5.

30. Ibid.

31. Ibid.

32. Ibid.

33. Eltis, *Rise of African Slavery*, pp. 117–18.

34. Tinker, *A New System of Slavery*, p. 146.

35. Klein, *The Middle Passage*, pp. 143–5.

36. B. Mangru, *Benevolent Neutrality* (London: Hansib, 1987), p. 123.

37. Falconbridge, *An Account of the Slave Trade*, p. 28.

38. Evidence given before the Police Magistrate, colonial Guyana, 13 November 1885. Enc.7 in Des. 56.

39. CO 386/186, Agent General of Immigration's (AGI) *Report*, 3 January 1893, Enc. in British Guiana Despatch 9, Viscount Gormanston to the Marquis of Ripon, 10 January 1893.
40. CO 386/91, CLEC Letter Book, Murdoch to Rogers, 14 April 1858.
41. Eltis, *Rise of African Slavery*, p. 66.
42. Falconbridge, *An Account of the Slave Trade*, p. 20.
43. Ibid.
44. *Adventures of an African Slaver*, pp. 75–6.
45. *An Exposition of the African Trade*, pp.150–2.
46. Ibid.
47. Enc. 3 in Des. 56, Extracts from the Official Logbook of the Ship *Allanshaw*, Friday 24 July 1885.
48. Falconbridge, *An Account of the Slave Trade*.
49. M. Seenarine, 'Indentured Indian Women in Colonial Guyana: Recruitment, Migration, Labor and Caste', in M. Gosine and D. Narine. eds., *Sojourners to Settlers: Indian Migrants in the Caribbean and the Americas* (New York: Windsor Press, 1999), p.56.
50. An Exposition of the African Trade, p. 152.
51. Curtin, *Atlantic Slave Trade*, pp. 275–86.
52. Eltis, *Rise of African Slavery*, p. 185.
53. Ibid., p. 159.
54. CO 386/95, Murdoch to Elliot, CLEC Correspondence, 31 October 1863.
55. CO 386/135,Walcott to Hunt Marriot, CLEC, 26 February 1863.
56. CO 384/169, *Report* of the AGI, 5 January 1888, Enc. in British Guiana Des. 15, Governor of British Guiana to Secretary of State Holland, 16 January 1888.
57. CO 384/169, AGI's Report, 26 November 1888. Enc. in British Guiana Des. 398, Gov. Bruce to Secretary of State Knutsford, 7 December 1888.
58. CO 384/60, Enc. 7 in Des. 56, Logbooks of Dr Hardwicke and Capt. Wilson.
59. Tinker, *A New System of Slavery*, p. 157.
60. Captain's Logbook, Enc. 7, Des. 56.
61. Protector of Immigrants' *Report*, Jamaica, 18 June 1891, Enc. in Des. 196, [?] Black, Administering the Government, to Knutsford, 22 June 1891.
62. CO 384/186, AGI's *Report*, 10 February 1893, Enc. in British Guiana Des. 35, Gormanston to Ripon, 21 February 1893.
63. Look Lai, *Indentured Labor, Caribbean Sugar*; K.O. Laurence, *A Question of Labour* (Kingston: Ian Randle, 1994).
64. CO 386/95-105, Correspondence/Letter Books, CLEC.
65. CO 386/97, Murdoch to R.H. McCade, CLEC, 8 January 1873.
66. CO 384/144, Enc. in Des. 52, Irving to Derby, 21 February 1883.

67. CO 386/135, Vol. 2, Walcott of the CLEC to A. McGregor of the CO, 26 Febuaryy 1861.
68. Ibid.
69. CO 386/93, Murdoch to Herbert, CLEC, 10 December 1874.
70. CO 384/144, British Guiana Des. 57, Irving to Derby, 20 February 1883.
71. CO 384/155, Enc. in British Guiana Des. 40, Irving to Derby, 19 February 1885.
72. CO 384/155, Protector of Immigrants' *Report*, 1885.
73. This case is more fully explored in my forthcoming book, *Maharani's Misery: Narratives of a Passage from India*.
74. CO 386/95, Murdoch and Rogers to Herman Merivale, 24 March 1860.
75. Report of Dr Robert Grieves, 13 January 1886.
76. Ibid.
77. Ibid.
78. CO 384/161, Report of the AGI to Governor Irving, 11 November 1886, Enc. in Des. 303, Irving to Stanhope, 11 November 1886.
79. Interestingly enough, Asserum's age was misrepresented on the ship's list as 18; and this would have been known to the Surgeon-Superintendent.

CHAPTER

17

Ethnicity and Economic Behaviour in Nineteenth-century Guyana

BRIAN L. MOORE

One of the interesting features of composite multiracial colonial societies has been the apparently close correlation between economic activity and ethnicity. There was a general tendency for economic or occupational specialisation along ethnic lines in such societies. Each ethnic group seemed to act as a corporate entity and soon found itself (whether by design or otherwise) occupying a specific niche in the economy where it sooner or later established a position of 'dominance'. Although this was accompanied by some measure of inter-group competition, there was also a high degree of economic interdependence among these groups. By and large these societies were dominated by one or two economic institutions (plantations, mines or settler farms), which were owned and controlled by one of the ethnic groups, usually the ruling minority. This pattern of economic organisation, however, created the popular perception that economic behaviour was intrinsically linked to ethnicity, that each ethnic group had inherent racial and cultural attributes which qualified it for certain kinds of occupations and economic roles. This chapter will attempt to determine the validity of this perception, using Guyana in the period after slavery as a case in point.

Arising out of this perception that economic behaviour is linked to race and culture is the tendency to reduce everything to ethnic stereotypes. These abound in all multiracial societies, both in the Caribbean and elsewhere. Nineteenth-century Guyana was a classic example. Starting with two primary ethnic groups (White/European and Black/African Creole) and an intermediary Coloured or mixed category at emancipation in 1838, large-scale government-sponsored immigration to meet the labour demands of the plantations led to the introduction of new ethnic groups mainly from Africa, Madeira, India and China. By far the largest of these new immigrants were Indians who at the end of the nineteenth century constituted about 40 per cent of the total population. With the exception of the Madeirans (hereafter called Portuguese), all of these immigrants were compelled to work under contract on the sugar plantations for a term of years (between three and five) before they could embark on any other form of economic activity. Under this contract system, therefore, the plantations cast a long shadow of dominance over the colonial economy by commandeering the services of the workers of all ethnic groups, and that dominance persisted well into the twentieth century.

In this multiracial environment, ethnic stereotyping was commonplace. These were related not only to attributed social and cultural characteristics and attitudes, but also to economic behaviour and roles. Whites (especially Anglo-Saxons) were reputedly endowed with the work ethic and were inherently intelligent, among other things, which made them the natural creators and leaders of industry; their Latin counterparts (Portuguese) were thrifty and hardworking, with shrewd business acumen. Blacks and coloureds (hereafter also called Creoles) by contrast were indolent and improvident, loved to party and consequently were unsuited to independent economic enterprise; with close supervision, however, they could make good unskilled workers. Indians were penurious, seeking to save every penny in order to accumulate capital to remit to India or to buy land. Chinese were industrious and smart with a special talent for business.

Such stereotypes reflect subjective, and often racist, perceptions of different ethnic groups in society and their economic activities, attitudes and values.[1] But the extent to which they were ingrained in the popular mind is clearly revealed in the following conversation in a Portuguese shop:

> *Black man:* 'Wha' make awe Blackman no keep shop? Because awe no able foo make money like them Portogee fella'.
>
> *Portuguese shopman:* 'I'll tell you why: when Portuguese makes nine dollars he spends six and puts by three; but when Blackman makes nine he spends eighteen'.[2]

In reality, economic behaviour in Guyana after emancipation was largely influenced by, first, the country's colonial status; second, the economic primacy of the plantation system; and third, by the cultural values and institutions of the several ethnic groups which made up the society. The political and economic systems effectively established the framework and the parameters within which the ethnic groups had to function. In the colonial context, White political hegemony was used to ensure that the plantation system remained dominant in the economy, and laws were passed to circumscribe economic opportunities outside of that system. This in effect imposed finite limits on the economic activities of the subordinate ethnic groups. Within the parameters set up by the power structure, however, economic behaviour was to some extent influenced by cultural difference. This determined how each subordinate ethnic group, and individuals within it, reacted to similar circumstances of restricted economic opportunity.

After the abolition of slavery in 1834, the dominance of the plantation system was supported by the Colonial State as the only viable means of ensuring long-term economic prosperity for all concerned, and also for the preservation of 'civilisation' in the colony. After a decade and a half under threat for its very survival, the plantation system reasserted its dominance (by the late 1850s) largely through immigration. With the injection of new capital and the use of modern steam equipment, production levels rose spectacularly well into the twentieth century (notwithstanding periodic recessions); and the sugar industry remained the backbone of the Guyana economy, employing the largest amount of labour.[3]

More importantly, it was capitalised and controlled entirely by the White ethnic minority either on their own account or, increasingly as the nineteenth century wore on, on behalf of metropolitan principals or companies. Through its absolute control of the State, this minority also controlled the allocation of jobs, licences, contracts and investments in the public sector, which was used to bolster continued White economic dominance. This all-pervasive dominance[4] reinforced the stereotypical perception that Whites were inherently gifted as rulers and leaders of industrial and commercial enterprise.

One important concomitant of this lopsided development was that the state sought to restrict the growth of alternative economic activity. Laws were passed to push the ex-slaves back into estate employment (for example, the Masters' and Servants' Ordinance), to restrict their acquisition of land, and to prevent their unauthorised movement into the hinterland. High indirect taxes or duties were imposed on articles of common consumption to force them to work for wages;[5] and the retail trade was soon closed to them (see below). Attempts by the ex-slaves to establish themselves as small farmers were severely hampered by the refusal of the State to assume the cost of draining their lands (these consequently suffered from regular floods);[6] as well as by the absence of a large market (either overseas or locally) for their produce (mainly ground provisions, plantains and fruit). Altogether this combination of adverse factors severely restricted the economic opportunities of the ex-slaves and their descendants and reduced them to chronic poverty off the plantations or dependence thereon.[7]

There was some alleviation for a small number of Creoles largely through the development of the gold and balata industries towards the end of the nineteenth century which provided alternative and fairly lucrative employment. But capitalised and run mainly by the dominant (British) Whites under state-issued licences (and to a lesser extent by Portuguese and Chinese investors), even these new economic sectors maintained the pattern of Black economic dependence on wage labour.[8] Moreover, their seeming inability to accumulate enough capital to make successful investments in new and expanding areas of the colonial economy reinforced the prevailing stereotypical impression that Blacks lacked drive and enterprise, were dissolute and improvident.

By the 1850s, the retail trade was more or less the preserve of the Portuguese. In the years immediately after emancipation, this was one major avenue which offered the prospect of prosperity relatively independent of the plantation system. But in order to restrict the economic options of the ex-slaves and to retain their labour for the plantations, every effort was made to prevent them from entering that economic sphere. Through a system of licences governing all aspects of retailing (groceries, cloths, liquors, drugs, butcheries, huckstering, etc), and credit practices which overtly discriminated against the ex-slaves, the Portuguese immigrants were encouraged and assisted by the dominant (British) Whites to take control of the retail trade. To facilitate this further, the Portuguese were from 1857 even exempted from the obligations to serve their indentures on the plantations despite being brought to the colony at public expense.[9]

Consequently, they were able to move unimpeded into the retail trade, and rapidly established their dominance over it. Within a decade of the emancipation, the Portuguese immigrants had taken control of this commerce and were already beginning to threaten the British wholesale merchants themselves. This lucrative service sector served as a vital base for the massive accumulation of capital by the Portuguese,[10] and enabled them to expand into other economic areas (import-export trade, forestry and balata gathering, gold mining, pawnbroking, banking and insurance, transportation, etc). Capital from these diverse enterprises was also used to purchase considerable amounts of landed property both in towns and country. But not all Portuguese were successful in business, and several joined the ranks of rural small farmers cultivating ground provisions, plantains, garden vegetables and fruit for the local market.[11] Nevertheless, by the later nineteenth century commercial business in Guyana became automatically associated with the Portuguese in the popular perception.

As regards the Indian immigrants, until the 1920s when the system of indenture terminated, many of these were literally tied to the plantations; and given the limits imposed on alternative economic enterprise, it is not surprising that the Indians remained the core of the labour force of the sugar plantations. However, from the 1870s onwards, the Colonial Government began to realise that one method of keeping the Indian immigrants in the colony and thus accessible to the plantations was by offering them grants of land in lieu of the contractual obligation to pay their return passage to India after ten years' service on the estates. This opened a window of opportunity previously closed to them. Indians thus began to acquire land, and like their Black counterparts just after slavery, sought to become independent small farmers.[12]

They did, however, enjoy two advantages not available to the Blacks: first, their principal crop, rice, could be grown locally on the ill-drained coastal lands of Guyana; second, rice enjoyed a market both locally and overseas which the ground provisions of the Black farmers did not.[13] This offered an opportunity to accumulate capital outside the framework of the plantations, mining or commerce, and provided a firm base from which the Indian population could later expand their activity into other areas of the economy. Capital accumulation through agricultural enterprise, however, was slow and, as we shall see below, required a disciplined pattern of saving which earned the Indians the stereotyped image of being miserly.

The Chinese, likewise, were restricted by the indentured system; but given their willingness to convert to Christianity, they were assisted by the government and the Anglican Church to acquire land after the termination of their indentures. Thus began their move during the 1860s into small farming (livestock rearing, rice cultivation and market gardening), wood cutting and charcoal manufacture. These became the bases for capital accumulation by the Chinese which they used to launch themselves into business as retail traders. By the turn of the twentieth century, the Chinese were well on their way to becoming very successful small businessmen in direct competition with the longer-established Portuguese, and they began to invest in gold mining as well.[14] This earned them credit in the popular perception as being naturally endowed with shrewd business acumen.

Thus without oversimplifying, it is reasonable to assert that the economy of nineteenth-century Guyana exhibited a strong tendency towards occupational specialisation along ethnic lines. The dominant (British) Whites owned and operated the plantations (the primary economic institution) and controlled the import-export trade and the public sector; the Portuguese dominated the internal retail trade though they later had to share space with the Chinese; the Blacks and Coloureds were peasant farmers and dependent labourers; and the Indian immigrants were estate wage labourers and later on small farmers as well.[15] This pattern persisted well into the twentieth century. There were of course some exceptions: for instance, some Portuguese engaged in small farming, a few Blacks and Coloureds in commerce, the professions and the public service; and some Indians in commerce. But the bigger picture presented a close correlation between economic behaviour and ethnicity.

Given the broad ethnic lines along which economic activity was structured, it would be tempting to assert that culture played a major role in determining this pattern. While from widely differing great traditions, both the Portuguese and Chinese came from cultures in which buying and selling of goods and services were commonplace. Although the Chinese who migrated overseas represented a mixture of 'peasants, working people and urban déclassé elements', Walton Look Lai estimates that about 96 per cent who came to the Americas originated from the province of Kwangtung, particularly from and around the bustling urban centres of Canton, Macao and Hong Kong.[16] As such commercial transactions were an integral part of their everyday lives, M. Freedman has asserted that familiarity with the handling of money, borrowing loans, repaying with interest and so on equipped Chinese migrants with the skills to enter business wherever in their diaspora such opportunities existed.[17]

Likewise, specifically with respect to Guyana, K.O. Laurence has asserted that:

Possibly the Portuguese were on the whole rather better educated, and in particular more familiar with figures and arithmetic, than the negroes. Certainly their general cultural background, including as it did a lifelong experience of a free as opposed to a slave society, was likely to have inculcated a greater familiarity with the attitudes needed for independent success in business than the emancipated slaves were likely to have. The Portuguese were also likely to be better acquainted with general business methods and more familiar with some of the imported goods which the new shopkeepers needed to handle, while the native negroes were more familiar with locally produced goods. These factors would have given the Portuguese a substantial advantage.[18]

Perhaps, but is this cultural familiarity with commerce sufficient to explain why first the Portuguese and later on the Chinese too were able to dominate the retail trade? Some slaves themselves had acquired rudimentary commercial skills, particularly those who engaged in the Sunday markets and those who lived in the urban centres; and indeed several Blacks and Coloureds did enter the retail trade after emancipation with varying degrees of success. Richard Haynes, for instance, was Coloured and earned his wealth as a merchant; he became mayor of Georgetown during the 1840s.[19] In 1870, Creoles still held 15 per cent of retail shop licences[20] although most of these were probably just 'cake shops' which, as the name implies, sold mainly cakes, sweets, ginger beer, 'mauby',[21] and a few other odds and ends. Nevertheless, the point is that the skills and inclination for commerce existed among the Creoles; yet very few were able to compete effectively with the new immigrants. Surely, therefore, factors other than cultural attributes are required to explain this.

Even Laurence recognises 'that the European community would have preferred to see Portuguese rather than Negroes enhancing their status through retail trade, because of their racial affinity'.[22] So whatever their cultural orientation, it could only have achieved positive results where favourable socioeconomic conditions existed. Race and colour clearly played a vital role in this; but it is only one part of the picture. In Guyana it was also the already alluded to determination of the colonial authorities to prevent the ex-slaves from leaving plantation labour for economic reasons that, to large extent, created the opportunity for the Portuguese and Chinese to enter and dominate the retail trade. This was effected mainly through preferential credit and the licensing system which both operated in favour of these immigrant groups.[23] However, in Bermuda, although the racial factor was present, the perceived economic imperative did not exist. So Portuguese immigrants there did not find commerce nearly as rewarding as in Guyana, and they remained mainly small farmers until relatively recently.[24] Racial prejudice and economic interest thus went hand in hand in Guyana; but it was the race and colour factor more than anything else which determined why it was the Portuguese and Chinese in particular who were encouraged and assisted by the British Whites to take control of the lucrative retail trade. Cultural attributes, therefore, were not sufficient to account for the commercial success of these two ethnic groups.

The Indians' relative success at estate wage labour and small farming was in part due to their economic and cultural background. It is estimated that over 60 per cent of Indian immigrants were from agricultural and low castes in India.[25] When given the opportunity to acquire their own lands, they reverted to occupations with which they were familiar, most notably the cultivation of rice and garden vegetables, and livestock rearing. But their access to land for these purposes was determined mainly by the need of the planters and government to retain their services, at least part-time, on the estates. Again, therefore, cultural factors were not sufficient on their own to explain the continuous involvement of the Indians in agriculture.

Culture, therefore, played only a small part in determining the economic activities of the different ethnic groups in Guyana. It was the political and plantation-dominated economic environment which primarily determined what place each group would occupy in the economy. In a hypothetically open economy free of sociopolitical interference and constraints, individual members of each ethnic group would most likely have engaged in different occupations as the market determined without regard to their ethnicity. In post-emancipation Guyana, however, the state played an important role, directly and indirectly, in the allocation of economic space and opportunity along ethnic lines. The very fact that power was monopolised by an ethnic minority in itself imposed certain imperatives which demanded that economic life in the colony should be aligned to ethnicity. It was an integral feature of the divide-and-rule policy pursued by the British.[26]

Having said that, however, it is important to recognise that culture did play a supporting role in influencing how each ethnic group (and individual members thereof) responded in order to function within their 'prescribed' space. This was in some measure also related to their perception of their length of residence in the colony. Of all the ethnic groups in the plantation society, only the Creoles had a sense of Guyana as their permanent home. This meant that their primary objective was to put down tangible roots in the soil, and acquire a real stake in the economy – in the form of land. This did not preclude capital accumulation with a view to becoming wealthy, but that seemed to have assumed secondary importance to the ex-slaves. All other groups, including the dominant (British) Whites, perceived their presence in Guyana as a temporary sojourn and made their economic decisions in that light. Their primary emphasis, therefore, was on accumulating as much capital as possible in the shortest time before returning to their respective homelands.[27]

These differing perceptions had a profound impact on the economic behaviour of members of the several ethnic groups. Land, for instance, was invested with rather more than mere economic significance by the Creoles. Raymond Smith (1964) noted that Blacks were especially reluctant to part with freehold rights in land even though it might be idle and they had to pay rates on it. Land to them provided independence and security. It was therefore handed from generation to generation whether or not it was in productive use. By the same token the village where the family land was located had special significance to individual Blacks. It was the place where one's 'navel string was buried'; and it was home no matter how long an individual had not been resident there.[28]

At the same time, however, there was a strong tendency within the Black community to seek individual ownership of plots of land whether or not this was backed by legal title. The communal spirit that had led to the purchase of whole plantations by combinations of ex-slaves immediately after emancipation disappeared soon thereafter as they sought to partition these lands. In the interest of fairness to all the shareholders, these estates were subdivided in a manner which gave each party small portions of land in different sections.[29] Alan Adamson notes that the result was small uneconomic plots which were further subdivided later on through inheritance. Village lands soon became no more than mini-subsistence plots producing very little surplus for the market. This, added to poor drainage and limited markets, reduced Black villagers to chronic poverty.[30]

Smith further observes that even within a single family, individual members tended to claim separate rights to provision and grazing lands and thus the family did not constitute a cooperative economic unit. No single family head, whether male or female, controlled the economic activities of the unit's members.[31] There is some evidence of this for the post-emancipation period.

Contemporary elite observers claimed that once children were big enough to work and earn money, they thought only of themselves and failed to contribute to the support of the household.[32]

Because of the impoverishment of village lands, Creole household incomes and capital accumulation seemed to be low.[33] This was to some extent reflected in their small bank deposits during the nineteenth century, which were consistently the lowest among all ethnic groups in the colony.[34] At the same time, however, it must be pointed out that this was not the only method by which Creoles saved. Money was also deposited in friendly and burial societies. In addition, they saved in community by 'throwing box'. By this system several persons agreed to subscribe money to a fund (the 'box'). Depending on their contribution, they were entitled to a given number of shares. The 'box' was kept by one of the subscribers. Each week participants 'threw up' a few shillings per share, and each contributor drew in turn weekly in an order that was previously determined by lottery. The 'box' was maintained until each participant received his/her accumulated share contributions, and the box-keeper was usually given a small commission by each drawing party. 'Box' allowed the participants to save regularly and to access a relatively larger sum of money at a given time than they would normally; but it was part of the informal economy for which there were no formal records.[35]

The pattern of fragmented land distribution, far from promoting an environment that favoured the generation of individual wealth, fostered instead a sense of shared poverty notwithstanding the development of a strong ethic of individualism in response to the dominant societal ethos. This was vividly demonstrated in the very layout and physical condition of the Black villages. Compare these descriptions:

> A negro village . . . is not a picturesque object . . . The cottages, or houses . . . stand in extreme disorder, one here and another there . . . There seems to have been no attempt at streets or lines of buildings and certainly not at regularity in building . . . There are no roads, and hardly a path to each habitat. As the ground is not drained in wet weather the whole place is half-drowned. (1860).[36]
>
> most of the negro villages present a rather drab appearance to casual observer. The houses do not vary greatly in size or appearance . . . Few houses are painted and because of the livestock that wanders freely about there are few gardens around the houses. The uniformly dismal appearance reflects the underlying sense of equality of the villagers; an equality of poverty and low status ... Most house yards are open and there is a constant bustle on the road which runs through the village. (1964).[37]

As Smith notes, this shared poverty meant that there was very little status differentiation based on material wealth. Social mobility among Blacks and Coloureds was linked more to their acquisition of White culture than material wealth.[38] By the end of slavery, most ex-slaves were already creolised or assimilated to accept the notion of the superiority of British culture, and they placed a premium on the attainment of those attributes. Greater recognition was therefore given to those who were acculturated, and the socially mobile educated Blacks and Coloureds sought to gravitate away from the land into higher status White-collar jobs even if low-paying. They fully absorbed the social philosophy of the colonial elites that manual work of any kind, whether in agriculture, commerce, forestry or mining, was socially demeaning. Thus although the vast majority had no option (because of poor education and social discrimination) but to engage in manual jobs, their ambition was to become clerks in stores and offices, messengers, etc. The more educated would seek to become teachers, nurses, clergymen and low-level civil servants. The ideal, achieved only by very few, was to become lawyers and doctors.[39]

For the other ethnic groups, Guyana was not home and this materially influenced their economic behaviour and attitudes. Since their primary orientation was to accumulate capital rapidly, the acquisition of land was important only as a means to that end. Land for them was largely an economic resource to be bought and sold as their economic interests demanded. In so far as land had any greater significance, it was regarded as an asset to underscore their status either within the colonial society at large, or within their ethnic grouping. But land was not equally accessible by each group. Access was directly related to the possession of political and economic power. This placed the dominant (British) Whites at a distinct advantage: hence, the largest estates and most land were owned by them as individuals and as a group. Large landed estates, the plantations, were the basis of their social and economic dominance.

The other immigrant groups were initially denied equal access to land through the discriminatory exercise of political power by the dominant landed Whites, the planters, in collusion with the colonial government. For the immigrants, the acquisition of land was either a reward for success in accumulating material wealth by other means (the Portuguese), or the result of patronage dispensed by the planters (the Indians and Chinese). In both instances, however, land was largely an economic resource to be used both to measure and to augment their material assets. They did not invest it with the same meaning and significance that the Blacks and Coloureds did.

The immigrants thus had a radically different attitude to wealth and progress from the Creoles. Although for each of them the first objective (regardless of cultural difference) was to accumulate capital, how they went about that might have been to some extent culturally determined. Unlike the other ethnic groups, Portuguese women migrated in almost as large number as the men[40] and thus facilitated intra-ethnic cohabitation and family or household formation. The family and the Catholic Church play a major role in Latin cultures, and it is not surprising that in Guyana the household unit should have been the basis on which the Portuguese built their fortunes. Initially, though, the male started the business by packing a sack of goods on his back and peddling these from door to door. Goods were generally obtained on short-term credit from the major import merchants (British Whites), who preferred to deal with the Portuguese than with the Creoles. The essence of Portuguese business habits was the quick turnover of stock and low profits. As peddlers they had no overheads.[41]

After accumulating some capital in this way, they opened a shop and involved the entire household in the business. Unlike the Creoles, therefore, the Portuguese household constituted a cooperative economic unit under the control of the male head. Goods continued to be obtained on credit from the big merchants in the city; and the Portuguese expanded their business by serving as moneylenders, pawnbrokers and rudimentary bankers to the estate workers and peasants. Lines of credit were extended to the latter who became increasingly dependent on the shopkeeper, and that in turn enabled him to increase his profits by charging higher prices and exorbitant rates of interest on loans. These unsavoury practices earned the Portuguese as an ethnic group the opprobrium of the mass of creoles who attacked their businesses in 1848, 1856 and 1889.[42]

Some Portuguese became extremely wealthy from the retail trade, and entered the import-export trade as rivals of the English merchants. Even so, they did not as a rule consider themselves permanent residents in Guyana until the twentieth century. In keeping with their perception as aliens, the Portuguese acquisition of landed property generally came after they had accumulated capital from the retail trade. By the later nineteenth century, however, they already owned a considerable amount of land and some of the most imposing buildings in the colony;[43] but rather than an indication of an intention to settle permanently, land for them was largely an economic investment and a status symbol. Their economic behaviour continued to be centred on the household as an economic unit, with the blessings of the Catholic Church, which benefited considerably from that wealth. Social status within the Portuguese community was largely related to accumulated wealth and property.

The other entrepreneurial immigrant group was the Chinese, although like the Portuguese some were also small farmers. Unlike the Portuguese, however, the Chinese, in keeping with their migratory patterns to all parts of their diaspora, migrated to Guyana mainly as single males. The proportion of females was extremely low.[44] As has already been noted, after leaving the estates they tended either to settle in small communities pursuing agriculture, wood cutting and charcoal manufacture, or engage in shopkeeping.

Not much is known about the internal organisation of the Chinese immigrant community, but religion seems to have played a major part in their ethnic bonding in the alien society. Ironically that religion was not one of the great Chinese religions, but Christianity. Of all the immigrants who went to Guyana, the Chinese had the least chance of returning to their homeland because they were not granted government assistance for return passages as were the Indian immigrants. Whether this played a part in their mass conversion to Anglicanism (the state religion) is difficult to say, but by the 1880s virtually all the Chinese had converted. This had the effect of breaking down the primary divisions between the *Punti* and *Hakka* Chinese, and moulding a sense of ethnic solidarity. The first Chinese settlement off the estates was composed largely of Christians.[45]

But it is also very probable that the traditional clan and/or secret society may have played an important part in the reorganisation of the Chinese in Guyana as an ethnic community, and more importantly in organising their economic activities both on and off the estates. While indentured on the estates during the 1860s, the Chinese earned notoriety for organising themselves in large nocturnal armed gangs which rampaged the stores of estates and provision grounds of neighbouring villages. This behaviour displayed some of the criminal, but cooperative, characteristics of Chinese secret societies overseas.[46]

There is also evidence of cooperative activity in the establishment of some of the earliest Chinese shops; and even when individual Chinese opened their own shops in different locations there may have been a fair degree of cooperation and assistance forthcoming from others.[47] Capital for starting commercial ventures may also have come from informal community saving schemes similar to the creole 'box'. Freedman notes that in China such a system of saving, called 'money-loan associations' thrived,[48] and there is no reason why the Chinese immigrants should not have maintained the practice in their new environment. But the data are too sparse to draw any definitive conclusions.

What is most clearly a legacy of their cultural background was their willingness to work literally seven days a week. Coming as they did from a culture with few holidays, they took with them overseas the habit of working all year round, and in Guyana seldom took days off while indentured on the estates.[49] This, coupled with their familiarity with commerce, fostered success in trade overseas and not least of all in Guyana.

Although the Chinese did accumulate a fair amount of capital, they did not hoard it. They were allegedly big spenders on both consumer goods (they were reputed to have expensive tastes in food and drink), and on narcotics (opium and marijuana); and they were big gamblers as well. It was reportedly not unusual for an individual to gamble away his accumulated savings or assets in one night. The Chinese also spent lavishly on their cultural festivals, particularly the lunar new year celebrations when they staged exotic and expensive lantern parades.[50] Nevertheless their savings per head in the banks were among the highest for any ethnic group.[51]

Finally, the largest of the immigrant groups, the Indians. Most of these, as pointed out before, remained agricultural workers, either on the sugar estates or on their own lands. On the estates, they worked as individuals in gangs controlled by the planters. When in the late nineteenth century they began to move off the estates on to their own lands, they had a chance to recreate a family unit patterned on their traditional Indian joint family where the sons and their wives lived under the same roof as the father. In those circumstances, the family functioned as a cooperative economic unit under the control of the eldest male. Land was owned by the father who thus controlled the labour of all dependents in the household. The incomes of all individuals who made up the household was considered family income, over which the father had control.[52]

Because Indians had for a long time considered Guyana as a temporary abode, they were pre-conditioned to save. Before the spread of modern banking facilities, they simply hoarded their money, literally under the mattress, or converted coins into jewellery which the women primarily, but also some men, wore all over their bodies. Some deposited their money with

Portuguese or fellow Indian shopkeepers, but this was a very risky practice. Others invested in livestock, mainly cows, sheep and goats; or lent money to fellow Indians at high rates of interest. 'Throwing box' was also very popular among the Indians. When land became more readily available from the late nineteenth century onwards, many sought to invest in it.[53]

Smith has observed that among the Indians there was a greater degree of forward financial planning which was in part related to their cultural obligations. This centred on the family and marriage, but was also connected to religious celebrations, which required expenditure.[54] During the nineteenth century, for instance, the annual celebration of the *tadja* festival required a reasonably significant financial contribution from Indians, both Hindu and Muslim, since it was regarded as an ethnic festival. They therefore saved towards this celebration.[55]

Likewise in the life cycle of Indians, marriage necessitates an enormous expenditure. Within the Indian community, the more money outlaid on the wedding festivities, the higher the status that was accorded the family. Indian weddings, both Hindu and Muslim, were lavish and expensive affairs which could exhaust the accumulated savings of the parties and their families. During the nineteenth century when women were in scarce supply, males had to provide an ample dowry (in the form of gifts of gold and silver jewellery and/or livestock) for their prospective spouses. And at the weddings, the guests were expected to make generous cash gifts both to the couple and to the officiating *pandit*.[56]

Although it later became customary for the sons and their families to live with the sons' father, in Guyana that was not an indefinite situation. Sooner or later the son and his family would set off on their own. According to Smith, however, most Indian fathers considered it incumbent on them to provide their sons with a start by giving them land. Thus Indian fathers had to save in order to accumulate capital to buy land for their sons. When the sex ratio began to equalise, the dowry arrangements began to be reversed and instead the women had to pay dowries. This, and the cost of the wedding, became the responsibility of the girl's father, and thus necessitated enormous forward planning and fiscal discipline.[57]

Likewise, the cultivation of rice as the principal crop meant that income came in only once a year, and that too required a great deal of long-term financial management to get through the leaner months. Thus for both economic and cultural reasons, the Indians had good reason to save in order to accumulate capital; but this emphasis on saving merely served to reinforce the stereotypical impression that Indians as a group were miserly and land grabbing.[58]

From the foregoing, it would appear that culture does influence the economic behaviour of ethnic groups in multiracial societies. But it is by no means the only, or even the most important, factor. What clearly emerges from the study of nineteenth-century Guyana is that there were no intrinsic racial and/or cultural attributes that qualified one ethnic group for certain economic roles over another. More important in defining ethnic roles were the overarching political and economic structures which set the limits of ethnic participation in the economy. It was the intervention of the state, and of the ruling group, that established the broad parameters within which the several subordinate groups (and individuals within them) functioned.

The tendency towards occupational specialisation so prevalent in multiracial societies is thus more a consequence of the artificial manipulation of the ruling elite than any natural group inclination based on ethnicity. An integral aspect of this manipulation is the emphasis placed on ethnic stereotyping, which seeks to classify groups according to some perceived inherent cultural and racial attributes. An environment is thus created which encourages members of ethnic groupings to act as corporate entities within the pre-set boundaries carved out by the state and the elites. In this way, the idea of ethnic identification is allowed to influence the economic behaviour and attitudes of the members of the different ethnic groups.

Notes

1. B.L. Moore, *Cultural Power, Resistance and Pluralism: Colonial Guyana 1838–1900* (Kingston: The UWI Press, 1995), pp. 12–13; see also B.F. Williams, *Stains on My Name, War in my Veins: Guyana and the Politics of Cultural Struggle* (Durham, NC: Duke University Press, 1991), pp. 127–74.

2. H.V.P. Bronkhurst, *The Colony of British Guiana and its Labouring Inhabitants* (London: T Woolmer, 1883), p. 102.

3. A.H. Adamson, *Sugar Without Slaves: The Political Economy of British Guiana, 1838–1904* (New Haven, CT: Yale University Press, 1972), pp. 160–213.

4. W. Rodney, *A History of the Guyanese Working People, 1881–1905* (Kingston: Heinemann Educational, 1981), pp. 125–7.

5. For a full discussion of the economics and subordination of the ex-slaves in post-emancipation Guyana, see Moore, *Race, Power and Social Segmentation in*

Colonial Society: Guyana after Slavery 1838–1891 (New York: Gordon and
Breach, 1987) chapter 6.

6.   Ibid., pp. 95–105.
7.   Ibid., pp. 111–21.
8.   Rodney, *A History*, pp. 92–102.
9.   See Moore, 'The Social Impact of Portuguese Immigration into British
     Guiana after Emancipation', *Boletin de Estudios Latinoamericanos y del Caribe*,
     No. 19, (1975).
10. Ibid.
11. Rodney, *A History*, pp. 108–9.
12. Moore, *Race*, pp. 176–8.
13. Rodney, *A History*, pp. 83–9.
14. Moore, 'The Settlement of Chinese in Guyana in the Nineteenth Century', in
     Howard Johnson, ed., *After the Crossing: Immigrants and Minorities in
     Caribbean Creole Society* (London: Frank Cass, 1988), pp. 46–7.
15. Moore, *Race*, p. 214; *Cultural Power*, pp. 12, 14.
16. W. Look Lai, *Indentured Labour, Caribbean Sugar: Chinese and Indian Migrants
     to the British West Indies, 1838–1918* (Baltimore: The Johns Hopkins
     University Press, 1993), pp. 40–2.
17.   M. Freedman, 'The Handling of Money: A Note on the Background to the
     Economic Sophistication of Overseas Chinese', *Man*, 59 (1959).
18. K.O. Laurence, 'The Establishment of the Portuguese Community in British
     Guiana', *Jamaican Historical Review*, 5:2 (1965), p. 55.
19. Moore, *Race*, p. 62.
20. *Official Gazette*, 1871, CO 115/38. In 1870, out of 1,271 shop licences, the
     creoles held 194.
21. Ginger beer and mauby were sweetened non-alcoholic beverages made from
     the ginger root and the bark of the carob tree, respectively.
22. Laurence, 'The Establishment', p. 65.
23. Portuguese traders were provided goods for retail on easy terms of credit by
     the leading British wholesale merchants, while Creole traders were granted no
     credit at all or on very stringent conditions (see *Royal Gazette*, 30 October
     1843). Furthermore, the imposition of licenses was clearly designed to keep
     creole participation in the retail to a minimum. In 1845 Governor Light
     indicated that without these licences, the creoles would have engaged in such
     trade in much larger numbers rather than remain in agricultural labour (Gov.
     Henry Light to Secretary of State Stanley, No. 70, 7 April 1845, CO
     111/227). In 1850, his successor Governor Henry Barkly agreed that the retail
     trade licences had indeed restricted creole enterprise in that sector (Barkly to
     Sir George Grey, No. 173, 31 December 1850, CO 111/227). For a full
     discussion of the impact of the licences on the Creole, see Moore, *Race*, pp. 142–3.

24. T. Tucker, *Bermuda: Today and Yesterday, 1503–1973* (London: Robert Hale, 1975), p. 132.

25. R.T. Smith, 'Some Social Characteristics of Indian Immigrants to British Guiana', *Population Studies*, 13:1 (1959), p. 39.

26. Moore, *Race*, p. 193.

27. Ibid., pp 149–150, p. 162; and *Cultural Power*, pp. 25–26, pp. 151–52, p. 238, p. 292, pp. 297–300.

28. Smith, 'Ethnic Differences and Peasant Economy in British Guiana', in R. Firth and B. Yamey, eds., *Capital Savings and Credit in Peasant Societies* (London: Allen Unwin, 1964), pp. 311, 316.

29. Moore, *Race*, pp. 94–5.

30. Adamson, *Sugar Without Slaves*, pp. 63–6.

31. Smith, 'Ethnic Differences', p. 314.

32. Callier to General Secretary, No. 74, 23 December 1869, MMS/W.v/2.

33. Adamson, *Sugar Without Slaves*.

34. See the *Blue Books of Statistics*. These sources provide data for savings only in the Government and the Post Office Savings Banks whose depositors represented only a very small sample of the total population. Nevertheless, they serve as a useful indicator of ethnic savings patterns. In 1891, the average savings per depositor in these two banks were as follows: Creoles, £11.32; Indians £15.93; Chinese £28.28; and Portuguese £48.26.

35. This method of saving is known as *susu* in Trinidad and according to M. Herskovits is derived from the Yoruba *esusu* and the Dahomean *gbe* and *so* (Herskovits, *The Myth of the Negro Past*, Boston: Beacon Press, 1969, p. 165). There is however, documentary silence about this among the Creoles in nineteenth-century Guyana, largely because they were very suspicious about the taxation intentions of the Colonial Government. For that reason, many creoles did not register to vote either even though they were qualified on the basis of their incomes. There is a fuller reference to this practice among the Indian immigrants, however, over whom the planters and immigration agents had greater scrutiny. See E.A.V. Abraham, 'The East Indian Coolie in British Guiana', *West Indian Quarterly*, 2 (1886), pp. 400–1; D.W.D. Comins, *Note on Emigration from India to British Guiana* (Calcutta, 1893), p. 100. See also Smith, 'Ethnic Differences', p. 322.

36. A. Trollope, *The West Indies* (London, 1860), pp. 183–4.

37. Smith, 'Ethnic Differences', p. 312.

38. Ibid.

39. Moore, *Race*, pp. 122–31.

40. Laurence, pp. 72–3. The ratio of females to males was always high, and improved from 1:1.5 in 1851 to 1:1 by 1891. See Moore, *Race*, p. 157.

41. Moore, 'The Social Impact', pp. 7–8.

42. Ibid., pp. 10–14.
43. Moore, *Race*, pp. 142, 149–50.
44. At the peak of Chinese migration to Guyana, 1859–66, only 17 per cent of the migrants were female; and as late as 1891 when the last census of the century was taken Chinese women formed only 30.5 per cent of that ethnic group. See Moore, *Cultural Power*, pp. 265–6.
45. Ibid., pp. 279–80.
46. Ibid., pp. 273–7.
47. Moore, 'The Settlement of Chinese', p. 46.
48. Freedman, *The Handling of Money*.
49. Yen Ching-Hwang, 'Early Chinese Clan Organisations in Singapore and Malaya, 1891–1911', *Journal of Southeast Asian Studies*, XII (1981), pp. 79–80; Moore, *Cultural Power*, p. 282.
50. Moore, *Cultural Power*, pp. 269, 284–5, 287–91.
51. Deposits by Chinese in the Government and the Post Office Savings Banks averaged about £28 between 1864 and 1891, second only to the Portuguese among the subordinate ethnic population. See the *Blue Books of Statistics*.
52. Moore, *Cultural Power*, pp. 168–79; Smith, 'Ethnic Differences', p. 317.
53. Moore, 'Social and Cultural Complexity in British Guiana, 1850–1891', (PhD thesis, UWI, 1973), pp. 230–1.
54. Smith, 'Ethnic Differences', p. 320.
55. Moore, *Cultural Power*, p. 222.
56. Ibid., pp. 182–7.
57. Smith, 'Ethnic Differences', pp. 320 1.
58. Ibid.

'Young Woman from the Country'
A profile of domestic servants in Jamaica, 1920–1970

MICHELE A. JOHNSON

*I*n the last quarter of the twentieth century, Jamaicans became all too familiar with the stereotypical profiles that have been constructed about domestic servants. Many are the citizens who have listened, partly with interest and partly with amusement, to various radio programmes, as servants use this medium to seek employment.[1] The recurring image that accompanies many of the pleas for work is that of the 'young woman from the country' seeking to enter domestic service in order to support herself and, very often, her family. This chapter recognises that profile as one which, with repetition, has become a stereotype, and uses another medium to investigate whether or not that profile was one which obtained earlier in the century. The chapter seeks to understand the message behind the constructed image which was present and further, it tests the construction of that profile.

Similar to many other groups of workers engaged in low-status occupations, domestic servants did not leave many written documents either about their personal or their work lives. In order to answer that problem, it is possible to use non-traditional sources for investigating domestic service in twentieth-century Jamaica. One such is the newspaper classified advertisements which provide consistent and systematic written insight into the island's domestic service sector. Newspaper advertisements were particularly useful to those operating in the sector because of their general accessibility: they listed for anybody who was interested, the persons and the positions which were available. Newspapers played an important part in the recruitment process, and as the only surviving systematic written source, have to be taken seriously.

There are, however, some limitations to the use of this source. The advertisements did not include the large number of employers and servants who used other means to recruit for, and to find positions within, the sector. Newspapers also excluded those who could not read or those who could not afford the price of the advertisements.[2] In spite of this, the newspaper has the advantage of spanning the entire period, and provides unbroken data unattainable in any other source. As the following indicate, classified advertisements provided a wealth of information.

> A decent young woman seeks employment as a cook, butleress or nurse; can make cakes and puddings, with good experience in any line of work, satisfaction is sure from a tidy, disciplined young woman, has uniform and references. Please call at No. 8 Charles Street.[3]
>
> A young woman just from the country seeks employment as cook, washer, maid or butleress; can furnish recommendation and will stop on premises. Please call to 'Willing' at 107 Orange Street.[4]

In addition to stating the positions, skills and special attributes sought or offered, by employers and servants, they often included details from both groups on the age, sex and place of origin of those who worked in service.

For the purposes of this discussion, which forms part of a larger study, a sample of advertisements was taken from *The (Jamaica) Daily Gleaner*.[5] The sample of *The Daily Gleaner* was drawn from the second Saturday or Sunday of every month, for five year intervals between 1920 and 1970. Prior to the introduction of *The Sunday Gleaner* in 1946, Saturday was the most popular day for the placement of advertisements for both employers and employees. After its introduction, Sunday became most popular. A total of 132 issues of *The Gleaner* between 1920 and 1970 yielded a total of 10,215 advertisements which formed the core of the study. From these advertisements, a mass of information was gleaned, and a system of coding and computer analysis was used to give order to the data and to make them manageable. This chapter highlights three of the 26 variables which were isolated in that larger study.

The chapter also makes use of oral histories which provide an opportunity for the servants' voices to give a qualitative dimension to the quantitative data. In spite of the difficulties of accuracy, of selective memory and the ravages of age which the oral history methodology has to address, the (ex-)servants who were interviewed furnished a face to the experiences which were captured by other means. These memories, along with the classified newspaper advertisements, provided the basis to investigate whether Jamaica's servants were indeed 'young women from the country'.

'Young . . .'

According to Barry Higman, domestic service has always employed 'large proportions of young people'.[6] This was partly because domestic servants were expected to work hard and were sought primarily as workhorses of the household, 'to wash and cook and clean and to be generally useful'.[7] Because the work was often difficult and monotonous, employers were inclined to hire young people because it was believed that they could manage the work better. Some of the tasks were decidedly difficult. The washing of clothes, for example, in this period largely followed the pattern of the previous century: clothes were washed by hand, in cold water and often with bars of harsh soap. The conditions surrounding cooking varied in households according to incomes. Some used the new gas and electric stoves, others used kerosene stoves or coal pots, but some households, especially in the rural areas, still used open fires, on a hearth, in a small kitchen, separated from the house. And the cleaning that so many servants did involved gruelling and dirty work. There was furniture to dust, there were windows to wipe, but perhaps the most difficult part of cleaning was the floor which servants had to wipe, polish and shine, most often on their hands and knees. Employers wanted 'young' persons for their households since they knew only too well what difficult work they had in store for them.

Another attraction of the young domestic was that employers believed that, as Herbert DeLisser puts it, she could be 'trained in the way she should go in the future'.[8] Employers were able to create exactly the kind of servant they wanted when they were dealing with young persons, controlling every aspect of their lives and getting them to work hard, sometimes without pay. Emerging from these circumstances was the 'schoolgirl system' which accounted for a large number of very young women and girls involved in service. Farmed out by their parents, often because of dire poverty, youngsters were assigned to domestic work rather than the agricultural work which their parents had known. They were 'given' to a mistress who taught them how to cook, wash and clean, as well as other household chores. The mistress was often proud of the girls she had trained and spoke of them as girls who 'now [according to her uncontradicted version of the story] are a credit to Church and State, and spend much of their time in congratulating themselves that in early life they came under the tuition of so good a mistress'.[9]

Some employers, however, objected to the younger servants, because of their lack of training and experience. Other employers were concerned about young servants' personal lives and feared that they would be more inclined to bring mates, family and friends into the employers' homes. These employers and those who placed great value on experience solved their problems by hiring older servants, confident in their belief that age, experience and appropriate behaviour went together. On the whole, though, middle-aged and elderly servants were not as popular because they were thought to be susceptible to illness and exhaustion and were sometimes difficult to control, being, like their US contemporaries, 'too set in their ways'.[10]

The sample of the classified advertisements in *The Gleaner* between 1920 and 1970 produced 77 different age references for the period. Some included numerical references ('young woman aged 19½' or 'boy of about 14–16 years'[11]), while others were descriptive – 'young', 'middle-aged' or 'elderly'. It was possible to merge several of the references, resulting in ten age categories in which an attempt was made to separate the numerical and descriptive references.

The number of job offers stipulating the ages of domestic servants in the sample of newspaper advertisements reveals that employers listed the preferred ages of their prospective servants in just under 28 per cent of the sampled advertisements (Table 18.1). When the eight employers who wanted servants under 20 years to work for them are added to the 226 employers who sought 'girls' or 'boys' and the 104 employers who wanted 'young' women/men in their employ, the preference for youth is clear among employers who listed a favoured age range. More than 70 per cent of the employers in the sample who did mention age sought 'young' servants.

The advertisements by employers who included age sometimes bear testimony to the 'schoolgirl system' in operation in the domestic service sector. Requests were made for 'schoolgirls' to fill positions, and even more specifi-

Table 18.1:   Reference to age by advertising and servants

	Employers		Servants	
Categories	Number	% Total	Number	% Total
10–14 years	4	0.2	10	.01
15–19 years	4	0.2	70	.08
20–29 years	9	0.5	30	.03
30–39 years	13	0.7	20	.02
40+ years	7	0.4	–	–
Girl/boy	226	13.6	2,996	35.2
Young	104	6.2	3,226	37.9
Middle-aged	67	4.0	366	4.3
Elderly	24	1.4	60	0.7
No young	3	0.1	–	–
No age	1,191	72.0	1,849	21.7
Total with age	461	27.9	6,661	78.2

Source: Sample, *Gleaner*, 1920–70

cally in one case, for a very youthful 'girl around 12'.[12] That the issues of youth and control were linked was made even more explicit when some employers requested that vacancies be filled by controllable young servants: 'orphan preferred', 'motherless girl between 10 and 12' or 'unencumbered young widow'.[13] Many Jamaican employers wanted and sought control over persons who worked in the intimacy of their homes and they tried to ensure that their servants would not be influenced by kith or kin.

If Jamaican employers were inclined to seek young servants, it was young people who offered themselves for positions in domestic service. From the first census relevant to this study (1921) to the last in 1970, the majority of Jamaica's citizens have been under 25 years old and the labour supply has been characteristically dominated by youth. In Jamaica 59.4 per cent of the population in 1921 was under 25 years, 55.2 per cent in 1943, 57.9 per cent in 1960 and 61.9 per cent in 1970.[14]

That most Jamaican domestic servants laboured in their youth is a feature that cannot escape notice. According to DeLisser, some of the island's women took on service from their mid-teens, although, he stressed, 'it is when they are about twelve years of age that their mothers begin to think of having them learn something by which they will be able to earn their bread',[15] the most obvious choice being domestic service. Domestic servants have emerged from that large pool of youthful labour, usually unemployed and largely inexperienced. Unskilled in many circumstances, young people might have felt most hopeful in applying for a domestic position where skill, educational achievement and experience seemed to have no edge over youth. In spite of their youth and their lack of training, these young persons needed to work, needed to support themselves and their families in a difficult economy where the state provided little welfare. Where poverty took hold of families, they responded by encouraging household members to fend for themselves. Domestic service was one of the few areas outside agriculture where the young could be readily employed and, indeed, were sought by employers. The newspaper advertisements seem to support this view.

Within the sample of domestic servants more than 78 per cent mentioned age in their bids to gain employment (Table 18.1) and of that number the majority said they were young. Of the servants who included a numerical age, there were eight in the sample who were under 20 years old. These eight, added to the 2,996 who referred to themselves as 'girls' or 'boys', and the 3,226 'young' men or women, resulted in a total of 6,230 servants or 73.2 per cent of the sample's total who offered their youth to prospective employers.

The oral histories of the (ex-)servants who were interviewed, also support this view. Bell Davis began to work as a domestic servant at 17, Ethline Fraser began at 14, while Cou Meme began her career at 12 and Mr C. was 'given away at 9' to begin a job as a 'yard boy', a position which he held for his entire working life.[16] Servants were just as aware as were employers of the asset of youth in domestic service and it was the 'young' who flocked to service.

'Woman'

By the twentieth century, in most places, domestic servants were women. While every society, to one degree or another, allocates labour along a basic gender division, and while women's responsibilities in that division have centred on the children they bear, it does not follow that the entire set of processes which have come to be called domestic work should, of necessity, be assigned to women. More precisely, there is nothing intrinsic to domestic service that decrees that those who do it for pay must be women. That it has is the story of domestic service in twentieth-century Jamaica, where it is considered 'women's work'.

Scholars concerned with domestic service have often commented upon the domination of women in the sector, and some like Pamela Horn, talking about Victorian England, hasten to point out that this was not always so.[17] However, with the emergence of the middle classes and their increasing importance as employers of service, there was a change in the face of the sector. According to Cissie Fairchilds, referring to old regime France, '[a]ccompanying this "bourgeoisification" was a . . . shift in patterns of servant employment, which might be labeled a "femininisation" of the occupation'.[18] In Latin America and the Caribbean, this trend is even more evident in the twentieth century, as domestic workers have accounted for not less than 20 per cent of all women in the paid work force in the region and in many countries the proportions are much higher, from one-fifth to one-third of the female labour force.[19]

According to the available data, a significant proportion of Jamaica's female labour force between 1920 and 1970 was employed as domestic servants. According to the census of 1921, of the total population of 858,118 Jamaicans 443,937 were considered 'productive'. Of that number, 20.6 percent of the 219,593 working women were domestic servants.[20] By 1943, of a total population of 1,237,063, the 'gainfully employed' portion numbered 505,092. The proportion of women employed as servants had risen to 34.3 per cent of the 183,455 working women.[21] According to the island's census in 1960, there were 1,609,814 citizens, 203,081 of whom were women over 14 years who were 'at work or on leave'. Whereas 14,080 men provided 'personal services' in that census period, 74,084 (24.5 per cent) of working women were employed in that sector.[22]

A study of domestic service in Jamaica from 1920 to 1970 is primarily a study in women's labour. Women were sought for domestic employment for several reasons, not least among them the belief that domestic service was 'women's work'. In a society which, by its very colonial, marginal, exploitative genesis, has always functioned in the murky waters of ambivalence, Jamaica has had great difficulty in defining the place of women. At once the society, based as it had been on slavery, expected women to work, to contribute to its development and at the same time to embrace the qualities defined as 'feminine' by the ruling/hegemonic forces. While these twin expectations were not levelled at all groups equally, they filtered through to the largest constituent, poor, Black women, who in some cases responded to and helped to perpetuate both desires, who tried to work hard, while maintaining their 'femininity'. One way to accomplish this was to remain within the areas described and prescribed as women's work. Employment in a home, doing household chores – domestic service – seemed to fit right in with the patriarchal beliefs held by most employers and their servants both in Jamaica and elsewhere.[23]

Women were also sought as domestic servants because they were cheaper to employ. In this society and in others, the patriarchal structures which helped to limit the opportunities open to women were also responsible for the higher value placed on male labour within the sector and the wider possibilities open to men in these societies. In all essential ways, domestic service reflected these biases. Where there were households with more than one servant, males stood at the apex of the hierarchy, were given positions of authority and were paid more. As men moved into the modernising sectors of the economy, leaving women confined to the service sector by restrictive social values and their lack of training, the result was the increased value of male labour in domestic service and the oversupply and devaluation of female labour.[24] In Jamaica, the women who turned to domestic service, in many cases, had few alternatives, and their growing labour pool depressed wages and gave employers large amounts of power in the context of an oversupplied market, all in one stroke.[25]

The growing importance of the middle class as employers of service was also influential because they seemed to prefer female servants. In most situations, male servants made their appearance in multi-servant households, where they held relatively high positions.[26] In Jamaica, the emergence of the middle class as primary employers of service[27] has meant a decline in the numbers of men employed since the majority of middle-class employers did not have multi-servant households, and in the event that a single maid-of-all-work was to be employed, that servant would be a woman. Cheaper, allegedly more pliable female labourers, who could be required to perform a multitude of duties, became increasingly attractive.

In a society that gave great latitude to its male citizens' behaviour and much more closely defined women's actions, female domestic servants were pre-ferred because they were perceived to be, and sometimes were, more easily disciplined. Further, the inclination of many employers to have within their households servants who appeared to be meek and subservient made them lean towards female servants. By entering the personal space of their employers, servants' contact with those employers was of a very intimate nature. When the employer, therefore, felt a need to 'discipline' servants, that reprimand was often of a very personal nature. Some employers restricted leisure and controlled visiting hours, clothing, religious practices, and some even extracted punishment for specific misdeeds by immediate dismissal or corporal punishment.[28] Where males, by virtue of patriarchal hegemony, were more likely to resist that discipline, women were expected to absorb it in much the same way that they did in their private lives. And while some female servants resisted these attempts, many were trapped by their situation at the base of every imaginable hierarchical construct and sought to eke out their survival as best as they could.

Women were also sought for, and became numerically dominant in, domestic service because where certain positions were concerned, especially those associated with childcare, it was widely believed that only women could effectively fill them. Women have most often been labelled as the island's nurturers, taking care of their children (often by themselves), taking care of other people's children and even taking care of the society's men. Portrayed as long-suffering and patient, indulgent yet firm, Jamaican women have earned a reputation in childcare that makes them popular, even internationally, as domestic servants.[29] As a result, many servants found that their duties most often included childcare along with the general housework that they did.[30]

When these factors converged in twentieth-century Jamaica, it should not surprise that employers sought more and more female servants. The newspaper sample bears this truth (Table 18.2). In the 1920s, of the employers who listed a sex for the servant they sought, 61.6 per cent were advertisements for women. The proportion rose steadily throughout the period, so that by the 1960s, the proportion of women sought had risen to 95.7 per cent and to 96.3 per cent by 1970. For the entire period, of the 1,652 employer advertisements, 90.7 per cent of them were for female servants.

For many, domestic service provided the only avenue for any economic accumulation. Studies investigating the low showing of women in occupations other than domestic service, have tended to point out women's limitations. Their responsibilities for family care, and in particular childcare, have been the main reasons advocated for the restricted supply of trained women. However, these conclusions have paid insufficient attention to the demand for labour, and to the anti-female recruitment policy of many employers, particularly in the industrial sector in developing countries.[31] In Jamaica, the compe-

Table 18.2:   Reference to sex by advertising employers and servants

	Employers						Servants				
Year	Female		Male		No Sex		Female		Male		No Sex	
	No.	%	No.	%	No.	%	No.	%	No.	%	No.	%
1920–25	98	61.6	16	10.0	45	28.3	80	93.0	6	6.9	–	–
1930–35	111	86.7	15	11.7	2	1.5	881	92.2	70	7.3	4	0.4
1940–45	110	85.2	19	14.7	–	–	1,269	91.6	114	8.2	2	0.1
1950–55	164	92.1	13	7.3	1	0.5	1,660	90.9	162	8.8	4	0.2
1960–65	544	95.7	21	3.6	3	0.5	2,945	94.9	156	5.0	2	0.6
1970	472	96.3	11	2.2	7	1.4	1,095	94.8	57	4.9	3	0.2
Total	1,499	90.7	95	5.7	58	3.5	7,930	93.1	565	6.6	15	0.1

Source: Sample, *Gleaner*, 1920–70.

tition for well-paid employment was often brutally intense as a result of a sizeable labour surplus to which, in the case of women, have been added negative stereotypes which penalise all women and keep them out of many occupations except those oversupplied, depressed 'female' sectors.[32]

According to the newspaper sample for the period 1920–70, it was women who sought jobs as domestic servants. In the sample for the 1920s, 93.0 per cent of the advertising servants were women and though the proportions may have fluctuated in some decades, the proportion of female servants seeking employment in the sample never fell below 90 per cent, ending the period in 1970 with 94.8 per cent. Of the 8,510 servants in the entire sample, 93.1 per cent of them identified themselves as women. As far as the patriarchal structures dictated and the enduring legacies of slavery demanded, domestic service in twentieth-century Jamaica was, indeed, women's work.

'From the country'

Employers of domestic service have often sought servants from rural areas to fill positions in their homes. For a variety of reasons, many employers did not want servants from their own areas. In reference to Victorian England, Horn claimed that servants with rural origins, being far removed from home, were ideal: to prevent them telling household secrets to friends, to deter frequent visits from servants' families and, in some societies, to stop the young women from running home.[33] By being in this manner recruited, according to Leonore Davidoff discussing service in Victorian and Edwardian England, 'the majority of girls moved from parental control, in their parents' home, into service and then into their husband's home – thus experiencing a lifetime of personal subordination in private homes'.[34] With a few qualifications, this held true for nineteenth- and twentieth-century Jamaican servants as well.[35]

Most Jamaican employers perceived the typical servant as being 'from the country'. Although the demand for servants rose rapidly with the growth of the urban middle classes, whenever alternative employment opportunities arose, as they sometimes did in urban centres, the supply of urban servants tended to dry up. In addition, many urban Jamaican employers shared with their international counterparts the feeling that the servants who were available in the city were unacceptable because they were, according to Lewis Coser, 'rebellious, recalcitrant, untrustworthy [and] fickle'. Hence, a large number of urban employers turned to the countryside for recruitment of 'suitably reliable and pliable servants'.[36]

That rural Jamaica was seen as the ideal place from which servants should be recruited, was a common perception and employers often asked their own rurally based relatives to help them in their search for the perfect servant. High-status, high-profile citizens in the country (teachers, pastors) were also asked to recommend young women for employment and, of course, some were sought through the newspapers.[37]

Some employers' newspaper advertisements insisted that the servants should be directly from the country (Table 18.3). The image of the trustworthy, if naive, willing but blundering girl of peasant stock, was romantically maintained by many employers, notwithstanding the fact that some of them had recently emerged from such stock themselves. Other employers were willing to accept servants who were not newly arrived from the country but who, instead, had lived in urban areas for some time. Servants in this situation were inclined to be more 'refined' than their rural-based counterparts, but were not as 'sly and treacherous' as the ones who were city born or bred. Employers who resided in the rural areas appeared to be less concerned about the origin of their servants, and did not state any specific preference for rural workers, but simply asked that such applicants be 'willing to work in the

Table 18.3:   Reference to country by advertising employers and servants

Categories	1920–5	1930–5	1940–5	1950–5	1960–5	1970	Total
For the country	7	8	3	–	1	–	19
Willing to go to country	3	1	3	5	5	2	19
Not long/recently from country	–	–	–	1	5	1	7
From country	5	5	8	7	23	47	95
Country preferred	7	3	4	–	9	12	35
No country	–	–	–	–	–	–	–
Did not list	137	111	111	165	525	429	1,478
Total with country	22	17	18	13	43	61	174
Country as percentage of total	14	13	14	7.4	7.5	12.4	10.5

Source: Sample, *Gleaner,* 1920–70

country'. The likelihood that city-dwellers would go to the rural areas was smaller than the possibility that rural-based persons would pursue such positions.

The number of advertisements which expressed a preference for country-bred servants remained above 13 per cent for the 1920s, 1930s and 1940s. After 1950 there was a considerable decline in employers seeking servants of rural origin. Perhaps by that time there were enough new rural migrants in the city to supply the demand for domestic servants without direct recruitment from rural areas. And, perhaps as the demand for servants grew, employers could not be too particular about their origins. In addition, when the new class of less affluent employers began their search for domestic help, they often could not afford the expense of the long-distance recruitment, which included transportation into town and usually room and board.

In as much as some Jamaican employers sought rural servants, many were the servants who looked to urban areas for their employment partly because of the impression that a real income differential existed between rural and urban Jamaica. Also, the employing classes tended to congregate in the urban areas and, based on the proportion of advertisements offering positions in

Kingston, employment opportunities abounded compared with most of rural Jamaica. Additionally, in a bid to leave unemployment and destitution behind, rural Jamaicans fled to the city.

In the twentieth century, rural Jamaicans attempted to escape into urban centres because of increased difficulties resulting from the contraction of the sugar industry, accompanied by the improvements in production techniques and the mechanisation of agriculture, which caused a reduction in the need for labour; the higher fertility of the rural population, which led to overpopulation in parts of rural Jamaica; and the difference in levels of income between the rural and the urban areas. As a result, between 1920 and 1970 Jamaica experienced more incremental increases in migration than at any earlier period. There were pulls into the emerging tourist industry of the north coast, into the banana industry of Portland and St Mary, but by far the greatest portion of the migration was into Kingston and St Andrew. Aspiring domestic servants formed part of this migratory flock.

The newspaper advertisements give a good indication of the persons who had moved into the urban centres in the hope of getting domestic employment. The advertisements which mentioned origins were usually those coming 'straight from the country'. These servants sought to assure their potential employers that they possessed the basic honesty and wholesomeness which were supposed to be part of the rural persona. Since they had not long parted with their moral base, they had not yet had a chance to be 'contaminated' with the aggressive, independent and wily ways of 'Kingston people', and therefore were perfect candidates for domestic employment.

Among the sample's applicants for domestic positions, the servants who said they were 'recently from the country' or 'from the country', constituted a significant proportion (Table 18.3). In the 1920s, 18.6 per cent of the servants' advertisements mentioned that they were from the country. The numbers increased to 23.2 per cent of the servants in the 1930s and then declined steadily, although never below 18 per cent.

Up to 1940, those with a rural claim were more likely to insert the fact that they were 'lately from the country' in their advertisements. After 1945, however, there was a change in the phrasing of advertisements where 'from the country' increasingly replaced 'lately from the country'. This alteration, though apparently slight, could very well portray wider changes in the supply of domestic servants. It could indicate a reduction of persons recently from the rural areas, and an increase in those who were originally from the country, but who had (long) settled in the urban centres. It is also quite plausible that the style of advertising changed, so that sharper and more businesslike advertising techniques dictated that the inclusion of the word 'lately' was no longer necessary.

Some applicants (120 servants, 1.4 per cent of the sample) assured their employers of their willingness to work in rural areas. Many of these might have been from the rural areas themselves, while others from urban centres might have felt enough in need of employment to accept it in any available region. A smaller number (23 servants, 0.2 per cent of the sample) stated explicitly that they would not work in rural areas. It might have been the attractions of urban life – the tendency for higher remuneration, as well as commercial and entertainment possibilities – which made servants reluctant to take jobs in the countryside. Other possibilities were the perception of faster social mobility and family ties which prevented them from leaving the urban areas.

The proportion of servants who stated their willingness to go to rural positions declined sharply after 1945. It is very likely that the differences apparent between the urban and rural working conditions had grown stark in Jamaica after the Second World War. Servants were, therefore, far less willing to leave the advantages of working in Kingston, Montego Bay and even Mandeville for the more rural offers of employment. The lack of electricity (and therefore of electrical gadgets) in many rural areas before 1970 implied the use of traditional methods of housework within the rural households. Washing in the running river and ironing with fire-heated irons compared very badly with the modern conveniences of most urban homes. As a consequence, servants were far less 'willing to go to country'.

The effects of internal migration were felt strongly in the urban destinations, and most especially in the growing Kingston and St Andrew metropolitan area. There was in these areas, by the 1950s, overcrowding, unemployment and depression. Opportunities for better employment which had pulled potential servants to Kingston often failed to materialise and in the absence of any system of social security, the results of growing unemployment were fully manifested.

The housing situation was perhaps the best indicator of the destitution which defined the lives of some of the rural migrants living in the capital city. Forced into the construction of shelters from flimsy materials, a large proportion found themselves squatting on parcels of government land, their dreams of employment and mobility shattered. After all, according to Colin Clarke, in Kingston '[s]quatting is not only an expression of extreme population pressure, it is also a way of life. Because of the stigma attached to inhabitants of the shantytowns and the poorer tenements, it is very difficult for people from these areas to find employment'.[38] Under conditions such as these, says Clarke, 'the personal service industry is as an employer of domestic servants, gardeners, yard-boys, and odd-job men, but at wages which only slightly exceed subsistence rates'.[39]

Conclusions: 'Young woman from the country?'

The focus of this discussion has been on the stereotypical profile of the 'young woman from the country', who allegedly defined the domestic service sector in twentieth-century Jamaica. As the chapter has demonstrated, according to the newspaper sample, the profile is substantiated by the evidence investigated, regarding the focus on youth in the sector (by both employers and servants) and the dominance of women in domestic service. Much more open to question is the assumption that servants were coming from the island's rural areas. To be sure, a significant proportion of the sample's employers (10.5 per cent) and an even larger percentage (21.4 per cent) of the servants made some reference to the country in their advertisements. But were the 'young women' who dominated service from the country? An investigation of the addresses which were attached to the advertisements did not indicate rurally based servants. Instead, the majority who offered themselves for employment were based in the Kingston and St Andrew metropolitan area (see Table 18.4). In some ways, the urban concentration of the servants might be explained by the fact that the persons most likely to use the newspaper would be those who were closest to it: the head offices of the newspaper in question (*Gleaner*) were located in Kingston. But there was more at work.

In the 1920s, 62.7 per cent of advertising servants in the sample included addresses in Kingston-St Andrew as their points of contact. By the 1930s that proportion had soared to 92 per cent, after which time there was some fluctuation, ending the period with 89 per cent of the sample's servants seemed to be based in the main urban area. What is even more significant is that the proportion of servants who gave rural addresses, or who seemed to be still 'in the country' fell steadily throughout the period, from 19.7 per cent in the 1920s to 0.4 per cent in 1970.

Table 18.4:   Location of advertising employers and servants by address

| | Employers | | | | Servants | | | |
| | Urban | | Rural | | Urban | | Rural | |
Years	No.	% Total	No.	% Total	No.	% Total	No.	% Total
1920–5	119	74.8	28	17.6	54	62.7	17	19.7
1930–5	91	71.0	10	7.8	879	92.0	15	1.5
1940–5	93	72.0	9	6.9	1,306	94.2	22	1.5
1950–5	145	81.4	5	2.8	1,617	88.5	19	1.0
1960–5	495	87.1	10	1.7	2,886	93.0	20	0.6
1970	439	89.5	5	1.0	1,029	89.0	5	0.4
Total	1,382	83.6	67	4.0	7,771	91.3	98	1.1

Source: Sample, *Gleaner*, 1920–70

The question of whether these 'young women' who dominated service were really 'from the country' seems open. This is especially true when the claims of 'from the country' (Table 18.3) are measured against the addresses which form the basis of Table 18.4. Whereas 1,165 servants said that they were 'from the country' (13.6 per cent of servant sample), and 520 servants said they were 'lately from the country' (6.1 per cent of servant sample), only 98 servants (1.1 per cent of servant sample) gave rural addresses with their advertisements. Perhaps the difference was to be found in the fact that many servants who claimed to be 'from the country' had in fact left their rural origins, perhaps for some time, or had never had these origins. This discrepancy suggests that domestic servants recognised that within the sector, for all the reasons examined, rural origin had value, and in an attempt to procure employment they claimed those origins, whether true or not.

This investigation suggests that the reasons for the emergence of the profile of the 'young woman from the country' in domestic service had a great deal to do with issues of control and servitude.[40] The young, the women, the persons with alleged rural origins were much more easily forced into the mould of subservience that Jamaican service demanded. Marginal and often vulnerable, these made the best servants in a sector and society built on exploitation.

Notes

1. *Citizens' Advice Bureau* (hosted by Mrs Hazel Monteith) and *Jamaica Today* (hosted by Dorraine Samuels) both aired for years on one of the nation's major AM stations, RJR, and allowed listeners to call in with concerns or problems. A significant proportion of these callers were domestic servants.
2. In the 1930s and 1940s, the advertisements in *The Daily Gleaner* cost '1/- per insertion of Five Lines (30 words)' and in the late 1960s and in 1970, each advertisement cost 50 cents. References to *The Daily Gleaner* are hereafter noted as *Gleaner*.
3. *Gleaner*, 13 July 1935.
4. *Gleaner*, 13 July 1940.
5. Several newspapers were surveyed in the initial stages of the study, for example, *West Indian Review, The Jamaica Standard, Planters' Punch, Public Opinion, Jamaica Times, Plain Talk* and *The Daily Gleaner*. It was quite clear that *The Daily Gleaner* was the best choice: it had the most advertisements for domestic service, it was consistent and accessible and it was the only newspaper to span the entire period.
6. B.W. Higman, 'Domestic Service in Jamaica, since 1750', in B.W. Higman, ed., *Essays Presented to Douglas Hall: Trade, Government and Society in Caribbean History 1700–1920* (Kingston: Heinemann Educational Books Caribbean, 1983), p. 126.
7. *Gleaner*, 10 January 1925 and 10 August 1935.
8. Herbert G. DeLisser, *Twentieth Century Jamaica* (Kingston: Jamaica Times, 1913), p. 100.
9. DeLisser, *Twentieth Century Jamaica*, p. 100.
10. E.R. Haynes, 'Negroes in Domestic Service in the United States', *The Journal of Negro History*, VIII, No. 4 (October 1923), p. 391.
11. *Gleaner*, 10 July 1920; 14 June 1930; 13 January 1945.
12. *Gleaner*, 14 December 1940; 8 August 1965; 10 August 1935.
13. *Gleaner*, 9 March 1940; 13 April 1940; 14 June 1930.
14. *Census of Jamaica and its Dependencies*, 1921, 1943, 1960, 1970.
15. DeLisser, *Twentieth Century Jamaica*, p. 99.
16. Bell Davis, personal interview, Golden Age Home, Kingston, October 1988; Ethline Fraser, interview with Franklene Frater, Golden Age Home, Kingston, November 1987; Cou Meme, interview with Erna Brodber, Walderston, Manchester, July 1973, Erna Brodber, *Life in Jamaica in the Early Twentieth Century: A Presentation of Ninety Oral Accounts* (Kingston: Institute of Social and Economic Research 1978); Mr C., interview with Erna Brodber, Rennock Lodge, St Andrew, January 1973, *Life in Jamaica*.

17. P. Horn, *The Rise and Fall of the Victorian Servant* (Dublin: Gill and Macmillan; New York: St Martin's Press, 1975) has pointed out that in pre-industrial England young men of 'gentle birth' were apprenticed as servants within the households of the aristocrats.

18. C. Fairchilds, *Domestic Enemies: Servants and Their Masters in Old Regime France* (Baltimore and London: The Johns Hopkins University Press, 1984), p. 2. This point is also discussed by Horn, *The Rise and Fall*, p. 4.

19. For a detailed discussion of domestic service in the region, see the various articles in E.M. Chaney and M.Garcia Castro, eds, *Muchachas No More: Household Workers in Latin America and the Caribbean* (Philadelphia, PA: Temple University Press, 1990).

20. Section 37: Occupations, Abstract G: Occupations, *Census of Jamaica and Its Dependencies, Taken on the 25th April 1921* (Kingston: Government Printing Office, 1922) pp. 7, 28–47.

21. Table 78: Gainfully employed population, occupation, sex, *Eighth Census of Jamaica and Its Dependencies, 1943* (Kingston: Government Printers, 1945), pp. 148–57.

22. *Census of Population of Jamaica*, Vol.1, Part D, pp. 5–1488, 6–1634, 8–1866, XVII–XVIII (Kingston: Government Printers). The 1960 census incorporated domestic service under the category 'personal services', which included domestic service, restaurants and taverns, hotels and rooming houses, launderers and cleaners, barbers and beauty shop attendants, photographic services, 'other personal services' and odd jobs.

23. For discussions around these issues, see P. Branca, 'A New Perspective on Women's Work: A Comparative Typology', *Journal of Social History*, Vol. 9, No. 2 (Winter 1975), pp. 136–7; D.E. Hojman, 'Women in Domestic Service in Santiago, Chile', *Bulletin of Latin American Research*, Vol. 16 (1987), p. 67; Fairchilds, *Domestic Enemies*, p. 15; J. Rollins, *Between Women: Domestics and Their Employers* (Philadelphia, PA: Temple University Press, 1985), p. 31.

24. The devaluation of female labour and the low wages paid to female servants are discussed by C. Fairchilds, 'Masters and Servants in Eighteenth Century Toulouse', *Journal of Social History,* 12, 3 (Spring 1979) pp. 369–70; S.C. Maza, *Servants and Masters in Eighteenth Century France: The Uses of Loyalty* (Princeton, NJ: Princeton University Press, 1983), p. 280; T. McBride, *The Domestic Revolution: Modernisation of Household Service in England and France, 1820–1920* (London: Croom Helm, 1976), pp. 60–2, 38; Horn, *The Rise and Fall*, pp. 4–5; C. Lascelle, *Urban Domestic Servants in Nineteenth Century Canada*, Studies in Archaeology, Architecture and History (Canada: Ministry of Supply and Services, 1987) p. 100.

25. Where the sample is concerned, the majority of employers did not list their wage offerings in their advertisements, but of those who did, male servants

were offered the highest wages. M. Johnson, 'Domestic Service in Jamaica, 1920–70' (unpublished MPhil thesis, Department of History, UWI, 1990), pp. 187–9. The censuses in the period also corroborate this trend.

26.   An important exception to this can be found in Zambia where men provided the bulk of the servant class. This is because Zambian families were wary of exposing their girls to the vulnerability that service often meant, because of the lack of alternatives for Zambian men, because Zambian women preferred the autonomy of work at home and because the European women, who dominated the employer class, viewed African women as probable competitors for their husbands' sexual favours. See K. Tranberg Hansen, *Distant Companions: Servants and Employers in Zambia, 1900–1985* (Ithaca, NY, and London: Cornell University Press, 1989).

27.   For this discussion see Higman, 'Domestic Service in Jamaica', pp. 117, 122.

28.   See DeLisser, *Twentieth Century Jamaica*, pp. 103, 105; D. Austin, 'Symbols and Ideologies of Class in Urban Jamaica: A Cultural Analysis of Class' (DPhil. thesis, Dept of Anthropology, University of Chicago, June 1974), p. 135; M. Hughes, *The Fairest Island* (London: Victor Gollanez Ltd, 1962), pp. 16–17; M. Macmillan, *The Land of Look Behind: A Study of Jamaica* (London: Faber and Faber, 1957), p. 36; Higman, 'Domestic Service in Jamaica', p. 132.

29.   Many of the Jamaican and other West Indian women who go to the United States and Canada in domestic service employment schemes are sought for childcare. See S. Cohen, '"Just a Little Respect": West Indian Domestic Workers in New York City', *Muchachas No More*; M. Silvera, *Silence: Talks with Working Class Caribbean Women about their Lives and Struggles as Domestic Workers in Canada* (Toronto: Sister Vision, 1989).

30.   Of the 1,377 servants who sought positions as nursemaids or mothers' helps, 99 per cent were women. Source, Sample, *Gleaner*, 1920–70.

31.   R. Anker and C. Hein, 'Why Third World Urban Employers Usually Prefer Men', *International Labour Review*, 124, No.1 (1985), pp. 73–90.

32.   G. Standing, 'Unemployment and Female Labour: A Study of Labour Supply in Kingston, Jamaica' (Kingston: Macmillan Press, 1981), p. 79. Also, G. Standing, 'Labour Force Participation and Development', 2nd edn (Geneva: International Labour Organisation, 1981).

33.   Horn, *The Rise and Fall*, p. 32.

34.   L. Davidoff, 'Mastered for Life: Servant and Wife in Victorian and Edwardian England', *Journal of Social History*, (1974), Vol. 7, No. 4, p. 409.

35.   Urban employers in nineteenth century Jamaica made complaints about servants' 'laziness, impudence and dishonesty'. Higman, 'Domestic Service in Jamaica', p. 121. Complaints about servants could be found in: 'Is It a Racket?', *West Indian Review*, Vol.1, No. 18 (3 September 1949) p. 6; M. Donaldson, 'Servant Problem', *West Indian Review*, Vol.1, No. 26 (29

October 1949), p. 4; P. Leach, 'Liberation from Tyranny of Servants', *Gleaner*, 3 October 1963, p. 3; 'Jottings', *Gleaner*, 18 April 1964, p. 3, examined some of the complaints about their servants.

36.   L.A. Coser, 'Servants: The Obsolescence of an Occupational Role', *Social Forces*, 52 (September 1973), p. 39. These sentiments are echoed by Davidoff, 'Mastered for Life', p. 41.

37.   According to Higman, in the entire history of domestic service, 'personal contact was most important' in the recruitment process. Higman, 'Domestic Service in Jamaica', p. 126.

38.   C. Clarke, 'Population Pressure in Kingston, Jamaica: A Study of Unemployment and Overcrowding', Institute of British Geographers, *Transactions*, No. 38 (June 1966), p. 177.

39.   Clarke, 'Population Pressure in Kingston, Jamaica', p. 171.

40.   For a look at other means of exerting control over Jamaican servants see M. Johnson, 'Intimate enmity: control of women in domestic service in Jamaica, 1920–1970', *Jamaica Historical Review*, Vol. XVIII (1993), pp. 55–65.

Restrictions and Freedoms for Women in Northern Cameroons to 1961

An examination of the liberating influences

R I C H A R D   G O O D R I D G E

Rationale, limitations and geographic context

The role and status of women in African society have become established and serious objects of enquiry among scholars. This fact may generally be linked to the demand for greater democratisation of human society which has characterised the twentieth century. Yet it is recognised that women still remain in unenviable positions in many African countries. This chapter focuses attention on the northeastern corner of modern Nigeria during the period when Britain assumed responsibility for that region's inhabitants on behalf of the international community.

A study of women in Northern Cameroons is useful for at least two reasons. For one, it helps to complement research done on the subject in the Southern Cameroons[1] and consequently serves to offer some basis of comparison between the two halves. Second, as will be seen, it will be possible to simultaneously perceive the various facets of women's lives in Africa since there must be an assessment of women in the traditional, Islamic and Western milieux that together constituted British Northern Cameroons.

Yet this study is of necessity circumscribed by various limiting factors. A principal restriction concerns the fact that the bulk of the source material, especially the colonial material, is derived from male officers many of whom were anxious to preserve and extend the patriarchal nature of Northern Cameroonian society. There is also a geographical limitation. The term 'Northern Cameroons' as used in this chapter does not refer to the northern area of the modern Republic of Cameroon but to the northern half of Britain's share of the ex-German colony, Kamerun (See figure 19.1).

Northern Cameroons was administered as part of three provinces of Northern Nigeria until 1960[2] when it was organised into a single Trusteeship or Sardauna Province. It stretched for 500 miles from Lake Chad to the border of Southern Cameroons. The territory, consisting of two strips of land lying north and south of the Benue River, varied in width from 5 miles on the shore of Lake Chad to around 100 miles on the border with Southern Cameroons. The vegetational and physical variations were equally significant. The Chad Basin portion of Northern Cameroons was arid and the areas contiguous or in close proximity to the border with the Southern Cameroons were thickly wooded. The portion south of the Benue was mountainous but closer to Lake Chad the terrain became increasingly flat. Within the 17,570 square miles of land that constituted Northern Cameroons,[3] there were important social and cultural differences.

The problematic

The argument of this chapter is that women's experiences in Northern Cameroons, especially in the Adamawa districts, were shaped by a mixture of several influences which were specific to different cultural milieux, but the influence of each milieu both modified and was modified by the others. It is also suggested that during the period 1919–61 Northern Cameroons women made what is best described as 'curtailed progress', for several social, economic and political restrictions remained in place and limited reforms were introduced. This discussion then, is an examination of the transformation in the status of Northern Cameroons women from that of slaves to one whereby they were allowed to vote.

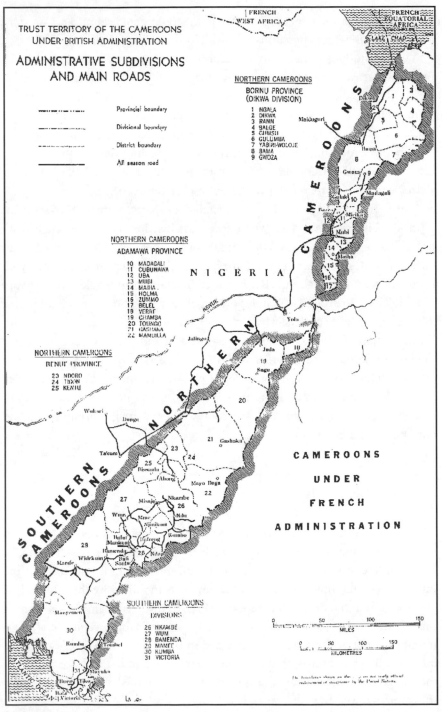

Figure 19.1

There were several restrictions applied to women in Northern Cameroons; but the nature and level of restriction varied according to the level of Islamic or Western influence. It is further suggested that there were major critical influences which served to undermine these restrictions over the period from about 1919 (the year of the completion of the partition of Kamerun) to 1961 (the date of the final plebiscite which determined the political future of Northern Cameroons). Although these influences were present from a fairly early stage – certainly by the 1930s in terms of Western-style influences – the major positive developments concerning females occurred fairly abruptly and largely in the decade after 1950.

This is not to argue, however, that women progressed from a highly restricted to a favourable or positive position over the period under discussion due to a process of modernisation arising from the intervention of the Colonial State. Although it is suggested that there were significant shifts in the structural position of women, this chapter asserts that not all changes were favourable nor were they entirely due to the colonisers.

Theoretical framework

A useful summary of the discriminatory practices against African women is provided by Robert Mugabe, President of Zimbabwe and himself no stranger to controversies over the treatment of African women. Mugabe stated:

> custom and tradition have tended more to favour men than women, to promote men and their status and demote women in status, to erect men as masters of the home, village, clan and nation. Admittedly, women have . . . been allowed . . . a significant, but at other times a deplorably insignificant role to play. The general principle governing relationships between men and women has, in our traditional society, always been that of superiors and inferiors. Our society has consistently stood on the principle of masculine dominance – the principle that the man is the ruler and the woman his dependant and subject.[4]

The literature suggests that the position of African women was not an enviable one. In general, women suffered from discrimination resulting from a gendered division of labour under conditions of patriarchy. Although, as M.J. Hay and S. Stichter observe, women in sub-Saharan Africa traditionally played a major role in food cultivation and trade, and in some states even enjoyed control over the fruits of their labour and wielded substantial political power, 'even in [sub-Saharan] Africa . . . women's power and status were always in some major ways less than those of men'.[5]

While women in Africa did the bulk of subsistence agricultural labour – and were expected to provide all the food for the family's daily consumption – the tendency was for others to control much of the surplus produced by that labour.[6] The explanation often advanced for this undemocratic, exploitative state of affairs is tied to an understanding of traditional socioeconomic institutions. Thus, Jeanne Koopman argues that male appropriation of the surplus generated by female labour stemmed from the fact that traditional African households were based on the control exercised by senior males over the labour of women and junior males (that is, patriarchy in its natural state) and the existence of female social and economic dependence on males.[7]

One major trend in the literature on women in Africa concerns the central place of male migration and the impact upon the family or household. During the twentieth century, the creation of dependent colonial structures and their continued operation under conditions of neo-colonialism led to the production of agricultural commodities for export and mass migration of males to the urban or production centres; a process which, therefore, held enormous implications for the male-female relationship.[8] Colonial rule also had an impact on Islam and its adherents and the treatment of women in Islam is an important theme in the literature.[9]

I. Lapidus suggests that the coming of Islam and the Qu'rán transformed the values of the family and of women as part of the process of establishing the general norms of Islamic society.[10] Before the advent of Islam Arab society was characterised by a firmly embedded patriarchal system in which women were assigned an inferior status, marriages were arranged without the consent or interests of the would-be bride, and various types of polygamous arrangements were common. In these conditions of 'institutional confusion and individual disregard for family obligations' which characterised Arabia, Quranic teachings strengthened patriarchy and simultaneously provided for reform and the introduction of a new dignity to family members.[11] Thus, for example, women (and children) were no longer regarded as mere chattels but as individuals with rights and needs of their own including the right to hold property in their own name.

As Lapidus points out, despite the emphasis on security and status of women, the Qu'rán did not establish equality of rights for men and women, although the Quranic ideal was much more favourable to women than later Arab and Muslim practice.[12] Moreover, Lapidus suggests that an understanding of women's roles and especially of subjective factors is still very limited and the issues are clouded by intense (ideological) debate. Lapidus issues one other caveat: the difficulty faced by outsiders in separating their own values from the conceptions of dignity, security and love which prevail in Islamic societies.[13]

At the turn of the twentieth century, there was a sharp division between the roles of men and of women in theory, ideology and in practice; with the public sphere assigned to the man while the house and the family was woman's domain. Islamic societies then assumed the dominance of men over women and public deference of women (and girls) to male authority. This male dominance was supported by social and legal structures (and strictures) and rested on the notion that men were physically stronger, more intelligent, and more suited to action. Consequently, men had to rule over women 'who were more subject to their emotions'.[14] Yet this patriarchal system was, in practice, modified for several reasons.

Women played a significant economic role in agriculture and animal husbandry, in crafts and cottage industries. Further, women tended to be custodians of the family social status, and in the direct relations between husbands and wives, wives' personal influence or their manipulation of husbands 'worked to subvert the domestic power of males'. Given the existence of symbols and rituals that belittled and excluded men, while from an outsider's perspective Muslim men were dominant, 'women cannot be thought of as an oppressed class. They did not see themselves as forming a collectivity with interests opposed to those of men'.[15] Lapidus' view that a gulf existed between the myth and reality of women in Muslim societies is not a universally acclaimed one. Indeed, there were calls for a reform of the status of Muslim women early in the last century, largely from Western sources.

Within Muslim societies, a Western intelligentsia emerged which demanded social and political reforms including the 'emancipation' of women and their integration into society as full equals of men. The central argument of this intelligentsia was that education was necessary to transform the lives of women, for only through education and freedom of women could the entire society be emancipated or modernised. Thus, calls for transformation in the status of Muslim women were intimately bound up with the attempt to secularise Muslim states and provided a symbol of demands for change in the entire social order.[16] The call for the education of female Muslims was mirrored by demands for an emancipation of (female) slaves especially, since the link between Islam and slavery was assumed.

Slavery in Africa

The question of slavery in Africa has stimulated tremendous debate over several issues: definition and character of slavery; origins of slavery in Africa; the relationship between the transatlantic slave trade and African domestic slavery; and the importance of women in slavery. Claire Robertson and Martin Klein commenced their important study by stating that 'most slaves in sub-Saharan Africa were women. But many accounts of African slavery are written as though slaves were exclusively men'.[17] While the weight of historical research clearly indicates that the bulk of the slave population was female, there is no agreement on why this was so.

Paul Lovejoy, in articulating several broad characteristics of domestic slavery in Africa, found that female slaves fetched higher prices and the physical attractiveness of females was a primary consideration influencing the price and the popularity of the female slave. Lovejoy also found that masters had the right of sexual access to female slaves who became wives and concubines, but in Islamic societies, including the Sokoto Caliphate, these concubines could not be sold once they had given birth.[18] While there is general agreement in the literature that the bulk of slaves in Africa were females, there is no consensus on the primary reason for this phenomenon, although the reproductive functions of the female slave as a prime factor behind their desirability as slaves are stressed. Here, we accept the definition of reproduction offered by M. Strobel,[19] which includes biological reproduction; daily reproduction or the servicing of workers; and the reproduction of the relations of production through the transmission of the ideology supporting the entire social structure. Reproductive functions apart, females in Africa are said to have been more readily enslaved because they were more easily assimilated than men.[20] Here we shall limit ourselves to the case of the Marghi of Northern Cameroons.

J.H. Vaughan states that women were the principal captives, for

> not only were they easier to capture than men but they were more desired, being more likely to accept their new status, which differed little from that of a wife acquired without benefit of bridewealth. It is said that their new relationship became so normal that they would return to their homes for visits.[21]

Moreover, the status of *mafa* (slave) was not transmitted from female *mafa* to her children, but *mafakur* (slavery) was heritable on the male offender and extended to his descendants,[22] a fact which made females better adjusted to slave society. Yet Robertson and Klein argue that 'stressing reproduction and assimilation . . . distorts the position and functions of female slaves by underestimating their productive functions'.[23]

In their reassessment of the literature about the rationale for enslaving females rather than males, Robertson and Klein suggest that there were important social and economic reasons why female slaves were more desirable. Females, particularly girls rather than males, were used as pawns, as gifts to soldiers as war booty and as payment of fines. However, Klein and Robertson insist that the real value of female slaves stemmed from a gender-based division of labour in pre-colonial Africa in which much of the productive labour was assigned to women. According to them, women slaves and most free women in pre-colonial Africa performed both productive and labour-intensive tasks in agriculture and craft work; and that this provides the fundamental explanation why most African slaves were women.[24]

These views were supported by Lovejoy's research on the Sokoto Caliphate in which he found that female slaves performed agricultural tasks, were needed to prepare and cook food for the large palace establishment, and were called upon to do the more labour-intensive work of carding and spinning cotton, while men did the weaving.[25] For all these reasons, females were heavily enslaved across Africa. The chapter now focuses attention on the role and status of women in pre-1919 Northern Cameroons.

The traditional socioeconomic formation was transformed during the nineteenth century largely on account of the activities of Muslim reformers. In that part of Northern Cameroons between Lake Chad and Gwoza, the actions of Muhammad el-Amin el-Kanemi and Rabeh Fadl Allah[26] were crucial. Similarly in the rest of what became Northern Cameroons, the Muslim *jihad* after 1809–11 is largely held responsible for the restructuring of society and economy. Thus, the Fulbe or Fulani incorporated the area into the Sokoto Caliphate, became the new elite displacing the autochthonous, basing their dominant position on the enslavement of those whom they had displaced.[27] Yet several groups managed to retain their freedom and to continue their pre-*jihad* social and economic institutions.[28]

Pre-colonial role and status of women

Some idea of the pre-colonial role and status of women in Northern Cameroons is necessary. In many respects, these were evident even in the

1930s when some of the data were collected. While J.H. Vaughan suggests that Marghi wives worked hard, had their own farms and accumulated wealth,[29] Protestant missionaries (Messrs Kulp and Fleming) in 1933 found that in the societies of the Marghi and the Higi women generally suffered from 'certain disabilities' which they held in common with women of 'practically all groups of the same cultural level' across Northern Cameroons. The missionaries pointed specifically to the lack of economic independence, a characteristic of pre-colonial African women's status, as well as to the non-refund of bride price,[30] for the latter was a major concern of Christian missionaries across Africa.

Anthropological and ethnographic studies undertaken by the British provide some clues about the status of women in the Northern Cameroons. In the case of the Mambilla of the southern extremity of Northern Cameroons, 'the mother [was] looked upon as the sole head of the family and the father has little authority. Anything done by the mother is accepted by the family without question'.[31] The economic importance of women was highlighted by one of the few visitors to the area who in the early 1920s found that the Mambilla women were critical participants in agriculture.[32] To the north of the Mambilla were the Chamba groups and among them, at least among the Donga Chamba, there existed the very important and influential role of the *mala* whose importance – if not her duties and powers – may be gauged from the fact that if she were married, her husband was an obscure, 'comparatively unimportant person'. As the Donga Chamba had a chief as the highest political institution, the religious and political duties of the *mala* would seem to make her his equal.[33]

Marriage and inheritance practices among the Chamba and other groups also provide some clues about the status and treatment of women in Northern Cameroons before the 1920s. Although the Chamba were organised into patrilineal kindred and descent was patrilineal, there were certain rights and privileges to be claimed on the mother's side. Thus, for example, a maternal uncle could, in times of distress, pawn or sell any of his sister's children and could exercise the right to custody of first-born nephews. Moreover, the Dakka Chamba[34] believed that 'a rich man may be wifeless, but an industrious farmer never'.[35] This offers some clues about the importance of agriculture, although by itself it is not conclusive about women's role in that agriculture.

Among the Higi the role and status of the female reflected the situation across much of sub-Saharan Africa. Thus, on the one hand, Higi religious beliefs recognised a supreme being or *Hyel* who had a female counterpart in *ikhi* (earth), whom he fertilised by sending rain upon. On the other hand, inheritance was based on patrilineage with the eldest surviving brother or eldest son inheriting property and using it on behalf of the whole family. In terms of marriage (that is, in theory, of virgin girls to youths their age[36]) the Higi were exogamous and gifts were made to both parents of the intended bride. Finally, wives had to work on their husbands' farms for they had none of their own except the 'cabbage patches' around their husbands' compounds.[37]

Although the Gwoza area had been claimed by the Muslim ruling family of Madagali in the nineteenth century and was administered as part of Dikwa Emirate after 1922, the area was largely 'pagan' and, as such, its marriage and economic practices fell into the pattern identified by Hay and Stichter. In fact, acquisition of wives, necessary for the continued success of agriculture in Gwoza region, continued to be dependent on the acquisition of wealth. Under colonialism, acquisition of British currency, qualifications and jobs became the means to amassing such wealth. As part of a campaign to increase taxes, British officials in Gwoza District pointed to the youth from Guduf ward who, after leaving to work in Maiduguri in 1934, had by 1937 not only learned to foxtrot – to the amazement of his elders – but had also acquired 'a large compound, 2 wives, 4 cows, 7 separate farms' at a total value of £20'.[38] Indeed, cows were often used in the Gwoza area to purchase a wife.

The nineteenth century spread of Islam had major implications for women, especially in the Adamawa area, given the freedoms of women in the Mambilla, Donga Chamba and Marghi societies and the tendency of the Fulbe to desire *habe* wives and/or concubines.[39] The oral sources suggest that Islam destroyed the pre-existing freedoms which were incompatible with its own ideals. Consequently, the British tended to make gloomy, often simplistic, pronouncements on women in the Islamic areas of Northern Cameroons: they were in slavery or in purdah.[40] Consequently, something had to be done; tackling the slavery question was an obvious measure.

The changing role of women in the economy to the 1950s

One major trend in the literature on twentieth-century African women, which is conspicuous by its absence in Northern Cameroons, concerns male migration. The institutions associated with male migration – mines, plantations, railways, large towns – were never a feature of twentieth-century Northern Cameroons economy. Thus, the colonial economic stimuli to transformations in the status of women were less frequent and less direct.[41] This is not to suggest, however, that economic considerations were not important in bringing about changes to the position of women in Northern Cameroons.

Expansion of the colonial economy including increased consumption of British manufactured goods by people in Northern Cameroons was a cardinal aspect of British policy. Women were central to the fulfilment of these desiderata. As the draft report for 1928 on the increase in internal and external trade in the Adamawa districts of Northern Cameroons indicated,

> The women are an important factor in this. They undoubtedly have great influence . . . and having begun to taste the delights of cheap and showy cloth, beads, jewellery and so on, they will not allow their men to revert to the leisure of past days but urge them on to produce more and more wealth.[42]

Yet this report was wrong to suggest that men alone were producers and women simply consumers of goods of doubtful economic value to Northern Cameroons.

As early as 1923 the Permanent Mandates Commission of the League of Nations discussed the issue of liquor traffic in Northern Cameroons. Sir Frederick Lugard, the *rapporteur* for the subject, found that the consumption of European spirits by Africans was 'practically unknown' and in the Islamic districts was actually an offence.[43] Yet he and other members of the Commission did not confine themselves to imported liquor but were concerned with the measures to control the sale and manufacture of 'ruinous native fermented liquors', for it was believed that these 'native-made intoxicants were probably more injurious than European spirits'.[44] The Commission was primarily concerned with the moral and social implications of males consuming liquor rather than with the process of its production. It, therefore, failed to recognise that most of the home brew, derived from the cereal crops of Northern Cameroons, was the work of women and any controlling measures would affect the women producers.

Women were heavily involved in agriculture in Northern Cameroons, although in the hill areas of Gwoza District they were prevented from owning land as late as the 1950s.[45] The involvement of women has been confirmed by colonial reports[46] and may be gauged from the fact that 1933 Forced Labour Ordinances Provisions restricted forced labour to males and tried not to recruit labour away from farming.[47] While it may be argued that the framers of the ordinance were seeking to avoid disrupting agriculture, it is equally possible to suggest that they were guided by the heavy participation of women in farming.

The more direct evidence on women's role in the agricultural economy is provided for the post-1945 period. In the Kentu, Ndoro and Tigon districts which were administered as part of Benue Province, in the early 1950s the British wanted to interest the population in 'better husbandry'. According to the British, the people in these three districts planted the land with maize, pepper and guinea corn for two years, after which 'the land was left to return to forest but sometimes was cropped for a third year by women with ground-nuts and sweet potatoes'.[48] The desire for the better husbandry of plants and animals was not limited to these three districts and both the discussion and implementation held implications for male-female relations.

The British sought to promote a profitable coffee industry on the Mambilla plateau by establishing a nursery and sending three male farmers from the area for training in Bamenda (Southern Cameroons) in methods of coffee cultivation. In the Dikwa Division emphasis was to be placed on cotton cultivation for export which was likely to be dominated by men. For the Adamawa districts, apart from Mambilla, and for Dikwa Division (the latter administered as part of Bornu Province), the emphasis after the 1950s was on increasing groundnut production for export as well as improving the health of the cattle herds – in order to increase the export of hides and skins – whose ownership was exclusively in male hands.[49]

The 1952 census provides some indication of economic organisation in Northern Cameroons. Here the discussion is limited to distribution of popu-lation by occupation and sex. For this reason the assessment must be incom-plete. The total population of the area was 687,190 (331,990 males and 355,200 females). Data taken from the census reveal that 336,800 (155,200 males and 181,600 females) were engaged in the agriculture and fishing category, with the fishing subsector being a male preserve, while 13,300 were occupied in trading and clerical categories, including 8,400 females. However, most of the clerical employees were male, given the limited level of female education; a point reinforced by the fact that the 2,500 employed in the administrative, professional and technical category were males only. Finally, according to the census, 5,700 were listed as craftsmen, all of whom were males.[50]

428   *Working Slavery, Pricing Freedom*

There was a clear need to effect changes in women's status, especially in the economic sphere. In the opinion of many, education offered the best possibilities for promoting that change, but this was postponed until the late 1940s. Before then, abolition of slavery was the issue which dominated the discussion.

British policy and attitudes to women and slavery

The European conquest of Africa and the establishment of European ruling systems had been justified on the grounds of 'civilising' and Christianising Africa, a process to which abolition of African slavery was central. The campaign against slavery had been motivated by the desire to reduce or end the economic disruption associated with slave raiding; by the need to take control of labour resources out of African, and transfer it into European, hands; and by the consideration of converting slaves into free labourers who would then provide a market for British goods and/or a source of raw materials for British industry. As a first step, Europeans envisioned the cessation of slave raids. Yet the Europeans were in practice unwilling to move quickly against slavery or even slave raiding for reasons connected to the process of establishing the colonial rule systems.[51]

It has been demonstrated for Africa,[52] Northern Nigeria[53] and Northern Cameroons[54] that European interests, fears and perceptions militated against a quick or radical conclusion of slavery. In the first place, Europeans were generally of the opinion that slavery in Africa was mild whereas slave raids formed the really brutal aspect of the African slave regime. More importantly, however, early European administrators feared provoking those owners who would be denied a major source of accumulating power and wealth and were reluctant to disrupt either the fragile peace that accompanied colonial conquest or the growing production and commerce by a swift abolition of slavery.[55] Initially, therefore, European policy towards slavery was characterised by the enactment but non-enforcement of anti-slavery legislation. Thus, for example, Ralph Austen found that the Germans in Kamerun (out of which Northern Cameroons emerged) outlawed slave trading in 1895 but only sought to enforce the law from 1901.[56]

Following Germany's defeat in the First World War, its Kamerun territory was divided between France and Britain.[57] Slavery in Northern Cameroons attracted the attention of British officials largely as part of the anti-slavery effort in Northern Nigeria, for the British were convinced that Northern Cameroons was a principal source of slaves for Northern Nigeria and liquidating this slave trade was essential to the larger task of abolishing slavery itself in Northern Nigeria.[58] Thus effecting social and economic reform in Northern Nigeria *per se* was a factor behind the anti-slavery effort in Northern Cameroons.

A more obvious stimulus to the anti-slavery campaign was provided by the terms of the mandate agreed upon by Britain and the League of Nations which took effect in 1922. The provisions on slavery of the mandate agreement were unambiguous: Britain was required to emancipate all slaves, to speedily eliminate domestic slavery and to suppress all forms of slave trade.[59] Yet the British, official and non-official, offered several reasons why there should be no speedy emancipation of the slaves, some of which were gender-specific in nature.

In the first place, the British in Northern Cameroons, as Europeans elsewhere on the continent, were reluctant to radically disrupt society by a quick or wholesale emancipation of the slaves. The British continued to follow the policy laid down by Sir Frederick Lugard whereby the position of the Emirs was not threatened or undermined by any quick abolition of slavery.[60] This policy was motivated by the promotion of British interests, for the British needed these local aristocrats to help erect the system of indirect rule on which British colonialism in Northern Nigeria, including Northern Cameroons, was based.[61] Apart from the fear of undermining royal authority, the British feared a general societal disturbance for 'too precipitate action would throw large numbers of "ex-slaves" onto the labour market with unfortunate consequences to the entire social framework'.[62]

In Northern Cameroons, the British affirmed that slaves were in effect 'a class of rather worthless dependants' who had been raised to look to their owners for everything and had little incentive to work for themselves. It was argued that even when freed, the members of this class exchanged a master for a patron and 'swell the number of lazy hangers-on, male and female, in towns and hamlets'.[63] Thus, as domestic slavery declined in importance the absence of welfare services would clearly be a problem in Northern Cameroons, as it had earlier been in the post-emancipation period in the British Caribbean.[64] Perhaps nothing more strikingly exemplified societal disruption in British eyes than the likelihood of vagrancy and prostitution.

The prevention of vagrancy had been a primary factor behind the adoption of Lugard's policy towards the Fulani Emirs. Yet the British, influenced by

Victorian Christian values,[65] viewed prostitution with trepidation. According to a retired British civil servant who made a tour of Northern Cameroons in the mid-1920s, women in and around Northern Cameroons preferred the free life of the prostitute in the big towns to the drudgery of married life. F. Migeod's description of the arrival and treatment of the prostitutes, as well as his explanation for the same, is worth quoting.

As a response to the activities of prostitutes, the Emir was occasionally advised to decree that they be expelled; a decree to which the 'ladies' submitted only to move to the next town and 'an equal number come thence in their place'. According to Migeod,

> They land from the steamer in gaily coloured cloths with a smile and glad eye for all, and the drab toiling wives are filled with envy and jealousy. One way to deal with these ladies has been for the chiefs to decree forced marriages within a month. This is some check, as the new husband if dissatisfied loots them of their fine cloths and ornaments, pronounces the simple 'I divorce you', which Islam provides for the purpose, and drives them out naked. So they are compelled to behave themselves. The hordes of prostitutes are really an administrative [sic] problem; as low as 3 [pence] a visit is sometimes accepted.[66]

In Migeod's view this 'administrative problem' was due to the 'debased condition of women under Islam with its plurality of wives' and to the clash of sociolegal systems as these related to concubines.

As late as 1955, a United Nations mission to Northern Cameroons found that polygamy, that is, polygyny, 'was still widely practised' and was so inextricably woven into the social system that to abolish it without disrupting the system would be impossible.[67] Yet neither the mission nor Migeod sufficiently explained the problem as it affected women.

The Germans had in their time sought to reform polygamy and 'wife purchase' but had met with little success.[68] During the Lugardian regime the British had passed their anti-slavery law under which no one born in or brought into Northern Nigeria after 1 April 1901 could be a slave. By 1924, when Migeod visited, the legal status of slavery had been abolished in Northern Cameroons and there were 'officially' no young women in a state of slavery. Yet Islamic law required that a concubine be a slave and provides that a man may have concubines; while the 'big men' in Northern Cameroons (and Northern Nigeria) desired concubines 'in increasing numbers as they ascend the scale to that of Emir'.[69] This contradiction was not corrected until 1936, when legal-status abolition completed its final phase, and after that date there was no legal foundation under Islamic law as practised in Nigeria which could rationalise or justify any demand for slavery.[70]

The Slavery Ordinance of 1936 represented the culmination of anti-slavery legislation in Northern Nigeria by removing the proviso that freedom applied to persons born in or brought into the area after 1 April 1901. While this restriction had not been made applicable to Northern Cameroons, the fact that the territory was administered as part of three Northern Nigeria provinces meant that in practice slavery continued into the 1930s and served to reduce the status of women. At the same time, the British argued that the emancipation of slave women in Northern Cameroons had been an ongoing process, since all transactions in slaves had been made illegal in 1919 and slaves, particularly women, had acquired their freedom. Thus, 32 people, of whom 26 were female, were emancipated in 1923 and the British suggested that this was the trend rather than the exception in the 1930s.[71] The end of women's enslavement did not, of course, imply any immediate or drastic change in their socio-economic and political status. Lack of proper education was a major obstacle.

Education

Given the importance attached to education as a barometer of the status of women and an agent for transforming that status, several prominent features of education need to be stated at the outset. The education policy laid down for Nigeria (including Northern Cameroons) in the early 1920s recognised that education should: first, conserve all healthy and sound elements in the social fabric of the population and adapt them to changed circumstances and progressive ideas as an agent of natural growth and evolution; second, promote the advancement of the entire community through improved agriculture and the development of 'native industries'; and thirdly, 'raise up capable trustworthy, public-spirited leaders of the people, of their own race, thereby narrowing the hiatus between the educated classes and the rest of the community'.[72] However, educational facilities throughout Northern Cameroons were limited and were in turn monopolised by males.

After perusing the first report submitted to the League of Nations on Northern Cameroons, the rapporteur for education on the Permanent Mandates Commission (Madame Bugge-Wickel of Belgium) remarked with respect to government schools that a single youth was acquiring secondary education and 25 boys were attending elementary school. This poor record was also reflected in the Islamic schools, since there were 805 such schools with a total of 3,470 pupils 'which would appear to indicate that the schools were not of very great importance'.[73] Indeed Governor Clifford of Nigeria even argued that a smaller number of schools was not necessarily disadvantageous for, as he found in the case of Southern Nigeria:

> it is not by any means of the bulk of the schools there maintained that any real enlightenment of the population can be effected; and His Excellency is convinced that in the majority of cases attendance at such schools is harmful to the average pupil.[74]

However bad the educational situation or standard was for boys, it was much worse for girls.

As late as 1948 the Chief Women's Education Officer found it necessary to ask that girls should not be neglected even when in school,[75] a clear sign that women were present but invisible. A decade earlier, when the Women's Training Centre (WTC) at Sokoto opened in 1939 it excluded women in purdah but welcomed candidates 'of good family' from 12 years old, who were expected to follow 'a curriculum [that] will be essentially practical, including all sorts of *aikin mata sosai*' (purely women's work). Yet the WTC was not expecting any candidates from Adamawa, Bornu or Benue provinces, the areas to which Northern Cameroons administratively belonged.[76] This is not surprising since girls were not then admitted to the elementary schools run by the government and where church schools existed these catered primarily to boys. Thus, by 1938 Britain had built no schools in the Kentu, Tigon and Ndoro districts, and the school at Gurumpawo run by the Sudan United Missions had 40 pupils with a boy:girl ratio of 9:1.[77]

Yet there was some improvement in educational development in Northern Cameroons beginning towards the end of the 1940s. In 1949 'a new departure' in women's education occurred when a small class for Fulani women was opened in Mubi. This represented 'the first attempt . . . to reach the better-class Muslim woman, and the future of the class will be watched with some interest'. The anxiety stemmed largely from the fact that women's education throughout Northern Cameroons was severely hampered by indifference, obsolete social customs, lack of staff and by the belief amongst the population that 'the education of girls is still an idea which parents abhor, and children strenuously resist'.[78] It is difficult to accept that Northern Cameroonian girls detested or resisted what was unavailable to them.

In the 1950s both Bornu and Adamawa provinces established provincial girls' schools to parallel similar institutions for boys. The school for Adamawa started in 1955 with 53 girls, of whom ten came from Northern Cameroons. The Bornu Girls' School, which had been created in 1952, had a roll of 103 in 1955, including 21 from Northern Cameroons.[79] Indeed Bornu Province would continue to outstrip Adamawa in the provision of education for females.[80] This is somewhat surprising given the early advanced status of women in Adamawa and the greater strength of Islam in Bornu.

The increased educational opportunities for females were not limited to government-run facilities; the proportion of girls attending mission schools in the Chamba areas ran from one-fifth to one-half of the total roll after about 1952.[81] The high figures for the Chamba area ought not to be considered freakish but should instead be related to pre-Islamic, pre-colonial practices that held women in fairly high esteem and may also be seen as a favourable response to the British effort to enhance the status of women through education.

Yet increased facilities did not mean a qualitative transformation of women's education. The Elementary Teacher Training Centre at Mubi was designed for males, but after the second year of their four-year programme the students were allowed to bring their wives to live with them (on the compound but in individual houses) and 'the wives attend[ed] domestic science, reading and writing classes'.[82]

The curriculum and career path followed by pupils of the Adamawa and Bornu Provincial Girls' Schools remained limited. At the former, needlework and tropical hygiene were emphasised and at the latter, apart from academic subjects, 'the girls receive practical training to enable them to run a home – needlework, knitting, cooking, spinning, weaving, domestic science and gardening'. After graduating from either school, the girls could enter a WTC to become nurses or teachers.[83] Although, as has been demonstrated, restrictions upon women remained clearly in place, there remains the need to explain why increased educational opportunities were made possible. Indeed, the basis for attempting any improvement in women's status must be explored.

Changing political status of women

In this final section some effort is made to explain the largely political attempts, however limited or unsuccessful, to transform the situation of the Northern

Cameroonian woman. The process of deconstructing African history is laying greater emphasis on women actively enhancing their position through direct and indirect effort. The evidence that Northern Cameroons women were essential players in their own liberation is not strong.

The impetus to reform came from external sources, even though the British colonial regime, as the principal external agent, might have been reluctant to press for too quick an emancipation of women. Yet the ruling class in Northern Cameroons – British officials and their local accomplices – had to take cognisance of the demand for change from women's groups and missionaries, together with the needs of the Colonial System and the example of British Southern Cameroons.

In a sense, the purpose of reform had been laid down by 1921, as the following quote suggests:

> One might urge 'leave well alone', but if the good of the people is our first consideration and not our own convenience, then something should be done to develop individual and social personality and to emancipate the women; they will then also be better customers for our goods.[84]

Reforming the situation of women in Northern Cameroons would, therefore, seem to be understood within a limited economic context, that is, in terms of the promotion of colonial imports from Britain.

However, there were important health considerations, most of which were present from the outset of British rule. Health problems in terms of dietary deficiencies also exercised some influence on the desire to transform women's status. Across Northern Cameroons 'many signs which result from minor degrees of malnutrition, can be seen in almost all the rural population'. The population suffered from a number of mineral and vitamin deficiencies and was also infested with 'chiggers'; the leading causes of death in the mid-1950s were malaria, malnutrition and gastro-enteritis in children.[85]

A high incidence of venereal diseases, especially syphilis, was compounded by an ignorance and negligence in treating it which was widespread in Northern Cameroons. Then, too, one other health problem was linked to the influence of Islam in Northern Cameroons. A dispensary had been erected at Uba in Nigeria, which mainly served Northern Cameroonians partly because it had a good pre-natal clinic. The effective use of this clinic was hampered by the practice of Muslim women who 'preferred to come after sunset in order not to be seen by others'.[86]

The sources are replete with accusations that Muslim patriarchal practices merely served to reduce the women to a very low status with disastrous consequences for the social order. This may be illustrated by the example of the members of a United Nations Visiting Mission, who pointed out to the leaders of public opinion in Mubi that Muslim delegates to the United Nations General Assembly and Trusteeship Council had denied that Islamic systems of law denied women equality of rights with men, but the Northern Cameroonians insisted that Muslim law did forbid women appearing in public.[87] Together with the problem of the low status of the (Muslim) woman was the issue of prostitution, for the oldest profession continued to be practised in the Northern Cameroons, especially in the towns or administrative quarters which had grown up.[88] Education was offered as the panacea for all these varied social ills.

Generally, it was assumed that development of education would 'have as one of its results the spreading of a higher conception of the role of women in society, giving them a consciousness of their status and dignity which will lead them to resist the requirements and usages of old and harmful customs'.[89] More specifically, while the British insisted that prostitution existed on an insignificant scale, the measures taken to combat it included the following:

> among the local indigenous communities, there are the efforts to improve their economic and social condition by developing the co-operative movement; educa-tion (particularly of girls and in the teaching of domestic science) and a rural health service with particular emphasis on the care of women.[90]

In more explicit terms, the United Nations Visiting Mission of 1955 posited that in respect of any and all 'unwholesome' customs vis-a-vis the place of women in society, 'their [that is, women's] evolution through education should bring about the desired change without causing the social upheaval that would result from unduly forcing the issue'.[91]

Yet the agencies of the United Nations, in particular the triennial missions that visited Northern Cameroons between 1949 and 1958 and the commissioner who conducted the plebiscites in 1959 and 1961,[92] did force the issue. The various bodies of the United Nations – particularly the General Assembly, UNESCO and the Trusteeship Council – frequently deliberated on the subject of women's status globally and the methods for its improvement.[93] In the specific case of Northern Cameroons, the annual discussion on the reports submitted by Britain and discussions on petitions presented by or on behalf of Northern Cameroonians provided the Trusteeship Council with the opportunity to goad Britain into ameliorating the status of women. However, it was the members of the visiting missions and the Plebiscite Commissioner who were the most direct UN agencies in championing the cause of Northern Cameroonian women.

According to the rules of procedure of the Trusteeship Council and Article 87c of the UN charter, provision was made for missions to visit and report upon the political, economic, social and educational conditions in trust territories. One condition to which the four visiting missions devoted some attention was the (Muslim) women's right to vote, which was ultimately viewed as critical to improving the debased status of women. The first mission of 1949 recommended as a first step towards the improvement of women's status that Britain should 'proclaim, and effectively protect, the right of women and girls to refuse to take part in any forced union, and to release themselves from any such unions in which they have been compelled to take part' and should also 'allow the wives of polygamists to withdraw from their marriages when it appeared they no longer wished to accept their position as additional wives'.[94] Certainly, the mission could not have been unaware that the pressure that would be brought to bear on any woman availing herself of such rights would be so enormous as to render such an idea impracticable. It should come as no surprise that the mission instead insisted upon an expansion in all areas of education, especially in the provision of higher educational facilities for girls.

Another visiting mission repeated the demand for increased and improved educational facilities for girls and unambiguously called for greater access to education for Northern Cameroonian females. Moreover, the members of this mission highlighted the patriarchal pre-colonial practices, entrenched by British rule, as a prime explanation for the limited access.[95] At last, the real source of the problem had been identified although a subsequent mission would appear to accept the traditional views that Islam rather than patriarchy militated against the progress of women.

The issue of women's right to vote came to dominate the debate on improving the status of women. The British had, of course, done nothing to promote women's rights in this area under the early Nigerian constitutions. Indeed, the 1958 Visiting Mission took the opportunity to question the decision of the Northern Nigeria government not to extend the vote to women in the forthcoming 1959 elections.

At Mubi, the mission was informed by the Consultative Committee of the Northern Cameroons (CCNC)[96] that the Islamic religion kept women out of public life and, consequently, they were not in a position to express their views on public affairs. In addition, postulated the Committee, women could not be allowed to vote because most of them were uneducated and, in any case, only an adult – defined as one who had assumed civic responsibilities and had paid taxes – could be reasonably entitled to vote 'and that was not yet the case of the women of the north'. Finally, the CCNC argued that some countries more advanced than Northern Cameroons[97] had delayed the introduction of female suffrage or had decided against it. While the CCNC was not ruling out the possibility that the vote could be extended to women, it was felt that time would resolve the issue. Yet the mission accepted the position of the CCNC, for in its own words, this was 'a view which in the present circumstances seems well founded, at least in regard to the Moslem women'.[98] Fortunately, this position was not accepted by the mission's parent body or by the women themselves – at least some of them.

The UN Trusteeship Council was quick to call for an end to electoral discrimination against Northern Cameroonian women, especially since Northern Nigeria, with which Northern Cameroons was administered, adopted electoral reform in 1959, which resulted in elections being direct and secret though restricted to male suffrage. Recalling UN General Assembly resolutions 1352 (XIV) of 16 October 1959 and 1473 (XIV) of 12 December 1959 which dealt with the future of British Northern and Southern Cameroons – 'and in particular the organisation of forthcoming plebiscites in the southern and northern parts of the Trust Territory on the basis of universal adult suffrage' – the council expressed the hope and desire 'that steps will be taken to extend the principle of universal adult suffrage to all future elections in the territory'.[99] The limited transformation of women was in many respects completed by their acquisition of the vote.

The pressure of the UN agencies in calling for the right of women to vote was part of a general process of reform under way since the Second World War, in which extending the franchise was seen as a means of alleviating the status of underprivileged groups.[100] Yet the pressure for change in Northern Cameroons was rooted in the contest between the fallacy of the argument presented by the CCNC and women mounting a challenge to their low status in Northern Cameroons.

The argument that women were not educated and, therefore, should not vote was clearly a fallacious one for the 1952 census indicated that men were also illiterate, since out of the total Northern Cameroons population (aged seven years and older) of 474,000, 456,900 were counted as illiterate.[101] For some women the only route to progress was to actively participate in 'men's work', that is, politics, and they took part in the decisive 1961 plebiscite campaign.

It is no surprise that the women championed the cause of the Northern Kamerun Democratic Party (NKDP), which was opposed to the governing party of Northern Nigeria, the Northern Peoples Congress (NPC).[102] Women's political participation was particularly upsetting to the patriarchs. On 28 January 1961 three women supporters of the NKDP 'had created a disturbance grave enough to lead to their arrest' and when they were brought to trial in the native court on the following day 'their husbands and numerous other men' gathered outside and sought to force their way in. Yet Djalal Abdoh, the Commissioner appointed by the UN to supervise the entire plebiscite operations, was unable to ascertain the reasons for trying the three women in the native court,[103] which was regulated by 'native law and custom', rather than in a British-style court which had proper jurisdiction for the case. This suggests that the idea had been to teach the women a lesson for seeking to undermine or challenge male dominance in society and the dominant position of the NPC.

By the 1950s, developments in Southern Cameroons were helping to exert pressure for change in the status of Northern Cameroonian women. The annual reports to the United Nations on British Cameroons clearly articulated the backwardness of the Northern Cameroonian woman vis-a-vis her Southern Cameroonian counterpart. There was evidence of changes in marriage practices in the south in which the woman had greater say in her choice of husband, divorce was more easily obtained and polygyny was on the decline. Educational facilities for girls and the enrolment of girls in schools were far greater in Southern Cameroons. In the opinion of the 1955 Visiting Mission, while women in both Southern and Northern Cameroons were the pivot of the local economy, those in the former region had managed to acquire 'a considerable degree of independence'.[104] Although this should not be interpreted to mean that Southern Cameroonian women were liberated from patriarchal practices, the need to bring the situation in Northern Cameroons more in line with that of the south was not lost upon the members of the 1955 mission nor upon those who annually examined the British reports at the Trusteeship Council.

The work of the United Nations bodies was a continuation – albeit more structured and potent – of the effort of the League of Nations to improve the lot of women especially in the area of labour. Thus, for example, the League of Nations had adopted a resolution in 1935 which demanded that the terms of the 1933 Equal Rights Treaty should be examined in relation to the existing political, civil and economic status of women under the law. Further, recognising that employment conditions of women fell within the sphere of operations of the International Labour Organisation (ILO), the resolution wanted that organisation to examine the question of equality of women under labour legislation, primarily the question of legislation which affects discrimination, some of which might be detrimental to women's work.[105] However, given the nature of the economy of Northern Cameroons in the mid-1930s, this recommendation hardly applied to the situation there. Yet the resolution did also call upon women's international organisations to continue with their study of the entire question of the political and civil status of women.

One such organisation was the Roman Catholic St Joan's Social and Political Alliance which sought 'to obtain information on the status of native women in different parts of the world'. The alliance primarily favoured the use of legislation to stamp out the various customs and practices affecting women, such as slavery, polygamy and ritual murder, but the limitations of this approach were obvious: it was impossible to legislate on attitudes. Yet the St Joan's Alliance did achieve some success, for the Colonial Office responded to pressure for effecting change in the status of women by investigating the welfare of women in tropical Africa and enquiring of the governor of Nigeria in 1936 whether coercion, including physical force, was used to persuade women and girls to contract marriages.[106]

It is unlikely that the St Joan's Alliance and other similar organisations had much direct impact on matters affecting women in Northern Cameroons. The significance of the alliance's work lay in highlighting the issue of the status of African women and placing the subject clearly on the agenda, in the forefront of international issues. The era of reform after the Second World War which characterised British colonialism was partly engendered by the work of organisations such as the alliance.

Conclusion

While one can justifiably argue that the status of Northern Cameroonian women in 1961 was not an enviable one, their situation had been somewhat ameliorated when compared with the early part of the twentieth century. This was exemplified by the fact that women had been transformed from slaves to voters in the brief period of 40 years between 1919 and 1961. Yet there remained enormous restrictions upon women.

The period 1919–61 was dominated by the conflict between retaining the restrictions upon women, especially in the critical areas of concubinage and marriage, and enhancing their socioeconomic status, which would undercut the control which males exercised over them. The conflict arose partly because the British colonialists were reluctant to undermine the position of those males upon whom the exercise of British authority rested but were simultaneously desirous of fostering their own commercial and economic interests. The conflict involved numerous questions pertaining to the control over women's labour and the surplus generated or likely to be generated by that labour.

The decision to allow Northern Cameroons women to vote in 1961 was a momentous one and it seemed to imply that women had made significant progress. Yet granting women the vote was based on the myth that mere exercise of this right would democratise the system; for male domination of Northern Cameroons society was not ended by this single development. Similarly, while figures for the education of girls and women showed an improvement by 1961, the overall situation was less than impressive. Thus, we can see the continuing duality in which progress or freedoms for women competed with the effort to retain the restrictions upon them.

It is significant that the bulk of the pressure to ameliorate the status of women in Northern Cameroons came largely from external sources. This suggests that economic growth and activities had been insufficient to create the conditions whereby internal demands for change would have emerged, particularly to threaten the position of the Muslim patriarchs. The persistence of slavery until the 1930s in Northern Cameroons – in spite of emancipation legislation as early as 1919 – and the territory's limited educational facilities, militated against real social or economic advancement which would have produced the pressures for change.

These pressures were ultimately exerted from sources outside Northern Cameroons, with the United Nations, especially its Visiting Missions to the territory, taking a leading role in recommending an improvement in the status of women. That the UN did not exist until 1945 meant that restrictions on women remained in force for a long time. Finally, the Southern Cameroons exerted pressure for change by shaming the record of Northern Cameroons on its treatment of women. Southern Cameroons had produced the level of economic activity that in turn promoted social change, including improving the status of women.

Notes

1. On women in Southern Cameroons see S. Nana Fabu, 'The Status of Women in Cameroon: A Historical Perspective' (PhD, Milwaukee 1987); E. Konde, 'Cameroonian Women in Nationalist Politics since the Second World War 1945–1985: a Historical Study of Women and Politics in a Male Dominated Society' (PhD, Boston 1991); R. Goodridge 'Women and Plantations in West Cameroon Since 1900', in V. Shepherd, et al., eds, *Engendering History: Caribbean Women in Historical Perspective* (Kingston: Ian Randle, 1995), pp. 384–402.
2. That is, Adamawa, Benue and Bornu provinces.
3. Nigeria, *Information on the Cameroons under United Kingdom Administration Prepared for the Visiting Mission of the Trusteeship Council, 1958* (Lagos, 1958).
4. Mugabe's view is quoted in S. Urdang 'Women in National Liberation Movements', in M.J. Hay and S. Stichter, eds, *African Women South of the Sahara* (London: Longman, 1995), pp. 215–16.
5. Hay and Stichter, *African Women*, p. xi.
6. Hay and Stichter do examine this issue; see also E. Boserup *Woman's Role in Economic Development* (New York: St Martin's Press, 1970), Part I; and J. Davison, ed, *Agriculture, Women, and Land: The African Experience* (Boulder, CO: Lynne Rienner, 1988).
7. J. Koopman, 'Women in the Rural Economy. Past, Present and Future', in Hay and Stichter, *African Women* pp. 3–22.
8. There is a wide body of literature on the twentieth-century economy in Africa; see, for example, R. Austen, *African Economic History* (London: James Currey/Heinemann, 1987); C. Coquery-Vidrovitch, *Africa: Endurance and Change South of the Sahara* (Berkeley: University of California Press, 1988); and P. Wickins, *Africa 1880–1980: An Economic History* (Cape Town: Oxford University Press, 1986); on the issue of migration in Nigeria, S. Osoba 'The Phenomenon of Labour Migration in the Era of British Colonial Rule', *Journal of the Historical Society of Nigeria*, 4, 4 (1969), pp. 515–38 remains relevant.

9.   N. el Saadawi, *The Hidden Face of Eve: Women in the Arab World* (London: Zed Books, 1980), and M. Kimball and B von Schlegell, *Muslim Women Throughout the World. A Bibliography* (Boulder, CO: Lynne Rienner, 1996).

10. Much of the following discussion of Islam and women is derived from an excellent work of synthesis I. Lapidus, *A History of Islamic Societies*, (London and New York: Cambridge University Press, 1988).

11. F. Mernissi, *The Veil and the Muslim Elite: A Feminist Interpretation of Women's Rights in Islam*, (Addison Wesley, 1991).

12. Lapidus, *A History of Islamic Societies*, pp. 29–31.

13. Ibid., p. 890.

14. The comparisons with patriarchal Western societies should be obvious; see, for example, J. Lorber and S. Farrell, eds, *The Social Construction of Gender* (London: Sage, 1991).

15. Lapidus, *A History of Islamic Societies*, pp. 891–2.

16. Ibid., p. 893.

17. See the introduction in C. Robertson and M. Klein, eds, *Women and Slavery in Africa* (Madison: University of Wisconsin Press, 1988).

18. Paul Lovejoy's views are set out in *Transformations in Slavery: A History of Slavery in Africa* (Cambridge: Cambridge University Press, 1983); and 'Concubinage and the Status of Women Slaves in Early Colonial Northern Nigeria', *Journal of African History* 29, 2 (1988), pp. 245–66.

19. M. Strobel, 'Slavery and Reproductive Labour in Mombasa', in Robertson and Klein, *Women and Slavery in Africa*, pp. 111–29.

20. Lovejoy, ed, *The Ideology of Slavery in Africa* (Beverly Hills: Sage Publications, 1981); see also S. Miers and I. Kopytoff, eds, *Slavery in Africa: Historical and Anthropological Perspectives* (Madison: University of Wisconsin, 1977), chap. I.

21. J.H. Vaughan, '*Mafakur*: A Limbic Institution Among the Marghi (Nigeria)', in Miers and Kopytoff, *Slavery in Africa*, pp. 85–102.

22. Vaughan, 'Mafakur', pp. 89–91.

23. Robertson and Klein, *Women and Slavery in Africa*, p. 8.

24. Their views are set out most clearly on pp. 5–11 of the 'Introduction' to the text.

25. Lovejoy, *Transformations*. pp. 195–6.

26. L. Brenner, *The Shehus of Kukawa: A History of the al-Kanemi Of Borno* (Oxford: Oxford University Press, 1974); W.K. Hallam, *The Life and Times of Rabih Fadl Allah* (London: Stockwell, 1977).

27. S. Abubakar, *The Lamibe of Fombina: A Political History of Adamawa 1809–1901* (London: Oxford University Press, 1977); M. Njeuma, *Fulani Hegemony in Yola (Old Adamawa) 1809–1902*, (Yaoundé, 1978).

28. C.K. Meek, *Tribal Studies in Northern Nigeria*, 2 vols (London: Frank Cass, 1931).

29. Vaughan, 'Mafakur', p. 91.

30. Nigeria National Archives, Ibadan (NAI), CSO 26/3 28570, Rev. Culp of the Church Brethren Mission to Resident Adamawa, 3 February 1934, and W. Fleming of the Sudan United Mission to Resident Adamawa, 12 March 1934.

31. (NAI) CSO 26/2 13977, Vol.II 'Ethnological Notes on the Mambilla Tribes' by Maj. Glasson (1924).

32. F. Migeod, *Through British Cameroons* (London: Cranton, 1925).

33. Meek, *Tribal Studies*, Vol. II, pp. 328–33.

34. This subgroup, unlike the Donga Chamba, was found largely in Northern Cameroons.

35. Meek, *Tribal Studies*, Vol. II, pp. 338–46, 348–402.

36. Personal communication from Mu'azu Ardo Hamman of the Mubi Traditional Council, who is of Higi origin.

37. Meek, *Tribal Studies*, Vol. II, pp. 221–65.

38. Nigeria National Archives, Kaduna (NAK) Gwozadist 18, Memorandum on Native Taxation, August 1937.

39. Lovejoy and J. Hogendorn, *Slow Death for Slavery: The Course of Abolition in Northern Nigeria, 1897–1936*, (Cambridge: Cambridge University Press, 1993), p. 38.

40. Colonial Office, *Reports on the British Sphere of the Cameroons. Presented to Parliament by Command of His Majesty May 1922* (London: HMSO), Cmd 1647; see also B. Calloway and L. Creevey, *The Heritage of Islam: Women, Religion and Politics in West Africa* (Boulder, CO: Lynne Rienner, 1994).

41. Several issues dealing with the colonial economy and women are dealt with in N. Nelson, ed, *African Women in the Development Process* (London: Frank Cass, 1981).

42. (NAI) CSO 26/3 21347, Vol. I, Draft Report for League of Nations (LON) on Portions of Mandated Territories included in Adamawa Province.

43. A. Olukoju, 'Race and Access to Liquor: Prohibition as Colonial Policy in Northern Nigeria, 1919–1945', *Journal of Imperial and Commonwealth History*, 24, 2 (1996), pp. 218–43.

44. League of Nations Permanent Mandates Commission (PMC), Minutes of 2nd and 3rd Meetings of Third Session, 1923.

45. (NAK) Gwozadist 687/S.1, pp. 89–92.

46. See (NAK) SNP 17 series, for various intelligence reports on groups in Northern Cameroons.

47. (NAK) SNP 17/1 9318, Vol. II contains the provisions of Forced Labour Ordinance No. 22, 1933.

48. (NAK) WukariProf Series for Annual Report Benue Province 1953.

49. Colonial Office, *Report to the General Assembly of the United Nations (GAUN) on the Administration of the Cameroons under United Kingdom Trusteeship for the year 1952*; and (NAK) MaiProf 1136E.

50.   *Report to GAUN* . . . 1952 Statistical Appendix Table 1B.
51.   S. Miers and R. Roberts, eds, *The End of Slavery in Africa* (Madison: University of Wisconsin Press, 1988); P. Manning, *Slavery and African Life. Oriental, Occidental and African* (Cambridge: Cambridge University Press, 1988); Miers and Kopytoff, *Slavery in Africa*, Part VII; and Lovejoy, *Transformations*, chaps 11 and 12.
52.   Miers and Roberts, *The End of Slavery*, Introduction, pp. 3–68, and Manning, *Slavery and African Life*, Chap. 8.
53.   See Lovejoy and Hogendorn, *Slow Death for Slavery*.
54.   Goodridge, 'The Issue of Slavery in the Establishment of British Rule in Northern Cameroun to 1927', *African Economic History*, 22 (1994), pp. 19–36.
55.   Miers and Roberts, *The End of Slavery*, p. 20.
56.   R. Austen, 'Slavery among Coastal Middlemen: The Duala of Cameroon', in Miers and Kopytoff, *Slavery in Africa*, pp. 305–33.
57.   A useful discussion is given in A. Osuntokun, *Nigeria in the First World War* (London: Longman, 1979).
58.   Several bulky files located in the Kaduna Archives contain the views of Northern Nigeria officials from 1919 to 1936: SNP 17/2 20216, 'Slavery in Nigeria'; SNP 17/2 12577, 'Slave Dealing in Nigeria and the Cameroons'; ZariaProf 1171, 'Slave Traffic in the Cameroons and Nigeria'.
59.   Treaty provisions, including the Mandate Agreements, of the Paris Peace Conference concerning Africa are found in the Appendices to G. Beer *African Questions at the Paris Conference*, edited L.H. Gray (New York: Negro University Press, 1923).
60.   On this see Hogendorn and Lovejoy 'Keeping Slaves in Place: The Secret Debate on the Slavery Question in Northern Nigeria 1900–1904', in J. Inikori and S. Engerman, eds, *The Atlantic Slave Trade: Effects on Economies, Societies, and Peoples in Africa, the Americas, and Europe* (Durham, NC: Duke University Press, 1992), pp. 49–75.
61.   Goodridge, 'The Issue of Slavery', pp. 31–3.
62.   (NAK) YolaProf 1563, Vol. II, Thomas to Bourdillon, 4 May 1936.
63.   Great Britain, *Report to the Council of the League of Nations* (Hereafter *Rep to LON) on the Administration Of British Cameroons for the year 1926* (London, 1928), para. 119.
64.   See W.A. Green, *British Slave Emancipation: The Sugar Colonies and the Great Experiment 1830–1865* (Oxford: Clarendon Press, 1976).
65.   J. Mackenzie, ed, *Imperialism and Popular Culture* (Manchester: Manchester University Press, 1986).
66.   F. Migeod, *Through British Cameroons*, pp. 208–9; on the general question see K. Little, *African Women in Towns: An Aspect of Africa's Social Revolution* (London: Cambridge University Press, 1973).

67. United Nations Trusteeship Council (UNTC), T/1226, *United Nations Visiting Mission to the Trust Territories of the Cameroons under British Administration and the Cameroons under French Administration 1955. Report on the Cameroons under British Administration* (Hereafter *UN Visiting Mission*) New York, 1956), para. 264.

68. Among the measures proposed were a ban on the sale of any girl not sexually mature and the prohibition of the re-sale of wives; see H. Rudin, *Germans in the Cameroons: A Case Study in Modern Imperialism* (New York: Greenwood Press, 1968), pp. 300–3.

69. Migeod, *Through British Cameroons*, p. 210.

70. Lovejoy and Hogendorn, *Slow Death for Slavery*, chap. 9.

71. Figures were provided in the annual reports made by Britain to the League of Nations; the 1923 figures are taken from (NAI) CSO 26/2 11524, Vol. II.

72. Education policy had been heavily influenced by the Imperial Advisory Committee on Native Education in British Tropical Dependencies; correspondence relating to the committee may be followed in (NAI) CSO 26/1 03527, Vols. I-III.

73. LON PMC (Provisional) minutes 5th Meeting 5th Session of PMC October 1924; also see copies of minutes of the PMC meetings for 1923 and comments thereon by officials responsible for Northern Cameroons in (NAI) CSO 26/2 11524 and (NAI) CSO 26/2 13977, Vol. I.

74. (NAI) CSO 26/1 03527, Vol. I Secretary Southern Provinces to Chief Secretary to Government, 10 May 1922, in which Clifford's minute is quoted.

75. (NAK) MaiProf 1464A, Vol. III, p. 189.

76. (NAK) SNP 17/1 11133/ S./1; in 1945 Northern Cameroons sent one girl to the WTC.

77. See *Rep to LON 1938*, chapter on education.

78. (NAK) SNP 17/4 32350, Vol. II, pp. 258–90.

79. UNTC, T/1226 *UN Visiting Mission 1955*, p. 339.

80. United Nations General Assembly A/4314, *Report of the United Nations Plebiscite Commissioner for the Cameroons under UK Administration 1959*, paras 28–33; UNTC, T/1556, R*eport of the UN Commissioner for the Supervision of the Plebiscites in Southern and Northern Parts of the Trust Territory of the Cameroons under United Kingdom Administration 13 April 1961*, para. 412.

81. UNTC, *UN Visiting Mission 1952* provides reliable and useful information.

82. Ibid., p. 31.

83. *UN Visiting Mission 1955*, para. 339.

84. (Cameroon Archives, Buea) Ba series for *Annual Report Cameroons Province*, 1921.

85. *Report to GAUN 1955*, paras 660–5, (NAK) MaiProf 4646/S.4 and MaiProf 4646/S.7.

86. *UN Visiting Mission 1952*, para. 260, p. 27.

87. *UN Visiting Mission 1955*, pp. 30–1.

88. On several visits to the former Northern Cameroons between 1986 and 1989, I was informed that prostitution had been prominent.

89. This was the official view presented to the UN Visiting Missions of 1949, 1952 and 1955.

90. *UN Visiting Mission 1955*, para. 266.

91. Ibid., para. 263; and Robertson, 'Women's Education and Class Formation in Africa, 1950–1980' in Robertson and I. Berger, *Women and Class in Africa* (New York: Africana, 1986), pp. 92–113.

92. Two useful works on the plebiscites are V. le Vine, *The Cameroons from Mandate to Independence* (Berkeley: University of California Press, 1964) and C. Welch, *Dream of African Unity: Pan-Africanism and Political Unification in West Africa* (New York: Cornell University Press, 1966), chaps. IV and V.

93. See UN *Yearbook of the United Nations* (New York: Columbia University Press and the UN, various dates) for brief annual reports of the various UN agencies.

94. *UN Visiting Mission 1949*, p. 113.

95. *UN Visiting Mission 1955*, para. 322.

96. Created in 1955 by the Northern Nigeria government as an organ to promote and represent Northern Cameroons interests.

97. The members of the CCNC were referring to Switzerland; see Annex iv, p. 11 to *UN Visiting Mission 1958* .

98. The views of the CCNC and the mission's response are contained in *UN Visiting Mission 1958*, pp. 69–70.

99. UNTC, *Official Records*, 26th Session.

100. On this point see F.R. Augier, 'Before and After 1865' *New World Quarterly* 2, 2 (1965).

101. *Rep to GAUN 1952*, Statistical Appendix Table 1C.

102. Personal interview with Umaru Micika at Micika in mid-1989; Umaru campaigned on an anti-NPC platform.

103. UNTC, T/1556 *Plebiscite Commissioner's Report 1961*, paras 470–1.

104. *UN Visiting Mission 1955*, p. 30.

105. LON, A.14. 1937.V, Minutes and Resolutions of League Assembly, Geneva 1937.

106. The correspondence over the St Joan's Alliance may be followed in (NAI) CSO 26/4 30302, Vol. II; Britain issued Cmd paper 5784 of 1938 as a result of the information collected from the colonies on the welfare of women in British tropical Africa.

SECTION VII

The Legacy of Slavery:
Race, labour, politics and protest

CHAPTER 20

Politics at the 'Grassroots' in Free Jamaica

St James, 1838–1865

SWITHIN WILMOT

St James before 1838

The parish of St James formed an important part of Jamaica's western sugar belt and was at the centre of the 1831 slave rebellion that hurried the process towards the abolition of slavery in 1834.[1] Before this, the free Blacks and Coloureds in 1830 and then the Jews in 1831 were granted full civil rights. The juxtaposition of these three important events was not accidental, as the ruling planter class was eager to build alliances with the Coloured and Jewish elites who had been previously accorded second-class status in the slave society.[2] Thus, emancipation in 1834 was part of a process of social change that was soon mirrored in the politics of St James, as the Black and Coloured classes, urban and rural, jockeyed for political influence with the entrenched, mostly White planter and Jewish mercantile interests. Some notice has been taken of the Jews and Coloured elites as they challenged the planters for political office but less attention has been paid to the more humble members of the Black and Coloured communities: artisans, shopkeepers and rural freeholders, many of whom were former slaves. This discussion of politics in the parish underscores the extent to which the post-emancipation society adjusted to new social formations which deepened its creole nature and established a political culture that incorporated the urban artisans and the rural settlers.

Economy and early politics after abolition

Despite the difficulties experienced by the proprietors as a result of emancipation and free trade, St James in 1854 still had 41 sugar estates; only the neighbouring parish of Trelawny had more. Although sugar cultivation dominated the coastal areas of St James, in the mainly mountainous interior the estates held their own in the valleys and competed with the new settlements of the freed people that dotted the rural landscape. Many of these new settlements had mushroomed in the areas where sugar estates, 18 of which had been abandoned between 1832 and 1848, had previously dictated the daily routines of slaves.[3] Montego Bay, the chief port town of the parish, was second only to Kingston with a slave population of 2,237 in 1832 and a total population of 4,553 in 1861. It conducted a vigorous trade by land and by coastal shipping with its sugar hinterland, and the merchants and professionals there were really an extension of the sugar economy. Nonetheless, sections of the free Black and Coloured populations in Montego Bay had endorsed the 1831 rebellion and when Joseph Sturge visited the town in 1837 he referred to the 'liberal opinion' there that represented a challenge to the decaying slave order.[4]

The first indication in the parish that electoral politics was changing came in 1831 when John Manderson, a Coloured merchant and wharfinger in Montego Bay, won one of the two seats in the Assembly. Although Manderson put up bail for the Baptist missionaries who were imprisoned after the 1831 rebellion, he endorsed the planters' views on emancipation and distanced himself from some of the more progressive demands of the Coloureds on the south side of the island, particularly those in Kingston. Thus, the change in 1831 was more one of colour than of political content and Manderson represented St James with Richard Barrett, the Speaker of the Assembly. However, in September 1835, Governor Sligo, eager to challenge Barrett and other opponents in the Assembly, called an election, and a pro-government coalition of Blacks, Coloureds, Whites and Baptist missionaries in the towns of Falmouth, Lucea, Savanna-la-Mar and Montego Bay endorsed White and Coloured candidates who were more supportive of Sligo's policies. The coalition was successful in Trelawny where Matthew Farquharson, who was described as 'one of the number of prudential managers of properties' under the apprenticeship, won with the support of the Free Coloureds and William Knibb, the Baptist missionary. In Hanover, the Free Coloureds failed by one vote to win a seat but shared the representation in Westmoreland.[5]

However, in St James, the 1835 election was bitterly contested as Robert Osborn, a leading Coloured politician from Kingston, tried to unseat Barrett. In order to drive a wedge between the Coloured and White voters in St James, Osborn's backers revived accusations about Barrett's lukewarm support for the campaign for Free Coloured civil rights in the 1820s. However, once Manderson and the remainder of the Coloured mercantile and planting interests endorsed Barrett, his return was never in doubt. Manderson polled 156 votes and Barrett received 154, thereby thrashing Osborn, who only managed 40 votes. The minority who endorsed Osborn's candidacy reflected the class cleavages in the Black and Coloured community in Montego Bay. Since the Coloured and White planters and the Coloured, Jewish and White mercantile interest in Montego Bay all voted for Barrett and Manderson, the planter press insisted that Osborn had been defeated by 'men of character, intelligence, and property'. In contrast Osborn's 40 supporters, who were drawn primarily from the Black and Coloured artisans in the town, as well as from the Baptist community, including the Rev. Thomas Burchell, were dismissed in the press as the 'gang of the Watchman'. Further, given their relatively humble status among the voting community in the parish, the minority was taunted as being 'the ignorant, the reckless and the penniless'.[6] If the Black and Coloured artisans and Baptists in Montego Bay failed to make their mark in 1835, they would soon strengthen their political leverage once they mobilised the growing class of freeholders in the St James countryside, most of whom were ex-slaves.

Baptists: foundations and political mobilisation

After 1838 the Baptist ministers in Jamaica's western sugar belt were the first to extract political advantage from the new class of Black and Coloured freeholders. The missionaries focused on issues such as the State Church, immigration and new taxes on imported goods for mass consumption as well as additional taxes on land and on small settler animals. However, this brand of the politics of Christianity was halted in its tracks by the 1844 snap election which deprived many of the new class of small freeholders of the opportunity to exercise the franchise, as they had not registered their claims to vote for the 12 months as required by law.[7] Nevertheless, this mobilisation laid the foundations for future challenges, and the small freeholders scattered throughout the network of Baptist stations in St James determined the outcome of the 1849 election in the parish.

By that time, Baptist roots were deeply embedded in the St James human landscape. The White Baptist missionaries built on the foundations laid by Moses Baker, a free mulatto, who came from North America in 1783 and was a member of George Liele's Native Baptist Church. Between 1788 and 1822, when the European Baptists took over his ministry, Baker had established important cells of Christians among the slave population throughout rural St James as well as in Montego Bay. After 1822, Thomas Burchell carried the Baptist standard in the parish, and soon after the repression of the Colonial Church Union in 1832, Walter Dendy joined Burchell in expanding the Baptist influence in the parish. Together, these two European missionaries solidified the Baptist presence in St James.[8] Thomas Burchell's main area of activity focused on the Montego Bay mission as well as the Mount Carey settlement, eight miles to the south, which lay in the heart of the 1831 rebellion in which all the works and buildings on the nearby estates had been destroyed. In 1843, Burchell handed over the Montego Bay mission to the Rev. Philip Cornford and focused exclusively on the rapidly expanding settlements of freed people in the hills of southern St James. Accordingly, he established another Baptist station at Shortwood, near Cambridge, and he lived at Mount Carey until he left Jamaica for the last time in 1846.[9] Walter Dendy's area of work centred on the church at Salters Hill, nine miles to the southeast of Montego Bay. Dendy had first arrived in 1832, four days after the planters, masquerading under the banner of the Colonial Church Union, had destroyed the original chapel which had been built near the Crooked Spring area where Moses Baker had earlier established a small 'society'. Dendy rebuilt the church and re-dedicated it on Good Friday 1833, when it was estimated that over 5,000 persons were present. Clearly, repression had strengthened the appeal of the gospel in the area. After 1838, as the members of the Salters Hill congregation scattered throughout the mountains adjoining the sugar estates of southeast St James, Dendy established other stations at Johns Hall, Maldon and Sudbury. In addition, by 1843, another Baptist minister, the Rev. Thomas Picton, had taken over the church at Bethetephil, near the Trelawny border, which had been initially a station attached to Salters Hill. Thus, so rich was the Baptist harvest that where one minister had toiled up to 1832, four were labouring a decade later and by 1847 St James had ten Baptist places of worship which seated 10,500 people. The Presbyterians, with five stations offering seats for 3,150, were a distant second and vying for the third position were the Anglicans and the Methodists who each had four stations that offered accommodation for a total of 2,000 persons respectively. Rural St James had been truly baptised.[10]

Both Burchell and Dendy were more than church builders, as they were part of the Baptist tradition of establishing free villages. Burchell founded Carey Town, adjacent to the Mount Carey church, and Dendy pioneered one of the first free villages in western Jamaica at Maldon, just south of Maroon Town on the edge of the Cockpit Country. The Maldon residents still laboured on the nearby estates as the lots were insufficient to develop a livelihood totally independent of estate labour.[11] However, there were other freed people, connected to either Burchell's or Dendy's congregations, who purchased larger holdings on which they grew sugar-cane and manufactured sugar from small crude mills, as well as producing minor export crops such as ginger and arrowroot. Others also concentrated on provision growing and coffee cultivation which afforded them some degree of independence from estate work. Clearly, many freed people from the Mount Carey and Salters Hill circuit of churches had created a thriving economy that contrasted with some of the nearby struggling sugar estates.[12] The 1849 election in St James then, was the first political contest between the sugar planters and the pen-keepers and this new class of peasants and small farmers that dotted the uplands of rural St James in the heartland of the Baptist church.

The tone of the 1849 campaign was influenced by a decade of hostile relationships between the planters and the freed people. In the first months of full freedom, the St James planters, like their counterparts elsewhere in the island, had adopted coercive strategies of low wages and high rents to extract consistent labour from former slaves. When the workers resisted, some of the more aggressive overseers pulled down cottages and let loose estate stock in the provision grounds that fuelled the freed people's autonomy. Those that could left the estates and settled on the surrounding mountain land.[13] Forced to compromise, the planters adopted more conciliatory strategies which improved labour relations until another confrontation took place in the summer of 1841 when the planters, alarmed at declining sugar prices, unilaterally reduced wages by 50 per cent. The workers retaliated with a strike that forced their employers to restore the agreed wages. In the vanguard of this strike were the Baptist workers attached to the Salters Hill church, where an estimated 2,000 freed people met in September 1841 and determined to resist the reduced wages. Although the planters relented, Baptists who were leaders in the strikes, were later singled out for reprisal. For example, in 1845, one such 'leader' was driven from his estate when the planters tried again to curb militancy among the workers, which was traditionally blamed on Baptist influence. When the free trade crisis hit the Jamaican sugar industry in 1847, St James' labour relations were further unsettled as wage cuts and wild talk of re-enslavement generated fears of a re-enactment of the 1831 Baptist war in the summer of 1848.[14]

This whole undercurrent of strained labour relations surrounded the 1849 election, especially when the planters endorsed the candidacy of Henry Groves, who was a former overseer and had moved up the ranks to become a sugar planter. By 1849, he was the proprietor of Belvedere estate and he also owned lands that adjoined Lethe and Hazelymph estates, all of which were in the vicinity of the parish served by the Baptist church at Mount Carey. The Baptist influence was very strong in this area and the planters blamed them for the poor labour relations that prevailed there after 1838. While it is unclear as to exactly what role Groves played in these controversies, his property at Belvedere had earned a terrible reputation for cruel management on the eve of the 1831 rebellion. Further, Groves was known for his conservative principles, a euphemism for his renowned dislike of Free Coloureds and his firm hand with labourers. Indeed, Groves' reputation remained with him throughout the period; in 1863 Governor Eyre described him as 'very preju-dicial, violent and overbearing'.[15] It speaks volumes of the state of panic induced by the free trade crisis, that the planters in St James turned to an extremist such as Groves to be their standard bearer to unseat John Samuel Brown, a Coloured merchant from Kingston, who had won the seat in 1844 with the backing of the artisans and retail shopkeepers in Montego Bay as well as some of the planters. However, between 1847 and 1849, Brown had jeopardised whatever planter support he had in St James by voting with the town party in the Assembly against the extreme retrenchment policies that were orchestrated to embarrass the government into restoring protection to the sugar industry.[16] While the planters were now hostile towards Brown, the Coloured artisans in Montego Bay, led by seasoned activists such as Neil

Malcolm and Lawrence Hill, both of whom had voted for Robert Osborn in 1835, were determined to keep the seat for Brown, thereby ensuring that the Coloured community maintained a share in the representation of the parish. Since the planters enjoyed the support of Jewish mercantile interests, the outcome of the election hinged on the participation of the freed men in rural St James. It was left to Israel Levy Lewin, a Jew who had converted to the Baptist church, and who was Brown's election agent, to unleash the reservoir of voters scattered in the new mountain settlements of St James.[17]

Lewin's long record of supporting abolitionists' and workers' causes provided him with the ideal political pedigree to be in the vanguard of the new politics in St James after 1838. A shopkeeper, he settled in Montego Bay in 1824, where he developed a 'lucrative business'. However, he developed strong anti-slavery views and was boycotted by the planters, so that his business fortunes declined. Moreover, he was snubbed by the Jewish community because of his conversion to Christianity and was further ridiculed when he espoused the Baptist faith. Despite having to pay such a high price for his convictions, Lewin remained faithful to his principles and in his unofficial role as a protector of slaves, he persisted in reporting slave owners to the authorities whenever he could adduce proof of their sadistic treatment of slaves.[18] During the period of the apprenticeship, Lewin was a crucial ally of the embattled Stipendiary Magistrates and it was because of his vigilance that nearly 300 apprentices in St James were granted full freedom before 1838 because they had not been properly registered. One month before the apprenticeship ended, the governor, Sir Lionel Smith, appointed Lewin to the magistracy. He immediately became known as the people's magistrate and his support for the government in the dying days of the apprenticeship system further widened the gulf between himself and the St James planters.[19]

Even before his conversion, Lewin had established very strong links with the Baptists when he offered his house to Thomas Burchell to use as a chapel during his early ministry in Montego Bay. When the planters under the umbrella of the Colonial Church Union destroyed Burchell's church in 1832 and forced him into exile, Lewin again opened his home for services that were conducted by Samuel Vaughan, a Coloured deacon, who deputised in Burchell's absence. Suitably, Lewin was among those who laid foundation stones for the new Baptist chapel in 1835 soon after Burchell's return to the island. On that occasion Burchell paid public tribute to Lewin whom he described as 'the unflinching advocate of civil and religious liberty, and the undaunted defender of the oppressed'.[20] Lewin's public association with and support of the Baptists' programmes in St James continued into the post-emancipation period. For example, in September 1838, he chaired meetings held in the Baptist chapels in St James to promote education. In 1841, Lewin chaired the mammoth meeting of over 2,000 workers at the Salters Hill Baptist church to protest against the arbitrary reduction of wages. On that occasion, he revived memories of the 1831 rebellion which he described as a 'just means' to terminate the slavery that had been 'inflicted by cruel and bloodthirsty planters'. Moreover, he urged the workers to leave the estates rather than accept any reduction of their wages, since they alone should not bear the costs of years of poor management and extravagance on the part of the overseers and planters. He also reminded the ex-slaves that they were the 'main props of the country' and without them 'the country cannot stand'. Further, Lewin urged them not be 'daunted nor care what they say of you; but always be steady; all of you holding to one word, and not breaking off till you get everything you wish for'. Clearly, Lewin's antagonisms towards the planters survived intact into the post-emancipation period and, describing himself as 'The Esquire of the People', he frequently clashed with other magistrates over the administration of justice in the courts and their labour recruitment policies.[21]

In April 1849, four months before the election, Lewin was elevated to the post of deacon of the Baptist church in Montego Bay. By then, his over 20 years of consistent opposition to the planters and his links with the Baptists made him a most suitable person to mobilise the votes among the freed people scattered in the settlements in rural St James. Moreover, Lewin had close political links with the Black and Coloured voters in Montego Bay, who had first elected him a vestryman in 1832, and it was he who had nominated Robert Osborn in his failed election bid in 1835. Thus, in the campaign to re-elect Brown and to defeat Groves, Lewin was ideally placed to pioneer a coalition of Black and Coloured voters from both the urban and rural areas of St James.[22]

Henry Groves' supporters, intent on wooing the votes of small settlers in St James, organised ten rural committees of planters who, exploiting Brown's residence in Kingston, stressed that he was an outsider who could not be relied upon to promote the interests of St James. In addition, the planters emphasised that during the retrenchment debates in the Assembly, Brown had opposed various measures to reduce expenditure in order to lighten the tax burden, including that of the small settlers. To rebut this strategy, Lewin, who was Brown's accredited agent and representative, used the Baptist stations in the parish to conduct election meetings. There he countered the planter propaganda campaign against the 'absentee' Brown, by emphasising that although Groves was then resident in St James, he, unlike Brown, was not a 'native' of the island. Rather, Groves was described as yet another of the many 'adventurers' who had come to Jamaica 'to try their fortunes'. Significantly, Lewin and his supporters utilised not only appeals to creole nationalism that were calculated to impress especially the free Coloureds, they revived the colour and class issues to woo the small freeholders, who were reminded that Groves, when an overseer, had wielded 'undivided powers' against the 'oppressed' and he had 'exploited the Black people'.[23]

Politics at the 'Grassroots': the 1849 election

Given the spirited and at times bitter contest, Montego Bay was a scene of excitement on election day Friday, 10 August 1849. Small settlers poured into the town from the rural districts determined to exercise their franchise for the first time and to carry the election for Brown. Together with the locals from the town they made up the 'massive crowd' that assembled outside the courthouse for the polling. The poll opened at 8.00 am, but by 9.10 am, the returning officer adjourned proceedings until the following day because he claimed to have been 'obstructed and interrupted by open violence'. On the following morning, the crowd again assembled but a strong police detachment guarded the hustings and voting proceeded up until 4.00 pm, by which time Brown had defeated Groves by two votes to one, the former receiving 140 votes to the latter's 70.[24]

Lewin's campaign strategy that brought together the rural freeholders with the Black and Coloured urban artisans had paid handsome dividends as it was the Baptist network that formed the core of Brown's remarkable victory in St James, and this in the core of the sugar heartland in western Jamaica.

Prominent among the Baptist votes in Table 20.1 were Reverends Walter Dendy and James Reid, Baptist ministers. At least 16 of Brown's supporters were attached to the Baptist church at Mount Carey. Three of these, Alexander Haughton, a mason, William McIntosh, a carpenter, and John Palmer, formerly a slave on Childermas estate, resided at Carey Town which Thomas Burchell had established near the church. The other 13 Baptist voters from

Table 20.1:   Church Affiliation of Voters, St James, 1849

| | Brown | | Groves | |
| | Affiliation Known (N=83) | | Affiliation Known (N=49) | |
Church	Number	% of N	Number	% of N
Anglican	14	16.9	43	87.8
Baptist	59	71.1	0	–
Methodist	2	2.4	1	2
Presbyterian	7	8.4	1	2
Jew	1	1.2	4	8.2
Not Known	57	–	21	–
Total	140	100	70	100

Sources: House of Assembly Poll Book; Anglican Registers of Baptisms and Marriages; Dissenters' Marriage Registers; Synagogue Records

the Mount Carey church owned freeholds in nearby districts; Anchovy, Bickersteth, Cambridge, Childermas, Comfort Hall, Ducketts, Unity Hall and York. Five of these men owned freeholds in the Comfort Hall settlement, to the south of Roehampton estate. Thomas Bernard, described as a 'Leader' in the Montego Bay Baptist church, was among them and may have been an important organiser for the Baptist voters in this area of St James. In addition to these 16 Baptist voters, two other small freeholders who supported Brown owned land in two of the settlements mentioned above, Cambridge and York, and another resided at Fustic Grove. All these 19 freeholders were located in the general vicinity where Groves operated his properties at Belvedere, Hazelymph and Lethe. Their vote against Groves was an unequivocal statement of the altered social relations in rural St James and underscored the significance of the franchise for ex-slaves intent on asserting their autonomy and citizenship.[25]

Similarly, among the Baptist voters in Table 20.1 at least 25 men were connected to the Salters Hill church, including six from the Maldon area where Dendy had established a free village. These men had freeholds in settlements such as Aberdeen, Cold Spring, Endeavour, Johns Hall, Latium, Paisley, Potosi, Springmount, Somerton, Sudbury, Tangle River, Vaughansfield and Williamsfield. Five of these men merit individual mention as they reveal the nature of the rural constituency around the Salters Hill church that supported Brown. William Allen, a Blacksmith, who had been a slave on Virgin Valley estate, resided at Latium and called his freehold 'Happy Land'. Francis Munroe, a carpenter, had been a slave headman on Paisley estate but had relocated to the nearby Sudbury settlement after 1838 because of the oppressive rent and wages policies. Both freed men enjoyed sufficient standing among their community that they addressed the meeting of workers at Salters Hill in 1841. Lewin had chaired that meeting and Allen and Munroe, as influential freed men in the Salters Hill area, may have been important to Lewin's organisational efforts in the 1849 election. The third, Samuel Finlayson, was a long-standing member of the church, having been baptised by Burchell in 1828; he was the deacon at Maldon church when he died in 1861. His endorsement may explain the support that a Kingston merchant received from the settlers in the Maldon area, deep in rural St James. Henry Hunter, a Coloured Blacksmith, managed Latium estate during the apprenticeship system and from that time had been a strong financial supporter of the Baptist school at Salters Hill. William Melvin was a free Black and in 1848 was the teacher at the Sudbury school, an outpost of the Salters Hill church. Clearly freed men, as well as free Blacks and Coloureds, comprised the electoral base in the rural Baptist areas that ensured Brown's electoral victory. The expressive sobriquets that some of these freeholders gave to their individual settlements confirm this: 'At Last', 'Comfort Victoria', 'Fathers Gift', 'Giliad', 'Happy Freedom', 'Happy Land', 'Happy Valley', 'Littleman Feeling', 'Never Expect' and 'Trysee'.[26] Allen and Munroe, the two mentioned freed men above, were among the 28 artisans, or 48 per cent of those identified as being affiliated with the Baptists in Table 20.1. Only three of these artisans resided in Montego Bay, while the remainder lived in the new settlements scattered throughout rural St James. No doubt they were among the masons, carpenters and coopers who were vital to the working of the sugar properties. But their freeholds, while not always guaranteeing them full autonomy from the estates, provided them with important political leverage that was used to defeat their employers' candidate in 1849.[27]

The support that Brown received from the Presbyterian freeholders in Table 20.1 also underscores the extent of the solidarity between them and the Baptists in St James. When Knibb pioneered the Jamaica Anti-Church-State Convention in 1844, both George Blythe and Hope Waddell, the Presbyterian ministers in St James, had also endorsed the principles of voluntarism. These links were further cemented just five months before the 1849 election when Baptist, Congregational and Presbyterian ministers in St James and Trelawny launched the Jamaica Educational Society to promote the voluntarist principle in education. Given such renewed links and Lewin's own popularity with the Presbyterians, all six voters identified as freeholders in the Presbyterian free villages at Goodwill and Rose Hill, respectively, voted for Brown.[28]

Furthermore, Brown's support among the artisans in Montego Bay emphasised how class and colour solidarity had cut across sectarian boundaries in the 1849 election. Besides Samuel Vaughan and Thomas Williams, the two senior Baptist deacons in Montego Bay, at least 11 other Black or Coloured artisans drawn from the Anglican and Methodist congregations, respectively, voted for Brown. The most prominent among these Anglicans was Neil Malcolm, a Coloured cabinetmaker, who held the office of church warden on several occasions during this period.[29] But Groves' solid support (Table 20.1) among the Anglican community in the parish reflected the backing from the White and Coloured sugar planters, attorneys and overseers, as well as the professionals and merchants in Montego Bay. At least nine Coloureds who were connected with sugar properties or pens in various capacities as owners, managers or master craftsmen, respectively, supported Groves over the Coloured candidate. In addition, 13 Montego Bay Coloureds, including wharfingers and merchants, and three artisans who had been characterised before 1830 as being 'White by law', voted for Groves.[30]

The Jewish fraternity in Montego Bay voted along both ethnic and class lines. While Samah Corinaldi and Moses Gedelia jointly nominated the other incumbent candidate, George Lyons Phillips, a Jewish merchant and planter, they divided their loyalties between Brown and Groves. Also, all the other four Jewish retailers backed Groves. This may have reflected both their links with the plantocracy in the parish as well as their antipathy towards Lewin, who they saw as an apostate. Indeed, the level of Jewish support for Groves would have been even more significant had not five other Jews been prevented from voting for him because their names were not on the approved voters' list.[31]

While class, colour and ethnicity all influenced the voting pattern in 1849, class was the underlying factor. From 1831, the sugar interests in the parish had been content to share the two Assembly seats with the Coloureds, once they adopted the planters' positions on emancipation. When the Coloured artisans in Montego Bay challenged this arrangement by importing Osborn from Kingston in 1835, they were thrashed, as the better-off Coloureds maintained their support for Barrett. Thus, the planter strategies to oust Brown in 1849 might well have worked had the constituency remained as restricted as it had been in 1835, because the Coloureds and the Jews linked to the embattled sugar interest supported Groves. However, unlike 1835, the Montego Bay artisans in 1849 had the crucial support of the enlarged constituency in rural St James, most of whom were former slaves. Mobilised under the auspices of the network of Baptist churches in rural St James and marshalled by Lewin, Jew turned Baptist deacon, the Black and Coloured small freeholders exercised their political leverage for the first time in St James and the planters lost. Consequently, Groves' 70 voters paid £474.75 in taxes in 1848; Brown's 140 voters had paid £150.2 in the same year. Clearly, the freeholders in rural St James had combined with the urban Black and Coloured artisans and defeated the White and Coloured planters and Jewish merchants of St James.[32]

After 1849

This ascendancy in the electoral politics of St James was temporary, for even though four Black or Coloured artisans and small shopkeepers in Montego Bay were elected to the St James vestry up to 1854, the planters continued to dominate. Various explanations account for this. The cholera epidemic followed by an outbreak of smallpox in the early 1850s lowered the morale and size of the Baptist communities in rural St James and Lewin's death in 1855 deprived them of bold political leadership. Moreover, as income and property values declined in the wake of the crisis in the sugar industry, the Rev. Edward Hewitt, who took over the Mount Carey circuit in the 1850s, adopted a more conciliatory attitude towards the planters since he believed that his survival was intertwined with the sugar industry that provided employment for his members. In addition, dissension and strife in the Montego Bay Baptist community in the 1850s undermined the unity and cohesion that had been important to the 1849 victory. Moreover, as more of the freed men filed for tax relief because of 'poverty' and 'distress', they lost the franchise, and the 1858 stamp tax discouraged others from its exercise. Given these factors, Groves finally achieved his political ambition to sit in the Assembly in 1861 and with Wellesley Bourke, a conservative Coloured solicitor, they represented the parish until the Assembly's abolition in 1866. By then, representational politics in St James had gone full circle back to 1834 when it had been the domain of the very privileged elite, White, Coloured and Jew.[33]

Shut out of the electoral process whether by circumstances or by design, the small settlers resorted to public meetings and petitions to force their views on public issues and proposed legislation. This was not new, as during the strike of the Assembly in late 1838, Burchell had organised petitions among the ex-slaves supporting the suspension of the Assembly until the time when 'the great body of the people' attained the franchise. In the 1840s Burchell had also joined other ministers of the Baptist Western Union in organising meetings of labourers to protest the Assembly's 'class legislation' that limited alternatives to estate labour. Also, in the run up to the 1844 general election the ex-slaves in St James were drawn into the Baptist-led islandwide campaign that organised meetings protesting partisan taxation to support the Established church and immigration.[34]

After declining health forced Burchell to leave Jamaica in 1846, Dendy maintained the meetings of small settlers in the 1840s and 1850s where issues that affected their livelihoods and their churches were ventilated and petitions organised. Dendy defended his involvement in political education via public meetings on the grounds that 'There are times and seasons when ministers may legitimately step forward as advocates for the oppressed, and as champions for the Civil and Religious Liberties of mankind'. For Dendy, that time had arrived when his mission's viability was threatened by the extension of state-sponsored schools and the erection of Anglican chapels in districts that were already serviced by Dissenters. Similarly, immigration in the midst of declining wages and irregular work opportunities was attacked, as were the proposals to limit education in orphanages to 'agricultural labour' and the 'doctrines of the Church of England'. Therefore, when the small settlers' electoral influence declined, popular meetings were used to involve the men and women with no franchise in the discussion of public issues.[35]

Thus, in May 1865, the people of St James assembled in Montego Bay for one last time before the suppression of the Morant Bay Rebellion silenced protests and closed the doors to political institutions for Black and Coloured Jamaicans. This gathering was one of the Underhill meetings, where Baptist ministers and others highlighted the poverty, the growing unemployment, the excessive taxation and the recklessness of the Jamaican authorities that squandered public funds on immigration schemes and denied political rights for the people. At the St James Underhill meeting, the Rev. John Henderson, Baptist minister at Montego Bay, mentioned that the stamp tax on the franchise was designed specifically for the small settlers and it had 'shut their mouths'. However, there was clearly one Black ex-slave, Samuel Holt, a Baptist minister at Fyfes Pen in the neighbouring parish of St Elizabeth, who was neither intimidated by legislation nor by the presence on the platform of magistrates and planters. Articulating the sentiments of the St James Blacks and also those of the men and women who later marched into Morant Bay in October 1865, Holt warned, perhaps prophetically:

> We are poor. Have we got the same property, the same quantity of clothing and money as we had in times past? A reduction of taxation must take place. We shall have it made. We won't submit to be crushed down any longer.[36]

Therefore, if the freeholders had failed to sustain their influence in electoral politics in St James after the 1849 election, public meetings had provided some outlets for their views. By 1865, they were not only signing and endorsing petitions prepared by European Baptist missionaries, but now through Samuel Holt they were speaking for themselves.

Notes

1.   B.W. Higman, *Slave Population and Economy in Jamaica, 1807–1834* (Cambridge: Cambridge University Press, 1976), pp. 30–5, 229–31; M. Turner, *Slaves and Missionaries: The Disintegration of Jamaican Slave Society, 1787–1834* (Chicago: University of Illinois Press, 1982), pp. 148–78;

2.   G. Heuman, *Between Black and White: Race, Politics and the Free Coloreds in Jamaica* (Westport, CT: Greenwood Press, 1982), pp. 44–53; C. Holzberg, *Minorities and Power in a Black Society: The Jewish Community of Jamaica* (Lanham, MD: North-South Publishing, 1987), pp. 27–9.

3.   CO 137/330, Henry Barkly to Henry Labouchere, No. 35, 6 March 1856, enclosed letter of Richard Hill to Hugh Austin, 25 January 1856; Edward Underhill, *The West Indies: Their Social and Religious Condition* (London: Jackson, Walford and Hodder, 1862), pp.387, 394–9.

4.   J. Sturge and T. Harvey, *The West Indies in 1837* (London, 1838), p. 232; K. Brathwaite, 'The Slave Rebellion in the Great River Valley of St. James, 1831/32', *Jamaica Historical Review*, XIII (1982), p. 11; Higman, 'Jamaican Port Towns in the Early Nineteenth Century', in F. Knight and P. Liss, eds, *Atlantic Port Cities: Economy, Culture, and Society in the Atlantic World, 1650–1850* (Knoxville, TN: University of Tennessee Press, 1991), pp.121–35.

5.   Heuman, *Between Black and White*, pp.57–8, 100; *Falmouth Post*, 7 October 1835.

6.   Jamaica Archives (JA) 1B/11/23/18, House of Assembly Poll Book, 1803–43, folios 141–5; *Kingston Chronicle*, 14 and 19 September, 9 and 10 October 1835. The *Watchman* was the Kingston-based newspaper owned by Edward Jordon and Robert Osborn, the political leaders of the Coloureds for most of this period.

7.   CO 137/280, Earl Elgin to Lord Stanley, No. 108, 7 September 1844; *Baptist Herald*, 23 June 1843, 9 July, 3 and 10 September 1844; P. Curtin, *Two Jamaicas: The Role of Ideas in a Tropical Colony* (New York: Atheneum, 1970), pp. 182–3.

8.   Underhill, *The West Indies*, pp. 388–90, 395.

9.   Ibid., pp. 391, 399–400; Sturge and Harvey, *The West Indies in 1837*, p. 227; W. Burchell, *Memoir of Thomas Burchell; Twenty Two Years A Missionary in Jamaica* (London, 1849), p. 374.

10.   National Library of Jamaica (NLJ) MS 378, Baptist Missionary Society, 1844–54, Walter Dendy to Joseph Angus, 19 April 1847 and 1 January 1848; *Jamaica Almanac 1843*, p. 92; Underhill, *The West Indies*, pp. 389, 395–6.

11.   Island Record Office (IRO) *Land Deeds*, Liber 884, folio 144; Liber 833, folio 215; Liber 887, folio 146; D. Hall, *Free Jamaica, 1838–1865: An Economic History* (New Haven: Yale University Press, 1959) pp. 23–4.

12.   CO 137/322, Barkly to Duke of Newcastle, 26 May 1854; Underhill, *The West Indies*, pp. 394–6.

13.   Underhill, *The West Indies*, p. 387; J.J. Gurney, *A Winter in The West Indies* (London, 1840), pp. 140–1.

14.   CO 137/248, Gov. Charles Metcalfe to Lord John Russell, 30 March 1840; *Jamaica Standard and Royal Gazette*, 25 September 1841; Underhill, *The West Indies*, p. 387; L. Simmonds, 'Civil Disturbances in Western Jamaica, 1838–1865', *Jamaica Historical Review*, Vol. XIV (1984), p.8.

15.   CO 137/376, Gov. Edward Eyre to Newcastle, No. 277, 2 December 1863; *Land Deeds*, Liber 845, folio 157; Liber 925, folio 222; Liber 930, folio 208; Sturge and Harvey, *The West Indies in 1837*, pp. 230–1; Gurney, *A Winter in the West Indies*, pp.140–2; *Falmouth Post*, 17 July 1849; *Morning Journal*, 18 September 1849.

16.   JA 1B/11/23/19, House of Assembly Poll Book, 1844–66, folios 23–4; Heuman, *Between Black and White*, pp. 142–7; T. Holt, *The Problem of Freedom: Race, Labor, and Politics in Jamaica and Britain, 1832–1938* (Baltimore, MD: The Johns Hopkins University Press:, 1992), pp. 224–9.

17.   *Morning Journal*, 16 July 1849; *Falmouth Post*, 17 and 24 July, 3 and 8 August 1849, 11 September 1855. The date of Israel Lewin's conversion to the Baptist church is not certain but he had a migratory religious sojourn. Raised a Jew, he married either a Coloured or Black woman in the Anglican church in

1829 and their Coloured daughter was baptised in that church in 1832. In 1849 he was appointed a deacon of the Montego Bay Baptist church. When he died in 1855, his funeral service was jointly conducted by Revs. Walter Dendy (Baptist) and Thompson (Presbyterian). Lewin's body was laid to rest in the Presbyterian burial ground.

18. CO 137/191, Lewin to Thomas Gray, Senior Magistrate of St James, 26 July 1833; JA 2/3/3, St. James Vestry Minutes, 1852–5; *Falmouth Post*, 11 September 1855.

19. Sturge and Harvey, *The West Indies in 1837*, pp. 205, 232; *Morning Journal*, 2 and 31 July 1838.

20. Burchell, *Memoir of Thomas Burchell*, pp. 274–6, 290. Lewin's account of Sam Sharpe's last words before his execution for leading the great slave rebellion of 1831 were later used by Baptist ministers to rehabilitate Sharpe as a freedom fighter. Furthermore, Lewin assisted the Baptists in removing Sharpe's remains from the original seaside grave to a vault in the Baptist church in Montego Bay.

21. CO 137/238, Sir Lionel Smith to Lord Glenelg, 23 April 1839, enclosures; *Morning Journal*, 3 October 1838; *Jamaica Standard*, 9 January 1839; *Jamaica Standard and Royal Gazette*, 25 September 1841.

22. NLJ MS 378, Dendy to Angus, 9 April 1847; *Kingston Chronicle*, 10 October 1835; *Falmouth Post*, 11 September 1855.

23. *Falmouth Post*, 17, 24 July and 3 August 1849; *Morning Journal*, 24 July and 18 September 1849.

24. JA 1B//11/23/19, House of Assembly Poll Book, 1844–65, folios 64–7; *Morning Journal*, 6 and 17 September 1849.

25. JA 2/3/2 and 3, St James Vestry Minutes, 1837–45, 1852–59; NLJ MS 378, Resolution of Baptist Church, Montego Bay, 2 July 1848; IRO Dissenters Marriage Registers, Vols 1–4; *Land Deeds*, Liber 827, folio 43; Liber 833, folio 121; Liber 845, folio 157; Liber 852, folio 16; Liber 869, folio 147; Liber 870, folios 12 and 61; Liber 872, folio 74; Liber 882, folios 75 and 144; Liber 883, folio 121; Liber 887, folio 146; Liber 888, folios 151 and 155; Liber 925, folio 222; Liber 930, folio 208; Liber 931, folio 109; Underhill, *The West Indies*, pp. 391, 395.

26. JA 2/3/3, St James Vestry Minutes, 1852–59, Tax Relief Lists; IRO Dissenters Marriage Registers, Vols 1–4; NLJ MS 378, Reports on Salters Hill and Maldon Churches, 31 December 1848 and 1861; *Land Deeds*, Liber 833, folio 25; Liber 841, folio 148; Liber 861, folio 5; Liber 870, folios 61 and 62; Liber 878, folio 201; Liber 882, folios 74 and 75; Liber 883, folio 74; Liber 896, folio 150; Liber 902, folio 58; *Jamaica Standard and Royal Gazette*, 25 September 1841; Sturge and Harvey, *The West Indies in 1837*, p. 223.

27. The artisans were as follows: eight masons, eight carpenters, seven coopers, four Blacksmiths and one bricklayer. Seventeen of the remaining 31 voters who were Baptists were described as 'labourers', a nomenclature used to describe both skilled and unskilled workers. For the specific categories above see *Land Deeds*, Liber 830, folio 78; Liber 860, folio 157; Liber 872, folio 76; Liber 884, folio 19; Liber 918, folio 73; *Jamaica Gazette*, 9 October 1845, 15 October 1846, 31 May 1849 and 7 July 1859; Dissenters Marriage Registers, Vols 1–6; Underhill, *The West Indies*, p. 405.

28. NLJ MS 378, Dendy to Angus, 19 March 1849; *Land Deeds*, Liber 843, folios 8 and 10; Liber 854, folio 186; Liber 858, folio 58; *Baptist Herald*, 28 May 1844; *Falmouth Post*, 11 September 1855.

29. JA 1B/11/8/8/4 and 5, St James Registers of Baptisms, 1826–64: JA 1B/11/23/18 and 19, House of Assembly Poll Books, 1804–66; JA 2/3/2, St James Vestry Minutes, 1837–45; NLJ MS 378, Dendy to Samuel Vaughan, 16 January 1849.

30. IRO St James Registers of Baptism, 1770–1841; JA 1B/11/8/8/4, St James Registers of Baptism, 1826–46; *Jamaica Gazette*, 19 February and 2 July 1846, 5 October 1848, 17 October 1850, 23 October 1851, 13 January 1852, 6 July 1854; *Jamaica Almanac 1845*, Returns of Proprietors, pp. 69–73.

31. JA 1B/11/23/19, House of Assembly Poll Book, 1844–65, folios 64–7; *Jamaica Gazette*, 9 October 1845, 1 January, 9 April and 2 July 1846, 21 January 1847 and 13 January 1852; *Land Deeds*, Liber 890, folio 183; *Morning Journal*, 17 September 1849; *Falmouth Post*, 11 September 1855.

32. *Kingston Chronicle*, 9 October 1835; *Falmouth Post*, 3, 8 August and 11 September 1849.

33. JA 2/3/3, St James Vestry Minutes 1852–59; NLJ MS 378, Dendy to Underhill, 22 February 1851 and 4 May 1852; Rev. J.E. Henderson to Rev. Thomas Trestrail, 9 December 1856; Curtin, *Two Jamaicas*, p. 188; Heuman, *Between Black and White*, p. 62; *Falmouth Post*, 18 December 1851 and 11 September 1855.

34. Burchell, *Memoir of Thomas Burchell*, pp. 350–1, 359–60; Curtin, *Two Jamaicas*, pp. 182–3; *Baptist Herald*, 27 May 1840 and 28 May 1844; *Falmouth Post*, 7 September 1844.

35. NLJ MS 378, Dendy to Angus 19 April 1847, 6 October 1847 and 16 January 1849; Dendy to Trestrail 24 May 1851; Dendy to Underhill, 4 May 1852.

36. CO 137/391, Eyre to Edward Cardwell, No. 137, 6 June 1865, enclosures. *Parliamentary Papers (PP)* 1866, (3683–1), XXXI, *Report* of the Jamaica Royal Commission, Part II, Minutes of Evidence, p. 1043. For a fuller discussion of the Underhill Meetings see Heuman, '*The Killing Time': The Morant Bay Rebellion in Jamaica* (London: Macmillan Press, 1994), pp. 44–63.

'A Brave and Loyal People'

The role of the Maroons in the
Morant Bay Rebellion in 1865

JOY LUMSDEN

*I*n the late 1730s the two groups of Maroons in Jamaica, in the east and the west, both signed treaties with the British authorities committing them to assist the Jamaican government in maintaining law and order, and the security of the island. They agreed to return runaway slaves, help to put down slave rebellions and defend the island against foreign invasion. In exchange the Jamaican government guaranteed the Maroons their freedom, possession of certain lands and a special relationship with the government through White officials permanently resident in the Maroon towns. By and large, both sides abided by the terms of these treaties, and even after the general emancipation of the slaves had changed the status of the Black population in general, the Maroons still believed that they had a special relationship with the British authorities. When the Morant Bay Rebellion broke out in October 1865, the Maroons of the eastern parishes rallied to the support of the colonial authorities, apparently without any reservations.[1]

A 'Black gendarmerie': 1738–1838

The Maroons' support of the British government for more than a century, from 1738 to 1865, has caused much debate, since they have often been identified as freedom fighters on account of their struggles against the Colonial Government in Jamaica before the treaties of 1738–9. Their struggle at that period is seen as part of a wider Black struggle against White colonial oppression. However, the Maroons' almost totally consistent fulfilment of their treaty obligations has made it difficult, if not impossible, for advocates of a freedom fighter hypothesis to explain and justify Maroon actions during the greater part of their history. No events have been more unpalatable than the Maroon refusal in 1865 to support the rebels in St Thomas, their enthusiastic cooperation with government forces in the suppression of the 'Rebellion' and their capture of the leader, Paul Bogle. Although some attempts have been made to modify the freedom fighter image of the Maroons, there is need for further objective consideration of their actions and motives, both before and after the signing of the treaties. Without such consideration, further discussion of the role of the Maroons will only involve reiteration of previous arguments about the treachery and perfidy of a group of people who have, from another viewpoint, been described as 'a brave and loyal people'.[2] Here an attempt will be made to review the involvement of the Maroons in the events of 1865, and to set that involvement, briefly, into the context of the whole history of the Maroons and their relationship to the British Colonial System.[3]

There can be no doubt that during the eighteenth century the Maroons, starting with Cudjoe, the leader of the Leeward Maroons in the First Maroon War, enthusiastically carried out their treaty obligations; within a year of the treaties, Maroon assistance was offered against the Spaniards in the newly declared war between Britain and Spain. Throughout the eighteenth century the Maroons were involved in other operations in conjunction with Jamaican government forces. They took part in the suppression of Tacky's rebellion in 1760 in St Mary, and were paid for their part in the suppression of this and other episodes of unrest in the eastern parishes. In 1779–80 the Maroons were called upon to be ready to defend the island against possible French invasion, and accounts of Maroon involvement in military operations indicate the expense involved in keeping them in the field; payments for Maroon parties were a regular and substantial item in the Assembly's annual accounts.[4]

The only occasion when the Maroons' loyalty to their treaty obligations was called into doubt was during the Second Maroon War in 1795. Then, the Trelawny Town Maroons took up arms against the Jamaican Government, but their neighbours from Accompong assisted government forces against them. The Windward Maroons were apparently more ambivalent; Scotts Hall kept out of the conflict, while Moore Town was rumoured to be inclined to support the rebels. Charles Town offered assistance to the government, then withdrew, and later had to make gestures of submission and reassertion of loyalty. After the disturbing events of 1795–6, the Maroons seem largely to have returned to their previous policy of full cooperation with the authorities; along with free Black and Coloured troops, as well as slaves, they continued to operate against rebels and runaways, always maintaining their reputation as the most effective fighters.[5]

The last major operation during slavery which involved the Maroons was the suppression of the Christmas rebellion of 1831. The leaders of that rebellion tried unsuccessfully to persuade the Accompong Maroons not to oppose the revolt, even if they would not join it. By 31 December, Maroons were arming and offering their services to assist in putting down the rebellion, and in mid-January 1832 a contingent of 107 Windward Maroons arrived at Falmouth and were used in the general mopping-up operations. These men were from Moore Town and Charles Town, and were led by the White superintendent of Charles Town, Captain Fyfe (later Colonel). They were considered effective and enthusiastic fighters, and their use seemed a valuable way of reinforcing their loyalty at a critical time. However, the abolition of slavery in 1834 and the ending of apprenticeship in 1838 brought about a fundamental change in the relationships within Jamaican society, and, in theory at least, ended the Maroons' special status; but they could not readily accept such a change.[6]

In 1842 the Jamaica Assembly passed an Act, the Maroon Lands Allotment Act, which placed the Maroons on the same legal footing as all other British subjects in Jamaica. They no longer had special obligations in dealing with internal and external threats; payment for work on roads ceased; their corporate ownership of their lands was to end; and the special representatives of the government in the Maroon towns were to be withdrawn. The main effect of the Act was to deprive the Maroons of their two main sources of income: from the parties organised against internal unrest, and from road building and maintenance. It is hardly surprising that the Maroons refused to accept the

Act; at the time and, generally, ever since they have maintained that the 1842 Act could not abrogate their treaties of 1739. They were not prepared to accept that they had now become ordinary British subjects, like the rest of the White, Coloured and Black population, including the newly freed slaves. They still considered themselves to be a special people, with a distinct relationship with the British authorities. Interestingly, in light of later events, this view of the Maroons was supported by George William Gordon, who noted, in the House of Assembly in 1864, their claim to be 'a superior class of people', and asserted that 'There was no class of people to whom the country was more indebted than the Maroons . . . They had distinguished themselves as great men in war; they had distinguished themselves as faithful subjects of the King or Queen, as the case might be'.[7] Although there is little information for this period, it seems reasonable to assume that the Maroons wished to continue to assert their special status in any way that remained open to them. They still assumed that they would be called upon to fulfil the role of a 'Black gendarmerie', as Richard Hart describes them, under their old commanders, if the need arose. The British may have thought that the old arrangements had been abrogated, but the Maroons certainly did not think so. In 1865 the colonial authorities were to be very thankful for this stubborn loyalty.

Uncertain loyalties

There was, however, no absolute certainty that the Maroons would remain true to their old allegiance. There were those, apparently including Bogle himself, who thought that the Maroons would rally to the side of the rebels in the eastern parishes, but it is not clear from any records why Bogle expected Maroon support. It seems that there was only one group of Maroons who might have considered joining the rebels: the little studied, secondary Maroon settlement of Hayfield, near Bath, which was probably established in the mid-eighteenth century as an offshoot of Moore Town. The Rev. William Clarke Murray, a Coloured Wesleyan minister, gave evidence to the 1866 Royal Commission that the Hayfield Maroons were very different from the Moore Town Maroons, whom he characterised as 'revengeful' and 'savage'. He claimed that the Hayfield Maroons warned him of threats to his life by the Moore Town Maroons because he had criticised their actions in the suppression of the rebellion. Bogle appealed to the Hayfield Maroons on behalf of the Black smallholders of St Thomas, assuming a commonality of interests, but to obtain Maroon support he had to get past the ingrained attitudes of the Maroons towards the rest of the Black population. A young non-Maroon Jamaican, I.E. Thompson, writing an account of the Moore Town Maroons in the 1930s, set out their traditional attitude:

> So they claim that they were not slaves, and are therefore distinct from the rest of Black people in Jamaica. They also claim to be more dignified and of a higher blood as their ancestors were not slaves . . . They call the rest of the Blacks 'Neagres' meaning a down-trodden race whose ancestors were slaves. It should be noted that the term 'neagre' is not used by them to mean 'negro', as they claim all Black people are negroes of which they form a part. Neither is the term a complimenting one, but is disrespectfully used by them to describe all the Blacks of Jamaica who cannot claim Maroon lineage.[8]

If the Hayfield Maroons shared these views at all, it is hardly surprising that Bogle received no comfort from their leaders, who claimed to have rejected his overtures when he visited them in September 1865, and warned him not to approach the Moore Town Maroons either. Francis Dean, from Moore Town, claimed to have responded, two weeks before the rebellion, to a man who said the Maroons were going to join in the fight against the White people, 'That is a thing we cannot do'. No Maroon, however, did anything to inform the authorities about Bogle's activities.[9]

In spite of these discouraging reactions, Bogle seemed to have hoped for Maroon support, even after the outbreak of violence in Morant Bay. On 17 October 1865, he and others reportedly signed a call to arms, which included the claim that the Maroons had sent a proclamation to them to 'meet them at Hayfield at once without delay, that they will put us in the way how to act'. On the same day an anonymous letter to the Custos of St Mary from a would-be rebel claimed 'We have received a letter from the captain of the Buff Bay Maroons, as soon as they are ready we will be'. There is no documentary evidence of any actions of, or communications from, the Maroons which would have substantiated these claims, but given the uncertainties of the time, some offer of Maroon support cannot be entirely discounted. On 13 October Major-General Forbes Jackson, a retired East India Company officer living in the Blue Mountains, wrote urgently to nearby Newcastle, the army's hill station, for reinforcements, since 'The insurrection of the Black population is rapidly increasing, and the Maroons are reported as marching to join the rebels'. In Portland, W. Wemyss Anderson, the Clerk of the Peace, was anxiously seeking protection for Port Antonio, not apparently from the rebels whom he barely mentioned, but from the Maroons of Moore Town. There was no general certainty about the course the Maroons were likely to take; the fear that they might back the rebels was clearly in the forefront of the minds of those nearest to the outbreak in St Thomas.[10]

The tradition sustained

As it turned out there was no need for the authorities to be concerned; as soon as news of the rebellion in St Thomas spread, the Maroon towns in the eastern parishes speedily volunteered their support to the authorities in their various localities. James Sterling, the Major at Hayfield, sent two men down to Bath on Thursday 12 October when he saw fires on the plain in the early hours of the morning, and received the report that rebels had entered and plundered the town. William Kirkland, a Magistrate in Bath, asked the Maroons for help, and early on Friday morning a group of Maroons went down to the town to take up the duty of protecting it. On the same day a letter was sent out to the Maroons by the Executive Committee in Kingston informing them of the rumours that they were siding with the rebels, and there was an immediate response from Moore Town offering the Committee every support. Within three or four days of the uprising Samuel Constantine Burke, a Coloured lawyer and Member of the Assembly, received an offer of help from the Scotts Hall Maroons, and by 20 October Captain Skyers of the St George's Volunteers was reporting the good response from Charles Town and Scotts Hall to the call for volunteers. There was very soon no doubt as to the Maroons' loyalty to their old treaty allegiance; it then remained to be seen what role they would actually play in the operations against the St Thomas rebellion.[11]

The participation of the Maroons in the suppression of the Morant Bay Rebellion has been attacked on two major grounds. The first is the ideological ground that they ought not to have joined with the White colonial regime to suppress their fellow Blacks; this is an attempt to force nineteenth-century Maroons into a twentieth-century model of Black solidarity, which it is clear was not a part of their *Weltanschauung*. The second ground is the extreme ferocity of their actions against the people of St Thomas; this charge needs closer investigation than it has received, and an attempt will be made to review the evidence for and against it, while outlining the Maroons' involvement.

In 1865, the Maroons operated mainly in three clearly defined groups. The most active group was that from Moore Town, and their activities will be considered in greatest detail. First, however, the actions of the Hayfield Maroons on the one hand, and the Charles Town and Scotts Hall groups on the other, can be considered separately and fairly briefly. There are not many references to the services performed by the Hayfield Maroons, about 30 of whom moved down into Bath on the morning of Friday 13 October. Their arrival was a great relief to the population of Bath, especially the Coloured residents, who had panicked on the previous day at the arrival of some 200 armed 'rebels'. Kirkland and many others fled precipitately into the surrounding woods in fear for their lives. The marchers from Morant Bay plundered the shops, and remained in the town until the Maroons' arrival on the following morning, when they fled on hearing their horns. These 30, poorly armed Maroons were able to protect the people of Bath until Fyfe's arrival with a contingent from Moore Town on 20 October. Meanwhile, they began to go out and bring in prisoners, with the help of the local constables, who had regained their confidence. According to Sterling, his men only brought in prisoners, and escorted those accused of major crimes down to Morant Bay. He denied that he and his men were involved with any burning of houses or flogging of prisoners, although he agreed that he had seen prisoners flogged on Kirkland's orders. After the arrival of Fyfe, the Hayfield Maroons came under his orders, but the implication seems to be that they continued their previous activities and were not involved with the forays of the Moore Town Maroons who had come with Fyfe. There appear to have been few complaints about these Maroons in Bath, and the general opinion as expressed in newspapers at the time and in evidence to the Commission was that the presence of the Hayfield Maroons in Bath had prevented loss of life among the residents of the area, and there were no accusations of any atrocities by them. The activities of the Maroons in St George and Metcalfe seem to have been of a similar nature and produced similar responses.[12]

Maroons from Scotts Hall and Charles Town do not appear to have been used in operations in St Thomas. On 16 October Skyers, in charge of the volunteers in St George, was ordered to muster volunteers and all loyal Maroons, inform the authorities in Port Antonio as to the number of men at his disposal and then put himself under the orders of the regular officer who would arrive in Buff Bay with a strong force on 17 October. On 20 October Skyers reported having Charles Town and Scotts Hall Maroons among the 86 men he had sworn in, and that 21 of them had gone to Port Antonio to collect 50 firearms for the Maroons. Forty Scotts Hall Maroons remained in

Metcalfe, seeing no action and being kept there 'to control the people'. There is little further information about the movements of the Maroons from Charles Town. According to the instructions received from Port Antonio on 19 October, they were to be issued '50 stand of arms, and 1,500 rounds of ammunition'. They were then to patrol southwards from Charles Town towards Newcastle, and eastwards along the coast as far as Hope Bay, guarding the Swift River Pass and scouring the woods in the area. These patrols numbered some 42 and their purpose was to prevent the 'rebels' spreading westwards out of St Thomas. Apparently a few people were taken on suspicion of being 'rebels', but they may well have been frightened people, especially Africans, fleeing from the Morant Bay area. The Maroons of Scotts Hall and Charles Town, therefore, did not play a very high-profile role in the suppression of the Morant Bay Rebellion, but were used in patrol and policing duties; like the Moore Town Maroons, however, they had made clear from the start where their allegiance lay.[13]

The leadership of Colonel Fyfe

The most useful sources for studying the activities of the Moore Town Maroons are the dispatches from Colonel Fyfe, which Governor Edward Eyre forwarded to the Colonial Office, and the evidence of Maroons and others given to the Royal Commission in 1866. Fyfe's dispatches, written on the spot and immediately after the events recorded, give information which is not influenced by the criticism of operations in St Thomas which surfaced once responses were received from Britain. It is important to realise that the suppression of the 'rebels' in St Thomas was completed long before Eyre had received any advice or reply from the Colonial Office. The response to his first dispatch of 20 October, which had reached London on 16 November, arrived in Kingston on 21 December and only then did Eyre begin to realise that he was going to have to defend his actions. Until then there was no reason for any camouflaging or excusing of actions, and it can reasonably be assumed that the information given was genuinely believed to be the truth.

Eyre, Fyfe and Brigadier-General Nelson arrived in Port Antonio during the morning of 15 October, coming from Morant Bay in *HMS Wolverine*. There were between 100 and 150 Maroons in the town, with about a half-dozen muskets. When Nelson ordered ten of them to act as guides to Captain Hole who was being dispatched towards the east, the Maroons refused. However, when Fyfe joined them, he was greeted with great enthusiasm and recollections of 1832; they declared themselves ready to follow him wherever he chose. Returning to Kingston, Eyre arranged for arms to be supplied to the Maroons by 18 October, and Fyfe could then lead them south over the mountains into St Thomas, as he and Nelson had agreed. Fyfe was 'authorised to follow his own judgement according to occurring circumstances, reporting as frequently as possible all movements', the same discretion he had been given in St James in 1832, and he soon had to start using it. On 20 October at Moore Town he decided to follow up a report of shooting heard some days earlier that might have come from a 'rebel' camp some 20 miles west of Moore Town and some 12 miles from Whitehall, on the Plantain Garden River. Fyfe then drew up a plan to split up his men, as he later reported to Eyre, including a 'hurried sketch' (map) of his planned movements:

> Starting from Moore Town No 1 party 23 men to march from Moore Town to Cambridge – thence to Kenney about 3 miles when they would leave 8 men – the rest to march through the interior, parallel with the coast to the back of Manchioneal entering the main road at Hector's River thence by main road to Amity Hall – No 2 Thirty men to march from Moore Town Westward through the woods towards the point marked 'supposed rebel Camp' (about 20 miles) so that there for the night & to be at Whitehall (distant about 12 miles) on the following afternoon.
>
> No 3 – 70 men to march to Bath & to proceed to Whitehall on the following afternoon taking Torrington on the way.
>
> I accompanied No 3.[14]

This plan was followed, and eventually the three groups were reunited in Bath on the night of 22 October.[15]

The march from Moore Town took place in the 'heaviest rain' Fyfe had ever seen, raising the problems of crossing rivers, exposure for the men and wet percussion caps. He reached Bath on the afternoon of 20 October, and confirming that Torrington had not yet been checked out by any troops, decided to move on it early on 21 October. The advance party was fired on, one Maroon being slightly wounded; they returned the fire and according to Fyfe's report at this time 'nine of the rebels were killed'. They burned the houses in the village, 'but leaving a small outbuilding at each place to shelter the women and children'. He ordered most of his party to spend the night in the hills, while he and 12 men went to Whitehall to meet the No. 2 party, which had seen no one on their march. The skirmish at Torrington was later cause for much concern and debate, and in his evidence to the Commission Fyfe stressed especially that the village was deserted by the time he entered it. At the time, however, he only reported two incidents. He arrested a Hayfield Maroon who had disobeyed his orders and taken a small party to Torrington during the night. He was also disappointed to find an old Maroon living at Torrington, who had been with him in 1832, but who had not informed other Maroons of the threatened uprising. The Maroons wanted to shoot him, but Fyfe limited them to burning down his house and sugar mill.

In spite of the continuing heavy rain, Fyfe planned further sorties for the Maroons, and reported to Eyre his intention to deploy them along the length of the Plantain Garden River Valley, making use of their tracking skills to flush the remaining rebels out of the woods. Their major success came on 23 October; receiving information of Bogle's whereabouts, Fyfe set off with a large party to sweep the area. After a hard day's work, moving silently, they took Bogle unawares, 'coming out of the bush with a sugar cane in his hand'. He was taken to Whitehall by about 7.30 pm and Fyfe sent an express messenger to Nelson with the news. Early the following morning Bogle was sent down to Morant Bay, presumably under Maroon guard. On 25 October the operations continued in the Stony Gut and Middleton areas, which were 'fired' and where seven men were killed. Fyfe left there and rode to Torrington where Maroons were scouring the hills for people whom he had told to surrender within 24 hours. One man was shot during the process, and those who came in were told that a day would be set for them to come in to Bath, when their offences would be dealt with. For the rest of the month Fyfe and the Maroons continued to 'scour' the valley, retrieving much plunder, search-ing for remaining rebels and holding a Court Martial at Monklands on 1 November, when two men were sentenced to be shot, and one to 100 lashes. Fyfe issued papers of protection to groups of people who surrendered, if they were not implicated in murder cases and had no plunder in their possession. He also issued papers to those who brought in stolen goods, so that others would not be afraid to do so.[16]

By the evening of 1 November he could call all the Maroons to assemble at Bath to hear his dispositions for the succeeding days, since an amnesty had been proclaimed. The plan, agreed with Eyre, was to take a body of some 200 Maroons, mostly from Moore Town, into Kingston and on round the island. The remaining Moore Town Maroons were to stay on at Bath as messengers and to continue patrols, also watching the road over the Cunha Cunha Pass, where some local people had been set to work as punishment for their participation in looting. Fyfe arrived in Kingston on 6 November, and the Maroons followed, being entertained in St Thomas and St David; joined by groups from Charles Town and Scotts Hall, they reached Kingston on 13 November. Maroon participation in suppressing the 'rebellion' in St Thomas was over; the controversy about that participation had not yet started.[17]

Aftermath of the Rebellion

There were three main consequences of the Maroons' activities – two were immediate and, for them, positive; the other started by the end of 1865, was negative and has to some extent continued ever since. The two immediate and positive consequences were the triumphal tour to Kingston, Accompong and the north coast, and the suggestions that the Maroons should be permanently reconstituted as a militia force; these can be dealt with fairly briefly. The much more important consequence was the barrage of attacks on the ferocity of the Maroons, which was extensively investigated by the Royal Commission in 1866 and has been debated ever since; this is a matter for more detailed consideration.

The suggestion of an island tour by Maroons first came from Fyfe in a dispatch on 29 October, when he wrote 'So soon as I can be spared I should like to take a party of the Maroons through St David, Kingston, Spanish town to Accompong detouring to some of the other parishes in the way. The sight of us might do good'. Eyre immediately responded with enthusiasm: 'Try arrange this expedition as soon as you can. It will have an immense moral effect in the parishes and the Westward where all is in a very uncertain and threatening state'. Fyfe went ahead with his plans to take about 200 men, including some 20 from Scotts Hall and 30 from Charles Town, into Kingston and on to Accompong. Details of the planned visit appeared in the press on 10 November, along with a notice announcing this tour by 'a large body of Armed Maroons', and inviting 'Custodes, Magistrates, and other Gentlemen of this Colony to afford every facility, and to show every attention in their power, to this brave and loyal people'. The Maroons were escorted into the city by various groups of volunteers and large crowds of citizens. The governor, many dignitaries and military formations greeted them at the court house where a reception took place, involving speeches and a 'sumptuous repast'. During the proceedings the governor presented Fyfe with his official commission as Colonel of the Maroons. Major McPherson, a Maroon officer, spoke for the Maroons, reaffirming to 'deafening cheers' that they 'were always prepared to place their services at the foot of the Crown, and to lose life and blood in the service of the country'. They went on to Spanish Town by train, and on foot to Accompong and over to Montego Bay. After being enthusiastically entertained there, the Maroons returned along the north coast, through the principal towns in the parishes, where they were received with equal enthusiasm. They eventually reached St George on Sunday, 17 December, and after a final round of celebrations, split up, going to their respective towns.

For the Maroons the tour was a success; they had been honoured and feted everywhere they went, and their services in helping to suppress the unrest in St Thomas were clearly appreciated by the authorities and many ordinary people of various classes. Whether the tour achieved the objectives hoped for by Fyfe and Eyre depends on whether there was any real risk of rebellion spreading to other parts of the island. Clearly Eyre believed there was such a risk and was 'throwing troops into different points' and 'surrounding the coast with men of war'. In fact the uprising did not spread, but there is little reason to think that it would have done so, even without Eyre's measures; evidence of an islandwide conspiracy is limited. Fyfe, however, like Eyre, believed in an islandwide threat and in a confidential report to Eyre just before Christmas, claimed that, 'In every step of my tour the conviction was firm that a rising would take place on the 24th or 25th of December'. If this analysis of the situation by Eyre, Fyfe and many others, was accurate, then the Maroons may well have played a role in thwarting further planned protests and restoring order.[18]

As early as 26 October Eyre had drawn up proposals for incorporating the Maroons into permanent arrangements for controlling the eastern end of the island. He proposed stationing Maroons at Morant Bay, Bath, Port Antonio, Buff Bay, Annotto Bay and Moore Town itself. He also suggested giving arms and payment to other Maroons who would be ready for service whenever they were required. He quickly deferred to Fyfe's greater experience when he raised objections to basing Maroons permanently on the plains. In a lyrical passage Fyfe set out his view of the Maroons:

> To employ Maroons in the occupation of Military posts in the plains would at once divest them of that distinctive nationality to which they owe their somewhat

mysterious power over the negro. The Maroons are 'the children of the mist' of Jamaica Romance. They have their haunted 'Nanny Town' in the interior fast-nesses which they never approach and even the White man who impelled by curiosity has tried to penetrate its mysteries has been scared by occurrences for which he has been unable to account. The sound of their wild war horns as they rush without warning and without apparent discipline to the plains strikes terror into the hearts of every one that hears it. Their charm consists in their very seclusion, bring them into every day contact with the people and that charm which in effect quadruples their numbers would be dispelled. Besides which the Maroons have a strong aversion to be employed with Troops. After the perfidy of the island to those who capitulated at the last Maroon war they have an inherent dread of remaining long in positions in which they know they are powerless to frustrate treachery.[19]

It is clear that Fyfe distinguished the Maroons sharply from the rest of the Black population for whom he had none of the affection and respect which he had for the Maroons. One of the sources of Fyfe's feelings for the Maroons becomes clear when he noted Eyre's intention of making him officially their Colonel, and added: 'in my formal Commission I should like to be also termed "& Chief" as I wish to consider them Jamaica Highlanders'.[20] It is ironic that Fyfe should be writing in such terms, since the original highlanders in Scotland had by this time all but disappeared. The terrible 'highland clearances' had depopulated the highlands to allow land to be turned over to sheep farming; the proud highland regiments which had helped to fight Britain's wars since the mid-eighteenth century had dwindled drastically, and recruits were almost impossible to find.

The 'Jamaica Highlanders' were to have no brighter future. Writing to Edward Cardwell, Secretary of State in the Colonial Office, on 20 November, Eyre said that a bill was about to be introduced into the legislature 'to embody and employ' the Maroons in a military capacity, 'to ensure their continued loyalty'. This bill was introduced on 22 November, and was read for the first time on 28 November as a measure 'for the formation of the Maroons of this island into septs or clans, and for their embodiment as a permanent military corps'. It was read for the second time on 5 December and referred to a committee. The reference to 'septs or clans', both terms connected with the highlanders, showed that Fyfe's idea had persisted, but in fact nothing more seems to have come of this measure. The House of Assembly was abolished and there is no indication that Sir John Peter Grant, the first governor under Crown Colony Government, showed any interest in maintaining the Maroons as a permanent force. Fyfe and the Maroons had failed to restore their old status; the Maroons were in future to be ordinary Jamaicans, like it or not.[21]

Assessment of Maroon activities in St Thomas

The most important consequence of the Maroons' activities, the accusations about their ferocity, began with a report sent to the Admiralty by Sir Leopold McClintock, the new commodore of the Jamaica station, who had arrived on 31 October to replace Captain Algernon de Horsey, who had commanded the ships throughout the operations against the 'rebels'. McClintock's report of 8 November included the statement: 'About 300 persons had been hanged, & at least 800 were shot, chiefly by the Maroons, who entered with fierce zeal into the bush hunt after rebel negroes'. Cardwell sent the report to Eyre, asking for an explanation, since Eyre's reports had not suggested such an unfavourable view of Maroon activities. When Cardwell's dispatch reached Kingston on 21 December, Eyre wrote hurriedly to Fyfe, to Vice-Admiral Hope, McClintock's superior, to Major General O'Connor, the commander of the forces, and to Cardwell. Fyfe insisted, both in person and in writing, that no more than 25 people had been shot by the Maroons, and that a number of those were killed in the skirmish at Torrington. He also queried strongly McClintock's use of the term 'fierce zeal' in an apparently derogatory sense; he saw rather the Maroons' 'unflinching energy that should mark the conduct of loyal men in the performance of their duty to their Queen and Country'. McClintock's response, via Hope, was to admit that his report was 'founded solely on the local press and upon the opinions of officers recently returned from Morant Bay etc and as accurately as I could gather it, upon current opinion'. He had obviously not intended to imply any personal knowledge. He concluded: 'I am very glad to find by His Excellency's letter on the authority of Colonel Fyfe that I have been misled by reports and that the actual number shot by the Maroons does not in his opinion exceed 25'. O'Connor, in his response, asserted that he had not heard such reports before receiving McClintock's statement and strongly affirmed his confidence that Maroons under Fyfe's command could not have carried out such actions with impunity. Officially the matter seems to have rested there, and the official count of persons killed by the Maroons stayed at 25. But the accusation remained, and was repeated and reinforced in reports in the foreign press; the Royal Commission in the following year heard much evidence of alleged Maroon brutality, though not a great deal to suggest that they had killed a number of persons greatly in excess of the official total.[22]

In considering the actions of the Maroons, it is important to consider also the role of their commander, Colonel Fyfe, who certainly held himself responsible for their activities. Fyfe, from his dispatches and the evidence to the Royal Commission, was a humane and moderate man, whose moderation was somewhat compromised by his belief that the 'rebels' in St Thomas were dangerous and brutal. Two indications of his humanity were his response to the terrible floggings that were taking place in Bath before his arrival, and his instructions to the Maroons under his command. The issue of the floggings in Bath lay both in their general severity and in the use of a particularly vicious type of cat with wire among the cords. Fyfe put a stop to all the floggings when he reached Bath, for the second time, on 22 October. He later found out about the wire cats, which clearly appalled him, and had them destroyed. It seems clear that he would never have sanctioned their use in any circumstances; in his evidence, he said: 'I made some exclamation, which I don't wish to repeat, but I stopped it'. The same humanity and moderation were obvious in the instructions to his men. From his reports to Eyre it appears that he had given his men orders not to shoot or molest women, children or men who surrendered, and that the order to burn down houses containing plunder was modified by the instruction to leave one building, even if the only one, as shelter for the women and children. The latter order appears in early reports, before any queries about Maroon actions had been raised, but the former appears in his response to McClintock's accusation. His Maroon officers insisted in their evidence that they had followed these orders and Fyfe seemed to have had total confidence that his orders were obeyed. In his evidence he discounted most of the reports of his men behaving otherwise. The great weakness of Fyfe's disavowal of any knowledge of misconduct is that many of the Maroon operations were carried out in his absence; he was only one man and could not be everywhere. It does seem surprising, even so, that of the 25 Maroon killings reported, he only actually witnessed one, that of a man called Patterson, who was executed at Stony Gut, without trial, on Fyfe's personal authority. He justified his action on the grounds that Patterson had in his possession a massive gold ring belonging to Baron von Ketelhodt, a personal friend of his, who had been killed in Morant Bay. Believing at the time the stories of mutilations and atrocities, Fyfe reacted irrationally and ordered an execution which he must have later realised was unwarranted. The

Commissioners' questions showed that they saw this as a very unfortunate example to set to the Maroon captains. There does certainly seem to be the possibility that shootings, floggings and burning of houses by the Maroons took place without Fyfe's knowledge, but it does not appear likely that the numbers killed by the Maroons could have been anywhere near the 800 that McClintock had suggested. The commissioners were very thorough and many witnesses were ready to make accusations against the Maroons, but none of the evidence suggests such an enormous discrepancy between reported and actual deaths.[23]

There are difficulties involved in dealing with the evidence of the Royal Commission, invaluable as it is, both in general and particularly in relation to the Maroons. Apart from discrepancies and inconsistencies inherent in such evidence, there are also problems in relating official statistics, dates and names in the lists of those killed by forces in action in St Thomas, to the evidence itself. A particular difficulty in assessing the culpability of the Maroons lies in the problem of identifying who was actually involved in the incidents reported. At the time, apart from White soldiers and sailors who were usually clearly identified, there were other groups of Black men involved on the side of the government besides the Maroons: these were Black volunteers, policemen, constables and soldiers of the West India Regiment. In addition there appear to have been opportunists who claimed to be Maroons, or acting under the orders of the Maroons or the military, in order to seize people's goods and produce or burn buildings. Various witnesses under questioning showed that they were not sure who the Black soldiers actually were, or had no real reason for saying they were Maroons. Fyfe indicated that he had to order Maroons to wear a cap and tie a red or White ribbon round their arms, so that they would not be shot in error by the soldiers; other witnesses indicated that there was no standard uniform for the West India Regiment men and that constables typically did not have any form of identifying insignia. In the chaotic conditions prevailing at the time there is at least a possibility that others were involved in incidents blamed on the Maroons.

There were four categories of activities that the Maroons were challenged about – theft, burning houses, flogging, and shooting or executing people, in all of which they were undoubtedly involved to a greater or lesser extent. Fyfe admitted in his evidence that Maroons had probably stolen what they thought they could get away with, and they sometimes took provisions and livestock. This was not behaviour that he or the Maroon captains could tolerate officially, and loss of property was a real disaster to smallholders, but this hardly falls into the category of an atrocity, the word used by some commentators. Burning of houses was carried out by the Maroons in various places up and down the Plantain Garden River Valley. Under Fyfe's instructions they were to leave one building in each yard, and they were only to burn the houses of those found with stolen property, or identified as known 'rebels'. Certainly Fyfe could not ensure that his orders were obeyed everywhere, and the burning of houses did get out of hand. The most serious complaints came from the area of Leith Hall, where the Maroon captains, Roberts and Briscoe, were to some extent guided by the local knowledge of John Woodrow, a White engineer, who lived at neighbouring Clifton Hill. Here, as in other places, the burning of houses was on a fairly arbitrary basis, and the opportunity was sometimes taken to settle old scores. The burning of houses, wherever it occurred, caused great hardship and loss, and in the rainy season, discomfort and a threat to health, but it was carried out on a wide scale by all the military groups, some of whom seemed to have been far more ruthless than the Maroons, who were possibly restrained by Fyfe's supervision.

Accusations made against the Maroons of carrying out floggings were limited; Fyfe believed that Briscoe had been responsible for the only instance, when he flogged a man at Airy Castle for preventing him from searching a house for stolen goods. There were a very few complaints of being flogged by, or at the orders of Maroons, in Bath and at Leith Hall. The more serious accusation would have to be that the Hayfield Maroons brought in the prisoners whom Kirkland had had flogged with wired cats, though Fyfe put a stop to that. They and other Maroons also took prisoners down to Morant Bay where they must have known of the floggings and hangings being carried out under the orders of the provost-marshal, Gordon Ramsay. The Maroons were implicated in those horrendous floggings by their bringing in of prisoners, but they themselves carried out very few of them. The most serious accusations concerned those killed by the Maroons.

The official total of the number of persons put to death in the suppression of the rebellion in St Thomas between 14 October and 13 November was 439; of that number the Maroons were responsible for 25. Both these totals were conservative, and the actual figures were probably larger, though estimates of 1,500–2,000 deaths which were made at the time, with the figure of 800 attributed to the Maroons, seem inherently impossible. That such an enormous discrepancy could have been concealed from the searching inquiries of the Commissioners, seems very unlikely, and there was a powerful lobby in Britain which was only too eager to find as much evidence as possible to indict Eyre. As far as the Maroons are concerned, it is fairly easy to attribute as many as six more deaths to them, when evidence is compared with the official listings. There is also a reference to further killings by Maroons in the evidence of James Stewart, a Black smallholder from Thornton, who charged that he was barely saved from being sent from Bath to Golden Grove with a group of 15 men who had been sentenced by Kirkland and were taken away and shot by the Maroons. This is a curious piece of evidence, which does not seem to have been followed up; the commissioners did not recall Kirkland to question him about the testimony, and there is no other reference to him issuing any death sentences. However, the charge does indicate the possibility that there were other unreported executions; adding this number to the other deaths attributed to the Maroons would make them responsible for some 46 deaths, so that it may easily be granted that they may have killed double the number of people officially listed.

The final issue to be considered is the circumstances and nature of the deaths caused by the Maroons. Fyfe was in command when seven men were shot at Stony Gut, and six men and one girl were shot at Torrington; Roberts and Briscoe were in command when eight men were shot and one man was hanged in the Leith Hall and Airy Castle area. The other two shootings to make up 25 were at Nutt's River and near Seaforth. There was most disagreement about what had happened at Torrington. Fyfe, as already described, had written of a skirmish when he attacked what was believed to be a 'rebel' hideout and that a number of bodies had been found after the attack. He claimed that the village was deserted when he entered it, but James Stewart and others, however, claimed that Maroons had entered the village before all the people had fled, and shot down men as they came out of their houses. The death of Amelia Stewart, the only woman shot by the Maroons, seems to have been unintentional; a young Maroon saw a movement and shot at what he thought was a man who might attack him. He hit her in the leg, and she died ten days later; the incident was not reported to Fyfe until just before he gave evidence to the Commission, as the Maroon was afraid he 'might have quarrelled', although the shooting was accidental. The truth about the shootings at Torrington presumably lies somewhere between the two versions. The Maroons were angered at being fired at, and having one of their number wounded in the eye, and probably did fire at stragglers trying to get out of the village; Fyfe admitted that he did not reach the scene in time to see any of the shootings, but only saw the dead bodies. Other killings raised similar questions.

At Stony Gut the Maroons were accused of shooting seven men in the area without reason, while Fyfe seemed to believe that four were shot, one on his orders and the others after 'trial' by the Maroons. The information about this episode is limited, and confused by uncertainty over dates; probably seven men were killed, in much the arbitrary fashion indicated by witnesses. At Leith Hall the issue is confused by questions over the role of Woodrow, who appeared to have given the orders for some of the executions. At Airy Castle two of the most reprehensible of the killings took place; two men, one a Creole and the other an African, but both called James Williams, were shot by a Maroon party led by Briscoe. One of the men, it was claimed, was an obeah man and it does appear that they shot both to make sure they got the right one. These killings may not have had any connection with the current unrest, though Briscoe claimed that the African, whom he identified as the obeah man, was working for the 'rebels'. The main reason for killing him was that he was a 'wicked man', who had gone to Moore Town pretending to be a doctor, had 'robbed' the people and given medicine to a woman who had subsequently died. Very clearly other factors were involved in the Maroons' activities, beyond concern with suppressing protests. There is much more evidence about the deaths attributed to the Maroons, but from these examples it is obvious that they did kill in a random fashion, with little concern for any niceties of court martial procedures, although Fyfe tried hard to argue that they did the best they could in the circumstances.

But however brutal the Maroons' activities were, they did not kill on the same scale as others. The operations of the troops sent from Port Antonio to Manchioneal involved the killing of 59 men; 77 died as a result of the operations in the Blue Mountain Valley. There were 56 executions in Port Antonio, and the officially supervised executions of 187 at Morant Bay, under the authority of Provost-Marshal Ramsay, were characterised by a deliberate, and yet, at the same time, manic ferocity, similar to the mood of the military in the Indian Mutiny in 1857–9, or of General Dyer at Amritsar in 1919. Within the total of 439 killed, the 25, or even 46, deaths due to the Maroons seem limited and explicable, while the executions at Morant Bay take on the aspect of nightmare.[24]

Conclusion: A long-established role

The Maroons were not directly involved in those executions and floggings at Morant Bay, but they did play a role as old as the history of European expansion, as auxiliaries to White military and civil authorities in the general operations in St Thomas. Other ethnic groups had allied themselves with Europeans and fought under their command against peoples of their own races, in many varied circumstances since the fifteenth century. In the nineteenth century, the British in Jamaica, as in India, could not have survived without locally recruited troops. In India, Punjabi Guides and Sikh and Gurkha regiments ensured British victory in the Mutiny; in the Ashanti Wars local troops, such as Wood's Regiment and Lord Gifford's Assin Scouts, fought on the side of the British. General O'Connor, who had served long in West Africa, saw the Maroons in the same light, honouring them for their loyalty and courage.[25]

In 1865, as in the past, the Maroons saw both their duty and their interest in continued loyalty to the British Crown. They had no commonality of interests with the people Bogle represented, and saw no advantage in allying with them. They must have been aware of the weaknesses of Bogle's situation; the muddled objectives and limited plans, and especially his lack of adequate arms. They themselves were without adequate arms, until supplied by the government, and it does not seem to have crossed their minds to take the arms and then switch sides; such a course would have been a betrayal of all their past history. Certainly they operated harshly, but not in as ruthless a manner as other forces operating in St Thomas. It hardly seems that a generation which has witnessed on television the internecine brutalities of the late twentieth century has much justification for singling out for special stigmatisation the actions of the Maroons in 1865.

The combination of sincere loyalty to sworn allegiances with the pursuit of narrow group self-interest is foreign to twentieth-century ideological interpretations and sensibilities, but it is the key to the actions of the Maroons and others like them. But for the Jamaican Maroons it was a way of viewing the world that had no future after 1865.

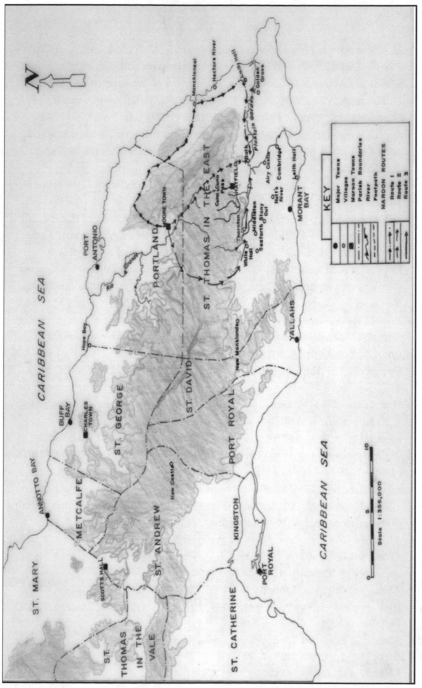

Eastern Jamaica in 1865

Notes

1.   M.C. Campbell, *The Maroons of Jamaica 1655–1796* (MA: Bergin & Garvey, 1988). Chapter 5 gives the texts of the treaties with both Leeward and Windward Maroons. The most recent account of the Morant Bay Rebellion is G. Heuman, *'The Killing Time': The Morant Bay Rebellion in Jamaica*, (London: Macmillan, 1994). Beverley Carey's *The Maroon Story* (Kingston: Agouti Press, 1997), which was published after this article was completed, gives a comparable account of Maroon involvement at Morant Bay, and a detailed account of Maroon history.

2.   See for example, Co 137/395, Gov. Edward Eyre to Edward Cardwell, 20 November 1865, Enclosure.

3.   K. Agorsah, ed., *Maroon Heritage* (Kingston: Canoe Press, 1994), especially C. Robinson, chap. 5, 'Maroons and Rebels (a Dilemma)'; R. Hart, *Slaves Who Abolished Slavery*, Vol. 2 (Kingston, UWI: Institute of Social and Economic Research, 1985); W.A. Roberts, *Jamaica; the Portrait of an Island* (New York: Coward-McCann, 1955), p 66; M. Craton, *Testing the Chains: Resistance to Slavery in the British West Indies* (Ithaca, NY: Cornell University Press, 1982), chaps 5 and 6.

4.   Campbell, *The Maroons of Jamaica; Journals of the Assembly of Jamaica* (*JHAJ*), Vol. V, pp. 226–7, 281.

5.   Campbell, *The Maroons of Jamaica*, pp. 220, 239–40; *JHAJ* Vol. IX, pp. 469, 476.

6.   Hart, *Slaves Who Abolished Slavery*, Vol 2, pp. 269–70, 288, 309–10, 313–4.

7.   B.K. Kopytoff, 'The Maroons of Jamaica: An Ethnohistorical Study of incomplete polities, 1655–1905' (unpublished dissertation, University of Pennsylvania, 1973), chap. 13; *Votes of the Assembly of Jamaica*, *JHAJ* 1864, pp. 45–7, 19 January.

8.   J. Williams, S.J., *The Maroons of Jamaica: Anthropological Series of the Boston College Graduate School*, Series 3 (Boston, MA: Boston College Press, 1938), p. 476, Appendix by I.E. Thompson.

9.   *Minutes of Evidence taken before the Jamaica Royal Commission*, 1866 (London, 1866), pp. 492, 1031–3; Williams, S.J., *The Maroons of Jamaica*, p. 476, appendix by Thompson.

10. *Minutes of Evidence*, 1866, pp. 861, 991, 993, 1119.

11. Ibid., pp. 265–6, 894, 924, 994, 1004, 1020, 1031; *Colonial Standard*, 23 October 1865, p. 2.

12   *Minutes of Evidence*, 1866, pp. 252, 894, 1031–2.

13. Ibid., 1866, pp. 544, 893–4, 994.

14. CO 137/394, Eyre to O'Connor, 26 October 1865.

15. CO 137/394, Col. Fyfe to Gov. Eyre, 22 October 1865.
16. CO 137/394, Fyfe to Eyre, 22, 28, 29, 31 October 1865; Fyfe to Edward O'Connor, 25 October, 1865.
17. CO 137/394, Fyfe to Nelson, 2 November 1865; *Colonial Standard*, 7 November 1865, p. 2, 15 November 1865, p. 2.
18. CO 137/394, Fyfe to Eyre, 29 October, 3 November, Eyre to Fyfe, 30 October 1865; CO 137/396, Fyfe to Eyre, 21 December 1865; *Colonial Standard*, 10 November 1865, p. 2, 15 November 1865, p. 2, 9 December 1865, p. 2, 12 December 1865, p. 2, 15 December 1865, p. 2, 19 December 1865, pp. 2–3.
19. CO 137/394, Eyre to O'Connor, 26 October 1865, Fyfe to Eyre, 29, 31 October 1865.
20. Ibid.
21. CO 137/394, Eyre to O'Connor, 26 October 1865, Fyfe to Eyre, 29, 31 October 1865; CO 137/395, Eyre to Cardwell, 20 November 1865; *JHAJ*, 1865–6, pp. 72, 97, 113–4; J. Prebble, *The Highland Clearances* (London: Penguin Books, 1963), pp. 295–304.
22. CO 137/394, Cardwell to Eyre, 1 December 1865; CO 137/396, Eyre to Edward Cardwell, Eyre to O'Connor, Fyfe to Eyre, McClintock to Hope, all 23 December 1865, O'Connor to Eyre, 24 December 1865; CO 137/397, McClintock to Admiralty, 8 November 1865. P. Sherlock and H. Bennett, *The Story of the Jamaican People* (Kingston: Ian Randle, 1997) repeats uncritically a version of McLintock's report, while suggesting, incorrectly, that he was involved in the suppression of the uprising; in his letter to the Admiralty, 8 November 1865, he stated that he arrived in Jamaica on 31 October 1865, by which time the suppression of the uprising was over. McLintock's 'evidence' is merely hearsay.
23. *Minutes of Evidence*, evidence of Fyfe, pp. 893–901; evidence of Joseph Briscoe, pp. 1028–31.
24. Ibid., pp. 307–8, 311–13, 479–80, 492, 893–901, 903–4, 955, 960, 1028–31, Returns Relative to Punishments pp, 1135–43. For a recent account of the suppression of the Morant Bay Rebellion, see C. Hutton, 'Colour for Colour: Skin for Skin' (PhD thesis, Dept. of Government, UWI, Mona, 1997).
25. *Colonial Standard*, 15 November 1865, p. 2; C. Hibbert, *The Great Mutiny: India 1857* (London: Penguin Books, 1978), pp. 284–5 and *passim*; B. Bond, ed., *Victorian Military Campaigns* (London: Hutchinson, 1967), pp. 190–1; B. Farwell, *Queen Victoria's Little Wars* (London: Allen Lane, 1973), pp. 357–8, 361–2.

CHAPTER

22

Dominican Plantations and Land Tenure in the Dominican Republic, 1900–1916

PATRICK BRYAN

*T*his chapter discusses the impact of the growth of sugar plantations on land tenure in the Dominican Republic. The studies of Bruce Calder, and others including Melvin Knight,[1] have given strong emphasis to the period of the United States (US) occupation; but that intervention can only be fully understood in the context of the preceding period.

The modern Dominican sugar economy, largely confined to the south and southeast of the republic, emerged after 1870 with capital inputs from Cuban, Italian, British, French and American investors. Sugar exports rose from 35,500 tons in 1893 to 122,300 tons by 1912,[2] and though the US occupation was to see even more dramatic increases, the issues and problems relating to the Dominican sugar industry had been placed on the agenda of Dominican history from before the close of the nineteenth century, and very definitely between 1900 and 1916. By 1905, nearly 50 per cent of the major plantations were controlled or owned by US capital. Sugar acreage had increased from 53,820 acres in 1892 (for seven plantations) to 123,335 acres by 1905 for the same seven plantations.[3]

Terrenos comuneros

Land acquisition in the Dominican Republic posed severe problems, however, and those problems were almost invariably associated with the structure of land tenure. Land had been passed from generation to generation on the basis of equal inheritance. The result was that the descendants of a former large land-owner could collectively own a large tract in common. Within the tract itself, the claims of the various *comuneros* were unadjusted among themselves in the legal sense. The *comuneros*, within the tract, enjoyed equal rights, including the right to sell through *acción de peso* sections of their land which they chose to make available to someone else. The *acción de peso* did not amount to an absolute transfer of property. On the contrary, it gave the 'purchaser' the right to enjoy the usufruct of the land.

There were reported to be certain districts in which there were 30, 50 or 100 proprietors, each having a claim on the tract, unadjusted among themselves, but independent of the rest of the world. These land claimants would be called small proprietors individually, but together they were owners of a large tract.[4] Although only one proprietor held the title, all proprietors shared equal rights with the owner of title to cultivate the land. This system operated successfully as long as land remained a relatively abundant resource, and enjoyed a natural rather than a commercial value. Up to the 1870s land in the Dominican Republic was not measured because it was regarded as uneconomic to do so.

The evidence suggests that the original grants of land, based on concessions of the Spanish Crown, were delineated quite roughly, and records were badly drawn and loosely kept.[5] Most of the records of original grants, as well as of transfers, have been lost or destroyed or at least were unavailable. *Peso* titles, or the concessions of land in exchange for a specific amount of money, did not necessarily indicate precisely any particular part of the whole original tract as passing to the purchaser.[6]

Government or municipal lands, the *ejidos*, were available for long-term lease. A citizen could pay a given sum ranging from $10 to $1,000 for the usufruct of extensive ('as far as a man can see') acreage. Lands belonging to the municipality were leased to the tenant for as long as they were put to productive use.

The capitalist mode of production introduced by the sugar plantation system came into conflict with this quasi-feudal system of land tenure and the search by the plantations for private undisputed titles which would solidify the stake of the US corporations in Dominican soil. The land question served to generate conflicts between formerly peaceful co-owners of *terrenos comuneros*, as with *latifundist* production the unscientific methods of distributing lands in the Dominican Republic could no longer bear the strain imposed by the radically new mode of production.

In the late nineteenth century plantations had gained access to land both by purchase and by an exercise of authority over *colonos* whose lands they steadily absorbed by a system of debt and advances.[7] Cattle estates, or *hatos*, had been converted into sugar *colonias*, small farmers had left their small provision grounds – *conucos* – to become peons on the new estates,[8] and, as President Heureaux noted, local production of foodstuffs had declined.[9]

Nevertheless, the major problem of sugar planters as far as land was concerned was the legal problem arising from the conflict between the quasi-feudal system of land tenure (*terrenos comuneros*) and the search by the plantations for private undisputed titles. During the period 1906–10, 40–50 per cent of recorded cases tried before the courts of the Dominican Republic arose out of conflicts between *agricultores* and *criadores*, that is, agricultural versus grazing interests.[10]

With the steady increase in the size of plantations and the growth of the population of the Dominican Republic, the situation of abundance of uncultivated land, upon which the *comunero* system had rested, changed substantially. It is true that in the late nineteenth century there had been conflicts of opinion between plantations and their *colonos*, but between 1900 and 1916 the problems became not only more acute but came to justify the interest of the US, and to create a demand for new legislation in the Dominican Republic to provide for securer titles.

It was always difficult to obtain a valid title to land in the Dominican Republic. The US minister did not, perhaps, exaggerate when he explained that 'there is no such thing as a perfectly valid title to land in the Republic under the communal ownership system'.[11] With the conferral of a market rather than a 'natural' value on land and the steady increase in landed property, the system of *terrenos comuneros* led to widespread fraud. Records of grants and of conveyances whether to families or individuals were inadequate or non-existent; and the ease with which property could be passed from one individual to another led to a situation in which 'The country has been flooded with false titles given by unscrupulous Notaries'.[12]

The process of acquiring land in 1911 was described in the following way:

> A purchaser appearing, a call was made for the survey of the land site indicated and for the presentation of titles. These titles only represented the money interest of the holder, and may or may not have been valid. In many cases they were pure fabrication. Survey was made of the commune tract, and the purchaser given a right in said tract in proportion to his money holdings, no accurate land boundaries being set. He had the right to settle on any portion of the tract that may have been occupied, and it can easily be seen how, by gradually extending their operations, the most influential inhabitants soon came to control the largest share of the commune land. Their best title consisted of a fence, and, indeed, in a majority of cases, it was the only title they had to the land occupied, and its completion generally resulted in the free and undisturbed possession of the property . . . With the above methods it naturally follows that trickery has been practised, and it is commonly stated that at least 80 percent of the large landholders in Santo Domingo are merely 'squatters' and hold their land by the force of a fence, and influence with the central government.[13]

US investors, whether sugar planters or not, found the system of land tenure an obstacle to the unimpeded development of their property. They either bought land – at their peril – or participated in the system of controlling areas of land by purchasing *acciones*. One such company was the Habanero Lumber Company. In an extensive report on its holdings, the company pointed out:

> it is not expedient for the Habanero Lumber Company to designate or take possession of any definite tract or tracts of land of any magnitude until same has been officially surveyed and allotted to it and as it now stands, the Habanero Lumber Company is simply a co-tenant with thousands of other people in vast tracts of undivided lands, and the only way that they can come into possession of these lands is to have some legally surveyed and their portion laid off to them.[14]

In a telling aside, the company indicated that the 'manufacture of false *Peso* Titles has been done in all parts of the Republic, in some places more than in others, and in some localities to a very great extent'. The company owned 552 acres of land in 1916, but worked 1 million acres.

From the late nineteenth century the Dominican sugar planters had had jurisdictional conflicts with *colonos*, and these problems, though tackled in the first 15 years of the twentieth century, found no easy solution. The problems remained of insecure and fraudulent titles and ill-defined boundaries. The indefinable nature of the boundaries was matched only by the indeterminate character of ownership. But the necessity to secure firm titles of ownership became more pressing as the estates expanded. For one thing, under the Dominican law in force, mortgages could only be placed on real property and not on personal property.[15]

Some sugar estates found their claim to a particular piece of property challenged. In November 1905 the Bartram brothers, owners of the estates Quisqueya, San Isidro and Santa Fe, producing 7,950 tons, 5,120 tons and 7,350 tons respectively in 1905, wrote to the US Minister, Mr Dawson, on the subject of 'damage to American interests'. The 'facts' of the case as presented by the Bartram brothers were that Juan Cruzado had ceded to the estate San Isidro, through José E. Hatton, administrator of the estate, the right of way through lands he claimed to own, and

> for several years the right has never been disputed and the dais road has continually been in use by the Estate. The document is in possession of Mr. Albert T. Bass at the Estate . . . We do not know by what authority this complainant claims to inherit this property for her sons, nor if it belonged to minor children when their father ceded the right of way, or if she has the right to demand payment for the land . . . As it looks at present, this complainant wants the court to enter a decree against the Estate and stop all communication between the Estate and the Ozama River without our having the opportunity of defending ourselves . . . [16]

The cloudy laws of property also made it possible for another Dominican citizen, Mr Romano, to defy the Central Ansonia Sugar Company in Azua in 1904. According to the company (managed by the Kelly North American interests), they had bought from Mr Romano (for a 'consideration') 'the strip of land that the canal runs through and 9 feet both sides of the said canal'. Mr Romano defiantly closed off the canal, fencing it and stationing an 'armed force preventing our entrance to *our* canal'. Since the waterway was the source for the irrigation of the cane fields, the company claimed that Mr Romano was causing 'severe damage to our crop'.[17] Although the company was convinced that it had a good case (since it had 'documents signed by Romano and registered here, giving us absolute right of way') it was reluctant to appeal to Dominican courts for redress. The sugar interests had very little faith in Dominican courts, evidently believing that there was little hope of justice from those tribunals. Judgements were known to have been affected by extra-legal considerations, by *honoraria* of various sums in exchange for favourable judgements. Yet the most incorruptible of courts would have found the entanglements of Dominican land tenure a severe strain on objective judgements.

The following letter received by the American minister from a photographer (Mr Waite) in Mexico bears out the difficulties of land transactions in the Dominican Republic. Mr Waite's concern was with the sugar estate San Cristóbal (3,937 acres) in the province of Santo Domingo, which Mr Waite had apparently helped to finance and upon which he now wished to stake his claim:

> I am enclosing . . . all the documents in my possession pertaining to San Cristóbal, consisting of deeds and receipts from the Tranquil? heirs, the Chevalier heirs, Malcolm Benit [sic] and the title from Paul Angenard which Mr. Stephenson declares was null and void because Mr. Angenard had no title from Mrs. Maria Chaner, and so Mr. Stephenson had this set aside and purchased direct from Mrs. Chaner and the deed from Mrs. Chaner to him is among some other papers in Toledo? Ohio and that he will write for them at once. However, there must be on record about 1875 or 1876 a file where he asked to have this contract annulled and which case was conducted by Lic de Castro, who if living will remember the case and if this can be found and is as Mr. Stephenson affirms, it will prove to the contrary that Mr. Angenard had no claim against Mr. Stephenson and the latter case in court was unjustly decided.[18]

The sugar interests, despite their occasional appeals to the 'American' minister in Santo Domingo, did at least recognise that the passage of laws was the business of the Dominican government, and did not hesitate on occasion, to use the tool of bribery to secure the passage of a law through the National Congress. Not that the tactic was used indiscriminately. In the case of land legislation, the government did make occasional efforts to remove abuses which the system of land tenure permitted. During the 1890s Heureaux's government had discussed the necessity to survey the idle lands in the nation, because no system of land tenure revised on the basis of individual ownership of title could be carried out without a general survey of lands. What was missing was not the desire to revise the land-tenure system, but the ability to put such a revised system into operation against the weight of a sanctified tradition.

The increase in the number of US-owned estates placed additional pressure on the traditional system of land tenure. The US minister and, indirectly, Washington made serious efforts to ensure that US proprietors in the Dominican Republic could obtain access to disputable titles.

The *modus vivendi* of 1905 and the Dominican-American Convention of 1907 introduced a period of control of Dominican customs through a US-appointed receiver of customs. Putting the receivership into the hands of a US nominee was partly intended to rectify the financial irregularities of the republic, to ensure repayment of European bond-holders and to keep the customs out of the reach of revolutionary movements. At the same time, however, the Dominican-American Convention convinced some US investors that the US had secured formal control over the republic, financially and politically. The US minister wryly denied suggestions that the convention equalled US control and the end of political violence.

Yet the belief that the Dominican Republic had the right investment atmosphere, with the 1905 and 1907 agreements, was held in the highest quarters, among others, by Mr Colton, the first receiver of customs who noted that land prices would, under the new agreements 'go up with a boom'. The Dominican government, however had accepted the convention largely on the grounds that they had little choice. 'It was impossible', declared the Dominican minister of finance in 1905, 'to pay [the bond-holders], and it was impossible to continue not paying'. As far as land was concerned, the Dominican government itself began to adopt measures to solve the problem of titles.

New laws of 1907, 1911 and 1915

On 22 June 1907 the government of Ramón Cáceres (1907–11) passed a law which was designed to regulate the measurement and survey of common lands in the republic. In its preamble, the law made it clear that its purpose was to remove the incidence of fraud in the sale of land. This law underlined the necessity to measure common lands before they were sold, a regulation that implied a practice of selling land before measurement and survey. Inevitably, a practice of this kind would and did lead to multiple abuses and injustices, and to conflicts between the *comuneros* themselves. The preamble of the decree makes it clear that: 'the lack of subdivision of the majority of the lands of the Republic gives opportunity for the perpetuation of numerous frauds which are the constant cause of conflicts between co-owners of communal lands'.

The law, which sought to remove this obstacle to the further development of Dominican agriculture, proceeded to forbid notaries 'or anyone acting in that capacity to carry out acts of sale or alienation of any portion of land in *terrenos comuneros* if they had not been previously measured by a competent surveyor in accordance with all the provisions of the law'. The law provided that before transfer of land could take place, information on the area of the land (in hectares), on the use to which the land was to be put, was to be provided. To reduce the possibility of fraud, a further check was imposed, namely that 'the officers in charge of the Civil Registers were to be "prohibited" from registering contracts made under private signature as touching the sale, the promise of sale, or the alienation of any portion of land, unless the plan of said property made out by a competent land surveyor is produced, in conformity with the terms of the previous article'.[19]

A further law was passed in 1911, coinciding with the 'active operations by Americans in the purchase of land during the past year in this country'.[20] The law of 1911 provided for the definition and partition of *terrenos comuneros* at the request of one or more shareholders. The court was required to commission a notary to act as depository of the titles. The notary was also required to make a record of, and award the portion of, land belonging to each shareholder after the land surveying had been completed. The rule of thumb was that the area which had been cultivated would pass to the petitioner in title, but co-owners were under no obligation to have their boundaries clearly defined. The law obliged any co-proprietor who was occupying more than his allotment of land to purchase the excess from the rightful owner, or to sell the improved part to the latter.

This law (1911) appears to have been concerned, above all, with the demarcation of property. Some doubt was expressed that the 'present landowners will ask for governmental survey, measurement, and delineation of their holdings for the simple purpose of having their boundaries recorded'.[21] The burden of boundary definition rested on the *comunero* who desired a quick survey in order to sell.

The law of 1911 did not meet the approval of US investors, either. The Habanero Company, regarding the law as too costly, noted that to survey 1 million acres at 20 cents per acre would cost them $200,000, in addition to government and legal fees.[22] The partition law of 1911 did not provide a 'settlement of the matter'.[23] According to the Habanero Company: 'While some of these laws, in intent, are excellent, they are very expensive, and even after the expense, vexations and litigations incident to such a survey and allotment of land, title to same is not quieted'.

The company pointed to the sugar interests as victims of the inappropriate laws:

This is evidenced by the numerous suits to upset such surveys and allotments brought against the sugar interests in the Dominican Republic, who have taken advantage of the law and had official surveys and allotments made, and gone to great expense to cultivate and improve the land.

The lawyer of the La Romana estate (owned by the South Puerto Rico Sugar Company, which in turn owned Guanica Central in Puerto Rico and which had evidently spent large sums to receive some form of title to land) complained to the US minister that the chaotic situation with regard to titles had frightened away investors from the Dominican Republic. Cuba and Puerto Rico were preferred destinations. 'Capital', mused the lawyer, Guy Lippitt, 'needs security'. Furthermore, it was almost impossible 'at present for owners of rural lands to obtain loans for development by means of placing mortgages on his property'. The titles to many lands, Mr Lippitt emphasised, were in 'precarious condition because of the system of *terrenos comuneros*'. The laws were difficult, and there was laxity and carelessness in the transfer of titles.[24]

In truth, to argue that millions of dollars worth of investment had been 'frightened' away from the Dominican Republic and had found refuge in Cuba or in Puerto Rico was to misrepresent the issue. Cuba, Puerto Rico and the Dominican Republic were in competition for capital and it is obvious that Puerto Rico's colonial status and the controls that the US exercised over Cuba would have made Cuba and Puerto Rico more attractive targets for US investment than Santo Domingo. The notion that capital was being frightened away also ignores the efforts made by the Dominican government to create the ideal 'investment atmosphere'.

Washington's growing interest in Dominican land reform was demonstrated by the decision of the Department of State to submit to Minister Russell, on 8 July 1914, a copy of the Land Registration Act (An Act to Provide for Adjudication and Registration of Titles to Lands in the Philippine Islands), enacted by the Philippine Commission. This act was inspired by the Torrens registration system developed, originally, in Australia. The Department of State was responding to a request from Minister James Sullivan to the effect that 'the time seems opportune for the passage of a land registration bill'. The department wished Mr Sullivan to bring the Philippine Bill unofficially to the attention of a member of the Dominican Congress. The Dominican lawyer, Francisco Peynado, among others, noted that whatever the advantages of the Torrens system it could only be applied in the Dominican Republic at the expense of or to the loss of land-owners of the Dominican Republic, and in particular the *campesinos*.

On 15 July 1915, the Dominican government, under continuing pressure from the sugar interests, passed a new law, *Ley para liberar títulos* (Freedom of Titles Law).

The aim of this law was to establish title *in dominio*. If this law (based upon a law put into effect in all Spanish colonies in the 1890s) were vigorously applied, it would enable a land-owner who had 'a title drawn in the regular form, together with an act of measurement and plan of his land, to begin an action in Court of First Instance of the Province where his land was located. The petitioner would request that the lands in question be declared his "sole and exclusive property from the date of the sentence"'. Challengers were entitled to sue in court. Where the petitioner did not present evidence that there was a mortgage or other lien on the property, the court could declare the petitioner owner of the land *in dominio*. All persons who claimed to have acquired title to land by virtue of 30 years prescription, could direct a petition to court for a *dominio* title.[25]

The general problem of *terrenos comuneros* was not solved by the laws of 1907 and 1911. In 1914 Listin Diario reported that there were still serious conflicts arising over the subdivision of *terrenos comuneros*:

> Apart from the labyrinth which the *terrenos comuneros* constitute in themselves, the cause of several judicial imbroglios, family disputes, some with the charac-teristic and tragic consequences of the Capulet-Montague vendetta, and other social evils, and which of themselves require methodical and decisive action on the part of the Public Powers, nothing is so frequent as to find oneself in the presence of titles whose validity is more than dubious.[26]

Among the conclusions that can be drawn about the land question between 1900 and 1916 are that, firstly, the US came to show a far more vigorous interest in rationalising land-tenure patterns in the Dominican Republic, and secondly, that up to 1916, the year of the US intervention, the problem of tenure remained unsolved. New estates still used a dual type of land possession combined with purchase and rental. In April 1916, for example, the Macorís Sugar Company established a new sugar estate in San Pedro de Macorís, capitalised at $400,000, renting land under a 29-year lease, on approximately 6,000 acres of virgin lands in 'the fork of the Iguamo and Casui Rivers'. An additional 2,400 acres adjoining was to be purchased.[27]

The US invasion and occupation, 1916–24, implemented the Torrens system of land tenure. The effect was to multiply sugar acreage even more radically than during the 1900–16 period. The new system and the adjustments made by the Dominican government before the 1916 occupation led to significant displacement of people, and to widespread violence.

Notes

1.   B. Calder, *The Impact of Intervention: The Dominican Republic During the U.S Occupation of 1916–1924* (Austin, TX: University of Texas Press, 1984); M. Knight, *The Americans in Santo Domingo* (New York: Vanguard Press, 1928).
2.   Bureau of the American Republics, *Handbook of Santo Domingo*, Bulletin 52 (1892, revised March 1894). Ex Doc. Pt 3, p. 15; Department of State (DS), Microfilm M-626, Internal Affairs, Industrial Matters (Roll 69).
3.   The 1892 figures are compiled from J. Sánchez, *La Caña en Santo Domingo* (Santo Domingo: García Hermanos, Biblioteca Taller, 1972) and the 1905 figures from Bureau of Insular Affairs (BIA), RG350, Dominican Convention (SD1–105) 'Review of the Organisation and Transactions of the Customs Receivership during the first year of its operation' (Exhibit N).
4.   Commission of Inquiry to Santo Domingo. *Report of the Commission of Inquiry to Santo Domingo with the Introductory Message of the President, Special Reports made to the Commission, and the Statements of over seventy witnesses* (Washington, DC, 1878), p. 234.
5.   A.W. Knapp, *Santo Domingo: Its Past and its Present Condition* (Santo Domingo, 1920), p. 27.
6.   Ibid., p. 28.
7.   Sánchez, *La Caña*, pp. 55–7.
8.   E. M. de Hostos, 'Falsa Alarma', in *El Eco de la Opinión* (1884).
9.   President Ulises Heureaux, quoted in *El Eco de la Opinión* (March, 1884).
10.   Archivo General de la Nación (AGN), *Hacienda y Comercio*, Estadísticas, 1906–10.
11.   DS M-626, Microfilm Roll 68, *Internal Affairs* (Economic Matters), W.L. Russell to the Secretary of State, 17 June 1911.
12.   Ibid. p. 4.
13.   Ibid., p.3.
14.   Ibid, See enclosure 'A Statement of the Pesos of Title and Cutting Rights Owned by the Habanero Lumber Co. in the Dominican Republic and the General Location of Same'.

15. DS General Correspondence, American Legation 1916, Pt VII. E. Clock (Central Romana) to Russell, 13 October 1916.

16. DS Miscellaneous Official Communications, Vol. 794/22, 1904–5. Bartram Brothers to Dawson, 7 November, 1905.

17. Ibid. José Lench (Acting US Consular Agent) to Dawson, 21 September 1904, enclosing letter of Ansonia Sugar Co., 21 September 1904.

18. DS Miscellaneous Official Communications, Vol. 795/23, 1907–11. Mr Waite to Fenton, 20 May 1907.

19. *Gaceta Oficial*, No. 1800, 29 June 1907. Also Enclosure, Shirley to Grey, 15 July 1907, Foreign Office (FO) 371/266, 1907, folio 153.

20. DS M-626, Roll 68, Russell to Sec. of State, 17 June 1911.

21. DS M-626, Roll 68, Enclosure Habanero Lumber Co.

22. Ibid.

23. Knapp, *Santo Domingo*, p. 28.

24. DS General Correspondence, American Legation 1915, Pt VI, Guy Lippitt to Russell, 20 November 1915.

25. DS General Correspondence, American Legation, 1915. Pt VI Russell to Sec. of State, Enclosure, 'Ley Para Liberar Títulos de Bienes Inmuebles'.

26. *Listín Diario*, 14 April 1914, 'Liberación de Títulos'.

27. BIA, RG350, SD55/8, Commercial Report submitted by C.J. von Zielinski (Vice-Consul), 24 March 1916.

Race, Labour and Politics in Jamaica and St Kitts, 1909–1940

A comparative survey of the roles of the National Club of Jamaica and the Workers League of St Kitts[1]

GLEN RICHARDS

The study of Caribbean history and the field of Caribbean studies are torn between the intellectual desire to emphasise the common sociohistorical experience of the region and the academic imperative of focusing upon the unique and distinct features of individual territories. While acknowledging the historical commonalties of the region, narrow academic specialisation has steadily reduced the field of Caribbean history to the historical study of individual Caribbean territories. The few studies which seek to produce a synthesis of the historical experience of the Caribbean as a whole, or even of the territories making up one of the four main language groupings, are dwarfed besides the specialised studies produced by the vast majority of Caribbean historians, including myself, who are specialists on single territories. This chapter seeks to arrive at a middle path by comparing the physical manifestation of a historical phenomenon which has appeared throughout the British-Colonised Caribbean in the context of two very distinct Caribbean islands, Jamaica and St Kitts.

St Kitts and Jamaica are very dissimilar Caribbean territories and these differences in themselves highlight the essential unity of the Caribbean historical experience, at least in the instance of the British-Colonised territories. In terms of territorial size and population the islands of St Kitts and Jamaica stand almost at opposite ends of the British-Caribbean experience. Jamaica has about half of all former British-Colonised population, and the population of St Kitts is among the smallest of the British-Caribbean islands. With a territorial size of 67 square miles, the island of St Kitts is marginally larger than the Windward district of Hanover, the smallest parish in Jamaica, which measures 66 square miles.

St Kitts in 1911 remained a monocultural economy dominated by estate cultivation of sugar, and agricultural workers (working exclusively on sugar estates) accounted for 57.23 per cent of the total labour force. The next largest category of workers was that of domestic servants at 14.65 per cent and general workers and porters at 7.2 per cent, some of whom may have supplemented their income by cutting estate cane during the harvest.[2] Of 12,993 acres in cultivation in 1905, 12,720 acres or 97.8 per cent were cultivated in sugar. In 1919 sugar exports valued at £32,556 accounted for 63.2 per cent of the value of total agricultural exports.[3]

Sugar had never dominated the economy of Jamaica as much as it did in St Kitts and by the beginning of the twentieth century the economic importance of sugar in Jamaica had declined dramatically. By 1900 sugar contributed only 10.8 per cent of the value of total agricultural exports already outstripped by bananas which contributed 25.6 per cent in that year.[4] In 1911 workers in sugar numbered 19,818, less than the 28,867 labourers employed in banana, and accounting for only 13.26 per cent of the total agricultural labour force.[5]

In spite of the marked geographical and economic divergence, the demographic composition and social structure of both islands bore some striking similarities. In 1911 the Jamaican population stood at 831,383, compared with a population of 26,283 in St Kitts, smaller even than the 35,463 persons in Trelawny, the parish with the smallest population in Jamaica. The White population of St Kitts formed a larger proportion of the total population, 5.12 per cent compared with 1.88 per cent in Jamaica. The Coloured populations, however, were 17.82 per cent and 19.6 per cent respectively and the Black populations stood at 77.04 per cent in St Kitts and 75.8 per cent for Jamaica.[6] Both remained plantation societies in which the dominant White upper class was led by individual sugar planters or individuals closely connected with sugar interests. The close identification of race with class also meant that the racial demography of each island was at the same time a fairly accurate reflection of class demography.

The British-Caribbean tradition of independent Black organisation and leadership

It is a striking feature of the politics of the British-Colonised Caribbean that the most successful of the early twentieth-century efforts at the political mobilisation of the Black working class, in order to achieve distinctly working-class objectives, were often led by individuals from the White and Coloured upper middle class. The most widely known example of this is Captain Arthur Cipriani of Trinidad, the French creole leader of the Trinidad Workingmen's Association, who was elected to that colony's Legislative Council in 1925. But the long list of White and Coloured individuals who became champions or spokespersons for the early labour movement also included Major Hugh Hole and Reginald Stevens of Antigua, Grantley Adams of Barbados, Nicholas Pollard and George Price of British Honduras, Phyllis Alfrey of Dominica, T. Albert Marryshow of Grenada and George McIntosh of St Vincent. To these names can be added those of Solomon Alexander Gilbert 'Sandy' Cox and H.A.L. Simpson, founders of the National Club of Jamaica, whose roles as White or Coloured labour leaders in that island prefigured those of Alexander Bustamante and Norman Manley, and Thomas Manchester and Edgar Challenger of St Kitts who founded the St Kitts Workers League.

The White and Coloured leaders who dominated British-Caribbean labour politics in the early twentieth century built upon a long tradition of independent Black political organisation and leadership. Indeed, the apartheid of slavery both dictated the need for and facilitated independent protest action on the part of Black slaves, sometimes in the form of marronage and open rebellion but also in the form of strikes and collective bargaining, as demonstrated by Mary Turner in her ground-breaking article 'Chattel Slaves into Wage Slaves: A Jamaican Case Study'.[7] In the post-emancipation period, the newly freed Black population quickly established independent social and political organisations. Swithin Wilmot's chapter in this volume as well as his earlier study of the political activism of the Black carpenter and small settler,

Samuel Clarke, reveals the vibrant political life of the free Black population of Jamaica, at times organised into independent Black Baptist Churches and Black political organisations such as the St David's Liberal, Recording, and Election Association.[8]

Later, in the 1890s, Jamaica again witnessed the emergence of an independent Black political movement engineered largely by the Black Bahamian cleric, lawyer and newspaper publisher, Robert Love. Love's political work helped to cement an electoral alliance of Black and Coloured politicians to contest the island elections of 1896. Subsequently, in 1898, Love established the People's Convention to commemorate the 50th anniversary of full freedom. Alexander Dixon, a Black cabinetmaker and municipal politician, was elected chairman of the People's Convention and in the following year, 1899, became the first Black man to win a seat in the Jamaican Legislative Council.[9]

Developing in parallel with this pattern of independent organisation by the Black population, slave or free, was a strategy of political cooperation between independent Black leaders and friendly and sympathetic White and Coloured individuals. This tendency can be seen in Jamaica in the cooperation between the Black Baptist slave preacher, Sam Sharpe, and the British Baptist missionary, William Knibb, in organising the general strike which preceded the Christmas slave rebellion of 1831, or in the subsequent alliance between the Black Baptist preacher, Paul Bogle, and the Coloured planter and vestryman, George William Gordon, in the Jamaican insurrection of 1865.[10]

It can also be witnessed in St Kitts during the general strike mounted by the newly freed Black population following the reading of the Emancipation Proclamation on 1 August 1834. Led by a Maroon, Marcus, King of the Woods, the ex-slaves' mass escape into the central mountain range in protest against the apprenticeship system was partly inspired by the impending return from England of the Coloured St Kitts politician, Ralph Cleghorn, whom the protesting ex-slaves declared would be returning with their 'free papers' which would show that they did not have to serve an apprenticeship.[11]

So cooperation between the Black labouring population and sympathetic White and Coloured political figures was not a new feature in the politics of the British-Colonised Caribbean. What was new in the colonial politics of the twentieth century was the assumption of top leadership roles by White and Coloured individuals in colony-wide nationalist and labour organisations created during this period with Black leaders assuming secondary positions.

Most of the White and Coloured Caribbean labour leaders of the early twentieth century had displaced the Black labour leaders who had preceded them. In Antigua, the 1937 electoral campaigns of Major Hole, a retired English army officer and estate owner, and Stevens, a well-to-do Coloured jeweller who became the first president of the Antigua Trades and Labour Union, the first legally registered trade union in the island, were managed and organised by Harold Wilson, a Black Barbadian-born newspaper editor, and Edward Mathurin, a Black Antiguan printer. These two pioneers in the attempt to organise workers in Antigua, having founded the Antigua Workingmen's Association in 1932, became lieutenants in the labour movement under White and Coloured leadership.[12]

When Cipriani assumed the leadership of the Trinidad Workingmen's Association in 1924, the organisation had already been in existence for 27 years under the leadership of Black men like Alfred Richards, the Afro-Chinese pharmacist; Sidney de Bourg, a Grenadian-born commission agent; and W. Howard-Bishop, a Guyanese journalist, school teacher and pan-Africanist.[13] Similarly, in Barbados, the political activities of the Black physician, Charles Duncan O'Neal, and his Democratic League co-founder, the Black newspaper editor, Clennel Wickham, were essential foundations for the subsequent leadership role of the Coloured barrister, Adams.[14]

The rise of White and Coloured leadership

The displacement of Black political and labour leaders by individuals from the White and Coloured upper class can possibly be explained by the prolonged economic depressions which affected the British-Caribbean sugar industry during this period; the openly racist colonial policies pursued by the British Colonial Office after the appointment of Joseph Chamberlain to the position of Secretary of State for the colonies; and the ingrained racism of colonial society in the British Caribbean.

The economic depression which commenced in the British Caribbean sugar industry in the 1880s, intensifying after 1896 and lasting until the outbreak of the First World War, would have threatened the prosperity of many Black middle-class individuals who had only recently achieved middle-class status. Many would have failed the property qualifications which would make them eligible for election to the Legislative Councils. Such a process could explain the failure of Dixon and other Black politicians to join Love in contesting the 1906 general elections in Jamaica. The prospect for the election of Black men to the legislature would also have been affected by the reduction in the ranks of Black artisans, tradesmen, skilled workers and peasants who could meet the income requirement to qualify for the franchise. In Jamaica the number of registered voters declined from 42,226 in 1887 to 16,256 by 1901.[15] Subsequently, the economic distress caused by the Great Depression could also help to explain the relative quiescence and lack of success of many Black politicians during the interwar years.

The attempt by Chamberlain to remove such constitutional advances as had been conceded to colonies with Black majority populations before his arrival in office also undermined Black political leadership in the British-Caribbean. In Jamaica, the most constitutionally advanced of the colonies, Chamberlain reinforced the power of the governor to name a nominated majority to the legislature, making it a permanent feature of the constitution in his effort to regain control of a legislature which was seen as coming under the influence of Black and Coloured men. In addition, the new doctrine of 'paramount importance' gave the governor the power to override any decision of the Legislative Council by declaring it to be a matter of 'paramount importance'. Such policies discouraged Black participation in colonial politics and made political success more unlikely.[16]

However, the embedded racism of British-Caribbean colonial society provides the single most powerful explanation for the relegation of Black politicians and labour leaders to a secondary role during this period. During both of his electoral campaigns in 1899 and 1900, Dixon, accused in the conservative pro-planter press of seeking to bring about racial strife, was maligned and attacked with racist slurs. One newspaper reported a White planter's description of him as 'an ignorant . . . who is hardly able to write his name' and quoted the planter as urging that rather than having such a man in the legislature, Jamaica should be returned to full Crown Colony rule.[17] In colonies like the Leeward and Windward Islands and Trinidad where the Legislative Councils were entirely nominated until 1924, there was little likelihood of Black men being nominated to the colonial legislatures. No Black native of St Kitts was nominated to the local legislature before 1937.

Racism in the British Caribbean also helped to shape the perceptions and judgements of the Black labouring population. The devaluation of the Black skin and the racial stereotypes directed against Blacks helped to undermine the confidence which Black workers held in individuals of their race. Additionally, it enhanced the value of White leadership. Governor Fletcher of Trinidad, in discussing the source of Cipriani's influence over the Black population, observed:

> I believe that the secret of Cipriani's influence lies, not so much in any personal ability, as in the colour of his skin . . . Labour, formerly accustomed to cringe before the White slave-driver, found in their strong and forceful White champion as it were a demi-god, and they placed him upon a pedestal accordingly.[18]

Most of the White and Coloured labour leaders who emerged in the British-Colonised Caribbean in the first three decades of the twentieth century had previously been involved in political campaigns for constitutional reform and representative government and their labour agitation was an outgrowth of their earlier political activities. Before becoming leader of the Trinidad Workingmen's Association in 1924, Cipriani had been a leading member of the Legislative Reform Committee formed in 1921 to support the cause of an elected majority in the Legislative Council and the introduction of a limited form of representative government.

The structure of colonial society aided the White and Coloured leaders of the National Club of Jamaica and the St Kitts Workers League. Their colour, class and education gave them an immense social and political advantage over contemporary Black labour leaders. They could not be dismissed casually or contemptuously by the ruling circles who came to recognise the value of having men with whom they could speak being accepted as leaders by the Black labouring population.

The National Club of Jamaica

The National Club was founded at a public meeting held on 3 March 1909. Its president, H.A.L. 'Corkfoot' Simpson, a solicitor, was 'Jamaican' White and S.A.G. Cox, first vice-president of the club and a barrister, was a 'high Coloured' man who could pass for White. The leading Black members of the club included Dixon, the club's second vice-president, and Marcus Garvey who in 1911 briefly became the club's secretary. Simpson and Cox had both been previously involved in the urban citizens' associations which were established in the leading towns of Jamaica during the first decade of the twentieth century to call for greater powers to be given to local government institutions. Simpson was a leading figure in the Kingston Citizens Association and Cox had been active in the Montego Bay Citizens Association. The National Club arose directly out of the agitation by some sections of the White and Coloured middle class for the introduction of representative government.

The White and Coloured leaders of the National Club of Jamaica built upon the earlier political activities of Black precursors like Love, Dixon and Josiah Smicle, the Black storekeeper, teacher and municipal politician. Between 1896 and 1900, these three men had attempted to create an independent coalition of Black politicians which would represent the interest of the disenfranchised Black labouring population. Their political campaigns achieved some success with the election of Dixon, Smicle and Love to the Jamaican Legislative Council in 1899, 1900 and 1906 respectively. The death of Smicle months after his election to the legislature in 1900, the failure of Dixon to contest the 1906 general election and the poor health of Love, who was 67 at the time of his election to the Legislative Council, served to undermine the legislative efforts of these men.[19] The collapse of this attempt at independent Black political organisation opened the way for White and Coloured middle class political leaders.

The call for constitutional reform and representative government was a principal plank of the platform of the National Club. At its founding meeting, the largely middle-class participants dedicated themselves to reforming the political structure of the colony and pledged 'to secure for the inhabitants of this island self-government, whereby we may be self-governing colonies of the Great British Empire'.[20]

The Club also turned its attention to the question of the conditions of labour and saw its role as the representative voice of labour. The labour activities of the National Club also built upon the earlier unionising efforts of independent Black trade unions. Attempts to organise trades and labour unions in Jamaica dated back to 1898 when the Carpenters, Bricklayers, and Painters Union (commonly referred to as the Artisans' Union) was founded. In 1907, the Jamaica Trades and Labour Union, affiliated to the American Federation of Labour, was established with W.G. Hinchcliffe, a carpenter and former secretary of the Artisans' Union, as president.[21] In November 1908, the Jamaican branch of the Typographical Union of America (also known as the Printers Union) called the printers out on strike. The young Garvey, a vice-president of one of the branches of the union, played a leading role in organising the strike.[22]

In pursuit of its working-class agenda, the National Club declared its intention of affiliating with trade unions in England and was in communication with Labour Members of Parliament.[23] At a monthly meeting of the National Club held on 17 June 1909 several resolutions on the labour situation were passed, notably one which denounced Indian indentured immigration as bordering 'closely on the slave trade' and called for an end to the importation of Indian immigrant labour which kept the wages of Jamaican labourers down to less than 1 shilling per day. Dixon, in supporting the resolution, went further, declaring that: 'Coolie labour did not border on slavery – it was slavery pure and simple . . . It was slavery that the people of this country contributed towards, to take bread from their own lips . . . In consequence of coolie labour, men had to work for 9d a day'. In other resolutions passed by that meeting the Club called on the government to 'introduce the several Employers Liabilities Acts of England into this island as our labour is absolutely unprotected, and it is not right that he should be so much at the mercy of the employer'. The government was also urged to introduce those laws presently in force in England which legalised and protected trade unions and Cox was authorised to secure the support of the labour unions in England to bring about the legalisation of trade unions in Jamaica.[24] The colonial government dismissed the Club's petition with the observation that the English statutes which it referred to were not 'under present conditions fully applicable to Jamaica'.[25]

Despite the absence of representative government, the existence of the elective principle in the Jamaican constitution since 1884 allowed the National Club to become involved in electoral politics. Under the 1886 Franchise (Amendment) Act, a voter had to own property on which rates and taxes of at least 10 shillings were paid annually.[26] This fairly liberal requirement enfranchised many middle-income peasant farmers in the rural areas. In 1909 the Jamaican Legislative Council consisted of the governor, 14 official and unofficial members nominated by the governor and 14 elected representatives of the various parishes. In November 1909, Cox was elected to the Jamaican legislature as the member for the St Thomas constituency through a by-election. Having achieved this early success the National Club aimed to increase its level of representation in the Legislative Council and, in the 1911 general elections, the Club contested three of the 14 elected seats. Simpson, president of the club, ran for the Kingston constituency; Cox ran as the incumbent in St Thomas; and F.R. Evans, a close ally of Cox, ran in Westmoreland.

Although the National Club candidates ran under the common banner of 'the red and green', they ran their campaigns as independents.

Despite the exclusion of the mass of the Black labouring population from the franchise, the National Club candidates put the labour question at the forefront of their electoral campaign. The disenfranchised labouring population responded enthusiastically to the National Club campaign and were fanatical in the devotion which they displayed towards 'Sandy' Cox, who had placed the depressed conditions of the Jamaican labouring population at the centre of his campaign. A correspondent in the *Gleaner* commented:

> The mass of the people of the interior believe in Mr Cox – men, women and children – and they absolutely refuse to listen to anything that is not Cox. Children, half-naked with the appearance of being strangers to a good meal and growing up without any education can all swell in shrillest notes a chorus of 'Vote for Cox' and the hillsides and valleys re-echo with the cry when the leader of the red and green or his opponent come by.[27]

Another *Gleaner* correspondent commented on the active participation of women in the 1911 electoral campaign, noting that at one of Cox's public meetings held in Bath on 14 January 'there was a large gathering of women and children'. The correspondent went on to comment, in a somewhat derogatory manner, that the 'women and children are playing an important part in these political meetings; indeed it seems to be a sort of free entertainment for them, and so they fail not to take advantage of it'.[28] The preponderance of women at the public meetings of the candidates in the 1911 election was widely commented upon and the rural women seemed even more vociferous in support of Cox than the men.

The three candidates of the National Club won their seats by convincing margins. Simpson won in Kingston with 838 votes and Evans also won in Westmoreland, but Cox had the largest margin of victory winning 446 votes to his opponent's 166.[29]

The St Kitts Workers' League

The St Kitts Workers' League was also formed at a public meeting, held on 9 September 1932. Thomas Manchester, president of the league, was the scion of a leading Coloured planter family which owned four small sugar estates. (His father, James Manchester, had been nominated to both the Legislative and Executive councils but the family, while retaining its social importance, had entered a period of declining fortunes.) Manchester's cousin, Edgar Challenger, a member of a leading Coloured merchant family, was vice-president of the league and W.A.H. Seaton, the Coloured managing director of a Portuguese-owned commercial establishment, was honorary secretary.[30] The only White member of the executive, Walter Davis, an engineer who was closely related to one of the island's leading planter families, was second only to Manchester in the popularity he enjoyed among the league's working-class supporters. The Black leaders of the league included Victor John, a pharmacist, who was second vice-president, and Joseph N. France, a printer and sub-editor of a working-class newspaper, the *Union Messenger*, who succeeded Seaton as the league's secretary.

Manchester and Seaton, like Simpson and Cox, had both been previously involved in middle-class political agitation for representative government. Manchester had been a member of the working committee of the Representative Government Association established in 1918 to press for 'popular representative government' and a founding member of the St Kitts Taxpayers' Association created in 1922 to oppose the introduction of income tax on incomes of £100 per year and over. Seaton had been secretary of the Representative Government Association and a leading member of the Taxpayers' Association.[31]

The St Kitts Workers' League was formed around the particularly middle-class concern of West Indian federation. The public meeting where it was founded had been called to listen to an address by Marryshow of Grenada who sought to encourage the island's participation in the Dominica conference of 1932. The conference had been convened by C.E.A. Rawle of Dominica, with the strong support of Marryshow and Cipriani, to discuss British proposals for the federation of the Windward and Leeward Islands with Trinidad. Manchester and Seaton were selected at a subsequent public meeting as delegates to represent St Kitts at the conference.[32] Constitutional reform remained the chief concern of the leaders of the Workers' League which declared as its principal objective the replacement of Crown Colony rule by a 'higher and more suitable system of government'.[33]

As its title denotes, improvements in labour conditions and representation of the interests of the Black labouring population was also a prime focus of the St Kitts Workers' League. Like the National Club, the league had a pre-existing tradition of working-class organisation to attach itself to when it was created in 1932. As early as 1916, a group of Black lower-middle-class labour activists had tried to form a labour union, the St Kitts Trades and Labour Union, publicly declaring their aim of securing a 'more satisfactory rate of wages for all classes of labour'. The union organisers included Frederick Solomon, a carpenter, undertaker and building contractor; Joseph Nathan. a small retailer; and George Wilkes, a barber. Seaton had originally associated himself with the attempt to form a trade union but soon disassociated himself after the colonial government hurriedly passed the Trade and Labour Unions (Prohibition) Ordinance which imposed a fine of £50 or six months' imprisonment on any person found guilty of involvement in the formation of trades or labour unions. The union organisers created instead a friendly society which they named the Universal Benevolent Association (UBA). By August 1917, the society reported a membership of 1,500 persons drawn mainly from among urban workers and a benefit fund of £208. The open hostility of the island administration and the employers severely limited its operations and its appeal to the island's labouring class. By 1932 its reported membership had declined to a mere 200 persons, falling further to 110 by 1935. Under the leadership of J. Matthew Sebastian, a Black head teacher who succeeded Solomon as president of the UBA, the organisation successfully established one of the earliest British-Caribbean working-class newspapers, the *Union Messenger*, which commenced publication in 1921. When the League was created, these early Black labour leaders were reduced to secondary roles as both Sebastian and Nathan became founding members of the League's executive accepting Manchester's leadership without demur.[34]

Soon after its formation, the St Kitts Workers' League initiated several public campaigns for improvements in the conditions of labourers. In November 1932, as part of its agitation for the introduction of trade union legislation, the League hosted a public meeting by Cipriani on the subject of trade unionism. A police report of the meeting noted that Cipriani introduced the large gathering of workers to: 'the weapon of striking as a means of bettering themselves and told them that it was necessary to have a Labour Union that was self-supporting from whose funds they would draw during strikes'.[35]

In December the Workers' League wrote to the secretary of state for the colonies urging the immediate introduction of workmen's compensation legislation. Although the Colonial Office was sympathetic to this call, any action along these lines was deferred in keeping with the advice of the Executive Council of St Kitts, which argued that the depressed economic conditions of the time made it inopportune for the introduction of such legislation.[36]

The Workers' League, like its Jamaican counterpart, also became directly involved in electoral politics. Between 1878 and 1936 the island of St Kitts had a wholly nominated legislature, which it shared with the island of Nevis, comprising of seven nominated official members and seven nominated unofficial members. The unrepresentative constitution of St Kitts and Nevis was one of the fundamental concerns of the St Kitts Workers' League. Like its fellow participants in the 1932 Dominica conference, the League insisted that some form of representative government had to be granted to each constituent part of the proposed federation of the Windward and Leeward Islands and Trinidad before such a federation could proceed. The meeting of the Closer Union Commission of 1933 had recommended the introduction or the strengthening of the elective principle in the constitutions of the Leeward and Windward Islands, but action on this had been delayed by strong planter opposition. The working-class disturbances in St Kitts in January 1935, and in St Vincent in October of that year, accelerated the introduction of the elective principle and in 1936 new constitutions were introduced providing for the introduction of elected members in the case of the Leewards and an increase in the number of elected members in the Windwards. The 1936 constitution of St Kitts and Nevis provided for a Legislative Council with five official members, three nominated unofficial members and a minority of five elected members, a much less liberal constitution than that enjoyed by Jamaica since 1884. The property qualifications for exercise of the franchise were equally restrictive requiring either an income of £50 per year or payment of at least 15 shillings annually in direct taxes.[37]

The election in St Kitts of 1937 produced similar sharp social divisions but did not yield the same level of passion and violence as had the 1911 Jamaican election. Manchester's political approach was conciliatory and he was never able to command the same level of undying devotion from the ordinary working people of the island as Cox.[38] The Workers' League fielded candidates in two of the three seats in the electoral district of St Kitts (the other two elected seats on the council represented the electoral district of Nevis) and endorsed an independent Coloured middle-class candidate, Clement Malone, in the third seat. The League was opposed by two candidates of the Agricultural and Commercial Society of St Kitts, the representative body of the planting and mercantile interests in the island, William Walwyn, a nominated member of the council and a leading White planter, and Patrick Ryan, a Portuguese merchant. The campaign of the Workers' League appealed directly to the vote of the Black lower middle-class and the more progressive elements of the Coloured middle-class who supported the call for representative government. The League's electoral platform focused on essentially middle-class concerns, including the call for the widening of the franchise with the ultimate goal of 'manhood suffrage'; the attainment of a federated West Indies with dominion status; and ensuring that the resources of the island were 'developed and distributed as to secure therefrom the maximum well being of all sectors of the inhabitants'. The league pledged to work towards the 'recognition of the principle of equal opportunities for every individual, irrespective of class and colour' and to introduce such legislative measures as will secure 'such public utilities and social services that will tend to raise the standard of community manhood and womanhood'.[39] Their studiedly neutral electoral platform had no specific programmes for the working class and was essentially a welfarist programme which could find general acceptance across the broadest band of progressive opinion in the island.

The two league candidates had significant victories over their candidates of the planter/merchant coalition. Manchester and Challenger gained 800 and 635 votes respectively and the independent candidate, Malone, won the largest number of votes with 934, making them the three elected members for St Kitts. The Agricultural and Commercial Society candidates trailed badly with Walwyn gaining 346 votes and Ryan obtaining 230.[40]

The social composition and political character of the National Club and the Workers' League

Both the National Club and the Workers' League took on the role of political representatives of the Black labouring populations and the White and Coloured leaders of these organisation saw themselves, and were accepted by their Black working-class followers, as the legitimate champions of Black labour. But they were not working-class organisations. Their active membership was drawn almost entirely from the middle class, with a several Black labour leaders and a few upwardly mobile workers providing a thin working-class veneer. The leadership hierarchy replicated the social stratification of contemporary West Indian colonial society with White and near-White individuals at the apex and dark Coloured and Black men occupying the middle rungs of leadership. The patriarchal structure of colonial society was also reproduced in these organisations, for no women occupied leading positions in either organisation. Thus there were no women in the leadership of the National Club and the only woman mentioned in connection with the Club was Miss G.C. Hay, an Englishwoman who was the sole owner of the Fort William and Roaring River estates in Westmoreland. She regularly made representations to the government about the poor conditions of the hospital and the poor house at Savanna-la-Mar and was a close associate and vocal supporter of Evans, but she was not directly involved in the activities of the Club.[41] One woman, Miss Isa Bradley, did play a prominent role in the political activities of the Workers' League. She was a former vice-president of the St Kitts Teachers Association, a founding member of the League and a leading platform speaker during the League's 1937 electoral campaign. However, she was not a member of the League executive.[42]

Despite their direct involvement in agitation on behalf of workers' rights, neither organisation attempted to establish trade unions, organise workers directly or engage in any form of direct action with and on behalf of workers. Nor did either seek to involve itself in the resolution of industrial disputes between workers and their employers. Like Cipriani and the Trinidad Workingmen's Association under his leadership, the focus of both organisations was political and they adopted a strictly constitutional approach to the labour question. Before 1919 in Jamaica and 1939 in St Kitts, trade union activity received no legal protection under the law. While they agitated for the legalisation of trade unions, the White and Coloured upper-class leaders of these organisations, some of whom were lawyers, refused to engage in any activity which threatened to place them outside the law. Nor did they make any special effort to recruit Black workers to their organisations or to encourage independent Black working-class action in defence of workers' rights. They saw themselves as the political representatives of the working class and sought to represent working-class interests through existing constitutional channels.

Elite leadership and Black working-class support

The White and Coloured upper-middle-class leaders of the National Club and the Workers' League established their unchallenged leadership over the labour movements of their respective islands with comparative ease. Their dominant role was challenged neither on a class or colour basis within their organisations nor within the labour movement as a whole. Existing Black labour leaders, such as Dixon, Garvey, Sebastian and Nathan, were success-fully incorporated into these organisations, holding important though secon-dary positions. Black working-class organisations which were already in existence and most contemporary Black labour leaders also acknowledged the leadership of the National Club and the Workers' League. In Jamaica, Hinchcliffe, the secretary of the Artisans' Union and president of the Jamaica Trades and Labour Union, was one of Simpson's nominees and supported his electoral campaign.[43] Perhaps the only leading labour figure of the time who refused to get involved with the National Club was A. Bain Alves. Alves came out in support of Simpson's electoral opponent, G.P. Myers, and was one of the main speakers on Myers' platform. Alves had indicated an earlier interest in running in the 1911 election as a representative of labour but had decided against it.[44]

The Black labour leaders who had pioneered the labour movement in St Kitts hoisted their flag on the Workers' League flagpole. The only note of dissent came with the approach of the 1937 elections from the old labour stalwart, Nathan, who was, perhaps, bitter at his growing marginalisation and his failure to win the levels of personal support which the *arriviste* White and Coloured leaders of the league had secured. He argued that the introduction of the elective principle did not go far enough to meet the representational needs of the island's working class who were largely excluded from the franchise, and petitioned the Secretary of State for the colonies for 'the labouring classes to be specially represented in the Legislative Council'.[45] During the 1937 general elections Nathan refused to participate in the League's electoral campaign and responded to queries about his absence with a letter to the press in which he declared that none of the electoral candidates appeared 'to be seriously talking about organised labour or getting more wages for the working people'.[46] However, Sebastian, the president of the UBA, remained loyal to the leadership of Manchester and devoted the pages of the association's newspaper, the *Union Messenger*, to the electoral campaign and activities of the Workers' League.

The Black labouring population, on whose behalf both organisations spoke, gave their unreserved loyalty and support, at least in public, to the White and Coloured leaders of both organisations. Governor Fletcher in explaining Cipriani's appeal to the Black labouring population of Trinidad had implied that the Black labourers' sense of racial inferiority made them elevate their benevolent White champion to the position of a demi-god. The entrenched racism of colonial society and the persistent positive affirmation of Whiteness would have made Black workers feel flattered at the unusual attention of a White or near-White man to their distress. The daily, petty impositions of the colonial situation fostered self-hatred and self-deprecation within the Black working class. These emotions would have been further entrenched by their personal experiences of fraud and theft by a minority of parasitic Black labour leaders whose level of poverty was not far removed from that of their working-class followers and whose venality led them to prey upon the Black working-class community.

But the Black labourers' understanding of colonial society would also have led them to realise that a White or near-White man would have much greater success in extracting wage concessions and moderate improvements in working conditions from White employers and a White government. So their support for the leadership of White or near-White men was also pragmatic. They had supported the earlier efforts of Black leaders to win wage concessions and labour reforms from racist employers and the colonial government and had felt the brunt of the punitive response of the state. Political wisdom and basic common sense would have suggested that a more conciliatory and constitutional approach under the leadership of colonial elites would have had a greater chance of success. The public neutrality of the colonial authorities and the electoral successes of the upper-middle-class leaders would have cemented Black working-class support. But the Black workers' support for White and Coloured leadership was conditional upon the achievement of material success and essentially strategic. The strategic nature of this support is amply demonstrated by the rapidity with which they turned from White and Coloured labour leaders, such as Cipriani, Challenger, Stevens and Adams, to Black leaders like Uriah Butler, Robert Bradshaw, Vere Bird and Errol Barrow. Indeed, Jamaica is the only West Indian island where White or Coloured leadership of the labour movement has persisted beyond the 1950s.

The motives of the White and Coloured labour leaders

The question may be – and has been – asked: why did these White and Coloured middle-class individuals take up the cause of labour? Was it a cynical attempt to manipulate the needs of the labouring classes in furtherance of their personal political aspirations, as was often suggested of Cox, or was it out of altruistic concern for the well-being of the Black labouring classes? During this period, in both Jamaica and St Kitts, the Black labourers were largely excluded from the franchise and could do little directly to secure the election of these self-proclaimed champions of labour. The fanatical support of the Black labouring class may have led some voters to support Cox or Manchester but may just as likely have alienated them. It would certainly have been a positive influence on those voters who met the minimum property qualifications, including artisans, well-to-do peasants and the more skilled sections of the labour force, but there are few clear indications of what proportion of the electorate was made up by these categories and how influential their role may have been.

The original involvement of most of these leaders in the campaign for constitutional reform and the primacy which they continued to accord to this objective does suggest that they recognised from personal experience that their political objectives could not be achieved without this strategic alliance with labour. Before the 1930s, the British Colonial Office had only grudgingly made political concessions to the demand for constitutional reform and some secretaries of state, like Chamberlain, had tried to revoke such concessions as had already been granted over the protests and petitions of progressive opinion in the colonies. By the early decades of the twentieth century, it was obvious that constitutional reform could not be won without widely supported popular protest in the British-Caribbean colonies. Middle-class leaders who were uncompromising in their demand for constitutional reform and representative government could easily see the strategic wisdom of connecting their constitutional objectives with the broader demands of Black labour.

Many of these leaders had political ambitions and would have seen themselves as the logical successors to British colonial officials and the White planter elite. But if political office was their sole personal goal, there were less costly ways to go about it. To see these White and Coloured upper-middleclass labour leaders as engaging in a Machiavellian manipulation of the Black labouring masses in a personal quest for political power ignores or belittles the personal cost to these individuals of taking up the mantle of working-class leadership. They each undertook this commitment at great personal sacrifice, either economic, in terms of lost income and financial opportunities, or social, in the case of the social ostracism which they all suffered from members of both their own class and the White upper class. After Cox's removal from the legislative council in 1911 on the grounds that he had not met the residential requirements to be the representative for St Thomas, he fled disillusioned into permanent exile to the US where he was apparently able to pass for White. Simpson remained in Jamaica, continuing his involvement in legislative politics, but his efforts, combined with Dixon's, failed to resuscitate the National Club which had collapsed following Cox's departure. Simpson, who was a prominent political ally of Garvey's Peoples' Political Party in the 1930 general election, was isolated by the members of his class.[47] In St. Kitts, the economic difficulties which had led to the collapse of Thomas Manchester's family fortune were compounded by the refusal of the members of his class to come to his financial assistance and were partly precipitated by the deliberate engineering of rival White planters who were opposed to his politics. His premature death in 1940, shortly before the registration of the first legal trade union in St Kitts, was hastened by the personal sacrifices and exertions which he had undertaken on behalf of the Black labourers of St Kitts.

The White and Coloured middle-class labour leaders do appear to have been motivated by middle-class philanthropy, their concern for the plight of the 'barefooted man' as described by Cipriani, and out of a sense of civic obligation. Labour leaders like Cox, Cipriani and Manchester again and again expressed their compassion for the plight of the poor Black workers and declared their desire to ease their suffering. The paternalistic traditions of these plantation societies, reinforced by religious teachings which emphasised good works and compassion for your social inferiors, provided the source of the philanthropic urge which guided these White and Coloured middle-class champions of Black labour.

Their altruism was combined with a deep sense of civic responsibility and their personal offence at and their desire to abolish the demeaning and dehumanising conditions, the need to wait at the office door of petty colonial officials for the granting of personal favours, which colonial status daily imposed.

Notes

1.   This chapter is a revised version of a paper submitted at the 28th Conference of Caribbean historians held in Barbados, 14–19 April 1996. My special thanks to Carl Campbell, Joy Lumsden and Patrick Bryan of the University of

the West Indies, Michael Craton of the University of Waterloo and Mary Turner of the Institute of Commonwealth Studies, London, whose comments, criticisms and kind advice have been invaluable.

2.   *Leeward Island Census,* 1911, St Kitts-Nevis report, table X.

3.   *Leeward Islands Blue Books, 1905,* section X2; *Report on the Agricultural Department St Kitts-Nevis 1919–1920,* Return of Agricultural Products Exported from the Presidency St Kitts-Nevis for the year ended 31 December 1920.

4.   P. Bryan, *The Jamaican People, 1880-1902* (London and Basingstoke: Macmillan, 1991), p. 7. For an elaboration of the issue of diversification in Jamaica compared with the rest of the English-speaking Caribbean, see B.W. Higman, *Slave Populations of the British Caribbean* (Baltimore: The Johns Hopkins University Press, 1984), V. Shepherd, 'Pens and Penkeepers in a Plantation Society' (PhD Dissertation., University of Cambridge, 1988) and her article in this collection.

5.   *Jamaica Census,* 1911, p. 8.

6.   An additional 2.69 per cent of the Jamaican population was categorised as East Indians, Chinese or unspecified. Although there had been imports of Asian immigrants to St Kitts their numbers had been so minuscule that by 1911 they had largely merged into the Black population and were no longer categorised separately. See *Leeward Islands Census, 1911*, St Kitts-Nevis Report, table VII; *Jamaica Census, 1911*, Abstract F.

7.   Mary Turner detailed the proto-trade union activity of the slaves on two Jamaican estates who protested working conditions by staging runaway strikes and sending slave delegates to represent their grievances and bargain their case with the absentee estate owner. See Turner, 'Chattel Slaves into Wage Slaves: A Jamaican Case Study' in M. Cross and G. Heuman, eds., *Labour in the Caribbean* (London and Basingstoke: Macmillan, 1988) pp. 14–31.

8.   See S. Wilmot, 'The Politics of Samuel Clarke: Black Political Martyr in Jamaica 1851–1865' *Jamaican Historical Review*, XIX (1996), pp. 17–29.

9.   For an account of the activities of Robert Love and Alexander Dixon see J. Lumsden, 'Robert Love and Jamaican Politics' (PhD dissertation, University of the West Indies, Mona, 1987).

10. For an account of these revolts see M. Craton, *Testing the Chains: Resistance to Slavery in the British West Indies* (Ithaca, NY: Cornell University Press, 1982) and G. Heuman, *'The Killing Time': The Morant Bay Rebellion in Jamaica* (London and Basingstoke: Macmillan, 1994).

11. See R. Frucht, 'Emancipation and Revolt in the West Indies: St Kitts, 1834', *Science & Society* 34:2 (1975), pp. 199–214.

12. For an account of the early history of the Antiguan labour movement see K. Smith, *No Easy Push-o-ver: A History of the Working People of Antigua & Barbuda, 1836–1994* (Scarborough, Ontario: Edan's Publishers, 1994).

13. K. Singh, *Race and Class Struggles in a Colonial State: Trinidad 1917–1945* (Kingston: The Press, 1994) p. 127; B. Brereton, *A History of Modern Trinidad 1783–1692*, (Kingston: Heinemann Educational Books (Caribbean), 1981) p. 160.
14. For a biographical sketch of the careers of Charles O'Neale and Clennel Wickham, see F. Hoyos, *Builders of Barbados* (London and Basingstoke: Macmillan, 1972).
15. Bryan, *The Jamaican People*, p. 14–15.
16. Ibid., pp. 15–16.
17. Lumsden, 'Robert Love and Jamaican Politics', p. 270.
18. Singh, *Race and Class Struggles*, p. 127.
19. See Lumsden, 'Robert Love and Jamaican Politics'.
20. *Daily Gleaner*, 4 March 1909.
21. See G. Eaton, 'Trade Union Development in Jamaica: Parts 1 and 2', *Caribbean Quarterly* 8 (1962) pp. 6–7; R. Hart, 'Origin and Development of the Working Class in the English-speaking Caribbean' in Cross and Heuman, eds., *Labour in the Caribbean*, pp. 43–4.
22. R. Lewis, *Marcus Garvey: Anti-Colonial Champion* (Trenton, NJ: Africa World Press, 1988), p. 41.
23. *Daily Gleaner*, 5 March 1909.
24. *Daily Gleaner*, 19 June 1909. For a wider discussion of anti-immigration, specifically anti-Indian agitation in Jamaica, see Shepherd, Transients to Settlers: The Experience of Indians in Jamaica 1845–1950 (Leeds: Peepal Tree Press, 1994).
25. CO 137/674/518, Colonial Secretary to Solomon Cox, 4 November 1909, Enclosure, Sidney Olivier to The Earl of Crewe, 20 November 1909.
26. R.N. Murray, 'The Road Back – Jamaica after 1866' *Caribbean Quarterly* (1960), p. 137.
27. *Daily Gleaner*, 19 January 1909.
28. *Daily Gleaner*, 18 January 1909.
29. *Daily Gleaner*, 20 January 1911.
30. One of Edgar Challenger's forebears, John Challenger, had been a signatory to an 1823 petition to the Crown appealing for the removal of all liabilities faced by the free people of colour in St Kitts. W.A.H. Seaton was descended from Mrs Lydia Seaton, a free woman of colour from Antigua, who had helped to spread Methodism in St Kitts and was instrumental in bringing the Reverend Thomas Coke to the island in 1787. CO 318/76, memorial and petition of the free people of colour, St Kitts 24 November 1823; Sir Probyn Inniss, *Historic Basseterre*, (1979), pp. 26–7.

31. See Richards, 'Masters and Servants: The Growth of the Labour Movement in St Christopher-Nevis, 1896–1956' (PhD dissertation, Cambridge, 1989), p. 34.

32. For a brief description of the Dominica conference see J. Mordecai, *The West Indies: The Federal Negotiations* (London: George Allen and Unwin, 1968), pp. 22–5.

33. *Union Messenger*, 23 November 1932, 'An Open Letter to the people of St Kitts-Nevis by Thomas Manchester'.

34. See Richards, 'Masters and Servants', pp. 198–261.

35. The Inspector of Police went on to say that although Capt. Arthur Cipriani had warned against disorder and violence, he was afraid that 'a large percentage of the listeners would only take in the suggestion of the strike (which was) greeted with much approbation amongst the labourers'. Richards, 'Masters and Servants', p. 277.

36. Ibid., p. 274.

37. C.A. Kelsick, 'Constitutional History of the Leewards', *Caribbean Quarterly* 6:3 & 4 (1960) p. 197.

38. Manchester's role in the 1935 disturbances in St Kitts revealed the limits of his influence. Before the outbreak of riot on 29 January in the capital town, Basseterre, he was called upon by the colonial administrator to persuade the riotous crowd to disperse. Manchester was able to convince about half of those gathered, mainly onlookers, to leave with him but his appeals had no impact on the disgruntled sugar workers who refused to disperse. See Cmd 4956, *Disturbances in St Christopher, January–February 1935* (London: HMSO, 1935).

39. *Union Messenger*, 27 February 1937, 'Workers League Appeal to the Electorate for the District of St. Christopher'.

40. *Daily Bulletin*, 25 June 1937.

41. CO 137/683/1, Olivier to Harcourt, 6 January 1911.

42. Richards, 'Masters and Servants', p. 309.

43. Eaton, 'Trade Union Development in Jamaica', p. 7; Hart, 'Origin and Development of the Working Class', pp. 43–4.

44. With a subtle suggestion that the National Club was elitist, Alves acknowledged that the National Club could 'do some good but, the moment it holds itself in seclusion, it fails to be of any use'. Cited in the *Daily Gleaner*, 16 January 1911.

45. CO 152/454/12, Joseph Nathan to Cunliffe-Lister, 8 March 1935.

46. *Daily Bulletin*, 24 June 1937, letter to the editor from Nathan, 8 June 1937.

47. J. Carnegie, 'Some Aspects of Jamaica's Politics, 1918–1938' (Kingston: Institute of Jamaica, 1973).

Contributors

Hilary McD. Beckles, Professor of History, who taught in the History Department at the University of the West Indies (UWI), Mona from 1979 to 1984 and subsequently at the Cave Hill campus, is Pro-Vice Chancellor and Chair of the Board of Undergraduate Studies at the Mona campus of the UWI. Among his numerous publications are *Centering Woman: Gender Discourses in Caribbean Slavery* (1999), *The Development of West Indies Cricket: The Age of Nationalism* (1998), *The Development of West Indies Cricket: The Age of Globalization* (1998), *A History of Barbados* (1990) and *White Servitude and Black Slavery* (1989).

O. Nigel Bolland, who has previously worked at the UWI's Mona campus, is Professor of Sociology at Colgate University in New York where he also teaches Caribbean Studies. He has published several books about colonialism and decolonisation in Belize. Among his publications are *The Politics of Labour in the British Caribbean: The Social Origins of Authoritarianism and Democracy in the Labour Movement* (2000), *Struggles for Freedom: Essays on Slavery, Colonialism and Culture in the Caribbean and Central America* (1997), *On the March: Labour Rebellions in the British Caribbean, 1934–1939* (1995) and *Colonialism and Resistance in Belize* (1988).

Patrick Bryan is Professor of History at the UWI, Mona. He is the author of several publications, including *Philanthropy and Social Welfare in Jamaica* (1994) and *The Jamaican People, 1880–1902* (1991). He has edited *August 1st: A Celebration of Emancipation* (1995) and co-edited (with Rupert Lewis) *Garvey: His Work and Impact* (1988).

Trevor Burnard, formerly a Senior Lecturer at the University of Canterbury, New Zealand, now teaches at Brunel University in the UK. He also previously taught at the UWI, Mona campus. He has published widely in scholarly journals. Among his important articles is 'Family Continuity and Female Independence in Jamaica, 1655–1734', published in *Continuity and Change*, 7 (1992).

Michael Craton is Professor of History at the University of Waterloo in Canada. He has published widely on Jamaican and Bahamian slave economy and society. He is currently researching the history of the Cayman Islands. Among his many publications are *Empire, Enslavement and Freedom in the Caribbean* (1997), *Testing the Chains* (1982), *Searching for the Invisible Man: Slaves and Plantation Life in Jamaica* (1978) and (with Jim Walvin) *A Jamaican Plantation* (1970).

Stanley Engerman is the John H. Munro Professor of Economics and Professor of History at the University of Rochester where he has taught since 1963. He is co-author (with Robert Fogel) of *Time on the Cross: The Economics of American Negro Slavery* (1974) which won the 1974 Bancroft prize in American history. He has co-edited several other books, including (with Seymour Drescher) *A Historical Guide to World Slavery* (1998) and (with Barbara Solow) *British Capitalism and Caribbean Slavery: The Legacy of Eric Williams* (1987).

Richard Goodridge is a Lecturer in African History at UWI, Cave Hill campus. He previously taught at the University of Maiduguri, Nigeria, and at the UWI, Mona. He recently co-authored (with Pedro Welch), *"Red" and Black Over White: Free-coloured Women in Pre-emancipation Barbados* (2000). He has several articles in scholarly collections and journals, including 'The Teaching of African History in Barbados Schools', *Journal of Education & Development in the Caribbean*, 2, 2 (1998) and 'Women and Plantations in West Cameroon', in V. Shepherd, et. al., eds., *Engendering History: Caribbean Women in Historical Perspective* (1995).

Allister Hinds lectures in African History at the UWI, Mona campus. Among his publications are 'Currency Unification in the British Caribbean, 1922–1951', in B. L. Moore and S. Wilmot, eds., *Before and After 1865: Education, Politics and Regionalism in the Caribbean* (1998) and (with June Wallace) *Our African Heritage* (1989). His current research focuses on the economics of decolonisation in the British empire.

Michele Johnson is a Lecturer in History at the UWI, Mona. Her publications include 'Intimate Enmity: Control of Women in Domestic Service in Jamaica, 1920–1970', *Jamaican Historical Review*, 18 (1993) and 'Century of Murder in Jamaica, 1880–1980', *Jamaica Journal*, 20, 2 (1987).

Joy Lumsden, former President of the Jamaica Historical Society, lectures at the UWI, Mona. Her publications include 'The People's Convention: Celebrating the Diamond Jubilee of Full Freedom in Jamaica', in Patrick Bryan, ed., *August 1st: A Celebration of Emancipation*. Her research interests include women's history and the political and social history of Jamaica between 1865 and 1914.

Brian L. Moore, Senior Lecturer and former Head of the Department of History at the UWI, Mona 1996–9, is author of *Cultural Power, Resistance and Pluralism: Colonial Guyana, 1838–1900* (1995) and *Race, Power and Social Segmen-*

tation in Colonial Society: Guyana After Slavery 1838–1871 (1987). He edited
(with Swithin Wilmot) *Before and After 1865: Education, Politics and Regionalism
in the Caribbean* (1998).

Kathleen E. A. Monteith is a Lecturer in History, UWI, Mona. She is the
author of 'Local Pressures vs Metropolitan Policy: The Clash over the Banking
Policy in the West Indies', in Moore and Wilmot eds., *Before and After 1865:
Education, Politics and Regionalism in the Caribbean* (1998) and 'The Victoria
Jubilee Celebration of 1887 in Jamaica', in *Jamaica Journal*, 20, 4 (November
1987–1988). Her research interests include Caribbean business and economic
history.

Glen L. Richards is a Lecturer in History at the UWI, Mona. He has several
published articles, including 'The Pursuit of "Higher Wages" and "Perfect
Personal Freedom": St Kitts-Nevis, 1836–1956', in Mary Turner, ed., *From
Chattel Slaves to Wage Slaves* (1995).

Veront Satchell is Senior Lecturer in History at the UWI, Mona. He is the
author of *From Plots to Plantations* (1990), and has also published articles in
scholarly journals and chapters in edited books on systems of land tenure, the
peasantry, slavery and technology.

Gail Saunders, President of the Association of Caribbean Historians, is
currently the Director of Archives, Nassau, Bahamas. She is author of
Bahamian Society after Emancipation (1994), *Slavery in the Bahamas* (1985)
and co-author (with Michael Craton) *Islanders in the Stream* (1 & 2).

Verene A. Shepherd is Senior Lecturer in the Department of History, UWI,
Mona. She is the author of *Transient to Settlers: The Experience of Indians in
Jamaica, 1845–1950* (1994), editor and compiler of *Women in Caribbean His-
tory* (1999) and (with Hilary McD. Beckles) co-edited *Caribbean Slavery in the
Atlantic World* (2000). She also co-edited (with Barbara Bailey and Bridget Bre-
reton) *Engendering History: Caribbean Women in Historical Perspective* (1995).

Richard Sheridan is Professor Emeritus of Economics, University of Kansas,
Lawrence. He is the author of many books, including *Doctors and Slaves* (1985)
and *Sugar and Slavery* (1974). He has also written numerous journal articles
and chapters in books.

Mary Turner retired from the University of Dalhousie and is now attached to
the Institute of Commonwealth Studies in London. She previously taught history in Jamaica. She is author *of Slaves and Missionaries* (1982) and editor of
From Chattel Slaves to Wage Slaves (1995).

Jim Walvin is Professor of History at the University of York and joint editor (with Gad Heuman) of the journal *Slavery and Abolition*. He is the author of numerous publications, including *Questioning Slavery* (1996), *The Life and Times of Henry Clarke* (1994), *Black Ivory: A History of British Slavery* (1993) and *England, Slaves and Freedom* (1986).

Waibinte Wariboko, formerly of the University of Port Harcourt, Nigeria, teaches African History in the Department of History, UWI, Mona. He is the author of *Planting Church Culture at New Calabar* (1998) and several articles, including 'The Status, Role and Influence of Women in the Eastern Delta States of Nigeria, 1850–1900: Examples from New Calabar', in V. Shepherd, et.al., eds., *Engendering History* (1995).

Swithin R. Wilmot is Senior Lecturer in History and former Deputy Dean at UWI, Mona campus. He is author, editor and co-editor of several publications on post-slavery Jamaica, including (with Brian Moore) *Before and After 1865: Education, Politics and Regionalism in the Caribbean* (1998), *Adjustments to Emancipation* (1994, by the Social History Project), and (with Claus Stolberg) *Plantation Economy, Land Reform and the Peasantry in a Historical Perspective: Jamaica 1838–1980* (1992).

Nuala Zahedieh teaches in the Department of Social and Economic History at the University of Edinburgh, Scotland. She is the editor of *Economic History Society* and author of several scholarly articles, including '"A Frugal, Prudential and Hopeful Trade": Privateering in Jamaica, 1655–1689', *Journal of Imperial and Commonwealth History*, 18 (1990) and 'Trade, Plunder and Economic Development in Early English Jamaica, 1655–1689', *Economic History Review*, XXXIX (1986). She is also on the Editorial Board of the *Economic History Review*.

Index